The Making of Chaucer's English

The Making of Chaucer's English undertakes a substantial reappraisal of the place Chaucer's English occupies in the history of the English language and the language of English literature. It attacks the widespread presumption that Chaucer invented literary English and argues instead that Chaucer's English is generally traditional. It shows that Chaucer's linguistic innovation was as much performance as fact, but it also traces the linguistic strategies that made (and make) the performance of 'originality' so believable. It includes a valuable history of every word Chaucer uses. The book also interrogates the theory and methodology of historicizing languages so even as it explores how Chaucer's words matter, it also wonders why these particular words have acquired such importance for poets and scholars alike – for 600 years.

DR. CHRISTOPHER CANNON is a Fellow of St Edmund Hall, and Lecturer in English, Oxford University. He is a contributor to the *Cambridge History of Medieval Literature*, and has published numerous journal articles on Chaucer and his use of language. *The Making of Chaucer's English* is his first book.

CAMBRIDGE STUDIES IN MEDIEVAL LITERATURE

General editor
Alastair Minnis, *University of York*

Editorial board
Patrick Boyde, *University of Cambridge*
John Burrow, *University of Bristol*
Rita Copeland, *University of Minnesota*
Alan Deyermond, *University of London*
Peter Dronke, *University of Cambridge*
Simon Gaunt, *University of London*
Nigel Palmer, *University of Oxford*
Winthrop Wetherbee, *Cornell University*

This series of critical books seeks to cover the whole area of literature written in the major medieval languages – the main European vernaculars, and medieval Latin and Greek – during the period c. 1100–1500. Its chief aim is to publish and stimulate fresh scholarship and criticism on medieval literature, special emphasis being placed on understanding major works of poetry, prose, and drama in relation to the contemporary culture and learning which fostered them.

A complete list of titles in the series can be found at the end of the volume.

The Making of Chaucer's English

A Study of Words

CHRISTOPHER CANNON

CABRINI COLLEGE LIBRARY
610 King of Prussia Road
Radnor, PA 19087

CAMBRIDGE
UNIVERSITY PRESS

PR
1940
.C36
1998
RW

#3742249

PUBLISHED BY THE PRESS SYNDICATE OF THE UNIVERSITY OF CAMBRIDGE
The Pitt Building, Trumpington Street, Cambridge CB2 1RP, United Kingdom

CAMBRIDGE UNIVERSITY PRESS
The Edinburgh Building, Cambridge CB2 2RU, UK   hhtp://www.cup.cam/ac.uk
40 West 20th Street, New York, NY 10011–4211, USA   hhtp://www.cup.org
10 Stamford Road, Oakleigh, Melbourne 3166, Australia

© Cambridge University Press 1998

This book is in copyright. Subject to statutory exception
and to the provisions of relevant collective licensing agreements,
no reproduction of any part may take place without
the written permission of Cambridge University Press.

First published 1998

Printed in the United Kingdom at the University Press, Cambridge

Typeset in Adobe Garamond 11.5/14pt [CE]

A catalogue record for this book is available from the British Library

Library of Congress cataloguing in publication data

Cannon, Christopher.
The making of Chaucer's English: a study of words / Christopher Cannon.
p.   cm. (Cambridge studies in medieval literature: 39)
Includes bibliographical references and index.
ISBN 0 521 59274 7 (hardback)
1. Chaucer, Geoffrey, d. 1400 – Language.
2. English language – Middle English, 1100–1500 – Glossaries, vocabularies, etc.
3. English language – Middle English, 1100–1500 – Lexicology.
4. English language – Middle English, 1100–1500 – Etymology.
5. Rhetoric, Medieval.   I. Title.   II. Series.
PR1940.C36   1998
821'.1–dc21   97–35262 CIP

ISBN 0 521 59274 7 (hardback)

For
Joel, Adrienne, Alyssa, and Tae

Contents

Acknowledgments

One of the chief pleasures of a first book is the opportunity to record long-standing debts publicly. First and foremost, I owe thanks to the remarkable triumvirate of teachers who have guided my study of Middle English and Chaucer. Derek Pearsall bore the brunt of this book, as the first reader of the doctoral thesis that began it, and the reader (and improver) of the most difficult steps of its journey to print. Larry Benson's unstinting generosity with computer versions of Chaucer's language and his constant insight into how that language might best be analyzed made this project possible. Jill Mann introduced me to the study of words, guided my work with a decade of helpful advice, and, then, in a moment of acute need, gave me the words themselves – by lending me her entire *MED*. At the eleventh hour she also gave my entire manuscript careful and widely improving scrutiny.

To many friends and acquaintances I know that I have seemed to be, for years, a crazed version of Mr. Ramsay, like him, convinced that success in life might be reckoned as a journey from "A to Z," but, unlike him, benighted enough to think that I might actually get past "Q." It is in fact only through the kind offices of the editors of the *MED* and, in particular, of the Editor-in-Chief, Robert Lewis, that I ever got any further than "T." I owe thanks to all of the fine scholars at work on this dictionary in the summer of 1994 for permitting me to paw through their carefully organized files, and for offering advice on many of the problems I encountered in my research. For their assistance in the archives of Oxford University Press concerning some of the points in chapter 5, I also owe thanks to Peter Foden, Jenny McMorris, Judith Pearsall, and John Simpson.

I could have found no better research assistant than Jessica Brantley (for whose assistance I also owe thanks to the Academic Senate of UCLA for the funds which paid her). I know all too well how tiresome studious attention to the data disposed as Part 2 of this book can be, and it must have been still more tiresome to check it so carefully. Readers of this book who find this material at all useful have her to thank for its accuracy – and if it is at all user friendly that is because its first user has been such a good friend.

I owe thanks to a great number of other friends and colleagues, many of whom peaceably endured years of description of my progress on this book and only rewarded that affront with the most kind advice and the most useful readings. Others met some form of this book before they met me, and, although confronted first with its unfinished and less convincing forms, still responded with invaluable generosity. I would like to thank, in particular, Charles Blyth, Jacqueline Brown, Douglas Bruster, John Burrow, Robert Dawidoff, Daniel Donoghue, A. S. G. Edwards, Lianna Farber, Elizabeth Fowler, Simon Gaunt, Scott Gordon, Ralph Hanna III, Sarah Kay, H. A. Kelly, V. A. Kolve, Jeffrey Masten, Anne Middleton, Donka Minkova, Jane Moody, Ad Putter, Elizabeth Scala, James Simpson, David Wallace, Luke Wenger, Barry Windeatt, and Nicolette Zeeman.

Juliet Fleming has been and will be this book's ideal reader.

A Jacob K. Javits Fellowship from the U. S. Department of Education and a Mellon Fellowship in the Humanities gave me time to do the research for this book when I was a graduate student. A Katharine Jex Blake Research Fellowship in Girton College, Cambridge gave me the opportunity, free from teaching responsibilities, to write it, and placed me in an intellectual environment so convivial as to make that extended process a great joy. Most of chapter 5 appeared earlier in article form and is reprinted here, slightly revised, with kind permission from *Speculum: A Journal of Medieval Studies* 71 (1996): 646–75.

Abbreviations

EETS OS   Early English Text Society, Original Series

EETS ES   Early English Text Society, Extra Series

MWME   *A Manual of the Writings in Middle English*, ed. J. B. Severs and Albert E. Hartung, 9 vols., New Haven, CT: Connecticut Academy of Arts and Sciences, 1967– (in progress).

MED   *The Middle English Dictionary*, Hans Kurath *et al.* (eds.), Ann Arbor: University of Michigan, 1954– .

OED   *The Oxford English Dictionary*, James H. Murray, *et al.* (eds.), Oxford: Oxford University Press, 1933.

OED2   *The Oxford English Dictionary*, J. A. Simpson and E. S. C. Weiner (eds.), 2nd edn, 20 vols., Oxford: Clarendon Press, 1989.

Abbreviations for Chaucer's works in all tables in Part 1 of this book conform to the system used in "Chaucer's writings" in Part 2 (see pp. 223–6 below).

Note on texts and lexical references

All quotations from the works of Chaucer are taken from the *Riverside Chaucer*, Larry D. Benson (ed.), 3rd edn, Boston, MA: Houghton Mifflin, 1987. Quotations from the *Canterbury Tales* are cited by fragment as well as line number.

When discussing particular words in Part 1 of this book, I am often relying heavily on information provided in the lexical index that comprises Part 2. Where such reference is straightforward I have simply referred to the word by the headword under which the relevant information is provided in Part 2. In such cases, this headword is the substantiating reference and no further reference is given in my text or notes.

Introduction

> Without those forerunners, Jane Austen and the Brontës and George Eliot could no more have written than Shakespeare could have written without Marlowe, or Marlowe without Chaucer, or Chaucer without those forgotten poets who paved the ways and tamed the natural savagery of the tongue.
>
> Virginia Woolf[1]

This book offers a complete lexical history of Chaucer's English as well as an analysis of that history and its implications. Its direct predecessor in subject is Joseph Mersand's *Chaucer's Romance Vocabulary* (1937), and, at root, this book simply extends and updates Mersand's work, describing the history of all the words Chaucer used instead of only his Romance borrowings, using material gleaned from the more recent survey of Middle English provided in the *MED* instead of the *OED* (on which Mersand had to rely). There are other, more general and widely known lexical studies from which I have drawn, if not my method, then certainly some comfort. The importance I accord lexis here also marks William Empson's *Structure of Complex Words* (1951), C. S. Lewis's *Studies in Words* (1960), and Raymond Williams's *Keywords* (1976), but, in the end, to describe the methodology of these studies in any detail would only define what my methodology is not. As attention to words in their history is a special kind of attention to texts, however, this study, like these other word studies, values the relations between a single lexical item and the variety of texts in which that item can be found more highly than the relations between lexical items in a single

---

[1] Woolf, *Room of One's Own*, pp. 84–5.

text. An inquiry that finds meaning in such historical movement may seem antithetical in its concerns to the kind of textual attention we call "reading." And yet I do understand my effort here to be reading, a word study above all in that the text read is not a single work but the history of the English language.

How such a reading may enter the current conversation about English writing, or, for that matter, any current conversation about Chaucer is a problem that both the unusual concerns and the very rarity of word study must itself immediately raise. It is true, I think, that no part of what has garnered the most attention and secondary reaction in recent scholarship on Chaucer has valued the study of words highly. It is symptomatic that the point of departure I claim for this book reaches back over fifty years and that the scholarship I will engage most closely in subsequent chapters is often many decades old. This book must arrive, even when it is new, like the dictionaries on which it is based, tarred with the brush of philology's past and its now-disreputable positivism. This may be a fundamental fault, and doubtless the reproduction of dictionary evidence in dictionary form as Part 2 of this book will seem to some to announce that fault. But it is my position (everywhere informing my discussion in succeeding chapters) that even an empirical philology provides the evidence for exploratory doubt, and, also, precisely the tools that Chaucer scholarship needs for challenging mistaken certainties. To those who would understand the old philology as "a desiccated and dogmatic textual praxis," to the image of the "dinosaur" that Cerquiglini calls "Monsieur Procuste, Philologue," I would return the words of explanation that introduce both the first and second editions of that lumbering brontosaurus of philological practice, the *OED*:[2]

> The Vocabulary of a widely-diffused and highly-cultivated living language is not a fixed quantity circumscribed by definite limits. That vast aggregate of words and phrases which constitutes the Vocabulary of English-speaking men presents, to the mind that endeavors to grasp it as a definite whole, the aspect of one of those nebulous masses familiar to the astronomer, in which a clear and unmistakable nucleus

---

[2] Fleischman, "Philology, Linguistics," 19. The phrases "Monsieur Procuste, Philologue" and "Gaston Paris et les dinosaures" are chapter titles in Cerquiglini, *Éloge de la variante*, pp. 33–54 and 73–101 respectively.

shades off on all sides, through zones of decreasing brightness, to a dim marginal film that seems to end nowhere, but to lose itself imperceptibly in the surrounding darkness. In its constitution it may be compared to one of those natural groups of the zoologist or botanist, wherein typical species forming the characteristic nucleus of the order, are linked on every side to other species, in which the typical character is less and less distinctly apparent, till it fades away in an outer fringe of aberrant forms, which merge imperceptibly in various surrounding orders, and whose own position is ambiguous and uncertain. For the convenience of classification, the naturalist may draw the line, which bounds a class or order, outside or inside of a particular form; but Nature has drawn it nowhere.[3]

It is true that the passage is saturated with the imperialism ("the highly-cultivated living language . . . of English-speaking men") of which positivism can be the scholarly form: the "aberrant" is called into existence here by the very penchant for "classification"; it is really the need "to draw the line" that renders "Nature" so incontinent. But, if this penchant and this need are widely enough perceived in recent discussions of philology's importance, what is too often missed is the way that they are themselves rooted in crushing doubt. As this passage shows, the project of classification posits its own failure: as it fervently hopes for order, it also acknowledges what order renders "imperceptible," what order leaves "ambiguous and uncertain." It has been one of my discoveries in writing this book with dictionaries like the *OED* and the *MED* at my side that they never pretend to the facticity we often attribute to them (when we pen phrases like, "according to the *OED* . . ."), and the very copiousness of a dictionary's historical witness – as dictionary-makers well know – furnishes its reader with the means to overturn dogmatism and startle the desiccated into new life. It is in this sense that the divagation between what is now sometimes called "theory" and the old philology is not only not great, I think, but, finally, nonexistent. As Paul de Man saw it, in fact, "a return to philology, to an

---

[3] "General Explanations," *OED*, vol. I, p. xxvii. These remarks are reprinted in the "General Explanations" for *OED2*, vol. I, p. xxiv. Murray (and, by extension, all the *OED* editors who had a hand in reprinting it) liked this particular point. He had already made it in slightly different terms in his first Presidential Address to the Philological Society. See Murray, "The President's Annual Address for 1880," 131.

examination of the structure of language prior to the meaning it produces" is "a turn to theory."[4] If this book has a theory then – and I think it must, because philology *is* a theory – it is the *OED*'s understanding that fixing quantities and circumscribing limits can only be a point of departure for the mind that endeavors to grasp ambiguity and uncertainty

My reading also intersects older conversations about Chaucer's language at an oblique angle, for where past scholarship has tended to talk of "style," and I will everywhere engage this category, my particular attention to words often moves just beneath the level of analysis that I often profess to correct. The historical misprision that results from understanding Chaucer's achievement as "stylistic" is dealt with at some length in chapter 1, but it is worth saying here that readers looking for an analysis of *all* the ways that Chaucer's English has been thought to have been "made" will be disappointed in this book. I do attend to words in the concatenated forms of verse lines, stanzas, prose sentences, and even of whole texts, but my perspective, simply put, is that we treat such large and complex linguistic constructs as objects themselves susceptible to historicization at our peril. Shot through what follows is a repeated confrontation with the ways that scholars and more casual commentators have described the structures of Chaucer's writing in terms of "style" on the assumption that they *know* how Chaucer's words comprise those structures – and, in that knowing, err. It may be true that a broader approach to Chaucer's English would offer insights that lexical analysis alone can never attain, but I also think this book demonstrates that word study has purchase on Chaucer's "style" precisely as that style has so generally been described as a historical achievement. It is in this limited but important sense that this book *is* stylistic analysis – an analysis, in short, of the whole of the making of Chaucer's English at the level of the word.

The relatively new claim this book makes as it engages past positions is that Chaucer's English is not "new," but generally "traditional." Ian Robinson's claim that "Chaucer *made* English capable of poetry" is the *donnée* that I everywhere try to undermine.[5] Part 1 of this book makes

---

[4] De Man, "Return to Philology," p. 24.
[5] Robinson, *Chaucer and the English Tradition*, p. 290. Emphasis Robinson's.

this effort discursively and chapter 2, in particular, is entirely devoted to defining the "traditional" in Middle English writing and describing how Chaucer's linguistic practices fit comfortably into this category. Chapters 3 and 4 extend this claim but in a different mode: they analyze how an English that *is* so traditional can seem to be "invented" to so many. They claim that the "new" in Chaucer's practice does not lie in any use of language, but in the linguistic performance that constitutes that use, in implicit, practical pronouncements that dress the old to advantage *as* the "new." Chapter 5 considers the complicated problem of why appearances have had power for so long, and it is here that I round completely on the dictionaries that furnish the evidence for preceding chapters and explore how the nature of their system – their "theory" – has made certain inaccurate conclusions inevitable. Before analyzing Chaucer's English in historical terms, chapter 1 offers an extended introduction of my method: it explores the various kinds of relations that have been proposed between Chaucer's English and the history of the language in the past in order to demonstrate the efficacy of lexical history as a method for specifying this relationship more clearly and richly. Part 2 of this book offers the evidence on which Part 1 is based: it is an index of all of Chaucer's vocabulary that can be historicized (that is, generally, excluding proper nouns) according to the system of Larry Benson's *Glossarial Concordance to the Riverside Chaucer*. It attaches a variety of information to each word culled from the *MED* and, where the *MED* remains incomplete (at the time of writing for words from *U–Z*), from the *MED*'s unpublished materials and the *OED*. This large body of evidence is included here because it is drawn upon so extensively in Part 1. But it is also included because I do not draw upon all of it, and I have hoped that other readers may find it helpful to interests and in directions I have not pursued.

The subject of this book, both in its scope and limitations, is defined by its moment: as the *MED* neared completion the time seemed ripe and the need seemed real for a study that would bring the new and full lexical history of Middle English it now disclosed to bear on long-standing assumptions. The reader who seeks a more capacious description of Chaucer's English will do better to consult works of different moments, in particular Ralph Elliott's exhaustive (although unsystematic) treatment in *Chaucer's English* (1974), or the synoptic analysis of the "architecture of Chaucer's language" in David Burnley's *Guide to Chaucer's Language* (1983). Unlike the descriptive impulse that animates these important studies I am most interested in prosecuting a particular historical argument. I have therefore deliberately ignored some obvious lines of inquiry in the hopes of making this argument compelling and persuasive, and I have doubtless overlooked other important issues in this single-minded pursuit. It is, of course, the fair and honest topos of the general study to assert that it is partial. But this study is partial, even in its aims, and its conclusions are therefore all the more tentative. Its main goal is to call attention to a set of relations that have been singularly and generally misunderstood and that studying Chaucer's words makes understandable. But I have hoped, most of all, to open certain interrogative doors. No final word is offered here.

PART I

The study of words

I

The making of English and the English of Chaucer

The share of Chaucer in the making of English must be passed over as not admitting of detailed illustration.   Henry Bradley[1]

Chaucer, it has often been said, "started a tradition."[2] The claim has had enough proponents to naturalize it into a presumption for Chaucerians, linguistic historians, and most speakers of the language alike. But what tradition did Chaucer actually start, and how did he start it? Confidence in Chaucer's linguistic originality has often been so great as to obviate the need to *pose* this crucial question, and, in many ways, it is a question that generally remains open in direct proportion to the certainty with which historical truth has been proclaimed. I have tried to employ a method here that does not beg this question, or, at the very least, a method that relates Chaucer's English to the history of the language by specifying very carefully what it leaves out. For my own method to speak clearly to past opinion, however, its relation to that opinion must be defined carefully first.

This, then, is a chapter of definitions. It is intent on stabilizing the *object* of scrutiny in the rest of this book by clarifying the two categories at whose intersection that object emerges: what I call in my title the making of English (on the one hand) and the English of Chaucer (on the other hand). These categories have been established carefully

---

[1] Bradley, *Making of English*, p. 226.
[2] Görlach, "Chaucer's English," 74. To be fair, Görlach's claim is more general. He says, in full: "the Ricardian poets, or rather Chaucer and Gower, *started* a tradition" (Görlach's emphasis). My point, however, is not to make Görlach responsible for the view expressed by the phrase I have extracted, but to describe how this phrase might mean in the context of Chaucer scholarship generally.

before, but rarely at one and the same time, and rarely in connection with an exploration of the nature of Chaucer's linguistic originality (how his English *matters* to the English language). In the remark I have taken as my epigraph, Henry Bradley observes this dense definitional haze and, quite reasonably, refuses to peer through it. His was a judicious reaction in 1904 and it remains a fair enough reaction now, but I also think the form of Bradley's abjection may itself be taken as a point of departure. As I will try to demonstrate here, we *can* explore the share Chaucer had in the making of English by means of the very tools Bradley dismisses ("lists of words and expressions which are used by Chaucer and, so far as we know, not by any earlier writer").[3] This chapter is meant to show the efficacy of such tools for historicizing Chaucer's English.

I

The problems that beset attempts to construe a relation between Chaucer's English and the history of English take clear shape in the earliest definitions we have, so it is worth broaching the problem in early days, in the fifteenth-century pronouncements that first proposed that relation. Hoccleve's claim in the *Regement of Princes* (c. 1412) that Chaucer was the "firste fyndere of our faire langage" may be taken as paradigmatic here because it seems to be the earliest pronouncement of this kind, and, like so many later remarks, it may be read in precisely two ways.[4] First, it may propose an originality for Chaucer's language that is virtually boundless. The "langage" to which Hoccleve refers may be the language that Hoccleve writes and that the "we" of his readership write too (*"our* faire langage") – in this reading it is *English* that is praised as "faire" and Chaucer is a "fyndere" because he deployed the whole of the English language in a way "firste" worthy of notice.[5] Second, however (and precisely because this reading is so broad), we

---

[3] Bradley, *Making of English*, p. 226.
[4] Hoccleve, *Regement of Princes*, Furnivall (ed.), line 4978.
[5] "Fyndere" seems to mean "inventor" in Hoccleve's use. The *MED* provides just such a definition ("One who invents, originates, or introduces [an art, craft, science, fashion, or way of living]; inventor, originator, author") and illustrates that definition with a passage from Trevisa's translation of Higden's *Polychronicon* that renders *inventorem* as "fyndere." See *MED*, s. v. "findere n.," 2a.

may detect a qualifying pressure on Chaucer's achievement in the adjective "faire" which could restrict the province of Chaucer's originality to one *kind* of English (Chaucer made English "faire" "firste"). This second reading of Hoccleve's phrase makes it only a shorter version of the description Lydgate offers of Chaucer's achievement in the *Life of Our Lady* (c. 1416):

> And eke my maister Chauser is ygrave
> The noble Rethor, poete of Brytayne
> That worthy was the laurer to haue
> Of poetrye, and the palme atteyne
> That made firste, to distille and rayne
> The golde dewe, dropes, of speche and eloquence
> Into our tunge, thurgh his excellence
>
> And fonde the floures, firste of Retoryke
> Our Rude speche, only to enlumyne
> That in our tunge, was nevre noon hym like . . .[6]

Here Chaucer is clearly not the inventor of "English," but its improver, the writer who only "enlumyne[d]" a "speche" that was formerly "Rude." Lydgate specifies the means Chaucer employed in this illumination (as Hoccleve does not) and he calls that means "Retoryke." Setting Lydgate's remarks cheek by jowl with Hoccleve's, however, also exposes a vagueness latent in Lydgate's specificity: "golde dewe, dropes, of speche and eloquence" as well as "excellence" mark the difference between Chaucer's English and other "speche" by *quality* and, in this way, Lydgate's terms open, even *as* they limit, the scope of his claim. The Lydgatian view also figures linguistic history as a function of "faire langage" and, in this sense, it makes Hoccleve's historical point by the same categorical extravagance: like Hoccleve's "langage" Lydgate's "excellence" has no clear bounds. Both claims license their esteem for Chaucer by gathering all the objective license of historical fact to that esteem, but, inasmuch as these claims specify *by means* of praise, they finally leave obscure just what Chaucer did.

Such early definitional terms matter very much because they actually sketch out a typology into which almost every subsequent definition of

---

[6] Lydgate, *Life of Our Lady*, Lauritis, Klinefelter and Gallagher (eds.), Book 2, lines 1628–37.

Chaucer's achievement fits. Hoccleve's brevity and Lydgate's greater length mark out two formal possibilities: claims for Chaucer's linguistic primacy take shape as either aphorism or description. The generality of Hoccleve's phrase and the specificity in Lydgate's lines also predict the two *claims* that subsequent commentators always make about Chaucer's English. On the one hand there is the Hocclevian arc toward the infinite – where the extent of Chaucer's primacy is limited only by the bounds the reader is inclined to impose upon it. The details of the Lydgatian view, on the other hand, mark out a tendency to limit Chaucer's achievement to a particular *kind* of English, although the category invoked for such limitation is always, as in Lydgate, itself vague at the edges. The form of these types must be separated from their claims because later remarks sometimes intermix these parts: as we shall see, there are aphorisms limiting the influence of Chaucer's English to a kind of English as well as elaborate descriptions of the importance of that English to the whole of the English language. Such typological variety is possible of course because the Hocclevian and Lydgatian strategies are, at root, substantially the same – both positions form themselves around a kernel of obscurity.

In the centuries between the fifteenth and our own the claim that Chaucer invented everything has survived best in Hocclevian brevity, gaining its suggestive power by claiming as much for Chaucer's linguistic primacy as it is actually possible to imply. We have, for example, Thomas Warton's suggestion in 1774 that "Chaucer manifestly first taught his countrymen to write English" and William Godwin's suggestion in 1803 that Chaucer "had to a certain degree to create a language."[7] John A. Weisse's claim that Chaucer was the "father of the English language" in the *Origin, Progress and Destiny of the English Language and Literature* (1878) occupies a similar space in the scheme, although Weisse makes the Hocclevian claim in Lydgatian form, offering an unusually detailed description of the changes that Chaucer made to English to become its "father"[8]:

> Chaucer, after rendering himself master of the situation as to Anglo-Saxon, French and Latin, resolved to bring some order out of this

[7] Warton, *History of English Poetry*, p. 226; Spurgeon (ed.), *Chaucer Criticism and Allusion*, vol. II, p. 9.
[8] Weisse, *Origin, Progress and Destiny of the English Language and Literature*, p. 270.

confusion: first he dropped the thirty-four senseless inflections of the Anglo-Saxon definite article, and replaced all by the one invariable monosyllabic word *the*. To complete this part of speech in his native tongue, he introduced *a* as an indefinite article. Also the seven inflections to denote the gender, number and case of adjectives disappeared. The ninety-seven absurd changes of the personal and possessive pronouns he reduced to about twenty-one. Of the twenty-three inflections that marked the gender, number, and case, in the demonstrative pronoun, he retained but two: *this* and *thise* (now *these*) . . . let us add that Chaucer dropped the inflections and substituted the invariable particles *of*, *from*, *to*, *in*, *by*, and *with*, to denote the genitive, dative and accusative, which obviates declension in English. To form the plural of nouns, he adopted the French rule, 'add *s* to the singular.'[9]

Weisse continues at some length in equally parlous detail, and he manages the difficult feat of grafting the Lydgatian form onto Hocclevian generality because he is only opening out the Lydgatian *claim* as it had taken definitive shape in the previous century. Weisse's suggestion that Chaucer is the "Father of the English language" is, of course, a clear echo of Dryden's suggestion in the "Preface" to his *Fables* (1700) that Chaucer was the "Father of English Poetry."[10] And while this latter phrase might almost seem specifying in the face of Weisse's Hocclevian generality (that is, it seems to limit the scope of Chaucer's achievement to the kind of English that is "poetry"), it is also Lydgatian as it installs imprecision in the very terms of its restraint. To call Chaucer "the Bard who first adorn'd our Native Tongue," as Dryden also wanted to is, at once, to split off "English Poetry" from English as a whole, to make Chaucer an improver of the "Tongue," *and* to place Chaucer's originality in a linguistic category that is itself ill-defined.[11] Dryden's definition rests on a presumption (Chaucer is first because he is good) that is only slightly different from the presumption behind Weisse's definition (Chaucer is good because he is first). And so, even after Weisse's errors might seem to bring the whole position into disrepute, the Lydgatian claim survives as Matthew Arnold reworks Dryden (in 1880) only two years after Weisse has pitched in: "Chaucer is the father of our splendid

[9] *Ibid.*, p. 278.   [10] Dryden, "Preface" to *Fables*, Kinsley (ed.), p. 528.
[11] Dryden, "To Her Grace The Dutchess Ormond" (the prefatory poem to "Palemon and Arcite" in Dryden's *Fables*), Kinsley (ed.), line 1.

English poetry; he is our 'well of English undefiled', because by the lovely charm of his diction, the lovely charm of his movement, he makes an epoch and founds a tradition."[12] The limit set to the "tradition" and "epoch" that Chaucer founds is marked out here by, of all things, loveliness ("the lovely charm of his diction, the lovely charm of his movement") and the category that walls in Chaucer's achievement is still confected by aesthetic evaluation (what is "splendid"). Vagueness survives here, not as Arnold refuses to specify what he means by "English poetry" (for his remarks introduce a two-volume collection of "selections" from the "English poets" that exemplify, at length, what he thinks "poetry" is), but as the terms of his specification require further limitation if anyone *else* should want to extend it (if "poetry" is "lovely" then what is *loveliness?*). Where the broadest definitions abrogate crucial definitional work by appealing to the reader's ready assent to Chaucer's primacy (it requires no proof, or, in Weisse's case, twists any fact into proof) even the narrowest definitions of that primacy abrogate that work by appealing to the self-evidence of the boundaries proposed for specifying duty.

Most pertinent to the definitional issues at hand in this history of claims however is the survival of such vagueness about Chaucer's achievement in our own century. Hocclevian brevity and generality survive, for example, in the popular study called *Chaucer* (1932) by G. K. Chesterton. Chesterton's stunning suggestions that he would have had to write "in French . . . if Chaucer had not chosen to write in English" or that Chaucer "did a number of rather remarkable things, including, for all practical purposes, tossing off a little trifle called The English Language,"[13] might be disregarded simply because they are popularizing, were it not that their strategy can be found in the scholarship of the time. Kittredge's famous lectures on "Chaucer and His Poetry," for example, only conceal their Hocclevian generality beneath the forms of Lydgatian specificity:

> [Chaucer's] native dialect was that which was to become, in the natural course of events, the English of literature. And it was a critical

---

[12] Arnold, "Study of Poetry," Super (ed.), p. 174. (This essay is a retitled reprint of Arnold's "General Introduction" to *The English Poets: Selections*, Ward, [ed.].)
[13] Chesterton, *Chaucer*, pp. 1 and 81.

moment, when nothing was needed to determine the tendency but a poet of commanding genius. Chaucer did not make the English language. His service was to write the Midland dialect with an ease, a polish, and a regularity which commanded immediate and unanimous admiration, and to use it as the vehicle for first-rate poetry. Nothing more was needed. Those who came after him had now an accepted standard.[14]

Kittredge doubtless has Weisse's claim that Chaucer *did* make the English language ringing in his ears when he writes this, but that echo is itself interesting, since Kittredge's correction is actually as inaccurate as Weisse's original claim. Kittredge also proceeds from the presumption of Chaucer's primacy to substantiating "facts" about the language, but Chaucer did not, as we now know, make "standard" English either. At the same time, the scholarship of Baugh and Cable, which can be looked to for correction of Kittredge's view, is itself interesting to the degree that it reproduces Lydgatian specificity by means of Lydgate's categorical vagueness:

> It was once thought that Chaucer's importance was paramount among the influences bringing about the adoption of a written standard. And, indeed, it is unbelievable that the language of the greatest English poet before Shakespeare was not spread by the popularity of his works, and, through the use of that language, by subsequent poets who looked upon him as their master and model. But it is nevertheless unlikely that the English used in official records and in letters and papers by men of affairs was greatly influenced by the language of his poetry. Yet it is the language found in such documents rather than the language of Chaucer that is at the basis of Standard English. Chaucer's dialect is not in all respects the same as the language of these documents, presumably identical with the ordinary speech of the city.[15]

Here, again, Chaucer's significance to the history of the language as a whole is denied by emphasizing his influence on a *kind* of language, on the "poetry" which he is said to have improved (as "the greatest English poet before Shakespeare") and which gave him influence in a particular

---

[14] Kittredge, *Chaucer and His Poetry*, p. 7. Baugh and Cable attribute the claim that Chaucer created the London standard to Brink. See their *History of the English Language*, p. 193 n. 1.

[15] Baugh and Cable, *History of the English Language*, p. 189.

linguistic continuum (the language of "subsequent poets"). The sequestration of Chaucer's English from linguistic history is a specifying gesture, but it is not the linguistic history it appears to be: Baugh and Cable also rely on the self-evidence of a linguistic category ("it is unbelievable that . . .") and Chaucer's primacy remains presumptive, a back-formation from a greatness that is itself taken for granted (he is a "model" for the "great" because he is "great" himself).

In fact, within the most authoritative modern claims, a slightly different typology, which might be characterized as disciplinary, has emerged, but this typology continues to preserve the characteristic vagueness of Hocclevian and Lydgatian types by making the hard historical issues some other subject's problem. On the one hand, where the history of the language is described, Chaucer's achievement is separated from that history as a "literary" achievement, and illustrative here are not only Baugh and Cable's remarks but the remarks that preface Robinson's first and second editions of Chaucer:

> A similar reminder might appropriately have been addressed to those writers who have called Chaucer the creator of English. Such a statement of course totally misrepresents the development of the language. Chaucer employed the London speech of his time, and a minute comparison of his usage with that of contemporary London archives shows the two to correspond in all essentials. He not only did not invent or alter the grammatical inflections, but he also appears to have added few words to the English vocabulary . . . But he did add greatly to its prestige and distinction. The very fact that he wrote in English instead of French was significant. He developed the resources of the language for literary use, and sent an example which was followed by a long line of poets.[16]

The aphorism of Robinson's last sentence is, moreover, only filled out by Norman Davis in the recent revision of Robinson that is the *Riverside Chaucer*:

> The influence [Chaucer] had on the language seems to have been more a matter of style than substance. He showed that English could be written with an elegance and power that earlier authors had not attained. Once his literary eminence was recognized, as happened

---

[16] "Introduction" to Chaucer, *Works*, Robinson (ed.), pp. xxv–xxvi. These remarks remain in Robinson's 2nd edn (p. xxx).

16

during his own lifetime, the type of language in which he wrote gained prestige. Yet this would concern the cultivation of literature more than the practical affairs of merchants or officials, and Chaucer's example cannot have had much effect in determining what kind of English would later develop into the generally accepted written standard.[17]

Robinson's move to "literary use" and Davis's emphasis on "style" offer clarity by means of firm negation – they define by correction – but they thereby continue to conceal the uncertainty of the category into which they place Chaucer's linguistic significance. "Elegance" and "power" stand in here for Arnoldian loveliness – as that loveliness stood in for Lydgatian "excellence" – and Chaucer's insignificance to the history of the language as a whole is still made to depend upon its significance to a category that is itself appreciated into existence.[18] On the other hand, when Chaucer's "literary use" or "style" is itself studied, the very appreciation that confects this subject places *history* itself out of categorical bounds. Thus, Norman Eliason's claim that "style in English poetry begins, in a sense, with Chaucer"[19] is confirmed, not by reference to history, but by "appraisal" or enumeration of the "delight afforded by . . . lines . . . singled out for admiration."[20] The power of this logic is nowhere more evident than in the peerless exploration of Chaucer's "stylistic heritage" in Charles Muscatine's *Chaucer and the French Tradition*.[21] Muscatine does have a particular historical concern, of course, but since this is to establish a connection between Chaucer's practice and *French* tradition he does not offer any historical analysis of Chaucer's relationship to English writing. At the same time, since Muscatine's concerns are "stylistic" he may stay within the categorical boundaries he sets and *still* claim that "in the history of the literature in English, Chaucer is an anomaly" because "he has no significant predecessors."[22] Where the object of historical analysis is

---

[17] Davis, "Language and Versification," p. xxx.

[18] The same definitional terms are in operation in the recent *Cambridge History of the English Language* as Chaucer is said to have "provided England with a new style which had completely revivified the literary scene." Blake, "Literary Language," p. 525.

[19] Eliason, *Language of Chaucer's Poetry*, 10.

[20] *Ibid.*, 12. For the term "appraisal" I am looking to Eliason's subtitle for his whole study.

[21] For the phrase see Muscatine, *Chaucer and the French Tradition*, p. 1.

[22] *Ibid.*, p. 244.

style, opinion is, of course, adequate grounds for such a claim, since opinion is precisely the thing that determines a style's significance – its excellence or loveliness.

It is true of course that a distinction between linguistic and literary accomplishment (between primacy in the "language" or in "poetry") ought to create the possibility for a stylistic "history" – for modern Chaucer studies to make good on the Lydgatian claim by describing Chaucer's literary "excellence" *and* specifying that excellence in linguistic terms. Indeed, in a way that completely distinguishes it from earlier praise for Chaucer's achievement, some modern studies of Chaucer have tried to historicize Chaucer's "golde dewe, dropes, of speche and eloquence." In a landmark article of 1966, for example, Derek Brewer copiously details how Chaucer "began a revolution in poetic diction" by identifying "his artistic formalisation of the language which is found in . . . the Middle English rhyming romances," the "vast number of new words of Latin, French, and Italian origin" that he added into that language, and the "good deal of rhetoric" Chaucer "absorbed direct from Machaut."[23] In a similar article in 1981 John Fisher describes the way Chaucer "naturalized in English a new poetic mode and language" by "developing a style modeled at the basic levels on French" as Chaucer "creat[ed] a metrical poetry adapted to the rhythms of the analytic grammatical idiom of Middle and Modern English."[24] And yet, the category of the "poetic," by the very nature of its constitution, remains vague even in these careful attempts. Since Brewer defines "literature" as "the formalization of language at its greatest intensity of meaning" he can comment on the "quality of feeling" that Chaucer adapts from Machaut. Since Fisher focuses on what he calls Chaucer's "tune and tone" he can show how "Chaucer's idiom and *music* are based upon the French model."[25] Brewer and Fisher do not indulge in these moments of critical appreciation *despite* a studious focus on linguistic questions for such indulgence is exactly what even historical study of the appreciated category of the "literary" demands. This is especially clear in an article by Alan Gaylord (also of

---

[23] Brewer, "English and European Traditions," pp. 1, 4, 26, and 29.
[24] Fisher, "Chaucer and the French Influence," pp. 178 and 191.
[25] *Ibid.*, pp. 190–1. Emphasis mine.

1981) that describes the way Chaucer decided "to invent a literary English."[26] Gaylord understands language – and *can* so understand it, since he speaks of "literary English" – not as a "style" that manifests itself in particular linguistic forms but as "a style that becomes its own subject."[27] Because Chaucer's writing is newly significant for Gaylord in its self-consciousness, in its "*idea* of language," Gaylord 's claim that Chaucer invented literary English does not require his discussion to take up linguistic history (or even the language of Chaucer) at all.[28]

It is also true that recent linguistic theory has more generally intensified the problem of setting any bounds at all to literary language. Although the concern of that theory has really been the status of statement or utterances (the possibility of distinguishing between the "ordinary" and the "literary") as opposed to the nature and function of particular linguistic forms that have most interested Chaucerians (rhetoric, borrowing, style), it has, nevertheless, been suggested that *any* observation about "literary" language is imprecise.[29] And so, although the category stood theoretically firm for most of this century, as Richards carefully defined it,[30] and as it was further refined by Wimsatt, Jakobson, Mukarovsky, and Riffaterre among others,[31] there have been recent attempts to show, as Stanley Fish puts it, that

---

[26] Gaylord, "The Moment of *Sir Thopas*," 311.   [27] *Ibid.*, 326.

[28] *Ibid.*, 311. Gaylord's emphasis.

[29] The best general consideration of the issues of this debate and a fundamental intervention in it is the chapter in Fish, *Is There a Text in This Class?* on "How Ordinary is Ordinary Language?," pp. 99–111.

[30] I. A. Richards makes a distinction between the "scientific" component of language "used for the sake of reference" and an "emotive" component in which language is "used for the sake of the effects . . . produced by the reference," Richards, *Principles of Literary Criticism*, p. 267. For a similar distinction between what are there called the "symbolic" and "emotive" values of words see Richards and Ogden, *Meaning of Meaning*. Josephine Miles provides a useful bibliography of other "critical contrasts of poetic and prosaic language," offered around the decades that Richard and Ogden were writing, in *Wordsworth and the Vocabulary of Emotion*, p. 2 n. 1.

[31] Representative claims by these writers are as follows: "What distinguishes poetry from scientific or logical discourse" is a "concreteness . . . enjoyable or valuable for its own sake," Wimsatt, *Verbal Icon*, p. 76; "Poetic language . . . concentrates attention on the linguistic sign itself," Mukarovsky, *Word and Verbal Art*, p. 4; "The literariness of the converted sentence lies in its double nature, which compels the reader to interpret it as a function of its form rather than as content. It conveys at the same time a message (the command) and a comment on that message," Riffaterre, *Semiotics of Poetry*, p. 64. For a representative claim by Jakobson, see p. 24 below.

"literature" as a category "is not definable."[32] In fact, according to Steven Knapp, there is "growing agreement, among literary critics and theorists, that literature's uniqueness is an illusion."[33] The rock on which the best definitions of Chaucer's achievement have been pitched, in other words, has shifted – or at least become radically unstable. To be sure, there have been aggressive defenses of the "literary" in recent years. Knapp himself defends the specificity of what he calls "literary interest," and Barbara Hernstein Smith and Derek Attridge have recently offered new, book-length definitions of the specificity of literary language.[34] But the problem is less that Chaucer studies has erred in employing the category of the "literary," than that, in the context of this general debate, the form of specificity it offers actually intensifies the very definitional problems that specificity should solve. In this sense, Chaucer studies has been simply but wholly improvident: the very terms it has chosen for historical and linguistic precision turn out to be those terms it is increasingly difficult to be historically and linguistically precise about.

And so, on the whole now, as in a lengthy past, comment on Chaucer's accomplishment defines an impossibility best of all. It even begins to seem that scholars have failed to produce a clear definition of what Chaucer achieved precisely because that achievement cannot *be* specified. That is, for all that it seems to offer a series of solutions, for all that it constitutes itself by sure claims, what the whole history of comment on Chaucer's English seems to discover most clearly is a constitutive vagueness. In order to identify the importance of that English, from the fifteenth century until now, it has been necessary to wedge it between impossible assertions grounded in clear definitions

---

[32] Fish, *Is There A Text In This Class?*, p. 109. Ronald Carter and Walter Nash also claim "that there is no such thing as literary language," in "Language and Literariness," 124, and E. D. Hirsch claims that "literature has no independent existence, aesthetic or otherwise" in *Aims of Interpretation*, p. 135.

[33] Knapp, *Literary Interest*, p. 1.

[34] "I propose to call 'literary' any linguistically embodied representation that tends to attract a certain kind of interest to itself, " Knapp, *Literary Interest*, pp. 2–3; "Fictiveness . . . is precisely what distinguishes the literary artwork from the more general class of verbal utterances and inscriptions," Smith, *On the Margins*, p. 10; The "literary" is "a diversion of attention away from the referent itself to the *activity* of referring carried out by language," Attridge, *Peculiar Language*, p. 153. Emphasis Attridge's.

("Chaucer tossed off a little trifle called The English language") and clear assertions grounded in impossible definitions (Chaucer is the "Father of English Poetry").

2

The *tertium quid* that might specify what so much scholarly effort has failed to find will be hard won – if it may be won at all – and the foregoing definitions do not mark out an obvious alternative. They are helpful however by making clear what that alternative would look like, what it would *take* to describe Chaucer's "share in the making of English." For if past remarks converge on a general claim about linguistic history – that the making of Chaucer's English had effects beyond the bounds of its own making – they have so converged by simplifying the object they intend to describe. They show, in the negative, that what linguistic history needs in order to give a complete account of the significance of Chaucer's English is a linguistic object identified *in* its complexity *as* that complexity is related to the other objects that comprise the history of the language. If the making of Chaucer's English exceeded its bounds to affect an English beyond its own making then we need a method that describes this *process*, that gives us the mechanism through which the salient linguistic objects affect each other. As I put it in the title of this chapter, the two linguistic objects at issue – the "English of Chaucer" and the "making of English" – must be kept stable while a third thing, the relation between them, is described with equal care.

Such a method needs to say first, then, just what Chaucer's English *is* – and this is not as simple a task as it might initially seem. It cannot be a matter of turning to the *Riverside Chaucer* for the "standard" text and inserting the textual forms found there into some broader linguistic history, since the definition required will not only identify Chaucer's linguistic forms, but their making (the determinate and contingent linguistic conditions that finally put *those* forms *there*) in the texts that we take to be Chaucer's English. I will claim below that there is a serious limit to the number of such conditions that a single analysis can compass at one time, but I want to approach that claim by considering the bulk of those conditions first, in part to show just how complicated

Chaucer's English as a linguistic object can be, in still larger part to make clear that the mode of analysis I choose for subsequent chapters is the most efficacious for defining the historical relation that is my – as well as Chaucer studies' – main concern. In isolating the linguistic object in terms of these conditions I will also try to isolate the *literary* forms of that English. This may seem a perverse decision given that I have just tried to demonstrate the definitional problems that inhere in any such attempt, but it is, I think, for two reasons, the only place to begin. First, Chaucer's literary achievement has a crucial claim on our attention because, despite their problems, past definitions of this achievement are still the most complex definitions we have – they have at least attempted to specify the linguistic object they historicize. Second, the literary must be revisited in whatever definition I offer if that definition is to speak to those aspects of Chaucer's English that so many scholars have thought mattered. For both of these reasons as well, however, my definition of the "literary" is only instrumental. It is not meant to fix categorical boundaries for the whole of this study but, rather, to establish – in a manner that can only slowly become clear – how an anatomy of "literary" forms will, by my procedure, finally collapse the distinctions that find those forms.

The general definition of the "literary" I want to begin with is, in fact, the definition Chaucer himself offers of this linguistic kind. The category of literary language was not one for which Chaucer's lexicon provided modern equivalents of course: the word "literature" is not recorded in English until the fifteenth century; the word "literary" is not adduced in Middle English at all.[35] Nor should any bounds Chaucer places on this shadowy category have greater descriptive authority because Chaucer proposed them. And yet Chaucer's identification of what we would call the "literary" in the case that interests me has an advantage over subsequent definitions because, unlike those definitions, it has a clear linguistic object for its referent. The definition I am referring to is offered by Lady Philosophy in Book 2 of the *Boece*:

---

[35] The *MED*'s earliest citation for "literature n." is c. 1425 in a manuscript of Trevisa's translation of Higden's *Polychronicon*: "Alurede . . . callede to hym seynte Grimbalde . . . nobly instructe in litterature [Trev.: lettrur; L litteratura] and in musyke." The *MED* contains no entry that would correspond to Modern English "literary."

> But now is tyme that thou drynke and ataste some softe and delitable thynges, so that whanne thei ben entred withynne the, it mowe maken wey to strengere drynkes of medycines. Com now forth, therefore, the suasyoun of swetnesse rethorien, whiche that goth oonly the righte wey while sche forsaketh nat myn estatutz. And with Rethorice com forth Musice, a damoysele of our hous, that syngeth now lightere moedes or prolacions, now hevyere. (Book 2, pr.1.37–47)

Particular English forms are identified here because Philosophy is referring to things she has just "said," and, the terms of that identification are also neatly congruent with terms used in later definitions of Chaucer's literary achievement. The "swetnesse rethorien" which Philosophy notes is very like the "floures . . . of Retoryke" which Lydgate said comprised Chaucer's "eloquence," and it is rhetoric as well to which modern scholars have pointed (Brewer, in particular) to identify Chaucer's contribution to "poetic diction." To be sure, the reference is not wholly an aspect of *Chaucer's* English since Philosophy's phrase derives from the French of Jean de Meun ("douceur de rethorique") and bears the stamp of the Latin of Boethius that Jean translated ("rhetoricae suadela dulcedinis").[36] On the other hand, sung "swetnesse" does have independent status in Chaucer's lexicon.[37] In the *Parliament of Fowles*, for example, in a passage that does not seem to be translated, Chaucer uses similar words to describe the same effect:

> Of instruments of strenges in acord
> Herde I so pleye a ravyshyng swetnesse,
> That God, that makere is of al and lord,
> Ne herde nevere beter, as I gesse. (197–200)

The "song" described here is distinctly nonverbal – the "swetnesse" of

---

[36] Jean de Meun, "Boethius' *De Consolatione*," Dedeck-Héry (ed.), 187 and Boethius, *Philosophiae Consolationis Libri Quinque*, Büchner (ed.), II, pr.1 (p. 21). I make the commonplace assumption here as throughout this chapter that Chaucer consults the Latin of Boethius for his translation but that he uses the French translation of that text by Jean de Meun as a trot. On the relationship between Chaucer's text and these sources see Machan, *Techniques of Translation*, p. 7 and the "Explanatory Notes" to the *Boece* in the *Riverside Chaucer* (pp. 1003–4).

[37] See also *The Romaunt of the Rose*, lines 714–15 and 719–20 ("These briddis maden as they sete./Layes of love, ful wel sownyng . . . The swetnese of her melodye/Made al myn herte in reverye.") and *The Book of the Duchess*, lines 294–7 (". . . for I was waked/With smale foules a gret hep/That had affrayed me out of my slep/Thorgh noyse and swetnesse of her song.")

melodies, not rhetoric – but this makes clear that what Chaucer understood by this term was not a meaning but a *function* that rhetoric is only one among many means for achieving. "Swetnesse" is Chaucer's general name for the tropic powers of "song," the way it may move its listener apart from its referential qualities. It is, in this sense, Chaucer's description of the *effect* that rhetoric is employed to produce in words.[38] "Swetnesse" for Chaucer is then what Lydgate called "eloquence," what Brewer called "poetic diction," and what Jakobson, in the most carefully analytic terms, called the "set toward the message" or the "poetic function" of language that makes it literary:[39] "Poeticity is present when the word is felt as a word and not a mere representation of the object being named or an outburst of emotion, when words and their composition, their meaning, their external and inner form, acquire a weight and value of their own instead of referring indifferently to reality."[40] It is *as* "swetnesse" that Chaucer named the process by which his own English acquired a weight and value of its own; it is his word for what precisely in language exceeds reference in order to say something more than indifferently.

However vague that quality may finally be, Chaucer's identification has the circumstantial result of isolating the particular linguistic forms that generate this effect in the *Boece*. In general terms, the "swetnesse" Lady Philosophy names is the procedure of her own speech in the whole of this text: it is all the strategies she employs (rhetoric, argument, the beauty of thought and statement) to ensure that her words *affect* their auditor, "Boethius." The "swetnesse" she isolates in the passage I quote is, in other words, only an example of the way that what Philosophy "says" will help Boethius "maken wey to strengere drynkes of medycines" in the whole of this "consolation" – how her verbal forms (as they allegorically represent "philosophy" as a cognitive mode) finally console. But, more specifically, this "swetnesse" is identified in the particular linguistic object that is the very *form* of this text. This

---

38 Elaine Scarry, in a fascinating discussion of the *Consolation*, analyzes Boethius's logic here: "Like the imagination and like music, rhetoric mediates between the material realm of the body and the immaterial realm of reason, for it is by appealing to the emotions that it leads its listener to the truth of its argument," Scarry, "The Well-Rounded Sphere," p. 159.

39 Jakobson, *Language and Literature* (from "Linguistics and Poetics"), p. 69.

40 *Ibid.* (from "What Is Poetry?"), p. 378.

correlative is specified in the slightly later passage where Philosophy, again, refers to "swetnesse of songe":

> But I se now that thou art charged with the weyghte of the questioun, and wery with the lengthe of my resoun, and that thou abydest som swetnesse of songe. Tak thanne this drawght, and, whanne thou art wel reffressched and refect, thou schalt be more stedfast to stye into heyere questions or things. (Book 4, pr.6.370–6)

This phrase also has a source in both Jean de Meun's French ("douceur de chançon") and Boethius's Latin ("carminis . . . dulcedinem"),[41] but, in all these texts, it describes the fact that Boethius's text is a *prosimetrum* in which lyrics in a variety of meters (referred to as *carmina* here but as *metra* more generally) alternate continuously with more discursive prose passages (*prosae*).[42] In Chaucer's English – as in Jean de Meun's French – this oscillation is suppressed and all *metra* are, in fact, translated as prose. But the distinction tends to survive as rubricated divisions in the manuscripts of the *Boece*[43] and it survives within the text as a kind of mime of formal change when Philosophy refers to this underlying structure (e.g., "It liketh me to schewe by subtil soong," Book 3, m.2, 1). Moreover, as Chaucer's Lady Philosophy makes a distinction between two different kinds of *prose* on the grounds of "swetnesse" she provides an even more nuanced conceptual framework. She makes the subtle (and, really, more modern) suggestion that differences in the "weyghte" of some words distinguish those words from other words that have an identical form. She identifies as the "literary" those procedures that transform the language of one *prosa* of the *Boece* into its matching *metrum*, even when that making is not the making of "poetry" in strictly formal terms.

[41] Jean de Meun, "Boethius' *De Consolatione*," Dedeck-Héry (ed.), 253; Boethius, *Philosophiae Consolationis Libri Quinque*, Büchner (ed.), IV, pr.6 (p. 91).

[42] Scarry's analysis again clarifies the function Boethius is attributing to language here: "Just as music is caused by motion, so it in turn causes motion, motion within the soul of the listener . . . Throughout the *Consolation*, the changes in the prisoner's psychological disposition are repeatedly attributed to the meters," Scarry, "The Well-Rounded Sphere," p. 150.

[43] Divisions between each "*prosa*" and "*metrum*" are attested in the two manuscripts of the *Boece* that have been fully transcribed and published: Cambridge University Library, Ii.iii.21 in Chaucer, *Boece*, Furnivall (ed.), and British Library, Additional 10340 in Chaucer, *Boece*, Morris (ed.).

Chaucer lends a further and helpful complication to this scheme by taking some of the prose forms Lady Philosophy identifies as "sweet" and working them up *into* meter elsewhere in his *oeuvre*. In this way, the balder distinction that is the source of Philosophy's remarks in the *Boece* actually survives alongside the more nuanced version of her claims. While Philosophy's distinction is probing within the *Boece* as it distinguishes between "resoun" and "song" in prose, in other words, it is also useful as it makes a distinction within Chaucer's entire *oeuvre* between unmetered and metered language. The framework that Lady Philosophy so carefully lays down for identifying the literary finally does make it possible to isolate the "swetnesse" of literary forms as a difference between linguistic objects in Chaucer's English. The language of one *metrum* in the *Boece*, for example, forms the basis for a poem:

> That the world with stable feyth varieth accordable chaungynges; that the contrarious qualites of elementz holden among hemself allyaunce perdurable; that Phebus, the sonne, with his goldene chariet bryngeth forth the rosene day; that the moone hath comaundement over the nyghtes whiche nyghtes Esperus, the eve-sterre, hath brought; that the see, gredy to flowen, constreyneth with a certein eende his floodes, so that it is nat leveful to strecche his brode termes or bowndes uppon the erthes (that is to seyn, to coveren al the erthe) – al this accordaunce and ordenaunce of thynges is bounde with love, that governeth erthe and see, and hath also comandement to the hevene. And yif this love slakede the bridelis, alle thynges that now loven hem togidres wolden make batayle contynuely, and stryven to fordo the fassoun of this world, the which they now leden in accordable feith by fayre moevynges. This love halt togidres peples joyned with an holy boond, and knytteth sacrement of mariages of chaste loves; and love enditeth lawes to trewe felawes. O weleful were mankynde, yif thilke love that governeth hevene governede yowr corages. (Book 2, m.8, 1–27)

And the poem in question here is generally called the *Canticus Troili* in Book 3 of *Troilus and Criseyde*[44]:

---

[44] While Boccaccio's *Filostrato* is generally Chaucer's source for *Troilus and Criseyde*, this inset lyric departs from the song Boccaccio gives to Troiolo and reproduces instead the meanings of the prose that is Book 2, m.8 of the *Boece*. Since there is no equivalent for the *canticus* in Boccaccio's *Filostrato*, Windeatt prints the passage from Boethius next

Love, that of erthe and se hath governaunce,
Love, that his hestes hath in hevene hye,
Love, that with an holsom alliaunce
Halt peples joyned, as hym lest hem gye,
Love, that knetteth lawe of compaignie,
And couples doth in vertu for to dwelle,
Bynd this acord, that I have told and telle.

That that the world with feith which that is stable
Diverseth so his stowndes concordynge,
That elementz that ben so discordable
Holden a bond perpetuely durynge,
That Phebus mote his rosy day forth brynge,
And that the mone hath lordshipe over the nyghtes:
Al this doth Love, ay heried be his myghtes! –

That that the se, that gredy is to flowen,
Constreyneth to a certeyn ende so
His flodes that so fiersly they ne growen
To drenchen erthe and al for evere mo;
And if that Love aught lete his bridel go,
Al that now loveth asondre sholde lepe,
And lost were al that Love halt now to-hepe.

So wolde God, that auctour is of kynde,
That with his bond Love of his vertu liste
To cerclen hertes alle and faste bynde,
That from his bond no wight the wey out wiste;
And hertes colde, hem wolde I that he twiste
To make hem love, and that hem liste ay rewe
On hertes sore, and kepe hem that ben trewe! (3.1744–71)[45]

As Philosophy would suggest, it must be "swetnesse" that distinguishes these two texts since their "resoun" is exactly the same ("love" binds the

to the *canticus* in his *en face* edition: Chaucer, *Troilus and Criseyde*, Windeatt (ed.), p. 338. For another extended comparison of Chaucer's *metrum* and the *canticus* see Baum, *Chaucer's Verse*, pp. 87–90. For the convenience of organizing my own analysis I assume here that Chaucer translated the *Boece* before he wrote *Troilus and Criseyde*, although it is often assumed that the two texts were composed simultaneously (on this see chapter 3, p. 100 n. 21 below).

[45] Although I take this text from the *Riverside Chaucer* I have deleted commas at the beginning of the second and third stanzas (after "That") to clarify the syntactic structures analyzed here.

contraries of "thynges" and should bind human hearts in the same way). Both texts call upon the same illustrative imagery to figure that "resoun": a providence both juridical (it governs) and physical (it binds, with bridles, the movement of the sun, the moon, day and night, the sea and, finally, without success, people) holds the raw "elementz," the "gredy see," the tension between Phebus's control over day and the moon's control over night, lest there be a "batayle" or "lepe asondre" should these tensions be loosed. And *metrum* and *canticus* even share a large number of linguistic forms. In the syntax of both prose and verse, a series of clauses beginning with "that" begins the *metrum* ("that the world . . . varieth . . . that Phebus . . . bryngeth forth . . . that the moone hath . . . that the see . . . constreyneth") and ends the *canticus* ("that the world . . . diverseth . . . that elementz . . . holden . . . that Phebus mote . . . forth brynge, . . . that the se . . . constreyneth"), and a succession of clauses concerning "love" ends the *metrum* ("with love . . . this love . . . this love . . . love . . . thilke love") and begins the *canticus* ("Love . . . Love . . . Love . . . Love . . ."). The subjunctives in the conditional sentence at the end of the *metrum* (". . . weleful were mankynde, yif . . . love . . . governede yowr corages") are matched by a similar subjunctive in the wish that fills the last stanza of the *canticus* ("wolde God . . . that from his bond no wight . . . out wiste"). Lexis is also shared in a large number of significant words ("all[y/i]aunce," "stable," "elementz," "constreyneth," "bridel[is]," "bounde/bynde," "bo[o]nd") and is very nearly shared in a number of others ("govern-aunce," "discordable," "durynge" and "rosy" in the *canticus* are related to "governeth," "accordable," "perdurable," and "rosene" in the *metrum*). In all these ways these two different texts are, in fact, identical both in what they say and how they say it.

But, as the similarities between these two texts enter them into the conceptual framework Philosophy lays out for identifying literary language – inasmuch as the *canticus* is the "song" that constitutes literariness in that framework – their differences can also be identified and defined as the "literary" linguistic object. To put it more mechanically, the linguistic differences that allow us to see that the *metrum* is *not* the *canticus* may also be taken as a record of the decisions Chaucer took to make the poem out of the prose. Set these two texts next to one another, determine how they *are* different, and, according to Philosophy, isolate the linguistic object that *is* "swetnesse." How such a method might actually work can be demonstrated most easily at the broad level of syntax. It is clear, for example, that the articulation of the first three stanzas of the *canticus* allows for several breaks in the period that structures most of the syntax of the *metrum* (excluding its final sentence), since important syntactic elements in verse can be emphasized by position, and the rigor of subordination and conjunction that organizes prose becomes superfluous. To isolate the terms of this diversion more particularly, the syntax of the period in the *metrum* can be represented in schematic terms as follows (with major sections numbered in bold):

1 That the world varieth . . . that the elementz holden . . . that Phebus bryngeth forth . . . that the moone hath commaundement . . . that the see constreyneth –
2 al this accordaunce of thynges . . . is bounde with love . . .
3 And yif this love slakede the bridelis, alle thynges . . . wolden make batayle . . .

The syntax of the *metrum* forms a loose but straight line in which two complex syntactic units (the sequence of clauses beginning with "that" [**1**], and the repetition of "love"[**3**]) are divided neatly by a third in the form of a delayed main clause ("al this accourdaunce of thynges . . . is bounde with love"[**2**]). In the syntax of the *canticus*, however, this line becomes a circle, beginning, in effect, at its end, moving toward a main clause that provides a center, and then moving outward again, revisiting the structures it has already used. This syntax can be represented by the following scheme (for the sake of comparison, I retain the numbers I used for the *metrum* as its structures reappear):

3 Love . . . Love . . . Love . . . bynd this acord . . .
1 that the world . . . diverseth . . . that elementz . . . holden a bond . . . that Phebus mote his rosy day forth brynge . . .
2 Al this doth Love –
1 that the se . . . constreyneth his flodes . . .
3 And if . . . that Love aught lete his bridel go . . . lost were al . . .

The units of the *metrum*'s period are broken up, expanded, and arranged concentrically around the bridging clause: the concerns of "love" begin and end these stanzas [3] and the delayed main clause ("al this doth love" [2]) now interrupts the "that" clauses [1], breaking them into two sets and, also, transforming them from the subjects they were in the *metrum* (there parallel to "al *this* accourdaunce of thynges . . . is bounde") to object clauses governed by "doth" (in the *canticus*, these clauses are equivalent to the "al this" that "love *doth*"). Within stanzas, in other words, the breaks the *canticus* introduces into the syntax of the *metrum* have clarifying effect, for they throw each important constituent of the period into prominent position: "Love" begins four of the seven lines in the first stanza; the important (because parallel) repetitions of "that" begin the two central stanzas; the coordinating sentence ("al this doth Love") concludes the second stanza (emphasized as it closes the final couplet) and sits at the center of this lyric, summarizing the general sentiment of what both precedes and follows it; the return to "Love" in the conditional sentence that ends this three-stanza unit allows this stanza to end, as I have said, where the first stanza began. Precisely because they derive from the stanzaic structure the poem lays over the prose's grammar, we can see how these particular changes in the syntax of the *metrum* constitute the "swetnesse" of the *canticus*. As the syntactic shape of the latter emerges from the form that makes it poetry and not prose these are some of the specific ways in which the *canticus* is (and the *metrum* is not) a "song."

Such identification of literary objects in the *canticus* can also be made by comparison with the *metrum* at the more basic level of lexis. Here the generally close contact between the first and second stanzas and the matter of the *metrum* they rework offer the best opportunity for examining differences minutely. For example, by comparing the important words of the first part of the *metrum*,

> . . . stable feyth . . . accordable chaungynges . . . contrarious ele-
> mentz . . . allyaunce perdurable . . .

with the forms they take in the *canticus*,

> feith . . . stable
> . . . stowndes concordynge,
> . . . elementz . . . discordable
> bond perpetuely durynge.

it can be seen that the *canticus* converts this important sequence of phrases into rhyme (and thereby lines them up prominently and in parallel at the end of successive lines) by a series of morphological and synonymic substitutions. If sequential composition of the *canticus* is assumed (not a necessary assumption at all, of course, but one that helps to organize discussion here), then the decision to retain "stable" in the initial rhyme position of this stanza constrains the possible forms subsequent words may take. Thus, "st*able*" forecloses the possibility of using "accord*able*" in the next rhyming position (since rhymes must alternate in this part of the rime royal), but its meaning can occupy that position once Chaucer has found a synonym for "accord*able*" with a different ending (that is, "concord*ynge*"). By the same logic "perdur-*able*" becomes "dur*ynge*" to make one rhyming pair and "discord*able*" is substituted for "contrari*ous*" to make another. "Chaungynges" became "stowndes" to prevent what would be awkward rhythm and a repeated participial ending (in the phrase "chaungynges concordynge") and "allyaunce perdurable" is expanded syllabically to "a bond perpetuely durynge" to fill out the last line of the quatrain (inasmuch as "holden an allyaunce durynge" does not provide a rhythmic line). Similar kinds of substitution also transform the material of the last sentences of the *metrum*,

> love . . . governeth erthe and see . . . love halt togidres peples . . . with an holy boond . . . and knytteth sacrement of mariages

into material for rhyme in the first stanza of the *canticus*:

> . . . governaunce,
> . . . hevene hye,
> . . . holsom alliaunce
> . . . gye,
> . . . lawe of compaignie,

Here "holy boond" becomes "holsom alli*aunce*" and "govern*eth*" becomes "govern*aunce*" to form one rhyming pair; "sacrement of mariages" becomes "lawe of compaign*ie*"; "hevene" becomes "hevene hye" and "g*ye*" is interpolated to prepare "compaign*ie*."

The isolation of the syntactic and lexical forms that make these two texts different finds more than the forms and structures that "swetnesse" entails however. The linguistic forms of both *canticus* and *metrum* may also be isolated insofar as Chaucer made both sets of forms out of Jean de Meun's French and Boethius's Latin – that is, as those forms sit on the cusp of the *making* of Chaucer's English itself, as Chaucer had to fit English forms to or had to *make* those forms in order to convey the "resoun" of his Latin and French sources. Interestingly enough, the joins of translation between Latin, French, and English remain extremely tight despite the wide linguistic divide they bridge:

> Ce que li mondes tourne diversement par estable foi ses acordables muances, ce que les contraires qualitéz des elemens tiennent entreus aliance pardurable, ce que li soleus par sa bele presence aporte le cler jour, ce que la lune a seignorie sus les nuiz que li vesprez amaine, et que la mer couvoiteuse de pourprendre la terre refrene ses floz par certain terme, et que les terres ne puissent trop estendre leur largez bonnes – ceste ordenance de chosez est liee par Amour gouvernant les terres et la mer et comandant neis au ciel. Se ceste Amour relascoit les frains, toutez les chosez qui s'entreaiment orendroit feroient tantost bataille et estriveroient de depecier la façon du monde, la quelle il demainent ore en acordable foy par biaus mouvemens. Ceste Amour neis constraint touz peuples par aliance sainte, ceste Amor enlace le sacrement de mariage par chastes amours, ceste neis donne et dite leurs droiturez aus compaignons loyaus. O, beneuréz fust li lignages humains, se celle Amour par quoy li cielz est gouvernéz gouvernast vox couragez.[46]

> Quod mundus stabili fide
> concordes variat vices,
> quod pugnantia semina
> foedus perpetuum tenent,
> quod Phoebus roseum diem
> curru provehit aureo,
> ut, quas duxerit Hesperos
> Phoebe noctibus imperet,
> ut fluctus avidum mare
> certo fine coherceat,
> ne terris liceat vagis
> latos tendere terminos,
> hanc rerum seriem ligat
> terras ac pelagus regens
> et caelo imperitans amor.

[46] Jean de Meun, "Boethius' *De Consolatione*," Dedeck-Héry (ed.), 204–5.

Hic si frena remiserit,
quicquid nunc amat invicem
bellum continuo geret
et, quam nunc socia fide
pulchris motibus incitant,
certent solvere machinam.
Hic sancto populos quoque
iunctos foedere continet,
hic et coniugii sacrum
castis nectit amoribus,
hic fidis etiam sua
dictat iura sodalibus.
O felix hominum genus,
si vestros animos amor,
quo caelum regitur, regat![47]

The extent of similarity is also, at this stage of analysis, much more interesting than any difference precisely because the presumption of translation is linguistic change. That Chaucer would adapt synthetic Latin grammar to analytic forms (as borrowed from Jean de Meun's similar changes), that he would rationalize French idioms to idiomatic English, and that he would use extant English vocabulary in place of French and Latin words is the expectation, so this comparison becomes interesting as it shows Chaucer deciding *not* to change but to borrow. It is in such a record of borrowing, moreover, that the isolation of linguistic objects in Chaucer's English begins to isolate them as they might have had effect on the English literary language, or even the English language as a whole – that is, as Chaucer may have actually invented forms and structures as he made these texts.

A comparison of syntactic similarities, for example, shows that the literary linguistic objects of *metrum* and *canticus* take distinctive shape as they are translated. The repetition of Chaucer's syntax across the whole of the *metrum* around the subject "love" derives directly from similar repetitions in Jean de Meun's prose ("*ceste Amour . . . ceste Amour . . . ceste Amor . . . celle Amour*"), and the *canticus* can be seen to *return* these repetitions to their original shape and, therefore, rediscover

---

[47] Boethius, *Philosophiae Consolationis Libri Quinque*, Büchner (ed.), II, m.8 (pp. 39–40).

their first cause. As I noted above, such repetition marks and is marked by the beginning of verse lines in the *canticus* ("Love . . . /Love . . . / Love . . . /Love . . .") just as it marks and is marked by line beginnings in the original Latin of Boethius (the sequence "*Hic* . . . /*Hic* . . . /*hic* . . . /*hic*" has "*amor*" as its referent). The fundamental continuity this reveals is of course the continuity of metrical form as Chaucer, in his *canticus*, also returns the "resoun" of the original *metrum* to the metrical forms of "song" that it had had in Boethius's Latin. The repetition that fits and shapes the meter of the *canticus* renders metrical form *as* syntax – reflecting the structural repetition of verse lines in a grammatical repetition of subject – just as metrical form was syntax in the original Latin. And this metrical arc (from the Latin *metrum* to the English *canticus*) also explains and arranges the second important syntactic unit in Chaucer's English, the sequence of clauses beginning with "that." Jean de Meun takes the substantival *quod* clauses, which function as objects in the Latin ("*Quod* . . . /*quod* . . . /*quod*" . . . parallel to "*hanc* . . . *seriem*" governed by *ligat*")[48] and converts them into subject clauses in his French ("*ce que* . . . *ce que* . . . *ce que* . . . *et que*"). Chaucer retains these subjects in his prose ("That . . . that . . . that . . ." parallel to "al this accourdaunce" governed by "is bounde"), but he makes them objects again in the *canticus* ("That that . . . That . . . That . . . doth Love . . . That that . . ."). In this way, the verse pairs that the Latin syntax originally made possible

> Quod mundus stabili fide
> concordes variat vices . . .

become verse pairs again:

> That that the world with feith which that is stable
> Diverseth so his stowndes concordynge . . .

That subject clauses in French and Chaucer's prose become object clauses in Chaucer's meter is finally less important historically (although it does result from the kind of poetic inversion that allows Chaucer to place the subject after the verb: "doth love") than that Chaucer's verse-

---

[48] On the "quod" in the sense of "that, the fact that" as in Boethius's Latin here see Greenough, Kittredge, Howard, D'Ooge (eds.), *Allen and Greenough's New Latin Grammar*, §572 and Woodcock, *A New Latin Syntax*, §241. I thank H. A. Kelly for help with this point.

form rediscovers the original syntactic structure of these clauses as he *again* adapts grammar to verse form. The correspondence between syntactic and stanzaic shape in Chaucer's verse results directly from that correspondence in Boethius's original. Put most simply, this comparison shows that the syntax of the *canticus* is literary as it is *borrowed*, a structure that has the shape it has because it is Latinate.[49]

The words of the *metrum* and *canticus* are also further explained by consideration of Chaucer's French and Latin sources, as the following chart, summarizing all important relations, shows:

Boethius > Jean de Meun		>	*metrum*	>	*canticus*
Phoebus			Phebus		Phebus
Hesperos			Esperus		
stabili	estable		stable		stable
	aliance		allyaunce		alliaunce
	elemens		elementz		elementz
	pardurable		perdurable		durynge
	gouvernant/gouvernéz/gouvernast		governeth/governede		governaunce
	acordables		accordable		discordable
	qualitéz		qualites		
	contraires		contrarious		
	ordenance		ordenaunce		
	bataille		batayle		
	estriveroient		stryven		
	muances/mouvemens		moevynges		
	sacrement		sacrement		
	mariage		mariages		
	couragez		corages		
variat			varieth		

It is true that only one word in the original Latin, "Phoebus," makes it all the way to the *canticus*, and only "Hesperos" and "variat" pass

---

49 Machan's detailed comparison of Chaucer's syntax with these French and Latin sources in the whole of the *Boece* finds Chaucer generally adopting a middle way between Latinization and complete naturalization: "To be sure, he has produced some syntactic oddities, but for the most part, Chaucer has naturalized constructions such as ablative absolutes, which are alien to English grammar; he has used the convenience of syntactic derivatives, when a construction which occurred in his sources was current in English; and he has occasionally clarified the syntactic relationships of his sources, particularly the Latin, since its synthetic nature allowed for an economy of expression which the analytic Middle English language could not imitate," Machan, *Techniques of Translation*, p. 82.

directly from the Latin to the *metrum* (although the Latin "stabilis" has an English form in Chaucer's texts, that form is clearly mediated through the French "estable"), and only two words, "alliaunce" and "elementz," survive from the French in Chaucer's poem. But, as I have already noted, "governaunce," "durynge," and "discordable" in the *canticus* are closely derived from the *metrum's* forms, and as this chart makes clear, derived significantly from forms that the English *metrum* shares with the French. On the whole, a huge number of the words in Jean de Meun's text are simply carried over into Chaucer's prose.

Isolation of these linguistic objects in Chaucer *in* the motion of their making is useful, I have suggested, because it allows us to ask historical questions about the relation between these clear objects and other English forms. Is Chaucer's Latinate syntax significantly new to English? Does that syntax, if it is new, survive in later English writing? Are the words Chaucer borrows significantly new to English? Do those words survive in later English after Chaucer borrows them? Is Chaucer's borrowing or its quantity with or without precedent in Middle English? Do the metrical constraints that encourage Chaucer's lexical and syntactic decisions bear on earlier or later English verse? These questions could be asked generally of course, but without the foregoing analysis they could not be asked about objects whose making is so visible. Chaucer's definition of "swetnesse" makes it possible to historicize his literary achievement because it isolates that "swetnesse" in linguistic objects *as* those objects sit in their historical context. Of course it is equally fair to note at this juncture that these objects are only a small part of what makes the *canticus* "song," that, in fact, my description of the "literary" here suffers woefully in comparison with the description Chaucer himself offers of the linguistic quality of both *metrum* and *canticus*. When "Boethius" has heard the meter I have just analyzed, for example, he recurs to, and nicely expands, the description of the literary with which I began:

> By this sche hadde ended hir song, whan the swetnesse of here dite hadde thurw-perced me, that was desyrous of herknynge, and I astoned hadde yit streyghte myn eres (*Boece*, Book 3, pr.1, 1–4)

In similar terms the narrator of *Troilus and Criseyde* anticipates the

Canticus Troili in Book 3 by describing the tropic effects he expects it to have:

> And by the hond ful ofte he wolde take
> This Pandarus, and into gardyn lede,
> And swich a feste and swich a proces make
> Hym of Criseyde, and of hire wommanhede,
> And of hire beaute, that withouten drede
> It was an hevene his wordes for to here (3.1737–42)

Decades of comment on Chaucer's English has shown with equal elegance that language which is a "hevene for to here" is best understood in its complexity and not by the kind of simplification I have attempted here. Chaucer's description of the literary in *metrum* and *canticus* is satisfying precisely *because* it is a Lydgatian description, specifying as it *avoids* detail. But Chaucer defines the literary so accurately because he replicates its tropic effects *in* his description: to say that language creates a "thurw-perc[ing] swetnesse" or that Troilus's words have been a "hevene . . . to here," is itself to create a kind of "swetnesse" that is a "hevene" to hear. And, if it is a fair objection to the textual history I have reconstructed that it is nugatory, my point would be that this discovery of *some* linguistic correlatives for literariness provides the satisfactions of precision in the very loss it entails. The systematic impoverishment of Chaucer's language which I have been engaged in here also enriches the *methodological* potential for defining its achievement with rigor. The linguistic objects I have isolated can now be firmly, and I think interestingly, entered into the history of literary English and the history of the English language as a whole.

3

There are several methods available for defining the relation between Chaucer's English and the history of the language that will measure effects, but, as my subtitle and preface make clear, the method I choose here is the study of words. Lexical analysis might simply be rationalized as a necessary, albeit arbitrarily, limiting focus, excluding syntax and meter from its purview because a historical study of every aspect of Chaucer's language would overwhelm a single argument. I would maintain, however, that words are not simply one linguistic object among many: they are the *best* objects for study and fundamentally distinct from other objects because of the greater analytic possibilities they extend. As I see it, in fact, there are *five* distinct advantages to lexical history that other forms of study do not provide, and these five advantages are themselves balanced by the distinct disadvantages that beset other modes.

First, lexical history isolates the linguistic objects that are Chaucer's words *in* their history without recourse to the elaborate analysis I have just pursued. There *could* be controversy about word boundaries of course: what constitutes a "word" for the purposes of history – how Chaucer's various spellings ought to be grouped as single lexical items for that history – are matters that, as Benson puts it, involve "the human eye, hand, and judgment."[50] But the various differences between the *MED*, the *OED*, and Benson's *Glossarial Concordance* (which I use as the basis for my analysis) are generally inconsequential with respect to the history that matters. Where the *MED* parcels out Middle English into lexical units that differ from Benson's for example (e.g. placing all Chaucerian instances of "graunt adj." under its entry for "gramerci n. & interj.," while Benson treats all these uses as a species of "graunt adj."), the very capaciousness of the *MED* is an assurance that the history of a particular form will be present in the subdivisions of some entry. Such differences will affect tabulations of course (how many new "words" Chaucer used, for example), but not significantly, since words are such simple objects that disagreements are rare.

Second – and this and all the remaining advantages of lexical study are also advantages over the detailed analysis I have just made for Chaucer's *metrum* and *canticus* – isolating all the lexical objects in Chaucer's English as their history is written in the *MED* attaches information to those objects that even the most detailed comparison of text and source would have to miss. In cases where Chaucer found his English in French or Latin (or any other language for that matter) etymologies in the *MED* align Chaucer's English with the *whole* history of borrowing in English; they effectively compare Chaucer's texts with texts in all the other languages from which Middle English took its words. The *MED*'s record shows, for example, that two of the words

---

[50] Benson, *Glossarial Concordance*, p. viii.

Chaucer absorbed from French in his prose ("accordable" and "perdurable") are new to English in Chaucer's writing, and, furthermore, two words in the *canticus* that source study does not show to be "borrowed" ("concordynge," "discordable") are also Chaucer's inventions:

MED headword	*MED* etymology	First English use recorded in *MED*
metrum:		
accordable adj.	OF	(c1380) Chaucer *Bo.* 2.m.8.2
perdurable adj.	OF & ML	(c1380) Chaucer, *Bo.* 1.m.5.3.
canticus:		
discordable adj.	OF & L	(c1380) Chaucer, *Bo.* 4.m.6.23
concorden v.	OF & L	(c1385) Chaucer *TR* 3.1752

Supplementing the *MED* with the *OED* also shows that yet another borrowing in the *metrum* was new to English in Chaucer's writing:

OED headword	*OED* etymology	First English use recorded in *OED*
metrum:		
vary v.	OF or L	c1369 Chaucer, *Dethe Blaunche* 802

Furthermore, if we associate the chronology of Chaucer's works with the lexical history taken from dictionaries (a procedure I pursue at length in chapter 3) we can also trace the history of invention in Chaucer's own English. In the cases just mentioned, for example, we discover that only one word in the *metrum* ("accordable") and one word in the *canticus* ("concordynge") appear first in English in *those* texts. Despite the French prompt for "perdurable adj." and the Latin prompt for "vary v." these words were already present in Chaucer's lexicon to do this translating work.

Third, lexical history discovers *kinds* of linguistic invention in the *metrum* and *canticus* that source study cannot. As the *MED* shows, there are other words in these passages that are not borrowings but are nevertheless new to recorded English in Chaucer's use:

MED headword	*MED* etymology	First English use recorded in *MED*
metrum:		
lefful adj2.	fr. leve n2	(c1380) Chaucer *CT.SN* G.5
mevinge ger.	(fr. meven v.)[51]	(c1380) Chaucer *HF* 812

---

[51] This etymology is my own conjecture since the *MED* gives none. On this procedure see Part 2, p. 230 below.

canticus:

cerclen v.	fr. cercle n.	(c1385) Chaucer *TR* 3.1767
perpetuelli adv.	fr. perpetuelle adj.	(c1380) Chaucer *HF* 1364

Although this process has rarely been discussed as a feature of Chaucer's new vocabulary, it is clear that Chaucer made some of the "new" out of the "old," both as he built on roots already present in English because of earlier borrowing ("perpetuelle adj.") or as he re-combined native English roots and suffixes ("leve n2." and "-ful suf.").

Fourth, lexical history makes it possible to situate Chaucer's achievement in the achievement of the English texts both anterior and posterior to his efforts, since the *MED*'s history is equally well (and equally fully) a history of the lexical activity of all other Middle English writers. The novelty of new borrowings *as* borrowings in Chaucer's *metrum* (such as "accordable adj." and "perdurable adj.") can be measured against (and qualified by) comparison with other borrowings in the *metrum* such as "accordaunce n.," which is not recorded for the first time in English by Chaucer, but in the earlier English of Robert Mannyng's *Handlyng Synne* (c. 1303):

> Se how þese wymmen *a-cordaunce*
> Plesyd god with lytyl penaunce.[52]

The novelty of a newly derived form like "lefful adj." in the *metrum* is qualified by the earlier use of the similar derivation "weleful adj.," also used in the *metrum*, as it appeared first in the record in *Hali Meiðhad* (c. 1200):

> For beo hit nu þet te beo richedom riue, ant tine wide wahes wlonke ant *weolefule* . . . [53]

On the other side of Chaucer's English, lexical history makes it possible to survey the fate of innovations and measure their influence on the later language. The *MED* shows that "perpetuelli adv.," for example, is taken up immediately in the vocabulary of Lydgate (and, of course, survives in Modern English):

---

[52] Mannyng, *Handlyng Synne*, Furnivall (ed.), lines 2003–4.
[53] *Hali Meiðhad*, Millett (ed.), p. 15, lines 20–1.

For God almy3ti, Iuge of Iuges alle
Hath sette a lawe, þe which may nat falle,
Amonge planetis *perpetuelly* tendure . . .[54]

but, by contrast, it also shows that "discordable adj." is hardly recorded in Middle English after Chaucer uses it.

The fifth and final advantage of lexical history over other analytic forms is the extent to which it directly confronts the definitional problems inherent in measuring Chaucer's role in fashioning *literary* English. James Murray, the first editor-in-chief of the *OED*, may well count as the first scholar forced to explore these difficulties as a feature of lexical history, when, early in the *OED* project, he was instructed by the Delegates of the Clarendon Press to limit his survey to literary language. Murray protested immediately – in ways that anticipate more recent critiques – that he could admit no such limitation precisely because he could not himself say "what is classed as literature."[55] Murray won the right to refuse this distinction from the outset (when the first fascicle of the dictionary was issued it claimed to include "English words now in general use"),[56] but the Delegates' wishes survive in a diagram in the completed dictionary's introduction in which the existence of the literary is asserted, but its inherently fluid boundaries – and the inherent fluidity of all linguistic categories – are exploited in order to suggest that a history of every English word is, perforce, *also* a history of literary English:

54 Lydgate, *Troy Book* (Part 1), Bergen (ed.), lines 1.1723–5.
55 Murray, *Caught in the Web of Words*, p. 221.
56 "Preface to Volume I," p. vi as collected in Raymond (ed.), *Dispatches from the Front*.

As the note accompanying this diagram glosses its implicit assertion: "it is not possible to fix the point at which the 'English language' stops along any of these diverging lines."[57] A dictionary's capacity for linguistic history becomes, in this view, its capacity to historicize *each* linguistic kind as it comprehends the history of all verbal forms. That capacity does not make it easier to say "what is classed as literature," but it does hold the distinction in abeyance while history is written.

Against these five advantages there is one serious objection that may be lodged against a lexical history derived from dictionaries and it is, of course, that any history reliant upon the record remains too credulous before evidence which must miss the history of the spoken language and from which, particularly in the case of Middle English, so much that *was* written has been lost. This is Bradley's greatest worry when he says that the "share of Chaucer in the making of English must be passed over": "it would be easy," he continues after the words I took as my epigraph above, "to give lists of words and expressions used by Chaucer, and *as far as we know*, not by an earlier writer," but we may never be sure "in individual instances" that "in the use of this or that word he had not some English example before him." Tim Machan has more recently referred this objection directly to the *MED*:

> Given the inadequate resources available, one can never be sure if the earliest citation in the *OED* or *MED* is in fact the first time a word was used. Probably more medieval literature has been lost than has survived, and, as notes in philological journals demonstrate every year, lexicographers do not always find the earliest occurrence in the works which have survived. [58]

While the troubles Bradley and Machan identify are real and certainly press acutely on the project of this book, they are limitable in terms of the claims dictionary evidence is understood to make. The moment when saying "according to the *MED*" becomes definitive history can be avoided by means of the qualifications that must be entered against *any* form of history. As recent scholarship on Middle English in very different modes has shown, the story the *OED* and *MED* make out of

---

[57] "General Explanations," *OED*, vol. I, p. xxiv and note (reprinted in "General Explanations," *OED2*, vol. I, p xxiv and p. xxiv n. 1). Diagram reproduced by permission of Oxford University Press.

[58] Machan, *Techniques of Translation*, p. 50.

textual fragments is no less hypothetical than *any* history because the eye turned to the past is not seeing the thing itself but a radically contingent trace.[59] It is only in the context of the authority dictionaries have been accorded in the past that we must remind ourselves of their "inadequate resources," but there is nothing inherent in dictionary evidence that forces us to regard it as anything but partial.

The more general forms of objection that might be lodged against lexical history would look to other modes and notice, in particular, that syntax and meter matter very much to Chaucer's achievement, and syntactic study, for one, could also take in the whole history of the language while deferring questions of linguistic kind. The fundamental disadvantage of syntactic analysis, however, is that it is much less easy (if it is even possible) to write a history of English syntax with anything like the iterative, historical detail of dictionaries. Olga Fischer has recently described the crucially disabling condition: "in syntax it is more difficult than in phonology, morphology and lexis to identify items to be compared" with the result that it is often impossible "to establish how far two surface structures actually represent the same construction."[60] In fact, most studies of English syntax compare surface structures precisely by pressing out the syntactic differences between texts in order to create a generic object that *can* be detailed. The examples Fischer herself chooses for their "illustrative" value are useless for historicizing Chaucer's forms, since, because of their "familiarity to the reader," Chaucer's are the forms she generally chooses.[61] As a back-formation of the very complexity of its historical object, syntactic history necessarily focuses, as Mustanoja does in his *Middle English Syntax*, on "the background of more general usage." And alongside Mustanoja's candid admission that his important study cannot be "definitive" there is the simple fact that even the complex history Mustanoja intended to provide (in a second volume meant to give a

---

59 I am thinking here of the account of the "fictionality" of documents comprising the historical record in Strohm, "False Fables and Historical Truth" in *Hochon's Arrow*, pp. 3–9. For an account of similar problems, focusing on the mediation of scribes in the making of that record, see Justice, "Inquisition, Speech, and Writing."

60 Fischer, "Syntax," p. 209.

61 *Ibid.*, p. 209. This point is made more generally about the *Cambridge History of English* in Howe (rev.), "*Cambridge History*," 126–7.

detailed account of "word-order and the structure of the complex sentence") has never been completed.[62]

The practical problem created by the difficulties of syntax becomes clear, however, in any attempt to enter a particular syntactic structure in the one syntactic history comparable to the *OED* and *MED* we have, Visser's *Historical Syntax of the English Language*. A historical survey of syntax more comprehensive than Visser's could hardly be imagined, but, notwithstanding this scope, Visser also acknowledges that "owing to the protean character of many constructions" the "lines of demarcation" and the "boundaries" he draws "are fluid and vague"[63] Confronted by Visser's monumental survey on the one hand, and such a vagueness with respect to syntactic objects on the other, the historian seeking to isolate the past of even a single one of Chaucer's structures must first *define* that structure and then coordinate his or her own definition with Visser's as it is schematized in Visser's table of contents. It will be useful I think to give an example of just the difficulty entailed here. If one wanted to historicize, say, the object clauses I discussed as they emerge from all the syntax of Chaucer's sources in the *canticus* of Book 3 of *Troilus*, it is possible to find some explanation of their form in Visser's history of "The heralding object þis" (§504) where the earliest example given comes from Laȝamon's *Brut*,

> Layamon 10950, þis iherde Coel þat icumen wæs Custance.

and the closest example to Chaucer comes from *Richard, Coer de Lion*:

> 13 . . . Coer de Lion 5035, Whenne kyng Richard wyst this, That ded was Jakes Denis, Allas, he sayde.[64]

But neither instance is precisely identical to Chaucer's syntax in form, if only because its most interesting feature is the inversion that actually places the "heralding object" in *secondary* position: "that the world diverseth . . . al *this* doth Love." In this sense, Visser's classification seems precisely inapposite in the case (since the object is not "heralded" by "this," but *explained* by it) so, of course, neither Chaucer's lines, nor anything like them, could appear as one of Visser's illustrations.

---

[62] Mustanoja, *Middle English Syntax*, p. 5.
[63] Visser, *Historical Syntax*, vol. I, p. vii.
[64] Visser, *Historical Syntax*, vol. I, pp. 459–60.

Furthermore, even if there *were* a precise characterization of the structure in the *canticus* (and I can find none), because Visser generally confines himself to "Syntactic Units with One Verb" (in Parts 1 and 2) and "Syntactic Units with Two Verbs" (in Part 3), the *repetition* of "that" clauses – the other interesting feature of Chaucer's syntax – could never be covered by Visser's survey. However copious that survey, in other words, it is still too limited to account for the very complexity that generates historical interest in this case. Or, to put it another way, to the very extent that Chaucer's syntax seems worthy of historicization – as it is "protean" in character and therefore "vague" of definition – it will escape Visser by the very bounds he must set himself in order to write syntactic history at all. For this same reason, even when a syntactic form in Chaucer's writing *is* actually described by Visser, the fundamental influence of, say, Latin or French on that form (in structures like those of the *canticus*) will remain undiscovered, since Visser's limits also keep him from examining anything but the influence of older English on later English forms. On the whole, then, and for these particular reasons, placing Chaucer's syntax in syntactic history can be nothing more than an anecdotal project.[65]

The disadvantages of metrical analysis and history as an analytic mode are even greater than the disadvantages of syntactic history. The development of English metrical patterns is easily viewed over a large space of literary time, and the same energetic scholarship that produced the *OED* and Visser's syntactic history also gave us Schipper's *History of English Versification* (1910) and Saintsbury's *History of English Prosody* (1906). More recently, Derek Attridge's *Rhythms of English Poetry* (1982) has given us a thorough analysis of Middle and Modern English meter in the light of generative linguistic theory. It is equally true that Chaucer's *historical* contribution to literary English has often been identified as metrical: as Fisher sees it, for example, the "movement toward metrical poetry" underway in English for more than 200 years before Chaucer culminates in Chaucer's poetry where we find "the first

---

[65] A recent exemplification of the anecdotal form is Roscow's *Syntax and Style in Chaucer's Poetry.* This study begins by calling itself a "selection" and proceeds by illustrations from early Middle English romance and contemporaneous alliterative poems of a select group of syntactic structures, and is therefore "by no means a comprehensive survey" (p. vii).

totally successful expression of the metrical system in English.[66] There are two problems with connecting Chaucer's meter to any history of English meter, however, and they are enormous problems. First, there is the well-documented doubt, arising from the progressive change in morphology that made Modern English out of Middle English, that Chaucer's meter, however identifiable in itself, actually *had* influence on later metrical writing. Derek Pearsall puts this problem succinctly: "The standard view is that the decline of sonant final –*e* after 1400 played havoc with Chaucer's versification, which made use of inflectional –*e* in a way that was already becoming archaic in his own day. The balance being lost, the artificial structure of the pentameter collapsed, and his successors fell back on rough four-stress native patterns."[67] Or, as Saintsbury puts it more mischievously, "the poet of the fifteenth century in England was a gamester, who suddenly found the dice to which he was accustomed loaded in quite a new fashion."[68] The effects of the decline of sonant final –*e* mean, first, that it is possible to elide Chaucer from an understanding of English meter altogether, to posit its "founding" not in Chaucer but in Tottel's *Miscellany* of 1567.[69] In this version of metrical history then, Chaucer's "invention" shouts into a wind of subsequent metrical practice that took a very long time to understand that Chaucer had achieved anything. This problem merges slightly with the second problem which is, again, the basic difficulty of identifying the linguistic object that *is* Chaucer's meter. Although Chaucer's poetry always figures prominently in histories of meter it is, more often than not, a *problem* for that history, and real uncertainty remains about what Chaucer's meter actually *was*. In recent decades, for example, James Southworth has explained that meter on the basis of the Latin *cursus*, Ian Robinson has claimed that Chaucer did not write regular iambic pentameter but, rather, lines that hovered between four and five stresses, and Susanne Woods has argued that

---

[66] Fisher, "Chaucer and the French Influence," p. 186. For a similar point see Eliason, *The Language of Chaucer's Poetry*, 26–7.

[67] Pearsall, *Lydgate*, p. 61. Pearsall gives this summary to note that this view, while "certainly true of what happened to Chaucerian verse in the sixteenth century" does not apply so well to Lydgate, "who uses final –*e* in much the same way under much the same conditions as Chaucer" (p. 61).

[68] Saintsbury, *History of English Prosody*, vol. I, p. 293.

[69] Thompson, *Founding of English Metre* (esp. pp. 2–3).

Chaucer never wrote iambic pentameter in the modern sense (but, rather, four-stress lines with one "promoted" secondary stress).[70] All these views may be credited or queried, but that is precisely the point. A history of Chaucer's meter cannot be written until study of that meter can say with some certainty what either a source for or a repetition of Chaucer's metrical practice would look like. In this important sense, a metrical history of Chaucer's achievement begins one considerable step behind a history of words and, even, of syntax – in a penumbra of contention.

I study words then, not only because lexical analysis knows its object in a history of great volume and breadth, but because its analytic certainties are greater and more promising than those provided by any other mode. Its simplicity is, in fact, its only real disadvantage, but, as the next four chapters will hope to show, the confusion that blinkers scholarly perceptions, although complex in formulation and layers of presumption, is itself often simple enough. Words are enough to cut through important misunderstandings and they also give us access to the more complex linguistic constructions they comprise and in which Chaucer's "invention" is more generally thought to reside. As I have worked here from reactions to these constructions, and from these constructions themselves to their history, it is equally possible to relate historical observations about Chaucer's words to their literary effects. The conviction that animates the next four chapters is, then, that words work by relating the English of Chaucer to the making of English, and they work precisely by keeping the complexities inherent in this relation both before us and clear from the very start.

[70] Southworth, *Prosody of Chaucer and His Followers*, pp. 25–72; Robinson, *Chaucer's Prosody*, pp. 109–31 and 151–85; Woods, *Natural Emphasis*, pp. 21–68. For a detailed survey of opinions about Chaucer's meter up until 1976 see Gaylord, "Scanning the Prosodists."

Traditional English

Thinkest thou there were no poets till Dan Chaucer?

Thomas Carlyle[1]

It will be well to begin here by acknowledging that, while the relation of Chaucer's English to tradition has generally been seen as one of innovation, the subject of this chapter has a perch in past comment. As far back as the "History of the English Language" which prefaces his *Dictionary* (1755) Samuel Johnson claimed that Chaucer's "diction was in general like that of his contemporaries."[2] Tyrwhitt concurred in his edition of Chaucer (1775),[3] as did James Lorimar in 1849,[4] and A. C. Champneys in his *History of English* (1893).[5] In our own century there has even been what Greenough and Kittredge characterize as an "active revolt . . . against the thesis that Chaucer 'made the English language.'"[6] As I noted in the last chapter, this revolt has never defeated the strong presumption of Chaucerian innovation, largely because it

---

[1] Carlyle, *Past and Present*, p. 112.

[2] Spurgeon (ed.), *Chaucer Criticism and Allusion*, vol. I, p. 411.

[3] "I think we may fairly conclude that the English language must have imbibed a strong tincture of the French long before the age of Chaucer, and consequently that he ought not to be charged as the importer of words and phrases, which he only used after the example of his predecessors and in common with his contemporaries." Spurgeon (ed.), *Chaucer Criticism and Allusion*, vol. I, p. 443.

[4] "Chaucer . . . took the language as he found it." Brewer (ed.), *Critical Heritage*, vol. II, p. 96.

[5] "Chaucer owes his language . . . to the writers of Middle English who preceded him." Champneys, *History of English*, p. 268.

[6] Greenough and Kittredge, *Words and Their Ways in English Speech*, p. 88. Greenough and Kittredge denounce the notion that "Chaucer actually imported many new words into our language" asserting that "almost every word that he used can be found somewhere at an earlier date" (p. 91).

dissents from the broad claim that Chaucer "made English" only to agree with the equally old claim that Chaucer made the *literary* language. But it is true that scholars such as Norman Davis emphasize Chaucer's "literary eminence" *by* suggesting that Chaucer's English is unremarkable in the history of the language ("Chaucer wrote in the English familiar to him from business as well as from court circles in London and Westminster").[7] When Davis enters his strongest opposition to Chesterton's suggestion that Chaucer had "toss[ed] off a little trifle called the English Language" (which he called Chesterton's "distorted account of the more general history of English") he does so by stressing the conservatism of even Chaucer's literary English:[8]

> When foreign-derived words do appear they are more often than not thoroughly naturalized in literary English before Chaucer used them . . . Innovations he certainly made, and in absolute terms they are fairly numerous as far as we can tell, but they are usually either discrete – and formed on well-known models and so inconspicuous – or strikingly designed to meet a particular situation.[9]

The view that Chaucer's English was "formed on well-known models" may be only a fitful one, but, in its recurrence, it does form a critical tradition of its own.

But how was Chaucer's English "traditional" and what, in that sense, does "traditional" mean? As in the competing claim, specificity is the rub here, and the definitional problems dogging attempts to describe the linguistic forms Chaucer originated emerge again, in a different form, in attempts to describe the forms he inherited. If we beat a retreat to the notion that Chaucer's linguistic innovation was only "occasional," as Elliott does in his compendious discussion of Chaucer's English, in what sense is the presumption of Chaucerian innovation to be so qualified?[10] To put it a different way, if Chaucer, in John Burrow's words, "cultivated an English style which is much more traditional than people realize," why have people *not* realized

---

7 Davis, "Language and Versification," p. xxx
8 Davis, "Chaucer and the English Language," 27.
9 *Ibid.*, 33. See also Davis, "Chaucer and Fourteenth-Century English," pp. 72–4. For Chesterton's claim, see my chapter 1, p. 14.
10 "Occasionally, though not very often, Chaucer even coined a new word." Elliott, *Chaucer's English*, p. 19.

it?[11] The problem for linguistic history is that the "tradition" of precedent writing to which Chaucer most frequently acknowledges some debt and whose filiations are most readily traced in his writing is not a tradition in English, but a tradition in French or Italian or Latin. As Norman Blake puts it, "Chaucer is different from many of his contemporaries, particularly in his acquaintance with foreign literature."[12] When Rossell Hope Robbins speaks of Chaucer's "models" he is not referring to an English past but a Continental one: for him Chaucer was "the Father of English Poetry" precisely because he began his career as a *"poète français."*[13] Although we have no sure evidence that the young Chaucer was a "writer of French court poetry" as Robbins claims he was,[14] his early writing gives clear evidence of a deep involvement with such poetry, and it is fair, in this sense, to understand Chaucer's poetics as emerging from that involvement, newly adapting "the skilled discipline, the polished speech, the elegance and the flexibility of Romance metres" to English idiom.[15] Lines of one of Chaucer's earliest works, the *Book of the Duchess*, have been shown to be direct imitation of the first lines of Froissart's *Le Paradys d'Amour.*[16] The most distinctive and skillful features of Chaucer's style, as Muscatine has amply shown,

---

[11] Burrow, *Ricardian Poetry*, p. 12.

[12] Blake goes on to say that Chaucer's "knowledge of French and Italian provided him with that sense of tradition which English could not and which his contemporaries lacked." *English Language in Medieval Literature*, p. 168. But Blake also doubles back on this distinction a little later in this same paragraph: "[Chaucer's] reaction was the same in essence if not in quality as that of most other writers in English. He attempted to introduce French linguistic habits into English and he extended the application of those features of language traditionally used by English authors" (p. 169). There is something irreconcilable I think in the joint positions that Chaucer is "different from many of his contemporaries . . . in his acquaintance with foreign literature" and the claim that he was like them as he introduced "French linguistic habits into English." In this contradiction I think Blake comes close to articulating the problem I am trying to describe here without acknowledging that he is doing so. Crucially absent from Blake's description of course is what "those features of language traditionally used by English authors" actually *were.*

[13] Robbins, "Geoffroi Chaucier Poète Français," 106.

[14] *Ibid.*, 100. For the survival of such early French poetry in one manuscript see Wimsatt, *Chaucer and the Poems of "Ch.".*

[15] Clemen, *Chaucer's Early Poetry*, p. 8.

[16] See Brewer's schematic of this imitation in "English and European Traditions," pp. 2–3.

can be explained by studious attention to French tradition.[17] All this evidence issues naturally in the view that the "great work" of Chaucer's life, as James Wimsatt puts it, was the "development of an English poetic tradition" that "involved the transference into English of the French tradition fed and supplemented by the greater literatures in Latin and Italian."[18]

The abundant testimony of Continental traditions gains still more force when studies of Chaucer turn their gaze – as Burrow recommends they do – to earlier English writing, since, however extraordinary some of this writing may be in its own right, Chaucer seems to owe little or nothing to it. As John Fisher puts it, there is "no evidence that [Chaucer] had ever read any literary English."[19] Chaucer's writing does not have precedent because, as David Wallace observes, there is "no antecedent tradition of English poetry for Chaucer to relate to."[20] The phrasing of both Fisher's and Wallace's claims is crucial here because they do not deny precedence to "literary English" nor do they really suggest that there was no "antecedent tradition" for Chaucer to draw upon; rather, they suggest that extant traditions do not *explain* what Chaucer did: he did not "read" what *may* have pre-existed him; he cannot be "related" to antecedent traditions *we* know of. But it is this dead end more than anything else that actually serves as evidence for the claim that Chaucer's formal and linguistic debts were wholly Continental. The widely accepted theory advanced by Laura Hibbard Loomis that Chaucer knew the texts of *Guy of Warwick*, *Horn Child*, and *Beves of Hamtoun* as he found them in the Auchinleck manuscript (a book she takes as one Chaucer plausibly had "in his hands") offers a clarifying case to this point.[21] It is true that P. M. Kean's study of Chaucer and the "making of English poetry" finds the roots of that poetry in the "English tradition" of "plain and easy verse style in

---

[17] I refer here to the whole of Muscatine's *Chaucer and the French Tradition*.
[18] Wimsatt, "Chaucer and French Poetry," p. 111. For expansions of this view in terms of particular texts see also two other articles by Wimsatt: "Guillaume de Machaut and Chaucer's *Troilus and Criseyde*" and "Machaut's *Lay de Confort* and Chaucer's *Book of the Duchess*."
[19] Fisher, *Importance of Chaucer*, p. 106.
[20] Wallace, "Chaucer's Continental Inheritance," p. 22.
[21] Loomis, "Chaucer and the Auchinleck MS," (for the quoted phrase see p. 111).

romance narrative" which she identifies, in particular, with the Auchinleck texts.[22] And Brewer's important study of the relationship between Chaucer's writing and both "English and European traditions" also focuses on these romances as the "source of [Chaucer's] first poetic nourishment," the "English tap-root of Chaucer's poetry." But Brewer also notes that these romances are, on the whole, "too simple" to be considered "great literature" and, at best, they "tell only half the story."[23] John Burrow tells us himself why this earlier English style prevents us from calling Chaucer's English "traditional" when Chaucer's knowledge of it is, nonetheless, so clear:

> Most of the 'lost literature of medieval England', after all, was lost as much to Chaucer and Gower as it is to us; and much of what we do know (Anglo-Saxon poetry, for example) they did not. Collections such as the Auchinleck MS, despite their great bulk, offered little work of sufficient distinction to command the respect of sophisticated London readers. If that was their native heritage (and where else are we to look for it?), then it was a poor thing – poorer by far than the inheritance of later English poets, and poorer even than that of some of their own English contemporaries.[24]

To see the Auchinleck romances as the "vigorous wild stock upon which were grafted Chaucer's other more literary and sophisticated styles" requires Burrow (like Brewer) to acknowledge that Chaucer records this debt most explicitly in the burlesque of *Sir Thopas*.[25] As Derek Pearsall puts it, "the only debt, in fact, which Chaucer can be proved to owe to earlier English poetry is one which he thought worth paying in withering scorn,"[26] or, to put it even more bluntly, as A. C. Spearing does, *Sir Thopas* "has the effect not just of biting the hand that fed but snapping it off at the wrist."[27] When it surveys what preceded Chaucer in Middle English, Chaucer scholarship finds precedent English lacking exactly those qualities that make Chaucer's English worth

---

[22] Kean, *Chaucer and the Making of English Poetry*, esp. vol. I, pp. 1– 23 (p. 9 for the quoted phrase).

[23] Brewer, "English and European Traditions," pp. 4 and 15.

[24] Burrow, *Ricardian Poetry*, p. 23. (Burrow's reference here is to Wilson, *Lost Literature of Medieval England*.)

[25] Burrow, *Ricardian Poetry*, p. 21.

[26] Pearsall, *Old English and Middle English Poetry*, p. 199.

[27] Spearing, *Medieval to Renaissance in English Poetry*, p. 35.

explaining. From collective frustration with traditions that are on the whole so "poor" it is a simple step back to the Continent where Chaucer's innovative engagement can again be strenuously confirmed.

There has been one other route to finding a tradition for Chaucer and it requires mention here because it solves the evidentiary difficulties I have been outlining by the simple expedience of eliminating the very *need* for evidence. This is the route that claims Chaucer was "traditional," not because he extended some lineage of precedent English writing, but because he imbibed an ambient "Englishness" necessarily present in all English literary making. Chesterton again provides an early and extreme example of this view when he describes Chaucer as an "Englishman" because he not only "made a national language," but "came very near to making a nation." For Chesterton, Chaucer was not only the "Father of English poetry" but the "Father of his Country, rather in the style of George Washington."[28] The breadth of this claim gives it its force and the self-evidence of its categorical distinctions means that "Englishness" itself requires no real definition: "Yet despite this close familiarity with French and Italian thought and expression, how very English Chaucer in essence remains! So English, indeed, that many passages from his work can still be quoted for their typical English quality."[29] Understanding the "typical English quality" of Chaucer's writing as an "essence" makes it possible to describe almost any aspect of Chaucer's writing *as* "English." This definition also precludes the need to posit any mechanism for the communication of this quality between different writers' works: Chaucer, like his predecessors, since he is English, simply breathes Englishness in. The view is a particularly exuberant form of literary nationalism that wills a tradition into existence as a simple function of geography. In John Speirs's words: "[Chaucer] became consciously an Englishman as distinct from a Frenchman or Italian, as he became conscious of the powers – particularly the dramatic power – of his English language as distinct from the powers of French, Latin, Italian."[30] In the face of such claims,

---

[28] Chesterton, *Chaucer*, p. 8 (for the chapter on "Chaucer as an Englishman" see pp. 186–216).

[29] Clemen, *Chaucer's Early Poetry*, pp. 7–8.

[30] Speirs, *Chaucer the Maker*, p. 29. Speirs's effort sits squarely (and explicitly) in the Leavisite attempt to outline the "Great Tradition" in English, and his concern is less to

the powers of Chaucer's poetry are the powers of English, and the tradition supporting Chaucer's writing becomes, not the roots that explain and prepare his literary achievement, but the name given to those achievements when they are identified.

In their own complexity, discussions of the traditional aspects of Chaucer's English stand in almost exact parallel to the discussion of its innovation I described in the previous chapter. English roots for Chaucer have been sought in a tradition where they have not been found (the Auchinleck romances) or they have been found in a tradition that is not actually there (Englishness). And it is the homologies in definitional method that really make possible the stunningly contradictory persistence of the view that Chaucer's English "started a tradition" in the face of the equally persistent view that Chaucer's English had native roots. The definitional and methodological deficiencies that characterize both views assure that neither can supplant the other because neither can muster sufficient evidence to establish an unequivocal claim. The Gordian knot may be cut, it would seem logical to suggest at this point, by conceding that *both* views are correct: Chaucer's English is innovative *and* traditional at the same time. This is really Brewer's unstressed but essential point (Chaucer, he says, "began a revolution in poetic diction" even as he employed a "traditional style"). But this chapter will suggest – as, really, will the whole of this book – that such a synthetic assessment is sufficiently over-simple to be itself essentially incorrect. To trace the history of techniques I described in the previous chapter in earlier English is to see that neither a "traditional" nor an "innovative" Chaucer is a complete Chaucer. Simply put, Chaucer's writing is traditional in precisely those linguistic forms that have often been thought to be most new. Proof for such an assertion comes when investigative emphasis is shifted away from what Chaucer may have had "in his hands" toward the particular continuities between Chaucer's linguistic *practice* and the practice of other Middle

connect Chaucer with what came before than with the "great English novelists" (p. 201). Similarly, Ian Robinson's *Chaucer and the English Tradition*, despite some attention to the *Owl and the Nightingale* (esp. pp. 36–41) concerns itself, not with the "English tradition" that preceded Chaucer but the "creation of a national literature" in Chaucer (p. 283). As Robinson revealingly notes, "the *Parliament of Fowls* belongs rather with D. H. Lawrence than with the modern critics" (p. 67).

English writers. In the words I take as my epigraph Carlyle ventures to shock his readers with the idea that there were "poets" before Chaucer because he assumes that they will not be able to name any. I take this as a starting point because I want to suggest that the search for such a poet (or for poetry equal to Chaucer's) has been the limiting assumption in perceiving the traditional nature of Chaucer's novelty. As I will argue in the following pages, Chaucer's language is not traditional by virtue of an interlocking line of influence – because he studied his predecessors the way Spenser studied him and Milton studied Spenser and Keats studied Milton – but by virtue of the set of common linguistic procedures employed by Chaucer and earlier Middle English writers. The connection is circumstantial, not patrimonial; the coercive force is not the strong example of earlier excellence but the common linguistic constraints of writing in the same language at roughly the same time. Chaucer employed the traditional procedures he did, not *because* they were employed in earlier texts, but because he found before him the same linguistic possibilities that made those procedures essential to Middle English literary making.

I

The chief obstacle which faces any discussion of the traditional nature of Chaucer's English is the long-standing presumption that the defining feature of that English was its innovative naturalization of Romance forms. Lexical study has, moreover, made a serious contribution to this presumption in the form of Mersand's *Chaucer's Romance Vocabulary*, and it is therefore worth examining Mersand's conclusions carefully at this juncture.[31] Mersand was not, as it happens, principally concerned with lexical innovation; as his title announces, he began by wanting to measure the "extent of Chaucer's Romance vocabulary." Mersand marshals most of his elaborate apparatus of tables, word-counts and percentages to take that measure, and, once he has it, he turns his statistics "to trace as definitely as possible the stages of [Chaucer's]

---

[31] Juliette de Caluwé-dor proposes such a reassessment in "Chaucer's Contribution to the English Vocabulary" but her article only treats a few letters of Chaucer's vocabulary in the *Canterbury Tales*.

linguistic development."[32] However, Mersand does devote a chapter to "Chaucer's Contribution to the English Vocabulary", which he calls Chaucer's "gifts to the English language," and, when he arrives, finally, at a series of "definite conclusions" the second of these points announces that Chaucer "introduced about 1,180 Romance words into the English vocabulary."[33] And it is this "fact" that has most intrigued Mersand's later readers.

It is fair to ask then whether Mersand's measure has any validity – whether, on the one hand, such figures count the "contribution" Mersand claims they do, and, on the other hand, whether such a count would mean anything to linguistic history even if it were accurate. In the half century since Mersand wrote, opinion has been decidedly mixed on this question. Mersand's figures have made their way into at least one history of the English language,[34] and they have been used to fortify two of what I considered in the last chapter to be the three more important attempts to describe Chaucer's originality in recent decades. Derek Brewer relies on Mersand's numbers to substantiate his claim that Chaucer "began a revolution in poetic diction," and John Fisher uses them to substantiate his claim that "Chaucer naturalized in English a new poetic mode and language."[35] But even Brewer has reservations about the accuracy of Mersand's numbers ("his details," he says, "are not always unquestionable").[36] And, with the advent of the *MED*, Norman Davis criticized Mersand's figures on the simple ground that they had now become outmoded: "The details given in Joseph Mersand's book about the priority of particular words are often unacceptable, partly because views of the dating of numerous works have changed since it was written, partly because new information, especially that collected

---

[32] Mersand, *Chaucer's Romance Vocabulary*, p. vii.

[33] For the chapter see pp. 53–7, for "General Conclusions" see pp. 137–8, and for the quoted phrases see pp. 56 and 137 in Mersand, *Chaucer's Romance Vocabulary*.

[34] Barbara Strang must rely on Mersand's statistics in her *History of English* when she claims that "over a thousand French words, for instance, are first recorded in Chaucer's work" (p. 184).

[35] See Brewer, "English and European Traditions," pp. 3 (and n. 1), 24 n. 2, 27, and 36; and Fisher, "Chaucer and the French Influence," pp. 180 n. 11 and 181 n. 16.

[36] Brewer, "English and European Traditions, p. 24 n. 2.

for the [*MED*] supersedes what he could learn from the [*OED*]."[37] But the most sweeping objections entered against Mersand's "definite conclusions" are theoretical. One of Mersand's reviewers weighed in with an attack on the blind faith in dictionaries *Chaucer's Romance Vocabulary* seems to embody:

> Part, if not most, of the reason that Dr. Mersand did not evaluate his evidence properly, is due to his misunderstanding of the results that lexicography obtains, and of the way in which to use such a dictionary as the *Oxford*. His method is to check Chaucer's Romance words with the *OED*, and whenever a quotation from Chaucer is earlier than any other given, to list it as an importation made by Chaucer. He states: "Chaucer used, at least in the opinion of the editors of the *New English Dictionary*, 1,180 Romance words for the first time." It is far from true that the editors of the *OED* had such an "opinion." The lexicographer hasn't "opinions"; he is merely doing the best he can with the evidence at hand.[38]

This objection speaks directly to Mersand's presentation of his evidence – his habit of calling "first uses" in the record "contributions" – but goes as well to his book's founding faith: the consistent belief that the Middle English record provides secure evidence for the lexical practice of Middle English speakers or writers. I noted Tim Machan's objection to neologisms gleaned from dictionaries in the previous chapter,[39] but as Norman Eliason makes the fundamental point simply, " 'first usages' like this," he says, "signify little."[40]

And yet, Mersand's figures are not so dubious as his most exacting critics have suggested. When checked carefully against the *OED* Mersand's evidence shows surprising accuracy, especially given its complexity and volume. An examination of every one of the 1,180 words Mersand describes as Chaucer's "contribution" to English in relation to its respective entry in the *OED* finds only ten words that Mersand mistakenly described as a "first use" in Chaucer.[41]

---

[37] Davis "Chaucer and Fourteenth-Century English," p. 73.
[38] Hulbert (rev.), "*Chaucer's Romance Vocabulary* (J. Mersand)," 302.
[39] See p. 42 above. [40] Eliason, *Language of Chaucer's Poetry*, 104.
[41] These words (which I give, first, as Mersand lists them in his appendix and, second, parenthetically, according to the headword in the *OED* that treats them) are "accion n." (action sb.), "allegeaunce n." (allegeaunce sb1.), "caytif a." (caitiff sub. & a.), "luxures n." (luxury sb.), luxurious a. (luxurious a.), "pencel n." (pencel sb.), "preys

Re-examining Mersand's statistics in the *MED*, as Davis suggests ought to be done, also finds that his figures generally hold. Although many of the "first uses" in Mersand's total are eliminated by *MED* evidence (193 because they are cited in earlier texts, 240 because Mersand classes some words as "Romance" which it does not seem right to so classify, 72 by the simple redefinition of word boundaries between the *OED* and the *MED*), an additional 427 Romance borrowings that Mersand does *not* cite are recorded for the first time in Chaucer in the *MED*.[42] Instead of the 1,180 Romance words that Mersand finds first record of in Chaucer's work, then, the *MED* itself shows 1,102 such words. The theoretical objections to Mersand's figures are an equally – if more understandably – unfair reaction to what might be called Mersand's numerical intensity. It is true that Mersand's statistics may not conduce to the conclusion he says they do: they are not (as Mersand puts it) "objective, scientific scholar-

n." (price sb.), "skarmish n." (skirmish sb.), "solsticium n." (solistice sb.), "staunchen v." (stanch v.). The discrepancies here are often the result of incorrectly matching forms in Chaucer's texts to their appropriate headwords in the *OED*. Mersand seems not to have noticed, for example, that there was a separate entry for "pencel sb." (which has early Middle English witnesses) and resolved Chaucerian "pencel" to modern "pencil sb" for which there is an *OED* entry showing no witnesses earlier than Chaucer. Mersand similarly looks for Chaucer's "solsticium" under "solstitium sb." without noticing that the entry for "solstice sb" in the *OED* subsumes similar forms. Mersand is not always completely in the wrong in these cases either. There is clearly room for debate in the location of Chaucerian "preys n.," which Mersand seems to have located under "praise sb." which is, in fact, the word's meaning in the context of the line of the *Monk's Tale* (VII, 2647) from which he draws it. The *OED* groups similar meanings under "price sb.," another potential significance of the Middle English word, but the division is confusing, I think, within the *OED* itself.

42 Mersand finds 4,189 Romance words in a total vocabulary of 8,072 words. He is, on the whole, more eager than I have been to call a word of "Romance origin." In addition to words derived from "Old French," "Anglo-French," and "Latin" he includes "compound nouns of which only one element is Romance" and "words with a Romance suffix." (*Chaucer's Romance Vocabulary*, pp. 39–43). Using the *Riverside Chaucer* and the *MED* I use a larger total for Chaucer's vocabulary (9, 117 words) but a smaller total of Romance words (3, 820 words). For my own definition of "Romance languages" I have followed the consensual definition offered by the *OED* (s. v. "Romance sb. & a.," I.,1.): ". . . commonly used as a generic or collective name for the whole group of languages descended from Latin." My total for Chaucer's Romance vocabulary collects every word in Part 2 of this book containing the following etymological designations: "AF" (Anglo-French), "AL" (Anglo-Latin), "CF" (Central French or Continental French), "L" (Latin), "NF" (Northern French), "OF" (Old French), "It." (Italian), "ML" (Medieval Latin), and "ONF" (Old Northern French).

ship" or an "answer" precisely because, as Machan and others note, first recorded uses are not complete evidence of linguistic practice.[43] On the other hand, Mersand's intensity leads him to grasp the horns of a dilemma that Chaucer scholarship has, on the whole, failed to discern. Mersand's use of dictionaries may reveal a naive faith, but the faith itself is the *same* faith so many Chaucer scholars have themselves professed – that Chaucer's borrowed Romance forms substantially account for the primacy of his English. The only difference between Mersand and these scholars is the level of detail Mersand is willing to commit to in making the standard assertion: where Chaucer criticism has developed a kind of politesse about specifying Chaucer's "contribution" too carefully, Mersand commits the sin of speaking plainly. He investigates mechanisms of linguistic creation that studies of Chaucer evoke but have preferred, on the whole, to leave occulted. In this sense, *Chaucer's Romance Vocabulary*, doubtless unwittingly, but nonetheless emphatically, gets into real trouble because it calls a bluff.

Mersand's work is useful, then, precisely because it embarrasses a body of Chaucer scholarship that has been woefully short on details in its own claims. Like Wimsatt later, Mersand understands Chaucer's "development of an English poetic tradition" to involve "the transference into English of the French tradition fed and supplemented by the greater literatures in Latin and Italian," and his copious figures enumerate that transference in their every lexical detail. Mersand's figures are dangerous because they open presumptions to all-too-careful scrutiny – they make a central assumption of Chaucerian appreciation look ridiculous by voicing it. Accept this danger, however, take Mersand at his word (or at his words), and Mersand's details are boldly and helpfully confirming of the *kind* of originality so much scholarship has credited Chaucer with. In large, the 1,180 words in Mersand's list give a careful account of Chaucer's linguistic activities as they survive in the record: they follow the footprints of his novelty as carefully as those prints could be followed in 1937. In each detail, Mersand's list writes the story of Chaucer's

---

[43] Mersand, *Chaucer's Romance Vocabulary*, p. 20.

lexical invention in the instance of each of his newly recorded words. They give procedural flesh to the gauzy portrait of a young Chaucer, recently or concurrently, *poète français*, who, in his infatuation with French writing, decides to translate the *Roman de la Rose* into English. So, for example, Mersand's story shows this young Chaucer translating the first four lines of the French *roman* without relying heavily on borrowed forms (and here I will make the convenient assumption that Chaucer translated seriatim, beginning with line 1):[44]

Many men sayn that in sweveninges	Maintes genz dient que en songes
Ther nys but fables and lesynges;	N'a se fables non et mençonges;
But men may some swevenes	sen Mès l'en puet tex songes songier
Whiche hardely that false ne ben . . .	Qui ne sont mie mençongier . . .
(*Romaunt*, 1–4)	(*Roman*, 1–4)[45]

It shows Chaucer reaching line 5, needing to supply a deficiency in English in anticipation of the rhyme-word "warraunt," which he wants to use in line 6 (this word is earlier adduced in English, although it is doubtless inspired here by its Old French root, "garant"),[46] and importing "apparaunt adj." from the French text for the first time in English:[47]

---

[44] "Fable" is the one exception here, although it is unremarkable in Mersandian terms since it is often adduced in the English record before Chaucer. See *MED*, s. v. "fable n" and (because Mersand would only have had the *OED* entry available to him) see also *OED*, s. v. "fable sb."

[45] I quote the *Roman de la Rose* from Sutherland (ed.), *The Romaunt of the Rose and Le Roman de la Rose*. For his text Sutherland uses Paris, Bibliothèque Nationale, MS Fr. 1573 and emends it heavily with Copenhagen, Royal Library, MS Fr. LV, on the presumption that these manuscripts give a text close to the one Chaucer had before him when translating Fragment A (pp. xv–xxii). I quote Chaucer's *Romaunt* from the *Riverside Chaucer*, however, since Sutherland takes his text from Thynne (see his edition p. xxxix). Hereafter all quotations from the *Roman* and the *Romaunt* will be quoted from these two editions and cited by line-number in my text.

[46] See the etymology in *OED*, s. v. "warrant sb1."

[47] Because I readjust the date of composition of the *Romaunt* (see Part 2, p. 232) I take Chaucer's use of "apparaunt adj." as first although the *MED* cites it first in "a1393 Gower CA."

But afterward ben *apparaunt.*	Ainz sont après bien *aparant.*
This may I drawe to warraunt . . .	Si en puis traire a garant . . .
(*Romaunt,* 5–6)	(*Roman,* 5–6)

As a constituent of the 1,180 "contributions" in Mersand's appendix "apparaunt adj." shows *how* Chaucer used French to make English in the writing of his poetry.[48] The other 1,179 words in the list simply repeat this implicit anecdote with enough accretive force to establish such neologizing as a practice defining Chaucer's vocabulary throughout his career, even allowing for the deficiencies of the record. As far as they go, in other words, Mersand's numbers have a claim.

In fact, the fairest criticism that might be addressed to Mersand's conclusions is not that his "first usages signify little" but that they are not made by him to signify quite enough. When the procedure that opens a window in the record onto Chaucer's significant borrowing is applied to *all* of Chaucer's vocabulary it not only threatens Mersand's concluding claims but the crucial *donnée* that both subtends and issues from them. That is, pushed still further, the statistical procedures that recover Chaucer's "gifts to English" also recover the larger Middle English lexical activity that puts those "gifts" in a general shade. Looking carefully at dictionaries shows that Chaucer's other Romance vocabulary derived from a second and equally voluminous pattern of borrowing; it shows that Chaucer got most of his Romance vocabulary from the store of extant Middle English, not from French or Latin or Italian. More of Chaucer's Romance vocabulary (2,718 words) was borrowed by his Middle English predecessors than by Chaucer himself, and to set out the "contributions" these other texts make to the record (as I do for the most frequently recurring texts in the following list) is to construct the very canon of earlier English that survives before Chaucer:

[48] Mersand, *Chaucer's Romance Vocabulary,* p. 160.

Number of new romance borrowings used by Chaucer	General date and text	*MED* title stencils[49]
338	c. 1200–75 *Ancrene Wisse*	(?a1200) Ancr.; a1250 Ancr. (Nero); c1225 Ancr. (Tit); c1230 (Corp-C); c1275 Ancr. (Cleo)
47	c. 1225–1300 *King Horn*	(?c1225) Horn; c1300 Horn (Ld)
42	c. 1250–1300 *Floris and Blauncheflur*	(c1250) Floris; (c1250) Floris (Auch); (c1250) Floris (Suth); a1300 Floris (Vit)
356	c. 1280–1325 *South English Legendary*	(?c1280) SLeg (Eg); (c1280) SLeg (Pep); (c1290) SLeg (Ld); c1300 SLeg (Ld); c1300 SLeg (Hrl); a1325 SLeg (Corp-C))[50]
104	c. 1300 *Kyng Alisaunder*	(?a1300) KAlex. (Auch); (?a1300) KAlex. (Ld)
64	c. 1300 *Arthur & Merlin*	(?a1300) Arth.& M.
13	c. 1300 *Bevis of Hamtoun*	(?c1300) Bevis
29	c. 1300 *Guy of Warwick*	(?c1300) Guy (1); (?a1300) Guy (2)
80	c. 1300–25 Robert of Gloucester's *Chronicle*	(c1300) Glo.Chron.A.; (a1325) Glo.Chron.B
96	c. 1303 Robert Mannyng's *Handlyng Synne*	(c1303) Mannyng HS
97	c. 1325 *Cursor Mundi*	(a1325) Cursor
14	c1330 *Seven Sages of Rome*	c1330 7 Sages(1); (?a1350) 7 Sages(2)
88	c.1338 Robert Mannyng's *Chronicle*	(a1338) Mannyng Chron.Pt.1; (a1338) Mannyng Chron.Pt.2
74	c. 1340 *Aȝenbite of Inwit*	(1340) Ayenb.
22	c. 1333 William Shoreham's *Poems*	(a1333) Shoreham Poems
55	c. 1340 Richard Rolle's Psalter	(c1340) Rolle Psalter (UC 64); (c1340) Rolle Psalter (Ld); (c1340) Rolle Psalter (Sid)

[49] I give *MED* stencils here to make clear the degree to which the "text" of each of the works for which I offer tabulation is assembled from a variety of witnesses.

[50] For the sake of concision I have elided the indications of individual saint's lives that accompany each *MED* citation for this collection (though they are given in full in Part 2 below). The stencils I give here do, however, reflect every difference in date and manuscript in which tabulated words appear.

These 16 texts account for 1,519 of Chaucer's Romance words alone. Without even suggesting that Chaucer knew these texts (for he probably knew only a fraction of them), it is possible to see that, in precisely this *kind* of "innovation," Chaucer's practice rested squarely on a precedent tradition.

Mersand's method, if not his conclusions, puts this second category of vocabulary before us then, and it also, if even more implicitly, proposes that a second pattern of word acquisition was crucial to Chaucer's practice. Take, for example, the Auchinleck text *Guy of Warwick* which can be examined for its "contributions" exactly as Mersand examines Chaucer's writing. Such scrutiny finds the anonymous translator of the English text arriving at the lines of French *Gui de Warwic* in which Felice refuses to marry Gui, as she had promised she would after he has earned renown:

> "Ne vus hastez mie, sires Gui!
> Uncore n'en estes tant preisé,
> Que alsi bon n'ait el regné.
> Preuz estes mult e vaillant,
> En estur hardi e cumbatant;
> Si sur totes riens vus amasse,
> E l'amur de mei vus grantasse,
> Tant devendirez *amerus*
> Que tut en serriez pereçus;
> Armes ne querriez mes porter,
> Ne vostre pris eshalcier;
> Jo mesfereie, ço m'est avis,
> Se par mei perdisez vostre pris."
> (*Gui de Warewic*, 1056–68)[51]

In forming his Middle English version of these lines this translator generally sticks very close to his source and so, on the whole, he simply finds extant English equivalents for the French here. At "amerus," however, he simply imports the word in his source – to make "amorous adj." – according to the record, for the first time in English:

> "No rape þe nouȝt so, sir Gij;
> ȝete nartow nouȝt y-preysed so,
> Þat me ne may finde oþer mo;

---

[51] I quote this text here and throughout this chapter from Ewert (ed.), *Gui de Warewic*.

> Orped þou art and of grete miȝt,
> God kniȝt & ardi in fiȝt:
> & ȝif ich þe hadde mi loue y-ȝeue,
> To welden it while þat y liue,
> Sleuþe þe schuld ouercome:
> Namore wostow of armes loue,
> No comen in turnament no in fiȝt.
> So *amerous* þou were anon riȝt."
> (*Guy of Warwick*, 1132–42)[52]

After "amorous adj." appears here, the *MED* shows, it finds its way into Mannyng's *Handlyng Synne*, where it is also drawn from that English text's French source (in this case William Wadington's *Manuel des Pechiez*),[53] and, when Chaucer is translating the *Roman de la Rose*, he also uses the word, as he sets the scene of the "swevenyng":

Than yonge folke entenden ay	Lors estuet ioines genz entendre
Forto ben gay and *amorous* –	A estre gais e *amoreus*,
The tyme is than so saverous.	Por le tens bel e savoureus.
(*Romaunt*, 82–4)	(*Roman*, 78–80)

If we only compared Chaucer's *Romaunt* with the *Roman* we would be inclined to think that Chaucer "borrows" this word anew from his source, as it is prompted by the French. If we set the lexical history of this word in *Guy of Warwick* behind this use, the comparison would still suggest that Chaucer *thought* he was using the word for the first time, since we cannot be sure, although Chaucer eventually knew *Guy*, that he knew that text at this stage in his career. But this lexical history must frame *our* understanding of Chaucer's borrowing, since the implacable (because recorded) fact of the earlier borrowing makes Chaucer's borrowing not an invention, but a repetition. It is by telling the story of such repetition, moreover, as Mersand's lexical history tells it, that we must also say that the "new" borrowings Chaucer used when translating the *Roman de la Rose* were "traditional": the precedent course of this practice that can be traced before Chaucer in text after text is a "tradition." It is, in this sense, that even *new* borrowing,

[52] I quote this text here and throughout this chapter from Zupitza (ed.), *The Romance of Guy of Warwick*.

[53] For Mannyng's text as well as his French source see the *en face* edition in Mannyng, *Handlyng Synne*, Furnivall (ed.) line 7987 (English) and line 6269 (French).

although always understood as the basis of Chaucer's "making of English," can be understood to be the opposite of innovation in Middle English – in fact, it was the *general* practice of the literary language that Chaucer's English simply joined.

2

The traditional nature of Chaucer's new Romance borrowings can also be established by approaching them through ends and not means – that is, through the *effects* that a linguistic capacity expanded by new vocabulary would produce. A useful point of departure here would be the achievement of one of Chaucer's predecessors, and effects rich enough for the purposes of this analysis are easily found in the early thirteenth-century treatise on the devotional life called *Ancrene Wisse*. Of particular interest in the passage I want to examine is the process by which the conventions of the *genre* of romance become an extended metaphor for this life, stressing its appeal, and, in that process, making the very *act* of borrowing itself constitutive of the claim:

> A leafdi wes mid hire fan biset al abuten, hire lond al destruet, & heo al poure, inwið an eorðene castel. A mihti kinges luue wes þah biturnd up on hire swa unimete swiðe þet he for wohlech sende hire his sonden, an efter oðer, ofte somet monie; send hire beawbelez baðe feole & feire, sucurs of liueneð, help of his hehe hird to halden hire castel. Heo underfeng al as on unrecheles, & swa wes heard iheortet þet hire luue ne mahte he neauer beo þe neorre. Hwet wult tu mare? He com him seolf on ende, schawde hire his feire neb, as þe þe wes of alle men feherest to bihalden, spec se swiðe swoteliche & wordes se murie þet ha mahten deade arearen to liue, wrahte feole wundres & dude muchele meistries biuoren hire ehsihðe, schawde hire his mihte, talde hire of his kinedom, bead to makien hire cwen of al þet he ahte. Al this ne heold nawt. Nes þis hoker wunder? For heo nes neauer wurðe forte beon his þuften. Ah swa, þurh his deboneirte, luue hefde ouercumen him þet he seide on ende: Dame, þu art iweorret & þine van beoð se stronge þet tu ne maht nanesweis wiðute mi sucurs edfleon hare honden, þet ha ne don þe to scheome deað efter al þi weane. Ich chulle, for þe luue of þe, neome þet feht up o me & arudde þe of ham þe þi deað secheð. Ich wat þah to soðe þet ich schal bituhen ham neomen deaðes wunde; & ich hit wulle heorteliche forte

ofgan þin heorte. Nu þenne biseche ich þe, for þe luue þet ich cuðe
þe, þet tu luuie me lanhure efter þe ilke dede, dead, hwen þu naldes,
liues. Þes king dude al þus: arudde hire of alle hire van & wes him
seolf to wundre ituket & islein on ende; þurh miracle aras þah from
deaðe to liue. Nere þeos ilke leafdi of uueles cunnes cunde, ȝef ha
ouer alle þing ne luuede him her efter?

Þes king is Iesu, Godes sune, þet al o þisse wise wohede ure sawle
þe deoflen hefden biset; ant he as noble wohere efter monie messagers
& feole goddeden, com to pruuien his luue & schawde þurh
cnihtschipe þet he wes luuewurðe, as weren sumhwile cnihtes iwunet
to donne; dude him i turneiment & hefde for his leoues luue, his
scheld i feht as kene cniht on euche half iþurlet.[54]

The terms of this metaphor are conventional enough; they have ample
warrant in scripture and affective religious writings in a variety of
linguistic traditions.[55] But the language of the passage is extraordinary
as it animates Christian doctrine by evoking the conventions of courtly
service not only by turning to a kind of text borrowed from French, but
by turning to some of the *words* that are characteristic of that textual
kind in its source language. It is true, of course, that many of the words
that evoke courtliness in this passage are of Old English origin ("ladie n.
[leafdi]," "knight n. [cniht]," "knightschipe n. [cnihtschipe]," "love n1.
[luue],") or are derived in Middle English using Old English roots
("loveworthi adj. [luueworthe]"),[56] and that some of those words
derived from French are previously adduced in English ("povre adj."
and "castel n."). It is also true that a word that would have to be
attached to the language of devotion here, "maistrie n." ("He . . . dude
muchele meistries biuoren hire ehsihðe"), is an Old French word
borrowed in *Ancrene Wisse* for the first time in the record of Middle
English. Still, five of the words that most clearly evoke romance here are

---

[54] I quote this passage from Shepherd (ed.), *Ancrene Wisse*, pp. 21–2. For this passage in
the full text of the treatise see the diplomatic edition of the manuscript Shepherd uses
as his base text in Tolkien (ed.), *Ancrene Riwle*, pp. 198–9.

[55] For a history of this "allegory of God (or Christ) as a king wooing the individual soul
as bride," see Shepherd (ed.), *Ancrene Wisse*, p. 55. For a general discussion of the
compelling images in the whole of this text see the introduction to this edition,
pp. lxviii–lxxiii.

[56] The *MED* treats "luueworth" as a compound s. v. "love n1.," 4f where it cites the
passage I quote as the earliest recorded use of the word. The components of this
derivation are, however, Old English. See *OED*, s. v. "love-worth a. Obs."

new Romance borrowings ("beaubelet n. [beawbelez]," "debonairete n.," "preven v. [prouvien]," "socours n. [sucurs]," and "tournement n. [turneiment]"). These words enter this devotional context not only as constituents of the language of a borrowed genre but as constituents of the language from which that genre was itself borrowed; these "R/romance" borrowings are, in this respect, borrowings twice over.

There is a descriptive language available for *Ancrene Wisse*'s conceit that speaks to its expressive power and, from that angle, makes a case for the literary significance of the borrowing this conceit entails. Such a description stays within the confines of a single language and explains such extended metaphor as a function of "fields of discourse" or "registers," mixed in such a way that the language proper to one field or register is transferred to another, where it stands out precisely because of the transference. David Burnley has used this language to describe Chaucer's writing, and, in its particularly lexical form, Burnley roots the practice in the linguistic theory that Latin rhetoricians called *"proprietas."*[57] In Burnley's account the simple manipulation of vocabulary of the kind I have just described in *Ancrene Wisse* is tropic:

> Psychologically, the effect of the intrusion into a particular discourse of words from a widely different register is one of linguistic shock; for one's expectancies, which have become attuned to the collocation of "termes" from a recognizable register, and to one set of proprieties, are suddenly disrupted . . . Although the allusions of some uses of "termes" may be difficult for the modern audience to grasp they form a technique by which Chaucer lends conceptual density to an admittedly economical style.[58]

[57] Burnley gives his fullest account of Chaucer's linguistic practice in these terms in chapter 7 ("Register and Propriety") of *A Guide to Chaucer's Language* (pp. 156–76). He roots his understanding of Chaucer's practice in Latin rhetoric: "The conception of propriety of use which is analogous to 'register' occurs . . . in Chirius Fortunatianus, III, 3; *Rhetorica ad Herennium*, IV, 17; and is fully explained in Quintilian, VIII, ii. 8. Geoffrey of Vinsauf makes only a brief reference to it, *Poetria Nova*, IV, 1087–93" (p. 240 n. 14). It is worth noting that Burnley sees *proprietas* as a particularly lexical phenomenon: "Whereas the term 'register' connotes features of style proper to a given field of discourse, and takes account of syntax and pronunciation as well as lexicon, *proprietas* is usually understood only as a function of vocabulary" (p. 167). See also two other articles by Burnley: "Chaucer's 'Termes'" and "Picked Terms."

[58] Burnley, "Chaucer's 'Termes,'" 62. Burnley also notes: "A great many of Chaucer's references to 'termes' are to the languages associated with the scientific exposition of his time: he refers to the 'termes' of natural science ("physik," *Troilus and Criseyde*,

In this view, it is the "shock" administered by driving together human love and the love of Christ for all men and women by the "termes" of romance that gives "conceptual density" to the passage in *Ancrene Wisse*. In fact, the effects of much Middle English writing before Chaucer are well accounted for under this particular rubric. In the introductory verses to the *South English Legendary* (c. 1300), for example, readers are told that the saintly lives that follow will be spiced up with the "batailles" readers might also expect (and prefer) in the knightly combat of romance:

> Men wilneþ muche to hure telle of batailles of kynge,
> And of kniȝtes þat hardy were þat muchedel is lesynge
> Wo so wilneþ muche to hure tales of suche þinge
> Hardi batailles he may hure here þat nis no lesinge
> Of apostles & martirs þat hardy kniȝtes were.[59]

These earlier texts must, of course, be entered as a qualification to Burnley's further claim that Chaucer's use of such intra-lingual borrowing was particularly new in the context of Middle English linguistic practice:

> The recognition of *proprietas* by Chaucer and his contemporaries was a recognition that English now possessed a vocabulary of sufficient complexity to enable one topic to be seen simultaneously in the light of another, and this opened the way to a literary use of analogy, allusion and irony, enabling Chaucer to write secular poetry of a greater degree of conceptual complexity than before. If he can truly be called the Father of English Poetry, it is clearly not for his employment of French themes and poetic forms, but more justly for his discovery and exploitation of a newly developed potential in the English language.[60]

II.1038), to the 'termes' of alchemy (G 752), astrology (F 1266), medicine (C 311), the 'termes' of rhetoric and the schools (E 16), and the Latin 'termes' of theology and the law (A 639; B1 1189) . . . the 'craft of fyn lovynge' has its 'loves termes', mentioned in *Troilus and Criseyde* (II.1067) . . . finally, 'termes' may belong to the distinguishable language habits of different social classes (A 3917), to the 'brode' or 'faire' speech of the churl or the courtier," "Chaucer's 'Termes,'" 55.

59 D'Evelyn and Mill (eds.), *South English Legendary*, vol. I, p. 3, lines 59–63. For a good example of this promised mixture of proprieties see the legend of St. Augustine of Canterbury and the description of his "bataille" against the devil (vol. I, p. 215, lines 39–46).

60 Burnley, *Guide to Chaucer's Language*, p. 176. Burnley's rhetoric here seems to depend

But Burnley's description of *proprietas* is useful to a description of Chaucer's language as it crucially connects the activity of borrowing to "literary use." The "complexity" of the extended metaphor in *Ancrene Wisse* that "enable[s] one topic to be seen simultaneously in the light of another," the "linguistic shock" that yields such extraordinary expressive power results, Burnley shows, *from* the mixing of linguistic kinds. If intra-lingual exchange produces "conceptual density" *inter*-lingual exchange must produce such density too, and the mechanics of borrowing, the simplicity of Mersandian "first uses," must also have *literary* effect – whether they be Chaucer's "first uses" or those of the authors of *Ancrene Wisse* or the *South English Legendary*.

This matters to the argument I have been advancing here, because approaching borrowing in an earlier period in these terms helps to find the *general* literary end of the wide body of Middle English writing that Chaucer's English only continued. As the *Ancrene Wisse* and the *South English Legendary* show in little, Middle English literature constituted itself *as* literature by borrowing from Latin and French because these were the other literary languages in wide use in England in the Middle Ages. Long before Chaucer, a linguistic border, on the one side of which lay status and capacity (in French and Latin), and on the other side of which lay obloquy and limitation, made abundantly clear that Romance languages had what English needed, and, as a result, border crossings – borrowings – became English literature's *moyen d'être*. Indeed, in the twelfth and thirteenth centuries writing English literature involved such a thorough interdependence on French and Latin that it has been described by Elizabeth Salter as a period of "internationalism,"[61] and such breadth of linguistic embrace was made possible, as M. T. Clanchy observes, because those "who read or wrote" in this period, "passed from English to French or Latin . . . frequently without

on the kind of drama that the pronouncement that Chaucer is the "Father of English Poetry" creates, because the sequence of his points vitiates the primacy he finally accords Chaucer. There is a contradiction, in other words, between Burnley's first suggestion that Chaucer held the "recognition of *proprietas*" in common with his "contemporaries" and his later suggestion that this potential was Chaucer's "discovery."

61 See Part I ("An Obsession with the Continent") in Salter, *English and International*, pp. 1–101.

comment and perhaps without effort."[62] The textual circumstances of the *Ancrene Wisse* in particular testify loudly to the fluidity Clanchy describes, since its readers soon made good on its author's reliance upon French forms by translating that English twice into French (and, even, once into Latin) in the thirteenth and early fourteenth centuries.[63] The roughly contemporary version of the *Brut* by Laȝamon (c. 1200) testifies best to the internationalism of the earliest period, however, as it finds its "English" history in Wace's Anglo-Norman *Roman de Brut* which is itself a translation of Geoffrey of Monmouth's Latin *Historia Regum Britannie*.[64] The crucial fact here, however, is that, after the Norman Conquest, English writing *used* internationalism as a mode of cultural advancement, to make itself *out* of Latin and French in order to compete with these dominant literary languages in their own terms. The effect of such an end on means can be illustrated in precisely Mersandian terms: surveys in the *MED* of the new loan-words entering English from French show that it was in the 150 years between 1200 and 1350, and not after, that these words were pouring into English at the greatest rate.[65] The dependence of Middle English on French and Latin

---

[62] Clanchy, *From Memory to Written Record*, p. 223. Clanchy gives a comprehensive account of the linguistic situation in England from 1066–1307. See, in particular, his chapter on "Languages of Record" (pp. 197–223).

[63] For discussion of the possible purpose of the translations of *Ancrene Wisse* see Dobson, *Origins of Ancrene Wisse*, pp. 286–304 (Dobson gives a *stemma codicum* that includes these translations on p. 287). The Latin translation ("by a man who was an M. A. of Oxford by 1280 and died in 1315") survives in four manuscripts and is edited as D'Evelyn (ed.), *Latin Text of the Ancrene Riwle*. The earlier French text ("made in the earlier thirteenth century") is edited as Herbert (ed.), *French Text of the Ancrene Riwle*. The later text (part of "a vast Anglo-Norman 'Compilation' . . . probably made between 1257 and 1274") is edited as Trethewey (ed.), *French Text of the Ancrene Riwle*). For the attributions of date that I quote for these translations, see Dobson, *Origins of Ancrene Wisse*, pp. 296–7, 298 n. 2, and 300.

[64] Laȝamon gives Wace as a source in the first lines of his text (Brook and Leslie [eds.], *Laȝamon's Brut*, lines 19–21). Françoise Le Saux gives a detailed account of Laȝamon's use of Wace's *Roman* (and other possible French sources) in *Laȝamon's Brut: The Poem and Its Sources*, pp. 24–93. She also makes a case for Laȝamon's direct reliance on Geoffrey's *Historia* (pp. 94–117).

[65] Dekeyser, "Romance Loans in Middle English," esp. pp. 258–9. Dekeyser is here reassessing work done using the *OED* in Jespersen, *Growth and Structure of the English Language*, pp. 93–4, and Baugh, "Chronology of Loan-words in English." Dekeyser points out the circularity involved in Jespersen and Baugh's count, since the flood of loan-words they trace coincides with "the ever increasing amount of available source material" (p. 258). His reassessment according to relative frequencies flattens their

writing meant that the voluminous use of Romance borrowings by so many early Middle English writers was not a choice but a given since "trilingualism was not uncommon" among the lettered in twelfth- and thirteenth-century England.[66]

There is, of course, an important distinction to be made between the trilingualism of the twelfth and thirteenth centuries as one period and the fourteenth century as another, but the nature of that qualification only reinforces the degree to which Chaucer's borrowing followed rather than led any trend. I refer here to the extent that writers in England were becoming what V. H. Galbraith called "vernacular-conscious" in the later century so that, even if written English continued to coexist with written French and Latin, it increasingly had the status it sought earlier as the *primus inter pares* even in literary culture.[67] While Denis Piramus (fl. 1173–1214) writes his life of St. Edmund in French because, he says, "en franceis le poent entendre/Li grant, li maien e li mendre," near the end of the fourteenth century the *Speculum Vitæ* is in English because "Boþe lered and lewed, olde and ȝonge,/alle vnderstonden english tonge."[68] Later in the century (1386–7), Thomas Usk insists that "Englishmen" (who he tellingly describes as "us") are best served by English words, while Latin must be restricted to clerks and French to "Frenchmen":

> The understanding of Englishmen wol not strecche to the privy termes in Frenche, what-so-ever we bosten of straunge langage. Let than clerkes endyten in Latin, for they have the propertee of science,

graphs but generally reproduces their results, showing only that the trend of heavy borrowing ends around 1375 and not 1400 (as Baugh and Jespersen report). For an earlier attempt to refine Baugh and Jespersen see Mossé, "On the Chronology of French Loan-words in English."

[66] Wilson, "English and French in England," 59. I am here broadening a phrase that Wilson is using to describe the "higher clergy."

[67] Galbraith, "Nationality and Language in Medieval England," 124.

[68] Piramus, *La vie Seint Edmund le Rei*, Kjellman (ed.), lines 3269–70. I quote the *Speculum Vitæ* (lines 77–8) from Ullmann, "Studien zu Richard Rolle de Hampole," 469 which prints the first 370 lines of this text. As the title of his article suggests, Ullmann attributes the text to Rolle, but see *MWME*, vol. VII, pp. 2261–2 (which also dates the text to "the third quarter of the fourteenth century"). For an account of "The Decline of Anglo-Norman" with many useful quotations from contemporary sources see Vising, *Anglo-Norman Language and Literature*, pp. 18–27. Rothwell also argues that French "was a widely-used language of culture" (p. 455) in "The Role of French in Thirteenth-Century England."

and the knowinge in that facultee; and let Frenchmen in their
Frenche also endyten their queynt terms, for it is kyndely to their
mouthes; and let us shewe our fantasyes in suche words as we lerneden
of our dames tonge.[69]

English became prized as, in the phrasing of the Wycliffite *De Officio
Pastorali*, the "modir tunge" of "þe comyns of engliȝschmen."[70]
English became the "ordinary means of communication in the urban
communities of fourteenth-century England" and, despite the fact that
the royal family and its attendants remained the strongest holdouts
against English, "proficiency in English, justifiably to be assumed in the
case of Edward I and Edward II, is directly evidenced for Edward III,
his sons, Edward, Prince of Wales (1330–76), and Thomas, Duke of
Gloucester (1355–97), and Richard II (1367–1400)."[71] This shift in
status finally had an effect that can itself be measured in terms of
Mersandian quantities, for, if we count the Romance borrowings
entering English after 1375, we find a dramatic slowing of the process.
All of which means of course that the period in which Chaucer wrote
was the very opposite of the watershed for Romance borrowing in
Middle English; it was actually the trickle after the flood.

French and Latin written traditions were not marginalized in
fourteenth-century England because they were supplanted by different
English traditions, however, but because English writing made itself
substitutable for French and Latin traditions by, in effect, becoming
them. This meant, of course, that translation itself became a tradition
such that, even in the fourteenth century, much Middle English writing
still had an immediate French source. Particularly in the genre of
romance the process of translation occurred on such a massive scale that
this entire *kind* of French writing was made over into a parallel body of
English writing. As Susan Crane points out, "virtually every Anglo-
Norman romance had a Middle English descendent."[72] Of the 18
romances in the Auchinleck MS (that "wild stock" on which Chaucer

---

[69] Usk, *Testament of Love*, p. 2.
[70] Cited in Berndt, "The Final Decline of French," 365 n. 40 from Matthew (ed.),
English Works of Wyclif, 430. Berndt attributes this text to Wyclif but see *MWME*, vol.
II, p. 368 and Hudson, *Premature Reformation*, p. 20 n. 71.
[71] Berndt, "The Final Decline of French," 350 and 363.
[72] Crane, *Insular Romance*, p. 6.

"grafted" his own style) all but five have extant French originals.[73] So close are the links between many of these English romances and their French sources that their "authors" were not so much writers, but, as Loomis terms them, "translator-versifiers."[74] The dominant position of English as the "ordinary means of communication" in fourteenth-century England must be distinguished then from the circumstance of Middle English *written* communication which remained afloat by the very means of its growing success on a subsidiary sea of Latin and French. If trilingualism was in real decline by the end of the fourteenth century, it was only because trilingualism had been such a success and, as a result, the primacy that literary English achieved by the end of the fourteenth century remained mortgaged to the French and Latin traditions it had used for its achievement. It is in this sense that the secure place independent English writing earned by the end of the fourteenth century was no simple triumph over a translating culture from which it emerged: it was, because of its roots, a *translated* literary culture that defeated French and Latin by absorbing it. All this matters of course because the significant linguistic result of that massive absorption – its *English* sign – is the sizeable number of Romance borrowings already in fourteenth-century English *as* the means by which English texts *were* French and Latin texts.

Fourteenth-century Middle English writing retained the traces of these general cultural ends even in those texts that finally had no connection to any French or Latin source. The Romance borrowings that were the tools of the translated culture's trade remain tools of an emergent English literature independent of translation. This means, first, that this literature inherits such borrowings as a now *naturalized* part of an autonomous English, as can be clearly seen in Chaucer's writing at the moment he liberates himself from French sources. As later fourteenth-century English writing is to earlier Middle English so too is Chaucer's *Book of the Duchess* to his *Romaunt*. Here then, by way of example, are the first lines of Chaucer's departure with its French borrowings identified (by italics):[75]

---

[73] Loomis, "The Auchinleck MS," 607.   [74] *Ibid.*, 608.

[75] In *Chaucer's Dream Poetry* Windeatt distinguishes the *Book of the Duchess* from straightforward translation, describing Chaucer as having "seized on some of the more expressive, more striking, and more strongly visualized component scenes or sections

I have gret wonder, be this lyght,
How that I lyve, for day ne nyght
I may nat slepe wel nygh noght;
I have so many an ydel thoght
Purely for *defaute* of slep
That, by my trouthe, I take no kep
Of nothing, how hyt cometh or gooth,
Ne me nys nothyng leef nor looth.
Al is ylyche good to me –
Joye or sorowe, wherso hyt be –
For I have felynge in nothyng,
But as yt were a mased thyng,
Alway in *poynt* to falle a-doun;
For sorwful *ymagynacioun*
Ys alway hooly in my mynde.
(*Book of the Duchess*, 1–15)

All four of these borrowings ("defaute n.," "joie n.," "pointe ni.," "imaginacioun n.") are recorded in English before Chaucer records them here. Second, however, the long-term dependency of Middle English on Romance originals had also made borrowing *habitual*, the fundamental means of the literary even at the point (in general and in Chaucer's writing) when Middle English had freed itself from the translation that had been the habit's originating necessity. The close linguistic contact between so many Middle English texts and their sources had, in other words, created an engine for new borrowing that steamed on even after there was no textual contact with Romance languages to stoke it. So Chaucer continues to use inherited borrowings in the *Book* until he describes Morpheus's cave, and, then, without any direct prompting from a Romance source, he borrows anew according to the pattern inscribed in the older borrowings he had already used (Romance borrowings are italicized here again):[76]

of his sources, and then pu[t] them together within his own distinctive forms" (p. ix). Windeatt also provides translations of pertinent passages of these sources (Machaut's *Le Jugement dou Roy de Behaingne*, *Le Dit de la Fonteinne Amoureuse*, *Remede de Fortune*, and *Le Dit dou Lyon*, and Froissart's *Le Paradys d'Amours*) and places the appropriate lines in Chaucer as a running commentary (pp. 3–70). Brewer examines parallels between the lines of the *Book* I quote and Froissart's *Paradys* as noted above p. 50 n. 16.

[76] Windeatt notes a reference to Morpheus and Enclimpostair in the lines of Froissart's

They had good *leyser* for to route,
To *envye* who myghte slepe best.
Somme henge her chyn upon hir brest
And slept upryght, hir hed yhed,
And some lay naked in her bed
And slepe whiles the dayes laste.
(*Book of the Duchess*, 172–7)

"Leiser n." is an inherited borrowing, but "envien v2." is recorded here, in this passage, for the first time in English writing, as it is borrowed from French "envier" without any direct textual prompting.[77] One might suppose in this instance that this word is only recorded for the first time in Chaucer's writing because it does not survive in the earlier texts in which it was used *because* of such prompting. It could also be supposed that this word was comfortably present in the spoken language long before Chaucer ventured to write it down. In either case, however, the novelty of this word is significantly representative of the general permeability of the Middle English *record* to Romance words at this point. That is, the textual moment at which liminal distinctions between English and French give way is less significant than the broader fact that these distinctions are *evidently* giving way as Chaucer makes texts like the *Book*. Like the other thirty-seven Romance words appearing for the first time in the English record in this poem, the word "envie" suggests that Chaucer is still borrowing to make literary English even when the real pressure to do so has subsided.

The line between English and French is not crossed continually in Chaucer because he was the "Father of English Poetry" but because to

Paradys that parallel *Book of the Duchess*, lines 166–9 (*Chaucer's Dream Poetry*, p. 42). The notes to the *Riverside Chaucer* (p. 968) point to parallels for *Book of the Duchess*, in Machaut's *Fonteinne Amoureuse*, line 174 ("ses mentons a sa poitrine") and Ovid's *Metamorphoses* lines 619–20 ("vix oculos tollens iterumque iterumque relabens/ summaque percutiens nutanti pectora mento . . ."), but there is no lexical borrowing involved. For the line from Machaut see the *Riverside* note. For the lines from Ovid see Ovid, *Metamorphoses*, Miller (ed. and trans.).

77 The *MED* distinguishes the verb in this passage, which it calls "envien v2." and defines as "to contend," from the verb it calls "envien v1.," from the same French root, which it defines as "to feel ill-will or enmity toward someone." "Envien v1." is cited first in the *MED* in "(a1382) WBible(1)," later than the use of "envien v2." I cite here (but earlier than Chaucer's first and only use of "envien v1. in the *Wife of Bath's Prologue*, III, 142).

write English in the fourteenth century was to cross this line. That Chaucer's practice was the literary habit I say it was – that all Chaucer's new words are themselves only part of larger patterns of literary culture – becomes more clear if these passages from the *Book of the Duchess* are themselves set in the context of earlier English writing. The Auchinleck romance *Guy of Warwick* again provides a useful example:

Now goþ Gii sore desmaid,	Gui s'en va, qui forment s'esmaie
His woundes him han iuel *afreyd*.	Mult li anguisse el cors sa plaie;
To an *ermite* he is y-go	A un *heremite* s'en est alé
Þat he was ere aqueynted to;	U il ert anceis acointé
His woundes þer hele he dede	Ses plaies fait iloec saner
Wiþouten noise in þat stede.	Celeement, sanz demorer;
Miche he him drade þe *douk* Otoun,	Mult par crient le *duc* Otun,
So ful he was of tresoun.	Qui tant est cruel e felun.
(*Guy of Warwick*, 1645–52)	(*Gui de Warewic*, 1489–96)

Two of the borrowings highlighted here, "heremite n." and "duk n.," illustrate the point I made before with Chaucer's use of "amorous" in *Guy* and the *Romaunt*: these words, although clearly prompted here by the English text's French source, already existed in the English record. The verb "affraien vi." in the English text is, however, exactly the kind of borrowing we have just seen in the *Book of the Duchess*: there is no immediate prompting for it in a French source, although the word comes to English from French and this word is recorded in this passage for the first time in the English record. Here then, and in a period much earlier than Chaucer's composition of the *Book of the Duchess*, the mechanism for linguistic exchange cannot be the pressure of a source text – precisely because, in this case, the source text exerts no pressure – but is necessarily the pressure of a literary culture that generally and particularly demands the use of Romance forms. The translator of *Guy* may have drawn this verb directly from his own knowledge of Anglo-Norman, or he might even have known it as a part of spoken Middle English before he committed it to writing in this earliest surviving form. By either of these models, however, such new borrowing is witness to both a general dependency and significant process. "Affraien vi." stands here, in little, for the larger means Middle English literature used to achieve the ends of its literary success, means and ends in which even Chaucer's newest borrowings and most successful poems could only follow. Chaucer's new Romance borrowings were traditional then, not only because such borrowings were already in place for him to use, but because the very novelty of borrowings was constitutive of Middle English literature.

3

The historical circumstance of Middle English literary culture which made the process of borrowing new words one of its necessary attributes had a further extensive and, therefore, significant ramification for lexical novelty in the literary language, and this ramification also requires comment here. Simply put, the problems posed by the continual adaptation of texts in other languages to English form created a need for novelty in Middle English writing that was both voracious and incessant. The practical need for new Romance words to meet the exigencies of translation was finally so habitual that even where French and Latin words were not immediately at issue lexical novelty became a formal attribute of Middle English poetics. As a result, new borrowing extended to languages that were not the primary source languages for translated Middle English texts. The seventeen words of Middle Dutch or Middle Low German origin that Chaucer's predecessors use but that also show up in Chaucer's writing are the tradition that Chaucer's eight new borrowings from those languages inhabit.[78] At the same time, as it was a language ever in progress, Middle English literary language finally became such a maw for the new that even borrowings of *every* kind could not satisfy its need for novelty. Other methods were therefore pressed into equally voluminous service.

The nature of these other methods is revealed by pushing Mersand's quantities just one step beyond the limits he sets for them. To look in

---

[78] For Chaucer's eight new borrowings from Middle Dutch and Middle Low German see *MED*, s. vv. "courte-pi n.," "kiken v2.," "lake n2.," "reie n.," "reisen v2.," "rore n2.," "rumbelen v.," "tricen v." For the seventeen words of Middle Dutch and Middle Low German in Chaucer's vocabulary cited in earlier Middle English texts see *MED*, s. vv., "clinken v.," "Duch adj.," "fraughten v.," "grot n3.," "herre n2.," "labben v.," "mite n2.," "pekken v.," "pit n.," "queken v.," "reken v2.," "scome n.," "sledde n.," "sparre n.," "speren v1.," "takel n.," "tuken v." On the Dutch influence on Middle English see Burnley, "Lexis and Semantics," p. 438 and Bense, *Dictionary of the Low-Dutch Element in the English Vocabulary*.

the *MED* for the lexical history, not only of words of Romance origin, but of *every* word in Chaucer's English, finds another 996 newly recorded words – that is, almost as many other new words as Mersand's survey of Romance vocabulary found. Mersand gives some small indication of where the great majority of these words came from as he unwittingly absorbs a few of them into his list. "Maister-hunte n.," for example, does occur, as Mersand suggests, for the first time in the record in the *Book of the Duchess*:[79]

> The mayster-hunte anoon, fot-hot,
> With a gret horn blew thre mot
> At the uncouplynge of hys houndes. (375–7)

And Mersand includes this word in his list of Romance borrowings because the *OED* describes its primary term, "maister," as a Romance derivation. In order to do this, however, he also ignores the Old English origin of "hunte n.," the word's second component, and he also ignores a fact that the *OED* tells him: "maister," although a borrowing, had been borrowed in the Old English period. What seems much more likely than new borrowing in this instance, in other words, is that Chaucer made the word by compounding its two essentially English elements.[80] A similar circumstance surrounds "convertible adj." which, Mersand also rightly notes, has its earliest citation in the *OED* in the *Cook's Tale*:[81]

> His maister shal it in his shoppe abye,
> Al have he no part of the mynstralcye.
> For thefte and riot, they been convertible,
> Al konne he pleye on gyterne or ribible. (I, 4393–6)

---

79 For Mersand's listing of this compound as a new borrowing see his appendix (*Chaucer's Romance Vocabulary*, p. 167).

80 *OED*, s. v. "master sb1." gives the Old English forms "mæзester" and "maзester" as derivations of Latin "magister" and "magistrum." *OED*, s. v. "hunt sb1." (meaning "hunter," as opposed, in Chaucer's use, to "hunt sb2." meaning "the act of hunting) gives the Old English root "hunta."

81 See Mersand's appendix in *Chaucer's Romance Vocabulary*, p. 162. For the *OED*'s earliest citation in Chaucer see "convertible a.," 1. The *MED*, s. v. "convertible adj.," a, cites "(c1385) Usk TL (Skeat)" as the earliest for this word (it dates the *Cook's Tale* c. 1390). This correction is not relevant to my point here, however, which is not to correct Mersand's lexical history but, rather, to examine the interpretation he gives to the evidence he rightly reads from the *OED*.

Mersand takes this word as a new Romance borrowing because the *OED* offers roots in both French ("convertible") and Latin ("convertibil-is"), but to do so he must also ignore a cross-reference in this etymology to the entry for the suffix "-ble," which, if taken, would obviate the need for borrowing this word at all.[82] According to the *OED* (in a citation confirmed by the *MED*), "converten v." is a Romance borrowing (taken from the Latin root from which French "convertible" comes) recorded in English from c. 1300.[83] Although it is not at all necessary that "convertible" was derived from this naturalized root, Mersand's list here again ignores the possibility that Chaucer could have used this root to make an adjective using the available ending – as he had in fact already done to make a number of Middle English words recorded much earlier than the *Cook's Tale*.[84] Finally, "fortunen v.," which Mersand also rightly finds Chaucer using for the first time in the record in the *Book of the Duchess*, exemplifies a third qualification to be entered against borrowings:[85]

> (He that wrot al th'avysyoun
> That he mette, kyng Scipioun,
> The noble man, the Affrikan –
> Suche marvayles fortuned than) . . . (285–8)

The *OED* and the *MED* offer French "fortuner" and Latin "fortunare" as roots for the Middle English word, but it is again true that "fortune n.," from which this verb can be seen to derive, had already been

---

82 In the *OED* the etymology for "convertible a." reads "a. F. 'convertible' . . . ad. late L. 'convertible-is', fr. 'convertere' to convert: see -ble." The etymology for "convert v." reads "a OF. 'convert-ir' . . . pop. L. '*convertire', for cl. L 'convertere' . . ." The *OED* discussion of "-ble" notes that "many" words with the suffix "were from the 12th to the 15th c. adopted in Eng. from Fr., and here served as models for the direct adoption or formation of others from Latin, a process which has gone on to the present day." The *MED* notes some Middle English derivatives and also suggests that the suffix is "rare in ME formations" (s. v. "-ible suf."). Even with the warrant of the Romance form of the adjective, however, it seems important to note the previous English naturalization of its root. Even if there is every likelihood that "convertible" *was* a borrowing, it matters that it didn't *have* to be.

83 For the earliest citations of this verb see *OED*, s. v. "convert v.," I, 9, a and I, 9, d in "a1300 *Cursor Mundi*." The *MED* cites the *Cursor Mundi* as well but, since it dates that text "a1325," the earliest citation it gives (s. v. "converten," 2a) is "c1300 SLeg. (Ld)."

84 E.g., "horrible adj.," "pesible adj.," "invisible adj."

85 *OED*, s. v "fortune v.," 3. The *OED*'s history is confirmed in the *MED*, s. v. "fortunen v.," 3a.

borrowed according to the English record as early as c. 1325.[86] Here again, Chaucer might well have looked beyond the bounds of naturalized English to find this word, but he might just as easily have used what had already become a native resource to convert the grammatical function of a noun by the simple addition of a verb ending.

To put it more generally, the claim that Chaucer's "development of an English poetic tradition" involved "the transference into English of the French tradition fed and supplemented by the greater literatures in Latin and Italian" ignores the general fact that the earlier transference of French traditions to English itself provided Chaucer with abundant resources for lexical making: borrowed forms naturalized into English that might themselves be developed within English to fashion new words. Chaucer need not have borrowed words from French even when he had the French before him that contained the very words he used. Early on in the *Romaunt of the Rose*, for example, it seems that Chaucer borrowed "Menouresse n." directly from his source:

Amydde saugh I Hate stonde	Enz en le mileu ui Haïne,
That for hir wrathe, yre, and onde,	Qui de corroz e d'ataïne
Semede to ben a *mynoresse*,	Sembla bien estre meneresse;
An angry wight, a chideresse;	Coroceuse e tançoneresse,
And ful of gyle and fel corage . . .	Et plaine de grant cuuertage . . .
(*Romaunt*, 147–51)	(*Roman*, 139–43)

However, "Menour n. & adj." was already adduced in Middle English from the beginning of the thirteenth century,[87] and the suffix "-esse," although also a Romance borrowing, exists in the English record from the earliest Middle English texts.[88] Accordingly, although the *MED* proposes a Romance root for "Menouresse n." (giving Medieval Latin "minorissa" not a French example), it also proposes "Menour n." as a root for this word.[89] Chaucer may himself have understood that his

---

[86] See *OED*, s. v. "fortune sb.," 1, and *MED*, s. v. "fortune n.," 1b citing "(a1325) Cursor." Interestingly enough, the *OED* etymology for "fortune v." also says "see fortune sb."

[87] According to the *MED*, s. v. "Menour n. & adj.," 2a, this root is first recorded in "c1230 Ancr. (Corp-C)."

[88] The *MED* entry for "-esse suf." gives no historical examples and notes that this suffix is a borrowing from Old French. Models available to Chaucer (that is, words with this same ending, recorded earlier in Middle English, which Chaucer's writing shows he knew) include "countesse n." and "emperesse n."

[89] Although the *MED* cites "Menouresse n." first in "(1395) EEWills" (a collection of

procedure here was borrowing of course; but it matters, I think, that he did not *need* to borrow "meneresse". Or, to put it another way, the long-attested presence of the suffix "-esse" in the language should have acted as some sort of license for Chaucer's translation, a now-native lever that made perceived borrowing easier (and therefore different) since the word was half-way into English already.

As such use of Romance resources suggests, Chaucer could also rely on purely native roots to make new words, and he could even use the resulting new words as a means for increasing his linguistic capacity so that he could translate *French*. This is exactly what he does when he uses "lenenesse n." slightly further along in his translation of the *Romaunt* to render "maigreice" in his original:

Hir semede to have the jaunyce.	El sembloit auoir la iaunice,
Nought half so pale was Avarice,	Si n'i feïst riens Auarice
Nor nothyng lyk of *lenesse*;	De palecé ne de maigreice.
(*Romaunt*, 305–7)	(*Roman*, 295–7)

"Maigreice" has no English (or no surviving English) form,[90] but Chaucer's alternative is no less lexically bold than borrowing this French word would have been. "Lene adjı." is an Old English word (and Chaucer actually uses it prior to these lines in the *Romaunt*) and "-nesse" is a suffix that also derives from Old English too, but root and suffix are here combined for the first time in the English record to render the French form.[91] Chaucer even makes reference to this procedure later in the *Romaunt*, when he does the same kind of lexical work to render the French "seraines" with the compound "mere-maiden n.":

Sich swete song was hem among	Tant estoit cil chanz doz e biaus
That me thought it no briddis song,	Qu'il ne sembloit pas chant d'oisiaus,

---

early English wills compiled for the EETS by Furnivall) my redating of the *Romaunt* means I regard Chaucer's use as first (on this procedure see Part 2, p. 232).

90 The closest Middle English version of "maigreice" is "megrenes n." but the *MED* cites only one use of the word in "(?a1425) Chauliac(1)" (the anonymous English translation of Guy de Chauliac's *Grande Chirurgie*).

91 The Old English root the *MED* gives for "lene adjı." is "hlæne" and the Old English root it gives s. v. "-nesse suf." is "-nes," "-nis," "-nys." Chaucer uses "lene" earlier in the *Romaunt of the Rose*, line 218 ("And thereto she was lene and megre") to render *Roman de la Rose*, line 206 ("E auec ce que ele ert meigre"). The *MED* cites "lenenesse" first in "(a1382) WBible(1)" but, as I redate *Romaunt* citations I take Chaucer's use as earlier. Again, see Part 2, p. 232 for this procedure.

But it was wondir lyk to be

Song of *mermaydens* of the see,

That, for her syngyng is so clere,

Though we *mermaydens* clepe hem here

In English, as is oure usaunce,

Men clepe hem sereyns in Fraunce.

(*Romaunt*, 677–84)

Ainz les peüst l'en aesmer

Au chanz des seraines de mer,

Que, pour leur voiz qu'eles ont saines

E series, ont non seraines.

(*Roman*, 669–74)

Chaucer undermines his very acknowledgment of the Frenchness of "seraines" by taking the word into his text in the context of such explanation, and this is in fact the path of least resistance in English since "siren n." was already in recorded use. But he is also over-modest – or, perhaps, more subtly disingenuous – when he says that the compound he wants to substitute for this word is "in English . . . oure usaunce," because the record shows no earlier use of "mere-maiden n." than this passage.[92] The components of this compound, "mere n2." and "maiden n.," are also of Old English origin, but these native materials are again joined here to make a word for the first time in the record.

The literary transference of French forms into English – the cultural translation constitutive of Middle English literary culture – was not simply a source of raw material for lexical invention then, but a goad *demanding* invention, even if that invention was wholly native in its materials. Moreover, that goad produced, not only the instances I have just adduced, but an entire procedure. The examples I have just given show this procedure in action and the materials and methods it employed, but it is worth emphasizing its breadth as it constituted Chaucer's English even *as* he translated. This procedure plays a large role, for example, even in making the English of the *Romaunt* out of the *Roman de la Rose*. Of the 135 words in Fragment A of the *Romaunt* that appear there for the first time in the record, 37 words are new by derivation. In addition to "lenesse n.," and "mere-maiden n.," Chaucer coins another 16 words in the process of translation out of unborrowed materials (Old English roots and detachable morphemes).[93] I give these

92 The *MED*'s dating of the *Romaunt* places its citation of this passage after its citation of this word in "(a1398) Trev.Barth." However, since Chaucer also uses the compound in the *Boece* (1.pr1.69), dated "c1380" in the *MED*, this *MED* entry still shows Chaucer as the first writer to record this word.

93 It would be possible to include in this count (raising the total of native derivations to nineteen and the sum of all derivations in the *Romaunt* to forty) "Pope-Holi adj."

words in the following table in the order of their appearance in the *Romaunt*, in the form they have in that text (marked with their grammatical function). In an attempt to reconstruct Chaucer's procedure in forming these words I give, along with the available native roots, the prompt for each word in the French of the *Roman* (unless the word seems to have no particular source in the given line).

Roman (line) >	*Romaunt* (line)[94]	etymology[95]
amee (43)	biloved ppl. (46)	(bi- pref2. [OE] & loven v. [OE])
d'aigniaus (217)	lombe-skynnes n. (229)	(lomb n. [OE] & skin n1. [OE])
proesce (277)	worthinesse n. (287)	[worthi adj. [OE] & -nesse suf. [OE]]
gardast neant (281)	awri adv. (291)	(wrien v2. [OE])
amez (462)	biloved ppl. (473)	as above
de chanter. . . enuis(653)	forsongen ppl. (664)	(for- pref1. [OE] & singen v. [OE])
timberesses (754)	timbester n. (769)	timber n1. [OE] (& -estre suf. [OE])
grailles (811)	smalish adj. (826)	small adj. [OE]
encisee (824)	toslitered adj. (840)	(to- pref2. [OE] & slitten v. [OE])
enuoisiez (920)	lightsom adj2. (936)	light adj.2 [OE]
biaus ostiex (1112)	hous-holding ger. (1132)	(hous n. (OE *hus*) & holden v1. [OE])

(*Romaunt*, 415 from "Papelardie," *Roman*, 409), "Swete-Loking n." (*Romaunt*, 415 and 1331 from "Douz Regart," *Roman*, 906 and 1305) and "Newe-Thought n." (*Romaunt*, 982 from "Nouiaus Pensers," *Roman*, 968). Benson treats these as "words" in his *Glossarial Concordance* in these forms, but, although I have generally followed Benson in such decisions (as in the compounds in this and the next chart), the proper nouns in these formations place them, I think, in a separate category from "new *words*." The *MED* does give a separate entry to "pope-holi adj." but treats the other two compounds s. vv. "swete adj.," 8 and "neue adj.," 5.

94 My redating of *Romaunt* citations in the *MED* means that the *MED* cites the following words in this list "first" in another text: "awri" in "(a1393) Gower CA," "hempene" in "(1392) *MS Wel.564," "proud-herted" in "(c1378) PPl.B (Ld)," and "shittyng" in "(c1384) WBible(1)." On this procedure see Part 2, p. 232.

95 Etymologies in this list are either taken from the *MED*, my own conjecture (enclosed in parentheses), or taken from the *OED* (enclosed in brackets). In general I follow the procedure outlined for etymologies in Part 2 (see pp. 229–30), although, for clarity's sake, I have sometimes included etymologies for suffixes and roots that the *MED* omits, and that I generally do not add in Part 2.

	overgret adj. (1229)	(over adv. [OE] & gret adj. [OE])
boraz (1211)	hempen adj. (1233)	hemp n. [OE]
amie (1250)	biloved ppl. (1272)	as above
riant (1260)	lustinesse n. (1282)	lusti adj. (fr. lust n. [OE] & -nesse suf. [OE])
au cuer farasche (1459)	proud-herted adj. (1491)	proud adj. [OE] & herted adj. (fr. herte n. [OE])
saut (1531)	[walm v.] (1561)	[walm n1. [OE]]
enclouse (1568)	shittinge ger. (1598)	(shitten v. [OE])

Another twenty-one words in Fragment A of the *Romaunt* are, like "Menouresse n.," derived from borrowed words or morphemes which were naturalized into English long before Chaucer gets to them. To survey these words and the procedure of their making I give them, again, in the form and order of their appearance in Chaucer's text with any apparent prompt in Chaucer's source and their root or roots. In this case I also give the date in which the already-borrowed root first appeared in the English record.

Roman (line) >	*Romaunt* (line)[96]	etymology[97]
couertement (19)	covertli adv. (19)	c1303: covert adj. [OF]
corroceuse (142)	angri adj. (150)	c1250: anger n. [ON]
tançoneresse (142)	chideresse n. (150)	chidere n. [OE] (& a1160: -esse suf. [OF])
paletiaus (211)	beggerli adv. (223)	c1225: beggere n. [OF, ult. MDu.]
em borneant (282)	baggingli adv. (292)	c1350: baggen v3. [?cp. OF]

[96] My redating of *Romaunt* citations in the *MED* means that the following words are cited in their *MED* entry "first" in another text: "tempere n." in "(a1387) Trev.Higd.," "closing" in "(c1384) WBible(1)," "fetisly" in "a1375 WPal," "desiryng" in "(c1378) PPl.B (Ld)," "tasseled" in "(?a1370) Winner & W.," "mesuryng" in "(a1398) *Trev.-Barth," "date-tree" in "(c1390) Susan," "strayne" in "(c1384) WBible(1)," and "cristall" in "(?c1380) Pearl." On this procedure see Part 2, p. 232.

[97] Etymologies are determined here as in the previous table (see n. 95) for individual roots as for the words in the *Romaunt*. Roots mentioned here that Chaucer does not otherwise use (which means that they will not appear in Part 2), are as follows (according to their *MED* headword, the subheading for the first recorded use of that word, and its citation): "besaunt n.," 3b ("?c1200 Orm."), "covert ppl. & adj.," 2a ("[c1303] Mannyng HS"), "cracchen v.," a ("c1330 Orfeo"), "date n1.," 1 ("c1300 SLeg. [Ld]"), "tassel n.," a ("[?c1300] Guy [1]"), "tempre adj.," a ("[c1340] Rolle Psalter [Ld 286]"), "tempren v.," 3a ("?c1200 Orm."). For "-esse suf." see n. 88 above.

esgratiner (315)	forcracchen v. (323)	for- prefi.[OE] & (c1330) cracchen v. [?MDu.]
amoler (336)	tempere n. (346)	c1340: tempre adj. [prob. OF, AF] or c1200: tempren v. [OE, OF, L]
sechiez (350) or *aneantiz* (351)	forwelked ppl. (361)	(for- prefi. [OE] & c1250: welked adj., fr. welken v. [prob. fr.MDu.])
clooison (515)	closing ger. (527)	(c1280: closen v. [OF])
apertement (560)	fetisli adv. (570)	(c1350: fetis adj. [AF])
	fetisli adv. (577)	as above
desirasse (712)	desiringe ger. (725)	(c1200: desiren v. [OF])
	semelihede n. (777)	c1200: semeli adj. [ON] (& -hede suf. [OE])
	fetisli adv. (837)	as above
orfrois (1059)	ribaning n. (1077)	c1325: riban n. [OF]
naelee (1061)	tasselen v. (1079)	c1300: tassel n. [OF & ML]
.i. besaunt (1086)	besaunt-wight n. (1106)	(c1200: besaunt n. [OF] & weghte nı. [OE])
grant biauté (1110)	semelihede n. (1130)	as above
iointe (1213)	fetisli adv. (1235)	as above
compasseüre (1323)	mesuringe ger. (1349)	(c1325: mesuren v. [OF])
datier (1339)	date-tree n. (1364)	(c1300: date nı. [OF] & tre n. [OE])
destraindre (1441)	streinen v2. (1471)	c1300: distreinen v. [OF]
cristal (1538)	cristal adj. (1568)	c1250: cristal n. [L & OF & OE]
cristal (1547)	cristal adj. (1576)	as above
cristal (1560)	cristal adj. (1589)	as above
fist . . . enuiron (1591)	cerclen v. (1619)	c1121: cercle n. [OF]
doutasse (1631)	endouten v. (1664)	(en- prefix [OF] & c1200: douten v. [OF])

"Cristal adj." appears to be a direct borrowing, of course, just as "Menouresse n." did, and "covertli adv.," "date-tree n.," and "besaunt-wight n." are very close calques of the French. But, while we may presume that such words were borrowings, we can also say, as in the case of "Menouresse n.," that native materials give the crossing of the linguistic divide between French and English here a much easier path. As a whole, these tables show how Chaucer could invent his English *out* of English. They show that, even when that English was made in the service of transferring French traditions, it involved the *re*-making of English by the recombination of its extant parts.

Such derivations in Chaucer are traditional as they use English *from* the tradition to make new words, but these words are also traditional as products of a procedure that was also in earlier use, as they replicate techniques that Middle English writers had steadily employed before Chaucer even began translating the *Roman de la Rose*. That is, the derivations Chaucer uses can all be seen at work in Chaucer's Middle English predecessors. His use of "communeli adv." in the *Romaunt*, for example, looks very much like a new derivation coined as a calque for the French "comunement" which it translates, since "commune adj." exists in the English record prior to the *Romaunt*, and adding "-li suf2." to English adjectives to make adverbs is a process with precedent in Old English:

Ful hende folk and wys and free,	Franches genz e bien enseignies,
And folk of faire port, truëly,	E gent de bel afaitement
There weren alle *comunly*.	Estoient tuit comunement.
(*Romaunt*, 1306–8)	(*Roman*, 1282–4)

But if "communeli adv." is a calque it is already present in Chaucer's English *as* a calque and the linguistic circumstance of its use in the *Romaunt* is almost exactly the circumstance that leads to the first recorded use of this word in *Guy of Warwick*:

Now þai smitte togider *comonliche*,	Atant i ferent communalment,
& fiȝt þai agin ardiliche	En l'estur tuit hardiement.
Þer men miȝt se Gij smite,	Qui veist Gui tant ben ferir!
& þe Sarrazins heuedes of strike . . .	Tant Sarazins fist le jur morir . . .
(*Guy of Warwick*, 2965–8)	(*Gui de Warewic*, 3041–4)

Prompted by an Old French variant for "comunement," the translator of *Guy of Warwick* fashions "communeli adv." to effect the same translation that Chaucer later uses it for.[98] Such precedence need not suggest that Chaucer was imitating *Guy* when he used this adverb, since he may, of course, have *re*-derived it. But such an ostensibly new derivation would still be traditional as the English before Chaucer gives the process a historical frame. A similar linguistic circumstance stands behind Chaucer's use of "nighten v." in the *Parliament of Fowles*.

---

[98] For the relationship of "comunement" and "communalment" see Tobler and Lommatzsch, *Altfranzösisches Wörterbuch*, s. v. "comunal adj.," cols. 644–5. and Wartburg, *Französisches Etymologisches Wörterbuch*, s. v. "communis," I, b, α.

Yit was there joye more a thousandfold
Than man can telle; ne nevere wolde it *nyghte*,
But ay cler day to any mannes syghte.
(*Parliament of Fowles*, 208–10)

The *MED* tells us that this verb is derived from "night n.," but, again, Chaucer's conversion has precedent in Robert Mannyng's *Handlyng Synne* (c. 1303), where the conversion of the noun for the first time in the record is prompted by the French word "enuespra" in Mannyng's French source:

Fyl so, he *nyghted* yn a wasteyne,	Vn iur quant en chemin ala,
Þere he sagh no stede certeyne	En vne wastine li enuespra
he sagh no stede where wast best	Quant hure vint de herbeger,
To lygge a nyght and take hys rest.	Pensa ou il pout reposer.[99]

Chaucer's new derivations are even rooted in tradition by the very words that accompany them, as, for example, in Chaucer's compounding of "maister n." and "hunte n." to form "maister-hunte n." In the very same line of the *Book of the Duchess* that the *MED* cites as the first use of this compound, Chaucer also uses "fot-hot adv." in rhyme position:

The mayster-hunte anoon, fot-hot,
With a gret horn blew thre mot
At the uncouplynge of hys houndes. (375–7)

"Fot-hot adv." is, by contrast, an old compound that is first recorded in *Guy of Warwick* where it is interpolated (because it does not directly translate a French word in this text's source):

& seþþe he badde he schuld him say	Gui li ad puis demandé,
Sum soþ tidinges of þe way,	Es regnes u il ad esté,
ȝif he herd neye oþer fer	S'il oit en nule terre
Speken of batayle & of wer	Parler ent de nule guere.
'Ichil þe telle' he seyd, '*fot hot*	'Sire,' fait il, 'jo vus dirrai
Of al þe wer þet y wot.'	D'une guere que jo sai.'
(*Guy of Warwick*, 1813–18)	(*Gui de Warewic*, 1633–8)

Generally speaking then, Chaucer's derivations reach back into English

---

[99] Mannyng, *Handlyng Synne*, Furnivall (ed.), lines 7729–32 (and 6117–20 of the *Manuel*).

tradition not only for their materials, but for the very method that confects them.

It is also true that linguistic history knows this. In explaining its etymological assumptions the *OED* provides a nice summary of the historical pattern I have been tracing, presenting derivation as a constitutive feature of English lexical history:

> If not the extant formal representative of an original Teutonic word, an English word has been *adopted* or *adapted* from some foreign language; i.e. it is a word once foreign, but now, without or with intentional change of form, used as English; or it has been *formed* on or from native or foreign elements, or from a combination of them. *Adoption* is essentially a popular process, at work whenever the speakers of one language come into contact with the speakers of another, from whom they acquire foreign things, or foreign ideas, with their foreign names.[100]

As Bloomfield and Newmark note in their history of English, a general account of the building of English vocabulary must describe procedures of suffixation ("worthinesse n." from "worthi adj."), conversion ("nighten v." from "night n."), prefixing ("biloved ppl." from "loven v."), and compounding ("lombe-skynnes n. from "lomb n." and "skin n1.").[101] It is therefore hardly surprising that 737 of Chaucer's words are new derivations. And yet it has been relatively unnoticed that these new

---

[100] *OED*, "General Explanations," vol. I, p. xxx. Italics are the *OED*'s. I have silently elided the identifying numbers and abbreviations for these italicized terms that the *OED* associates with some of the processes here. For general discussion of derivation see also Bloomfield, *Language*, p. 227: "[There are] three types of morphologic constructions which can be distinguished according to the nature of the constituents . . . composition, secondary derivation, and primary derivation" where "composition" refers to compound words, "secondary derivation" refers to words formed from components that otherwise stand free as words (e.g. door-knob), and "primary derivation" refers to words formed from roots and affixes that never stand free (e.g. re-ceive).

[101] Bloomfield and Newmark, *Linguistic Introduction to the History of English*, pp. 33–46. See also Jespersen, *Growth and Structure of the English Language*, pp. 160–77; Burnley, "Lexis and Semantics," pp. 439–50; and Marchand, *Categories and Types of Present-Day English Word Formation*. Marchand devotes large sections to "compounding" (pp. 11–127), "prefixation" (pp. 129–208), "suffixation" (pp. 209–358) and "derivation by zero-morpheme," a category more strictly defined but similar to what I am calling "conversion" (pp. 359–89). Marchand's discussion focuses on Modern English but it is generally historical as well. For discussion of Chaucer's derivations in particular see Donner, "Derived Words."

derivations entered an English vocabulary that was already significantly composed of them. Indeed, as I demonstrated above, the tradition of invention these derivations represent can again be surveyed in the broad canon of works that contributed significant numbers of the derivations Chaucer later used:

Number of new derivations used by Chaucer	General date and text	*MED* title stencils
39	c. 1121–60 *Peterborough Chronicle*	[various dates between 1121–1160] Peterb.Chron.
74	c. 1200 *Ormulum*	?c1200 Orm.
19	c. 1200 *Vices & Virtues*	(c1200) Vices & V.(1)
102	c. 1200–75 *Ancrene Wisse*	(?a1200) Ancr.; ?c1225 Ancr. (Cleo) a1250 Ancr. (Nero); c1225 Ancr. (Tit); c1230 (Corp-C); c1275 Ancr. (Cleo: Morton)
60	c. 1200–1300 Laȝamon's *Brut*	(?a1200) Lay.Brut; c1300 Lay.Brut (Otho)
16	c. 1225–1300 *King Horn*	(?c1225) Horn; c1300 Horn (Ld)
111	c. 1280–1325 *South English Legendary*	(?c1280) SLeg (Eg); (c1280) SLeg (Pep); (c1290) SLeg (Ld); c1300 SLeg (Ld); c1300 SLeg (Hrl); a1325 SLeg (Corp-C)
36	c. 1300 *Kyng Alisaunder*	(?a1300) KAlex. (Auch); (?a1300) KAlex. (Ld)
21	c. 1300 *Arthur & Merlin*	(?a1300) Arth.& M.
19	c. 1300 *Guy of Warwick*	(?c1300) Guy (1); (?a1300) Guy (2)
27	c. 1300–25 Robert of Gloucester's *Chronicle*	(c1300) Glo.Chron.A.; (a1325) Glo.Chron.B
51	c. 1303 Robert Mannyng's *Handlyng Synne*	(c1303) Mannyng HS
84	c. 1325 *Cursor Mundi*	(a1325) Cursor
11	c1330 *Sir Tristrem*	(?a1300) Tristrem
27	c. 1338 Robert Mannyng's *Chronicle*	(a1338) Mannyng Chron.Pt.1; (a1338) Mannyng Chron.Pt.2
37	c. 1340 *Aȝenbite of Inwit*	(1340) Ayenb.
29	c. 1340 Richard Rolle's *Psalter*	(c1340) Rolle Psalter (UC 64); (c1340) Rolle Psalter (Ld)

The 763 derivations anatomized in this list comprise roughly half of the 1,390 derivations in Chaucer's vocabulary that were coined by his predecessors.[102] These are the words that English writers made for themselves out of English prior to a single Chaucerian invention. They are the sea of invention on which even Chaucer's *native* English floated.

Derivations are the extreme category that prove the essential role new words played in Middle English literary endeavor. Furthermore, as they used the native to make the new *in order* to translate French texts, derivations were finally no different in function from the new borrowings they resembled. On the whole then, lexical invention constituted Chaucer's English because lexical invention constituted Middle English literary culture. The traditional was paradoxically new in Chaucer because novelty was precisely the method of Middle English tradition: the making of English as the means to writing literature was not something Chaucer exceptionally did, but, in fact, the only avenue open to him. So far from being the hallmark of his style, or his "gifts to English," the 1,102 new borrowings and the 737 new derivations that appear in Chaucer's writing for the first time in the record were, therefore, nothing new at all. Even if we add other categories of new vocabulary to these to account for the entire sum of 2,098 words Chaucer used for the first time in the record (categories I will analyze in subsequent chapters), all such lexical novelty *can* demonstrate is the degree to which Chaucer's English was traditional.

---

[102] The *MED* and *OED* sometimes offer English roots for derivations that enter the record after the words they are said to spawn and I eliminate these words from my figures here. I do count derivations based on my own conjectural etymologies (where the *MED* has no etymology), but I do not count such conjecture when the root I propose is attested later than a given derivation. See Part 2, pp. 229–30 for my procedures.

3

The development of Chaucer's English

In movement direction is everything, and the amazing fact is not that there was once a time (as Meredith has it) 'when mind was mud', but rather that mud in due course mounts to mind, and alligators and idiots and slimy seas become the stuff that dreams are made on.

John Livingston Lowes[1]

Several lexical practices transform Chaucer's traditional English into something that appears to be new and they are all interrelated. In this chapter I confine my discussion to the most subtle of these practices, one that furnishes a good starting point because its effects are as enormous and as frequently described as its procedures are difficult to see. In fact, reading Chaucer's writing carefully is as likely to obscure this practice as it is to expose it – for, as I will try to show, it is enabled by a common kind of readerly attention. Chaucer encouraged such attention generally (and it is to this extent that he may be understood to create the misapprehension this practice entails), but the lexical patterns that benefited from this encouragement are themselves so subtle that they probably lay just behind even Chaucer's awareness – or, if he was aware of them, he probably had other effects in mind. Whatever intent we project behind it, however, we must understand this practice since, more than any other, it has allowed critics to equate the making of Chaucer's texts with the making of English poetry, to conflate one poet's literary accomplishment, as P. M. Kean does, with the literary accomplishment of the entire fourteenth century:

> It will be necessary to give some indication of the state of English poetry at the time when [Chaucer] began to write. We can start from

[1] Lowes, *Road to Xanadu*, p. 48.

two generalizations: first, that there seems to have been very little change in attitudes towards poetry, and in the kinds of writing which were undertaken in the two hundred or so years before c. 1360; secondly that, during the second half of the fourteenth century, a change took place which certainly gaining momentum through Chaucer's work though not necessarily initiated by him, altered the whole aspect of English poetry.[2]

Kean may hesitate here in assigning Chaucer full responsibility in larger linguistic changes, but that hesitation is undone some pages later when she claims that Chaucer was responsible for "the development of a new manner of writing in English."[3] In a trice – and not just in Kean – the "momentum" provided by Chaucer's work becomes the "development" of an English tradition. It is the aim of this chapter to describe how this later conflation occurs as a *mis*reading of differently important (and therefore undetected) features of Chaucer's English.

This is a large task because, quite apart from separating the making of literary English from the making of Chaucer's English, it is also necessary, in this case, to separate Chaucer's writing from the idea that this writing comprises an *oeuvre*, from the overwhelming presumption that each of his texts represents a stage in the "development" of a towering "genius." The impulse toward biography exerts an implacable influence here, and Chaucer is uniquely susceptible to that impulse among his predecessors or contemporaries because there is such an unusual wealth of surviving documentary evidence from which to make his life into a story. The voluminous *Chaucer Life-Records* brims with biographical data, and it is a relatively straightforward task to involve those records in the *Complete Works*, to write a critical biography that puts before us, in Derek Pearsall's words, "an image of the man that may serve as a coordinate in refiguring certain expectations."[4] In the earliest period of Chaucer studies, there hardly seemed any other way. Furnivall for one thought that the "chief interest" of writing a commentary on the minor poems was observing "the growth of the Poet's mind and power from his earliest effort to the greatest triumph of his genius," and crucial to his perception of this "genius," he said, was ten Brink's description of the "development [*Entwicklung*]" of

[2] Kean, *Chaucer and the Making of English Poetry*, vol. I, pp. 3–4.
[3] *Ibid.*, vol. I, p. 32.   [4] Pearsall, *Life of Geoffrey Chaucer*, p. 8.

Chaucer's writing. According to Furnivall, this *Entwicklung* "let a flood of light in on the matter" and that light still guides us, with the last two decades alone having seen publication of biographies by John Gardner (1977), Derek Brewer (1978), Donald Howard (1987), and Derek Pearsall (1992).[5]

Chaucer himself abets this project by providing chronologies that give biography an impetus as well as a preliminary ordering for his writing. In fact, the *Introduction* to the *Man of Law's Tale* presents a Man of Law already engaged in biography, viewing Chaucer's work retrospectively and working to coordinate the canon of that work with the living that produced it:

> In youthe he made of Ceys and Alcione,
> And sitthen hath he spoken of everichone,
> Thise noble wyves and thise loveris eke,
> Whoso that wole his large volume seke,
> Cleped the Seintes Legende of Cupide . . . (II, 57–61)

The point of origin fixed in Chaucer's "youthe" grows into both canon (the "large volume") and life (the acts of "speaking" that happen "sitthen"), and sequences the two in lock-step. That sequence is confirmed, moreover, *within* the large volume to which the Man of Law refers, since the "Seintes Legende of Cupide" is, of course, what we now call the *Legend of Good Women*, and the *Prologue* to that work offers similar biographical moments (here, as Cupid accuses Chaucer of "mysseying"),

> Thou hast translated the Romaunce of the Rose,
> That is an heresye ayeins my lawe,
> And makest wise folk from me withdrawe;
> And of Cresyde thou hast seyd as the lyste,
> That maketh men to wommen lasse triste, (F 329–33)

(and, again, as Alceste defends Chaucer against Cupid's charges):

---

[5] Furnivall, *Trial-Forewards*, 5–6. Furnivall refers here to ten Brink, *Chaucer: Studien zur Geschichte seiner Entwicklung und zur Chronologie seiner Schriften*. Furnivall also speaks of a "decline – in accordance with Nature's law – to its poorest" in the period of writing "before the Poet's death" (p. 6). Gardner, *Life and Times of Chaucer*; Brewer, *Chaucer and His World*; Howard, *Chaucer and the Medieval World*. For Pearsall's biography see n. 4 above.

> He made the book that hight the Hous of Fame,
> And eke the Deeth of Blaunche the Duchesse,
> And the Parlement of Foules, as I gesse,
> And al the love of Palamon and Arcite
> Of Thebes, thogh the storye ys knowen lyte;
> And many an ympne for your halydayes,
> That highten balades, roundels, virelayes;
> And, for to speke of other holynesse,
> He hath in prose translated Boece,
> And maad the lyf also of Seynt Cecile.
> He made also, goon ys a gret while,
> Origenes upon the Maudeleyne.
> Hym ought now to have the lesse peyne;
> He hath maad many a lay and many a thing. (F 417–30)

Cupid presents Chaucer's work in an order that modern Chaucerians have come to accept (the *Romaunt of the Rose* early, *Troilus and Criseyde* late), and, although Alceste departs from that order (we tend to assume, for example, that the "Deeth of Blaunche the Duchesse" precedes the "Hous of Fame") it is still important that Alceste assumes there *is* such an order. Some works are made in the distant past ("goon ys a gret while") while others have been written more recently. More important than the particular sequences offered in these sketches, then, is the way that such sketches place the *Legend of Good Women* in a particular position within an even larger sequence. The *Legend* will be written, according to its own fiction, as Chaucer obeys Alceste's command in his life ("while that thou lyvest, yer by yere") as the primary occupation of his living ("the moste partye of thy tyme spende/In makyng of a glorious legende") *subsequent* to all the works listed here. This chronology is, then, both real and useful: we can be sure that the works it lists preceded the *Legend* and, from that, we may follow Alceste's assurance that the "makyng of a glorious legende" will be a development of that earlier effort.

Not only have Chaucerians continued to elucidate and refine such chronologies according to more oblique references in his poems, but critical studies of Chaucer's writing have read Chaucer's work according to that sequence, committing their own structures to its scheme and understanding the particular feature of Chaucer's writing they are concerned with as ramifying from – growing according to – that order.

Kittredge's important early lectures, for example, trace the "whole process of Chaucer's career" by working through the accepted chronology of Chaucer's work.[6] And Lowes, who had already described what he called the mounting of mud to mind in Coleridge's career (this is the context of the remark I take as my epigraph in this chapter), gave the view both a theory and its most confident language in the series of lectures he called, significantly, *Geoffrey Chaucer and the Development of His Genius*. Those lectures essentially translate Tatlock's earlier description of *The Development and Chronology of Chaucer's Works* into a sensitive and sequential reading of the "passage of [Chaucer's] powers from morning into noon" in the early works, "the spoils of a reading which had grown *pari passu* in breadth and depth" that produce *Troilus and Criseyde*, and the "unfolding of Chaucer's genius" in the "crowning achievement" of the *Canterbury Tales*.[7] Even when less confident about the development of "genius" (that is, in the context of much more carefully defined critical concerns), Chaucerians have remained committed to developmental schemes. Here, for example, is Muscatine two decades after Lowes's lectures in *Chaucer and the French Tradition*:

> Traditional criticism has made much of the progressive technical accomplishment and the widening sphere of interest, nourished by reading and observation, that [the *Book of the Duchess*, *The House of Fame*, and the *Parliament of Fowls*] display. We may safely accept these and focus our attention on a third factor, the development of Chaucer's feeling for the adjustment between style and meaning.[8]

Two decades after Muscatine, Alfred David "traces the metamorphoses of Chaucer's conception of poetry as these are reflected in his works" and organizes his treatment of that conception according to the

---

[6] Kittredge, *Chaucer and His Poetry*, p. 27. After an introductory lecture on "The Man and His Times," Kittredge works through the *Book of the Duchess*, the *House of Fame*, *Troilus*, and the *Canterbury Tales*, in that order, in lectures 2–6.

[7] Tatlock, *Development and Chronology of Chaucer's Works*. Lowes, *Geoffrey Chaucer and the Development of His Genius*, pp. 115, 191–2 and 198. The title of these lectures is itself an illustration of the thinking I am describing here.

[8] Muscatine, *Chaucer and the French Tradition*, p. 98. Muscatine analyzes Chaucer's, "Early Poems" first (chapter 4, pp. 98–123), then *Troilus and Criseyde* (chapter 5, pp. 124–65) with the *Canterbury Tales* seen finally as an "outgrowth of the long story" of Chaucer's entire career (p. 172) and analyzed at length last (chapter 6, pp. 166–243).

standard chronology.[9] Even more recently, Carolyn Dinshaw has claimed that this standard chronology forms a "coherent narrative sequence" for the sexual poetics she defines.[10] And Lee Patterson's *Chaucer and the Subject of History* understands Chaucer's earlier texts (*Anelida and Arcite* and *Troilus and Criseyde*) to "define the problematic of history" and "explore . . . the complex subjectivity that constitutes the inner dimension of selfhood," while examination of his texts in a chronological sequence demonstrates how these issues emerge, finally, "at the heart of the *Canterbury Tales*."[11] These well-spaced works, particularly notable for their quality, and worth comparing for the diversity of their critical concerns, take the broad measure of the durability of this critical mode. "Development" still matters in some of the best writing on Chaucer's work we have.[12]

So Chaucer's English, of course, develops too. As C. S. Lewis put it with characteristic pugnacity in the broad terms of "style," there is a "development" from "the old, bad manner" of the *Book of the Duchess* to the "preludings of the new style" in the *Complaint of Mars* akin to "passing from the engine-room of a ship to the deck."[13] Muscatine is of

---

[9] David, *Strumpet Muse*, p. 6. See also pp. 22, 26, 30, 37, and 77 where David also places his reading in the context of this chronology. See p. 245 n.1 and p. 248 n. 1 for David's explicit reliance on Tatlock's datings. There is an exception to David's general reliance on the chronology of Chaucer's works in his treatment of the *Second Nun's Tale* in his last chapter for thematic reasons, although he notes this displacement from standard chronological schemes (p. 232).

[10] Dinshaw, *Chaucer's Sexual Poetics*, p. 26. Dinshaw does begin her study with a framing discussion of *Adam Scriveyn* (out of its conventional place in the standard chronology of Chaucer's writing). Subsequent chapters, however, work through the standard chronology sequentially.

[11] Patterson, *Chaucer and the Subject of History*, p. 26. Patterson begins his discussion with *Anelida and Arcite* and then moves through *Troilus and Criseyde*, the *Knight's Tale*, the *Legend of Good Women*, and various *Canterbury Tales*. This order, of course, displaces the *Knight's Tale* from what some would take to be its appropriate position, before *Troilus*. But see Tatlock, *Development and Chronology of Chaucer's Works*, p. 82 and n. 23 below.

[12] Payne's *Key of Remembrance* is an important exception to the general reliance on chronology. Payne describes his scheme as "more categorical than chronological," and he, therefore, displaces the *Prologue* to the *Legend of Good Women* and *Troilus and Criseyde* from their biographical sequence (see his p. 8). Hansen's *Chaucer and the Fictions of Gender* is a more recent example of a book that uses no chronological scheme (she treats the *Legend of Good Women*, then the *Wife of Bath's Prologue and Tale*, and then the *Book of the Duchess* in her first three chapters).

[13] Lewis, *Allegory of Love*, pp. 164–5.

course amplifying this view in his description of Chaucer's "progressive technical accomplishment" and that accomplishment is specifically located in the "language of Chaucer's poetry" by Norman Eliason: "Roughly speaking, the development was from the artificial to the simple and then to the colloquial. This does not mean that Chaucer replaced one by the other. It means rather that he relied more on the artificial in his early poems and then gradually introduced the colloquial, relying heavily on it in his late poems."[14] Eliason's pattern is unusual in its emphasis on Chaucer's progressive use of the "colloquial" (a separately interesting observation that I will return to in the next chapter), but it is otherwise typical in understanding Chaucer's language as a steady course. When R. W. V. Elliott focuses on lexis in his compendious study of Chaucer's English he makes that course a progress of lexical invention: the "valuable practice [the] *Boece* afforded," he says, led to "further lexical inventiveness in *Troilus and Criseyde* and the *Canterbury Tales*."[15] Similarly, Tim Machan's detailed consideration of the *Boece* finds that Chaucer used that translation as an "opportunity to explore and expand the means of expression he had used theretofore" with the result that, after the *Boece*, "Chaucer's powers of expression were necessarily wider than they had been before."[16] In terms of Chaucer's lexis as a whole, however, the touchstone, as we might expect, is again Mersand, who proposes that the shape of Chaucer's language precisely confirms existing chronologies as it grows *pari passu* by its use of Romance borrowings:

> It has been shown, therefore, that the accepted chronology is fortified, rather than challenged, by the theory that Chaucer's Romance vocabulary was enlarged with each stage of his literary career. As his reading advanced from French to Italian literature, his vocabulary

---

[14] Eliason, *Language of Chaucer's Poetry*, 117. More recently David Wallace traces a similar pattern for Chaucer's career: "The mature Chaucer strove not to gild his diction with Latinate qualities, but rather to liberate and organize those natural rhythms and energies which were peculiar to his own native tongue. The experimental *Anelida* was left incomplete, and thereafter we see Chaucer's diction becoming ever less Latinate and ever more finely attuned to the various registers and natural nuances of an English-speaking voice," Wallace, "Chaucer's Continental Inheritance," pp. 25–6.

[15] Elliott, *Chaucer's English*, pp. 160–1.

[16] Machan, *Techniques of Translation*, p. 126.

increased and expressed more vividly the thoughts and emotions he found so perfectly described in Dante, Petrarch and Boccaccio, and which he later imparted to his own literary creations.[17]

Mersand's claim is picked up in the key studies of Chaucer's language that I have been mentioning. Brewer, for example, speaks of the way, "the increasing use . . . of a language of wider vocabulary of ideas, of intellectual discriminations, of items of luxury, of more sophisticated entertainment, of deeper thought" and how "Chaucer revolutionized 'poetic diction' by 'augmenting'. . . . English with a vast number of new words of Latin, French and Italian origin."[18] And Fisher traces a similar expansion: "As [Chaucer] progressed . . . more and more of his French words were taken from the administrative and cultural vocabulary with which he and his bilingual audience were so familiar."[19] In criticism, then, Chaucer's very words have become, in effect, another *form* of his life: as the textual traces of the growing sophistication of the man, Chaucer's English is not simply a body of work but a lexical biography in its own right.

Such wide-spread belief in Chaucer's development matters to this chapter because it is my central claim here that Chaucer's English, and particularly Chaucer's vocabulary, does *not* develop. In fact, I want to show that Chaucer's vocabulary is static in precisely those attributes in which it has been said to "grow." Chaucer's readers have seen a language increasing in its powers, enlarging crucially in its vocabulary, *by* looking for that growth, but it is actually sequential arrangements of Chaucer's writing that create the impression of progress, not the other way around. In that sense, exposing the stasis in Chaucer's lexis ought to call the very project of chronological readings – and all the claims that ramify from them – into question. And yet, these readings are true in an unexpected sense because, *in* its stasis – or, better, in the particular nature of that stasis – Chaucer's lexis also encourages readers to *see* progress; the organizational complexities that govern this stasis them-selves necessitate the sequential reading that creates the developing genius. In this sense developmental views are a significant back-

---

[17] Mersand, *Chaucer's Romance Vocabulary*, p. 81.
[18] Brewer, "English and European Traditions," p. 26.
[19] Fisher, "Chaucer and the French Influence," p. 181. For a more recent version of this claim see Fisher, "Chaucer's French," 42–3.

formation from Chaucer's language, a reading his English breeds, not one brought to it under biography's separate impetus. We focus on Chaucer's biography for the same reason we focus on the novelty of his language: because "progressive technical accomplishment" becomes as thematic in his work – an aspect, finally, of its *meaning* – as the idea of the poet "Chaucer" and his lived life.

The method I will use for defining the techniques that encourage developmental readings involves what may seem – at least initially – a paradoxically close reliance on the standard chronology of Chaucer's works. For that reason I should first make clear that I do not intend my argument to question either the standard chronology of Chaucer's work or the possibility of crafting such a time-line. I employ a chronology because that is the only method (or so it has seemed to me) for testing the ramifications of chronology, for showing how reading according to this standard scheme conduces to certain misunderstandings, how, what I will call a developmental hermeneutic is bred by Chaucer's lexical techniques and therefore misses what is precisely *anti-developmental* in Chaucer's language. Instead of engaging in the circular project of making arguments *about* chronology while arguing *for* a particular chronology itself I have tried to move the particular out of court by relying on an order constructed by others.[20] For the sake of clarity, I have set out that chronology at the beginning of Part 2 of this book where it is prefaced by a more copious explanation of my rationale for its determination. The order I use is most speculative as it places the *ABC* early, most of the *Monk's Tale* before the *House of Fame*, the *Boece* not parallel to but before *Troilus and Criseyde*, and *Troilus and Criseyde* before the *Knight's Tale*.[21] I think it is fair to be free with these

---

The chronology I choose is loosely laid out in the *Riverside Chaucer*, pp. xxvi–xxix (esp. p. xxix). There is further discussion of dating in the *Riverside's* "Explanatory Notes" and I give relevant page references for individual works in the ordered table of "Chaucer's Writings" in Part 2 of this book (pp. 223–6). For a convenient summary of scholarship on the dating of Chaucer's works before 1907 see Tatlock, *Development and Chronology of Chaucer's Works*, pp. x–xi.

21 Pearsall recently confirmed much of the *Riverside's* chronology in his *Life of Geoffrey Chaucer* (see esp. his "Chronological Table," pp. 306–13) as does Howard in his biography (*Chaucer and the Medieval World*), but the schemes proffered by both of these writers have important points of disagreement with each other and with the *Riverside's* chronology. Pearsall thinks the *ABC* "was probably composed in the late 1370's" (p. 152), although the *Riverside* places it before the *Book of the Duchess* (which it

presumptions precisely because I do not attempt to test any specific chronological arrangements here but, rather, the ramifications of chronological order *per se*. My end will, I think, justify my means since I am working here toward the claim that Chaucer's lexical techniques encourage his readers to see "progressive technical accomplishment" when his works are placed in *any* order. In that sense, the order I choose here only shows what any order would finally show.

I

The developmental hermeneutic that governs so much of Chaucer studies is abetted not only by chronological schemes in Chaucer's work, but by self-referential tendencies in Chaucer's English. These networks of allusion – as it is sometimes put, Chaucer "borrowing from himself" – have a catalytic effect on chronology: they do not themselves imply any particular priority of composition for Chaucer's texts, but they lend powerful support to any order once that order has been posited.[22] Believe the chronology that Chaucer's texts offer for themselves in the *Introduction* to the *Man of Law's Tale* and the *Prologue* to the *Legend of Good Women*, in other words, respond to the biographical impulse that those passages inject into the process of reading the texts Chaucer mentions, and Chaucer's language will demonstrate the forward

dates "c. 1368–72") as does Howard (pp. 87–91). Pearsall places the *Knight's Tale* before *Troilus and Criseyde* (p. 153), as does Howard (pp. 260–81) where the *Riverside* chronology has the opposite order. Pearsall presses the notion that Chaucer translated the *Boece* "during the period of composition" of the *Knight's Tale* and *Troilus* (p. 154) and Howard also assumes that Chaucer translated Boethius "while working on the *Troilus*" (p. 353). This is of course the fundamental objection that might be lodged against *any* chronological sequence of Chaucer's works (even an experimental one like my own), since it brings out the absence of firm evidence that Chaucer's texts were written sequentially in any sense, that their composition did not actually (and often) overlap. Indeed, although the *Riverside* places the *Boece* in a sequence, it groups it with the *Knight's Tale* and *Troilus and Criseyde* in a general range of dates ("1380–7") that admits the possibility of simultaneous composition. On the other hand, it is difficult for discussion of Chaucer's work (as in *reading* Chaucer's work) to keep the possibility of such simultaneity always in view. Pearsall, for example, must discuss the *Boece* sequentially, between his discussion of the *Knight's Tale* and *Troilus* (pp. 159–68), an organizational expedience that my own order can be seen to respond to.

22 For two other examples of Chaucer's "self-indebtedness" see Pratt, "Chaucer Borrowing From Himself."

movement you have been impelled to see.[23] Since each of Chaucer's texts is linked to the texts that precede and follow it, these texts can easily become the textual correlative of Chaucer's remembering and developing mind, linked (in an image Coleridge used and Lowes favored) by "hooks-and-eyes of the memory."[24] Read Chaucer's work according to the standard chronology and these hooks-and-eyes join Chaucer's writing into an *oeuvre*: "later" linguistic activities benefit from "earlier" textual experiences because those "earlier" activities are "recalled" and brought to bear on later textual situations.

It is the agenda that surrounds the static object, the imported presumption of a chronological pattern, that makes that object move, that creates the evidence of the development it purports to register. Take, for example, the famous double presence of the line "Allone, withouten any compaignye" in both the *Knight's Tale* (I, 2779) and the *Miller's Tale* (I, 3204). Reading through Fragment I of the *Tales* in sequence makes the Miller's use of the line a repetition of the Knight's, a development of the Knight's language, a trivializing riposte to his solemnity (as is, by this reading, the whole of the *Miller's Tale*): as the story of the *Tales* figures it, in other words, the Miller is *remembering* the Knight's words and reworking them because the fixed sequence of Fragment I tells a story that positions the *Miller's Tale* "after" the *Knight's Tale*, making the one an emphatic response to (a "quitting" of) the other *in time*. The form of the tale-telling contest in the *Canterbury Tales* offers a local developmental model which sequences homologous elements of the Knight's and Miller's tales, but it is precisely because that sequence *is* fiction that, apart from it, all that can be certainly said about these lines is that they are exactly the *same*. Since readers have other reasons to assume that the *Miller's Tale* was written after the *Knight's Tale* (in particular, the lines of the *Prologue* to the *Legend of Good Women* that place "Palamon and Arcite" outside of the *Canterbury Tales*), this fiction does not have substantially determinate effects. But take, by contrast, the phrase "Passen as dooth a shadwe upon the

---

[23] For the use made of such repeated lines as grounds for dating the *Knight's Tale* after *Troilus and Criseyde* see Tatlock, *Development and Chronology of Chaucer's Works*, pp. 76–9.

[24] Coleridge uses the image in *The Friend*, vol. I, essay 3. See *Collected Works*, vol. IV, Rooke (ed.), p. 21. See also Lowes, *Road to Xanadu*, p. 44.

wal," which appears (with slight variation) in the *Merchant's Tale* (IV, 1315), the *Shipman's Tale* (VII, 9), and the *Parson's Tale* (X, 1068), texts whose compositional sequence other evidence does not so easily secure. The story of the *Tales* make it possible to say that the Parson's recollection of this phrase helps him to "knytte up" previous tales and "make an end" to the whole Canterbury pilgrimage by reworking and "quitting" memorable (because repeated) phrases from the texts that "precede" his own. [25] In the case of the phrase "Passen as dooth a shadwe upon the wal," however, our sense of this sequence, our developmental reading rests only on the *Tales'* story. The use the Parson makes of this line is only "repetition" (a "quitting") because the frame narrative of the *Tales* places (or, in its unfinished form, implies placement of) the *Parson's Tale* last.

Repetition, in other words, exists to be "perceived" by virtue of a temporal structure external to the ("repeated") items in question, as can be seen most clearly when standard chronologies actually conflict with what we might call "Canterbury" chronology. For example, to read Chaucer's work in the order of standard chronologies finds the phrase "Pitee renneth soone in gentil herte" for the "first" time in the *Knight's Tale* (I, 1761) and "subsequent" uses of that line in the *Prologue* to the *Legend of Good Women* (F 503; G 491), the *Merchant's Tale* (IV, 1986), and the *Squire's Tale* (V, 479). But the narrative of the *Canterbury Tales* puts the origin of the line in the *Legend of Good Women*, not the *Knight's Tale*, because the Man of Law makes the "Seintes Legende of Cupide" prior to the whole of the tales (as above, in II, 61) while the *Tales*, of course, gathers the *Knight's Tale* into its narrative and temporal fold. At the same time, the reference to the story of "the love of Palamon and Arcite" in the *Legend* (F, 420) is one of the grounds on which the composition of the *Knight's Tale* may itself be placed prior to the *Tales* as a sequence. The narrativity of these chronologies and the fissures that

---

[25] For the extensive "quitting" of the other *Canterbury Tales* performed by the *Parson's Tale* see Patterson, "The 'Parson's Tale' and the Quitting of the 'Canterbury Tales.'" Patterson is more interested to position the *Parson's Tale* within the ideational and formal development of the *Tales* than in a chronological sequence *per se*. Still, he classes the phrase "a shadwe upon a wal" with other phrases that "*echo* passages in the preceding tales" (p. 357). Emphasis mine. Patterson also helpfully describes the widespread opinion that the *Parson's Tale* is "a journeyman's work completed early in the poet's career" (p. 332 and p. 332 n. 2).

comparing them will open expose the narrativity of all chronology. The evidence that puts this line in motion, that understands its textual filiations as aspects of a chronological order, is brought to it and cannot inhere anywhere in these lines. Identity produces memory – repetitions become what Tatlock calls "reminiscences"[26] – only when identical objects are *put* into time, when one identical object is tagged as a beginning and other identical occurrences (now *re*currences) become "second," or "third," and so on. Once the process is set in motion, however, identity becomes a powerful argument *for* chronology.

This argument matters especially at the level of lexis since words are even more often identical than lines and therefore more often repeated. It is a logic very much at work in all views of the "growth" of Chaucer's vocabulary, and, not surprisingly, it is a logic very much at the heart of Mersand's copious study of Chaucer's words. In fact, although Mersand's work has been most frequently remembered for its tabulation of Chaucer's Romance "contribution" to English, as I noted in chapter 2, Mersand had larger purposes, and chief among them is what he described as the "evolution" of Chaucer's Romance vocabulary.[27] The evolution of Chaucer's contributions ("Chaucer imported fewer new Romance words in his earlier works than in his later ones") is really a subset of his larger claim that "Chaucer's Romance vocabulary was enlarged with each stage of his literary career."[28] At the same time, the

---

[26] Tatlock, *Development and Chronology of Chaucer's Works*, p. 76.

[27] Mersand's interest in this is most prominent in the title to chapter 10, "The Evolution of Chaucer's Romance Vocabulary," *Chaucer's Romance Vocabulary*, pp. 90–122. But evolution is Mersand's steady concern beginning with chapter 6, "Romance Words in *Romaunt of the Rose*" (pp. 58–61) and continuing through two of his "General Conclusions": "8. Chaucer used few Romance words in his early works, increased his store of them after his acquaintance with Italian literature, and used most of them at the height of his popularity at the Court. This was probably at the time of his composition of the *Legend of Good Women*. 9. After Chaucer's reversal of fortune in 1386, he abandoned many of his Romance words which he used, in all probability, to satisfy the Gallic tastes of Court circles" (*Chaucer's Romance Vocabulary*, p. 138). The late abandonment of Romance words Mersand observes is an odd twist here that essentially contradicts the trajectory he describes in the passage I quoted above (pp. 97–8). It is, however, an observation that confirms points I will make below.

[28] For the first phrase see Mersand, *Chaucer's Romance Vocabulary*, p. 73. For the second, see p. 97 above. Mersand tends to mix these levels of analysis as is particularly evidenced by the fact that his description of the development of Chaucer's "contributions" occurs in the "summary" conclusions to the chapter called "Romance Words in Minor Poems" (pp. 62–74).

equation of "contribution" and "evolution" of Romance vocabulary puts a powerful chronological engine beneath Mersand's more general observation of lexical enlargement: it privileges the moment a word enters English (thereby turning the moment of each borrowing into an origin) and thereby frames the story of Chaucer's English with the story of *English*, using the more general chronology as a lever to impel the smaller chronology forward. Mersand pretends that his method begins by keeping lexis and chronology apart, that "contributions" will be counted in individual texts and, "if these statistics are granted evidential value, we may then proceed to their interpretation and their application to matters of Chaucerian chronology and literary development."[29] But the statistics he provides (that precede these very remarks) are set out in a table that shows the "number of words used first by Chaucer" in each of his texts as those texts are *already* ordered chronologically.[30] On closer reflection his analytic sequence ("we may then proceed . . .") is an impossibility, since "matters of Chaucerian chronology and literary development" must already be settled before *any* word that is used "first" in a particular text can be listed. Take, for example, the occurrence of the new borrowing "executen v." in a line from the *Knight's Tale* ("The destinee, ministre general, That executeth in the world over al . . .," I, 1663–4) and a line from *Troilus and Criseyde* ("But execut was al bisyde hire leve/The goddes wil," 3.622–3).[31] Assume that the *Knight's Tale* precedes *Troilus* and this chronology makes it possible to say that the "first" borrowing of the verb from French or Latin (as its source languages are identified in the *MED*) occurs in the *Knight's Tale*, that Chaucer's vocabulary "increased" in the earlier text and this increase was remembered and exploited in *Troilus and Criseyde*.[32] On the other hand, since the order of these texts is

---

[29] Mersand, *Chaucer's Romance Vocabulary*, pp. 56–7.

[30] For this chart see *ibid.*, pp. 54–5. Its order generally conforms to the standard chronology of Chaucer's work I am relying on here, although Mersand groups all the *Canterbury Tales* together at the end of the chart, even those like the *Knight's Tale* he elsewhere assumes were written earlier.

[31] Mersand actually lists (and, therefore, counts) these two forms as separate words ("execut adj." and "executeth v.") in his appendix (p. 164). However, I am not examining evidence Mersand adduces here (because, had he worked through these details, he might not have reached the conclusions he did) but the specific patterns that underlie the numbers and contributions he sets out in his tables.

[32] Chaucer's lexical decisions in these lines are independent of his sources. There is no

unstable, it is possible to assume that *Troilus* was written before the *Knight's Tale*, at which point the "contribution" and the "increase" Mersand describes are upended: rearrange the chronology of Chaucer's works in this common way and "executen v." is now borrowed "first" in *Troilus*, "contributed" to English there, and "enlarges" the vocabulary of the *Knight's Tale*. Mersand can only count "*first* uses" because he has already decided what *is* "first."

There is a further strand to the circularity of this thinking which is evident in Mersand's claim that Chaucer's increasing vocabulary made it possible for him to express his thoughts and emotions "more vividly" as well as Brewer's more general claim that the "augmenting" of Chaucer's English provided him with a "wider vocabulary of ideas . . . of deeper thought." The presumption in both cases is that "first uses" are progressive not only by repetition but by accretion. Thus, "influence n." may be seen to develop, like "executen v.," as it is borrowed for the "first" time in the English of Chaucer's *Troilus and Criseyde*,

> O *influences* of thise hevenes hye! (3.618)

and as it is repeated (by standard chronologies) in the *Astrolabe* and the *Merchant's Tale*,

> . . . or elles whan the planetes ben under thilke signes thei causen us by her *influence* operaciouns and effectes like to the operaciouns of bestes. (*Astrolabe*, part I, 21.59–62)

> Were it by *influence* or by nature . . . (IV, 1968)

This word enlarges Chaucer's vocabulary because it adds to the store of words he may "later" draw upon, but, further, according to the Mersandian and Brewerian schemes, Chaucer's vocabulary is enlarged because the process of new borrowing that produces this one word is repeated *alongside* its use to produce other new words – and therefore *more* new words in aggregate. These schemes must note that the repetition of "influence n." in the *Astrolabe* is itself accompanied by the "first" borrowing of "operacioun n." which also appears in that text

parallel passage for this line of the *Knight's Tale* in the *Teseida*. See the table of correspondences between the *Teseida* and the *Knight's Tale* in the *Riverside Chaucer* (p. 827). There is also no parallel passage in the *Filostrato* for this line in *Troilus*. See Chaucer, *Troilus and Criseyde*, Windeatt (ed.), p. 280.

(twice, in the passage I quote above) for the first time according to standard chronologies. And they must note as well that this word has its own evolution as it is repeated in a whole series of subsequent texts:

> Sith folk ne doon hir *operacion* . . . (*Wife of Bath's Tale*, III, 1148)
>
> Er he had doon this *operacioun* . . . (*Squire's Tale*, V, 130)
>
> Which book spak muchel of the *operaciouns* . . . (*Franklin's Tale*, V, 1129)
>
> Acordaunt to his *operacioun* . . . (*Franklin's Tale*, V, 1290)

Chaucer's English develops in this sense because the hooks-and-eyes of a linguistic memory push Chaucer's *oeuvre* forward as a single, accumulating whole, each text in the service of the language of the texts that precede it, *as* they build on that earlier language. In this view, each text gives more to the works that follow it than it got from the texts that came before. The methodological premise here of course is that Chaucer continues to use all his new words after they are new (a point I will return to at greater length below) and the definitional premise is that even repeated *novelty* allows the elements of repetition to be called "new." At root, in other words, such schemes ignore the possibility that a technique of lexical invention used so steadily and identically from text to text may actually represent a kind of *stasis*.

That stasis is a significant feature of Chaucer's lexical invention can indeed be observed by recreating exactly the kind of table Mersand provides to illustrate the growth of Chaucer's vocabulary in its new borrowings. Once again, if Mersand's methods are used, if his figures for the Romance "contributions" of each of Chaucer's texts are updated with word-counts taken from the *MED*, and if those text-by-text contributions are determined and organized according to a standard chronological scheme, the general contours of Mersand's results are confirmed. (In place of Mersand's density calculation of the "percentage of vocabulary" the number of new words in each text represent I include figures based on total vocabulary and total number of headwords; the figures on which my calculation is based will be given below where they are analyzed.)[33]

---

[33] "Words per new word" takes the total number of words in each text (*counting* all repetitions, declined forms, proper nouns – that is, every semantic unit that can be

Table 3.1. *Romance words recorded first in Chaucer's writing*[34]

	New Romance words	Words per new word	Headwords per new word		New Romance words	Words per new word	Headwords per new word
ROMA	69	155	26	GP	34	196	48
ABC	13	110	37	AST	67	190	16
BD	38	228	36	LGW G (rev.)	2	626	221
PITY	9	102	37	MILPRO	1	603	251
LADY	2	522	173	MILT	12	428	94
SNPRO	7	129	52	RVPRO	0	–	–
SNT	10	336	76	RVT	5	661	164
MKT (w/o MI)	49	107	24	CKPRO	0	–	–
HF	97	137	20	CKT	1	450	207
ANEL	8	347	97	INTMLT	4	248	109
PF	21	263	59	MLT	8	982	175
BO	257	200	12	EPIMLT	0	–	–
TR	124	529	29	WBPRO	8	851	167
ADAM	0	–	–	WBT	1	3218	755
MARS	3	774	226	FRPRO	0	–	–
VENUS	0	–	–	FRT	5	576	145
KNT	49	350	47	SUMPRO	1	346	173
FORMAGE	3	159	83	SUMT	9	512	118
FORT	2	289	138	CLPRO	1	422	209
TRUTH	0	–	–	CLT	7	1290	195
GENT	0	–	–	MERPRO	0	–	–
STED	1	193	111	MERT	9	1014	166
LGW F	8	565	125	EPIMERT	0	–	–
LGW	8	2113	246	INTSQT	0	–	–

(cont'd)

called a "word") and divides it by the number of new Romance words in that text. The resulting figure gives a kind of frequency (170 "words per new word" for the *Romaunt* suggests that, statistically speaking, every 170th word in that text was a new borrowing). "Headwords per new word" takes the total number of headwords in each text (that is the number of entries in Benson's *Glossarial Concordance* that account for the words in the text – *excluding* repetitions and declined forms) and divides it by the number of new Romance words.

34 The tabulation given for "LGW G (rev.)" in this and subsequent tables only counts words in the revised parts of the "G Prologue" of the *Legend of Good Women* (that is, where lines in this prologue are not also present in the "F Prologue"). " MkT (MI)" refers to the "Modern Instances" in the *Monk's Tale* (lines 2375–462) and only tabulates words in those lines. "MkT" therefore excludes those lines.

Table 3.1. (*cont'd*)

	New Romance words	Words per new word	Head-words per new word		New Romance words	Words per new word	Head-words per new word
SqT	10	546	117	NPT	8	606	141
FranPro	1	147	99	EpiNPT	0	–	–
FranT	8	864	154	CYPro	3	446	148
PhyT	3	729	206	CYT	31	193	37
IntPardT	1	335	176	MancPro	1	856	334
PardPro	1	1032	395	MancT	1	1992	596
PardT	8	491	120	ParsPro	0	–	–
ShipT	5	723	164	ParsT	42	724	62
ProPrT	0	–	–	Scog	0	–	–
PrT	2	784	251	Buk	0	–	–
ProThop	0	–	–	Purse	0	–	–
Thop	5	307	113	Prov	0	–	–
Mel	12	1401	129	Ros	3	62	36
ProMkT	2	392	168	WomUnc	0	–	–
MkT (MI)	0	–	–	WomNob	2	112	63
ProNPT	0	–	–	MercB	0	–	–

These figures show that Chaucer's vocabulary steadily "increased" if they are read as Mersand says they should be: most of Chaucer's texts "contribute" some new Romance word to the language, so that the cumulative effect of the constant importation of new words will be a steady increase. Indeed, the very process of charting new vocabulary, text by text *as* a chronological march, begs for addition: the iteration of each text looks like a step *toward* a final total, and the very succession of numbers makes Chaucer's vocabulary seem to burgeon. But if this table may be read for this total, it also need not be so read; for the numbers that can be added here may also be compared to one another for their identity, and in that comparison, a stasis may be detected at the root of any growth – precisely because the growth here is steady. And it must be clearly borne in mind that what this table does *not* show is that the words borrowed in each of Chaucer's texts were, in fact, passed to the texts that followed them, that iterative use was, in fact, successive use. Mersand assumes that more is simply more, that a constant increase in new vocabulary is necessarily an aggregation in that all new vocabulary is subsequently available for use. But these numbers do not themselves offer evidence that *could* support this assumption, an assumption that is itself, of course, an application of the developmental hermeneutic (addition is the mathematical activity that developmental assumptions demand). If we refuse to add these first uses – even *as* they are determined by chronological presumptions – we may note, first, that the individual numbers in this table are *not* identical, either with respect to the raw count of new words in each text, or with respect to "density." But we may notice, second, that most of the texts Chaucer wrote resemble each other *in that* they contributed new Romance words. The density of new words, although it varies considerably from text to text (most notably, however, from prose to verse and from long to short texts), only helps to underscore this point.[35] Chaucer is still borrowing at virtually the same *rate* in his early texts as he is borrowing in his later ones (the one new word for every thirty-six he used in the *Book of the Duchess* is virtually identical to the one new word for every thirty-seven he used in the *Canon's Yeoman's Tale*). Like the repetition of the borrowing of "operacioun n." next to the repetition of "influence n." in the *Astrolabe*, the similar numbers next to each text in this table show a lexis at procedural rest. It shows a vocabulary that, *as* it borrows, is not really growing at all.

2

Mersand finds evolution when he counts Chaucer's words because the presumptive chronology he employs must transform stasis into development, but he is persuaded to presume development by still deeper and more complex patterns in Chaucer's vocabulary. If a developmental hermeneutic led Mersand down a primrose path there were even more primroses lining that path than he could see, and the increase he makes

---

[35] It is true that an unusually large number of words entered Chaucer's writing in the constellation of Boethian texts (the *Boece*, the *Knight's Tale*, and *Troilus and Criseyde*), but this is part of a separate story that is discussed later in this chapter. Mersand observes this in two different ways: "The *Boethius* and the *Troilus* contain the largest numbers of new words, respectively" (*Chaucer's Romance Vocabulary*, p. 73); "Chaucer did not begin to use a large percentage of Romance words until his middle period" (*Chaucer's Romance Vocabulary*, p. 83).

in Chaucer's vocabulary could have been made by using two other kinds of evidence his analysis does not even discern. There are, first, other new words in Chaucer's vocabulary that Mersand ignores because they have nothing to do with borrowing. There is, second, a kind of expansion in the vocabulary of each of Chaucer's texts that a measure of novelty using the history of the language as its ruler (when a word enters the English record "first") simply cannot see. The first of these lexical categories is transformed into growth by the same kind of chronological presumption I have just examined. But the second of these categories of novelty only exists *by means* of this presumption. It is the extreme example of this presumption and the power of a developmental hermeneutic to create its own evidence, but it illuminates still more than this power, since pressing hard on this second category also helps to uncover how Chaucer's vocabulary itself encourages a developmental hermeneutic.

What matters again then is the repeated use of the other important lexical technique I described in the previous chapter for the creation of new vocabulary in Chaucer's English and Middle English as a whole. As I noted there, Chaucer provided his writing with words new to English not only by borrowing Romance words, but by deriving them anew from elements already present in the language (e. g. "maister-hunte n.," "convertible adj.," "fortunen v."). Mersand ignores these words, but setting them out in the kind of text-by-text table he provided for Chaucer's new Romance vocabulary shows how he could have used them, since, in this iterative form, they trace exactly the same pattern as new borrowings.

Mersand could have added up these numbers just as he added up Chaucer's new Romance borrowing, and such a treatment of these figures would have nearly doubled the aggregate novelty of Chaucer's lexis. But, as above, these numbers only testify to an accumulation by imposing the shape of a career upon them, because Chaucer's derived vocabulary is as static in its procedures as are his borrowed words. Derivation occurs at a slightly slower rate than new borrowing, but its constancy in so many of Chaucer's texts counts as an important identity between them. And it is again true that significant differences in such novelty between texts follows no general trend: new derivations can appear as often in late texts (for example, the thirty derivations in the

Table 3.2. *Derived words recorded first in Chaucer's writing*

	New derived words	Words per new word	Headwords per new word		New Derived words	Words per new word	Headwords per new word
Roma	43	248	41	SumPro	0	–	–
ABC	1	1425	484	SumT	4	1152	266
BD	29	299	47	ClPro	0	–	–
Pity	0	–	–	ClT	8	1129	171
Lady	4	261	87	MerPro	0	–	–
SNPro	8	113	46	MerT	10	913	150
SNT	4	841	190	EpiMerT	0	–	–
MkT (w/o MI)	9	581	129	IntSqT	0	–	–
HF	31	428	63	SqT	10	546	117
Anel	11	252	71	FranPro	0	–	–
PF	16	345	78	FranT	7	987	176
Bo	157	328	20	PhyT	1	2186	620
Tr	105	625	34	IntPardT	1	335	176
Adam	0	–	–	PardPro	1	1032	395
Mars	3	774	226	PardT	5	786	192
Venus	0	–	–	ShipT	7	516	117
KnT	37	464	62	ProPrT	0	–	–
FormAge	8	60	31	PrT	0	–	–
Fort	4	145	69	ProThop	0	–	–
Truth	2	111	65	Thop	4	383	142
Gent	0	–	–	Mel	15	1121	103
Sted	1	193	111	ProMkT	3	261	112
LGW F	6	753	167	MkT (MI)	0	–	–
LGW	19	890	104	ProNPT	1	435	212
GP	28	238	58	NPT	5	970	226
Ast	17	750	61	EpiNPT	0	–	–
LGW G (rev.)	5	250	88	CYPro	1	1338	445
MilPro	0	–	–	CYT	9	664	127
MilT	13	396	87	MancPro	3	285	111
RvPro	3	177	84	MancT	4	498	149
RvT	10	330	82	ParsPro	1	558	249
CkPro	1	322	162	ParsT	30	1014	87
CkT	2	225	104	Scog	1	392	214
IntMLT	2	495	217	Buk	0	–	–
MLT	9	873	156	Purse	0	–	–
EpiMLT	1	208	125	Prov	0	–	–
WBPro	9	757	148	Ros	0	–	–
WBT	5	644	151	WomUnc	0	–	–
FrPro	1	275	143	WomNob	1	223	125
FrT	1	2878	726	MercB	0	–	–

Parson's Tale) as in early texts (for example, the twenty-nine derivations in the *Book of the Duchess*).

The second category of new vocabulary Mersand misses is, curiously enough, vastly larger than either new borrowings or new derivations or, even, the sum of these two categories taken together; had Mersand seen it he might have turned almost the whole of Chaucer's vocabulary into evidence of growth. In one sense, however, it is not surprising that Mersand overlooked it since the definitions necessary to discern the category have nothing to do with his purpose. In another sense, however, these definitions *are* directly relevant to that purpose because they demand a deep immersion in chronological presumptions if they are to be perceived, and, as we have seen, Mersand was emphatically immersed in those presumptions. It will probably help to effect the necessary immersion here, however, to generate this category out of a few of its constituent words as they emerge from a particular textual moment in the posited sequence of Chaucer's career. The *Envoy to Scogan* provides a compact site for such analysis, not least because P. M. Kean gives it great importance in her developmental scheme by calling it "a good example" of the "urbane manner" that she considers the "new manner of writing in English" which Chaucer fashioned.[36] Kean's concerns are not specifically lexical but her claim makes it especially interesting to note the various ways in which the lexis of this poem was new. In the first five of its seven stanzas there are six words that appear in Chaucer's English for the first time in the record, and all of this novelty results from the procedures I have examined so far: these words are either new foreign borrowings ("creat ppl.," "mortal adj.," "proceden v.," "eterne adj.," "causen vi.") or new derivations ("rakelnesse n."). But closer examination shows that these words are not so interesting at the moment of the *Envoy* in Chaucer's "career" since, according to standard chronologies, all of these new words are recorded first in some text by Chaucer that preceded this poem.[37] The last two

---

[36] Kean, *Chaucer and the Making of English Poetry*, vol. I, pp. 32–3 (see p. 3 for the last phrase quoted). This poem is generally placed late. See the notes in the *Riverside Chaucer* (p. 1086) for a convenient summary of careful discussion in Chaucer, *Complete Works*, Skeat (ed.), vol. II, pp. 556–7 (dating the poem to 1393) and in Brusendorff, *Chaucer Tradition*, p. 292 (dating the poem to "July or August 1391").

[37] For the first uses of these words according to standard chronologies see the *ABC*, line 56 ("eterne adj."), *Second Nun's Tale*, line 328 ("proceden v."), the *House of Fame*, line

stanzas of this *Envoy*, on the other hand, show a purer kind of lexical novelty:

> Nay, Scogan, say not so, for I m'excuse –
> God helpe me so! – in no rym, dowteles,
> Ne thynke I never of slep to wake my muse,
> That rusteth in my shethe stille in pees.
> While I was yong, I put hir forth in prees;
> But al shal passe that men prose or ryme;
> Take every man hys turn, as for his tyme.
>
> [*Envoy*]
> Scogan, that knelest at the stremes hed
> Of grace, of alle honour and worthynesse
> In th'ende of which strem I am dul as ded,
> Forgete in solytarie wildernesse –
> Yet, Scogan, thenke on Tullius kyndenesse;
> Mynne thy frend, there it may fructyfye!
> Far-wel, and loke thow never eft Love dyffye. (36–49)

While some of the lexical novelty here is also recycled ("Muse n." and "worthinesse n." appear for the first time in English in earlier texts by Chaucer), and some of it conforms to activities I have already discussed ("prosen v." is derived in this text for the very first time in English), the words "ded n." and "minnen v." occur here, in this stanza, for the first time, not in English, but in *Chaucer's* writing. That is, these words are invisible to the measures of novelty I have so far used because each one is recorded in English long before Chaucer began to write. On the other hand, these words do more here than fill a semantic gap, since Chaucer's vocabulary already contained exact synonyms for "ded" ("deth n.") and "minnen." ("remembren v.").[38] These words are reached off the shelf of English lexical possibility at this late point in Chaucer's career, departing from those forms that, especially if we view Chaucer's writing as a career, this career had habituated. Each of these departures shows Chaucer mining *English* for words that he had not used yet, thereby

---

3 ("causen vi."), *Boece*, Book 3, pr.ii, line 179 ("creat ppl.") the *Complaint Unto Pity*, line 61 ("mortal adj."), the *Manciple's Tale*, line 283 ("rakelnesse n.").

38 Chaucer had used "deth n." 306 times and "remembren v." 69 times before he first used these synonyms in the *Envoy*. See Benson, *Glossarial Concordance* (although Benson's citations are not in the strictly chronological order I have used, as in Part 2, pp. 223–6, to determine my figures).

creating a separate category of novelty for vocabulary of this kind. As a crucial moment in the fashioning of a "new manner of writing in English" this last stanza of the *Envoy* shows that Chaucer could fashion the "new" simply by turning anew to the "old."

When viewed at the particular moment of emergence it is simplest to say that Chaucer used extant English words like "ded" and "minnen" late in his career because he had had no previous cause to use them before. When we look at Chaucer's career as a whole, however, this cannot be the end of the story since, with all the hindsight of everything Chaucer has done and all the foresight of everything he will do, such vocabulary acts like a delay – even a calculated one. If we care about "progressive" novelty, in other words, we have to see that these words *can* provide additional novelty at a late stage because they were held in "reserve" before. Since this is the perspective that interests me I will call this vocabulary "reserved" hereafter. It is a category of lexis that, to my knowledge, readers who have separately described the growth of Chaucer's vocabulary have never noticed. On the one hand, this is perfectly reasonable since "reserved" words are not novel but "old" by standard measures. On the other hand, the omission is odd because, as I have said, it is only a developmental hermeneutic that can create this category: "reserved" words are *only* new if Chaucer's works are read in a chronological scheme. What seems clear is that, even though this pattern in Chaucer's vocabulary has not been named, it exerts a strong pressure on presumptions of growth since, once chronology creates "reserved" vocabulary, its novelty vastly exceeds other kinds of novelty in each of Chaucer's texts. In fact, if data for the progressive enlarge-ment of Chaucer's vocabulary is sought, a text-by-text table of the 5,414 "reserved" words Chaucer uses offers the largest possible body of evidence that Chaucer's vocabulary steadily "grows".[39]

---

[39] This tabulation should include all those words that are not new in Chaucer's English (i.e. the 9,117 words analyzed in Part 2, minus these 2,098 new words) minus all the words remaining from this calculation used in Chaucer's "first" text, the *Romaunt of the Rose* (in this case 1,449 words). By definition, this category must exclude all words in Chaucer's "first" text (since no word used there *could* have been "reserved" from an earlier text). Another 156 words have been eliminated from this category, because this is the number of words only treated by "specimen" in Benson's *Glossarial Concordance* (and so this is the quantity of vocabulary not analyzed for the "first use in Chaucer" in my Part 2).

Table 3.3. *Reserved vocabulary in Chaucer's writing*

	Reserved words	Words per reserved word	Head-words per reserved word		Reserved words	Words per reserved word	Head-words per reserved word
RomA	0	–	–	SumPro	3	115	58
ABC	163	9	3	SumT	71	65	15
BD	435	20	3	ClPro	8	53	26
Pity	45	20	7	ClT	61	148	22
Lady	33	32	11	MerPro	3	83	47
SNPro	69	13	5	MerT	44	208	34
SNT	148	23	5	EpiMerT	1	174	114
MkT (w/o MI)	235	22	5	IntSqT	1	67	47
HF	465	29	4	SqT	32	171	37
Anel	59	47	13	FranPro	0	–	–
PF	181	31	7	FranT	17	407	72
Bo	770	67	4	PhyT	8	273	78
Tr	644	102	6	IntPardT	3	112	59
Adam	8	7	6	PardPro	11	94	36
Mars	33	70	21	PardT	32	123	30
Venus	9	66	29	ShipT	23	157	36
KnT	237	72	10	ProPrT	0	–	–
FormAge	20	24	13	PrT	12	131	42
Fort	5	116	55	ProThop	3	57	37
Truth	7	32	19	Thop	35	44	16
Gent	3	52	28	Mel	74	227	21
Sted	6	32	19	ProMkT	14	56	24
LGW F	46	98	22	MkT (MI)	0	–	–
LGW	113	150	17	ProNPT	3	145	71
GP	247	27	7	NPT	47	103	24
Ast	96	133	11	EpiNPT	3	40	29
LGW G (rev.)	14	89	32	CYPro	19	70	23
MilPro	3	201	84	CYT	66	91	17
MilT	90	57	13	MancPro	13	66	26
RvPro	13	41	19	MancT	11	181	54
RvT	75	44	11	ParsPro	4	140	62
CkPro	10	32	16	ParsT	256	119	10
CkT	13	35	16	Scog	4	98	54
IntMLT	11	90	40	Buk	1	268	149
MLT	53	148	26	Purse	2	104	58
EpiMLT	6	35	21	Prov	2	23	22
WBPro	90	76	15	Ros	1	185	108
WBT	27	119	28	WomUnc	2	88	52
FrPro	5	55	29	WomNob	2	112	63
FrT	34	85	21	MercB	1	318	111

Since this calculation measures every text against the text that precedes it the *Romaunt of the Rose* (as Chaucer's first text) must act as control: none of its words can be "reserved" from use in a previous text because, according to developmental schemes, the *Romaunt* has no precedent. But the interest of the list is greater "later" rather than "earlier" as it demonstrates the degree to which Chaucer was *still* turning to words he had never used before, even at the end of his career. It is of course equally true that this table, like all the ones so far discussed, testifies to another kind of procedural stability in Chaucer's lexis. Although we must read with chronological schemes to *have* this list, its steady numbers (every single one of Chaucer's texts after the *Romaunt* uses reserved vocabulary) are another kind of iterative identity: Chaucer's texts are generally the same *as* they use reserved words.

But pressing as hard on chronological thinking as it is necessary to do to generate these reserved words also helps to bring into view the ways that a developmental hermeneutic must limit the cumulative novelty of Chaucer's vocabulary in ways that it never acknowledges. That limit is simply this: if a substantive body of new but extant English vocabulary is created simply by viewing Chaucer's use of words as necessarily "progressive," the very path of progress must also *antiquate* words by the very re-use (in accumulation) that it assumes. The novelty that may issue from Chaucer's early *dis*use of some words, in other words, is balanced by his copious later *use* of others: as Chaucer's vocabulary is put in forward motion, subtraction must take its place next to addition in the tabulation of the aggregate. Another short passage – this time from the *Summoner's Tale* – finds exactly such antiquation at a revealing textual moment:

> Oure Lord Jhesu, as hooly writ devyseth,
> Yaf us ensample of fastynge and preyeres.
> Therfore we mendynantz, we sely freres,
> Been wedded to poverte and continence,
> To charite, humblesse, and abstinence,
> To persecucioun for rightwisnesse,
> To wepynge, misericorde, and clennesse.
> And therfore may ye se that oure preyeres –
> I speke of us, we mendynantz we freres –
> Been to the hye God moore acceptable
> Than youres, with youre feestes at the table. (III, 1904–14)

These lines contain none of the seventeen words that appear in the English record for the first time in the *Summoner's Tale*,[40] but they do contain three words from its reserved vocabulary ("mendinaunt n.," "persecucioun n.," and "acceptable adj."). The weight of these words in this short passage can stand, in little, for the weight of the seventy-one reserved words in the *Summoner's Tale* as a whole, and the counter-vailing tendency to progressive use is equally well represented in this passage by "humblesse n." This word is a new borrowing, appearing first in the record in Chaucer's writing, but it appears there for the first time in Chaucer's career in the *ABC*, so that, by the time the word appears in this passage, the chronological reading that would place the passage late must also acknowledge that Chaucer has already used this word twelve of the twenty times he was to use it in his career.[41] Such a "new" word must be counted among any of Chaucer's contributions to English (as Mersand so counts it),[42] but it has grown very long in the tooth by the time it reaches this poem. Precisely to the extent that we care about novelty in the development of Chaucer's English then, we must acknowledge that this word is *not* new in this passage. The "development" that chronological reading makes of identity may recognize that a certain degree of "growth" is also "habituation," and that one distinct result of the frequent repetition of this word is that, eventually, it will not seem new at all.

---

[40] These words are "blasfemour n." (III, 2213), "buf interj." (III, 1934), "contemplaunce n." (III, 1893), "dagoun n," (III, 1751), "demoniak n." (III, 2240 and 2292), "demon-stratif adj. & n." (III, 2272), "distemperen v." (III, 2195), "effectual adj." (III, 1870), "equalli adv." (III, 2237 and 2273), "goune-clooth n." (III, 2247 and 2252), "incon-staunce n." (III, 1958), "nifle n." (III, 1760), "perturbinge ger." (III, 2254), "reverber-acioun n." (III, 2234), "rumbelinge ger." (III, 2232), "trippe n3." (III, 1747), and "village n." (III, 2165).

[41] Chaucer uses "humblesse n." (according to the chronology I employ here) in the *ABC* (line 108), *House of Fame* (line 630), *Anelida and Arcite* (line 248), *Boece* (Book 3, pr.8.13), the *Complaint of Mars* (line 178), the *Complaint of Venus* (line 18), the *Knight's Tale* (I, 1781 and 2790), the *Former Age* (line 55), the *Legend of Good Women* (line 2269), the *Man of Law's Tale* (II, 165), the *Summoner's Tale* (III, 1908), the *Clerk's Tale* (IV, 932 and 936), the *Squire's Tale* (V, 544), the *Franklin's Tale* (V, 753), the *Prologue of the Prioress's Tale* (VII, 470), the *Melibee* (VII, 1236), and the *Parson's Tale* (X, 481 and 1046). See Benson, *Glossarial Concordance*.

[42] Mersand lists the word as one of Chaucer's "contributions" and cites it in the *Former Age* (noting as well that it occurs "earlier in *ABC*"). See *Chaucer's Romance Vocabulary*, p. 166.

Such retrograde "progress" has enormous implications of course for any presumption of progress in Chaucer's *oeuvre*, but developmental readings routinely ignore it by making the point of entry of the new into the chronology of Chaucer's works the moment for measure. What they also ignore, in that process, is the still deeper stasis in Chaucer's lexical patterns that becomes clear when we look at the figures I have been using to compute lexical density. To compute a general density for each of Chaucer's texts in the following table I take the total number of words in each text (its length), the number of dictionary headwords represented by that total (how many different "words" are present in the text when repetitions and different forms are resolved to a single lemma), and divide the one by the other to give the number of words per headword in each text. This final figure gives the average number of times Chaucer actually used a given word in each of these texts, a "density," in this sense, because it describes the frequency of lexical re-use. I lay these figures out in chronological order because I have done so in previous tables although they do not depend on chronology at all.

Table 3.4. *Words and their density in Chaucer's writing*[43]

	Total words	Head-words	Words per head-word		Total words	Head words	Words per head-word
ROMA	10659	1760	6	VENUS	597	265	2
ABC	1425	484	3	KNT	17168	2286	8
BD	8677	1375	6	FORMAGE	478	249	2
PITY	915	335	3	FORT	578	276	2
LADY	1043	346	3	TRUTH	222	130	2
SNPRO	904	365	3	GENT	156	83	2
SNT	3363	758	4	STED	193	111	2
MKT (w/o MI)	5228	1163	5	LGW F	4519	1002	5
HF	13261	1951	7	LGW	16904	1971	9
ANEL	2772	775	4	GP	6659	1617	4
PF	5517	1243	4	AST	12755	1039	12
BO	51528	3142	16	LGW G (rev.)	1252	442	3
TR	65625	3612	18	MILPRO	603	251	2
ADAM	56	45	1	MILT	5141	1125	5
MARS	2322	678	3	RVPRO	530	252	2
							(cont'd)

---

[43] For the raw figures (of "total words" and "headwords" for each of Chaucer's texts), based on the texts in the *Riverside Chaucer*, I am greatly endebted to Larry Benson.

RvT	3303	818	4	ShipT	3615	820	4
CkPro	322	162	2	ProPrT	261	150	2
CkT	450	207	2	PrT	1568	502	3
IntMLT	990	434	2	ProThop	170	112	2
MLT	7859	1401	6	Thop	1533	567	3
EpiMLT	208	125	2	Mel	16816	1547	11
WBPro	6810	1333	5	ProMkT	784	336	2
WBT	3218	755	4	MkT (MI)	696	299	2
FrPro	275	143	2	ProNPT	435	212	2
FrT	2878	726	4	NPT	4848	1129	4
SumPro	346	173	2	EpiNPT	120	88	1
SumT	4607	1064	4	CYPro	1338	445	3
ClPro	422	209	2	CYT	5980	1145	5
ClT	9033	1367	7	MancPro	856	334	3
MerPro	249	142	2	MancT	1992	596	3
MerT	9128	1498	6	ParsPro	558	249	2
EpiMerT	174	114	2	ParsT	30423	2609	12
IntSqT	67	47	1	Scog	392	214	2
SqT	5459	1167	5	Buk	268	149	2
FranPro	147	99	2	Purse	208	115	2
FranT	6911	1230	6	Prov	46	43	1
PhyT	2186	620	4	Ros	185	108	2
IntPardT	335	176	2	WomUnc	176	104	2
PardPro	1032	395	3	WomNob	223	125	2
PardT	3928	960	4	MercB	318	111	3

The nature of the calculation performed here makes the figures in the third column inversely proportional to the degree of lexical variety a particular text exhibits: or, to put it more simply, a high number in the third column means that Chaucer repeated words often (a "12" means that Chaucer used one new word for every twelve words in the text), a low number means that he repeated words rarely, that practically every word in the text differed from all the others (a "1" means that every word in that text – or nearly every word since I have rounded decimals off – was different from all the others). These figures are also interesting because, although they do not emerge from a posited chronology, they too follow no trend. Their movement correlates most closely to the text's form (density decreases markedly in prose texts) or to its length (texts with high word totals generally have lower densities), but, in the vast majority of texts, the average density hovers close to one side of the four words-per-headword that is the average for all of Chaucer's texts. In fact, the *general* density of Chaucer's lexis for the beginning to the end of his career hardly moves at all. (The *Boece* and *Troilus and Criseyde* are exceptional but I will account for these anomalous figures below.)

When read chronologically, however, the stability in these figures creates a serious problem for developmental views since they show that Chaucer's vocabulary *did not grow more dense*, that Chaucer did not use more words in later texts than he had in his earlier texts, even though, as we have seen, the novelty of his vocabulary increased significantly with almost every successive text. How can this be so? If Chaucer's vocabulary steadily increased then the result of that increase must produce a steady increase in lexical density across Chaucer's career: if Chaucer had constantly provided himself with more words, if he had had a "wider vocabulary of ideas" as Brewer says, he should have *had* to crowd this wider language into later texts thereby making them more dense. To restate the question in its more lexically specific form: where, then, did all the new words Chaucer borrowed, derived, and mined from extant English in nearly every one of his texts *go*? The answer of course is that Chaucer simply threw them away, that his lexical procedures got rid of words he had already used precisely because new words were entering his vocabulary to take their place. This process can be substantiated further, but before doing so it is worth noting the series of anti-developmental possibilities that are suddenly before us. At the same time that Chaucer was progressively antiquating the very lexical novelty he had fashioned in earlier texts he may also have been throwing away the very new words on which notions of lexical growth have been based. To put the possibilities for such contraction in the more acute form these statistics suggest: Chaucer's vocabulary may have been shrinking at exactly the same rate it was growing; it may have been *only* iteratively novel.[44]

3

At this point it is worth looking at all the categories of lexis I have entered into this analysis at a particular moment in the presumptively

[44] The most acute form in which the possibility could be stated is, of course, that Chaucer's vocabulary was shrinking *faster* than it was growing. But the density calculations I give in my text make this unlikely, since they should then show Chaucer's vocabulary becoming *less* dense – which they generally do not.

developing career of Chaucer. This will help to clarify the local importance of all these categories to Chaucer's language as it is disposed in textual constructs, but it will also offer a chance to answer the question I have just posed, to see what Chaucer *did* with the different kinds of novelty he employed "after" he used them in a particular text. I want to return briefly, then, to the *Boece* and the kind of close reconstruction of its lexical procedures that I employed in chapter 1. An extract from Book 3, *metrum* 9 of the *Boece* offers a particularly compact example of all the varieties of lexical novelty I have examined so far, and it is helpfully situated in the middle of a text that is itself usually placed in the middle of Chaucer's career (giving, then, the before and after in Chaucer's career a roughly equal chronological weight). In the following quotation from this *metrum* I have leveled all the categories of novelty I have so far addressed by italicizing all new borrowings, derivations, and reserved vocabulary:

"O thow Fadir, soowere and creatour of heven and of erthes, that governest this world by *perdurable* resoun, that comaundest the tymes to gon from syn that age hadde bygynnynge; thow that duellest thiselve ay stedefast and stable, and yevest alle othere thynges to ben meved, ne *foreyne* causes *necesseden* the nevere to *compoune* werk of *floterynge* matere, but oonly the forme of sovereyn good *iset* within the withoute envye, that moevede the frely. Thow, that art althirfayrest, berynge the faire world in thy thought, formedest this world to the lyknesse semblable of that faire world in thy thought. Thou drawest alle thyng of thy sovereyn *ensaumpler* and comaundest that this world, parfytely ymakid, have frely and *absolut* his parfyt parties. Thow byndest the elementis by nombres *proporcionables,* that the coolde thinges mowen accorde with the hote thinges, and the drye thinges with the moyste; that the fuyer, that is purest, ne fle nat *over-heye,* ne that the hevynesse ne drawe nat adoun *over-lowe* the erthes that ben ploungid in the watris. Thow knyttest togidere the mene soule of *treble* kynde moevynge alle thingis and divydest it by membrys accordynge; and whan it es thus divyded and hath assembled a moevynge into two *rowndes* it gooth to torne ayen to hymself, and envyrouneth a ful deep thought and turneth the hevene by semblable ymage. Thow by *even-lyke* causes enhauncest the soules and the lasse lyves; and *ablynge* hem heye by lyght *waynes* or cartes, thow sowest hem into hevene and into erthe." (*Boece,* Book 3, m.9.1–35)

In this form the vocabulary of this passage seems densely novel, but, as I have been stressing, the place of this novelty in Chaucer's vocabulary as a whole – the contribution it makes to Chaucer's English – changes when we attend to the history of each of these words, which I provide in the following table. Reading it from left to right traces each word from its source language (that is, Latin and/or French for borrowings and roots for derivations), through its first appearance in Middle English (if any), and, finally, through every appearance it makes in prior passages of the *Boece* (again, if any). In every case, the text in which the word first appears in Middle English – when it first crosses the divide of novelty – is marked in bold type. For derivations I have also given the date on which the word's root was first recorded in English.

Headword	Root/Source language > Textual history			
ablen v.	fr. able adj. (c1338)	>	**B01 m6.18**	> B03 m9
absolut ppl.	L	>		**B03 m9**
compounen v.	L & OF	>		**B03 m9**
ensamplere n.	L & OF[45]	>		**B03 m9**
evenli adv.	OE	> **c1250 Prov.Alf**	>	B03 m9
floteren v.	OE	> **c1290 SLeg.Mich**	>	B03 m9
forein adj.	OE	> **(c1250) Floris**	>	
			> B01 m2.4, pr4.113; B02 pr2.25, pr5.73, pr5.96, pr5.126, B03 pr3.63, pr3.70, pr3.80, pr6.37, pr6.45, pr9.29, pr9.71 > B03 m9	
isetten v.	fr. setten v. (OE)	> **a1121 Peterb.Chron**		
			> B02 pr5.125 > B03 m9	
necessen v.	L	>		> **B03 m9**
overheighe adv	fr. 'heigh' adv. (OE)	> **c1225 Ancr.(Tit)**	>	B03 m9
overloue adv.	fr. 'loue' adv. (c1200)	>		**B03 m9**

---

[45] In Part 2, following my general rubric where the *MED* gives no etymology, I have suggested that "ensamplere n." could have been derived from "ensample n." because this potential root is adduced in English earlier (according to the *MED*, s. v. "ensample n.," 2b in "c1290 SLeg. [Ld]"). It is very likely, of course, that Chaucer borrowed this word directly from his source texts (for these texts, see n. 47 below) given that "exemplo" is present in the Latin and "examplaire" is present in the French. On the other hand, the presence of "ensample n." as a documented part of Middle English must count as a licensing influence, not least because Chaucer had already used this possible root in earlier texts (*Romaunt of the Rose*, lines 1181, 1539, and 1584, *Book of the Duchess*, line 911, *Anelida and Arcite*, line 197) and even in earlier lines of the *Boece* (Book 1, m.3.4; pr.4.23; Book 3, pr.5.5.) See Benson, *Glossarial Concordance*.

perdurable adj.	OF & ML	>	> **Bo1 pr1.21**, m5.2, m3.21,	
			m4.2, m8.4	> Bo3 m9
proporcionable adj.	OF; ML	>		> **Bo3 m9**
rounde n.	OF, AF[46]	> (?a1200) Ancr.		> Bo3 m9
treble adj.	OF	> (?c1280) SLegOTHist (Ld 622)		> Bo3 m9
wain n1.	OE	> ?c1200 Orm		> Bo3 m9

This is a complicated history but its detail gives some idea of the numerous contingencies that frame the novelty of any of Chaucer's "new" words. In fact, in many cases these contingencies drastically qualify the novelty that these words can be said to bring to Chaucer's *metrum*. Some new borrowings appear first in the *Boece* but they have already appeared in Chaucer's writing prior to this passage ("ablen v.," "perdurable adj."), and even some of the reserved vocabulary, while it appears first in Chaucer's English in the *Boece*, has already been used within this text before this passage ("forein adj.," "isetten v."). A contingency not visible in this chart, but relevant to the assessment of novelty, comes into view if we compare these Romance borrowings to the words that prompt their use in Chaucer's French and Latin sources.[47] Some of these words are simply lifted from those sources

[46] The *MED* also proposes "rounde adj." as a root for "rounde n." even though it cites "rounde n." first in "(?a1200) Ancr." and cites this putative root for the first time in Middle English *after* it (s. v. "rounde adj.," 1a) in "c1300 SLeg.Mich. (Ld)."

[47] The parallel passages in the Latin and Old French sources for the *Boece* are as follows: "O qui perpetua mundum ratione gubernas,/ terrarum caelique sator, qui tempus ab aevo/ ire iubes stabilisque manens das cuncta moveri,/ quem non externae pepulerunt fingere causae/ materiae fluitantis opus, verum insita summi/ forma boni livore carens, tu cuncta superno/ ducis ab exemplo, pulchrum pulcherrimus ipse/ mundum mente gerens similique in imagine formans/ perfectasque iubens perfectum absolvere partes./ Tu numeris elementa ligas, ut frigora flammis,/ arida conveniant liquidis, ne purior ignis/ evolet aut mersas deducant pondera terras./ Tu triplicis mediam naturae cuncta moventem/ conectens animam per consona membra resolvis;/ quae cum secta duos motum glomerauit in orbes,/ in semet reditura meat mentemque profundam/ circuit et simili convertit imagine caelum./ Tu causis animas paribus vitasque minores/ provehis et levibus sublimes curribus aptans/ in caelum terramque seris . . .," Boethius, *Philosophiae Consolationis Libri Quinque*, Büchner (ed.), III, m.9 (p. 56). "O tu peres, createurs du ciel et de la terre, qui gouvernes cest monde par pardurable raison, qui commandez que li temps aille de pardurableté (des lors que aagez out commencement), qui es estable et ne te meuz et faiz toutez chosez mouvoir, ne onques estrangez causez ne te esmurent a former euvre de matere flotant et transmuable, mais la forme du souverain bien assise en toy sans envie te meut tant seulement; tu traiz toutez chosez de ton souverain exemplaire; tu, tres biaus, portez le biau monde dedens ta pensee et formes cestui monde a l'ymage et a la semblance de celui et commandez que cist mondez parfaiz ait ses partiez delivres et parfaitez. Tu lies les elemens par certains nombres pour ce que les froidez chosez se puissent acorder aus chaudez et les sechez aus moistez, si que li feu plus purs ne vole pas trop hault et que li faiz ne face pas trop abessier les terres plungiees es eaues. Tu enlaces et conjoins au corps l'ame moienne de treble nautre qui toutez chosez muet et la devisez par

("ensaumplere n." from Latin "exemplo" and/or French "examplaire," "absolut ppl." from Latin "absolvere") but three of them are not: "compounen v. (prompted by Latin "fingere" and/or French "former"), "necessen" (prompted by Latin "pepulerunt" and/or French "esmurent"), and "proporcionable adj." (prompted by French "certains nombres"). The novelty of two of these borrowings is therefore further framed by the fact that Chaucer did not really *need* them since "formen v." (which could be used to render "former") and "certain adj." as well as "nombre n." (which could be used to render "certains nombres") were all words imported into English long before Chaucer even began to write. Chaucer had even used these borrowings numerous times in his writing prior to this passage of the *Boece*, and, indeed, he uses "formen v." in this very passage.[48] The novelty in Chaucer's lexis here therefore resembles the novelty of the reserved vocabulary in the *Envoy to Scogan* – in both cases, since *less* novel words could have been used, novelty itself seems to be part of the lexical function. In this sense as well as generally, these words demonstrate the importance of the novelty that Mersand and so many others have thought so crucial to Chaucer's English. But these words also expose the contingencies that must *qualify* such novelty, if we look carefully at the other side of the coin – where these words go after this passage.

In the following table, then, I continue the history given above as it extends beyond the *metrum* (for ease of comparison, I have marked all those words recorded for the first time in Chaucer's writing in bold type). Constraints of space preclude giving a full account of these words in later Middle English, but I include a representative example for those words that are attested anywhere in the record after Chaucer uses them.

acordables membrez. Et quant elle est ainsi devisee et a assemblé son mouvement en deus manierez de rondes esperes, elle trespasse a retourner a soi meismes et avironne et enquiert la parfonde pensee de dieu et tournoie le ciel par ymaginacion semblable, si comme elle voit que dieu le veult. Tu par semblables et par pareillez causez essaucez les ames et les vies meneures et, quant tu les as ajusteez en hault par legiers veictures (par raison et entendement), tu les semes ou ciel et en la terre," Jean de Meun, "Boethius' *De Consolatione*," Dedeck-Héry (ed.), 220–1.

48 According to standard chronologies Chaucer uses "formen v." first in the *Romaunt of the Rose*, line 1189 and has used it seven times before its appearance in this passage of the *Boece*. He uses "certain adj." first in the *Book of the Duchess*, line 1222 and has used it nineteen times already (eleven times in the *Boece*) before this *metrum*. He uses "nombre n." first in the *Romaunt*, line 1412, and has used it twelve times (nine times in the *Boece*) already. See Benson, *Glossarial Concordance*.

Boece, 3 m9 >	All textual issue in Chaucer	>	Later textual issue
ablen v.	none	>	Lydg. *FP* 3.3123
absolut ppl.	Bo3 pr10.28, pr11.22; Bo5 pr 4.55, pr4.105, pr5.105,		
	pr5.18, pr6.176, pr6.203, pr.6.236	>	Walton *Boeth.*, p. 175
compounen v.	Bo3 pr10.196	>	Lydg. *ST* 735
ensaumplere n.	none	>	Gower *CA* 7.4026
evenli adv.	Bo4 m6.22, Bo5 pr2.22	>	Lydg. *TB* 1.1402
floteren v.	Bo3 pr11.210	>	Mirk *Fest.* 260/4
forein adj.	Bo3 pr12.191; Bo4 pr3.25, pr3.105, pr4.199;		
	Bo5 pr4.216	>	Lydg. *FP* 3.1334
isetten v.	Bo4 pr1.62, pr4.234, pr6.48; Tr3.1488, 1731;		
	Tr4.184, 674 KnT, 1.1635; CKPRO, 1.4337;		
	ClT,4.409; SQT, 5.173 PARDPRO 6.392	>	Lydg. *TB* 2.5724
necessen v.	none	>	Walton *Boeth.* p.304
overheighe adv.	none	>	*Ludus C.* 356/32
overloue adv.	Mel 7.1465	>	Pecock *Fol.* 93/6–7
perdurable adj.	Bo3 pr11.186; Bo4 pr4.57, pr4.167, pr4.193, m6.20;		
	Mel.7.1509, 11510; PARST 10.75, 120, 124, 184, 234 ,		
	240, 241, 243, 247, 335, 669, 811, 847	>	Lydg. *FP* 2.3957
proporcionable adj. none		>	Pecock *Rule* 449
rounde n.	none	>	Lydg. *ST* 4312
treble adj.	Bo4 m7.37	>	Gower *CA* 3.159
wain ni.	Bo4 m1.32, m5.6	>	Lydg. *TB* 1.630

The powerful point of this "progress" is, of course, that these new words do not get very far. Of the words Chaucer borrowed anew here, only "perdurable adj." makes it out of the *Boece*, and it is subsequently confined to prose. The novelty of this word in this passage of the *Boece* is already qualified, moreover, since, as the previous table shows, it is well worn in Chaucer's usage by the time it reaches this *metrum*. "Isetten" is, in fact, the only word here that figures in a variety of subsequent texts and it is, of course, part of Chaucer's reserved vocabulary, hardly novel as an English word at all. Four of Chaucer's reserved words never make it beyond this passage ("ablen v.," "floteren v.," "overheighe adv.," and "rounde n.") and three of Chaucer's six new borrowings never appear in his writing again ("ensaumplere n.," "necessen v.," and "proporcionable adj."). In fact, the largest function these words can be said to perform is to increase the novelty of *this* passage of the *Boece*. "Proporcionable adj." is, in fact, the word that most emphatically proves this point. It shows Chaucer most committed to novelty *for novelty's sake*, using new words at this textual moment, not to enlarge his vocabulary on the whole, but to enlarge his vocabulary *here*. It is the extravagance, *in extremis*, that figures forth the extravagance at the heart of Chaucer's lexical practice. It shows that lexical novelty was not Chaucer's point of departure for later development, but an end in itself. After this word had been novel here, Chaucer throws it away.

So much of Chaucer's vocabulary in the *Boece* is discarded in fact that the activity I have anatomized in this *metrum* has been observed before. As I noted above, Elliott regards the *Boece* as a ground for "practice," not so much lexically enriching as lexically experimental; Tim Machan also calls it Chaucer's "opportunity to explore."[49] But the characterization of this pattern by these other writers is at best instrumental (Elliott sees the text as preparation for "further" inventiveness), and, at worst, simply pejorative (Machan writes of the "unnecessarily large vocabulary" Chaucer's experimentation led him to).[50] Such views also derive from and, finally, further underwrite developmental schemes for Chaucer's writing. "Having written *Boece* the way he did," Machan concludes, "Chaucer's powers of expression were necessarily wider than they had been before."[51] The latter may be true, but, as the previous example makes clear (and as subsequent statistics will make more broadly apparent), Chaucer simply did not put those wider powers to wider *use*. These writers are right about what Chaucer is doing in the *Boece*, but because they understand the lexical practices they observe as a function of the *Boece* (in Machan's phrase one of Chaucer's "techniques of translation"), and because they understand the *Boece* itself as an exploration, they cannot see how the lexical practices of the *Boece* are general in Chaucer's English. In fact, so far from being "unnecessary," Chaucer's simultaneous invention and abandonment of words was generally constitutive of his style.

David Benson has gone some way to demonstrating this more general point by describing what would have to be the effects of this practice on a text like the *Canterbury Tales*. As he sees it, the language of each of the *Tales* is so distinctive that it amounts to a "special kind of poetry," written, for all intents and purposes, by a different poet.[52] In order to identify the kind of poetry in individual tales Benson

---

[49] See p. 97 above.
[50] Machan, *Techniques of Translation*, p. 55.
[51] *Ibid.*, p. 127.   [52] Benson, *Chaucer's Drama of Style*, p. 20.

frequently focuses on vocabulary, and his most thorough study focuses on the *Reeve's Tale* where, he observes, "unique words and phrases often have a particular appropriateness," where a "distinct vocabulary" demonstrates the *"Reeve-*poet's particular skill with language."[53] The vocabulary of the *Reeve's Tale* bears out Benson's claim very nicely, since so many of its unique words are the Northernisms characteristic of the two clerks' speech (e.g. "hethen adv. [hence]," "hething n. [mockery]," "emelle prep. [among]") or words describing key objects and events in its story (e.g. "hoppere n. [hopper]," "pekke n. [peck, a dry measure]," "routinge ger2. [whirring]"). In lexical terms, Benson's claim also works nicely in many more of the *Tales* than he analyzes, as can be easily illustrated by a list of the words Chaucer only uses in a single *Tale* and nowhere else in his writing (the following list is by no means exhaustive and it deliberately excludes those *Tales* that my chronology places earlier than the Canterbury scheme).

GP	Caunterbury-ward n. (1 time)
MᵢₗT	ferting ger. (1), gnof n. (1), kimelin n. (2), shot-windoue n. (2)
CₖT	vitailer n. (1)
MLT	constable n. (17), soudan n. (13), soudanesse n. (6), virago n. (1)
WBPro	bishreuen v. (2), octogamie n. (1), sufferable adj. (1), tormentrie n. (1)
WBT	disfigure n. (1), lothli adj. (1), overbiden v. (1), twelve-month n. (1)
FᵣT	rebekke n2. (1), viritrate n. (1), wicchecraft n. (1)
SᵤMT	cartwheel n. (2), equalli adv. (2), glosinge ger. (1), nave n. (2), possessiouner n. (1), reverberacioun n. (1), rumbelinge ger. (1)
CₗT	buxomli adv. (1), reverentli adv., (2) , sad adv. (1), wiven v. (2)
MₑᵣT	cliket n1. (5), pirie (3), untrust n. (1)
SₒT	peregrine adj. (1), plumage n. (1), trillen v1. (3)
FᵣₐₙT	serment n. (1)
PₐᵣDT	hasard n. (4), sermounen v. (1), tavernere n. (2), win-yevinge ger. (1)
SHIP T	creauncen v. (3), counting-bord n. (1), countour-dore n. (2), countour-hous n. (1), port-hors n. (2)
PᵣT	clergeoun n. (1), gramere n. (1), primere n. (2), scoleward (1)
THOP	amble n. (1), dappel-grai adj. & n. (1), doggerel adj. (1), love-druri n. (1), love-likinge n. (1)

---

[53] *Ibid.*, p. 99. In his discussion of the language of the *Reeve's Tale* Benson relies on Frank, "The *Reeve's Tale* and the Comedy of Limitation," pp. 62–3 and Chaucer, *Reeve's Prologue and Tale*, A. Spearing and J. Spearing (eds.), pp. 62–3. For Benson's word counts for individual *Canterbury Tales*, see *Drama of Style*, pp. 84, 106, and 139–40.

MEL   conversacion n. (1), examinacion n. (1), supportacioun n. (1), vengeaunce-taking ger. (5)

NPT   chukken v. (1), cotage n. (2), col-fox n. (1), daie n. (1)

CYT   crosselet n2. (9), elixir n. (1), vitriol n. (1)

ParsT   accidie n. (18), concupiscence n. (9), evene-Cristene n. (5), gostli adj. (6), obedience n. (4), penitencere n.(1), presthede n. (1), spiritualli adv. (2), theologie n. (1), venial adj. (17)

As Benson predicts, defining objects and crucial narrative themes are trapped by this *Tale*-specific vocabulary, but Benson's predictions come true, I would further suggest, not because such lexical tailoring was inherent to the *Canterbury Tales*, but because it was inherent to all of Chaucer's writing. The kind of defining vocabulary that Chaucer uses anew and then throws away in each tale can also be found in equally restrictive use in almost all of his pre-*Canterbury* works, as can be illustrated by another selective list of such words (here I insert the *Tales* which are thought to precede the Canterbury scheme).

RomA   chapelet n. (4 times), passage n. (2), pome-garnete n. (1), sweveninge ger. (2)

BD   halouen v. (1), igreten v. (1), maister-hunte n. (1), mot n2. (1), on-huntinge adv. (1), rechasen v. (1)

SNPro   chastnesse (1), whitnesse n. (1)

MkT   misgovernaunce n. (1), mishap n. (1)

HF   airish adj. (2), clariouninge ger. (1), famous adv. (1), lapidarie n. (1), unfamous adj. (1)

PF   hei-sugge n. (1), stork n. (1), queken v. (1), tercel n. (7), water-foul n. (4)

Bo   arbitre n. (5), blisfulnesse n. (86), destinal n. (6), eternite n. (7), fortuit adj. (2), fortunous adj. (8), future n. (7), perturbacion n. (5), preterit n. (5), welefulnesse n. (31)

TR   augurie n. (2), congeien v. (1), disaventure n. (4), doutance n. (3), em n1. (18), fate n. (3), feithed ppl. (1), mistrust n. (2), poesie n. (1), rape n2. (1), remede n. (1), remorse n. (1), reufulli adv. (3), sobbe n. (2), twinninge ger. (1), uncle n. (19), unkist adj. (1), unloven v. (1), unmanhede n. (1), zel n. (1)

KnT   armipotent (2), brest-plate n. (1), dereinen v. (4), foinen v. (3), justes n. pl. (1), pomel n. (1), sparre n. (2), unhorsen v. (1)

LGW   bitraisinge ger. (1), devourer n. (2), enamoured ppl. (2), sikeren v. (1)

Ast   alititude n. (65), elevacioun n. (2), meridian adj. (5), mid-dai n. (9), plum-rule n. (1), zodiak n. (37)

It might be possible to understand the restrictive use of such words mechanically: necessitated to describe the crucial "uncle" in *Troilus and Criseyde*, the "pirie" in the *Merchant's Tale*, or the various kinds of bird in the *Parliament of Fowls*, only because such objects did not need description where they did not occur in other texts. But the decisions that produce such differing narrative necessities must themselves be related to a poetics of *le mot juste* (the former is just the latter in large). And even better proof of Chaucer's commitment to narratives, styles and a lexis constantly novel in this way can be found in the following list of those words with no obvious relevance to a particular text that are nevertheless restricted to that text.

RoMA	ther-amonge adv. (1 time)	IntMLT	erect adj. (1)
ABC	adversaire n. & adj. (1)	MLT	seriousli adv. (1)
BD	flat adj. (2)	WBPro	preferren v. (1)
HF	her-withal adv. (2)	WBT	burgh ni. (1)
PF	unto conj. (1)	SuMT	whal n. (1)
Bo	whosoevere pron. (4)	MerT	never-the-mo adv. (1)
TR	rosi adj. (3)	FranT	hou-ever adv. (1)
KnT	northerne adj. (1)	SqT	no-mo adv.
LGW	nedes-cost adv. (1)	PardT	never-a-del n. & adv. (1)
GP	no-mo adj. (1)	Thop	tellinge ger. (1)
Ast	whether adj. (1)	Mel	overmuchel adj. (2)
MiLT	bet adj. & adv. as n. (1)	NPT	messe-dai n. (1)
RvPro	half-wei adv. (1)	CYT	biforen-hond adv. (1)

Sufficient ingenuity could probably produce arguments to demonstrate the circumstantial necessity of most if not all of these words to their respective texts too. But Chaucer's lexical practice *in general* (that is, when we consider every one of his words) provides the final evidence that these nonce words are not wedded to the texts in which they occur by semantic need but by a still-larger lexical imperative. Nonce usage was, in other words, a basic principle of Chaucer's English *regardless* of the narrative content of that English.

To put this back into the statistical terms I have been using throughout this chapter is to see that Chaucer's nonce vocabulary is numerically greater than the aggregate of all words new to the record in his writing (2,098). The categories overlap of course, and new words are often nonce words too: of the 1,102 Romance words Chaucer used for the first time in recorded Middle English 683 appear in only one of his

Table 3.5. *Nonce words in Chaucer's writing*

	Nonce words	Words per nonce word	Head-words per nonce word		Nonce words	Words per nonce word	Head-words per nonce word
RomA	189	56	9	SumPro	2	173	87
ABC	6	238	81	SumT	58	79	18
BD	79	110	17	ClPro	3	141	70
Pity	6	153	56	ClT	48	188	29
Lady	4	261	87	MerPro	1	249	142
SNPro	11	82	33	MerT	47	194	32
SNT	10	336	76	EpiMerT	1	174	114
MkT (w/o MI)	44	119	26	IntSqT	0	–	–
HF	146	91	13	SqT	43	127	27
Anel	13	213	60	FranPro	1	147	99
PF	63	88	20	FranT	30	230	41
Bo	558	92	6	PhyT	11	199	56
Tr	436	151	8	IntPardT	4	84	44
Adam	5	11	9	PardPro	8	129	49
Mars	20	116	34	PardT	32	123	30
Venus	5	119	53	ShipT	27	134	30
KnT	186	92	12	ProPrT	0	–	–
FormAge	21	23	12	PrT	13	121	39
Fort	6	96	46	ProThop	2	85	56
Truth	4	56	33	Thop	45	34	13
Gent	2	78	42	Mel	61	276	25
Sted	4	48	28	ProMkT	18	44	19
LGW F	33	137	31	MkT (MI)	0	–	–
LGW	96	176	21	ProNPT	5	87	42
GP	177	38	9	NPT	57	85	20
Ast	133	96	8	EpiNPT	3	40	29
LGW G (rev.)	12	104	37	CYPro	18	74	25
MilPro	2	302	126	CYT	105	57	11
MilT	86	60	13	MancPro	17	50	20
RvPro	9	59	28	MancT	14	142	43
RvT	69	48	12	ParsPro	7	78	36
CkPro	5	64	32	ParsT	334	91	8
CkT	9	50	23	Scog	5	78	43
IntMLT	9	110	48	Buk	1	268	149
MLT	58	136	24	Purse	2	104	58
EpiMLT	4	52	31	Prov	2	23	22
WBPro	62	110	22	Ros	4	46	27
WBT	23	140	32	WomUnc	1	176	104
FrPro	4	69	36	WomNob	5	45	25
FrT	31	93	23	MercB	1	318	111

texts,[54] and of the 737 derived words Chaucer used first in the record, 578 appear in only one of his texts. In the category of reserved vocabulary too, 2,122 of the 5,414 such words appear in only one of Chaucer's texts. On the whole, then, of the 9,117 words I survey as Chaucer's entire vocabulary 3,676 (or 40 percent of these words) appear in only one of his texts. If we are inclined to count, in other words, *local* novelty is the novelty that matters most in Chaucer's vocabulary, and, as the table makes clear, nonce words are also evenly distributed across Chaucer's entire *oeuvre*.

Such statistics are not entirely new since Walter Scheps made a similar calculation using Tatlock's concordance, although, in every case, Scheps's figures are substantially smaller than the figures I give here.[55] Scheps also excludes the *Romaunt of the Rose*, the *Boece*, and the *Astrolabe* from his calculations,[56] a crucial difference since Chaucer's use of nonce words is near an absolute high in these works. Nevertheless, although Scheps's table shows a relatively steady frequency of nonce uses in Chaucer's texts (he computes density as nonce words per line), he still reads it as a measure of development: "the table," he says, "indicates a general, although not unmixed, tendency for Chaucer to use increasing quantities of nonce words as his career progresses."[57] As I read my figures as well as those of Scheps, however, they indicate exactly the opposite. Both tables show that Chaucer's use of nonce words was as steady as his use of the other lexical procedures I have described: nonce words occur at substantially the same rate in later texts as they occur in earlier ones. There is a much higher rate of nonce usage in some texts, but there is still no trend here. Moreover, the higher rate of this procedure precisely matches the higher rates of innovation that previous tables have shown in the *Romaunt of the Rose*, the long Boethian texts (the *Boece*, *Troilus and Criseyde*, and the *Knight's Tale*), the *Astrolabe*, the *Canon's Yeoman's Tale*, and the *Parson's Tale*. And nonce vocabulary

---

54 Mersand also noticed the large extent to which Chaucer's new words were used only once: "Almost 60 per cent of the new Romance words are dropped by Chaucer after their first use," *Chaucer's Romance Vocabulary*, p. 74. Mersand does not make much of this data but he includes a table that breaks down these nonce usages in each of Chaucer's texts in his Appendix I (pp. 154–5).

55 Scheps, "Chaucer's Use of Nonce Words." Benson relies on Scheps's statistics in his discussion of Chaucer's vocabulary in *Drama of Style* (see p. 169 n. 23).

56 Scheps, "Chaucer's Use of Nonce Words," 70 n.8.   57 *Ibid.*, 76.

is not only inherently *non*developmental – since it is the opposite of accumulation, bricking words into the span of an individual text – it is also emphatically *anti*-developmental as Chaucer uses it: his nonce usage grows in intensity precisely to the extent that development is threatening to occur, thereby curbing that development. In fact, Chaucer's nonce vocabulary does not correlate with the "progress" of Chaucer's career (*when* a work was written), but to the extent of lexical innovation a text otherwise evinces (*how* it was written). The profile of Chaucer's nonce usage does indeed explain why significant innovation in each of Chaucer's texts does not, over time, increase the lexical density of his style: Chaucer planes flat the highest peaks of the new exactly *as* his vocabulary grows.

But a nonce vocabulary is more than anti-developmental for Chaucer in the moments of his greatest lexical exuberance; it is also anti-developmental *by definition*. Although I present the preceding table according to the standard chronology of Chaucer's works so that it might match other surveys in this chapter, I might have presented this table in any order. Nonce words cannot be added, cannot be turned into Mersandian patterns of accumulation, cannot be made "progressive," because nonce vocabulary exists as a category precisely as its constituents *do not move* from text to text. Read Chaucer's career from end to beginning and the data reported above would not change. Sort Chaucer's texts according to *any* chronology whatsoever – or simply sort them at random – and these figures will not change either. A nonce vocabulary may be a vocabulary containing extraordinary innovation as, indeed, Chaucer's nonce vocabulary is, but it is also a vocabulary that *sequesters* innovation from subsequent use, whatever the "subsequent" is deemed to be. Nonce words are exempt from the developmental hermeneutic that influences so much of Chaucer scholarship because nonce words simply cannot *be* developed.

Paradoxically, however, a nonce vocabulary also encourages as well as provides evidence for a developmental hermeneutic. Once a developmental reading is underway, a nonce vocabulary provides the evidence that this reading needs in exactly the form it needs it. This is to say that, if an identical object develops in a developmental view, not only because it is seen to repeat, but because it is associated with other objects that are successively identical to it in *form* (one new word is the same as another new word because they are both new) the consequence of a new object *becomes* the advent of the similar object. This is how one new word in the *Romaunt of the Rose* and another new word in the *House of Fame* can be seen to outline an "increase" in vocabulary; the separate events, because they are the *same* event (although producing different verbal objects) can be seen as accumulation in Chaucer's *oeuvre* because all views of "increase" care about is the aggregated whole. Nonce words may not themselves repeat, in other words, but every one of Chaucer's texts includes a significant number of nonce words such that *nonce vocabulary* repeats. Where iterative formal recurrence is all that is counted, where static practice is made to move because constant novelty is measured as constant *growth*, a nonce vocabulary is a growing vocabulary. And a nonce vocabulary encourages addition of this kind because it makes a reader notice lexical difference *as* a function of chronology: that is, its very nature is to privilege the nature and moment of the "new." Since its primary effect is novelty (it assures that each text contains what was not in the text that came before), a nonce vocabulary *makes* novelty the attribute that most wants measure in Chaucer's words. It also works to diminish those antiquating processes of re-use that ought to be the primary limitation on "growth" in a chronological reading since nonce vocabulary makes each of Chaucer's texts look (*be*) lexically distinctive. When placed in a sequence, in other words (as developmental views always do prior to collecting evidence), a nonce vocabulary gives development the consequences it wants (a steady supply of new words) and expunges consequences that would be problematic (the antiquation of words "later").

It is according to this same logic that Chaucer's nonce vocabulary also works, finally, to proffer the making of Chaucer's English as the making of English as a whole. A nonce vocabulary limits the extent to which the English of each of Chaucer's texts partakes of the English of those texts that are thought to precede it; it makes the vocabulary of each of Chaucer's texts begin, to a large extent, as if *ex nihilo*. In lexical terms, in other words, every text in Chaucer's *oeuvre* stands to every precedent text as Chaucer's *oeuvre* has been made to stand to each text (and all texts) in precedent Middle English. A nonce vocabulary means that every text in Chaucer's English *is* new, if not with respect to earlier

Middle English (as I argued in the previous chapter) then at least with respect to every text in *Chaucer's* English. Thus, if Chaucer has "no significant predecessors" in English, as Muscatine puts it, Chaucer's nonce vocabulary, as analyzed by a developmental hermeneutic, proves this claim *text by text*, since his English in, say, *Troilus and Criseyde*, has no significant precedent in, say, the *House of Fame*. Chaucer is the " first fyndere of our faire langage" (Hoccleve), he "naturalized in English a new poetic mode and language" (Fisher), he decided "to invent a literary English" (Gaylord), he "began a revolution in poetic diction" (Brewer), not so much with respect to Robert Mannyng in *Handlyng Synne* then, but, in each of his texts, *with respect to himself.* A developmental hermeneutic, ruled by addition and the progress it shapes, must work by this analogy. It must transform each of Chaucer's texts into a little step toward the larger leap forward Chaucer's English is thought to effect. It must make the novelty that nonce vocabulary provides for each of Chaucer's texts represent his entire *oeuvre* within the context of Middle English linguistic history and make that *oeuvre* represent all of Middle English linguistic history in its turn. It must do all this because it makes Chaucer's English do duty for the larger history of English by making his *oeuvre* conform to exactly the shape it also says that larger history has.

Many of the subsidiary lexical techniques I have described in this chapter also contribute to this crucial conflation of Chaucer's accomplishment and English linguistic history, of course. New borrowing and new derivation also tend to differentiate each of Chaucer's texts from the texts that came before and therefore accentuate the novelty of each of these texts over against the texts that are thought to precede it. Chaucer's substantial reservation of native words until later texts promotes those words into real novelty with respect to precedent works too. What unifies borrowings, derivations and reserved vocabulary and makes them in turn like nonce vocabulary is that they help Chaucer's English to gather the *quality* of novelty to itself and to present that novelty as constitutive of its own making. On the other hand, since the words Chaucer uses to do this are, as I have said, either traditional at root (because native) or traditional in technique (because made using well-worn procedures), the constitutive novelty they imply is very substantially, and powerfully, a performance. A developmental hermeneutic is such a constant feature of Chaucer studies in this sense because Chaucer's readers are always encouraged to see novelty as the salient feature of Chaucer's English *by* Chaucer's English. To call this a "performance" is to suggest of course that Chaucer had some hand in the misunderstandings that ramify from these lexical patterns. It is not an unwarranted supposition given the dramatic difference between the effects of techniques and their inherent nature, but it would require further substantiation to claim that Chaucer actually *meant* the misprision I have tried to unpack here. There is such evidence in the particular claims for his English and its effects that Chaucer entered alongside these patterns. These claims, however, warrant careful study all on their own and they are, therefore, the subject of the next chapter.

4

Invented English

> O for a Muse of fire, that would ascend
> The brightest heaven of invention!　　　　　William Shakespeare[1]

The subtle movements of Chaucer's words encouraged the view that his English was new, but Chaucer also had a direct hand in this encouragement – although his touch was exceedingly light. Daring statements were hemmed in by qualification and great ambition was couched in significant reserve. The careful reader may search but will search in vain for lines in which Chaucer *says* that he "invented" English literary language, but that same reader will be equally likely to come away from Chaucer's texts with the impression that he has claimed precisely this. Such a complex result is possible because Chaucer always comports himself as if the claim had not only been entered but were self-evidently true. The indirection was crucial for two reasons: first, Chaucer's English was not invented in any historical sense, and, second, given the high memorial stakes of the game, overt claims would be less efficacious (or positively dangerous in the invitation to scrutiny they would give) than insistent implication. Rather than proclaim himself the "firste fyndere of oure langage" then, Chaucer simply created the opportunity for those he wanted to see him as such to say as much *for* him. Rather than extend a direct invitation, Chaucer simply left the door ajar.

Chaucer could achieve such a complicated result because he had two distinct traditions to choose from, as Brewer terms them in his own analysis of their importance to Chaucer, the "English" and the

---

[1] *Henry V,* Prologue, lines 1–2 in Shakespeare, *Riverside Shakespeare*, Evans (ed).

"European," and Chaucer carefully played the one off against the other.[2] The filiations of the amalgam that resulted are finally less important then than the way Chaucer disposed the traditional parts of his style so that *disposition* itself made a claim. The broad terms of that claim are visible in the relation between the two tales Chaucer gives "Chaucer" to tell in the *Canterbury Tales*. In the simplest terms, as *Sir Thopas* recalls native romance traditions it is Chaucer's embrace of the "English," and as the *Melibee* is "a close translation" of the *Livre de Melibée et de Dame Prudence* by Renaud de Louens it is Chaucer's embrace of the "European." The form of each embrace may also be said to confuse traditional distinctions as English romance is itself, at root, a "European" tradition and as prose was, in fact, the one Middle English form with strong native roots.[3] But that confusion is itself an aspect of Chaucer's technique since it is equally true that the style and language of these two texts *is* drastically different even as *each one* mixes the two traditional kinds of Middle English writing. The difference between these texts shows Chaucer choosing both modes in his English and moving between them *as if* they were distinct. So it is also true that, in the context of the *Tales*, such formal differences, however their roots may be understood, are also presented as qualitative differences. *Sir Thopas* is demonized as "drasty speche" and "rym dogerel" (VII, 923, 925) and the *Melibee* is embraced as a "murye tale" replete with "sentence" (VII, 963–4). This valuation and the differences that make it possible are in the service of a joke, but the method of this joke is precisely the method Chaucer everywhere uses to annex traditional filiations to his own achievement. By presenting traditional forms as alternatives and grading them, Chaucer presents *his* English as the salvific form that can extract the good from the bad and become the best. It is his *general* method, as here, to evoke one linguistic mode scornfully and to present it as a platform from which "drasty" speech will be repaired by "murye" virtues. In this way, Chaucer everywhere presented himself as the poet who could save English from itself.

---

2 Brewer, "English and European Traditions."
3 This is of course a tradition of *religious* prose as it is definitively traced in Chambers, *On the Continuity of English Prose* and Zeeman, "Continuity in Middle English Devotional Prose." No suggestion is made in either of these studies that Chaucer was influenced by this tradition, and it seems unlikely that he even knew of its existence.

Contrasts of a similar sort have, of course, been noticed in Chaucer's writing before, although, as I mentioned in chapter 3, they have usually been noticed as evolutionary patterns of "style" (the "new" issuing from the "old") which make it possible to distinguish one of Chaucer's works from another as its traditional roots change in degree and kind.[4] Such distinctions may clarify the forms of Chaucer's style, but they lose sight of the linguistic components of that style since, as I argued in chapter 2, no stark distinction between the traditional and the new can be made in a Middle English literary practice where the new so often *is* the means of tradition. The stylistic analysis that sees a sequence in Chaucer's traditional filiations must miss the degree to which different kinds of such filiation sit cheek by jowl in Chaucer's English and particularly Chaucer's words, and, therefore, the degree to which the constant conjunction of difference works throughout Chaucer's writing to make an implicit (but large) linguistic claim. As I wish to show here, Chaucer's English breaks down into contrastive parts precisely because *both* terms of the bifurcation are traditional. It is the double possibility that equips Chaucer's English with the capacity to move from one linguistic kind to another and present this movement as "invention," while the deep traditional roots of this very division assure that, however startling the apparent novelty, it is only apparent. For, again, Chaucer's English only *is* "invented" *as* it is "traditional."

---

[4] The contrast I return to here is C. S. Lewis's distinction between the "old bad manner" and the "preludings of the new style" which I mentioned in the previous chapter (Lewis, *Allegory of Love*, pp. 164–5). It is worth recalling this and a number of the other schemes for Chaucer's stylistic development I discussed there, to make clear that, although these schemes also divide Chaucer's language into two or three parts, the division I want to discuss is a different one. In particular, I would distinguish my scheme from Kean's distinction between the "narrative style" and the "urbane manner" (*Chaucer and the Making of English Poetry*, vol. I, pp. 1–30 and 31–6), from Eliason's discussion of the "artificial, simple and colloquial" (*Language of Chaucer's Poetry*, 113), and from Muscatine's analysis of the two modes he calls "conventionalism" and "naturalism" (*Chaucer and the French Tradition*, pp. 166–243). My point is not that these distinctions are incorrect (the unanimity with which these disparate analyses see stylistic distinction itself argues generally for the validity of dividing Chaucer's style into parts) but simply that my distinctions work at a level of detail that subtends the contrasts of style in passages or whole poems, which is the level of analysis at which all these other studies work.

I

To say that Chaucer exploited linguistic contrasts is to seem to make the distinction that classical rhetoric makes between levels of style. As John Manly demonstrated long ago, and as Robert Payne described in more detail subsequently, Chaucer knew rhetorical traditions and drew upon them.[5] However, the contrasting modes that interest me in his English differ crucially from Cicero's linguistic scheme for description of the "plain (*humilis*)," the "moderate (*mediocris*)," and the "high (*altus*)" as well as from the rewriting of that scheme by Augustine for the Middle Ages as three modes for conveying Christian truth "to instruct (*docere*)," "to please (*delectare*)," and "to persuade (*flectere*)."[6] If Chaucer was aware of any scheme for a tripartite, stylistic hierarchy, committed searching has found neither a language for its description in his use, nor any clearly tripartite distinction in his writing.[7] Chaucer does entertain general notions of linguistic propriety ("The wordes moote be cosyn to the dede," I, 742),[8] and he uses the term "heigh style" on more than one occasion.[9] The Host even contrasts that high style with a "plain" style in the *Clerk's Prologue*:

> Youre termes, youre colours, and youre figures,
> Keepe hem in stoor til so be ye endite
> Heigh style, as whan that men to kynges write.
> Speketh so pleyn at this tyme, we yow preye,
> That we may understonde what ye seye. (IV, 16–20)

[5] See Manly, "Chaucer and the Rhetoricians," Payne, *Key of Remembrance*, and Payne "Chaucer and the Art of Rhetoric." For Chaucer's use of more extended forms of rhetorical invention see Copeland, *Rhetoric, Hermeneutics, and Translation*, pp. 186–202.

[6] For these distinctions see Cicero, *Orator*, Hubbell (ed.), xxviii, 100 and Augustine, *De doctrina Christiana*, Green (ed.), IV, xix, 38. I draw these citations and my description of the theories of Cicero and Augustine from the useful discussion of the relationship between these schemes in Copeland, "Richard Rolle and the Rhetorical Theory of Levels of Style" (see esp. pp. 57 and 60). For her discussion of Augustine's adaptation of basic terms from the *Orator* Copeland cites McKeon, "Rhetoric in the Middle Ages," 4–5 (see her article p. 77 n. 6).

[7] See Burnley on "Levels of Style" in *Guide to Chaucer's Language*, pp. 177–200. See also Payne, *Key of Remembrance*, pp. 188–92 and 197–201.

[8] See also *Boece*, Book III, pr.12.206 (". . . that nedes the wordis moot be cosynes to the thinges of whiche thei speken").

[9] See the *Canterbury Tales*, IV, 18; IV, 1148; V, 106.

But it is as crucial to the Host's understanding of stylistic possibility as it is to Chaucer's work in general that Chaucer had, as David Burnley has suggested, *two* distinct levels of style, not three.[10] Admitting the third term of a middle way here would in fact weaken the contrastive force of the Host's demand: there is a right way and a wrong way for the Clerk to tell his tale.

Instead of "levels of style" Chaucer worked with the bipartite division of written modes that he inherited. The roots of this division lay in the stark social distinctions that resulted from the Norman Conquest, still remembered two and a half centuries after the fact by Robert of Gloucester in his *Chronicle* (c. 1300):

> & þus was in normannes hond þat lond ibroȝt iwis
> þat anaunter ȝif euermo keueringe þer of is
> Of þe normans beþ heyemen þat beþ of engelonde
> & þe lowemen of saxons as ich understonde.[11]

Robert's scheme, of course, does not account for the variety of social circumstance in centuries after the eleventh, and, as that various circumstance maps onto writing practice, surviving texts from the period show that knowledge of French was far from restricted to "heyemen," nor was it only "lowemen" who spoke and wrote English. But Robert is right that the political change effected by the Conquest represented a momentous change in the *status* of English, which "had achieved, by the eleventh century, an importance in relation to Latin which no other vernacular was to match for centuries."[12] If not in all practice then in fundamental principle, English became "low" because the "lowemen" who originally employed it had been conquered, Latin returned to its presumptive status as English was derogated, and French took its place as "high" next to Latin because the conquering "heyemen" originally employed it. The subjection that structured most personal relations in the Middle Ages was, thus, as a result of the

---

[10] "In this discussion of the levels of style in Chaucer's language, we have been able to demonstrate a very tangled skein of stylistic associations, complicated by shifting moral, social, and artistic values. It has been possible to discern in this a kind of polarization toward two distinct levels: a lower style and a higher style, both of which are further complicated individually," Burnley, *Guide to Chaucer's Language*, p. 199.

[11] Robert of Gloucester, *Metrical Chronicle*, Wright (ed.), lines 7498–501.

[12] Pearsall, *Old English and Middle English Poetry*, p. 86.

Conquest, given long-lasting and determinate linguistic relevance. A passage defining the form of such personal relations in the thirteenth-century *De Legibus et Consuetudinibus Angliæ* (commonly attributed to Henry Bracton) gives a usefully contemporary account of the pressures subsequently in play:

> But with men, in truth, there is a difference between persons, for there are some of great eminence [who] are placed above others and rule over them: in spiritual matters which belong to the priesthood, the lord pope, and under him archbishops, bishops and other less exalted prelates; in temporal matters which pertain to the kingdom, emperors, kings and princes, and under them dukes, earls and barons, magnates or vavasours and knights, also freemen and bondsmen.[13]

Whatever the mixed realities of the lived and written situation, a writer like Robert of Gloucester, even on the eve of the fourteenth century, understood language as a relation between "some of great eminence [*præcellentes*]" and the "less exalted [*inferiores*]":

> Þus com lo engelond in to normandies hond
> & þe normans ne couþe speke þo bote her owe speche
> & speke french as hii dude atom & hor children dude also teche
> So þat heiemen of þis lond þat of hor blod come
> Holdeþ alle þulke speche þat hii of hom nome
> Vor bote a man conne frenss me telþ of him lute
> Ac lowe men holdeþ to engliss & to hor owe speche ȝute[14]

Robert's is a record of his own, not merely past, cultural understandings, since he describes linguistic division in the present tense ("holdeþ") and lays distinct emphasis on its currency ("ȝute"). Since Robert's own "englissh" draws copiously from Latin and Anglo-Norman, his *Chronicle* belies its own claims, but, particularly in that conflict, these lines provide important witness to the durability of a powerful *idea*

---

13 "Apud homines vero est differentia personarum, quia hominum quidam sunt præcellentes et prelati et aliis principantur: dominus papa in rebus spiritualibus quæ pertinent ad sacerdotium, et sub eo archiepiscopi, episcopi, et alii prelati inferiores. Item in temporalibus imperatores, reges, et principes in his quæ pertinent ad regnum, et sub eis duces, comites, et barones, magnates sive vavasores, et milites, et etiam liberi et villani, et diversæ potestates sub rege constitutae," Woodbine (ed.) and Thorne (trans.), *Bracton: De legibus et consuetudinibus Angliae*, vol. II, p. 32.

14 Robert of Gloucester, *Metrical Chronicle*, lines 7537–43.

about language.[15] Indeed, certain kinds of fluidity between English and Anglo-Norman would have secured rather than attenuated the hierarchy Robert describes. Since the "language of official business" was so often French after the Conquest, "Englishmen [had to] learn to speak, and even more emphatically, to read and write French" in order "to gain entry into that world of affairs controlled by the ruling elite."[16] The prestige of French was in this way preserved by the very circumstances in which English speakers might have cause to know it.

That Chaucer bore something like this social map of linguistic practice in mind is given oblique but clear support in Dante's assertions on behalf of his own vernacular. Dante only had to contend with the prestige of Latin of course, but, for him as well as for an English writer like Chaucer, the problem of fashioning (what Dante termed) "vernacular eloquence" was also defined by the vernacular's presumptively lower status. *De vulgari eloquentia* acknowledges the very severity of the problem as Dante shows himself compelled to defend the vernacular *in* Latin. And the scheme Dante sets out in that Latin also shows that, for him, as for Robert of Gloucester, the problem of the vernacular's prestige was best understood and confronted in terms of social hierarchies.[17] A vernacular writer, Dante says, must use a "sieve in separating out the best words" taking care to see that "only the noblest words [*vocabula nobilissima*] are left in your sieve."[18] For Dante too the vernacular has two parts: one contains words that are "childish [*puerilia*]," "womanly [*muliebria*]," "rustic [*silvestria*]," "glossy [*lubrica*]," or "bristly [*reburra*]," and the other contains the "urbane [*urbana*]" words that are the "most noble [*nobilissima*]."[19] The fruit of "great eminence" –

---

15 Robert drew material from the Latin chronicles of Geoffrey of Monmouth, Henry of Huntingdon, Robert of Canterbury, Matthew of Westminster, and from Wace's *Roman de Brut*. On Robert's sources see *MWME*, vol. VIII, pp. 2617–21.

16 Burnley, "Lexis and Semantics," p. 426.

17 Rita Copeland reads the *De vulgari* similarly: "In attempting to theorize a place for the vernacular in a hierarchy of languages, Dante seems to accept, rather than challenge the given terms of that hierarchy," *Rhetoric, Hermenutics, and Translation*, pp. 180–1.

18 The language in the *De vulgari* is "ad exaceranda egregia verba te cribrare oportet" (II, vii, 3) and "sola vocabula nobilissima in cribro tuo residere curabis" (II, vii, 4). Dante, *De vulgari eloquentia*, Mengaldo (ed.). Translations from Dante, *Literature in the Vernacular*, Purcell (trans.), p. 47.

19 Dante, *De vulgari eloquentia*, Mengaldo (ed.), II, vii, 3–4 and Dante, *Literature in the Vernacular*, Purcell (trans.), pp. 47–8.

what Dante calls the *"stilus prelatus"* – remains when the husk of the "less exalted" is sifted away and the inherent nobility that remains may compete with the privilege that Latin, by definition, possesses. Dante's scheme is, in other words, the Bractonian social scheme applied to the vernacular as a set of recommendations for undoing the very divisions on which those recommendations are based.

Dante's scheme matters to Chaucer's English, not because Chaucer either knew or drew upon it, but because it foretells the English problem and makes explicit the solution Chaucer would also find.[20] And Dante's description is also important because it sets out in detail the confrontation that Chaucer would only stage. If we want to see Chaucer setting out his own scheme for vernacular eloquence, however, we will find it at its most explicit in that stanza at the end of *Troilus and Criseyde* where Chaucer's own vernacular efforts are brought into closest contact with great eminence:

> Go, litel bok, go, litel myn tragedye,
> Ther God thi makere yet, er that he dye,
> So sende myght to make in some comedye!
> But litel book, no makyng thow n'envie,
> But subgit be to alle poesye;
> And kis the steppes where as thow seest pace
> Virgile, Ovide, Omer, Lucan, and Stace. (5.1786–92)

This pageant resembles a similar one in the *House of Fame*,[21] but the stakes are raised here as Latin and Greek authors fill out a category called "poesye," and the subjected status of English "makyng" before this privilege is at once acknowledged (as this *"litel* tragedye" sits "subgit") and respectfully but emphatically questioned (as Chaucer elevates his own work high enough to "kis the steppes" on which Greco-Latinity processes). Bractonian hierarchies are still in place, mapped onto linguistic distinctions, but Chaucer enters his own name

---

[20] Howard Schless's exhaustive comparison of Chaucer and Dante offers no parallels between Chaucer's writing and any passage of the *De vulgari*. See his "Index of Comparisons" in *Chaucer and Dante*, pp. 249–52.

[21] In *House of Fame*, lines 1451–1512, Chaucer describes a pantheon that includes "Stace," "Omer," "Virgile," "Ovide," and "Lucan" each standing on an "yren piler" in a "rowe." There he also mentions "Dares and Tytus" (Dares Phrygius and Dictys Cretensis), "Lollius," "Guydo . . . de Columpnis" (Guido delle Colonne), "Englyssh Gaufride" (Geoffrey of Monmouth), and "Claudian."

into the hierarchy even as he confirms it. The gesture itself had a tradition in the *Roman de la Rose*, Dante's *Divina Commedia*, and Boccaccio's *Filocolo*, but that network of allusion simply extends Chaucer's claim beyond the privilege of Greco-Latinity to the privilege already gained by the vernacular writers who had previously proved their fitness in this august society.[22] These lines wallow in subservience and establish clear linguistic boundaries between privilege and its lack, but they also blithely transgress the very boundaries they establish.[23] The boldness of Chaucer's ambition here is the more obvious, too, when these lines are compared with Robert Mannyng's handling of similar boundaries in his *Chronicle* (c. 1338):

> Als þai haf wryten & sayd,
> haf I alle myn Inglis layd,
> In symple speche as I couthe
> Þat is lightest in mannes mouthe,
> I mad noght for no disours,
> ne for no seggers, no harpours,
> Bot for þe luf of symple men
> þat strange Inglis can not ken.[24]

The contents of Mannyng's categories, while different from Chaucer's,

---

[22] Jean de Meun mentions Tibullus, Gallus, Catullus, Ovid, and Guillaume de Lorris (Guillaume de Lorris and Jean de Meun, *Le roman de la rose*, Lecoy [ed.], lines 10477–500); Dante mentions Homer, Horace, Ovid, Lucan, and Virgil (Dante, *Inferno*, Petrocchi [ed.], IV.80–102); and Boccaccio mentions Virgil, Lucan, Statius, Ovid, and Dante (Boccaccio, *Filocolo*, Qualio [ed.], Book V, 97, 4–6). I draw this point and these citations from Wallace, "Chaucer's Continental Inheritance," pp. 29 and 36 n. 33. See also Wallace, *Chaucer and the Early Writings of Boccaccio*, pp. 46–53.

[23] In "Chaucer's 'New Men' and the Good of Literature" Anne Middleton describes a Chaucer who is much more troubled by the prospects he considers in these lines (see esp. pp. 34–9). In understanding "poesye" as a property of the "mighty dead" (p. 36), Middleton suggests, Chaucer creates serious problems for his own status as a poet and for any living poet's practice ("'Poetry' remains for [Chaucer] an enterprise that can only be thought of in the perfect tense" [p. 37]). I would agree with Middleton, but I concern myself here with the *linguistic* claims that are, I think, by definition, less troublesome for Chaucer. He may have difficulty saying whether he is "making," "enditing" or writing "poetry" (the terms Middleton shows Chaucer exploring) but he is unambiguously writing in English just as the authors he names unambiguously wrote in Latin and Greek. The simplicity of the linguistic contrast means that Chaucer can be firm in what he says about his language while failing of that certainty in confronting the larger issue of his status as "poet."

[24] Mannyng, *Story of England*, Furnivall (ed.), lines 71–8.

still conform to the same social lines. As Mannyng put it most directly, he wrote "not for the lered bot for the lewed."[25] He divides what can be "wryten & sayd" into two forms (although both here are identified as "Inglis"), one for "symple" men and the other reserved to a more specialized class ("disours," "seggers," and "harpours"). Quite unlike Chaucer, however, Mannyng is content to assign the "symple" function to his own making. Slightly later in this same poem, he even expresses some revulsion at attempts to make English appeal to the "lered" through the borrowing of French forms:

> If it were made in ryme couwee
> or in strangere or enterlace
> þat rede Inglis it ere inowe,
> þat couthe not haf coppled a kowe,
> þat outhere in couwee or in baston
> som suld haf ben fordon,
> so þat fele men þat it herde
> suld not witte howe þat it ferde.[26]

For Mannyng "ryme couwee" and "enterlace" are a kind of social climbing that threaten the "Inglis" simplicity he understands his vernacular project to be. In fact, Mannyng wildly misrepresents his own poem in that he borrows heavily from French,[27] but he uses the same socio-linguistic divisions Chaucer later reverses to make his point. Both Mannyng and Chaucer posit a written accomplishment different from their own, but, where Mannyng endorses his *Chronicle* by heaping scorn upon privilege, Chaucer endorses privilege and then sends *Troilus and Criseyde* forth in its company. Where Mannyng asserts a distinction to identify his writing with the familiar side of a divide, Chaucer asserts that distinction to edge his English writing across it. Chaucer turns the very linguistic difference that make his English "subgit" to eminence into the merit of that English and, hence, his (now) poetic achievement. If Greek and Latin writers count as "alle poesie" but *Troilus* at least

---

[25] Mannyng, *Story of England*, Furnivall (ed.), line 6. Mannyng also says he writes *Handlyng Synne* "nat to lered onely, but eke to lewed." Mannyng, *Handlyng Synne*, Furnivall (ed.), line 10804

[26] Mannyng, *Story of England*, Furnivall (ed.), lines 85–92.

[27] For evidence of Mannyng's extensive use of French, see the lists showing the quantity of Mannyng's original borrowings that appear in *Chaucer's* texts (above p. 62).

touches that rank, then Chaucer's "poesye" is also, necessarily, the first *English* "poesye."

Chaucer's position is finally more complex than Dante's however, because, even as he lays claim to the privilege of poetic "heyemen," Chaucer maintains his own claim, like Mannyng's, to the "lewed" simplicities of "lowemen." Against the pantheon in *Troilus* must be set the passage in Book 2 of the *House of Fame* in which Chaucer provides a nice echo of Mannyng as the Eagle extols the virtues of speaking "symply" to an audience of the "lewed":

> "Have y not preved thus symply,
> Withoute any subtilite
> Of speche, or gret prolixite
> Of termes of philosophie,
> Of figures of poetrie,
> Or colours of rethorike?
> Pardee, hit oughte the to lyke,
> For hard langage and hard matere
> Ys encombrous for to here
> Attones; wost thou not wel this?"
> And y answered and seyde, "Yis."
> "A ha," quod he, "lo, so I can
> Lewedly to a lewed man
> Speke, and shew hym swyche skiles
> That he may shake hem be the biles,
> So palpable they shulden be." (854–69)

The Eagle's clerkly pretensions mean that he must eat his linguistic cake and have it too: the disavowing of "prolixite" is itself, of course, a prolix *occupatio*. But the material of this joke matters fully as much as its form: the heights of "poetrie" may here be scaled, but that ascent does not leave behind an English virtuous in its simplicity. The Eagle – like Chaucer generally – distinguishes between two kinds of vernacular making – speaking "symply" and "gret prolixite" that is "encombrous" – as both kinds are ostentatiously present in the language that makes the distinction. The capacity of English is shown here to be great enough to use and reprehend – at once – the "hard langage and hard matere" that defines poetry's excellence.

The material of the Eagle's joke in the *House of Fame* is otherwise

deployed in Chaucer's writing with an insistence that lends it all the
weight of argument. In the *Clerk's Prologue*, moreover, the humor that
nearly conceals the serious point is shed for a more explicit consideration of linguistic hierarchies and Chaucer's place in them:

> "I wol yow telle a tale which that I
> Lerned at Padowe of a worthy clerk,
> As preved by his wordes and his werk.
> He is now deed and nayled in his cheste;
> I prey to God so yeve his soule reste!
>   "Fraunceys Petrak, the lauriat poete,
> Highte this clerk, whos rethorike sweete
> Enlumyned al Ytaille of poetrie . . ." (IV, 26–33)

Here, although behind the screen of the Clerk, we have a serious
statement of Chaucer's poetic ambitions akin to those made in *Troilus* –
what Anne Middleton has characterized as a "play upon the very terms
of literary value" in the form of what David Wallace has called a
"critique" of the "Petrarchan Academy"[28] – and this statement makes
its point in linguistic terms: the Latin of Petrarch, which the Clerk
translates, had itself been translated from the vernacular of Boccaccio's
Decameron, and so the very vernacularity of the *Clerk's Tale* delivers a
pointed rebuke to Petrarch's linguistic intervention by reversing it.[29]
But these lines also align Chaucer's efforts with the privilege of Latinity

---

[28] Anne Middleton, "The Clerk and His Tale," 122; Wallace, "'When She Translated
Was.'" For another important discussion of these lines see Lerer, *Chaucer and His
Readers*, pp. 26–34.
[29] Chaucer knew of Petrarch's linguistic gesture because he clearly knew the letter in
which Petrarch included and explained the purpose of his translation (*Seniles* 17.3).
The Clerk's explanation of his source and purpose in the *Clerk's Prologue* is itself an
echo of Petrarch's censure of Boccaccio by ostensible praise (that is by an abjection rife
with personal ambition). Chaucer's use of the material of this letter is described in
much greater detail in Middleton, "The Clerk and His Tale." The letter from Petrarch
to Boccaccio that includes Petrarch's translation is printed in Bryan and Dempster
(eds.), *Sources and Analogues*, pp. 296–330. For Boccaccio's story see *Decameron*,
Branca (ed.), X, x. For Wallace's discussion of the reversal of Chaucer's translation as
critique see "'When She Translated Was,'" p. 196.
   We know Chaucer knew Petrarch was a vernacular writer since he translated
Petrarch's lyric "S'amor non è" in *Troilus and Criseyde*. See Wallace, "'When She
Translated Was,'" p. 157 and p. 157 n. 2. The sonnet can be found in *Troilus and
Criseyde*, 1.400–20 and its Italian original is printed in *Troilus and Criseyde*, Windeatt
(ed.), p. 112 .

that Petrarch represents: as the Clerk remembers Petrarch as the poet *par excellence* of medieval Latinity (the "poete" crowned *laureatus*, in Rome, in 1341)[30], his translation makes a bid for the privilege Petrarch defines precisely by *noting* that privilege (the observation that Petrarch "Enlumyned al Ytaille of poetrie" trembles with the possibility that the *Clerk's Tale* will illuminate "al *Engelond* of poetrie"). Since it is here that the Host has urged the Clerk to "speken pleyn" and "keepe . . . in stoor" his "heigh style" and the Clerk has, as well, ostensibly agreed to "do . . . obeisaunce" to this request, the Clerk's rime royal seems of a piece with the Eagle's wit: the "heigh" is partaken of precisely as it is disavowed. But the claim entered here for the form and capacity of the Clerk's English (that is, *Chaucer's* English) in the lines I quote is no joke: Chaucer again marks out the line between eminence and the less exalted in order to claim the virtues of *both* for his own vernacular endeavor. Here, he suggests, his English can supplant Latin while partaking of its appurtenant privileges because the simplicity that is the vernacular's inherent virtue can be rendered as "heigh." Chaucer's writing will be "poetrie" but it will be *English* "poetrie," and since, here, as generally, Chaucer does not bother to remember any English

---

[30] Since Chaucer is leaning so hard here on Petrarch's fame and Petrarch's fame in the Middle Ages rested almost entirely on his Latin writings which, with the exception of the sonnet Chaucer translated (see previous note), were all that circulated outside Italy until well into the fifteenth century, it seems reasonable to assume that Chaucer knew Petrarch was crowned "precisely as the greatest living Latin poet." Foster, *Petrarch*, p. 28.

There is no direct evidence that Chaucer knew Petrarch's *Coronation Oath* but there is one indication that he might have. On the occasion of his laureation, among a welter of citations to the Latin poets of antiquity, Petrarch placed himself exactly where Chaucer later placed himself in *Troilus and Criseyde*, just after Statius in privileged poetic descent: "I recall that . . . in this very Roman Capitol where we now are gathered, so many and such great poets, having attained to the highest and most illustrious mastery of their art, have received the laurel crown they had deserved, but that now this custom seems to have been lost than to have been merely laid aside . . . For we do not read that anyone has been decorated with this honor since the illustrious poet Statius . . . [Recolo . . . in hoc ipso capitolio romano ubi nunc insistimus tot tantosque vates ad culmen preclari magisterii provectos emeritam lauream reportasse nunc vero morem illum non modo intermissum sed obmissum . . . Si quidem post statium pampineum illustrem poetam . . . nullum legimus tali honore decoratum]." For this translation see the appendix to Wilkins, *Studies in the Life and Works of Petrarch*, p. 304 (Wilkins gives a translation of the entire *Oath* on pp. 300–13). For the original see Petrarch, *Scritti inediti*, Hortis (ed.), p. 316.

predecessors (he only seems to have a Latin model) he presents the *Clerk's Tale* as the first English example in the laureate line he projects.

A vernacular writer's ambition could reach no higher in the Middle Ages, and even if these claims are distanced as the performance of the Clerk, the *Canterbury Tales* as a whole are a performance of this sort, and so, in defining the poetics of the *Clerk's Tale*, Chaucer is simultaneously defining the ambition of all the *Tales*. In fact, the performance of the *Clerk's Prologue*, along with the performance of *Sir Thopas* and the *Melibee*, represent Chaucer's complete absorption of Bractonian distinctions into the very structure of the *Tales* – as the linguistic correlatives for social distinctions construct both the pilgrims and the tales they tell. The pilgrims embody Chaucer's argument for the capacities of his own language, and their interactions simply play out language difference on a social stage. In this sense *every* description of an individual pilgrim's language matters. The Host's prejudice against the "heigh style" in the *Clerk's Prologue* (the "lewed man" himself preferring simplicity to subtlety) can be connected to the Squire's claim that he cannot match the "speche" of the knight that comes to Cambyuskan's court:

> Al be that I kan nat sowne his stile,
> Ne kan nat clymben over so heigh a style,
> Yet seye I this, as to commune entente:
> Thus muche amounteth al that evere he mente,
> If it so be that I have it in mynde. (V, 105–9)

This "heigh style" sits in parallel to the Pardoner's "hauteyne speche" (VI, 330), and they find their opposite in the "cherles termes" that the Reeve says he and the Miller employ:

> This dronke Millere hath ytoold us heer
> How that bigyled was a carpenteer,
> Peraventure in scorn, for I am oon.
> And, by youre leve, I shal hym quite anoon;
> Right in his cherles termes wol I speke.
> I pray to God his nekke mote to-breke. (I, 3913–18)

To be sure, none of these is a positive assertion: what the Host warns the Clerk to avoid, the Squire says he cannot "climb" to; the Pardoner impugns whatever might be "hauteyne" in his language insofar as that language is an instrument of deception; the Reeve is offended by the Miller's "termes" and employs them vengefully. And yet the socio-linguistic map that these distinctions make still matters, for, within these negatives the possibility of a "heigh" speech is reserved to the learned (the Clerk and, however venally, the Pardoner) and the noble (the Squire), while "cherles termes" attach to the clear opposites of cultural privilege, the self-described "cherles" themselves. And it matters still more that, with infinite nuance, the sequential linguistic performances of the pilgrims exist as an adequation of what Chaucer calls "hir wordes and hir cheere" (I, 728). It is equally true, of course, that any stark division between "heyemen" and "lowemen" is blurred in the *Tales* because it is part of Chaucer's point that such distinctions are blurred in social life. In the end, however, wherever the pilgrims are oriented with respect to the "high" and the "low," the *Tales* emphati-cally enfold both extremes and everything in between. In portraying the Canterbury pilgrims as a society in conflict over linguistic kinds, Chaucer trumps this conflict by making every one of its terms a part of *his* English. Chaucer's vernacular, the *Tales* as a whole maintain, can attain the virtues of the *stilus prelatus* while also remaining *inferior*: the pilgrims' linguistic plenty is the plenitude of Chaucer's success, for it shows Chaucer's English compassing all that the vernacular could possibly be.

2

Chaucer's claim for his own linguistic capacity is implicitly about linguistic "invention" in those passages from *Troilus* and the *Clerk's Prologue* I have just examined, but Chaucer argues most steadily for the novelty of his English – and that argument has its most extensive effects – in the very words that comprise his works. This English is constituted everywhere in the form of the more capacious contrast that shapes all the claims I have explored so far. It is bifurcated into high and low modes such that the high can be used as a fulcrum to vault it over precedent English to the privileged realm of French and Latin even as the low is made to root that achievement in the vernacular (to make it an achievement *of*, not in spite of, the vernacular). Both of these modes are traditional, but, at their extremes, they have also both been identified as Chaucer's salient invention. This was, of course, an appearance Chaucer encouraged. In fact it was precisely his linguistic means for proving true the claims I have just explored: the distance between the traditional nature of Chaucer's materials and the invented appearance of their result is the general form of Chaucer's claim that his English was "first." It is therefore crucial that an anatomy of what is "invented" in Chaucer's English looks most to combined forms, for it is in combination that the balance of high and low issues in the appearance of originality. To see this combination clearly, however, we must begin by pulling its two constituents apart.

We can begin with Chaucer's high mode, or, as Chaucer describes it, the "heigh style." As this style is most often understood, it matches the prestige of French and Latin with its own Franco-Latinity, incorporating Romance privilege into English by means of borrowed Romance lexis – English competes with the languages of status by becoming them. It is the making of this style that Brewer, for example, sees as the story of the development of English eloquence:

> It must first be recalled that at the Conquest the English language, the most highly developed vernacular of Northern Europe, was displaced as the language of the dominant classes by French and Latin . . . The result of this displacement was that almost the whole of the 'cultural superstructure' that had been developed in the Old English language gradually perished; that is, most of the general terms, the abstractions, the subtle poetic and prose diction, the words of government, the terms of art, disappeared. What remained was the main hull of the language, the words we cannot live without . . . The story of the language for the next few centuries is the story of how it created, largely by borrowing, a new superstructure of abstractions, words for new things, new ideas, new feelings, new arts, that were built on to the continuing basic language, and were modified to its essential, though changing nature.[31]

Brewer, like much stylistic and linguistic history of this development, gives a share in the provision of this new "cultural superstructure" to all those writers whose story is the "story of the language" after the Conquest, but he also gives Chaucer pride of place in the general process. When Chaucer "felt the lack of English to be a hindrance to his poetry,"

---

[31] Brewer, "English and European Traditions," p. 9.

Brewer says, he "beg[a]n to repair the lack," and "to enrich or 'augment' English" by "introduc[ing] . . . French words into literary English."[32] As Burnley refines this description, he makes this precisely the process by which Chaucer acquired his "heigh style." Chaucer, he says, "was ready to import new French, Latin and Italian loan words in order to lend grandeur to his diction and proclaim his erudition."[33] Burnley also connects the "grandeur" achieved through borrowing with principles advocated by Latin rhetoricians: "Chaucer to some extent prefigured the diction of the aureate poets of the fifteenth century by using elevated, polysyllabic, Latin-derived terms, the equivalent of the *verba splendida* or *nitida* of the rhetorics: *celebrable, ardaunt, columbyn, perdurable*." He calls such "*verba splendida*" a "conscious creation of stylistic elevation."[34] Elsewhere Burnley says that Chaucer's "complicated words of Latin, French or even Italian origin" were neologisms made for the express purpose of adding "dignity and ceremony to literary composition."[35]

Chaucer's English conduces to the view that Brewer and Burnley have of it. It can be divided neatly along a line that places new, polysyllabic borrowings on one side and native synonyms for those words – the "main hull of the language" – on the other. A list can be drawn up, for example, in which borrowings recorded for the first time in Chaucer's English (the words forming the first half of a pair) offer elevated equivalents for other words used by Chaucer that are recorded in Middle English from its earliest writing (the second half of these pairs): "difficulte n."/"hard n."; "disaventure n."/"unhap n."; "dishoneste n."/ "shendship n."; "edifice n."/"bildinge ger."; "existence n."/"being ger."; "ignoraunt adj."/"unconning adj."; "informacioun n."/"red n1."; "re-prehensioun n."/"wite n2."; "secre adj."/"derne adj."; "signifiaunce n."/ "mening ger1." Such pairs show that English *had* the words to do the basic semantic work that borrowings could do, and, therefore, they also show that part of the signifying importance of new words was precisely the "elevation" and "dignity" Burnley attributes to them. These words

---

[32] *Ibid.*, p. 24.

[33] Burnley, *Guide to Chaucer's Language*, p. 139. Burnley also notes, in connection with this observation, that Chaucer "was also ready to employ words of a far less estimable kind in the cause of stylistic propriety" (p. 139). I will take up this point – with which I agree – in the next section of this chapter.

[34] For this phrase and the preceding longer quote see Burnley, "Picked Terms," 202.

[35] Burnley, *Guide to Chaucer's English*, p. 136

fit out a style not least because they are *marked* with the work of augmentation they perform, in their novelty, as well as in the terminal morphemes that represent their borrowed nature and link them to other borrowings with similar endings. Because of their history these words comprise a lexical category and because of their shape they define a linguistic texture. That texture becomes both noticeable and particularly useful in poetry because such endings can be used repeatedly at a line's end to fashion rhyme. As Burnley points out, such "aureate" diction (to use Lydgate's term) came to define the lexical legacy that the fifteenth century understood Chaucer to have bequeathed to it. In that crucial sense, these new words are not only the salient feature of Chaucer's high style but precisely the contribution he was understood to make to English by those imitators who actually used his words.

The equation of Chaucer's lexical contribution with these polysyllabic borrowings is mistaken, however, as it must carry with it the assumption that polysyllabic borrowings are *necessarily* "novelty," and, therefore *all* that is new in Chaucer's English. Brewer and Burnley do not explicitly extend their thinking to this conclusion, but it is a logic that must inform any attempt to equate the "grandeur" of Chaucer's English with aureation, aureation with borrowing, and borrowing with "augmentation." It matters very much then that polysyllabic borrowings may also be as traditional *in* their grandeur as Chaucer's foreign borrowings generally, that, like the larger class which I examined in chapter 2, polysyllabic borrowings are also traditional insofar as they *are* borrowings. It is also possible, for example, to pair polysyllabic borrowings with native synonyms such that the borrowing *as well as* the synonyms are recorded in English long before Chaucer uses them: "commaundement n."/"heste nɪ."; "contenaunce n."/"fare nɪ."; "creature n."/"wight n."; "destruccioun n."/"overthrouinge ger."; "langage n."/"leden n."; "profitable adj."/"spedeful adj."; "serment n."/"oth n."; "servaunt n."/"thral nɪ."; "sustenaunce n."/"lif-lode n."; "vesture n."/"wede n." To suggest that Chaucer enriched Middle English diction while pointing to aureation as the different form this memorable enrichment took is to ignore the history of borrowing that confects these pairs. As generally in his borrowing, Chaucer only made common cause with precedent Middle English literary achievement by means of his aureation. It is even fair to say that such aureation was among the most traditional of Chaucer's linguistic practices – *itself* the "main "hull" of the precedent language of which his particularly novel contributions were only imitative. This larger point can be made by a more thorough history of those polysyllabic words in Chaucer's vocabulary that form what Burnley calls the *verba splendida*: words marked as borrowings by their borrowed, terminal morphemes. Chaucer's vocabulary is so filled with such words that they form a significant category of 1,023 words, representing more than a quarter of Chaucer's Romance vocabulary (27 percent of 3,820 words), and over a tenth of his entire vocabulary (11 percent of 9,117 words). In the following table I sort this category morpheme-by-morpheme, as its constituent words are both invented and traditional.

Ending	Romance source for ending[36]	Total words with ending	Words recorded earlier than Chaucer	Words recorded first in Chaucer
-able/-ible	[OF -*able*, -*ible*, L -*abilis*, -*ibilis*]	96	49	47
-age	[OF -*age* , L -*aticum*]	49	38	11
-ai(l)l(e)/-e(i)l	[OF -*aille*, -*ail*, L -*alia*, -*alium*, -*alis*]	28	23	5
-at(e)	[OF -*at*, L -*at-um* or L -*atus*]	14	5	9
-a(u)nce/-ence	[AF -*aunce*, CF -*ance*, -*ence*, L -*antia*, -*entia*]	131	92	39
-aunt(e)/ -ent(e)	[AF -*aunt*, CF -*ant*, L -*ant-em*, -*ent-em*]	104	64	40
-io(u)n	[OF -*ïon*, AF -*ioun*, L -*io(nem)*]	220	118	102
-ment	[OF -*ment*, L -*mentum*]	47	38	9
-our(e)	[OF -*ëor*, AF -*our*, -*ur*, L -*or(em)*]	107	90	17
-ous(e)	[OF -*os*, -*our*, -*eus*, -*eux*, L -*osus*]	78	50	28
-te(e)	[OF -*te*, L -*itatem*, -*itas*]	105	69	36
-ure	[OF -*ure*, L -*ura*]	44	31	13

[36] For the etymologies for these endings see *MED*, s. vv. "-able adj. suf.," "-ible suf.," "-age suf.," "-aille suf.," "-at suf1." and "-at suf2.," "-aunce suf.," "-aunt suf.," "-ioun suf.," "-ment suf.," "-our suf.," "-ous suf.," and *OED*, s. vv. "-ence suffix," "-ent suffix," "-ty suffix1." There is no entry in these dictionaries for "-ure suf.," but see, for example, the etymology in the *MED*, s. v. "creature n." For a more general history of these suffixes see also Marchand, *Categories and Types of Present-Day English Word-Formation*, pp. 229–32 ("-able"), pp. 234–6 ("-age"), pp. 248–9 ("-ance, -ence"), pp. 254–9 ("-at" and "-ate"), pp. 259–61 ("-ation"), pp. 251–2 ("-ant, -ent"), pp. 331–2 ("-ment"), pp. 339–45 ("-ous"), pp. 350–1 ("-ure").

Chaucer brought 356 words (or 35 percent of these words) to a language in which he found 667 of them already present (or 65 percent of the words surveyed). The length of such words may make them appear ornamental, particularly in the face of simpler synonyms, just as their origins may seem to mark them as additions to the language even as they are traditional, but if they do "lend grandeur" to Chaucer's diction than that is only because grandeur was *already* constitutive of Middle English lexical practice.

Chaucer's high style is rooted in tradition in other ways too, since Middle English also contained within itself the linguistic resources necessary to construct calques for polysyllabic loan-words. Such calques are already visible in the two sets of paired synonyms I have just given, where it is also true that some of the *native* words are polysyllabic. "Being ger.," "bildinge ger.," "lif-lode n.," "mening ger1.," "over-throuinge ger.," "shendshipe n.," "spedeful adj.," and "unconning adj." may not all look like *verba splendida*, and few of these particular words are used by Chaucer to shape that texture of the polysyllabic rhymes that marks his high style,[37] but Chaucer did use such native polysyllabicism in that texture, and, as he so used it, some of what is "heigh" in Chaucer's English is also "native," and, at the same time, some of what is "native" is also "new." The relation of this category to the one just examined can be seen in a lyric such as *Lak of Stedfastnesse*, where every one of the poem's twenty-five rhyme words is polysyllabic (some rhyme words are repeated over the poem's twenty-eight lines), and nineteen of these rhyme words are borrowings,[38] but six of them ("wilfulnesse n.," "up-so-doun adv.," "sted-fastnesse n.," "wrecchednesse n.," "fikelnesse n.," "worthinesse n.") are native in all their component parts. Two of

---

[37] Only a few of these words appear in rhyme position (see "meninge ger1." in the F Prologue, *Legend of Good Women*, line 474, and "unconninge adj." in *Romaunt of the Rose*, line 686); in fact these words generally appear in Chaucer's prose. For their other uses in Chaucer see Benson, *Glossarial Concordance*.

[38] These nineteen words (in the order of their appearance as rhyme words) are "stable adj.," "obligacioun n.," "deceivable adj.," "conclusioun n.," "variable adj.," "dissencioun n.," "unable adj." (derived from "able adj.," according to the *MED*, itself a Romance borrowing), "collusioun n.," "oppressioun n.," "fable n.," "dominacioun n.," "merciable adj.," "discrecioun n.," "permutacioun n.," "honourable adj." (derived from "honour n.," according to the *MED*, itself a Romance borrowing), "extorcioun n.," "reprevable adj." (derived from "repreven v.," according to the *MED*, itself a Romance borrowing, or from "OF" directly) "regioune n.," "castigacioun n."

the borrowings are used by Chaucer for the first time in recorded English ("conclusioun n.," "castigacioun n."), but so too is one of the "native" words ("fikelnesse n."). The novelty of this word along with the native polysyllabicisms in this poem root it in a precedent tradition which defines another large category of Chaucer's words. These words are all, essentially, calques of the aureate borrowings whose shape they have and alongside which they create Chaucer's most aureate verbal textures, and, as with polysyllabic borrowings, the category they comprise is large enough to warrant analysis in terms of the traditional and the invented, again, morpheme-by-morpheme.

Ending[39]	Etymology	Total	Words recorded earlier	Words recorded first in Chaucer
-ful(le)	fr. ful adj. (OE)	45	34	11
-hede/-hode	OE	18	10	8
-inge	OE	372	272	100
-li(che)	OE & ON	320	251	69
-nesse	OE	132	91	41
-shipe	OE	6	6	0
-ward	OE	30	26	4

In the 923 words analyzed here, the 233 words new to Chaucer's vocabulary are more interesting than the 690 words recorded earlier. They show that the wholly native can enrich and lend grandeur to a poem like *Lak of Stedfastnesse* by recombinant processes that never leave the borders of English. They are, in that sense, the mirror image of Chaucer's polysyllabic borrowings – not the new that is old but the old that is new. But they are similar to those borrowings as they show, in only slightly different terms, how tradition and invention were just different sides of the same coin in Chaucer's lexical practice. What matters much more than the provenance of any new word Chaucer

---

[39] For these endings see *MED*, s. vv. "-ful suf2.," "-hede suf.," "-inge suf1.," "-li suf1.," "-li suf2.," "-nesse suf.," "-shipe suf.," and *OED*, s. v. "-ward suffix." For a more general history see also Marchand, *Categories and Types of Present-Day English Word-Formation*, p. 291 ("-ful"), p. 293 ("-hood"), pp. 302–5 ("-ing"), pp. 329–31 ("-ly"), pp. 334–6 ("-ness"), p. 345–6 ("-ship"), pp. 351–2 ("-ward").

used is the precedent practice that had already made invention of precisely this kind traditional.

To turn from the complex components of Chaucer's high style to the low is not to flip this coin, but to find the same coin again, with its sides, in effect, reversed. That is, where Chaucer's high style is traditional precisely as its constituents are so inventive, the low style is inventive precisely as it remains so unusually rooted in tradition. Scholars have not described Chaucer's low style in this way, of course, although they have agreed – with a conviction that equals general confidence in the novelty of Chaucer's polysyllabicisms – that such a low style is an important contribution of Chaucer's English. Where Chaucer's "colloquialism" (as it is generally termed) is related to the aureate it is most often cast in the role of a mediating earthiness, a sensible restraint curbing the dangers of over-abstraction that polysyllabic borrowings pose. As C. S. Lewis understood it, it was "the Chaucerian style, imitated ill, and with gross exaggeration of its foreign and polysyllabic elements" that Lydgate brought to a "terrible perfection." Like the *House of Fame*'s Eagle, Lewis sees "fussy prolixity" as error and the real measure of Chaucer's achievement is the degree to which he managed, finally, to make prolix places plain.[40] This is also part of P. M. Kean's point (which I noted in chapter 3) when she describes the "urbane manner" (which she calls Chaucer's "new poetic technique") as a "plain, conversational style."[41] Brewer makes this low style the root from which elaboration branches: "In respect of language, therefore, Chaucer grafts onto his basic English style, found in the romances, a new diction, more elaborate, learned and formal, though also colloquial."[42] And Burnley makes the colloquial a constant foil for the aureate when he says that Chaucer's readiness "to import new French, Latin and Italian loan words" was matched by his readiness "to employ words of a far less estimable kind in the cause of stylistic propriety."[43]

In this category of achievement, however, scholarly certainty that Chaucer's colloquialism is worthy of praise has not been matched by

---

[40] Lewis, *Allegory of Love*, pp. 164–5.
[41] Kean, *Making of English Poetry*, vol. I, pp. 32 and 23.
[42] Brewer, "English and European Traditions," p. 27.
[43] Burnley, *Guide to Chaucer's English*, p. 139.

any certainty in identifying the forms in which that achievement resides. Brewer and Burnley have the least trouble here because they carefully shade the spoken into the written: Brewer's "spoken language of the court" is courtly writing *as* speech (the language of romance in daily use); Burnley's "words which have become old-fashioned, and would consequently have been shunned by a practitioner of courtly literature except for a specific stylistic purpose" are related to what Donaldson famously identified as the "idiom of popular poetry," written forms representing themselves *as* speech.[44] These are vague definitions that only approach a gray space that Norman Blake describes, in a neat (and telling) oxymoron, as a "form of literary colloquialism."[45] Still, eluding all of these definitions of the colloquial are those written forms that we might *know* Chaucer actually took from speech, forms that would have *been* colloquial to Middle English readers because they had never before been written.[46] Norman Davis sets out the methodological problem without actually identifying these forms:

> The appearance of so many colloquial or informal words first in Chaucer is no doubt largely to be explained by the comparatively few works before his time in which his kind of realistic dialogue found a place. It nevertheless makes clear how precarious it is to credit Chaucer (or any other) with the 'introduction into English' of particular words simply on the evidence collected by the lexicographers. All of the

---

[44] Brewer, "English and European Traditions," p. 25; Burnley, *Guide to Chaucer's English*, p. 139; Donaldson, "Idiom of Popular Poetry."

[45] Blake, "Literary Language," p. 536. Blake defines "literary colloquialism" as "linguistic features included in a literary text to suggest to the reader an informal style."

[46] Eliason makes a similar point when he says Chaucer's "colloquial style" contains "words more or less confined to spoken rather than written usage," although his equivocation shows the difficulty he has in finding such words himself. This is the fifth of ten characteristics of the "colloquial" Eliason identifies. The other characteristics are "1. Short sentences . . . 2. Frequent use of terms of address . . . 3. Use of familiar *thou* rather than *ye*; 4. Homely, not simply familiar, comparisons and proverbs . . . 6. Exclamations . . . 7. Name-calling . . . 8. Swearing . . . 9. Exuberance or exaggeration . . . 10. Indications of gestures or 'stage business,'" *Language of Chaucer's Poetry*, 114–15. By contrast, Elliott describes the "chief characteristics of . . . colloquial turns of speech" as "their monosyllabic quality and their heavy reliance upon stock phrases, clichés, tags, oaths, and sententious commonplaces often dressed up as proverbs," *Chaucer's English*, p. 191. Elliott also devotes an entire chapter to "Cherles Termes" (pp. 181–239).

words mentioned in the last paragraph are 'first found in Chaucer,' but none of them, except perhaps *wantrust*, can have been new to English, though they may well have been new to works of literary pretension.[47]

The historical problem in this part of Chaucer's style has not been misperceiving the linguistic history of an aspect of Chaucer's English, but in perceiving it in any detail at all. Even where Chaucer's "colloquial English" is not a purely lexical category the problem rears its head. Margaret Schlauch's important study of Chaucer's "colloquial English" gets the closest to fashioning a definition that can isolate forms, but the "deviations from the contrasting formal usages" she finds are defined against "formal usages of both Chaucer's age and *ours*" – so, not surprisingly, the normative in Middle English is actually traced in her study by means of *modern* grammars.[48] These definitional problems make it just as difficult as ever to separate the new from the traditional in Chaucer's English. For if that English is distinctive as it "grafts" colloquial forms onto precedent forms, but the only way to identify colloquial forms is by their precedent presence, then how is the graft to be distinguished from the root?

I offered a partial answer to this question in the last chapter by describing two interesting features of the disposition of Chaucer's words. First, the essentially "reserved" character of all of Chaucer's vocabulary: the way most native words only slowly silt into Chaucer's writings in a chronological scheme so that old words seem "new" as they appear for the "first" time in a given text. As Chaucer encouraged the chronological reading that creates this impression he also encouraged the renovation of the native that is its result. Secondly, as I also noted in the previous chapter, 2,122 of Chaucer's "reserved" words are nonce words: they are therefore as rare on the whole as they are new in their chronological advent. The habits that create both of these categories give even "old" Middle English the very quality of the new at the lexical level of each of Chaucer's texts. If these words are not traditionally new, they are refreshingly old, and, as a result, they are all

---

[47] Davis, "Chaucer and Fourteenth-Century English," p. 83.
[48] Schlauch, "Chaucer's Colloquial English," 1104. Emphasis mine. For Schlauch's references to modern grammars see this article, p. 1105 n. 4, p. 1107 n. 5, p. 1108 n. 6, p. 1110 nn. 8 and 10.

candidates for the paradoxical position of native novelty grafted onto native root.

But there is more to the novelty of Chaucer's low style than these patterns of presentation. In fact, the most noticeable lexical feature of this style is its vastly smaller part in numeric terms, although this small part is the emphatic gesture making obvious what larger patterns only more generally enforce. This smaller part was, I think, very clearly taken from speech, although Davis is right about the inherent difficulties in using written evidence as a means of demonstrating that this was so. On the other hand, the lexicographical evidence he dismisses is also richer and more complex than he grants. In fact, it is precisely because words deriving from speech *must* leave no written trace that dictionaries can give evidence of their existence, for a spoken history will necessarily result in the *failure* of the written record. It may be, of course, that any given failure in a dictionary's attempt to write a word's history is evidence of the loss of written forms. Such failure may even be evidence that Chaucer made a word up; but gaps in dictionaries are also the certain result if a word had only lived in speech until Chaucer wrote it down. In particular, speech would seem to be Chaucer's most likely source for the number of Old English words that the *MED* and *OED* find nowhere in Middle English until Chaucer uses them. In such cases these dictionaries are saying that a particular word existed before 1100 (the cut-off date for illustrations in the *MED* and the cut-off I have, therefore, applied to illustrations in the *OED*), that it existed *again* in written form when Chaucer used it, and that it survived for the intervening 270–300 years without leaving any written evidence of its use. Such words were not dead and then reborn but simply lived outside the surveillance of texts – until Chaucer recruited them again for his own. There are 36 words of this kind in Chaucer's vocabulary representing 109 different uses (I give the number of times each word was used by Chaucer in the following table).[49]

---

[49] My redating of the *Romaunt* (see Part 2, p. 232) means that I take the following words as used by Chaucer first despite the dating of *MED* citations: "cherlish adj.," although the *MED* cites it first in "(a1382) WBible(1)"; "lovinge ger1.," although the *MED* cites it first in "1372 Undo thi dore"; "restles adj.," although the *MED* cites it first in "(?c1380) Cleanness."

bere n3.	1	lerninge ger.	5
blosmi adj.	3	lifli adv.	2
brat n.	1	lovinge ger1.	16
cherlish adj.	2	ordal n.	1
chimb n.	1	oversloppe n.	1
chirken v.	2	rednesse n.	3
deden v.	1	restles adj.	4
drasti adj.	2	salu adj.	1
elf n.	4	shelfe n.	1
ermen v.	2	soulen v.	1
ferting ger.	1	swiven v.	7
fomi adj.	2	tape n.	1
fore-witen v.	4	tappester n.	2
frendli adj.	18	thurrok n.	2
harpe-stringe n.	1	wasp n.	1
hevenish adj.	5	wifli adj.	7
hoppestre n.	1	willingli adv.	1
last n2.	1	wonger n.	1

Some of them are certainly *re*-derivations from roots that are themselves recorded in intervening centuries ("lerninge ger.," "lovinge ger1."), but most of them look like exactly the kind of words that literature would have to work to capture ("ferting ger.," "swiven v."). Chaucer gives these words *back* to English because they are so old, as the cliché has it, that they are now new again.

These resolutely native colloquialisms are themselves parallel to a second category of words where dictionaries fail, not as they record the history of a word's use, but as they trace its etymology. Words sourced as "imitative" (by definition, then, having a source in the sounds of speech), words "probably" or "perhaps" derived from one language or another, or, most simply of all, words whose derivations cannot be found (where dictionary-makers, research culminates only in the graph of doubt, an etymology that consists of a question mark) are words with no certifiable past – in English or in the writing of any *other* language. Uncertainty about etymology may be the result of a failure of dictionary-makers or the mark of diffidence, when no firm etymological solution can be arrived at. And yet, diffidence is itself most likely to arise where normal patterns of naturalization and word-formation have been foiled by the irrecoverable workings of speech, by the mutation of

forms outside of that record which would make it possible to reconstruct necessary etymological connections. And the *MED* and *OED*
hesitate in writing etymologies for 74 of the words new to Chaucer's
vocabulary (representing 95 uses). In the following list of these words I
give the number of times these words appear in Chaucer's texts again,
but this time I also give their *MED* or *OED* etymologies (in brackets).[50]

a-caterwawed adv.	1	?
agroteien v.	1	?OF; ?MDu.
aline adv.	1	?cp. aright adv.
archangel n3.	1	?
ba v.	2	?
bismotered ppl.	1	?
blasen v2.	1	?cp. blasen v1.
bomblen v.	1	imitative
buf interj.	1	no etym.
canked-ort n.	1	?fr. cankred ppl. & ort n.
chuk n.	1	imitative
chukken v.	1	cp. chuk n.
claspen v.	1	prob OE
cok, cok! interj.	1	imitative
dagoun n.	1	?
druggen v.	1	prob. OE
gaitris n.	1	cp. gate-triu n.
ginglen v.	1	?imitative
gnof n.	1	?cp. EFris.
hait interj.	3	?
hamperen v.	1	?fr. hamper n.
hummen v.	1	prob. imitative
hust adj.	6	prob. imitative
jo v.	2	?OF
jossa n.	1	?fr. OF
jubbe n.	2	origin uncertain
jumperen v.	1	?Imitative
kempe adj.	1	?ON
marcien adj1.	1	?ML
motle n.	1	prob. fr. mot n1.
nodden v.	1	?MLG
panade n.	2	prob. AL or AF

[50] As in the previous note, because of my redating of the *Romaunt*, I take Chaucer's use of
"hamperen v." first, although the *MED* cites it first in "(a1375) WPal." and I take his
use of "poppen v2." first, although the *MED* cites it first in "c1400 St. Anne (1)."

phislias n.	1	? fr. phisike n.
piken v2.	1	?fr. MDu.
poetical adj.	2	? fr. poete n.
Poileis adj.	1	prob. AF
pol-cat n.	1	?AF
popelote n.	1	prob. OF
poppen v2.	1	prob. OF
poupen v.	2	imitative
prollen v.	1	?fr. prologen v. or proloinen v.
quakke n.	1	prob. imitative
qualm n2	1	?Cp. EFris.
radevore n.	1	?OF
raket n.	1	?OF
rebekke n2.	1	?fr. L
refuse adj.	1	?fr. OF
resport n.	2	prob. OF
ruggi adj.	1	prob. ON
scorklen v.	1	?fr. scorcnen v. by dissimilation
Scot n3.	2	?ON
semi adj.	2	prob. fr. semeli
seriousli adv.	1	prob. fr. ML
shrimpe n.	1	prob fr. MLG, MDu.
sippen v.	1	perh. fr. OE?
smateren v.	1	cp. bismotered ppl., smoterli adj., smotri adj., smotten v.
snurten v.	1	?ON
stellifien v.	3	prob. OF
sublimatori n.	1	prob fr. ML
te he interj.	1	prob. imitative
textuel adj.	3	?AL
thwitel n.	1	prob. fr. thwiten
tidif n.	2	origin unknown
toti adj.	1	prob. fr. toteren v.
trappour n.	1	prob. from AL or AF
trauncen v2.	1	perh. ult. from L
trippe n3.	1	cp. MnE dial.
troubli adj.	1	prob. fr. trouble n.
twiteren v.	1	prob. imitative
verie n.	1	[no etym.]
viritrate n.	1	[Of obscure origin]
vitremite n.	1	[?prob. L]
walshnot n.	1	[?MDu.]
wariangle n.	1	[?OE]

Some of these words do not look like colloquialisms either: "aline adv.," and "poetical adj." look very much like derivations from roots that the *MED* simply hesitates to propose. More trouble seems to be made of the origins of "marcien adjı." and "textuel adj." than is necessary. Still, the bulk of these words have what Davis called "a distinctly colloquial air"[51] for the very reason that this lexical category finds them: they cannot be related well enough to other forms in English or related languages for dictionaries to say where Chaucer got them from.

The 110 words in these two categories of evidence do not comprise a large proportion of Chaucer's vocabulary (scarcely more than 1 percent of 9,117 words), but the contents of these categories grow if the parameters I have been using are slightly relaxed, and, as they grow, these categories also begin to include the *history* of these colloquialisms in Middle English. Rolling back the boundary for the Old English words Chaucer uses from the edge of Middle English (c. 1100) to just inside its chronological boundary, taking words of Old English origin in Chaucer, then, that were not recorded again after 1250 before Chaucer used them, provides seventeen more words that seem to have survived in speech before Chaucer wrote them down. I cite these words in the following list (in the form of their *MED* headwords) along with the only recorded uses of these words in the pre-Chaucerian record (in the form of their "title stencils" in the *MED*):

	Pre-Chaucerian uses	Uses in Chaucer
fnesen v.	c1150 *PDidax.*	MancPro
fortreden v.	a1225 *Trin.Hom.*	Bo, ParsT
foryetelnesse n.	(?a1200) *Trin.Hom.*	ParsT
frendli adv.	(1155) *Chart.Hen.II*, (?a1200) *Lay.Brut*	BD, Tr, Mars, KnT, SumT
galen v.	(?a1200) *Lay.Brut*, c1275 *Ancr. (Cleo: Morton)*	WBPro, FrT
grimnesse n.	c1175 *Bod.Hom.*	ParsT
hamelen v.	(?a1200) *Lay.Brut*	Tr
haue nı.	c1250 *Owl & N.*	PardT
hei-sugge n.	c1250 *Owl & N.*	PF

[51] Davis, "Chaucer and Fourteenth-Century English," p. 82.

helmen v.	(?a1200) *Lay.Brut*	Mᴋᴛ, Tʀ
ihevien v.	c1150 *PDidax.*, (c1200) *Vices & V.(1)*,	Bo
	(?a1200) *Ancr.*	
ikissen v.	(?a1200) *Lay.Brut*	Tʀ
kechel n.	?c1200 *Orm* (2 citations)	Sᴜᴍᴛ
lefsel n. (s.v. lef n1.)	c1175 *Bod.Hom.*	RᴠT, Pᴀʀsᴛ
mast n2.	(?a1200) *Lay.Brut*	FᴏʀᴍAɢᴇ
mistiden v.	c1250 *Owl & N.*	Mᴇʟ
mixen n.	(?a1200) *Ancr.*, (?c1200) *St.Juliana*	Pᴀʀsᴛ

As this list expands the category of Chaucer's colloquialisms it also begins to suggest an upper limit (say, the words that appear closest in time to Chaucer, around 1250 in the *Owl and the Nightingale*) at which such vocabulary was forming what might be appropriately, if paradoxically, called a *written* colloquial tradition. Such a tradition could take (and, I think, took) two forms. First, it was what Blake called "literary colloquialism," a category of words so occasionally captured from speech in writing that, even when written, they retained their "colloquial air" (such, for example, might be the case with "haue n1.," which only appears between 1100 and 1400, twice in the *Owl and the Nightingale* and once in the *Pardoner's Tale*). Second, we have, not a tradition of particular words, but a tradition of *practice*, a habit or penchant for capturing words from speech which resulted in the iterative (and not continual) use of colloquialisms, each one newly captured. Of course, colloquialisms might have lost their "colloquial air" as they were repeated from text to text, but that "air" in an earlier text could have encouraged later writers to reproduce it (with different words). The importance of this habit becomes abundantly clear if we reverse the search for words of Old English origin in Chaucer to look, not for words that were absent from the record for a long time before Chaucer used them, but for words that were absent for a long time and then *appeared* in the record just *before* Chaucer used them. Sixteen words of Old English origin stand out in this category (again, I give the full *MED* history of these words according to "title stencils"):

	Pre-Chaucerian uses	Uses in Chaucer
clom n1.	c1350 *Ayenb.App.*	MilT
fane n1.	(?a1350) *Siege Troy(1)*	CiT
fanne n.	a1325 *Gloss. Bibbesw,* (a1382) *WBible* (1)	MilT, MancPro
halten v.	c1325 *Heye louerd,* (a1325) *Cursor*	BD, Tr
knoppe n1.	(c1353) *Winner & W.*	RomA
late-rede adj.	(c1280) *SLeg.Pass.(Pep)*	ParsT
leden adj.	(c1384) *WBible (1)*	CYT
loppe n1.	c1350 *MPPsalter*	AsT (twice)
mirili adv.	(?a1350) *7 Sages (2)*	RomA, Bo, GP, etc.
mirinesse n.	(a1325) *Cursor,* (?1348) Rolle *FLiving*	Bo
not adj.	a1325 *SLeg (Corp-C)*	GP
pose n.	c1300 *SLeg.Dunstan (Hrl)*	RvT, MancPro
ron n3.	a1300 *Hwi ne serve*	RomA
routen v3.	(a1325) *Ipotis*	HF, TR
saloue n.	(1373) *Lelamour Macer.,* (a1382) *WBible (1)*	WBPro
shipe n.	(1340) *Ayenb*	Anel, ParsT

These words probably retained their "colloquial air" even in Chaucer because they are so infrequently adduced before he used them, but they are mostly interesting as the extreme examples of the much larger category of 230 words in Chaucer's vocabulary that are of Old English origin but do not appear in the Middle English record until some time in the fourteenth century – even though, once they appear, they are used frequently. This tradition of colloquial use (and iterative novelty) also leads us to a similar tradition in the first category of words that I called colloquial (words that failed of etymological identification). When defining that category I listed only the words of this type that appear first in Chaucer, but it becomes especially meaningful now that dictionaries show equal uncertainty about the etymologies of another eighty-three words in Chaucer's vocabulary which appear first in the writing of his fourteenth-century predecessors. Since the contour of this second category of words might associate them continuously with the spoken (that is, since their imitative origins or uncertain relation to other English forms might amount to a constitutive property these words do not shed) it is probably also worth pointing out that Chaucer's vocabulary includes another 234 words with uncertain etymologies that appear in Middle English in the twelfth and thirteenth centuries. All these older colloquialisms have a double function. To a greater or lesser extent they come to Chaucer as a written tradition, but in their iterative use in precedent texts they also define the traditional procedure that licenses Chaucer's own colloquial words. They show Chaucer again making common cause with earlier practice as he joins his new colloquialisms to these older forms.

The variety of rubrics I have used to define Chaucer's low style makes it a more fluid category than the high style defined by polysyllabic words. Indeed, it would finally be difficult to say just how many colloquialisms Chaucer actually employed. If we were to count all the words I have so far mentioned, we would, however, have 657 words (or 5 percent of Chaucer's total vocabulary) – a significant enough number. And however strictly we might want to draw the line, whatever words remained would stand as a significant and contrastive foil to the polysyllabic borrowings whose novelty is thought to be so significant in "enriching" and "augmenting" the "main hull" of English. A language which had been made to stand *as* speech over against written languages of privilege (or at least was often thought to so stand) gained status by borrowing, but it also gained status *as* English by holding on to signs of that speech. Colloquialism was the proof of identity that all Middle English writers addressed to French and Latin as they also proved their right to its linguistic privilege. In this sense of course, it was precisely the *fully* traditional nature of Chaucer's English that equipped him with the means to take credit for this precedent practice, to assimilate this general accomplishment of all Middle English writing to his own efforts and to present it as his own invention. The lexical novelty of Chaucer's bifurcated English, by turns traditionally aureate and traditionally colloquial, compassed the entire proof that Middle English writers *could* offer of their capacity. Chaucer's only real contribution to this long-fought struggle was the extent to which he *marked* the difference between these two modes. In fact, Chaucer seems to have realized, as his predecessors did not, that, just as these modes had distinctly different roots in English lexical history, they also had distinctly different stylistic *effects*, and, furthermore, that these different effects were precisely the result of these different roots. In short, Chaucer saw that polysyllabic borrowings and colloquialisms held their history within themselves and that, by emphasizing the stylistic difference that ramified from this history, he could seem to make – he could, as I put it earlier in this chapter, stage – a *choice* about his own patrimony in his use and sequential presentation of these lexical styles. That choice could be used *within* his language to insist upon the same contrastive point that Chaucer made about his language in the rarer moments of linguistic self-reflection I analyzed above. At this level of contrast – at the level, that is, of the word – this point could be made in virtually every line of every poem Chaucer wrote. It could become the claim that *was* the whole of his English.

3

Chaucer, Lee Patterson has observed, while "no revolutionary" himself, remained "committed not just to innovation but to the understanding of innovation."[52] This is as apt a description of Chaucer's linguistic practices as it is of his politics, since Chaucer, while traditional in his language, was equally committed to understanding (and using) the invention inherent in tradition. The two different lexical styles Chaucer employed were his means to that end: they allowed him to explore the forms of innovation that had occurred in earlier English by continually embracing its variety. But this very variety also allowed him to skew that exploration so that his English might seem to *favor* novelty as it considered it, to reject what it figured as old in the very process of this procedural examination. It is in this way that an English that was not really "revolutionary" at all comes to *seem* revolutionary in its course. This curious process can be isolated in the language of a single but deeply searching passage from the *House of Fame* in which both the salient traditions and their constituent vocabulary are considered:

> Now herkeneth every maner man
> That Englissh understonde kan
> And listeth of my drem to lere,
> For now at erste shul ye here
> So sely an avisyon,
> That Isaye, ne Scipion,
> Ne kyng Nabugodonosor,
> Pharoo, Turnus, ne Elcanor,
> Ne mette such a drem as this.

[52] Patterson, *Chaucer and the Subject of History*, p. 25.

Now faire blisfull, O Cipris,
So be my favour at this tyme!
And ye, me to endite and ryme
Helpeth, that on Parnaso duelle,
Be Elicon, the clere welle.
O Thought, that wrot al that I mette,
And in the tresorye hyt shette
Of my brayn, now shal men se
Yf any vertu in the be
To tellen al my drem aryght.
Now kythe thyn engyn and myght! (509–28)

The first four lines of this passage evoke the typical opening of an "English" romance,[53] but subsequent lines turn immediately to the "European," in what Spearing has identified as the first invocation to the classical Muses in English poetry.[54] The words of the passage substantiate the filiations Chaucer here suggests: diction remains native for the evocation of English traditions (every word in these four lines has Old English roots), but it then turns decisively to polysyllabic borrowing in the rhyme of the fifth line ("avisioun n.") which opens a rhyming door for a large-scale embrace of Latinity in the long series of allusive proper nouns that follows (beginning with reference to the *Somnium Scipionis* as "Scipion"). The lexical turn is followed by more direct references to Biblical learning ("Isaye," "Nabugodonosor," "Pharoo") and the *Aeneid* ("Turnus"), which prepare the focusing invocation ("O Cipris"), at which point even simple nouns tend to become Romance borrowings ("favour n.," "enditen v.," "rime n3.," "tresourie n.," "vertu n.," "engin n."). In fact, the one word in this passage that is new to the record is "Parnaso n.," the very word that

---

53 See for example the opening of *Havelok the Dane*,
    Herknet to me, gode men,
    Wiues, maydnes, and alle men
    Of a tale þat ich you wile telle.
  or, even more notably the opening of the Auchinleck romance *Beves of Hamtoun*:
    Lordings, herkneþ to me tale
    Is merier þan þe niȝtengale
    þat y schel singe.
  For these quotations see Skeat (ed.), *Lay of Havelok the Dane*, lines 1–3, and Kölbing (ed.), *Sir Beues of Hamtoun*, lines 1–3.
54 Spearing, *Medieval to Renaissance*, p. 25.

marks the goal of Chaucer's strivings. As Chaucer mentions Parnassus, in other words, the base of his native diction allows him to scale its heights by giving him space to reconstitute his English in Franco-Latin forms. But there is also a slippage in the way what is "new" in Chaucer's words may map onto the shape of his allusions. First, the high style exists in later lines *because* it makes the absence of borrowed forms from earlier lines noticeable – not only is a high style fashioned here, in other words, but a low style emerges *as its retrospective result* in order to act as a contrastive foil for scaled heights. Second, not only are Romance borrowings in this passage *generally* traditional, but so too (as we have seen) is even a "new" borrowing such as "Parnaso." In fact, the salient lexical issue in this passage is that Chaucer's English demonstrates its capacity to "climb" to the "high" by sitting squarely in *both* of the traditions Chaucer fell heir to: it is not the lexical content of this passage that is so significant, but the sequence in which that content is taken up. As Chaucer's lexis moves between the stable points of the squarely traditional and traditional novelty, in other words, the traditional nature of both coordinates fades into the background of the agile *movement* to which the comportment of this passage (at every level) draws attention. It is this movement, the overturning of one tradition in favor of another, that is "revolutionary" here in every sense of that word. It is the direction of movement that presents one linguistic mode as old and another as new, and seems to proffer the novelty of the latter as Chaucer's particular accomplishment. But that accomplishment hardly lies in the "new" of the "European" but resides, rather, in the particular shape of the aggregation of this "English": as old procedures and words are everywhere employed, but so disposed as to create (to *invent*) the impression of a progress that is not really occurring.

Such a lexical performance of invention also subtends the important linguistic self-definition attempted in the *Clerk's Prologue* that I discussed above, and it is worth revisiting that passage now to note how it too relies on lexis to press its general point:

> "I wol yow telle a tale which that I
> Lerned at Padowe of a worthy clerk,
> As preved by his wordes and his werk.
> He is now deed and nayled in his cheste;
> I prey to God so yeve his soule reste!

Invented English

"Fraunceys Petrak, the lauriat poete,
Highte this clerk, whos rethorike sweete
Enlumyned al Ytaille of poetrie . . ." (IV, 26–33)

The marked lexical shift at the paragraph mark in this passage is more complex than the similar shift in the *House of Fame*. In the lines preceding the break the Clerk has already reached the kind of "European" proper noun ("Padowe") that signals a turn in the lines of the *House of Fame*. "Preven v.," also before this break, is a borrowing, although of long standing in the language, and "cheste n.," too, although an Old English word, comes to Old English from Latin. At the same time, the mention of "Fraunceys Petrak" – the naming of the source of the borrowing of the "tale" – also triggers a real concentration of borrowings in the last three lines ("laureate adj.," "poete n.," "rethorike n.," "enluminen v.," "Itaille n.," "poetrie n."), and three of them ("laureate," "enluminen," and "poetrie") are, in fact, new to English in Chaucer's use. Again, the novelty of these borrowings helps to press the point of "lauriat" claims by proving them: while the lexis of these lines remains largely native as the plan for an English translation is put forward, that lexis is immediately (and newly) Latinate as Chaucer offers his English as comparable to Latinity. Again, this sequence produces the high style by means of a turn from the native, just as it makes a low style emerge, by contrast, as new borrowings are embraced – rejecting the former as it proffers the latter. Again, the linguistic capacity demonstrated here takes credit for traditional forms and procedures as it makes those traditions particular to the project of making "Petrak's" tale into the *Tale* of the Clerk. Again, put on view here in both styles are only the general and traditional capacities of Middle English.

The constant potential for movement between the native and the borrowed, the "English" and the "European," in Chaucer's English made this kind of compelling argument possible not only in these bravura forms, at moments of implicit speculation about linguistic filiation and importance, but at *any* moment. For, as I have suggested, Chaucer's English was everywhere capable of those strategic uses of native and borrowed lexis that will implicitly argue for Chaucer's linguistic inventiveness. Another of Chaucer's famous invocations (this time to Venus) at the beginning of Book 3 of *Troilus and Criseyde* will help to illustrate this omnipresence:

> O blisful light of which the bemes clere
> Adorneth al the thridde heven faire!
> O sonnes lief, O Joves doughter deere,
> Plesance of love, O goodly debonaire,
> In gentil hertes ay redy to repaire?
> O veray cause of heele and of gladnesse,
> Iheryed be thy myght and thi goodnesse! (3.1–7)

The invocation is launched with a Romance borrowing ("adournen v.") that the record shows Chaucer using here for the first time in English, and that new word is nested in other borrowings ("cler adj.," "plesaunce n1.," "debonaire adj. & n.," "gentil adj." "repairen v." "errei adj.," "cause n."), fortified by native calques of polysyllabic borrowings ("blisful adj.," "gladnesse n.," "godnesse n2."). These borrowed words and native calques (which provide five of the seven rhyme words here) put this inaugural stanza squarely in the lexical texture of Chaucer's high style, and that texture is maintained by similar borrowings and calques in the remaining forty-two lines of this proem. By way of a general survey I list below all of the borrowings and calques in these lines in the order of their appearance (new borrowings are in italics, rhyme-words are in bold, and stanza divisions are marked with a space):

descerne	[discernen v.]
best	[beste n.]
herbe	[herbe n.]
vapour	[vapour n.]
eterne	[eterne adj.]
creature	[creature n.]
endure	[enduren v.]
Joves	[Jove n.]
effectes	[effect n.]
comeveden	[commeven v.]
amorous	[amorous adj.]
mortal	[mortal adj.]
ese	[ese n.]
adversitee	[adversite n.]
formes	[forme n.]

fierse	[fers adj.]
apaisen	[appesen v.]
ire	[ire n.]
digne	[digne adj.]
vices	[vice n.]
resygne	[resignen v.]
corteys	[courteis adj. & n.]
benigne	[benigne adj.]
entendeth	[entenden v.]
joies	[joie n.]
regne	[regne nɪ.]
unitee	[unite n.]
frendship	[frendshipe n.]
covered	[coveren vɪ.]
qualitee	[qualite n.]
construe	[construen v.]
universe	[universe n.]
stryveth	[striven v.]
benignite	[benignite n.]
reverence	[reverence n.]
serven	[serven vɪ.]
devyse	[devisen v.]
joye	[joie n.]
servyse	[servise n.]
sentement	[sentement n.]
swetnesse	[swetenesse n.]
vois	[voice n.]
present	[presente adj.]
destresse	[distresse n.]
gladnesse	[gladnesse n.]

As interesting as the studiously borrowed lexical texture of this proem, however, is the texture of the lines that actually begin Book 3 of *Troilus* when the narrative recommences and Pandarus and Criseyde come to find Troilus in bed:

> Lay al this mene while Troilus,
> Recordynge his lesson in this manere:
> "Mafay," thoughte he, "thus wol I sey, and thus;

Thus wol I pleyne unto my lady deere;
That word is good, and this shal be my cheere;
This nyl I nought foryeten in no wise."
God leve hym werken as he kan devyse!

And, Lord, so that his herte gan to quappe,
Herying hire come, and shorte for to sike!
And Pandarus, that ledde hire by the lappe,
Com ner, and gan in at the curtyn pike,
And seyde, "God do boot on alle syke!
Se who is here you comen to visite:
Lo, here is she that is youre deth to wite."

Therewith it semed as he wepte almost.
"Ha, a," quod Troilus so reufully,
"Wher me be wo, O myghty God, thow woost!
Who is al ther? I se nought trewely."
"Sire," quod Criseyde, "it is Pandare and I."
"Ye, swete herte? Allas, I may nought rise,
To knele and do yow honour in som wyse." (3.50–70)

The same contrast in styles I have been describing occurs here, but in reverse: in the first stanza I quote the high style is slowly released for the low as invocation and apostrophe give way to direct address ("Ye, swete herte?"), non-referential asseveration ("Ha, a"), oath ("Mafay," "God do boot," "O myghty God"), and the sequential assignment of speakers that presents most of these lines as direct speech ("seyde . . . quod . . . quod"). The text shifts (or sinks) to the colloquial in lines that suddenly and markedly function *as* speech. That shift in stylistic ambition is again matched in lexis. Although the four borrowings in the first two lines of the first stanza ("mene adj.2," "recorden v.," "lessoun n.," "manere n.") essentially leave those lines in the texture of the high style, such borrowings quickly thin out: there are only three in the remaining five lines of the first stanza here ("pleinen v.," "chere n1.," "devisen v."), and the next two stanzas contain only two borrowings each ("curtine n." and "visiten v." and then "sire n." and "honour n."). Parallel to this successive diminishment in the borrowed is the inclusion of the verb "piken v2." in line 60, one of the new colloquialisms that I mentioned in the previous section (because its etymology is uncertain) occurring here for the first time in English. The probable roots in speech of this newly written word stand in exact opposition to the new borrowing, "adournen," that launches the proem and sets its texture. It is a contrast that points the linguistic difference between the affiliations of the proem (firmly seated in the tradition of polysyllabicism and borrowing) and these opening lines of the book (slowly but surely seating itself in the tradition of the native as the colloquial exemplifies it). The two textures again create each other reciprocally: the plethora of borrowings, many of them rhymed and new, pushes out the native in the proem, while the predominance of the native precludes substantial borrowing in the book proper. It matters, of course, that the direction of movement here, from high to low, is exactly the opposite of the movement we have seen before, but this is precisely how Chaucer also claims the virtues of the low (the novelty of the *colloquial*) as a particular virtue of his style as well. Above all, of course, it is the movement between two textures – the distance Chaucer's English traverses between traditions – that proffers these textures as an *activity*, an activity occurring *here*, a movement and accomplishment of these lines and, therefore, a general accomplishment of Chaucer's English. But, as he is also capable of doing all through his English, Chaucer shows himself abandoning what, in this context, comes to seem the *over*-sophistication of polysyllabicism for the sure plainness of the native and quotidien. Here Chaucer claims the status of the borrowed along with the status of the native, making the latter in this case, the accomplishment for which the former is rejected.

On the whole, Chaucer's English exploits the potential of such movement for annexing the virtues of the two traditions it embraces, not through a noticeable exchange of lapidary styles but in the simultaneous embrace of the two forms of tradition – in *constant double employment*. As I have argued here, the whole of Chaucer's English is best described as a thorough intermixture of these inherited modes, and, in this sense, Chaucer's entire lexis enters his most persuasive claim for its invention. That is, while Chaucer has the Reeve describe the *Miller's Tale* as "cherles termes" (I, 3917) to set it against the "noble" *Knight's Tale* which was "worthy," in particular, for the "gentils" to "drawen to memorie" (I, 3111–13), the *Miller's Tale* in no way *consists* of "cherles termes." While the *Knight's Tale* contains forty-nine new borrowings, the *Miller's Tale* also contains twelve new borrowings and this is not significantly less when these figures are adjusted for the exceeding length of the *Knight's Tale*.[55] The contrastive argument I have been tracing in particular textual *loci* allows Chaucer to champion his own linguistic efforts generally because the common form of that effort is an alternation of native and borrowed lexis so frequent (and so graceful) that the alternation is *itself* the linguistic texture. The full illustration of that claim would involve a lexical history of every one of Chaucer's words (which I provide in Part 2 of this book) but the basic principle can be illustrated anecdotally by turning to the third passage of linguistic self-definition I mentioned above, that stanza at the conclusion of *Troilus and Criseyde* (I quote it here with some preceding lines to better illustrate the alternations of which it is part):

> And this commeveth me
> To speke, and in effect yow alle I preye,
> Beth war of men, and herkneth what I seye!
>
> Go, litel bok, go, litel myn tragedye,
> Ther God thi makere yet, er that he dye,
> So sende myght to make in some comedye!
> But litel book, no makyng thow n'envie,
> But subgit be to alle poesye;
> And kis the steppes where as thow seest pace
> Virgile, Ovide, Omer, Lucan, and Stace. (5.1783–92)

An alternation between the borrowed and the native prepares the stanza: "commeven v." is a new borrowing in Chaucer, but the next two lines are resolutely native, including – not incidentally, as preparation for the succeeding stanza – an allusion to the style of English romance ("herkneth what I seye!") of the kind that Chaucer also uses in the *House of Fame*. Both words in the first rhyming pair of the next stanza are new borrowings ("tragedie n." and "comedie n1.") but they bracket a line ("Ther God thi makere yet, er that he dye") that is itself wholly

---

[55] See the table in chapter 3 above (p. 107). One new borrowing for every 350 words or 47 headwords in the *Knight's Tale* does not greatly exceed the density of 1 new borrowing for every 428 words or 94 headwords in the *Miller's Tale*.

native in its lexical constituents.[56] The next line rhymes the native ("dien v.") with the borrowed ("envie n."). The subsequent line ("But subgit be to alle poesye") contains a borrowing only recently attested in Middle English ("poesie n.") and a word that (depending upon the available roots one opts for) can be regarded as a borrowing or a derivation closely related to a Romance root ("subget adj.").[57] This line is followed by a line that is wholly native until its rhyme ("passen v.,"), where the shift to Romance links this line to the next, which drops Latin and Greek names for its entire length.[58] The texture here, in other words, is neither borrowed nor native, old nor new, high nor low – but *all* these things at once. It is a "form of literary colloquialism," the "spoken language of the court," but it is also, in its supple duality, in the contrasts that it incorporates so fully into its movement, an implicit claim about the literary language it also, more explicitly, champions. It gathers up both of the written traditions to which Chaucer was heir and presents them with such plenitude and balance that their separate achievement is gathered to these lines – as to all of Chaucer's lines – as a separate and aggregate accomplishment *of* those lines. It does *in parvo* all that I have said Chaucer's English does on the whole: it presents that English as invented, not because that English departs from Middle English precedent, but because it fully partakes of *all* precedent.

Of course this view of Chaucer's English ignores the one thing that so many have thought matters centrally to (or even counts as) its attainment of the "brightest heaven of invention" (as Shakespeare conceived the process in the lines I take as my epigraph to this chapter): the "swetnesse" of its "song" (as Chaucer puts it) or its "excellence" (in Lydgate's formulation). And it is fair to acknowledge that none of what

---

56 For the earlier history of the words in line 5.1887 see *MED*, s. vv. "ther adv.," "God, god nı.," "thin pron.," "makere n.," "er adv.," "that conj.," "he pronı.," "dien v.," and *OED*, s. v. "yet adv." All of these are Old English words except "makere" (a derivation from "maken vı." first adduced in "[1340] Ayenb.") and "dien v." (an Old Norse borrowing first adduced in "c1175 HRood").

57 See *MED*, s. v. "subget adj.," 2a, for its earliest recorded use in "(a1338) Mannyng Chron.Pt.1" and an etymology "fr. subget n. & L & OF, AF." See *MED*, s. v. "subget n.," 1a, for its earliest recorded use in "c1330 7 Sages(1)" and an etymology in "L & OF, AF."

58 For the native status of all but the last word in line 5.1791 see *MED*, s. vv. "and conj. (& adv.)," "kissen v.," "the def. art.," "step n.," "as conj.," "thou pron.," "sen vı.," and *OED*, s. v. "where adv. & conj."

I have said here speaks to the reader of Chaucer who feels that Chaucer invented English because he wrote so *well*, so much more ably than his predecessors. Such a reader must respond to what I have claimed by pointing out that even if Chaucer *was* only traditional in his techniques, he certainly deployed those traditions *better* than any English writer who preceded him. I have not addressed this point because I do not think it is finally germane either to the historical task I have set myself or to the linguistic phenomena Chaucer himself placed at issue by the set of implicated claims I have extracted from his writing. If there is qualitative difference – and I would not mean in any way to deny it – its evaluation cannot do duty for historical account. Set Chaucer's English next to the English of any of his predecessors and you may well find it easy to say why Chaucer's English is better. But you could not, on the other hand, find a difference in degree or kind of linguistic invention between that text and any of Chaucer's writing that linguistic history could confirm. In that sense, the issue this chapter points – the question it leaves unanswered – is: how *does* evaluation become history? Or, as the question might be directed at Chaucer scholarship as a whole: how have Chaucer's attempts at linguistic self-definition become scholarly *données*? These are questions that I will try to answer in the next chapter, as I turn from the traditions that preceded Chaucer's English to the English tradition that followed it, to the set of the claims in which Chaucer's invention finally (and emphatically) sheds its cloak of implication and dons the mantle of historical "fact."

5

The myth of origin and the making of Chaucer's English

The language of England, upon which [Chaucer] was the first to confer celebrity, has amply justified the foresight which led him to disdain all others for its sake, and, in turn, has conferred an enduring celebrity upon him who trusted his reputation to it without reserve.

T. R. Lounsbury[1]

If his English is really traditional then a lot of Chaucer's readers have been gulled. If Chaucer carefully left a door ajar, poets, literary historians, and critics alike have rushed through it, eager and determined to see and describe the novelty inside. This is to say that the vagueness of the definitional types I described in chapter 1 is no more striking than their constancy over wide spaces of literary-historical time. Lydgate's bold assertion in the *Troy Book* (1412–20) that Chaucer "Gan oure tonge firste to magnifie,/And adourne it with his elloquence" may be interesting in itself *and* as it helps us discern similar definitional logic in Derek Brewer's claim that Chaucer "began a revolution in poetic diction" and John Fisher's conviction that Chaucer "naturalized in English a new poetic mode and language." But the association is also interesting as it shows that an identical view of Chaucer's English has endured for almost six hundred years.[2] As I noted in chapter 2, discussion of traditional features of Chaucer's

---

[1] Lounsbury, *Studies in Chaucer*, vol. II, p. 458.
[2] Lydgate, *Troy Book*, Bergen (ed.), lines 3.4242–3; Brewer, "English and European Traditions," p. 1; Fisher, "Chaucer and the French Influence," p. 178. Other claims along the same lines in modern Chaucer criticism which I have also noticed in earlier parts of this book include "Chaucer *made* English capable of poetry," Robinson, *Chaucer and the English Tradition*, p. 290. Robinson's emphasis; Chaucer's poems were the "vehicle . . . for the development of a new manner of writing in English," Kean,

English has, at times, intervened, although, as I also noted, that discussion gives such quarter to the generalities of Chaucer's "style" that it has often been unsuccessful in finding evidence for its own belief. In fact, the omnipotence of the view that Chaucer's English started something is best illustrated in the way that scholars have been able to maintain it *even as* they root that English in some tradition. Brewer, for example, describes the "revolution" in poetic diction that was Chaucer's writing in the same paragraph in which he describes a Chaucer who "inherited a particular English style."[3] T. R. Lounsbury suggests that Chaucer "can most justly be called the refiner and purifier of our speech," [4] but, only a few pages later, he says that "Chaucer wrote in the speech of his time and wrote in that only."[5] In registering the tenacity of the view that Chaucer's English was somehow "new" these doubled views also register the general condition responsible for such inveteracy: for reasons that I want to explore in some detail here, comment on Chaucer has somehow *needed* originality to attend that English. In a stunning confirmation of Derrida's suggestion that "the idea of writing . . . is meaningful for us only in terms of an origin (*origine*)" readers of Chaucer have held that his English is only meaningful as it is an origin of English literary language.[6]

The explanation for this need lies outside Chaucer's English itself, in the mechanisms by which a tradition forms or – to put the case as I want to advance it here – as a tradition is formed by retrospection. That is, for literary history, a tradition's "originals" are not strictly what was previously absent from literary practice, but what was previously absent *and* had subsequent effect. The past that literary history writes for a tradition (which tends to follow the past a tradition writes for itself) does not call novelty without influence "invention"; it calls it eccentricity. Two examples from Middle English pertinent in this respect would be the *Owl and the Nightingale* and Laȝamon's *Brut*. The linguistic practice of these texts is extraordinary and worthy of careful scrutiny,

---

Chaucer and the Making of English Poetry, vol. I, p. 32; "Style in English poetry begins, in a sense, with Chaucer," Eliason, *Language of Chaucer's Poetry,* 10.
[3] Brewer, "English and European Traditions," p. 1.
[4] Lounsbury, *Studies in Chaucer,* vol. II, p. 437
[5] *Ibid.,* vol. II, p. 452.
[6] "L'idée d'écriture . . . n'[a] de sens pour nous que depuis une origine," Derrida, *De la grammatologie,* p. 14; *Of Grammatology,* Spivak (trans.), p. 4.

and its isolation from other Middle English writing alone makes the language of each text "new" – and yet this language is rarely singled out for its novelty.[7] On the contrary, a standard literary history of the period notes how the *Owl and the Nightingale* "is often treated by English scholars as if it were some kind of freak" and itself calls Laȝamon's *Brut* a "massive erratic in the history of English poetry": indeed, it is simply true that neither of these texts has any detectable effect on the texts that come after them.[8] These poems are not "original" because they are as much *in nihilum* as they are *ex nihilo*; that they have no parents is to their credit but that they have no progeny is their misfortune. The same point can be made in two different ways by the "two sophisticated English literary languages" that sit in parallel with Chaucer's English in literary history, one, the finely-honed alliterative meter exemplified in *Sir Gawain and the Green Knight*, the other, the fluid and elegant prose style of the religious writing exemplified by Walter Hilton.[9] Alliterative meter is called a "tradition" in its fourteenth-century form, but its death in the fifteenth century means that literary history does not view its earliest examples for what they beget, but, as the standard term for the tradition goes, for what they "revive": that we class later exemplars of a tradition in documented existence for almost a century as part of a "revival" – as, say, in the case of the alliterative *Morte D'Arthur* – are the wages literary memory exacts from a tradition for its death.[10] As R. W. Chambers traces its course from Ælfric to More, sophisticated religious prose has no such problems with longevity.[11] But if this "continuity" is a "tradition," it is

---

7 Pearsall does note that Laȝamon's *Brut* had an effect on the later recension of Robert of Gloucester's *Chronicle* and he suggests (for this reason and others) that such preservation may well have formed the kernel of continuity around which the alliterative revival formed (see "The Origins of the Alliterative Revival," esp. pp. 7–10). The need for careful reclamation of such a lineage, however, shows just how fragile and unselfconscious the "tradition" it represents is or would be.

8 Pearsall, *Old English and Middle English Poetry*, pp. 94 and 112.

9 For this characterizing phrase and a consideration of these languages as Chaucer's literary options in English, see Pearsall, *Life of Geoffrey Chaucer*, p. 74.

10 "Despite the widespread popularity of alliterative poetry, it seems likely that little of any importance was written after the first decade or so of the fifteenth century." Turville-Petre, *Alliterative Revival*, p. 122.

11 For the subsequent influence of the prose tradition represented by Hilton (and its limitation to religious contexts) see Chambers *On the Continuity of English Prose*, pp. cx–clxxiv and Zeeman, "Continuity in Middle English Devotional Prose," passim.

also one with no inscribed view of its own beginnings, no acknowledged "father," unaware of its *own* existence because it lacks an inscribed theory of origination. Despite its scope, then, religious prose was not a "tradition" until bridges were built across the presumptive disruptions of the history it traversed by Chambers's landmark work. What makes texts of the alliterative revival and of religious prose function in the same isolation in Middle English literary history as the *Owl and the Nightingale* and La3amon's *Brut*, in other words, is not any absence of originality – a fecundity with potential – but the absence of champions, writers who will describe novelty as original and give a tradition both life and trajectory in their very proclamations. In this sense, it is certainly true, there *are* no "originals" in English before Chaucer.

If retrospection creates "originality," however, the process is exceedingly difficult to see because, by its very nature, it constructs a hermeneutic circle. Another description of Chaucer's language by T. R. Lounsbury, which I take as the epigraph to this chapter, describes this circle with helpful concision. In his intricate sentence Lounsbury proffers Chaucer as the cause of English excellence ("the first to confer celebrity . . .") and the passive recipient of the favors of English ("has conferred . . . celebrity upon him"). The involution of Lounsbury's syntax, in which perspective shifts three times (from "the language of England" to "Chaucer," from "Chaucer" to the "language of England," and, finally, from the "language of England" back to "Chaucer") and time rounds a full circle (the "foresight" of the past which led Chaucer to write in English is recognized in a future which looks backward, "in turn"), neatly traps the troublesome reflexivity of the linguistic and historical mechanisms in operation here. As in Lounsbury's remark, so too in the history of the language, it remains very difficult to say who ("Chaucer" or the "language of England") has done what ("conferred celebrity" or had it passively "conferred") to whom. In fact, as I want to show in this chapter, the significance of Chaucer's linguistic making cannot be addressed or solved by an "accurate" history of the language because it cannot be separated from the project of writing that history. The problem is epistemological not historical, a question finally of origination and how the history of a "beginning" may be written without determining it. To revisit the long history of comment on Chaucer for its effects as I will do in the first part of this chapter, or to review the lexical evidence that I have compiled from the *OED* and *MED* for its bias toward Chaucer as I will do in the second part of this chapter, is to discern not only what I will characterize as a "myth of origin" but also the *procedure* by which Chaucer's originality was post-positively constructed by abject praise and empirical scrutiny alike. Putting the material that has so far formed the background of this study at the center of its inquiry will show that even the most self-consciously objective forms of that material are implicated in the making of Chaucer's English. No account of such scope can be complete – the contingencies determining each proclamation of Chaucer's originality are as complex as the long tradition these proclamations form – but even a summary account can show how taking a position on Chaucer's achievement is an activity with determinate results.[12] In fact, my largest point here is that the myth of origin makes the truth it claims to find. The persistence of this myth in every genre of retrospection creates a linguistic history in which, to paraphrase a different Derridean catch phrase, there is no "outside-myth."[13] By the circular logic of this phenomenon an account of centuries of opinion on Chaucer's linguistic making is finally the most accurate account of that making that could be offered. It is, of course, a different account from the one I have so far given (particularly in chapter 2), not because it contradicts the claim that Chaucer's English is traditional, but because it explains how such traditional English came to *be* as new as Chaucer's most fervent champions say it is.

I

Like most good stories the myth of origin first takes compelling shape *in mediis rebus*, in this case, in the sixteenth century. It is in this period that Chaucer's English is really dead, or at least really dying, and memory of Chaucer grows increasingly haunted by an implacable

---

[12] For a more nuanced and detailed account of the contingencies of critical reaction to Chaucer's work in the fifteenth and early sixteenth centuries than I give here see Lerer, *Chaucer and His Readers*.

[13] The famous phrase is, of course, "il n'y a pas de hors-texte" (Derrida, *De la grammatologie*, p. 227). The pun that gives the remark its resonance foils straightforward translation and Spivak offers two possibilities: either "there is nothing outside the text" or "there is no outside-text." (*Of Grammatology*, p. 158.)

linguistic change.[14] In 1546 Peter Ashton is compelled to note that "by re[a]son of antiquitie" Chaucer's language is "almost out of use,"[15] and Sidney is acknowledging his "great wants, fit to be forgiven in so reverent antiquity."[16] By 1598 Chaucer's vocabulary has become so "old and obscure" that the edition of his work by Speght requires a glossary in which that vocabulary is "expla[i]ned" and its "difficulties opened."[17] *Troilus and Criseyde* receives the first of its many modernizations in 1630 by Jonathan Sidnam,[18] and so difficult has Chaucer's "unknowne tongue" become by 1635 that it was "Englisht" by translation into *Latin* as Sir Francis Kynaston's *Amorum Troili et Creseidae libri duo priores Anglico-Latini* (1635).[19] In these years it is still possible to hold the notion that "old Dan Geffrey," as Spenser labels him, is also "Dan Chaucer, well of English undefyled" as Spenser also calls him.[20] Speght's edition embodies this tension, "opening" the "difficulties" of Chaucer's English but prefacing that English with Francis Beaumont's recurrence to the view that Chaucer's English embodies "the pith and sinewes of eloquence."[21] The suspension is, however, an unstable one, and as the need to remember Chaucer *even if* "old" implicitly

---

[14] Lerer notes the seeds of this change earlier in Caxton's elegiac concern for a Chaucer who is emphatically dead, witnessed by his printing of Chaucer's tomb inscription in the epilogue following his printing of the *Boece* (see *Chaucer and His Readers*, pp. 147–75). My purely linguistic concerns are necessarily broader than Lerer's: where he marks what he calls a shift from "evocation to invocation," a change in the mode of "Chaucerian citation" (p. 151), I am marking, across a longer period, the moment when language change finally makes Chaucerian citation impossible.

[15] Spurgeon (ed.), *Chaucer Criticism and Allusion*, vol. I, p. 87.

[16] Sidney, *An Apology for Poetry*, Shepherd (ed.), p. 133.

[17] Spurgeon (ed.), *Chaucer Criticism and Allusion*, vol. I, p. 147.

[18] For introductory material to this translation see Spurgeon (ed.), *Chaucer Criticism and Allusion*, vol. I, p. 203 and Brewer (ed.), *Critical Heritage*, vol. I, p. 150.

[19] A great deal of the prefatory material to this translation is printed in Spurgeon (ed.), *Chaucer Criticism and Allusion*, vol. I, pp. 207–15. One prefatory poem by Edward Foulis is printed in Brewer (ed.), *Critical Heritage*, vol. I, pp. 152–3. The reference to Chaucer's "unknowne tongue" appears in prefatory verses written by William Barker in Spurgeon (ed.), *Chaucer Criticism and Allusion*, vol. I, p. 207. The reference to a translation "Englisht" in Latin occurs in the prefatory poem by Thomas Read in Spurgeon (ed.), *Chaucer Criticism and Allusion*, vol. I, pp. 214–15.

[20] The first phrase occurs in the *Two Cantos of Mutabilitie*, 7.7.9 which appeared posthumously, in 1609. The second phrase occurs in *The Faerie Queene*, 4.2.32 which appeared in 1596. I cite these phrases from Spenser, *Faerie Queene*, Hamilton (ed.). See p. 4 in this edition for these dates.

[21] Spurgeon (ed.), *Chaucer Criticism and Allusion*, vol. I, p. 146.

acknowledges, senescence has produced a crisis for literary memory. Why is Chaucer's English remembered *as* "undefiled" if the need for translation requires that memorial to be, in a sense, a defilement?

The faltering of Chaucer's English spelled trouble because of course, as I noticed at the beginning of chapter 1, from almost the moment of Chaucer's death, his English had been used by writers to define their poetic purpose, to claim privileged status for their own efforts by imitating Chaucer generally as well as in the very forms in which they praised him. Chaucer had made himself conduit to a hieratic literature by joining his own writing to a privileged line of earlier poets, and his successors were more than willing to endorse his claim because, in their endorsement, they, too, partook of the fruits of his achievement. Lydgate is quick to echo Chaucer's self-authorizing praise of Petrarch in the *Clerk's Prologue* in his *Life of Our Lady* (c. 1409–11), since, in according Chaucer the "laurer" crown "first," as a student to this "maister," he makes his own claims to English "excellence" second only to Chaucer's ("And eke my maister Chauser is ygrave/ The noble Rethor, poete of Brytayne/ That worthy was the laurer to haue/ Of poetrye"). [22] When Hoccleve describes Chaucer as the "firste fyndere of our faire langage" in the *Regement of Princes* (1412), he is indulging in a similar self-authorizing gesture, since he also calls Chaucer his "worthi maister" in that context. [23] Lydgate is still more ambitious in the *Fall of Princes* (1430) when he firmly places Chaucer in that pantheon with Virgil, Homer, and Ovid because Chaucer had placed himself there at the end of the *House of Fame* and *Troilus and Criseyde*. [24] In endorsing Chaucer's claim as the first "poet" of stature to "kiss" Parnassan steps, Lydgate firmly enters his own "poetrye" into this extraordinary company with what, in this light, can only be ostensible modesty:

---

[22] Lydgate, *Life of Our Lady*, Lauritis, Klinefelter and Gallagher (eds.), lines 2.1628–31. I quote a fuller version of these lines where I also discuss them in chapter 1, pp. 11–12.

[23] Hoccleve, *Regement of Princes*, lines 4978 and 4983. On this claim too see chapter 1, pp. 10–12.

[24] I take Lydgate to reconstruct the pantheon of "Omer," "Dares", "Virgile," and "Ovide," among others, standing on a "rowe" of "pilers" in the *House of Fame* (1451–96) and the "steppes" on which "pace/Virgile, Ovide, Omer, Lucan, and Stace" at the end of *Troilus and Criseyde* (5.1791–2). See chapter 4 above, pp. 143–4 and nn. 21–2, for discussion of these passages.

I nevir was acqueynted with Virgyle,
Nor with the sugryd dytees of Omer
Nor Dares Frygius with his goldene style,
Nor with Ovyde, in poetrye moost entieer,
Nor with sovereyn balladys of Chauceer
Which among alle that euere wer rad or songe,
Excellyd al othir in our Englysh tounge.[25]

As I have said, Lydgate and Hoccleve's words are interesting because
they predict so much that follows them, but their self-reflexivity – the
use they make of the Chaucerian accomplishment they describe – is
particularly relevant to the period before 1600 because it is only then
that this self-reflexivity had a real linguistic function. That is, in these
years before linguistic change had advanced so far as to make Chaucer
"old," praise of Chaucer could create a patrimony for English "poetrye"
by licensing studious *emulation* in what Lydgate tellingly calls "our
tunge;" it could posit an origin for English "poetrye" in Chaucer *as a
means* to finding a set of imitable linguistic objects in Chaucer's English
whose subsequent use could make the writing of imitators excellent
too.[26] Like Lydgate and Hoccleve, the anonymous writer of *The Book of
Curtesye* (1477) calls Chaucer the "founder of ornate eloquence" while
(and because) he describes Chaucer as "fader" and "maister."[27] John
Skelton is "bounde . . . with all deu reverence . . . to owe" Chaucer the
"servyce" of steady imitation in *The Garland of Laurel* (1523) because,
like Lydgate, he is also chasing after the "lawrell" Chaucer made
possible in English when he "oure Englysshe rude so fresshely hath set

<hr>

[25] Lydgate, *Fall of Princes*, Bergen, (ed.), lines 9.3401–7 (in vol. III).

[26] A measure of the success of this self-authorization is the way Lydgate's name is added
by subsequent poets to their praise of Chaucer. See George Ashby (1470): "Maisters
Gower, Chaucer & Lydgate,/ Premier poetes of this nacion," "Active Policy of a
Prince," Bateson (ed.), lines 1–2; Henry Bradshaw (1513): "To alle auncient poetes,
litell boke, submytte the . . . Fyrst to maister Chaucer and Ludgate sentencious," *Life
of St. Werburge of Chester*, Horstmann (ed.), lines 2.2020 and 2.2023; Stephen Hawes
(1506): "And after [Chaucer] my mayster Lydgate/ The monke of Bury dyde hym well
apply . . .," *Pastime of Pleasure*, Mead (ed.), lines 1338–9; William Dunbar (1503): "O
reverend Chaucere, rose of rethoris all . . . O morall Gower and Ludgate laureate,"
Goldyne Targe, Kinsley (ed.), lines 253 and 262; John Skelton (1523): "And maister
Chaucer, that nobly enterprysed/ How that our Englysshe myght fresshely be
ennewed/ The monke of Bury then after them ensuyd/ Dane John Lydgate," *Garlande
or Chaplet of Laurell*, Scattergood (ed.), lines 388–91.

[27] Furnivall (ed.), *Book of Curtesye*, lines 330–1.

out" (Chaucer is Skelton's "mayster" too).[28] There is even scope for this praise to attach itself to the reproduction of Chaucer's work, to authorize and make significant its preservation and even sale. In an "Epilogue" to his printing of Chaucer's *Boece* (1478) Caxton calls Chaucer the "worshipful fader & first foundeur & enbellisher of ornate eloquence in our englissh" and he describes Chaucer's "crafty and sugred eloquence" in the "Prohemye" to his printing of the *Canterbury Tales* (1483).[29] Praise of this kind showers distinct benefits on its purveyors because naming Chaucer as a linguistic origin renders present-day activity important by elevating the past that this activity memorializes. In praising a Chaucerian poetic they so assiduously preserve, these latter-day Chaucerians effectively praise themselves.

By this logic, then, the death of Chaucer's English ought to have foreclosed the possibility of subsequent praise, but it did not – and it did not because praise of Chaucer managed to absorb linguistic change into the argument for its still-insistent obsequies. The development of what we call Modern English bricked Chaucer's English off from imitation (for "affecting the ancients" in such imitation Ben Jonson said Spenser "writ no language"),[30] but writers who wanted to praise him after this crisis learned to praise him *as* "old." Gone after 1600 are the references to "our tunge" or "our Englysh" through which earlier poets had made common linguistic cause with Chaucer (and ensured that he made common cause with them) and in place of hopeful poetic community comes reverent retrospect. In this sense Dryden can describe the excellence of Chaucer's English in the "Preface" to his *Fables* (1700) precisely *because* he presents him as "our *old* English poet":[31] Chaucer's English was, he says (quoting Tacitus), "*auribus istius temporis accomodata*" and only "they who liv'd with him, and

---

[28] For Skelton's praise of Chaucer see *Garlande or Chaplet of Laurell*, Scattergood (ed.), lines 421–5. His bid for the laurel comes later in the poem when "Gower," "Chauwcer," and "Lydgate" conduct him into a room "Where all the sayd poetis sat in there degre/But when they sawe my lawrell rychely wrought/ All other besyde were counterfete they thought" (lines 1104–6).
[29] Caxton, *Prologues and Epilogues*, Crotch (ed.), pp. 37 and 90.
[30] Jonson, "Timber or Discoveries," Donaldson (ed.), p. 569. This essay or commonplace book appeared posthumously in 1640 (see this edition p. 614).
[31] Dryden, "Preface" to *Fables*, Kinsley (ed.), p. 521. My emphasis.

some time after him, thought it Musical."[32] Chaucer, of course, created the English precedent for this view as well:

> Ye knowe ek that in forme of speche is chaunge
> Withinne a thousand yeer, and wordes tho
> That hadden pris, now wonder nyce and straunge . . .
> (*Troilus and Criseyde*, 2.22–4)

When the form of speech *has* changed and Chaucer's prediction has become incontrovertible reality, Pope's echo of these lines in *An Essay on Criticism* (1709) shows how that reality not only becomes cause for lamentation but the very argument for literary memory. According to Pope, it is this change in "forme of speche" that ramifies in the equally incontrovertible prospect of lineal descent:

> Short is the date, alas, of modern rhymes,
> And 'tis but just to let them live betimes.
> No longer now the golden age appears,
> When patriarch-wits survived a thousand years:
> Now length of fame (our second life) is lost,
> And bare threescore is all ev'n that can boast;
> Our sons their fathers failing language see,
> And such as Chaucer is, shall Dryden be.[33]

That the father's language will fail for sons is time's imperious threat – but time's compensatory promise is that there will inevitably be sons.[34] By incorporating what Dryden called "process of Time" into the description of Chaucer's contribution to literary English the very difficulties that had to be excused in Chaucer's language ("we can only say, that he liv'd in the Infancy of our Poetry, and that nothing is brought to Perfection at the first") becomes the very ground for his subsequent importance ("We must be Children before we grow

---

[32] *Ibid.*, p. 528.   [33] Pope, *Essay on Criticism*, Rogers (ed.), lines 476–83.

[34] This is a point Dryden makes about his own translation of Chaucer: "I have not ty'd my self to a Literal Translation; but have often omitted what I judg'd unnecessary, or not of Dignity enough to appear in the Company of better Thoughts. I have presum'd farther in some Places, and added somewhat of my own where I thought my Author was deficient, and had not given his Thoughts their true Lustre, for want of Words in the Beginning of our Language . . . Another Poet, in another Age, may take the same Liberty with my Writings; if at least they live long enough to deserve Correction," "Preface" to *Fables*, Kinsley (ed.), p. 533.

Men").[35] In this sense, Chaucer's originary role actually expands insofar as it is immured in the past; no longer restricted to the particular poet praising him, Chaucer's paternity now extends to an entire line of poets (he is not to be called "*my* fadir" as Hoccleve called him, but, as James Harington put it in 1691, he is the "father of *our* Poets").[36] Dryden can arrive at the claim that Chaucer is the "Father of English Poetry" in the "Preface" to the *Fables*, then, precisely because he excludes Chaucer's achievement from "Modern Art" ("he wanted the Modern Art of Fortifying").[37] I remarked on this shift in definitions of Chaucer's primacy in chapter 1, but what might be newly noticed here is the degree to which this shift is a function of linguistic (and therefore historical) change. As Chaucer becomes a figure in the past, his importance remains constant but the grounds of that importance change too: where origination had been only a feature of the general linguistic excellence in which fifteenth- and sixteenth-century ephebes claimed their share (Chaucer was "first" because "excellent"), after 1600 Chaucer's originality must increasingly be the *reason* he is excellent (he is "excellent" because "first") as writers no longer can imitate him.

Historicizing Chaucer's importance in the seventeenth and eighteenth centuries made praising Chaucer an act of historical reclamation; it made him available to the mode of memory we now comfortably call "literary history." In 1754, Thomas Warton, the "first historian of English literature in the full sense of the term,"[38] set out the problem that historical understanding would solve:

> Chaucer seems to be regarded rather as an old poet than a good one, and that he wrote English verses four hundred years ago seems more frequently to be urged in his commendation than that he wrote four hundred years ago with taste and judgment. We look upon his poems rather as venerable relics, than as finish'd patterns; as pieces calculated rather to gratify the antiquarian than the critic.

Persuading the present day "that this neglected author . . . should be

35 *Ibid.*, p. 529.
36 Hoccleve, *Regement of Princes*, Furnivall (ed.), line 4982 and Spurgeon (ed.), *Chaucer Criticism and Allusion*, vol. I, p. 263. My emphasis in both cases.
37 Dryden, "Preface" to *Fables*, Kinsley (ed.), pp. 527–8.
38 Wellek, *Rise of English Literary History*, p. 201.

more universally and attentively studied,"[39] as Warton tried to do, made Chaucer's English verses an artifact that could be purposefully used to make a tradition. Thus Warton calls Chaucer the "father of English poetry" in an edition of Milton (1785) as he fits Milton into a poetic lineage extending from Chaucer through Spenser.[40] At the same time, the writers who award Chaucer this title subsequently are, like Warton, also poets – Wordsworth (1807), Walter Scott (1808), Robert Southey (1836), Leigh Hunt (1846), and Matthew Arnold (1880) – and, even though the title is bestowed by these poets in prefaces, biographies, and introductions to extracts in anthologies (that is, in literary history of some kind) they do so because the title has important ramifications for their poetry as well.[41] Urging antiquarian interest in Chaucer makes the writing of literary history possible (providing an origin into which later poets can be fit), but it also gives "Modern Art" its own purpose (providing a lineage into which later poets can also fit themselves). To describe Chaucer as "the Bard who first adorn'd our Native Tongue" writes a history of the "Native Tongue," but it also leaves Dryden a space to adorn the tongue as a "Bard" himself.[42] To describe "time-honored Chaucer" as a "great Precursor," as Wordsworth does, creates a role for Wordsworth as the dutiful ephebe of the great begetter.[43] Although "Modern" writers can no longer portray themselves as having a share in Chaucer's English, praising Chaucer as a historical monument still gives venerators a reflexive share in their praise since they can thereby create the possibility for their own entrance into the tradition they credit Chaucer with starting. But it does more than even this, as

---

[39] This phrase and the preceding longer quote are from Warton's *Observations on the Fairy Queen of Spenser* in Spurgeon (ed.), *Chaucer Criticism and Allusion*, vol. I, p. 409. See also Spurgeon (ed.), *Chaucer Criticism and Allusion*, vol. I, p. 423 for a slightly altered version of these remarks in a second edition (1762).

[40] The phrase occurs in a note to line 116 of *Il Penseroso* ("And if aught else great bards beside"): "From Chaucer, the father of English poetry . . . our author seems to make a very pertinent and natural transition to Spenser," Milton, *Poems Upon Several Occasions*, Warton (ed.), p. 83.

[41] Wordsworth, "Note" to *To the Daisy* in Spurgeon (ed.), *Chaucer Criticism and Allusion*, vol. II, p. 35; Scott, "Life of John Dryden" in *Works of John Dryden*, Scott (ed.), vol. I, p. 417; Southey (ed.), *Select Works of the British Poets*, p. 1; Hunt, *Wit and Humor*, p. 71; Arnold, "Study of Poetry," Super (ed.), p. 174.

[42] Dryden, "To Her Grace The Dutchess Ormond" (the prefatory poem to "Palemon and Arcite" in Dryden's *Fables*), Kinsley (ed.), line 1.

[43] Wordsworth, *Ecclesiastical Sonnets*, part 2, no. 31 ("Edward VI"), Sheats (ed.), line 12.

Scott illustrates when he fulfills Pope's hopeful prediction by placing Dryden next to Shakespeare and Milton (in introducing the work where he names Chaucer as the "father of English poetry") in "at least the third place" among "our most eminent English classics."[44] Such as Chaucer is shall Dryden be. Venerating Chaucer as a means to describing the history of English poetry proposes a *future* tradition in which "Modern" endeavor might eventually have a part when "process of Time" has finally made *it* historical: poets use Chaucer to create a place for themselves in history when "Modern Art" is itself consigned, as it must inevitably be, to the past.

But the historical understanding that used the past to define the present also contained the paradoxical possibility of neutralizing history, of bridging the difference created by "process of Time" by claiming that the past was somehow coincident with the present, that the excellence which made Chaucer worth remembering finally trumped the changes that had made him "old."[45] The seeds of this view are present in the fifteenth-century claim (which was the Chaucerian claim) that the memorialized writing of Virgil and Ovid is somehow parallel to the writing of Chaucer and Lydgate within a timeless pantheon of the "laureate": in this view, "poetrye moost entieer" exists out of time in the sense that age cannot wither nor changing custom stale its "excellence." But there is a crucial difference in the character of later formulations which emphatically *notice* the "process of Time" as a means to forgetting it. As Matthew Arnold updates these older procedures of literary memory, history is held at bay precisely *by* viewing Chaucer's originality as historical. "A poet or poem," he says,

---

44 Scott, "Life of John Dryden," Scott (ed.), vol. I, p. xi.
45 This is a point made in broader terms by Lee Patterson in his discussion of "Chaucer's foundational status" for later writers in *Chaucer and the Subject of History*, pp. 13–22. According to Patterson, "Dryden's Chaucer provides English literature with a new and definitive origin, a father at one with the transcendent source (the 'God's plenty' of character) who provides his heirs with a similarly immediate access" (p. 17). Patterson makes an important contrast between this view and that of Chaucer's immediate successors, such as Lydgate, who thought "not of origination but enhancement" (p. 16). Indeed, the whole subject of Patterson's crucial book – Chaucer's "making of himself as a man at once in and out of history" (p. 46) – articulates much more clearly than I can the roots for later representations of Chaucer's role in English literary history in Chaucer's own subtle and shifting engagement with history and historical understanding.

"may count to us historically, they may count to us on grounds personal to ourselves, and they may count to us really," but the "historic estimate," while always possible, actually obscures what our "benefit" from poetry should be:[46]

> Everything depends on the reality of a poet's classic character. If he is a dubious classic, let us sift him; if he is a false classic, let us explode him. But if he is a real classic, if his work belongs to the class of the very best (for this is the true and right meaning of the word *classic*, *classical*), then the great thing for us is to feel and enjoy his work as deeply as ever we can, and to appreciate the wide difference between it and all work which has not the same high character.[47]

In acknowledging the "*same* high character" across history – in the case of Chaucer, the change English had undergone to make him "old" and a "relic" – we remember history in order to forget it, to render the work "classic" *despite* its age. The salient difference between poets is measured by "quality," not by historical distance, by the old poet's capacity to function in the present (how it benefits "us," how we enjoy it "as deeply as ever we can"). According to this theory the qualities most valuable to "Modern Art" can be extracted from Chaucer's practice and his prophetic modernity becomes another ground for describing him as original. Dryden's word for Arnold's "reality of classic character" is "genius" and he says he sets his own "Original Papers" next to Chaucer's in the *Fables* (and, not incidentally Homer and Ovid's) because all the included works are united by "Resemblance of Genius" across the linguistic and temporal divide that his translation and modernization plane out.[48] Leigh Hunt also finds a transcendent "wit and humor" in Chaucer that, despite the "taint of his age" displays a "comic genius . . . so perfect that it may be said to include prophetic intimations of all that followed it."[49] Chaucer is still good, this argument goes, *because* he effaced history's change. As Wordsworth put it, Chaucer's language remained "affecting " because it is "almost always expressed in language pure and universally intelligible even to this day."[50] And pure and

[46] Arnold, "The Study of Poetry," Super (ed.), p. 163.
[47] *Ibid.*, p. 165. Arnold's emphasis.
[48] Dryden, "Preface" to *Fables*, Kinsley (ed.), p. 522.
[49] Hunt, *Wit and Humour*, pp. 67–8.
[50] Wordsworth, "Preface" to the *Lyrical Ballads* (1800 edition), p. 124, note.

universal intelligibility are exactly what Arnold has in mind when he says that Chaucer's English may be "a cause of difficulty for us" but it is "a difficulty to be unhesitatingly accepted and overcome": "in Spenser, Shakespeare, Milton, Keats," he says, "we can follow the tradition of the liquid diction, the fluid movement of Chaucer" – because he wrote "real poetry."[51] Chaucer, as Dryden put it otherwise, was a "rough Diamond, and must first be polish'd e'er he shines,"[52] and, from the seventeenth century onward, Chaucer was polished by evaluative terms so supple that they could sequester him from the very historical change that made polishing necessary.

The bracketing off of historical contingency by its acknowledgment (Chaucer is important because "old") or the dismissal of that contingency through an emphasis on Chaucer's proleptic modernity (Chaucer is important because modern *although* old) converged on the general presumption that remains with us today: Chaucer "began a revolution in poetic diction." But, in attending to Chaucer's role in history, literary memory never really took stock of the role such attention might itself play in constructing that role: in its iterative concern for what Chaucer could mean to later traditions writers never troubled themselves about what such concern might mean generally to Chaucer. Praise that worked so hard to banish history, not surprisingly, occluded its own history – that is, the tradition formed by comment on Chaucer itself. The very success with which Chaucer's putative origination of English poetry had detached itself from the "historic estimate" meant that claims about Chaucer's originality arrived in modern scholarship as neither an imitated procedure of Chaucerian self-fashioning (as in Lydgate) nor the method that a tradition of English poetry used to fashion and understand itself (as in Arnold). The rhetoric that proffered Chaucer as an origin was not likely to acknowledge the reflexive benefits of such praise of course: Lydgate could gain nothing by noting that the stature of *his* English was magnified by the claim that Chaucer "gan oure tonge first to magnifie"; English poets could gain nothing by acknowledging that they entered their own claims to veneration by calling Chaucer "venerable." In order to be self-authorizing the myth of

51 Arnold, "The Study of Poetry," Super (ed.), pp. 174–5.
52 Dryden, "Preface" to *Fables*, Kinsley (ed.), p. 533.

origin had to be entered as a *donnée*, but this is exactly why it is appropriate to characterize the claim that Chaucer was the "father of English poetry" as a "myth." In fact, Lévi-Strauss's analysis of this term works surprisingly well as a description of the long line of comment I have just summarized: "Myths [*les mythes*] have no author . . . whatever their real origins, they exist only as elements embodied in a tradition. When the myth is repeated, the individual listeners are receiving a message that, properly speaking, is coming from nowhere."[53] The myth of Chaucer as the origin of English literary language traveled so well, in other words, because it traveled so light, without the variegated baggage of its own historicity (or really, historicit*ies*) to qualify its claims: it had to come to Dryden and Arnold, as to Lydgate, as it was spawned by Chaucer, "from nowhere"; it had to exist *in* the tradition, "embodied" there as a constitutive property. But, precisely because it was "embodied in a tradition," this myth inevitably acquired a kind of historical validity: the "myth" became fact insofar as it accurately described the way the English tradition had constituted itself. This is exactly how Nietzsche predicts, in *The Birth of Tragedy*, that "real estimates" tend always to become "historic estimates" by "process of Time": "It is the fate of every myth [*jedes Mythus*] to creep by degrees into the narrow limits of some alleged historical reality [*historischen Wirklichkeit*], and to be treated by some later generation as a unique fact with historical claims."[54] When a scholarly machinery finally began to fashion a careful and detailed history of the English language at the end of the nineteenth century, the myth of Chaucer's originary importance had become the "historical reality" that this machinery took as its point of departure. As Lounsbury put it at this crucial moment, Chaucer is "most justly called the refiner and purifier of our speech" because "the words and the grammatical forms and the peculiarities of speech he used became largely the ones that were employed by the men who came after." This is a valid view of what Lounsbury also calls the "development of the English tongue" insofar as it accurately describes the effects of the myth of origin, but it leaves one

[53] Lévi-Strauss, *Le cru et le cuit*, p. 26. I adapt my translation from *The Raw and the Cooked*, John and Doreen Weightman (trans.), p. 18.
[54] Nietzsche, *Die Geburt der Tragödie* in *Sämtliche Werke*, p. 74; *Basic Writings of Nietzsche*, Kaufmann (trans.), p. 75.

thing out.[55] It ignores the work the myth itself did to bring this result about; it misses the vital part the myth played in affecting the very subject it purports to describe – the "development of the English tongue."

2

To see how the myth of origin had determinate effects it is necessary to return once more to the years around 1600 when linguistic history was first absorbed into its tenets. The rigorously positivist history of English that the nineteenth century began to write proceeded according to principles that had their roots in the changes that first made Chaucer's English difficult to understand and, therefore, emulate. The fervent debate over the improvement of English in the sixteenth century – and the efficacy of reviving old words and introducing new ones to effect that improvement – returned to first principles with Chaucer, since the myth of origin had already given him almost exclusive credit for earlier linguistic change.[56] Even more importantly, since Chaucer's "excellence" had long been tied to his learning (his "acquaintance" with "Virgyle," "Omer," "Dares Frygius," "Ovyde"), even Lydgate had figured that connection, just as it would be figured later, in the materiality of Chaucer's writing implements:

> My maister Chaucer. . .
> . . . ʒif I shal shortly hym discryve
> Was neuer noon to þis day alyue
> To rekne alle, boþe ʒonge & olde,
> Þat worþi was his ynkhorn for to holde.[57]

The worthiness of the "ynkhorn" was exactly what both vexed and enthralled the sixteenth century and, as a result, in the passionate controversy over what were often called "ink-horn terms," Chaucer became the lightning-rod of both praise and opprobrium.[58] A curious

[55] Lounsbury, *Studies in Chaucer*, vol. II, p. 437. My emphasis.
[56] This debate is summarized in introductory notes to extracts from its main participants in Moore, *Tudor-Stuart Views on the Growth, Status and Destiny of the English Language*.
[57] Lydgate, *Troy Book*, Bergen (ed.), lines 5.3521 and 5.3527–30.
[58] For a summary of the debate over the improvement of English and the "ink-horn

result of the venerable age that Chaucer's English had assumed by this stage was that it seemed to some to be an English free of ink-hornisms. As Peter Betham put it in 1543, Chaucer's English was notable for its "cle[a]nnes[s]" before later corruption by "termes borrowed of other tounges."[59] Simultaneously, if paradoxically, Chaucer's words were regarded as a kind of antiquarian ink-hornism, an English that writers and speakers were affecting to be pretentiously old-fashioned. As Thomas Wilson complained in his *Arte of Rhetorique* (1553), "the fine courtier will talke nothyng but Chaucer."[60] More typically and more aptly, however, Chaucer's English was the exemplar par excellence of early attempts to augment English with "termes" borrowed from Latin and French. As Holinshed notes influentially in the last volume of his *Chronicles* (1577):

> Geffreye Chaucer . . . for reducing our Englishe tong to perfect conformitie . . . hath excelled therein all other . . . for whereas before those dayes, the learned vsed to write onely in latine or Frenche, and not in Englishe, oure tong remayned very barreyne, rude, and unperfect, but now by the diligent industrie of Chaucer and Gower, it was within a while greatly amended, so as it grewe not only to be very rich and plentifull in wordes, but also so proper and apt to expresse that which the minde conceyued as any other usuall language.[61]

The problem here, of course, was that an English "rich and plentifull in wordes" from "latine or Frenche" was precisely what many writers in this period inveighed against. To the degree that Chaucer was credited

term" controversy see Baugh and Cable, *History of the English Language*, pp. 209–18. The earliest use *OED2* cites for "ink-horn term" is "1543, Bale *Yet a Course*, 59 b: Soche are your Ynkehorne termes" (s. v. "ink-horn," 2b). The locus classicus of the term is George Puttenham's definition (in 1589) in the short essay "Of Language": "We finde in our English writers many wordes and speaches amendable, & ye shall see in some many inkhorne termes so ill affected brought in by men of learning as preachers and schoolemasters: and many straunge termes of other languages by Secretaries and Marchaunts and travailours, and many darke wordes and not usuall nor well sounding, though they be dayly spoken in Court," *Arte of English Poesie*, Willcock and Walker (eds.), p. 145.

[59] Brewer (ed.), *Critical Heritage*, vol. I, p. 99.

[60] *Ibid.*, vol. I, p. 103. Although Wilson attacks foreign borrowings as "straunge ynkehorne termes," which he calls "Frenche English," the context of this remark makes clear that he is not, as others did, blaming Chaucer for "Frenche English."

[61] Spurgeon (ed.), *Chaucer Criticism and Allusion*, vol. I, pp. 114–15.

with borrowing, he was also blamed for the perceived affront. According to the antiquary Richard Verstegan in the *Restitution of Decayed Intelligence* (1605), "Geffrey Chaucer . . . is of some called the first illuminator of the English toung: of their opinion I am not . . . He was indeed a great mingler of English with French . . . Since the tyme of Chaucer more Latin & French hath bin mingled with our toung then left out of it."[62] And it is here, in the specific terms that linguistic history now used to remember Chaucer, that the occlusion of the point of departure of that memory begins to occur. Inasmuch as the constant concern of this long debate was the relative merit of borrowing, the validity of the claim that Chaucer *was* a borrower quickly passed – as it passes in Verstegan's protest – into secondary importance: it was very soon a universal assumption that Chaucer *had* been a great "mingler of English with French," and all that was at issue was whether that mingling was itself for good or for ill. This crucial transition is obvious in the way Thomas Fuller disagrees with Verstegan in his *Church-History of Britain* (1655):

> [Chaucer] was a great Refiner and Illuminer of our English tongue (and if he left it so bad, how much worse did he finde it?) . . . Indeed Verstegan, a learned Antiquary, condemns him, for spoiling the purity of the English tongue by the mixture of so many French and Latin words. But he who mingles wine with water, though he destroies the nature of water, improves the quality thereof.[63]

Fuller simply adopts Verstegan's claim that Chaucer had borrowed extensively and disagrees with Verstegan only about whether borrowing is itself a bad thing. It has been generally observed that early-modern controversies over language tended to resolve numerous subsidiary issues (the propriety of translating the Bible into English, for example) into simple questions of an appropriate "poetic vocabulary"[64] and, so too, the myth of Chaucer's origination was similarly resolved by the "ink-horn term" controversy into questions of diction. By the end of the seventeenth century, the historical view that helped fix Chaucer in

---

[62] *Ibid.*, vol. I, p. 176. For discussion of Verstegan as he is involved in problems of origination that have defined Anglo-Saxon studies, see Frantzen, *Desire for Origins*, pp. 27–35.

[63] Spurgeon (ed.), *Chaucer Criticism and Allusion*, vol. I, p. 230.

[64] See Jones, *Triumph of the English Language*, p. 120 (and generally pp. 94–141).

the past (and, thereby explained his originary project) understood his foundational "refining" of a "rude and unsettled language" to have occurred entirely by "foreign Correspondence," by means of the borrowed words that newly entered the language through his English.[65]

The beginnings of the myth of origin had focused on Chaucer's "excellence" in "poetrye" but the closest it had ever really come to specifying a linguistic mechanism for that "excellence" was Lydgate's reference to "Retoryke"; so it is indeed momentous that the sixteenth and seventeenth centuries fix Chaucer's English in history by specifying a new and different method for that achievement:

> They who attempted verse in English down till Chaucer's time made an heavy pudder, and are always miserably put to't for a word to clink . . . Chaucer found an Herculean labor on his Hands; And did perform to Admiration. He seizes all Provençal, French, or Latin that came his way, gives them a new garb and livery, and mingles them amongst our English: turns out English, gowty, or superannuated, to place in their room the foreigners, fit for service, train'd and accustomed to Poetical Discipline.[66]

The narrative Thomas Rymer offers here in his *Short View of Tragedy* (1692) makes the seizing of "Provençal, French, or Latin" the particular means by which Chaucer provided English with "Poetical Discipline," the linguistic change he worked to make himself important to literary history. The legacy of Chaucer's involvement in the controversy over the forms English could and should take refashioned the story of Chaucer's significance to English poetry as a master narrative of linguistic mingling, as a story, in particular, of poetic diction. With specific reference to Rymer, Dryden readily adopts that narrative in the "Preface" to the *Fables* ("Chaucer first adorn'd and amplified our barren Tongue from the Provencall");[67] in 1774 Warton carries it over into his *History of English Poetry* ("Chaucer . . . formed a style by naturalizing words from the Provençal");[68] and Arnold also describes Chaucer as "nourished" by a French poetry from which he gets "words, rhyme,

---

[65] These phrases are taken from James Harington's introduction to the *Athenae Oxonienses* in Spurgeon (ed.), *Chaucer Criticism and Allusion*, vol. I, pp. 263–4.
[66] Rymer, *A Short View of Tragedy*, Zimansky (ed.), pp. 126–7.
[67] Dryden, "Preface" to *Fables*, Kinsley (ed.), p. 522.
[68] Warton, *History of English Poetry*, p. 226.

metre."[69] Because this narrative has implications for the history of the language as well as the history of poetry, the view also had influence outside the line of poets I focused on above. Thomas Percy emphasizes Chaucer's borrowings in 1765 in his *Reliques of English Poetry* ("this great poet . . . introduced many terms and new modes of speech from other languages"),[70] and the second edition of the *Encyclopedia Britannica* describes those borrowings in 1778 ("he had also the merit of improving our language considerably by the introduction and naturalization of words from the Provençal").[71]

At the end of the nineteenth and the beginning of the twentieth centuries a newly empirical linguistic history continues to understand Chaucer's significance as a lexical issue – as, above all, an issue of borrowing – and it is in the rigor such history brought to this understanding that the myth of origin finally creeps confidently into history's facts. Investigation of the overwhelming presumption that Chaucer was original because he was a "mingler of English with French" meant, for positive practice, that Chaucer's presumptive originality could be reified by counting his newly borrowed words. Tabulation of these words begins, as near as I can tell, in George Perkins Marsh's *Origin and History of the English Language* (1862).[72] John Weisse offers further statistics in his *Origin, Progress and Destiny of the English Language* (1878).[73] But these early statistical forays pale in comparison of course to the numbers deployed on almost every page of the book I have been extensively examining in these pages: Mersand's *Chaucer's Romance Vocabulary*. As I have noted, Mersand's ally in his ambitious tabulation was the *OED*, which had reached completion just four years earlier, and his book may be viewed here as an attempt to transmute the huge survey of English lexical history the *OED* had amassed – what James Murray, the dictionary's principal editor, characterized as its "fabric of

---

[69] Arnold, "Study of Poetry," Super (ed.), p. 173.
[70] Spurgeon (ed.), *Chaucer Criticism and Allusion*, vol. I, p. 427.
[71] *Ibid.*, vol. I, p. 454.
[72] "Of the Romance words found in [Chaucer's English], not much above one hundred have been suffered to become obsolete, while a much larger number of Anglo-Saxon words employed by him have passed altogether out of use," Marsh, *Origin and History of the English Language*, p. 382.
[73] Weisse, *Origin, Progress and Destiny*, p. 272.

fact"[74] – into an empirical statement of the myth of origin. Inasmuch as Mersand wanted to offer "the final evaluation of our indebtedness to the word-wizard of the fourteenth century"[75] he was offering what Arnold called a "real estimate" of Chaucer's achievement – a measure of the present's debt to the timeless quality of the past – but Mersand's figures were also a "historic estimate" insofar as the *OED* styled itself as "A New English Dictionary According to Historical Principles."[76] Mersand leaned very hard on the *OED*'s imprimatur to endorse what I have been taking throughout this book as his most important conclusion: "Chaucer used, at least in the opinion of the editors of the [*Oxford*] *English Dictionary*, 1,180 words for the first time."[77] And the phrasing of that conclusion gives a concise account of the procedure through which a principle of poetic self-fashioning finally dons the dress of "objectivity." As I noted in chapter 2, Mersand's work received quick censure for "misunderstanding the results that lexicography obtains" precisely because Mersand said he followed the "opinion" of the *OED*'s editors, and "the lexicographer hasn't opinions."[78] But, of course, as Mersand's phrasing acknowledges in its naked bid for the *OED*'s authority, the lexicographer has nothing *but* opinions. Even if unwittingly, Mersand points out how a lengthy survey of a textual history pervasively governed by the opinion that Chaucer was the "firste fyndere of our faire langage" must be at the mercy of the "opinion" *as* "historical principle" that the myth of origin had become. *Chaucer's Romance Vocabulary* is the ne plus ultra of the myth of origin, an apotheosis of the long trend in the tradition of the myth to shift the issue of Chaucer's originality to lexis and lexis alone. But in its dependence upon the ne plus ultra of English linguistic history, the *OED*, Mersand's book also provides rigorous purchase on the myth's forms, curving backward along the involuted course of its own insistent tradition. Its paramount significance to the myth under examination here is its attempt to proffer that myth as a historical fact in such a way

[74] Murray, "The President's Annual Address for 1884," 509.
[75] Mersand, *Chaucer's Romance Vocabulary*, p. 2.
[76] For the subtitle see any title page of the twelve volumes of the *OED*.
[77] Mersand, *Chaucer's Romance Vocabulary*, p. 53.
[78] Hulbert, (rev.) "*Chaucer's Romance Vocabulary* (J. Mersand)," 302.

as to reveal that the myth actually confects the very authoritative linguistic history on which modern scholarship now relies.

The *OED* reproduces the myth, first, because it was designed to reflect back the kind of traditional understanding that writers like Lydgate, Dryden, and Arnold had constructed. It is true that the "Preface" of the *OED* proposes much broader aims (to survey "the words that have formed the English vocabulary from the time of the earliest records down to the present day"), but, by marked contrast, James Murray also described the dictionary's intention in its earliest stages in this different way: "to begin at the beginning, and extract anew typical quotations for the use of words, from all the great English writers of all ages."[79] The bias toward a "great writer" such as Shakespeare that results from a beginning so conceived has already been well documented.[80] In the case of Chaucer, moreover, the scholars who played a significant role in the *OED* made no secret of their belief in Chaucer's originary importance when they wrote elsewhere. F. J. Furnivall, the prime mover for the entire *OED* project as well as its "editor" from 1861 to 1877 (a period in which little editing was done, but a great deal of the material for the dictionary was compiled),[81] claimed that "one cannot say too strongly that Chaucer's originality is a fact."[82] W. W. Skeat, another key figure in the dictionary's inception and a "principal" contributor to the finished work,[83] in his separate description of the "origin and progress of the English language," thought that "much" of the "history of the language" was "effected by the genius of Chaucer."[84]

But the *OED* also reflects back the myth of origin in a second way, insofar as the very procedures that were the dictionary's "historical

---

79 For the first statement of the *OED*'s purpose see "Preface," *OED*, vol. I, p. v. (This phrase also appears in *OED2*, vol. I, p. vii.) For Murray's earlier and different statement of this purpose see "Preface to Volume I," p. v (originally published in 1888) as collected in Raymond (ed.), *Dispatches from the Front.*

80 Schäfer, *Documentation in the* O. E. D.

81 See "Historical Introduction," *OED*, vol. I, pp. vii–xii, and Murray, *Caught in the Web of Words*, pp. 135–70.

82 Furnivall, *Trial-Forewards*, 53.

83 For the list of "principal readers" in which Skeat appears, see "Historical Introduction," *OED*, vol. I, pp. xxi–xxiii. For Skeat's important role in the dictionary project, see Murray, *Caught in the Web of Words*, pp. 135–70.

84 Skeat, *Popular Sketch of the Origin and Progress of the English Language*, p. 40.

principles" rested heavily on ambient opinion. For the "beginning" of the *OED* *was* opinion inasmuch as its "typical quotations" were compiled by people the editors always and significantly called "readers." The language of the charge given these readers is worth reviewing:

> Make a quotation for *every* word that strikes you as rare, obsolete or old fashioned, new, peculiar or used in a peculiar way.
> Take special note of passages which show or imply that a word is either new and tentative, or needing explanation as obsolete or archaic, and which thus help to fix the date of its introduction or disuse.[85]

Readers were to look to their own understanding of the history of English in deciding which passages to select ("make a quotation for every word that strikes *you* as rare"), and "opinion" was precisely the ground on which the historical importance of a particular word was to be determined ("take special note of passages . . . which thus help to fix the date of [a word's] introduction"). In this way, the *OED* laid itself bare at its very foundation to wide-spread presumptions about the history of the English language and the history of literature. Readers surveying a tradition of "great writers" in English who returned quotations that confirmed their own belief in the myth of origin would have followed their instructions exactly. If the *OED* reflects back *as* history the mythic view that the written tradition had long had of itself and which, not incidentally, the *OED*'s compilers had of that tradition themselves, it would only have done exactly what it set out to do.

The *OED*'s reliance upon the kind of "opinion" that made the myth in the first place suggests that a different reading of textual remains might diminish Mersand's count of Chaucer's new words. As I noted in chapter 2, the different reading program conducted more recently by the *MED* finds, indeed, that 193 of the 1,180 words Mersand said Chaucer contributed to English on the basis of *OED* evidence were not, in fact, contributed by him because they are recorded first in earlier Middle English texts. Some of these discrepancies are owing, of course, to the increased availability of early Middle English texts since the *OED* was edited. But other discrepancies trace the very pattern of privilege

---

[85] "Historical Introduction," *OED*, vol. I, p. xv. *OED*'s emphasis.

that a dictionary open to the myth of origin would be expected to produce. To pick one representative example, it is clear that the *OED*'s readers and editors were most "struck" by two uses of the noun "lure" in Chaucer's *Legend of Good Women* and tge *Friar's Tale*, which are cited in the *OED* as the earliest use of the word "lure sb.":

> Thow sly devourere and confusioun
> Of gentil wemen, tendre creatures,
> Thow madest thy recleymyng and thy *lures*
> To ladyes of thy statly aparaunce . . .
> (*Legend of Good Women*, 1369–72)

> This false theef, this somonour, quod the Frere,
> Hadde alwey bawdes redy to his hond,
> As any hauk to *lure* in Engelond . . .
> (*Friar's Tale*, III.1338–40)

And yet this noun was used almost a century earlier in Robert of Gloucester's *Chronicle* (c. 1300):

> Þo þis gode tidinge com to þis noble arthure
> Mid gode herte he wolde such tydinge yhure
> He þo3te come bi hom & bringe some to *lure*
> & to winne al europe 3if he mi3te dure.[86]

It is appropriate to describe the absence of this citation from the *OED* as an "omission" because the edition of Robert of Gloucester's *Chronicle* from which I quote these lines was read for the *OED* (it appears in its bibliography) and was completed at least fifteen years before the *L* volume of the *OED* was prepared.[87] A number of other pre-Chaucerian citations are omitted from the *OED* in instances where every procedure of its compilation (the words appear in earlier texts, cited in the *OED*'s bibliography, dated there earlier than Chaucer) should have seen to their inclusion.[88] These citations include "roial adj." in *Floris and*

---

[86] Robert of Gloucester, *Metrical Chronicle*, Wright (ed.), lines 3757–60.

[87] The "L" volume was completed in "1901–3" (see "Historical Introduction," *OED*, vol. I, p. xix). See the listing of this edition in the "Bibliography," *OED*, p. 67 (this bibliography is placed at the end of vol. XII).

[88] As I noted in more general terms in my introduction, no one admitted with greater candor than James Murray the sheer impossibility of a thoroughly accurate account of a subject as large as the English language. Murray was also quick to heap scorn on the pedants who rushed "with a flourish of trumpets" to *Notes & Queries* with early citations the *OED* had missed: as he liked to point out the *OED* had only ever hoped

Blauncheflur (c. 1250), "amblen v." in *Guy of Warwick* (c. 1300), "lache adj." ("weary, dull") in *Kyng Alisaunder* (c. 1300), "passaunt adj." ("transitory") in *Sir Beues of Hamtoun* (c. 1300), "floute n." in glosses to Walter of Bibbesworth's *Treatise* (c. 1325), "murmuren v." in *Cursor Mundi* (c. 1325), "administracioun," "ardaunt adj." and "argument n." in Shoreham's *Poems* (c. 1333), "affect n." in Richard Rolle's *Psalter* (c. 1340), "solitude n." in Rolle's *Form of Living* (c. 1348), "commendable adj.," "feminine adj.," "masculine adj.," "preciouslie adv.," and "resistence n." in the Vernon MS *Saint's Legendary* (c. 1350), and "enhabiten v." and "indignacioun n." in the *Midland Prose Psalter* (c. 1350).[89]

These omissions are mistakes in an attempt to survey "the words that have formed the English vocabulary from the time of the earliest records" but they do "begin at the beginning" if that beginning is understood to be the "great writer" who is the "Father of English Poetry." That the myth was preferred to a more capacious historical view even as readers' quotations were edited – that the voicing of the myth by those involved in the making of the *OED* also mattered – is a supposition given further support by a set of omissions from "the earliest records" that the *OED* almost certainly did not have to make. The citation for the noun "lure" in Robert of Gloucester's *Chronicle* that the *OED* omits, for example, not only occurs in an edition of the chronicle in the *OED*'s bibliography, but in an edition edited by William Aldis Wright, a scholar whose assistance is frequently mentioned in prefaces to volumes of the *OED* and who is thanked, in one instance, for his help "in the investigation of the history . . . of words."[90] More interesting still, however, is the omission of the words (which I give according to their *OED* headwords), "fawn sbi.,"

to get within fifty years of the first use of any word (See Murray, "President's Annual Address for 1884," p. 516). On the other hand, it is also worth recognizing that some of the discrepancies I note are more on the order of one hundred years than fifty.

[89] For references to the editions of these texts available to the *OED* see its "Bibliography." For reference to what I call the "Vernon MS *Saint's Legendary*" (in the *MED*, the "Smaller Vernon Collection of Legends," abbreviated "*SVrn.Leg*") see the "*Sammlung Altenglischer Legenden*" entered under "Horstmann, Carl ed." in "Bibliography," *OED*, p. 39; for the "*Midland Prose Psalter*" see "*An early English psalter*" under "*Psalter*" in "Bibliography," *OED*, p. 65.

[90] For the quoted acknowledgment see "Preface to Volume V," *OED*, p. vii (originally published in 1901) in Raymond (ed.), *Dispatches from the Front*. For other acknowledgments of Wright's assistance see "Preface to Volume I," p. xiii and "Preface to Part I

"felonous a. Obs." (a variant of "felonious"), "ensure v.," and "infinite a." These four words are also cited for the first time in Chaucer in their respective *OED* entries, although "fawn" and "felonous" are recorded earlier in Robert Mannyng's *Chronicle* (c. 1338), "ensure" is recorded in the "A-text" (c. 1376), and "infinite" is recorded in the "B-text" (c. 1378) of *Piers Plowman*.[91] These texts were not only available to the *OED* (edited before the relevant volumes of the dictionary were prepared), and editions of these texts are not only listed in the *OED* bibliography carrying dates earlier than the texts by Chaucer in which the *OED* first cites these words,[92] but the editor of the cited edition of *Piers Plowman* and the editor of the cited edition of Mannyng's *Chronicle* were "principal readers" for the *OED* listed in the dictionary's "Introduction."[93] What is more, these editors were actually W. W. Skeat and F. J. Furnivall, scholars central to the *OED* from its inception and who, as I have noted, both gave voice to the myth of origin in their own writing. It is impossible to determine whether these editors read the texts for the *OED* that they edited (although they certainly might have). These errors are hardly significant to the linguistic history the *OED* generally offers, and it is easy to understand them as natural omissions from the welter of material the *OED* collected and sorted. Still, whatever the

(A-Ant)," p. vi also in Raymond (ed.), *Dispatches from the Front*. I owe thanks to Jenny McMorris for these references.

91 See Mannyng, *Story of England*, Furnivall (ed.), lines 488 and 15750; Langland, *Piers Plowman*, Skeat (ed.), A-text: vol. I, line 6.31 and B-text: vol. II, line 13.127 and, again, line 13.128.

92 Word by word, these omissions may be dissected thus: "ensure v." appears in the A-text of *Piers Plowman* published in 1867 (Skeat [ed.]), the "E" volume of the *OED* is prepared and published 1888–91, the *OED*'s bibliography dates the A-text "1362", but the *OED* cites "ensure v." first "c1385 Chaucer *L. G. W.*2115 *Ariadne*"; "fawn sb1." and "felonous a." appear in Mannyng's *Chronicle*, published in 1887 (as *The Story of England*, Furnivall [ed.]), the "F" volume of the *OED* is prepared and published 1893–7, the *OED*'s bibliography dates the *Chronicle* (as "*The story of England*") "c1330," but it cites "fawn sb1." first "c1369 Chaucer *Dethe Blaunche* 429" and "felonous a." first "c.1374 Chaucer *Boeth.*i.iv"; "infinite a." appears in the B-text of *Piers Plowman* published in 1869 (Skeat [ed.]), the "I" volume is prepared and published 1899–1901, the *OED*'s bibliography dates the B-text "1377," but cites "infinite a." first "c1385 Chaucer *L. G. W.* 1675 *Hipsipile*." For the date of preparation and publication of individual volumes of the *OED* see "Historical Introduction," *OED*, vol. I, pp. xvii–xix. For references to the editions of these texts available to the *OED* see its "Bibliography."

93 See "Historical Introduction," *OED*, vol. I, pp. xxi–xxii.

exact procedure of their making, the contour of these errors carefully details the course by which the myth of Chaucer as the origin of English literary language becomes lexical history according to the *OED*. In the entries for these words, despite every possibility for preventing it, the *OED* proffers the myth as the history of English.

We can see the hermeneutic circle I mentioned at the outset begin to close here insofar as the *OED* remains an important scholarly resource for linguistic history. The mythic understandings of Furnivall, Skeat, and Murray do continue to circulate with great authority: the recent second edition of the *OED* repeats all the errors I have described,[94] and this second edition still cites Chaucer more often than any other writer as the earliest recorded user of individual words (in 2,012 instances).[95] If the point is not that the *OED*'s editors were remiss (and given their herculean and epochal achievement I think it would never be worth saying that they were), the reproduction of the myth as "fact" on various levels of the *OED*'s empirical procedure simply confirms the myth's extensive power, and generates a different problem for any version of linguistic history that might now be written: is there any significant historical *alternative* to the myth of origin to which linguistic history might now turn? In fact, that problem is given an even finer point by the *MED*, the dictionary I have been using as a corrective for the *OED*. It is not possible to correct the *MED* of course – there is no later, larger survey that might discern its omissions – but some of its entries show, in themselves, that Chaucer's linguistic use is still privileged in its pages. I quote three of the more revealing of these entries here in full:

---

94 For an important discussion of the general dependency of this second edition of the *OED* on the first edition of 1933 see Brewer, "The Second Edition of the *Oxford English Dictionary*."

95 Willinsky, *Empire of Words*, p. 221. Willinsky's appendix shows the *OED2* finding the largest number of earliest citations in Chaucer (2,012 words). Willinsky gives a useful account of the "particular patterns of favored and neglected sources" in the *OED* and the "Victorian interests" they reflect and subtend (p. 5). In analyzing these earliest citations Willinsky discusses the implications of the second largest number of earliest citations in the *OED*, the 1,986 words in works attributed to John Wyclif (p. 221). According to Willinsky these citations combined with all the early citations from Chaucer allowed the dictionary's editors to portray the "heroic image" of "a nation forged out of well-turned verse and outspoken nay-saying" (see pp. 96–100).

brok n2. [Cp. OI **brokkr** trotting horse, **brokkari** cart horse.] Name of a horse. (c1395) Chaucer *CT.Fri*.D.1543: This cartere smoot and cryde. 'Hayt, Brok [vrr. broke, brake, liard]! Hayt, Scot! what spare ye for the stones!'

gat-tothed adj. Also **gate-**, **gaite-**, **gad-** & **gap-**, **gapt-**, **gaptothe**. [From **gate** n1. Some instances have been reshaped under the influence of **gap** & **gapen**.] Having teeth set wide apart. (c1387–95) Chaucer *CT.Prol*.A.468: She koude muche of wandrynge by the weye; Gat tothed [vrr. gate toþede, Gaptothe] was she soothly for to seye. (c1395) Chaucer *CT.WB*.D.603: Gat [vrr. Gayte, Gad, Gap, Gapt] tothed I was, and that bicam me weel; I hadde the preente of seynt Venus seel.

in principio phr. [L] In the beginning; – first words of a formula used by begging friars [cp. John 1.1]. (c1387–95) Chaucer *CT.Prol*.A.254: For thogh a wydwe hadde noght a sho, So plesant was his In principio, Yet wolde he haue a ferthyng er he wente.

The presentation of proper nouns, nonce compounds, and Latin phrases in separate entries in the *MED* – which, perforce, enters these forms as *hapax legomena* in Chaucer – pays extraordinary attention to Chaucer's lexical practice. Nor are these the only examples of such careful attention to Chaucer's "words."[96] Although "gat-tothed" might be subsumed into the entry for its simplex (there is a long entry for "gate n1." in the *MED*) and "brok n2." and "in principio" might be excluded from the *MED* altogether (as other proper nouns and Latin phrases are), the argument for giving these "words" separate entries in the *MED* must be that Chaucer's lexis is historically significant as it departs from other Middle English usage, that it is worthy of distinguishing note because Chaucer's use is distinctive. Further versions of this latent argument can be discerned in the way Chaucer's use of common words is singled out for separate attention within the individual entries for other words. For example, in the *MED*'s entry for the verb "moten" a separate subheading is devoted to the verb's use "in proverb[s]" (as the subheading is labeled) but under that subheading the *MED* cites only Chaucer's repeated use of the axiom "the wordes

---

[96] See *MED*, s. vv. "airish bestes phr.," "cok, cok!," "convers n3.," "feithed ppl.," "fortuna major n.," "quoniam n.," "rom n.," "ruf n2," and "Significavit n." for other unusual words cited only in Chaucer.

mote be cosyn to the dede" (*General Prologue*, 742, *Boece* 3.pr.12.206 and the *Manciple's Tale*, 8–10) or direct echoes of this phrase in his imitators.[97] The *MED* also gives Chaucer's practice *as* the etymology of a word: for example, according to the *MED*, the noun "contemplaunce" only occurs in Middle English in a rhyme in the *Summoner's Tale* (3.1893) and therefore the etymology of this word (the "origin" the *MED* posits for it) reads: "coined for rime's sake."[98] Following Chaucer's every linguistic move with such studious attention creates a bias toward the eccentricities of Chaucer's English in the *MED*'s pages, but the fundamental rationale for that attention lies in a fact far more significant than any of these remarkable entries: the completed portion of the *MED* still has entries that show 1,909 words recorded for the first time in English in Chaucer's writing.[99] Some of these "first-uses" are of course precisely a function of studious attention to Chaucer's practice – exclude the three entries quoted above and there would be 1,906 such words – but, liminal cases aside, the abundance of the *MED*'s evidence argues powerfully for the privilege it accords Chaucer's use by showing that Chaucer's language is eminently and constantly privileg*able*. Chaucer's English determines the lexical history of the language in these entries because, generally speaking, the *MED*'s survey shows Chaucer's

---

[97] *MED*, s. v., "moten v2.," 7a, b. The only non-Chaucerian use of this axiom cited by the *MED* here is Walton's direct echo of Chaucer's formulation in his translation of Boethius's *Consolation of Philosophy* (1410): "Plato seide . . . Þat wordes moste be cosyns kyndely/To þinges which þei ben referred to."

[98] *MED*, s. v. "contemplaunce n." Other etymologies for the words mentioned in n. 96 are also derived directly from Chaucer's use. The etymology for "airish bestes phr.," for example, which is cited only in *House of Fame* 932 (" 'These ben the eyryssh bestes, lo!' ") and 965 ("And beheld the ayerissh bestes . . ."), reads "rendering L *aeria animalia*," a claim for the influence of Augustine and Apuleius on these lines of the *House of Fame* put forward in Ker, "Chaucer, 'House of Fame' (ii.417–26)." The etymology for "feithed ppl." in the *MED*, "from the phrase 'strong feith,'" also points directly to Chaucer's use of that participle in the single line of *Troilus and Criseyde* cited to exemplify that participle in Middle English ("And strengest feythed ben, I undirstonde," 1.1007).

[99] In order to give an account of the published *MED*'s testimony this word count leaves aside the extrapolations on the basis of *MED* records (used in other chapters and Part 2) and tabulates only the 8,246 words in Chaucer's vocabulary covered in available fascicles of the *MED* (at the time of writing, through *T*). My count for even this curtailed portion of Chaucer's new vocabulary is still much larger than Mersand's because (as in previous chapters) I count derived, compounded, and converted forms as well as the Romance borrowings Mersand confined himself to.

English determining the history of the language. If we take the *MED* as a careful study of all Middle English, a more careful study on the whole than the *OED* (a fair enough assumption I think), then the implicit claim of its result is this: even when "the words that have formed the English vocabulary from the time of the earliest records" are examined they return a history in which Chaucer's English was significantly and (in numerical terms) dramatically "first."

Whatever bias the *MED* and *OED* may display toward Chaucerian originality arises, in other words, from overwhelming general evidence *of* Chaucerian originality in the record; it reflects the "fact" that the most an empirical survey can do is return evidence that confirms the truth the myth purveys. These dictionaries absorb the myth of origin into their lexicographic procedures, adapting the old lexical strain of the myth to twentieth-century rubrics of linguistic investigation – dressing Chaucerian achievement once again in the sanctioned values of "Modern Art." But these dictionaries have evidence with which to reify the myth because the evidence available to them has always been culled by the myth's shaping hand. As I noted above, some of the emphasis given to Chaucer's language in the *OED* is owing to the simple fact that its editors did not have access to certain Middle English writings which have since become available. The twenty-six-page list of texts in "Supplement I" to the first *MED* bibliography (issued as a separate volume in 1984) shows as well just how many new texts have become available since the *MED* itself first began to be published (in 1954). If Middle English texts were continually gathered and disseminated across the decades that the *OED* and the *MED* were being written, if the contours of published pre-Chaucerian Middle English continue to broaden even in the present day, Chaucer's language has benefited, because Chaucer's language has remained continuously and prominently in print all through this period.[100] This availability alone makes it impossible for a dictionary to avoid privileging Chaucer's words at the expense of other Middle English writing. But the myth has

[100] Skeat's important edition appeared in 1894, but the Moxon (1843), Aldine (1845), Bell (1854), Routledge (1860), Crowell (1880), Gilman (1880), and Blackwood (1890) editions of Chaucer assured the ready availability of Chaucer's writing through the latter half of the nineteenth century. See Hammond, *Chaucer: A Bibliographical Manual*, pp. 135–46.

encouraged the preservation of Chaucer's writing at the expense of earlier Middle English, not only in recent centuries, but since its inception. John Fisher has recently described what he calls a "Lancastrian language policy" under Henry IV and Henry V which sought to cement the authority of English by "publishing" Chaucer's works.[101] Whether the particular motivation Fisher proposes is believed or not, the "outburst of copying and composing in English . . . soon after 1400" which he describes is undeniable,[102] and the textual record has exactly the shape any language policy designed to privilege Chaucer's writing would have produced. Roughly 30 manuscripts of vernacular literature survive from the 75 years before Chaucer's death in 1400 and over 600 such manuscripts survive from the 75 years after 1400.[103] Whether or not we connect this efflorescence to a "language policy," or to the fifteenth-century poets who privileged Chaucer as a means of authorizing their own vernacular productions, or to a readership that learned to prize the vernacular by reading Chaucer and subsequently created a new demand for vernacular production, the record of Middle English that modern dictionaries might survey largely consists of writing proclaiming Chaucer the "firste fyndere" of the "faire langage" or writing written in the shadow (and effect) of such claims. And it is around this feature of the record that the hermeneutic circle I mentioned earlier finally constrains even scholarship's potential. The validity of any claim that Chaucer's language was original must be tested – no matter how it is tested – in a body of texts which largely presume this originality. No matter how much any attempt to evaluate the myth might succeed in freeing itself procedurally from the myth's influence, such a measurement could only assess a record of texts that respond to Chaucer as if the myth were "historical." In fact (in the "fabric of fact" itself), there *is* no linguistic history other than the myth of origin to which linguistic history *can* turn.

3

The omnipotence of the myth is a huge problem if we want to oppose "historical principles" to mythic understandings, but it is hardly a

---

[101] Fisher, "Language Policy for Lancastrian England."   [102] *Ibid.*, 1178.
[103] Edwards and Pearsall, "The Manuscripts of the Major Middle English Poetic Texts," p. 257.

problem at all if we credit the myth with its own historical claims as a feature of the history of English and the history of English literature. Theories of "origination" predict exactly the circularity I have just detailed: it is, in fact, exactly the set of postpositive relations that any process of origination inevitably produces. In his lengthy study of this process Edward Said observes that "beginnings" are not autonomous, but "designated in order to indicate, clarify or define a later time, place or action."[104] In this observation Said builds on the even broader, political scheme proposed earlier by Nietzsche: "The cause [*Ursache*] of the origin [*Entstehung*] of a thing and its eventual utility, its actual employment and place in a system of purposes, lie worlds apart; whatever exists, having somehow come into being, is again and again reinterpreted to new ends, taken over, transformed, and redirected by some power superior to it."[105] A formula that demands reciprocity between latter-day understandings and the "beginnings" of things explains a great deal of what I have been describing in the conventional understanding of Chaucer's achievement: the linguistic "beginning" Chaucer made could *only* be made insofar as what he began (the tradition of English poetry) posited its origins in his writing. Much as we might want to separate the "historical" estimation of Chaucer's originality from a poet's choice of his poetic father, it is in precisely such a choice (or such choices) that the history we wish to examine unfolds. To say that Chaucer "started a tradition" is to create that "start" and that "tradition" at a blow.[106] It is not under the mode of analysis, or its relative perspicuity, or its degree of accuracy that hermeneutic circles historically bend, but under the simple pressure of seeking some origin for a tradition at all.

The interest in calling attention to the operations of the myth of origin is not, then, so much in correcting the view this myth propounds as in emphasizing the vital *importance* of this myth to the history of English. The fullest possible understanding of the myth would not seek

---

[104] Said, *Beginnings*, p. 5. Said distinguishes "beginnings" from "origins" (see p. 380) in terms of "intention" (see p. 372). I am simplifying Said's terminology, in other words, but not, I hope, distorting his important and fundamental observation.

[105] Nietzsche, *Zur Genealogie der Moral* in *Sämtliche Werke*, p. 313. Translation from *Basic Writings of Nietzsche*, Kaufmann (trans.), p. 513. Cited in Said, *Beginnings*, pp. 174–5.

[106] Görlach, "Chaucer's English," 74. On this phrase see also p. 9 n. 2 above.

to sweep it away but to describe its workings with some care. These workings are necessarily complex and cannot be fully illustrated in the space of this chapter, but some indication of particular lexical mechanisms may be observed in the progress of those borrowings which have become, in the twentieth century, the very substance of the myth. It is possible to see that those borrowings which reify Chaucer's originality in modern dictionaries owe their contribution to the language to a cooperative process between Chaucer (who borrows those words) and his successors (who continue to use them as they imitate Chaucer). We can recur for an example to one of the new borrowings I discussed in chapter 4, "adournen v.," which Chaucer used for the first time in the English record in the apostrophe to Venus in *Troilus and Criseyde* ("O blisful light of which the bemes clere/*Adorneth* al the thridde heven faire!, 3.1–2). When Lydgate formulates the myth of origin he does so in a phrase that repeats this word (Chaucer "Gan oure tonge firste to magnifie/ And *adourne* it with his elloquence"). Lydgate might have drawn the word from elsewhere (from French or Latin as Chaucer did), but the presumption that Lydgate takes this word directly from Chaucer is strengthened by the fact that the *Troy Book* is itself a Trojan poem, generally inspired by the example of *Troilus and Criseyde*, and the very passage of the *Troy Book* in which Lydgate uses this verb looks directly to Chaucer as an inspiring muse ("My maister Galfride, as for chefe poete . . . / þe name of whom shal passen in noon age,/ . . . withoute eclipsinge shyne")[107] in much the way that Chaucer looks to Venus, his inspiring muse, when he uses the verb in the first place. Chaucer uses this verb only once in all of his writing, and, because it passes in the record from this nonce use in *Troilus and Criseyde* to Lydgate with only one intervening use in Usk's *Testament of Love* (another text heavily dependent on the example of *Troilus and Criseyde*), it is fair to say that the contribution of this word to English – its stability in the language as a word that others might use – is work done as much by Usk and Lydgate (who are willing and eager to treat this word as if it is a repeatable attribute of English lexis) as it is by Chaucer (who is never interested in this word again). It is the successive and derivative use of this verb as a confirmation of the myth of origin

---

[107] Lydgate, *Troy Book*, Bergen (ed.), lines 3.4256–9.

within that myth that actually makes Chaucer's borrowing successful, that secures a permanent place for this borrowing in English as an English word. "Adournen v." might have found its way into permanent English usage without the aid of the myth or its progenitors of course – or even without its use in Chaucer. But the history of this one word in the record traces the mechanism through which what "came into being" in Chaucer's language was "reinterpreted to new ends . . . taken over, transformed, and redirected" by a successor such as Lydgate, who performed this transformation and redirection precisely to confirm the originary role for Chaucer's English he uses this word to posit.

A more capaciously historical view of English, alive itself to the ways the myth of origin played a part in the history of that language, can use the kind of lexical investigation that has been used to evaluate Chaucer's contributions to English vocabulary to evaluate the contributions the myth has itself made to English. A few more statistics are informative here. Of the 1,909 words recorded in Chaucer's writing for the first time in English in the completed *MED*'s survey, 756 survive in later Middle English in the writing of Chaucer's most voluble imitators, Hoccleve and Lydgate. It is therefore possible to say that these words survive in English to some significant degree as a result of Lydgatian and Hocclevian imitation. The naturalizing work such imitative use performs can be measured more exactly by looking at the subcategory of 1,159 words recorded for the first time in Chaucer's texts but used only once by him. Hoccleve and Lydgate repeat 360 of these words, using them first *as* English words (and not as new coinages), wearing a lexical groove along the pattern Chaucer's verbal practice could only mark out (with his single new use), ensuring that these words stay in the language. By contrast, in this same category of new words Chaucer used only once, 262 of the 799 words that Lydgate and Hoccleve do not choose to imitate simply die. They never appear in the English record again.[108]

---

[108] These and some subsequent figures will differ from the version of this chapter published in *Speculum* 71 (pp. 646–75) because I include the last fascicles of *T* which were unpublished at the time of that article's completion. The difference in the second figure in this paragraph (756 instead of the previously reported 1,322 words) cannot, however, be accounted for in this way. Since that difference is almost exactly a factor of two, I can only think that I somehow doubled my calculation before. This figure should now supersede the previous one, however, and I apologize for any misconception that may have been fostered by this error.

The naturalization that the myth effects can be specified across an even longer span of time in some of the other vocabulary used to formulate the myth. As I have mentioned, Lydgate's claim that Chaucer "worthy was the laurer to have/ Of poetrye" because he "enlumyne[d]" English with his "Retoryke" was a direct echo of Chaucer's self-authorizing praise of Petrarch ("the lauriat poete . . . whos rethorike sweete/Enlumyned al Ytaille of poetrie"). But it is also true that the key words Chaucer uses to establish the category for his praise ("poetrie n.") its method ("enluminen v.), and the word that Lydgate adds when echoing the same sentiment ("eloquence n."), occur, like "adournen v.," for the first time in recorded English in Chaucer's writing, and pass as well into later English usage via the continuous repetition of the myth itself.[109] It is worth setting out some of these formulations again along with others like them to emphasize the persistence of these words in the myth.

Enluminen:

(1409–11) . . . And fonde the floures, firste of Retoryke
Our Rude speche, only to enlumyne . . .
(Lydgate, *Life of Our Lady*)

(1412) . . . With bookes of his ornat endytyng,
That is to al þis land enlumynyng.
(Hoccleve, *Regement of Princes*)

(1477) O fader and founder of ornate eloquence
That enlumened hast alle our bretayne
(*The Book of Curtesye*)

(1503) O reverend Chaucere, rose of rethoris all,
. . . This mater coud illumynit have full brycht . . .
(Dunbar, *The Golden Targe*)

---

[109] "Eloquence n." does not occur in a passage of Chaucer particularly devoted to establishing the myth, but it does occur in the *Clerk's Tale* to refer to Griselda ("so discreet and fair of eloquence," IV, 410) and, by the Clerk in his address to "archewyves" ("the arwes of thy crabbed eloquence," IV, 1203). It is elsewhere used by the Black Knight to describe the speech of Blanche (*Book of the Duchess*, line 925), by Philosophy in the *Boece* to describe the speech of "Boethius" (Book 2, pr.3.57), and by the Franklin to refer to the speech of the Squire (V, 678). For a full description of Chaucer's use of these words see their respective entries in Benson, *Glossarial Concordance*.

(1598) Geffrey Chaucer . . . the first illuminer of the English
tongue . . .
(Speght, "Life of Geffrey Chaucer" in Geffrey Chaucer, *Workes*)

(1600) The famous poet Geffrey Chaucer esquire, the first
illuminer of our English language . . .
(Stowe, *Annales of England*)

(1655) He was a great Refiner and Illuminer of our English
tongue . . .
(Fuller, *The Church History of Britain*)

Eloquence:

(1412) Mi maister Chaucer, flour of eloquence,
Mirour of fructuous entendement . . .
(Hoccleve, *Regement of Princes*)

(1412–20) . . . he cam, & þoruȝ his poetrie
Gan oure tonge firste to magnifie
And adourne it with his elloquence.
(Lydgate, *Troy Book*)

(1478) The worshipful fader & first foundeur & enbelissher of
ornate eloquence in our englissh . . . I mene Maister
Geffrey Chaucer . . .
(Caxton, "Epilogue" to *The Consolacion of Philosophie*)

(1484) Gefferey chaucer . . . made many bokes and treatyces . . .
sheweyng the pycked grayn of sentence vtteryd by
crafty and sugred eloquence.
(Caxton, "Prohemye" to the *Canterbury Tales*)

(1513)   Chaucer, principall poet but peir,
Hevinlie trumpat, horleige and reguleir,
In eloquence balmy, condit and diall . . .
(Douglas, *Eneados*)

(1523) O Noble Chaucer, whos pullisshyd eloquence
Oure Englysshe rude so fresshely hath set out . . .
(Skelton, *The Garland of Laurel*)

(1597) For the sweetness of his Poetrie . . . so may Chaucer bee
rightly called, the pith and sinewes of eloquence . . .
(Beaumont, "Preface" to Speght's edition of Chaucer's *Works*)

(1700) The Verse of Chaucer... 'tis like the Eloquence of one
whom Tacitus commends...
(Dryden, "Preface" to the *Fables*)[110]

The word "poetry" is so generally used after Chaucer that it can be less
closely linked to repetitions of the myth, although the entry for "poetrie
n." in the *MED* shows the word moving from Chaucer, through John
Trevisa's translation of Higden's *Polychronicon*, out into repeated uses by
Lydgate; and the entry in the *OED* for "poetry sb." cites the word in
subsequent uses by Caxton and Hawes (who imitates Lydgate's myth-
making praise of Chaucer, by using the term to praise his "mayster"
Lydgate). But, ultimately, "poetrie n." became even more crucial than
"enluminen v." or "eloquence n." to the myth of origin, inasmuch as it
establishes, as I explored in some detail in chapter 1, the very category
that Chaucer was later understood to have begun: it is the word Lydgate
uses (echoing Chaucer's use of "poesie n." in *Troilus and Criseyde*) to
establish Chaucer as that category's origin. As I have noted in this
chapter, the word becomes paramount in the myth when it is finally
codified in the eighteenth century as the claim that Chaucer was the
"father of English poetry."

In the case of "adournen v.," "enluminen v," and "eloquence n." it is
fair to say that the myth actually helped to make the very English it
attributes to Chaucer's making in retrospect, extracting the terms in
which it is couched from Chaucer's particular "eloquence," from the
words he is said to use to "illuminate" and "adorn" English. As the
myth flowed across the great divide of 1600 the ability of the myth to
make the language grew attenuated – as Chaucer could no longer be
imitated – but the myth still had formative power as a constitutive

---

[110] For these passages see Lydgate, *Life of Our Lady*, Lauritis, Klinefelter and Gallagher
(eds.), lines 2.1635–6; Hoccleve, *Regement of Princes*, Furnivall (ed.), lines 1973–4;
Furnivall (ed.), *The Book of Curtesye*, lines 330–1; Dunbar, *Goldyne Targe*, Kinsley
(ed.), lines 253–5; Speght, "Life of Chaucer" in Brewer (ed.), *Critical Heritage*, vol. I,
p. 142; Stowe, *Annales*, Spurgeon (ed.), *Chaucer Criticism and Allusion*, vol. I, p. 164;
Fuller, *History*, Spurgeon (ed.), *Chaucer Criticism and Allusion*, vol. I, p. 230;
Hoccleve, *Regement of Princes*, Furnivall (ed.), lines 1962–3; Lydgate, *Troy Book*,
Bergen (ed.), lines 3.4241–3; Caxton, *Prologues and Epilogues*, Crotch (ed.), pp. 37
and 90; Douglas, *Virgil's Aeneid*, Coldwell (ed.), lines 17–19; Skelton, *Garlande or
Chaplet of Laurell*, Scattergood (ed.), lines 421–2; Beaumont, *Preface* to Speght's
edition of Chaucer's *Works* in Brewer (ed.), *Critical Heritage*, vol. I, p. 138; Dryden,
"Preface" to the *Fables*, Kinsley (ed.), p. 528.

claim of the poetic tradition. When continued attention to Chaucer's language could no longer do the work of making specific elements of that language a part of English, the repeated praise of that work perpetuated the category (of "poetrie") that this work was understood to have founded. The myth of origin that made the reality of Chaucer's originality before 1600 continued, in other words, after 1600, to make the myth real. As generation after generation took that myth, repeated it, and handed it along to successive writers, the myth itself pieced out the very lineage of writers who form the tradition Chaucer has so generally been said to have founded. In the very process of positing their own origin in Chaucer, then, the proponents of this myth, not only described Chaucer's place in the history of the "language of England," they created that place.

There is reason to say, then, that the most scholarly view of the making of Chaucer's English that could now be offered *is* the myth of origin, that, if Lydgate was Chaucer's "scholler" as E. K. rightly describes him in the first lines of his commentary on the *Shepheardes Calendar*, and, if scholars of Chaucer in this century have remained thoroughly Lydgatian, positions converge at both ends of the time line because the position adopted is correct.[111] To say that Chaucer created English literary language and literature is to make a claim that the most "historical" survey can only confirm, certainly, at least, in the lexical terms by which this claim has generally been substantiated, and probably as well in the more general terms of rhetoric and meter that most concerned Chaucer's immediate successors. There is too of course – hence this book – some reason to lament the degree to which Chaucer scholarship remains Lydgatian out of purely Lydgatian motives: a scholarship that makes Chaucer's originality self-authorizing, gathering importance to his own endeavors by praising the poet it studies, is a scholarship deeply circumscribed by its own assumptions. It is no accident, in other words, that John Fisher is interested in emphasizing "Chaucer's importance in creating English literary language and

---

[111] Spenser, *Poetical Works*, Smith and Selincourt (eds.), p. 416. The epithet occurs in the first lines of the "Letter to Gabriel Harvey" that stands as preface to the *Shepheardes Calendar* (1579); it is signed by "E. K." but attributable by implication to either Gabriel Harvey or to Spenser himself.

English literature" in a book that he calls *The Importance of Chaucer*.[112] The damage that scholarly embrace of the myth of origin can do is even broadly visible in the contours of the entire enterprise that is the study of Middle English writing. A survey of the *MLA Bibliography* since 1981 (including dissertation abstracts as well as books and articles) finds thirty-one items on the *Ancrene Wisse* (c. 1200), thirty-one on the *Owl and the Nightingale* (c. 1250), forty-five on Laȝamon's *Brut* (c. 1200) thirty-seven on the *South English Legendary* (c. 1300), two on Robert of Gloucester's *Chronicle* (c. 1300), eleven on the writings of Robert Mannyng (c. 1303–38), and forty-three on the writings of Richard Rolle (c. 1340–50).[113] These are the surviving precedent texts whose language has offered the most generous opportunity for historicizing Chaucer's language in this book – the precedent Middle English texts that measure the relative novelty of anything that Chaucer did – and these studies are completely engulfed by the 2,754 articles and dissertations and books on Chaucer which have appeared since 1981.[114] As Charles Muscatine has bravely put it, "there is abroad in our time a sort of Chaucer religion."[115] It is a religion for which Lydgate and Hoccleve were apostles, for which Dryden served as a disciple, and in which Chaucer scholars still, often, profess their fervent faith. Piety in this religion, it almost goes without saying, is maintained by market forces – by students who find Chaucer more interesting to read than other writers, by institutions that need to hire qualified teachers of Chaucer to teach these students, by hiring practices that increasingly award jobs to those scholars who can certify their knowledge of Chaucer through publication on his writing. And here it is probably germane – and inevitable – that I acknowledge what this book gains from its circumscription in the very circle that I am trying to describe, and which I claimed earlier must circumscribe any study of Chaucer's English. My own scholarship, in its beginnings, was meant to offer a general history of what I called the "rise of English as a literary language": it was to

---

112 Fisher, *The Importance of Chaucer*, p. 29.
113 *MLA International Bibliography [computer file]*.
114 Chaucer even overwhelms his named contemporaries. Since 1981, only 169 articles have appeared on Gower and 384 on Langland (*MLA International Bibliography [computer file]*).
115 Muscatine, "Chaucer's Religion and the Chaucer Religion," p. 260.

culminate in a book that would focus most of all on the early Middle English writing that preceded Chaucer. My own capitulation to the necessities of the myth had much to do with my perception that this subject should be treated in a way that would speak to the general concerns of the field, but that capitulation was, of course, itself a way of gathering importance to *this* book. It may be true that the only way to have understood the over-emphasis on Chaucer's language in the history of the "language of England" was to focus on that over-emphasis, but that focus will only add this book to the horde of the 2,754 that embraces Chaucer at the expense of other truly important concerns. Whatever the rationale, the paradoxical result is a study that queries the long-standing emphasis of the importance of Chaucer's English by concentrating almost entirely *on* that English.

The general point of this study, however, is that *if* the myth of origin survives as a piety, however appropriate before a record shaped by its doctrine, then there *is* a ready method for leaping out of the analytic circle: we may carefully, but often, advance the heresy that Chaucer's English does not really matter very much, that Chaucer did not really begin anything at all – and we may try to believe ourselves when we say this. The belief, of course, will come less easily than its tenets are to discern. A book on, say, the making of Robert of Gloucester's English will probably never be written – and, if it were to be, it is unlikely to be a hot item in Middle English studies. The pleasure that reading *Troilus and Criseyde* or the *Canterbury Tales* affords will be greater than the pleasure afforded by reading Robert's *Chronicle* to almost every student and scholar alike, but this appeal is, of course, itself a product of a Chaucerian agenda dictating our estimations of poetic "excellence," demanding the kinds of elucidation scholarship provides. The problem lies only in letting the pleasure of the text – the extent to which Chaucer's writing remains "real" for us – do duty for the "historic estimate." And so, the ambiguity in the agency of the title of this book (*who* made Chaucer's English?) might issue, finally, in a more gentle recommendation: if Chaucer's English is made as much by our attempts to understand it as it was made by the Chaucer who wrote it, then the simple antidote to the myth of origin is some commitment to understanding early Middle English as something more then a tributary to the Chaucerian flood. This earlier English might now be accorded the historical significance that has so often been accorded Chaucer's English not least because its general practice – elucidated more fully than I have been able to elucidate it here – will finally allow us to understand *Chaucer's* English. The myth of origin may be right about Chaucer, in other words, but it is not right about everything. We may have no choice but a steady appreciation of the English that Chaucer made, but we need not remain conscripted to the understanding of linguistic innovation and tradition that this English wants us to have.

PART 2

Words studied

Chaucer's writings

The following list of Chaucer's works sets out the abbreviations used in the index to Chaucer's vocabulary in *Chaucer's Words* (pp. 226–460). For convenience of cross-reference these abbreviations match those used in Benson's *Glossarial Concordance*.

This list is also intended to make manifest the assumptions about the chronological order of Chaucer's writings that I depend upon and analyze in chapter 3, and that I have also used on occasion to adjust *MED* datings in compiling the subsequent index to Chaucer's vocabulary. Abbreviations are therefore given below in the chronological order for Chaucer's works that I consider "standard." This order generally conforms to the sequence given in "The Canon and Chronology of Chaucer's Works" in the *Riverside Chaucer* (p. xxix), but that sequence has been refined according to discussions of dating in the Riverside's "Explanatory Notes" (information from and references to that material are given in the rightmost column below). As I suggest in chapter 3, neither this list nor this book is intended to advance any *claim* about the probable chronology of Chaucer's writings. I defer to the *Riverside's* sequence because it summarizes a general consensus, but I acknowledge that there remains room and reason for debate in many instances.

The *Canterbury Tales* are grouped together at the end of this chronological sequence in "Ellesmere order" (again, as in the *Riverside Chaucer*) with the exception of the *Second Nun's Tale* and its Prologue, the *Monk's Tale* (except for the "Modern Instances" in that tale), and the *Knight's Tale*, since Chaucer places these texts outside the *Canterbury*-frame in the chronologies he gives in his own writings. Except in these cases this arrangement conforms to the general assumption that the *Tales*, as a project, came generally late in Chaucer's career, but it also gives Ellesmere order the force of chronology here, in chapter 3, and in the lexical index below. This is unfortunate, but it is a result that I have found impossible to avoid given the absence of any consensus about the compositional order of most of the *Tales*.

Lyrics for which the *Riverside* provides no dating (*Proverbs, To Rosemounde, Against Women Unconstant, Womanly Noblesse,* and *Merciles Beaute*) are grouped at the very end of this sequence where they least affect conclusions based upon it.

I only list here and analyze in this book the works that the *Riverside Chaucer* attributes to Chaucer with certainty (that is, all those works concorded in Volume I of Benson's *Glossarial Concordance*). I therefore exclude two of the "Poems not Ascribed to Chaucer in the Manuscripts" in the *Riverside* (the *Complaynt d'Amours* and *A Balade of Complaint*), the "Supplementary Propositions" to the *Treatise on the Astrolabe*, and Fragments B and C of the *Romaunt of the Rose*.

Here and throughout this book the *Retraction* is grouped with the *Parson's Tale* and the *Prologue* to the *Man of Law's Tale* is grouped with the *Introduction* to that tale because they are so grouped in Benson's *Concordance*.

Abbreviation	Text	Dates
	BEFORE 1372	
RomA	The *Romaunt of the Rose* (Fragment A)	
ABC	An *ABC*	
BD	The *Book of the Duchess*	[1368–72]
	1372–80	
Pity	The *Complaint Unto Pity*	
Lady	A *Complaint Unto His Lady*	
SNpro	Prologue to the *Second Nun's Tale*	
SNT	The *Second Nun's Tale*	
MkT	The *Monk's Tale* (lines 1991–2374 and 2643–766)	[except "Modern Instances," p. 929]
HF	The *House of Fame*	[1378–80]
Anel	*Anelida and Arcite*	
	1380–7	
PF	The *Parliament of Fowls*	[1380–2]
Bo	*Boece*	["late 1370's or early 1380's," p. 1003]
Tr	*Troilus and Criseyde*	[1382–6]
Adam	*Adam Scriveyn*	
Mars	The *Complaint of Mars*	[c1385]
Venus	The *Complaint of Venus*	[c1385, p. 1081]
KnT	The *Knight's Tale*	[after Tr, p. 826]
FormAge	The *Former Age*	
Fort	*Fortune*	
Truth	*Truth*	

GENT	*Gentilesse*	
STED	*Lak of Stedfastnesse*	
LGW F	The *Legend of Good Women*	[1386–8, p. 1060]
	(Prologue, Text F)	
LGW	The *Legend of Good Women*	
		1388–92
GP	The *General Prologue*	[late 1380's, p. 797]
AST	A *Treatise on the Astrolabe*	[1391–2, rev. 1393]
		1392–5
LGW G	The *Legend of Good Women*	[1394, p. 1060]
	(Prologue, Text G)	
MILPRO	The *Miller's Prologue*	
MILT	The *Miller's Tale*	
RVPRO	The *Reeve's Prologue*	
RVT	The *Reeve's Tale*	
CKPRO	The *Cook's Prologue*	
CKT	The *Cook's Tale*	
INTMLT	Introduction to (and Prologue of)	
	the *Man of Law's Tale*	
MLT	The *Man of Law's Tale*	
EPIMLT	Epilogue to the *Man of Law's Tale*	
WBPRO	The *Wife of Bath's Prologue*	
WBT	The *Wife of Bath's Tale*	
FRPRO	The *Friar's Prologue*	
FRT	The *Friar's Tale*	
SUMPRO	The *Summoner's Prologue*	
SUMT	The *Summoner's Tale*	
CLPRO	The *Clerk's Prologue*	
CLT	The *Clerk's Tale*	
MERPRO	The *Merchant's Prologue*	
MERT	The *Merchant's Tale*	
EPIMERT	Epilogue to the Merchant's Tale	
INTSQT	Introduction to the *Squire's Tale*	
SQT	The *Squire's Tale*	
FRANPRO	The *Franklin's Prologue*	
FRANT	The *Franklin's Tale*	
PHYT	The *Physician's Tale*	
INTPARDT	Introduction to the *Pardoner's Tale*	
PARDPRO	The *Pardoner's Prologue*	
PARDT	The *Pardoner's Tale*	
SHIPT	The *Shipman's Tale*	
PROPRT	The Prologue of the *Prioress's Tale*	
PRT	The *Prioress's Tale*	

ProThop	The Prologue of the *Tale of Sir Thopas*	
Thop	The *Tale of Sir Thopas*	
Mel	The *Tale of Melibee*	
ProMkT	The Prologue of the *Monk's Tale*	
MkT (MI)	The *Monk's Tale*, "Modern Instances" (lines 2375–462)	[p. 929]

1396–1400

ProNPT	The Prologue of the *Nun's Priest's Tale*	
NPT	The *Nun's Priest's Tale*	
EpiNPT	Epilogue to the *Nun's Priest's Tale*	
CYPro	The *Canon's Yeoman's Prologue*	
CYT	The *Canon's Yeoman's Tale*	
MancPro	The *Manciple's Prologue*	
MactT	The *Manciple's Tale*	
ParsPro	The *Parson's Prologue*	
ParsT	The *Parson's Tale*	
Scog	*Lenvoy de Chaucer a Scogan*	
Buk	*Lenvoy de Chaucer a Bukton*	[c. 1396, p. 1087]
Purse	The *Complaint of Chaucer to His Purse*	[c. 1399, p. 1088]
Prov	*Proverbs*	
Ros	*To Rosemounde*	
WomUnc	*Against Women Unconstant*	
WomNob	*Womanly Noblesse*	
MercB	*Merciles Beaute*	

Chaucer's words

The following list of Chaucer's vocabulary is at once an index to the *MED* according to the lexical analysis provided by Benson's *Glossarial Concordance* and a historical gloss on Chaucer's lexis as that history is surveyed in the *MED*. It summarizes the evidence deployed in the discursive part of this book so that readers may study my claims in their iterative detail. In the largest sense, as I suggest in my preface, this index is the *text* that the chapters of Part I read.

I also provide this evidence for readers who might wish to extend the study of Chaucer's lexis in directions I have not pursued. It is therefore designed to give readers a quick and direct path through the barriers of reference between a word in Chaucer's writings and a word's lexical history. Benson's *Concordance* has already accomplished a crucial part of this task by resolving the variety of lexical forms in the *Riverside* to

MED conventions of spelling and, from there, counting a given "word's" frequency of use. To Benson's work I have also added a lexical history that traces the word, through its roots, to its first use in English, and its first use in Chaucer. Much of this information is readily available in the published volumes of the *MED*, but it is not so readily extracted. Textual illustrations in the *MED*'s entries are organized by manuscript date, not proposed date of composition, and even manuscript date only organizes words chronologically under a given subheading (it is possible, in other words, and it does happen, that the earliest recorded use of a word will appear as the last illustration in an *MED* entry). The homogenous typography of *MED* entries (except in the most recent fascicles) makes searching still more difficult. And I have often supplemented the *MED* with historical information from other sources.

As a result, this index has had to reconcile a variety of serious differences in lexical system. Although Benson adheres to *MED* conventions, the boundaries he constructs between Chaucer's "words" often differ significantly from *MED* boundaries. In addition, *MED* conventions are sometimes internally inconsistent as they have changed over the decades of its production. The dating of Chaucer's texts in the *MED* is sometimes so different from consensual chronologies that I have had to intervene. Most importantly, however, as this book goes to press, the *MED* is still in progress. Inasmuch as the *MED* was *less* complete when Benson's *Concordance* was completed I have had access to some finished fascicles of the *MED* that Benson could not consult (and so there are differences between some of my headwords and his). The *MED*'s current incompleteness also means that I have had to turn to incompletely edited materials provided by the *MED* for *U–Z* and, where such information was unavailable (or too copious to cull properly myself), I have had to rely upon the *OED*. The particulars for *U–Z* here will therefore be slowly superseded by the completed *MED*; although I have hoped that my use of *MED* materials will make final differences minor in detail, and that my method for citing the *OED* (reconciling its citations to *MED* conventions and its headwords to projected *MED* forms) will make my data relevant and generally comparable to new *MED* fascicles as they appear.

Even where the different sources employed for this index meshed neatly there were sometimes problematic cases. In the general description of my procedures below I have tried to lay bare all the decisions I took in reconciling these problems. My goal, in every case, has been to keep my decisions as straightforward and transparent as possible. This sometimes means that I have had to split hairs (as I detail below), but adherence to rigid rules was often the only way to keep my own method simple and obvious before the complexity of the information I wished to dispose.

GENERAL PROCEDURES

Entries in this index dispose their information in the following form:

> **headword** reference *etymology* first recorded use FIRST USE IN CHAUCER Frequency

There are 9,117 **headwords** in this index, one for each word in Benson's *Concordance* for which the *MED* provides (or is planning to provide) a lexical history. Where these headwords are also headwords in the *MED* they follow the dictionary's form. For many compounds Benson's headword does not correspond to a headword in the *MED*, although the *MED* does give the word's lexical history under a subheading of the simplex. Of the 951 words in Benson's list but not in this index, most are proper nouns and the rest are compounds for which neither the *MED* nor *OED* gave any lexical history.

References direct the reader to the particular subheading in the *MED* where the *first recorded use* of the headword appears. Because the *MED* occasionally misses the particular citation that I understand to be the *first use in Chaucer*, my designation of that "first use" will not always match the *MED*'s citation at this reference. Occasionally the *MED* will miss a citation in Chaucer entirely, and in such cases, again, my reference will not point to the *first use in Chaucer* I cite, but to whatever "first use" the *MED* gives. Since not all *MED* entries have subheadings, some entries in this index offer no *reference*. Where the *MED* headword differs from my headword, the reference cites both the *MED* headword and the subheading in which the *first recorded use* appears (here, for example, "bedstrau n." appears under "1c s" in the entry for "bed n1."):

> **bedstrau n.** 1c s, bed n1. *(fr. bed n1 & strau n.)* a1200 Body & S.(2) MERT 1

228

Where there is no extant *MED* entry or I have drawn any information in the entry from the *OED* the *reference* gives the *OED* headword under which the word's lexical history may be found surrounded by brackets (here a history for *MED* "unarmen v."can be found in the *OED*, s. v. "unarm v."):

> **unarmen v.** [unarm v.] *fr. armen v.* c1300 SLeg.John (Ld) *SQT* 1

Occasionally I provide two references to subheadings, the second of which is included in curved brackets: { }. In all such cases there is also another reference for a *first recorded use*, the first of which results from an adjustment I have made to an *MED* date (see the section on *first recorded uses* below), the second of which (also in curved brackets) gives the subheading for the *first recorded use* if "first" were to follow the *MED* datings (here "a" is the subheading under which the *MED*'s citation in "(1422) Yonge SSecr." can be found):

> **alich adj.** b {a} *(fr. aliche adv.)* Chaucer {(1422) Yonge SSecr.} *LGW G* 1

Etymologies from *A–T* are generally taken from the *MED*, but I have recorded only source languages and not examples of forms. Because *MED* etymologies are not formally consistent I have silently emended them so that they are: forms of English roots (whether native or borrowed) have been expanded to fit extant (or planned) *MED* entries, elided notations to parts of speech for these roots have been added, and abbreviations for source languages have been standardized according to the norm established by later volumes of the dictionary. All abbreviations for Old English dialects (e.g. *WS* for West Saxon, *A* for Anglian) have been resolved to *OE*. For the expansion of all of these abbreviations see the *MED*'s "Plan and Bibliography" and its supplement.

Etymologies for *U–Z* were generally taken from unpublished but edited records of the *MED*, and, where such information was lacking or unavailable, etymologies were taken from the *OED*. Information from the *OED* is enclosed in square brackets: "[ ]." For the sake of cross-reference I have adapted all *OED* abbreviations to the *MED*'s standard (e.g. the *OED*'s "ad. OFr." becomes the *MED*'s "OF") and I have also so adapted the *OED* forms for roots to the headword this root has (or will have) in the *MED* (e.g. the etymology "f. WEIGH v.'" in the *OED* becomes "fr. weien vi." in this index).

The *MED* is silent on the etymology of a very large number of derived words, including compounds "whose elements are clear" ("Plan and Bibliography," 7), many participial adjectives, and (until recent fascicles) almost all gerunds. The portion of the *OED* I have relied upon is silent on etymologies in many of these same instances. I have, therefore, filled these lacunae in the following ways:

1. Where the *MED* or *OED* offers no etymology for derived forms, I have offered my own conjecture enclosed in parentheses:

    abaishing ger. *(fr. abaishen v.)* Chaucer *BO* 1

    Here, the parentheses around my etymology indicate that the *MED* gives no etymology for this word, and, also, that the root I propose here is recorded in Middle English before the *first recorded use* of "abaishing ger." (Such a conjecture is given even when, as here, the root in question does not otherwise appear in my index.)

2. I have also offered conjectural etymologies to obvious roots even though the root I propose is *not* recorded in either the *MED* or *OED* until after the given headword. All such conjectures are marked with a "*":

    assemblinge ger. 1a *fr. assemblen vi.** (c1280) SLeg.Pass. (Pep) *BO* 5

    Here, although "assemblinge ger." seems likely to have been derived from "assemblen vi.," this root is not, in fact, recorded in Middle English until after "c1280" (in this case, "assemblen vi." is first recorded "a1325").

3. Where either the *MED* or the *OED* give roots in their etymologies that are not recorded in the language until *after* the derived form I have also indicated this fact with angled brackets.

    apposen v. 1a *var. of <opposen v.>* c1300 SLeg.Inf.Chr. (Ld) *SNT* 1

    This etymology indicates that, although the *MED* gives it as a root, "opposen v." is not recorded in Middle English until *after* "apposen v."

The *first recorded use* cites texts and dates according to the *MED* "title stencil" for that text (as expanded in this dictionary's "Plan and Bibliography" and its supplement) and I understand "first" with respect to "recorded use" to be that text in an *MED* entry which has the earliest proposed date of *composition*. These dates of composition are enclosed in parentheses if the *MED*'s editors thought the date they had proposed was "at least 25 years earlier" than the date of the manuscript being cited. Manuscript dates that precede such dates of composition in *MED* title stencils are, however, *not* included in this index.

The lexical history for headwords from *U–Z* was collected from edited and unedited slips of quotations which I consulted at the offices of the *MED* in Ann Arbor. These citations are presented exactly as citations taken from the printed *MED*. Where *MED* slips were unedited and too voluminous for careful examination, or where *MED* information was unavailable to me, I have consulted the *OED*, converted its forms to *MED* conventions, and enclosed the citation (to indicate its source) in brackets:

unwit n. [unwit sb.] *[fr. wit n.]* [?c1200 Orm.] MARS 2

Here (in addition to the etymology, also drawn from the *OED* and re-solved to *MED* convention) I have drawn this *first recorded use* from the *OED*, s. v. "unwit sb." but converted the *OED*'s form "c1200 ORMIN" to the form of the *MED*'s "title stencil" for this text. Wherever I have drawn on the *OED* for any citation I have redated *all* the cita-tions in the given *OED* entry according to *MED* dating so that the *first recorded use* I am reporting *would be* the earliest citation in the *MED* were it relying only on the *OED*'s data.

Where the *MED* cites a number of texts whose date of composition is exactly the same I have arbitrarily (and silently) taken the first citation in the entry (i.e. the stencil under "1a" in preference to the identical citation under "1b"). When sorting texts with identical *years* of composition but different qualifying indications concerning the same date, I have taken citations according to the following chronological hierarchy: I understand texts whose manuscript date is identical to their composition date as "earlier" than texts whose composition date differs from (i.e. is earlier than) the manuscript in which it is cited; I understand "*ante*" datings to come before specific datings, specific datings to come before "*circa*" datings, and "*circa*" datings to come before questionable datings (those marked with a "?"). For the group of texts dated around 1200 (the date around which most of the texts requiring decision in this regard cluster) I have ordered *MED* citations as follows (with the first listed text as "earliest" and the last listed text as "latest"):

> a1200 Wor.Aelfric Gloss.
> c1200 Wor.Serm. in EGSt.7
> ?c1200 Orm.
> a1225 (c1200) Vices & V.(1)
> c1230 (?a1200) Ancr.

I also rely upon this hierarchy in my conjectural etymologies for determining whether a given root was recorded prior to a derived headword.

I have *departed* from *MED* datings in the case of certain texts by Chaucer. For citations from Fragment A of the *Romaunt of the Rose* (generally cited as "(?a1400) RRose" in the *MED*) and many citations from the *Astrolabe* (which, although dated to "1391" in some *MED* entries is often cited as "c1400 *Chaucer Astr. [Brussels]") I have adjusted *MED* datings to my own: so Fragment A of the *Romaunt* becomes "before 1372" and the *Astrolabe* is always "1391." All such redatings are indicated in the index as I give both forms of *first recorded use*:

> **almaunder n.** *OF* Chaucer {(a1382) WBible(1)} *ROMA* 1

Here, the *MED* cites "almaunder n." in "(?a1400) RRose" but my re-dating of the *Romaunt* (to "before 1372") makes the *MED*'s citation of that text the *first recorded use*. The secondary citation in this entry (in curved brackets) shows that the *MED*'s citation in "(a1382) WBible(1)" *would* be the *first recorded use* in the absence of my redating. In this case and throughout, the citation *not* in curved brackets is the one I use in all figures and examples in Part 1.

Where the *MED* cites a text with *exactly* the same date as a text by Chaucer, and this is the earliest work cited, I have taken the text that is *not* by Chaucer as the *first recorded use*. This was not, in fact, a common circumstance, but since the presumption this book generally addresses is Chaucer's "invention" of certain English forms it seemed important to record all the instances in which Chaucer's use was *not* first.

My general reliance on the *MED* for a history of English means that the Old English history of words is ignored in my citation of *first recorded use*. The cut-off date for Middle English in the *MED* (c. 1100) is the cut-off date for "first uses" in my list. I have allowed this arbitrary partitioning because my etymology everywhere shows when a Middle English word was also an Old English word. Moreover, the category of Old English words not recorded in Middle English until some time after 1100 turns out to be an interesting one (see chapter 4, pp. 160–167), and it is only possible to describe it by cleaving strictly to the *MED*'s barriers of reference.

The following kinds of citation in the *MED* are *disregarded* for the purposes of this index, even though the *MED* dates them earlier than the "first recorded use" I give:

1. Citations in the *MED* to texts that are (apart from the headword in question) *not* in English. Such citations are certainly valuable as evidence of the fluidity of linguistic boundaries in England and to a word's pre-English history, but since it was my purpose to measure Chaucer's language against precedent *English* lexical practice, I have understood such information to be irrelevant.
   [*Note A*: I have, however, taken non-English citations as *first recorded uses* where the language of the passage specifically identifies the word *as* English (e.g. I take the first recorded use of "cherl n." in the example "Lahslit, quem Angli vocant ceorlman" because the cited Latin describes "ceorlman" as an English word).]
   [*Note B*: By the same logic I have cited as a *first recorded use* any use of a word in a gloss, since, although the context of a gloss is essentially non-English, I take the implicit claim of glossing to be that a given word *is* English as it makes a non-English document intelligible to English speakers.]
2. Uses of a word as a proper noun (in place names or surnames) unless the word in question is used by Chaucer *as* a proper noun.

The *first use in Chaucer* gives the first time a given word appeared in a text by Chaucer as those texts are ordered according to the chronology I give above (pp. 223–6). Where Chaucer's use is too voluminous and Benson's *Glossarial Concordance* does not analyze the word in all its uses "GENERAL" is substituted for any indication of Chaucer's first use.

Where a word appears in only one of Chaucer's texts (even if it appears in that text several times) the text is italicized in this column:

absolut ppl. a *L* Chaucer *Bo* 9

Here, "*Bo*" indicates that this word only appears in Chaucer's *Boece* even though it is used nine times in that text. The *frequency* gives the number of times an individual word is used by Chaucer in the texts concorded in Volume I of Benson's *Glossarial Concordance*. These figures are taken directly from Benson.

a indef. art. 1a *OE* a1121 Peterb.Chron. GENERAL 5543
a interj. 1b *[?OF]* ?c1200 Orm. ROMA 41
a n1. a *no etym.* ?c1200 Orm. TR 22
abaishen v. 1b *cp. OF* (c1303) Mannyng HS ROMA 14
abaishing ger. *(fr. abaishen v.)* Chaucer *Bo* 1
abak adv. 1a *OE* ?c1200 Orm. MiLT 3
abakward adv. b *(fr. abak adv. & -ward suf.)* (c1280) SLeg.Pass (Pep) *Bo* 1
abandonen v. 2a *OF* Chaucer MEL 4
abaten v. 2a *OF* c1300 SLeg (Ld) ROMA 15
abaven v. b *OF* (c1303) Mannyng HS *BD* 1
abbeie n. 1 *OF* c1300 SLeg.Becket (Ld) SHIPT 4
abbesse n. *OF* c1300 SLeg.(Ld) *WBPRO* 1
abbot n. a *OE & ML* a1121 Peterb.Chron. GP 8
abedde adv. a *fr. on bedde phr.* ?c1200 Orm. TR 17
abeggeth adv. *fr. *on beggeth phr.* (?a1387) PPl.C (Hnt) FRANT 1
abette n. *OF & ML (fr. OF)* c1330 Adam & Eve(1) TR 1
abhominable adj. 2a *L & OF* (c1303) Mannyng HS SUMT 10
abhominacioun n. 1b *L & OF* c1350 MPPsalter INTMLT 3
abiden v. 7a b *OE* a1121 Peterb.Chron. ROMA 96
abiding ger. 1 *(fr. abiden v.)* (1340) Ayenb. *Bo* 2

abien v. 2a *OE* a1126 Peterb.Chron. ROMA 19
abilite n. 1 {1} *OF* Chaucer {(a1398) *Trev.Barth.} AST* 1
a-blakeberied ppl. *fr. on & blakberieth phr.* * Chaucer PARDPRO 1
able adj. 3b *OF; L* (a1338) Mannyng Chron.Pt.1 ROMA 21
ablen v. 2c *fr. able adj.; cp. OF* Chaucer *Bo* 2
ablucioun n. *L* Chaucer CYT 1
abod n. 1b *cp. OE & abiden v.* (?a1200) St.Juliana HF 4
aboundaunce n. 2 *L,OF* (1340) Ayenb. *Bo* 13
aboundaunt adj. 2a *L & OF* Chaucer *Bo* 7
aboundauntli adv. a *fr. aboundaunt adj.* (a1382) WBible(1) MLT 1
abounden vi. 1a *OF & L* c1325 Dream Bk(1) ABC 9
abouten adv. 6a *OE* a1121 Peterb.Chron. ROMA 79
abouten adv. as adj. 2 *(fr. abouten adv.)* (c1200) Vices & V.(1) ROMA 22
abouten prep. 1a *(fr. abouten adv.)* a1121 Peterb.Chron. ROMA 94
aboven adv. 1a *OE* (c1200) Vices & V.(1) HF 25
aboven adv. as adj. a *(fr. aboven adv.)* (c1250) Gen.& Ex. SNT 39
aboven prep. 1c *fr. aboven adv.* * ?c1200 Orm. ROMA 43
abreggen v. 4e *OF* (c1303) Mannyng HS TR 9

abregginge ger. 2a *(fr. abreggen v.)* Chaucer BO 3

abreiden vi. 1a *OE* c1175 Bod.Hom. BD 10

abrochen v. b *OF* (?c1380) Pearl *WBPRO* 1

abrode advi. 2a *fr. on brode phr.* (c1280) SLeg.Pass. (Pep) *SQT* 1

absence n. a *OF* (c1378) PPl.B (Ld) BO 16

absent adj. (& n.) a *L & OF* Chaucer ANEL 10

absenten v. c *OF & L* Chaucer *ABC* 1

absolucioun n. 1a *L & OF* (?a1200) Trin.Hom. GP 2

absolut ppl. a *L* Chaucer BO 9

absolutli adv. c *fr. absolut ppl.* Chaucer BO 1

abstinence n. 1 *OF & L* (1340) Ayenb. HF 12

abstinent adj. *L* Chaucer *PARST* 1

abusioun n. 3 *OF & L* (a1325) Cursor TR 4

a-caterwawed adv. *[?]* Chaucer *WBPRO* 1

acceptable adj. 1a *OF & L* (?c1378) Wycl. OPastor *SUMT* 1

accepten v. 1a *L* Chaucer SNPRO 11

accesse n. 1b *OF & L* c1300 SLeg. (Ld) TR 3

accident n. 2b *L* (c1380) Wycl.Papa HF 5

accidental adj. c *ML* (1386) RParl.FM *MEL* 1

accidie n. 1a *ML (fr. Gr.) & OF* (?a1200) Ancr. *PARST* 18

accioun n. 2a *AF & L* (a1338) Mannyng Chron.Pt.2 ABC 4

accomplisshen v. 1a *OF* Chaucer BO 19

accomplisshing ger. *(fr. accomplisshen v.)* Chaucer *PARST* 1

accord n. 1c *OF* a1250 Owl & N. BD 27

accordable adj. *OF* Chaucer BO 2

accordaunce n. b *OF* (c1303) Mannyng HS ROMA 4

accordaunt adj. 1d *OF* (c1280) SLeg.Pass. (Pep) PF 7

accorden v. 1b *OF* a1121 Peterb.Chron. ABC 63

according ppl. 2a *(fr. accorden v. & accorden v.)* c1300 SLeg.(Ld) BO 7

accounte n. 2a a *OF* (c1280) SLeg.Pass. (Pep) SHIPT 3

accounten v. 6 *OF* (c1280) SLeg.Pass. (Pep) BD 4

accountinge ger. *(fr. accounten v.)* Chaucer BO 1

accusacioun n. a *OF & L* Chaucer BO 2

accusement n. b *OF* Chaucer TR 1

accusen v. 1a *OF & L* c1300 SLeg.Becket (Ld) ROMA 21

accusinge ger. *(fr. accusen v.)* (?a1300) KAlex. BO 5

accusour n. a *OF* (a1349) Rolle MPass.(2) BO 16

accustomaunce n. *OF* Chaucer MKT 2

achat n. 1b *CF, AF* Chaucer BO 2

achatour n. *AF, CF* Chaucer GP 1

ache n1. *OE* c1150 Hrl.HAPul. TR 1

acheken v. a *OE* (?a1200) Trin.Hom. BO 2

achekked ppl. *(fr. acheken v.)* Chaucer HF 1

acheven v. 1c *OF* c1300 SLeg.Becket (Ld) HF 10

acloien v. 1b *cp. OF* c1330 Why werre PF 1

acoien v. b *OF* a1375 WPal. BO 2

acompas adv. *OF* Chaucer LGW F 1

acte n. 1a *OF & L* Chaucer HF 7

actif adj. 3 *OF & L* (1340) Ayenb. BO 1

actual adj. 2b *L & OF* (a1333) Shoreham Poems *PARST* 1

acursen v. 2a *cp. OE* (?a1200) *Ancr. ROMA 10

a dai, adai phr. & adv. a *fr. on dai phr.* (?a1200) Lay.Brut TR 3

Adam n. a *[Heb.]* ?c1200 Orm. ABC 22

adamaunt n. 2 *L & OF, fr. Gr.* Chaucer ROMA 4

adauen vi. 2a *(fr. dauen v.)* (?a1300)
KAlex. TR 2

adden v. 1a *L* Chaucer Bo 17

adieu adv. 1a *OF* Chaucer *TR* 2

adjeccioun n. *L* a1325 MS.Rawl.B.520
Bo 1

adjuracioun n. *L* Chaucer PARST 1

administracioun n. 2 *L & OF* (a1333)
Shoreham Poems Bo 1

administren v. 1a *OF & L* Chaucer Bo 2

adoun adv. 1a *OE* c1150 PDidax.
GENERAL 105

adoun prep. b *fr. adoun adv.* c1325 Horn
(Hrl) *TR* 1

adouren v. 1a *OF (fr. L)* Chaucer *MKT* 1

adouring ger. *(fr. adouren v.)* Chaucer
PARST 1

adournen v. a *OF & L* Chaucer *TR* 1

adreden v. 1a *OE* (?c1175) PMor. (Lamb)
ROMA 10

adressing ger. a *(fr. adressen v.)* Chaucer
Bo 1

adversaire n. & adj. a *OF* Chaucer ABC
1

adversarie adj. *L* (c1385) Usk TL (Skeat)
PARST 1

adversarie n. 3a *L* (1340) Ayenb. MKT
31

adverse adj. *L & OF* Chaucer *TR* 1

adversite n. 1a *OF* (?a1200) *Ancr. ABC
53

advertence n. 2 *OF* Chaucer SNT 4

advocacie n. b *OF & ML* Chaucer *TR* 1

advocat n. c *L & OF* (a1325) Cursor
ABC 10

afer adv. a *fr. on ferre phr. & of ferre phr.*
c1300 SLeg.Edm.King (Ld) HF 8

afered ppl. 1a *(fr. aferen v.)* c1150
Hrl.HApul. *TR* 13

affeccioun n. 2b *OF & L* (?a1200) Ancr.
SNPRO 27

affect n. 2 *L* (c1340) Rolle Psalter (UC
64) *TR* 1

affermen v. 1d *OF & L* (?a1300) KAlex.
Bo 9

affiaunce n. 1b *OF* (c1303) Mannyng HS
SHIPT 1

affilen v. a *OF* Chaucer *TR* 2

affinite n. 1a *OF & L* (c1303) Mannyng
HS Bo 3

afforcen v. 2 *OF* c1300 SLeg.(Ld) PARST
1

affrai n. 2b *OF* (c1303) Mannyng HS HF
7

affraien vi. 3a *OF* (?c1300) Guy (1)
ROMA 8

Affrike n. *L** (?a1300) KAlex. HF 5

afire adv. & pred. adj. 1b *fr. on fire phr.*
(?a1200) Lay.Brut ABC 12

afore-seid ppl. *fr. afore said phr.*
Chaucer MEL 2

afor-yen prep. 1b *fr. afore adv. & yen.*
(1340) Ayenb. *TR* 1

afounden v2. a *OF* Chaucer ROS 1

afrighten v. 1 *OE* c1175 Bod.Hom. *NPT*
1

after adv. 2b *OE* (c1125)
Vsp.D.Hom.Fest.Virg. ROMA 75

after conj. 1c *fr. after that phr.* ?c1150
PDidax. PF 39

after prep. 3a *OE* a1121 Peterb.Chron.
GENERAL 348

after-diner n. 2b, after- pref. *(fr. after
pref. & diner n.)* Chaucer FRANT 2

after-mete n. *(fr. after- pref. & mete n1.)*
(?c1350) SVrn.Leg. MERT 1

after-soper n. 2l, after- pref. *(fr. after
pref. & sopere n1.)* Chaucer SQT 2

after-ward adv. 1 *OE* ?c1200 Orm.
ROMA 32

agame adv. a *fr. on game phr.* c1300
SLeg.Magd.(2) (Ld) *TR* 3

agasten v. 1a *OE* (?a1200) Lay.Brut MKT
37

age n. 2b *OF* (?c1225) Horn ROMA 76

aggreggen v. 2a *OF* (a1349) Rolle
MPass.(1) MEL 5

agilten v. 1 *OE* c1175 Bod.Hom. ABC 20

agon v. 2a *OE* a1200 Body & S.(2)
ROMA 59

agonie n. b *L & OF, fr. Gr.* (c1384)
WBible(1) *MILT* 1

agreable adj. 1a *OF* Chaucer HF 8

agreableli adv. a *fr. agreable adj.*
Chaucer *BO* 2

agreablete n. *OF* Chaucer *BO* 1

agreen v. 2a *OF* Chaucer PF 3

agref adv. b *OF* (?a1300) KAlex. PF 6

agreven v. 1a *OF* (?a1300) Arth.& M. TR
5

agrisen v. 1a *OE* (?a1200) Lay.Brut HF
12

agroteien v. *?OF; ? cp. MDu.* Chaucer
LGW 1

ague n. 1 *OF, fr. L* (c1300) Glo.Chron.A
NPT 1

aguler n. 1a *OF* Chaucer *ROMA* 1

ai adv. 1b *ON* ?c1200 Orm. ROMA 230

aiel n. b *OF (fr. L)* (c1378) PPl.B (Ld)
KNT 1

air n1. 3c *OF (fr. L; ult. Gr.* (?a1200)
*Ancr. BD 37

airish adj. airish bestes phr. *(fr. air n1.)*
Chaucer *HF* 2

aisel n. 3 *OF* a1200 Hat.Gosp. *ROMA* 1

ajournen v. 2a *OF* (a1338) Mannyng
Chron.Pt.2 *ABC* 1

ajuggen v. 1c *OF* Chaucer *BO* 1

ajusten v. *OF* Chaucer *BO* 1

aken v. 1a *OE* c1150 Hrl.HApul. HF 5

aketoun n. a *OF (fr. Ar.)* (?a1300)
KAlex. *THOP* 1

aking ger. *(fr. aken v.)* (1373) *Lelamour
Macer *TR* 1

aknouen ppl. a *(fr. aknouen v.)* c1300
SLeg. (Ld) *BO* 2

akorn n. 1a *OE* a1150 PDidax. *BO* 3

al adv. & conj. 3 *fr.al lim. adj. & n.* * 1123
Peterb.Chron. GENERAL 783

al lim. adj. & n. 1a a *OE* a1121
Peterb.Chron. GENERAL 2709

al n. b *OE* (?a1200) *Ancr. *TRUTH* 1

alabastre n. *L & OF* (a1384) WBible(1)
KNT 1

alai n. 3 *AF* a1325 MS.Rawl.B.520 *CLT* 1

alambik n. *ML & OF, fr. Ar.* Chaucer
TR 2

alas interj. 1a *OF* (?a1200) *Ancr. ABC
370

alaunt n. a *AF* Chaucer *KNT* 1

albeit conj. 5b, al. adv. & conj. *(fr. al adv.
& conj. be it phr.)* (a1325) Cursor *BO* 4

albificacioun n. *ML* Chaucer *CYT* 1

Albion n. *no etym.* (?a1200) Lay.Brut
PURSE 1

al dai phr. & adv. a *(fr. al adj. & dai n.)*
c1175 Bod.Hom. ROMA 23

Aldeboran n. *ML, fr. Ar.* Chaucer *AST*
1

alder n1. 1a *OE* a1200 Wor.Aelfric Gloss.
KNT 1

alderbest adj. *(alder pref. & best adj.)*
not in MED BD 4

alderbest adv. 1, alder- pref. *(fr. alder pref.
& best adv.)* Chaucer BD 3

alderfirst adj. 1, alder- pref. *(fr. alder pref.
& first adj.)* ?a1160 Peterb.Chron.
BD 2

alderfirst adv. 1, alder- pref. *(fr. alder pref.
& first adv.)* ?c1200 Orm. ROMA 12

alderlast adv. 1, alder- pref. *(fr. 'alder'
pref. & 'last' adv.)* ?c1200 Orm. ROMA
1

alderlest adv. 1, alder- pref. *(fr. alder pref.
& leste adv.)* a1300 PMor. (McC) *TR* 1

alderlevest adj. 1, alder- pref. *(fr. alder
pref. & lef adj. & adv.)* Chaucer *TR* 2

alder-man n. 1a *OE* a1121 Peterb.Chron.
GP 1

aldermost adv. 1, alder- pref. *(fr. alder
pref. & most adv. sup.)* a1126
Peterb.Chron. BO 7

aldernext adv. [all a., n. & adv.] *fr. alder-
pref. & next adv.* * [?c1200 Orm.] *PF* 1

alderwisest adj. [all a., n. & adv.] *[fr. all
adj. & wisest sup.]* [(?c1350) Mirror
St.Edm.(4) (Thrn)] *TR* 1

aldiran n. *ML, fr. Ar.* a1223 Cmb.Hh.6.8
Stars *SQT* 1

ale n. 1a *OE* a1121 Peterb.Chron. GP 23

aleie n. 2b *ML (fr. OF) & OF* (a1382) WBible(1) TR 4

ale-stake n. 4e, ale n. *(fr. ale n. & stake n.)* Chaucer GP 2

Alexandrin n. *[OF & L]* Chaucer *ROMA* 1

al-gates adv. 3c *ON* (?a1200) Ancr. BD 61

Algomeisa n. *ML, fr. Ar.* Chaucer *AST* 1

Alhabor n. *ML, fr. Ar.* Chaucer *AST* 2

alich adj. b {a} *(fr. aliche adv.)* Chaucer {(1422) Yonge SSecr.} *LGW G* 1

alienen v. 2b *L & OF* c1350 MPPsalter *BO* 1

alies n. pl. *OF* Chaucer *ROMA* 1

alighten vi. 1a *OE* a1123 Peterb.Chron. ABC 10

aline adv. *? cp. aright adv.* Chaucer *AST* 1

alive adj. & adv. 1a *fr.on live phr.* (?c1175) PMor. (Lamb) *ROMA* 15

alkali n. *ML, fr. Ar.* c1330 SMChron. (Auch) *CYT* 1

alkamistre n. *OF & ML* Chaucer *CYT* 1

alkaron n. *cp. ML, fr. Ar.* Chaucer *MLT* 1

al-kinnes adj. *OE* ?c1200 Orm. *HF* 1

allegeaunce n2. 1 *AF* (?a1300) Arth.& M. *WomNob* 1

alleggen vi. 1 *OF; L* c1300 SLeg.Becket (Hrl) HF 4

alleggen v2. 1b *OF* (?c1280) SLeg.OTHist. (Ld 622) *BO* 1

alliaunce n. 2a *OF* (c1300) Glo.Chron.A ABC 17

allie n. 2c *fr. allien v.* Chaucer SNT 4

allien v. 2b *OF* (c1300) Glo.Chron.A PITY 8

allouen v. 5a *AF (fr. L)* (a1325) Cursor *BO* 2

Almageste n. *ML, fr. Ar. (ult. Gr.)* (c1386) Almanac (1647) MILT 3

almaunder n. *OF* Chaucer {(a1382) WBible(1)} *ROMA* 1

almenak n. *ML, fr. Ar.* (a1388) *Wallingford Exafrenon *AST* 2

almes-dede n. 1a *OE* c1175 Bod.Hom. MLT 2

almesse n. 1a *OE* ?a1160 Peterb.Chron. MLT 12

almicanteras n. *ML, fr. Ar.* Chaucer *AST* 31

al-mighti adj. 1a *OE* a1121 Peterb.Chron. ABC 23

al-most adv. 1 *fr. al adv. & conj. & most adv. sup.* a1123 Peterb.Chron. *ROMA* 52

almuri n. *ML, fr. Ar.* Chaucer *AST* 9

Alnath n. *Ar.* Chaucer *FRANT* 1

aloes n. b *ML (fr. Gr.), OE* c1150 PDidax. *TR* 1

alofte adv. 1a *fr. on lofte phr.* ?c1200 Orm. PF 3

alonde adv. 1a *fr. on londe phr.* (?c1175) PMor. (Lamb) *LGW* 2

al-one adv. & adj. 1a a *fr. al one phr.* ?c1200 Orm. *ROMA* 78

along adj. a *fr. OE* (a1325) Cursor *TR* 2

along adv. & prep. 1a *OE* (?a1200) Lay.Brut *ROMA* 2

alosen v. 2a *OF* (c1280) SLeg.Pass. (Pep) *TR* 1

aloude adv. a *fr. on loude phr.* (c1280) SLeg.Pass. (Pep) *HF* 1

alpe n. a *?* (c1353) Winner & W. *ROMA* 1

al-redi adv. 1b *fr. al-redi phr. & adj.* c1300 SLeg. (Ld) *AST* 1

also adv. 1c a *OE* a1131 Peterb.Chron. GENERAL 320

altercacioun n. 1b *L & OF* Chaucer MERT 2

alteren v. 2a *ML* Chaucer *TR* 1

alther-fairest adj. 1, alder- pref. *(fr. alder-pref. & fair adj.)* (?a1200) Trin.Hom. *ROMA* 3

alther-fastest adv. *(fr. alder- pref. & faste adv.)* MED Suppl *HF* 1

alther-worst adj. 1, alder- pref. *fr. alder pref. & worst adj.* *c1250 Owl & N. *BO* 1

al-though conj. 2 *(fr. al conj. & though*

conj.) c1325 Middelerd for mon.
ROMA 93

altitude n. 1 *L* (c1386) Almanac (1647)
AST 65

al togeder phr. & adv. a *(fr. al adv. &
conj. & togeder adv.)* c1150 PDidax.
BO 1

alum n. 2b *OF, fr. L* (1373) *Lelamour
Macer HF 2

al-wei adv. 1 *OE* (?1200) *Ancr. ROMA
234

amadriades n. pl. *L, fr. Gr.* Chaucer
KNT 1

amaien v. a *AF, CF* (?a1300) Arth.& M.
TR 2

amalgaming ger. *fr. amalgamen v.* *
Chaucer *CYT* 1

amased ppl. 2 *OE* (?a1200) Ancr. *CYT* 1

Amazones n. pl. *L, fr. Gr.* Chaucer *KNT*
1

ambages n. *OF, fr. L* Chaucer *TR* 1

ambassadour n. *OF* Chaucer TR 4

ambassadrie n. b *OF & ML* Chaucer
MLT 1

ambes-as n. b *OF & L* (a1250)
Harrow.H. *INTMLT* 1

amble n. *OF* Chaucer *THOP* 1

amblen v. b *CF, AF* (?c1300) Guy(1)
WBPRO 2

amblere n1. a *fr. amblen v.* Chaucer *GP* 1

ameled ppl. *cp. CF* Chaucer *ROMA* 1

amen interj. 1b *L, ult. Heb.* a1121
Peterb.Chron. ABC 11

amendement n. 4 *OF* c1230 *Ancr.
(Corp-C) RvT 6

amenden v. 1a *OF, fr. L* c1230 *Ancr.
(Corp-C) ROMA 49

amender n. a *fr. amenden v.* (c1395)
WBible(2) *WBT* 1

amendes n. 1a *OF* (?a1300) Tristrem BD
3

amenusen v. 1 *OF* a1325 MS Raw.B.520
BO 14

amenusinge ger. *(fr. amenusen v.)*
Chaucer *BO* 3

amerciment n. b *AF & AL* (a1325)
MS.Rawl.B.520 *PARST* 3

ameven v. 1a *OF* ?a1325 The grace of ihu
BO 4

amiable adj. {2} *OF* Chaucer {a1375
WPal.} ROMA 8

amidde adv. & prep. 2b *OE* (?a1200)
Lay.Brut ROMA 22

amie n. b, bel-ami n. *OF* (?a1200) *Ancr.
INTPARDT 1

amis adv. 3 *ON* (?c1200) HMaid. BD 43

amis pred. adj. a *fr. amis adv.* (c1300)
Glo.Chron.A TR 6

amonesten v. 1 *OF & ML* (1340) Ayenb.
BO 4

amonestinge ger. b *(fr. amonesten v.)*
(?1348) Rolle FLiving BO 3

amonges adv. 3a *(fr. amonges prep.)*
(?a1200) Lay. Brut ROMA 4

amonges prep. 3 *OE* a1121 Peterb.Chron.
GENERAL 127

amonicioun n. a *OF & L* Chaucer *BO* 1

amorous adj. 1b *OF* (?c1300) Guy(1)
ROMA 14

amorousli adv. a *(fr. amorous adj.)*
Chaucer *MERT* 1

amorwen adv. 1c *OE* c1150 PDidax. BD
12

amounten v. 1 *OF* c1275 Ken.Serm. KNT
6

amphibologie n. *ML, ult. Gr.* Chaucer
TR 1

ancille n. *L & OF* Chaucer *ABC* 1

ancle n. 1a *OE* c1150 PDidax. *KNT* 1

and conj. (& adv.) 1a a *OE* (1100)
Chart.St.Paul in RHS ser.3.58
GENERAL 17304

anelas n. a *cp. OF (fr. Gmc.)* (c1300)
Havelok *GP* 1

an-ende adv. 23, 5b, ende n1. *(fr. on ende
phr.)* (a1325) Cursor *ROMA* 1

angel-hok n. 1b, angel n. *(fr. angel n. &
hok n.)* (a1382) WBible(1) *MARS* 1

anger n. 1a *ON* (c1250) Gen.& Ex.
ROMA 18

angle n2. 1a *OF & L* Chaucer HF 10
angri adj. {2} *fr. anger n.* Chaucer
{(?c1380) Cleanness} ROMA 15
angrili adv. a *fr. angri adj.* (?a1387)
PPl.C (Hnt) PARST 1
angwisshe n. 2 *OF* (?a1200) Ancr. BO
12
angwisshen v. a *OF* (a1338) Mannyng
Chron.Pt.2 *BO* 1
angwisshous adj. 2a *OF* (?a1200) Ancr.
ROMA 13
anhongen v. 1a *cp. OE* (?a1200) Lay.Brut
ROMA 8
ani lim. adj. 3 *OE* (1100) Chart.St.Paul
GENERAL 567
anientishen v. 1a *OF* (c1340) Rolle
Psalter (UC 64) *MEL* 1
anightes adv. *fr. on night phr.* (?a1200)
Lay.Brut ROMA 16
animal adj. 1 *L* Chaucer *KNT* 1
ani-thing phr. & n. 1a *fr. ani thing phr.*
a1121 Peterb.Chron. LADY 7
ani-wher adv. (*fr. ani lim. adj. & wher*
adv. & conj.) Chaucer BO 4
anker n. 3b *OE, OF & L* (*ult. Gr.*) a1200
Wor.Aelfric Gloss. BO 3
annexen v. 3a *ML & OF* Chaucer PITY 5
annueller n. *OF* Chaucer *CYT* 1
annunciat ppl. *L* Chaucer *MKT* 1
anoi n. 1a *OF* (?a1200) *Ancr. BO* 8
anoiaunce n. *OF* Chaucer PARST 2
anoien v. 4b *OF* c1275 Ken.Ser. PF 37
anoiful adj. (*fr. anoi n.*) Chaucer *MEL* 1
anoious adj. c *OF* Chaucer BO 6
anoiousli adv. (*fr. anoious adj.*) Chaucer
BO 1
an-on adv. & conj. 3 *OE* a1121
Peterb.Chron. GENERAL 455
anon-rightes adv. & conj. a (*fr. an-on*
adv. adv. & righte adv.) (?a1200)
*Ancr. BD 25
another adj. 5b a, other adj. (*fr. on other*
phr.) a1121 Peterb.Chron. GENERAL
178
another pron. 4a f, other pron. (*fr. an*

other phr.) c1175 Bod.Hom. GENERAL
65
answere n. 1 *OE* c1175 Bod.Hom. ROMA
31
answeren v. 1a *OE* a1121 Peterb.Chron.
ROMA 200
answering ger. b (*fr. answeren v.*)
(?a1300) Arth.& M. SNT 3
antartik adj. & n. a {a} *ML* Chaucer
{(a1398) *Trev.Barth.} *AST* 2
Antecrist n. 1 *ML & OF, ult. Gr.* a1150
Vsp.D.Hom. PARST 1
anteme n. 1 *OE (thr. L fr. Gr.)* (?a1200)
*Ancr. PRT 1
antiphonere n. *OF & ML* Chaucer PRT
1
anvelt n. a *OE* (c1350)
Cmb.Ee.4.20.Nominale BD 1
aornement n. *[OF]* not in MED CLT 2
apaien v. 1a *OF* c1250 *St.Marg.(2) LADY
28
apallen v. 1b *OF* (a1333) Shoreham
Poems KNT 4
apart adv. 1a *OF* (a1325) Cursor SHIPT 4
apassen v. 1b *OF* c1300 SLeg.John (Ld)
BO 1
ape n. 2a *OE* a1250 Ancr. (Nero) HF 16
apeiren v. 1a *cp. CF, AF* c1300
SLeg.Kath.(Hrl) HF 6
apert adj. 1a *OF & L* (c1280) SLeg.Pass.
(Pep) HF 5
aperteli adv. 2a *fr. aperte adj. & adv.*
(c1280) SLeg.Pass. (Pep) BO 5
apiken v. (*fr. piken v1.*) (?c1380)
Cleanness GP 1
apocalipse n. 1a *L, fr. Gr.* ?a1200 Orm.
HF 2
apoplexie n. *L, fr. Gr.* (a1387) Trev.
Higd. NPT 1
aposteme n. 1 *ML (fr. Gr.) & OF* (1373)
*Lelamour Macer BO 2
apostle n. 1 *OE, L & OF (fr. Gr.)* (c1125)
Vsp.D.Hom.Fest.Virg. GP 23
apotecarie n. *ML; cp. OF* Chaucer GP 4
apparaunce n. 2a *OF & L* Chaucer HF 7

apparaunt adj. 1b {1c} *OF* Chaucer
{(a1393) Gower CA} *ROMA* 1
appareil n. 2a *OF* (?a1300) Rich. (Auch)
ROMA 7
appareillement n. c *(fr. appareillen v.)*
Chaucer *BO* 1
appareillen v. 1c *OF* c1275 Ken.Serm.
MKT 20
appareilling ger. a *(fr. appareillen v.)*
(a1333) Shoreham Poems KNT 3
appel n. 1a *OE* c1150 Hrl.MQuad.
ROMA 9
apperceiven v. 1a *OF* ?a1300 Fox & W.
BO 12
apperceiving ger. *(fr. apperceiven v.)*
Chaucer *SQT* 1
apperen v1. 1a *OF* c1275 Ken.Serm. ABC
18
apperen v2. *OF* Chaucer *LGW F* 1
appertenen v. 1a *OF & L* Chaucer BO 28
appesen v. 1a *OF* c1300 SLeg.(Ld) BO 13
appetit n. 2a *OF & L* (c1303) Mannyng
HS MKT 24
appetiten v. *fr. appetit n.* Chaucer *LGW*
1
applien v. 4b *OF* (?a1350) Castleford
Chron. *BO* 1
appointen v. 1a *OF* Chaucer TR 5
apposen v. 1a *var. of <opposen v.>* c1300
SLeg.Inf.Chr. (Ld) *SNT* 1
apprentis n. a *OF* (1307) Mem.Bk.York.
in Sur.Soc.120 ROMA 2
appreven v. 2a *OF* (?c1300) Amis BO 8
approchen v. 1b *OF* (c1280) SLeg.Pass.
(Pep) HF 23
approching ger. a *(fr. approchen v.)*
(1386) RParl.FM *PARST* 1
appropren v. 1a *OF & L* a1325
MS.Rawl.B.520 *GENT* 1
approuer n. *AF* Chaucer *FRT* 1
appurtenaunce n. 1 *AF* (?a1300) KAlex.
PARST 1
appurtenaunt adj. 2a *AF; cp. CF*
Chaucer PITY 3
april n. *L* c1150 Hrl.HApul. ANEL 8

Aquarie n. *L* Chaucer *AST* 3
aqueintaunce n. 2a *OF* c1230
*Ancr.(Corp-C) HF 11
aqueinten v. 2a *OF* (?a1200) *Ancr.
ROMA 5
aquiloun n. *L* Chaucer *BO* 2
aquitaunce n. 1 *OF & ML* (a1338)
Mannyng Chron.Pt.2 ABC 3
aquiten v. 4c *OF & ML* (?a1200) Ancr.
TR 5
Arabi n. & adj. d *OF, fr. Ar.* a1225
Lamb.Hom. BD 2
Arabien n. a *OF & L* (?a1300) KAlex.
MKT 3
Arabik adj. & n. b *OF & L* (c1325)
Recipe Painting(1) in Archaeol.J.1 *AST*
1
aracen v. 1 *OF* (a1333) Shoreham Poems
LADY 10
araisen v. 2 *(fr. reisen v1.)* (c1303)
Mannyng HS BO 9
arbitracioun n. 2 *L & OF* Chaucer *MEL*
1
arbitre n. *OF & L* Chaucer *BO* 5
archangel n3. *?* Chaucer *ROMA* 1
arche n. 1a *OF* c1300 SLeg.Patr.Purg. Ast
12
arche-bisshop n. 1a *OE* a1121
Peterb.Chron. *FRT* 1
arche-deken n. *OE (fr. L) & OF* a1121
Peterb.Chron. GP 5
archer n. 1a *OF* c1300 SLeg. (Ld) THOP 2
arche-wif n. *(fr. arche pref. & wif n.)*
Chaucer *CLT* 1
ardaunt adj. 2b *OF, L* (a1333) Shoreham
Poems *BO* 2
ardour n. b {c} *L & OF* Chaucer {?a1425
*Chauliac(1)} *PARST* 1
areden v1. 4 *OE* (?a1200) Lay.Brut BD 5
areste n. 3a *OF* Chaucer KNT 7
aresten v. 1c *OF* a1375 Al other loue BO 6
aretten v. 1a *OF* c1350 MPPsalter BO 5
argoille n. 1a *AF; ult. fr. Gr.* (c1325)
Recipe Painting(1) in Archaeol.J.1
CYT 1

The making of Chaucer's English

arguen v. 1a *L & OF* (c1303) Mannyng HS BD 6
arguing ger. 1 *(fr. arguen v.)* (c1340) Rolle Psalter (UC 64) *LGW F* 1
argument n. 1 *L & OF* c1330 7 Sages(1) PF 21
argumenten v. *OF & L* Chaucer TR 2
Argus n1. c *[L, fr. Gr.]* Chaucer TR 4
Aries n. *L* (a1338) *Wallingford Exafrenon TR 24
a-right adv. 1a *fr. on right phr.* (?a1200) Lay.Brut ROMA 44
arisen v. 11a *OE* c1150 Hrl.MQuad. ROMA 71
arising ger. 1a *(fr. arisen v.)* (1340) Ayenb. BO 16
arist n. 2a *OE* c1175 Bod.Hom. *AST* 1
arivage n. a *OF* Chaucer *HF* 1
arivaille n. 1b *AF* Chaucer *HF* 1
ariven v. 1a *OF* (?a1200) Lay.Brut ROMA 13
arm n. 1a *OE* 1123 Peterb.Chron. BD 94
armee n. b *OF, fr. L* Chaucer *GP* 1
armen v. 1a *OF* (?a1200) Lay.Brut PITY 16
Armenie n. *[L]* (1373) * Lelamour Macer *ANEL* 1
armes n. pl. 1a d *OF* a1250 Ancr. (Nero) MKT 43
arm-gret adj. *(fr. arm n. & gret adj.)* Chaucer *KNT* 1
arm-hol n. *(fr. arm n. & hole n2.)* a1325 Gloss.Bibbesw. *AST* 1
arming ger. a *(fr. armen v.)* (?a1300) Arth.& M. *THOP* 1
armipotent adj. *L* Chaucer *KNT* 2
armles adj. *(fr. arm n.)* Chaucer *MKT* 1
armoniak adj. b, armoniak n. *ML* c1330 SMChron. *CYT* 3
armonie n. 1a *L, fr. Gr.* Chaucer BD 5
armure n. 1a *OF, fr. L* c1300 SLeg.Fran.(1) (Ld) ROMA 10
armurer n. a *OF* Chaucer *KNT* 1
aroue adv. 1a *fr. on roue phr.* (?a1200) Lay.Brut. LGW F 3

aroume adv. 1a *fr. on roume phr.* (c1250) Prov.Hend. *HF* 1
Arpie n. *L, fr. Gr.* Chaucer MKT 2
arrai n. 2a *AF, CF* (a1338) Mannyng Chron.Pt.2 MKT 79
arraien v. 2b *AF* (?a1325) Bonav.Medit.(1) ROMA 31
arrerage n. 1a *OF* a1325 MS.Rawl.B.520 *GP* 1
arrogaunce n. b *OF & L* (c1303) Mannyng HS WBT 2
arrogaunt adj. *OF & L.* Chaucer *PARST* 1
ars n. 2a *OE* a1150 Hrl.HApul. MILT 9
arsenik n. 2 *OF & L* (a1393) Gower CA *CYT* 1
ars-metrike n. a *ML & OF (fr. L, ult. Gr.)* (c1250) Gen.& Ex. KNT 2
art n1. 7a *OF & L* (c1250) Floris. ROMA 44
artelrie n. b *OF & ML* Chaucer *MEL* 1
arten v. 1a *L* (a1382) WBible(1) *TR* 1
artificial adj. 1b *L* Chaucer AST 5
artik adj. & n. a *OF & ML* Chaucer *AST* 14
Artur n. 1a *L, fr. Gr.* Chaucer *BO* 2
arwe n. 4b *OE* (c1200) Vices & V.(1) ROMA 39
as conj. 1a *OE* a1150 Vsp.D.Hom. GENERAL 4389
as n. b *OF, fr. L* Chaucer MKT 2
ascaunce adv. & conj. 1a cp. *OF* (a1333) Shoreham Poems TR 5
ascenden v. 3a *L & OF* (a1382) WBible(1) AST 22
ascendent n. *L & OF* Chaucer HF 46
ascending ger. 3a *(fr. ascenden v.)* Chaucer *AST* 1
ascensioun n. 1b *OF & L* (?a1300) Arth.& M. AST 16
ascri n. 2 *AF* (c1333–52) Minot Poems *TR* 1
ashamed ppl. 1 *OE* (c1280) SLeg.Pass. (Pep) ROMA 14
Asia n. *L & OF* (?a1300) KAlex. HF 2

Chaucer's words

aside adv. 1b *fr. on side phr.* (?a1300)
Rich. (Auch.) BD 9

asken v. 1a a *OE* c1175 Bod.Hom. ROMA
157

askinge ger. 1a *OE* (?a1200) *Ancr.
ROMA 9

aslaken v. 1a *OE* (?c1300) Guy(1) KNT 2

aslepe adv1. 1a *fr. on slepe phr.* ?c1200
Orm. BD 9

asonder adv. & pred. adj. 3a *fr. on
sondren phr.* c1150 Hrl.HApul. BD 8

aspe n. 1a *OE* (?c1300) St.J.List Trees
ROMA 6

aspect n. 1 *L* Chaucer TR 7

aspie n. 1 *AF, & CF* (c1280)
SLeg.Pass.(Pep) TR 3

aspien v. 2b *AF, & CF* a1250 Ancr.
(Nero) ROMA 83

aspiinge ger. b *(fr. aspien v.)* (1340)
Ayenb. *VENUS* 1

aspre adj. a *L & OF* (a1338) Mannyng
Chron.Pt.1 ANEL 16

asprenesse n. *fr. aspre adj.* Chaucer BO 2

assai n. 1b *AF; CF* (c1303) Mannyng HS
BD 16

assaien v. 1a a *AF; CF* (?c1300) Arth.&
M. BD 43

assaillen v. 1a *OF* (?a1200) Ancr. ROMA
15

assaut n. 2a *OF* (?a1200) *Ancr. BO 5

asse n. 2c *OE* c1150 PDidax. MKT 13

assege n. a *cp. OF* c1380 Firumb.(1) TR 7

assegen v. a *OF* (c1300) Glo.Chron.A TR
2

assemble n. 1a *OF* c1300
SLeg.Inf.Chr.(Ld) ROMA 5

assemblen v1. 1 *OF* a1325 Flem.Insur.
SNPRO 25

assemblinge ger. 1a *fr. assemblen v1.* *
(c1280) SLeg.Pass. (Pep) BO 5

assent n. 2b *OF* (?a1300) KAlex. PF 29

assenten v. 1a *OF* c1300 SLeg.Becket
(Hrl) PITY 48

asshe n1. 1a *OE* c1300 SLeg.Kenelm (Ld)
ROMA 4

asshe n2. 1b *OE & ON* c1150 PDidax.
ANEL 12

asshi adj. b *fr. asshe n2.* Chaucer KNT 1

assignen v. 4b *OF, L* c1300 SLeg. (Ld)
BO 7

assise n. 3c *OF* c1300 SLeg.Inf.Chr.
ROMA 5

assoilen v. 1a *OF* c1275 Ken.Serm. BO
10

assoiling ger. b *(fr. assoilen v.)* (c1300)
Glo.Chron.A GP 1

assuraunce n. 4 *OF* Chaucer TR 2

assuren v. 1b *OF* Chaucer PITY 24

asswagen v. 1a *OF* c1300 SLeg. (Ld)
ROMA 7

asterten v. 1a *OE* (?a1200) Lay.Brut BD
18

astoned ppl. 1 *AF* c1300 SLeg.Marg.
(Hrl) HF 17

astonen v. 1 *AF* (1340) Ayenb. HF 3

astoninge ger. 1 *(fr. astonen v.)* Chaucer
BO 3

astoren v. 2a *AF* (c1200) Vices & V.(1)
GP 1

astrelabie n. a *ML & OF (ult. Gr.)*
(?a1300) KAlex. AST 55

astrologer n. b *fr. L* (a1382) WBible(1)
Pref.Jer. TR 1

astrologie n1. a *L & OF* (a1387)
Trev.Higd. AST 4

astrologien n. *OF* Chaucer AST 7

astronomie n1. 1a *L, fr. Gr.* (?a1200)
Lay.Brut BO 6

asur n1. 3b *OF & ML; ultim. Pers.*
(?a1300) Arth.& M. ROMA 5

asweved ppl. *(fr. sweven v.)* Chaucer HF
1

aswouen pred. adj. & adv. *OE* (?a1300)
Arth.& M. LGW 10

at prep. 1a a *OE* a1100 Chron.Tbr.B.4
GENERAL 808

ataken v. 1a *(fr. overtaken v.)* c1300
SLeg.Becket(Hrl) MARS 5

atasten v. 2a *OF* Chaucer BO 1

atazir n. *OF & ML* Chaucer MLT 1

243

a-temple adv. *fr. on- pref.2 & temple n.* *
not in MED *TR* 1
athinken v. a *fr.* *OE* c1300 Lay.Brut
(Otho) *TR* 3
atir n. 1 *fr. atiren v.* c1300 Lay.Brut
(Otho) PF 3
at one phr. a *fr. at prep. & on adv2.*
(?c1225) Horn *TR* 3
at ones phr. 1 *(at prep. & ones adv.)*
c1300 Havelok HF 23
at-reden v. *(fr. reden vi.)* Chaucer *TR* 2
at-rennen v. 1a *OE* c1175 HRood *TR* 2
attamen v. 1a *OF* (?c1300) Bevis *PRONPT*
1
atteinen v. 4 *OF* (?a1300) KAlex. RomA
21
attempraunce n. 1 *OF* (?a1375) Abbey
HG Bo 9
attempre adj. 1a *OF* (1340) Ayenb.
RomA 16
attempreli adv. a *fr. attempre adj.* (c1340)
Rolle Psalter (UC 64) SumT 6
attempren v. 3a *OF* (c1200) Vices &
V.(1) Bo 7
attempringe ger. *(fr. attempren v.)*
Chaucer Bo 1
attencioun n. *OF & L* Chaucer Bo 1
attendaunce n. 2b *OF* Chaucer Bo 3
attri adj. 1a *fr. atter n.* c1150 Hrl.HApul.
PARST 1
attricioun n. a *L & OF* Chaucer *TR* 1
atwein adv. a *fr. OE* (?a1200) Lay.Brut
BD 1
atwinne adv. 1a *fr. on twinne phr.* (a1250)
Bestiary Bo 5
atwixen prep. *cp. bitwixen prep.* (?a1300)
Guy(2) RomA 4
atwo adv. 2a *fr. OE* c1175 Bod.Hom.
SNT 22
auctorite n. 4a *OF* (?a1200) *Ancr. SNT
27
auctour n. 1a *OF & L* (?c1350) SVrn.Leg.
RomA 34
audience n. 2b *OF & L* (?c1350)
SVrn.Leg.Barlaam SNT 23

auditour n. 1 *AF & ML* (a1333)
Shoreham Poems GP 2
aue n. 3b *ON* ?c1200 Orm. MkT 6
augrim n. 1b *OF & ML (fr. Ar.)* (?a1200)
*Ancr. AST 4
augurie n. *OF & L* Chaucer *TR* 2
august n. *L & OF* a1121 Peterb.Chron.
AST 4
auncestre n. a *OF* c1300 SLeg.Becket
(Ld) RomA 8
auncestrie n. 1a *cp.* *OF* (a1338) Mannyng
Chron.Pt.2 *RVT* 1
aungel n. 1a *OF & OE* (c1125)
Vsp.D.Hom.Fest.Virg. RomA 43
aungelik adj. c *OF & L* (a1325) Ipotis *TR*
1
aungelik adv. *(fr. aungelik adj.)* Chaucer
LGW F 1
aunte n. a *AF, CF* c1300 SLeg.John (Ld)
MLT 1
auntren v. 3b *OF* (?a1300) Arth.& M.
RVT 2
aurora n. a *L & OF* Chaucer *LGW* 1
auster n. *L* Chaucer Bo 3
autentik adj. 1a *OF & L* Chaucer BD 1
auter n. 1a *OE & OF* ?c1200 Orm. PF 11
autumpne n. *OF & L* Chaucer Bo 4
availen v. 1b a *prob. AF; cp OF* c1300
Body & S.(5) PITY 57
avalen v. 1b *OF* (?c1300) Guy(1) Bo 3
avarice n. a *OF* (?c1300) Spec.Guy
RomA 34
avaricious adj. b *OF* Chaucer MEL 10
avauncen v. 2b *OF* a1250 Ancr. (Nero)
HF 13
avaunt n. 3 *fr. avaunten v.* (?c1378)
Wycl.OPastor *TR* 6
avauntage n. 2a *OF* c1300 SLeg.Becket
(Ld) KnT 10
avaunten v. 1 *OF* (c1303) Mannyng HS
HF 11
avaunting ger. b *(fr. avaunten v.)* (1357)
Gaytr.LFCatech. RvPRO 2
avauntour n. *OF* Chaucer PF 7
Ave Marie n. 1b *L* (?a1200) *Ancr. ABC 2

avenaunt adj. b *OF* (?a1300) KAlex. ROMA 1

avengen v. 2a *prob. AF; cp OF* (c1378) PPl.B (Ld) PARST 1

aventaille n. 1 *AF; cp. CF* a1375 WPal. TR 2

aventure n. 2a *OF & ML* (?a1200) *Ancr. ROMA 86

aventurous adj. 3a *OF* c1330 Degare BO 4

averil n. *OF* (?a1200) Lay.Brut WBPRO 1

avis n. 6a *OF & ML* c1300 SLeg.Becket (Ld) TR 11

avise adj. *OF* (?a1300) KAlex. LGW 1

aviseli adv. 1 *fr. avise adj.* (?a1325) Bonav.Medit.(1) AST 4

avisement n. 1b *OF* (a1338) Mannyng Chron.Pt.2 PF 13

avisen v. 1a *OF* (c1300) Glo.Chron.A ROMA 58

avisioun n. 1a *OF* c1300 SLeg.Becket (Hrl) ROMA 13

avoi interj. *OF* c1300 SLeg.Becket (Ld) NPT 1

avoue n. 1b *prob. fr. avouen v2.* (a1325) Cursor BD 7

avouen v1. 3a *OF, fr. L* c1300 SLeg. (Ld) CYPRO 1

avouen v2. 1c *cp. OF & L* c1300 SLeg.Bridget(1) (Ld) ANEL 2

avouter n. 1a *OF (L)* (c1303) Mannyng HS FRT 3

avoutrie n. 1a *OF* (c1303) Mannyng HS PF 15

awaite n. 2a *ONF* Chaucer MKT 7

awaiten v. 1a *ONF* c1250 Ancr. (Nero) ROMA 7

awaiter n. a *cp. CF* Chaucer BO 1

awaiting ger. c *(fr. awaiten v.)* Chaucer ANEL 1

awaken v. 1a *OE* c1175 HRood BD 40

award n. a *AF* Chaucer PARST 1

awarden v. a *AF* Chaucer PHYT 2

awei adv. 1b *OE* c1150 Hrl.HApul. GENERAL 164

awei-ward adv. 1a *fr. awei adv.* (c1200) Vices & V.(1) MANCT 1

awepe adv. *fr. on wep phr.* Chaucer TR 1

awerke adv. b *fr. on werke phr. & on warke phr.* Chaucer CKPRO 2

awhaped ppl. *cp. <wap n.> & <wappen v.>* (?a1300) Arth.& M. ANEL 5

awreken v. 1a *OE* (?a1200) Lay.Brut ROMA 4

awri adv. a {b} *(fr. wrien v2.)* Chaucer {(a1393) Gower CA} ROMA 1

axe n1. 1a *OE* c1175 HRood TR 5

ax-tre n. b *axe n2. & tre n.* * (?c1200) St.Juliana AST 2

ayen adv. 2a *OE* c1175 Bod.Hom. GENERAL 255

ayen prep. 4a *fr. <ayen adv.>* c1150 Hrl.HApul. GENERAL 96

ayenes prep. 1b *fr. <ayen adv.> & ayen prep.* ?a1160 Peterb.Chron. GENERAL 133

ayen-ledinge ppl. adj. 3a, ayen- pref. *(fr. ayen pref. & leden v1.)* Chaucer BO 1

ayen-ward adv. 1a *fr. ayen adv.* (?a1200) Ancr. BO 13

azimutz n. b *ML & OF, fr. Ar.* (a1388) *Wallingford Exafrenon AST 12

b n. a *no etym.* (1340) Ayenb. AST 2

ba v. *?* Chaucer MILT 2

babewin n. {a} *OF* Chaucer {(?c1380) Cleanness} HF 1

Babiloine n. *OF & L* Chaucer BD 5

bacheler n. 1a *OF* c1300 SLeg.John (Ld) ROMA 15

bachelerie n. 1 *OF* (c1300) Glo.Chron.A(Ld) CLT 2

Bachus n. *L, fr. Gr.* (?a1300) KAlex. PF 8

bacin n. 1a *OF* (?c1200) St.Marg.(1) ROMA 5

bacoun n. 1a *AF, CF* c1330 Why werre WBPRO 4

badde adj. 3a *?* (c1300) Glo.Chron.A ROMA 19

badde n2. a *fr. badde adj.* Chaucer LADY 4

baddeliche adv. c *fr. badde adj.* (c1300) Glo.Chron.A MEL 2

bagge n1. 1a *ON* (?a1200) *Ancr. FORMAGE 4

baggen v3. c *? cp. OF* c1350 Cmb.Ee.4.20 Nominale *BD* 1

bagge-pipe n. *(fr. bagge n1. & pipe n1.)* c1350 Cmb.Ee.4.20 Nominal *GP* 1

baggingli adv. *fr. baggen v3.* Chaucer *ROMA* 1

bai adj. *OF, fr. L* (c1350) Libeaus TR 4

baiard n1. a *OF* (a1338) Mannyng Chron.Pt.2 TR 3

baillif n. 1a *OF* c1300 SLeg.Becket (Ld) GP 4

baiten v. 2a *ON* ?c1200 Orm. ROMA 5

bak n. 9a *OE* a1121 Peterb.Chron. ROMA 36

bak-biten v. 1a *(fr. bak n. & biten v1.)* a1325 Ne mai no lewed *PARST* 1

bak-bitere n. *fr. <bak-biten v.>* (?a1200) *Ancr. PARST* 4

bakbiting ger. a *fr. bak-biten v.** (?a1200) *Ancr. PARST* 5

baken v. 1a a *OE* c1150 Hrl.HApul. BO 6

baken-mete phr. & n. *fr. baken v. & mete n1.* (c1353) Winner W. *PARST* 1

bakere n. a *OE* 1300 LSSerm. (Jes-O) *NPT* 1

bak-half n. 1c *(fr. bak n. & half n.)* (c1378) PPl.B (Ld) *AST* 2

bak-side n. 1a *(fr. bak n. & side n.)* Chaucer *AST* 2

bak-wardes adv. 1b *(fr. bak n. & -ward suf.)* (a1325) Cursor TR 6

bal n. 2a *prob. OE* (?a1200) Lay.Brut. KNT 3

balade n. 2a *OF* Chaucer LGW F 5

balaunce n. 1a *OF* ?c1200 Wor.Bod.Gloss. BD 7

bale n1. 3 *OE* a1200 Body & S.(2) BD 4

balke n. 2a *OE* a1325 Gloss.Bibbesw. LGW 3

balled adj. 1a *prob. fr. bal n.* c1300 SLeg.Mich. (Ld) KNT 2

bandoun n. a *OF* (?a1200) *Ancr. ROMA* 1

bane n. 1a *OE* (?a1200) Lay.Brut HF 15

banere n. 1a *OF* (?a1200) *Ancr. ANEL 7

banishen v. 2b *fr. OF* (a1376) PPl.A(1) (Vrn) KNT 2

banke n1. 1a *ON* ?c1200 Orm. LGW 2

bapteme n. 1 *OF & ML* (c1303) Mannyng HS *PARST* 6

baptisen v. 1a *OF & L* (c1280) SLeg.Pass. (Pep) SNT 4

baptist n1. *OF & L* ?c1200 Orm. *PardT* 1

bar adj. 14b *OE* (?c1175) PMor. (Lamb) ROMA 28

baraine adj. 1a *AF, CF* (?a1200) Trin.Hom. BO 8

barbar adj. & n. 3 *OF & ML* (c1350) Alex.Maced. *MLT* 1

barbarie n. 3a *OF & ML* (?a1300) KAlex. *FRANT* 1

barbe n. 2 *OF* Chaucer *TR* 1

barbour n. 1a *OF* (?a1300) Tristrem *KNT* 1

barel n. 1a *OF* c1300 SLeg.Judas (Hrl) *CLPRO* 2

barel-ful n. *fr. barel ful n. phr.* Chaucer *WBPRO* 1

bar-fot adv. *OE* (?a1200) Lay.Brut HF 4

bargaine n. 2a *OF* (a1338) Mannyng Chron.Pt.2 GP 2

bargaining ger. 2b *fr. bargainen v.** Chaucer *PARST* 1

barge n. 1b *OF* (?1300) KAlex. LGW 11

bark n. 1 *ON* (a1325) Cursor BO 7

barli-bred n. 3a, barli n. *(fr. barli n. & bred n1.)* (a1376) PPl.A(1) (Vrn) *WBPRO* 2

barm n. 1a *OE* (?a1200) Lay.Brut MKT 4

barmcloth n. 2, barm n. *(fr. barm n. & cloth n.)* Chaucer *MILT* 1

barnage n1. 2a *OF & ML* (?c1225) Horn KNT 2

baroun n. 1 *OF* (?a1200) Lay.Brut ROMA 3

barre n. 1a *OF* (?c1200) St.Kath.(1)
ROMA 5

barren v. 1a *OF* (c1280) SLeg.Pass. (Pep)
ROMA 2

barringe ger. c *(fr. barren v.)* Chaucer
PARST 1

basilicok n. *OF* (1340) Ayenb. PARST 1

basket n. 1a *AF* ?a1300 Jacob & J. HF 2

basten vi. *OF* Chaucer ROMA 1

bataille n. 3 *OF* (?c1225) Horn SNT 49

bataillen v. 1a *OF* (a1338) Mannyng
Chron.Pt.2 *BO* 2

bateren v. 1a *OF* c1330 Degare PARST 1

bath n. 1a *OE* c1150 Hrl.MQuad. SNT 8

bathen v. 1a b *OE* (c1125)
Vsp.D.Hom.Fest.Virg. TR 10

batild ppl. a *OF* c1330 Orfeo NPT 1

baude n. a *OF* (a1376) PPl.A(1) (Vrn) TR
5

bauderie n1. a *fr. baude n.* Chaucer TR
2

bauderie n2. *OF* Chaucer KNT 1

bauderik n. 1 *cp. Cat., MHG & OF*
(?a1300) KAlex. GP 1

baudi adj. *prob. fr. <bauded ppl.>*
(c1378) PPl.B (Ld) CYPRO 1

baume n. 1a *OF* (?a1200) *Ancr. HF 2

be n. 1a *OE* a1131 Peterb.Chron. SNT 11

beau adj. 1a *OF* c1300 SLeg.Becket (Ld)
ROMA 2

beaute n. 1a *OF* a1325 Ichot a burde
ROMA 129

beche n. 1a *OE* a1300 Owl & N. (Jes-O)
KNT 2

bechen adj. *OE* c1150 HApul. CYT 2

bed n1. 1a a *OE* c1150 PDidax. ROMA 121

bedden v. 1b *OE* c1150 PDidax. TR 1

bedding ger. 1a *(fr. bedden v.)* a1200
Wor.Aelfric Gloss. KNT 1

bede n. 1a *OE* c1175
Bod.Hom.Dom.Quadr. GP 1

beden v. 4a a *OE* a1121 Peterb.Chron.
ROMA 12

bed-reden adj. & n. a *OE* c1175
Bod.Hom. SUMT 2

bedstrau n. 1c s, bed n1. *(fr. bed n1 &
strau n.)* a1200 Body & S.(2) MERT 1

bef n. 1a *OF* c1300 SLeg.Magd.(2) (Ld)
SUMT 2

beggen v. a *AF* (?a1200) *Ancr. INTMLT
5

beggere n. 1b *fr. OF (ult. MDu.)* (?c1225)
Horn GP 4

beggerli adv. *fr. beggere n.* Chaucer
ROMA 1

beggestere n. *fr. beggen v.* Chaucer GP 1

being ger. 2b *(fr. ben v.)* (?1300) Arth.&
M. SNT 16

bek n3. a *OF* (a1250) Bestiary PF 4

bekken v. a *fr.bekenen v.* Chaucer TR 3

bel adj. 1a *OF* (?c1300) Guy(1) HF 6

belding ger. 2 *(fr. belden v.)* (?c1375)
NHom.(3) Leg. *HF* 1

beli n. 3a *OE* (c1125)
Vsp.D.Hom.Elucid. SUMT 3

Belial n. a *L, fr. Heb.* (?c1200)
St.Kath.(1) PARST 2

beli-naked adj. 1c, beli n. *(fr. beli n. &
naked adj.)* Chaucer MERT 1

belle n1. 1a a *OE* a1131 Peterb.Chron. BD
17

belle n2. *fr. belle n1.* (a1387) Trev.Higd.
GP 1

belt n. a *OE* a1325 Maximian (Hrl) GP
2

belwen v. a *OE* c1175 Bod.Hom. *HF* 1

bem n. 7b *OE* a1121 Peterb.Chron.
ROMA 20

beme n1. b *OE* a1200 Body & S.(2) HF
2

ben v. 1c *OE* a1121 Peterb.Chron.
GENERAL 14459

benche n. 1a *OE* a1200 Body & S.(2)
ABC 9

benched adj. b *fr. benche n.* Chaucer TR
3

bende n1. 1a *OE & OF* a1121
Peterb.Chron. ROMA 2

benden vi. 1a *OE* c1300 SLeg.Edm.King
(Ld) ROMA 15

bending ger2. *fr. benden v2.* * Chaucer
PARST 1

bene n1. 1c b *OE* ?c1125 Dur-C.Gloss. TR
9

benedicite interj. a *L & OF* (?a1200)
Lay.Brut TR 18

benedight n. a *L* (?a1200) Lay.Brut GP 2

benefice n. 4a *OF & L* c1300
SLeg.Becket (Ld) GP 4

bene-straw 1c b, bene n1. *(fr. bene n1. &
strau n.)* Chaucer MERT 1

benigne adj. 1a *OF* (?a1325)
Bonav.Medit.(1) BD 30

benigneli adv. 2b *fr. benigne adj.* (c1378)
PPl.B (Ld) PF 9

benignite n. 1b *OF* Chaucer SNPRO 21

benisoun n. 3 *OF* a1300 Floris (Vit)
MERT 3

bent n1. 2b *OE* (?c1350) Jos.Arim. KNT
2

berd n1. 1a *OE* (?a1200) Lay.Brut ROMA
27

bere n1. 1c *OE* c1150 Hrl.HApul. MKT
14

bere n3. *cp. OE* Chaucer BD 1

bere n8. 2 *OE* a1200 Wor.Aelfric Gloss.
PITY 18

beren v1. 2b *OE* a1121 Peterb.Chron.
ROMA 331

berere n. 2a *fr. beren v1.* c1275
Ancr.(Cleo: Morton) BO 1

berie n. 2a *OE* ?c1125 Dur-C.Gloss.
(Cokayne) ROMA 4

beril n. a *OF, L* a1300 A Mayde Cristea
HF 2

bering ger. 6a *fr. beren v1. & v2.* (c1250)
Gen.& Ex. MERT 6

berken v. 1b *OE* c1150 Hrl.HApul. BO 1

berking ger. a *(fr. berken v.)* (?a1300)
KAlex. NPT 1

berme n. c *OE* ?c1200 Orm. CYT 1

bern n2. 1a *OE* c1175 Bod.Hom. MKT 5

besaunt-wight n. 1b, besaunt n. *(fr.
besaunt n. & weghte n1.)* Chaucer
ROMA 1

best adj. (sup.) a *OE* a1121
Peterb.Chron. ROMA 35

best adj. as n. 1a *(fr. best adj. (sup.))*
(?c1175) PMor. (Lamb) ROMA 110

best adv. (sup.) 1a *OE* (c1200) Vices &
V.(1) ROMA 108

beste n. 2b *OF* (?a1200) *Ancr. ROMA
120

bestialite n. *OF & L* Chaucer TR 1

bet adj. & adv. as n. a *OE* c1330 Otuel
MILT 1

bet adv. & adj. 3a *OE* 1123 Peterb.Chron.
ROMA 114

beten v1. 5a *OE* c1150 Hrl.MQuad.
ROMA 44

beten v2. 1b *OE* a1131 Peterb.Chron.
LADY 8

beting ger1. 1 *(fr. beten v1.)* (?a1200)
*Ancr. HF 2

bettre adj. 1a *OE* 1131 Peterb.Chron.
ROMA 66

bettre adv. 1a *fr. bettre adj.* ?a1160
Peterb.Chron. ROMA 34

bettre n. a *fr. bettre adj.* c1175 Bod.Hom.
WBPRO 2

bever n1. 1b *OE* c1150 PDidax. GP 1

bi adv. 1a *(fr. bi prep.)* (?a1300) Tristrem
ROMA 33

bi conj. 3 *fr. bi prep. <& bi adv.>* a1225
Vsp.D.Hom. LGW 3

bi prep. 1a c *[OE]* (1100) Chart.St.Paul in
RHS ser.3.58 GENERAL 2287

bibben v. *fr. L* (?c1380) Cleanness RVT 1

bible n. 1a *OF & ML (ult. Gr.)* (a1325)
Cursor BD 9

bibleden v. b *(fr. bleden v.)* (?a1200)
*Ancr. BO 2

biblotten v. *fr. blotten v.* * Chaucer TR 1

bicause conj. 1a *fr. bi cause phr. & adv.*
Chaucer BO 5

bi cause phr. & adv. {b} *(fr. bi prep. &
cause n.)* Chaucer {(?c1380) Cleanness}
BO 4

bicched ppl. adj. *fr. bicche n.* c1225
Wooing Lord PARDT 1

biclappen v. *(fr. clappen v.)* Chaucer
SNPRO 1

bicomen v. 1a *OE* c1150 PDidax. ROMA
21

bidaffed ppl. *(fr. daffe n.)* Chaucer *CLT*
1

bidden v. 1b *OE* a1121 Peterb.Chron.
ROMA 119

biddinge ger. 1a *(fr. bidden v.)* (?a1200)
*Ancr. LGW 3

bidelven v. a *OE* (c1280) SLeg.Pass.
(Pep) *BO* 1

biden v. 8a *OE* 1131 Peterb.Chron. TR 11

bideuen v. a *(fr. deuen v.)* (1340) Ayenb.
BO 1

bidoten v. *(fr. doten v.)* Chaucer *LGW*
1

bien v. 1a a *OE* a1121 Peterb.Chron.
ROMA 51

bifallen v. 4b a *OE* (?c1175) PMor.
(Lamb) ROMA 74

bifallinge ger. a *(fr. bifallen v.)* Chaucer
TR 2

biforen adv. 1a a *OE* a1200 Body & S.(2)
GENERAL 113

biforen conj. a *fr. biforen adv. or biforen
prep.* ?c1200 Orm. BO 6

biforen prep. 7 *OE* ?a1160 Peterb.Chron.
GENERAL 119

biforen-hond adv. b *(fr. biforen prep. &
hond n.)* (?a1200) *Ancr. CYT 1

big adj. 1a a *orig. obs.?* (c1300) Havelok
TR 4

bigamie n. a *OF* a1325 Gen.& Ex. ANEL
5

bigilen v. 1a *(fr. gilen vi.)* (?c1225) Horn
ROMA 38

bigiler n. *fr. bigilen v.* (a1382) WBible(1)
PARST 1

biginnen v. 4a *OE* a1121 Peterb.Chron.
ROMA 207

biginner n. 1 *fr. biginnen v.* Chaucer *BO*
1

biginninge ger. 2c *(fr. beginnen v.)*
(?c1175) PMor. (Lamb) SNPRO 49

bigon v. 4a *OE* c1175
Bod.Hom.Dom.Quadr. ROMA 19

bihalve n. 2a *fr. bi halve phr.* (c1303)
Mannyng HS TR 3

bihated ppl. *fr. hated ppl.* Chaucer *BO* 1

biheste n. 1a a *OE* (?a1200) Lay.Brut PF
21

biheuen v. a *OE* c1175 HRood *HF* 1

bihinde prep. 3 *fr. bihinden adv.* ?c1200
Orm. ROMA 16

bihinden adv. & pred. adj. 1b *OE*
(?c1175) PMor. (Lamb) ROMA 20

biholden v. 1a c *OE* (c1125)
Vsp.D.Hom.Fest.Virg. ROMA 109

biholdere n. a *fr. biholden v.* Chaucer *BO*
2

biholding ger. 1a *(fr. biholden v)*
(?a1200) *Ancr. BO 1

bihoten v. 2b *OE* a1121 Peterb.Chron.
BD 30

bihove n. 1a *OE* (?c1150) Prov.Alf.
(Jes-O) *ROMA* 1

bihoveli adj. c *OE* (c1125)
Vsp.D.Hom.Gest.Virg. TR 3

bihoven v. 1a b *OE* 1131 Peterb.Chron.
ROMA 44

biinge ger. 1a *(fr. bien v.)* a1250 Ancr.
(Nero) *BO* 2

bijapen v. 1a *fr. japen v. or jape n.* (c1378)
PPl.B. (Ld) TR 5

biker n2. a *cp. MDu.* (c1300)
Glo.Chron.A *LGW* 1

biknouen v. 1a *OE* (c1200) Vices & V.(1)
BO 14

bilden v. 2a a *OE* c1175 Body & S.(1)
ABC 8

bildere n. a *fr. bilden v.* (c1280)
SLeg.Pass. (Pep) *PF* 1

bildinge ger. 2a *(fr. bilden v.)* (c1300)
Glo.Chron.A *SUMT* 1

bile n1. 1a *OE* (?a1200) Trin.Hom. HF 2

bileve n. 1a *cp. OE* c1175 Bod.Hom.
SNPRO 7

bileven vi. 5a *OE* (?c1150) Prov.Alf. TR
9

bileven v2. 1a *LOE* a1150 Vsp.D.Hom.
SNT 15
bille n. 2c *AF (CF) & AL (ult. ML)*
Chaucer ABC 14
bilongen v. 4a *(fr. longen v3.)* (1340)
Ayenb. ROMA 4
biloved ppl. b *fr. biloven v.* Chaucer
ROMA 14
binden v. 4a *OE* (c1125)
Vsp.D.Hom.Fest.Virg. ROMA 72
bindinge ger. 3 *(fr. binden v.)* ?c1200
Wor.Bod.Gloss. BO 3
binethen adv. 2a *OE* a1126
Peterb.Chron. AST 3
binethen prep. 1a *fr. binethen adv.* c1150
PDidax. BO 8
binimen v. 2 *OE* a1121 Peterb.Chron.
ROMA 17
binne n. a *OE* 1372 In bedlem is *GP* 1
bi-path n. 1a *(fr. bi adv. & path n.)*
(?a1325) Bonav.Medit.(1) *TR* 1
biquethen v. 1 *OE* (c1200) Vices & V.(1)
TR 5
birche n. a *OE* ?c1300 in James MSS.
St.Johns, Camb. *KnT* 1
birde n1. 3 *fr. OE* ?c1200 Orm. *ROMA* 1
bireinen v. b *fr. reinen v1.* Chaucer *TR* 1
bireven v. 1 *OE* a1126 Peterb.Chron.
LADY 43
biriels n. 1a *OE* a1200 Wor.Aelfric Gloss.
SNT 1
birien v. 1a *OE* ?a1160 Peterb.Chron. BD
15
biriing ger. 2 *(fr. birien v.)* (c1280)
SLeg.Pass. (Pep) SNT 4
birthe n. 7e *cp. OE* c1175
Bod.Nativ.Virg. BO 10
birthen n. 1a *OE* ?a1160 Peterb.Chron.
BO 1
biscornen v. *fr. scornen v.* (a1325) Cursor
PARST 1
bisechen v. 1a *OE* (c1200) Vices & V.(1)
ABC 86
bisegen v. *fr. assegen v.* c1300
SLeg.Edm.King (Ld) MKT 9

bisen v. 2b *OE* (c1125)
Vsp.D.Hom.Fest.Virg. ROMA 5
bisetten v. 2 *OE* ?a1160 Peterb.Chron.
BD 22
bishenden v. a *fr. shenden v.* Chaucer
LGW 1
bishetten v. 1 *fr. shitten v.* (?a1300)
KAlex. *TR* 1
bishop n. 1a *OE* a1121 Peterb.Chron. TR
10
bishreuen v. 1a *fr. shreue n.* (?c1280)
SLeg.Advent, etc. (Eg) *WBPRO* 2
bisi adj. 4 *OE* (c1125)
Vsp.D.Hom.Fest.Virg. ROMA 41
bisi adv. *(fr. bisi adj.)* Chaucer *BO* 1
bisides adv. 1 *fr. OE* (?a1200) Lay.Brut
ROMA 13
bisides prep. 1a *fr. <bisides adv.>*
(?a1200) Lay.Brut ROMA 33
bisien v. 1b *OE* c1175 Bod.Hom. PF 11
bisili adv. 1 *fr. bisi adj.* (?a1200) Lay.Brut
ROMA 29
bisinesse n. 3a *fr. bisi adj.* (a1333)
Shoreham Poems BD 58
bi-smare n. 2 *OE* (?c1150) Prov.Alf.
(Trin-C) *RvT* 1
bismoken v. b *fr. smoke n.* Chaucer *BO* 1
bismotered ppl. *?* Chaucer *GP* 1
bispeten v. *OE* (c1125)
Vsp.D.Hom.Fest.Virg. *PARST* 2
bispotten v. *fr. <spot n1.>* (?a1200)
*Ancr. *BO* 1
bisprengen v. a *OE* c1150 Hrl.HApul.
PITY 1
bistad ppl. 3a a *(fr. stede n1.)* (c1303)
Mannyng HS ROMA 2
bistouen v. 2b *fr. stouen v.* (a1333)
Shoreham Poems ROMA 10
bistriden v. b *OE* (?a1200) Lay.Brut
THOP 1
bitaken v. 1 *fr. taken v.* (?a1200) Lay.Brut
SNT 10
bite n. 2a *OE* c1150 Hrl.HApul. *LGW* 1
bitechen v. 5a *OE* 1121 Peterb.Chron.
THOP 1

biten vi. 2a *OE* (?c1150) Prov.Alf. ANEL 21

bithinken v. 1b b *OE* a1131 Peterb.Chron. ROMA 23

bitiden v. 1b *OE* (?c1150) Prov.Alf. (Mdst) ROMA 93

bitidinge ger. *(fr. bitiden v.)* Chaucer BO 21

bi-time adv. b *fr. bi time phr.* (?c1225) Horn TR 3

biting ppl. 2c *(fr. biten vi.)* (?c1300) Arth.& M. BO 6

bitinge ger. 1a *(fr. biten vi.)* c1300 SLeg.Mich. (Ld) BO 2

bitingli adv. *(fr. biting ppl.)* Chaucer BO 1

bitoknen v. 1 *OE* (c1125) Vsp.D.Hom.Rest.Virg. ROMA 5

bitour n. 1 *OF* (?a1300) Arth.& M. WBT 1

bitraien v. 2b *fr. traien v.* (?c1225) Horn HF 11

bitraishen v. 1 *fr. traishen v.* (a1325) Cursor ROMA 14

bitraisinge ger. *(fr. bitraishen v.)* Chaucer LGW 1

bitrenden v. b *fr. trenden v.* c1250 Louerd asse thu ard TR 2

bitter adj. 1a a *OE* c1175 HRood ABC 27

bitter adj. as n. 1a *(fr. bitter adj.)* a1200 Body & S.(2) TR 1

bitterli adv. 2a *OE* ?c1200 Orm. TR 4

bitternesse n. 1a *OE* c1175 HRood PF 18

bitwene adv. 1a *OE* ?c1200 Orm. TR 6

bitwene prep. 3a d *OE* a1121 Peterb.Chron. HF 16

bitwixe prep. 1a a *OE* a1121 Peterb.Chron. GENERAL 115

biwailen v. 1a *fr. weilen v.* (?a1300) KAlex. (Auch) BD 26

biwaren v. a *fr. waren vi.* *c1330 Pennyw.Wit(1) TR 1

biwepen v. 3 *OE* c1175 Bod.Hom. BO 6

bi-word n. *(fr. bi prep. & word n.)* a1131 Peterb.Chron. TR 1

biwreien v. 1b *fr. wreien v.* (?c1225) Horn SNT 23

biwreiing ger. a *(fr. biwreien v.)* Chaucer MEL 3

biyeten v. 1a *OE* a1121 Peterb.Chron. MKT 5

biyonde prep. 1b *OE* a1121 Peterb.Chron. ROMA 4

bladdre n. 1a *OE* c1150 Hrl. HApul. SNT 1

blade n. 3d *OE* (c1300) Havelok GP 2

blak adj. 4d *OE* ?c1125 Dur-C.Gloss. (Cokayne) ROMA 55

blak n. 4 *OE* (?a1200) *Ancr. BD 17

blaken v. 1a *fr. blak adj.* (?c1200) St.Juliana MKT 1

blame n. 1b *OF* (?c1200) HMaid. ROMA 29

blameful adj. *fr. blame n.* Chaucer MEL 1

blamen v. 1a *OF (fr. L)* ?c1200 Wor.Bod.Gloss. (Hat 116) ROMA 44

blanket n. a *OF* c1300 SLeg.Becket (Ld) SUMT 1

blank-manger n. *OF* (c1378) PPl.B (Ld) GP 1

blase n. a *OE* c1150 Hrl.Apul. TR 1

blasen v2. *? cp. blasen vi.* Chaucer HF 1

blasfemen v. 1a *L & OF* (1340) Ayenb. SUMT 1

blasfemie n. 1a *OF & L* (?a1200) Ancr. PARDT 2

blasfeminge ger. *(fr. blasfemen v.)* Chaucer PARST 1

blasfemour n. *OF* Chaucer SUMT 2

blast n. 2a b *OE* (c1200) Vices & V.(1) BO 6

blasten v. 2a *OE* c1300 SLeg.Chris. (Ld) HF 1

blaundishen v. a *AF* (c1340) Rolle Psalter (UC 64) BO 4

blaunk adj. 1a *OF* (c1250) Floris TR 1

blechen vi. a *OE* (?a1200) Trin.Hom. FORMAGE 1

bleden v. 1a *OE* (?a1200) Lay.Brut MKT 18

bledinge ger. 1 *(fr. bleden v.)* (?c1350)
SVrn.Leg. *LGW* 1

bleine n. 1a *OE* (?c1200) St.Marg.(1)
ROMA 1

blemishen v. 2a *OF* (?a1350) Nicod.(1)
BO 1

blenchen v. 1a *OE & ON* (?a1200)
Lay.Brut TR 3

blenden vi. 2a *OE* ?c1200 Orm. ROMA
21

bleren vi. 1a *OE* ?a1325 Elde makith me
RvT 3

bleringe ger1. c *(fr. bleren vi.)* Chaucer
RVPRO 1

blessed ppl. 1b *OE* c1175 Bod.Hom.
FORMAGE 7

blessen v. 2a *OE* a1121 Peterb.Chron.
ROMA 49

blessinge ger. 1b *(fr. blessen v.)* a1123
Peterb.Chron. MEL 3

bleu adj. 1a *OF* (?a1300) Tristrem ROMA
10

bleu n. 1a *fr. bleu adj.* (a1325) Cursor
WOMUNC 4

blind adj. 5a *OE* ?c1125 Dur-C.Gloss.
(Cokayne) ROMA 50

blind n. a *fr. blind adj.* c1175 Bod.Hom.
SNPRO 1

blinden v. 1a *fr. blind adj.* c1225 Ancr.
(Tit: Morton) CYT 2

blindnesse n. a *OE* c1175
Bod.Hom.Dom.Quadr. SNPRO 3

blinnen v. 1a *OE* ?c1200 Orm. TR 2

blisful adj. 1a *fr. blisse n.* (?a1200)
Trin.Hom. ROMA 115

blisfulli adv. a *(fr. blisful adj.)* (?a1200)
*Ancr. TR 3

blisfulnesse n. a *(fr. blisful adj.)* Chaucer
BO 86

blisse n. 1a *OE* a1121 Peterb.Chron. BD
94

blithe adj. 1a *OE* c1175 HRood ROMA
18

blithe adv. a *OE* c1175 Bod.Hom. *ROMA*
1

blitheli adv. 2a *OE* a1121 Peterb.Chron.
BD 2

blithnesse n. *OE* (?c1150) Prov.Alf.
(Trin-C) *BO* 1

blive adv. 1a *fr. bi live phr.* ?c1200 Orm.
ROMA 29

blo adj. 1c *ON & OF* (?a1200) *Ancr. *HF*
1

blod n1. 1a a *OE* c1150 PDidax. ROMA 93

blodi adj. 2a *OE* a1121 Peterb.Chron. HF
23

blod-shedynge n. 1b a, blod n1. *(fr. blod*
n. & shedinge ger.) (c1300)
Glo.Chron.A *HF* 1

blonderen v. b *ON* (a1349) Rolle
MPass.(2) CYPRO 2

blosme n. a *OE* c1150 Hrl.HApul. LGW
F 3

blosmen v. *OE* Chaucer {(c1378) PPl.B
(Ld)} ROMA 2

blosmi adj. *OE* Chaucer PF 3

blot n. a *? cp. OF* (1373) *Lelamour
Macer *PARST* 1

blouen vi. 4a *OE* a1131 Peterb.Chron.
BD 51

blouing ger1. b *OE* (?a1200) *Ancr. *CYT*
1

bobaunce n. 1 *OF* (?c1280) SLeg.Pass.
(Pep) ABC 2

bocche n. 4a *ONF* c1330 Body & S.(5)
BO 1

boce n. 2 *OF* a1325 Lord that lenest MILT
2

bocher n. 1 *OF* (?a1300) KAlex. *KNT* 1

bod n1. 2a *fr. abod n.* (?a1200)
Trin.Hom. *ANEL* 1

bod n2. 1a *OE* a1121 Peterb.Chron. *PF* 1

boden vi. 1 *OE* a1121 Peterb.Chron. BO 2

bodi n. 1a *OE* a1200 Wor.Aelfric Gloss.
ROMA 280

bodilich adj. 1 *fr. bodi n.* (c1300)
NHom.(1) Gosp. BO 19

bodiliche adv. 1 *fr. bodi n.* (c1300)
NHom.(1) Giezi *PARST* 1

Boetes n. *L, fr. Gr.* Chaucer *BO* 2

boidekin n. a *?OF* (?c1300) Reinbrun
MᴋT 3
boie nɪ. 1 *OF* (?c1225) Horn FʀT 4
boillen v. 1a *OF* c1300 SLeg.John (Ld)
Bo 5
boillinge ger. 3a *(fr. boillen v.)* Chaucer
Bo 1
boiste n. 1a *OF* (a1200) *Ancr. HF 3
boistous adj. 1a *OF* c1300 SLeg.Fran.(1)
(Ld) *MᴀɴcT* 1
boistousli adv. 1a *fr. boistous adj.* (c1350)
NHom.(2) PSanct. *CLT* 1
bok nɪ. 1a *OE* a1121 Peterb.Chron.
RoᴍA 181
bokel n. 2a *OF* (?c1300) Reinbrun *RoᴍA*
1
bokelen v. 1b *fr. bokel n.* (c1353) Winner
& W. *KɴT* 1
bokeler nɪ. 1a *OF* (?a1300) KAlex. GP 6
boket n. a *OF* a1300 Fox & W. *KɴT* 1
bolas n. a *prob. AF* a1325 Gloss.Bibbesw.
RoᴍA 1
bold adj. 4a *OE* ?c1200 Orm. RoᴍA 21
bolde adj. as n. a *(fr. bolde adj.)* (?a1300)
Tristrem *PʜʏT* 1
boldeliche adv. 2a *OE* (?a1200) Lay.Brut
SNT 16
bolden v. 1a *OE* (?a1200) Lay.Brut *PF* 1
boldnesse n. c *fr. bold adj.* (a1338)
Mannyng Chron.Pt.2 BD 3
bole nɪ. 1a *ON* ?c1200 Orm. Bo 13
bole n3. *ML (fr. Gr.)* a1300 Hrl.978
Vocab *CYT* 1
bolle n. 1a *OE* c1150 Hrl.HApul. LGW
2
bolt n. 1b *OE* (?c1150) Prov.Alf. (Trin-C)
MɪʟT 1
bolt-upright adj. & adv. b *(fr. bolt n. &
upright adv.)* Chaucer RᴠT 2
bomblen v. *imitative* Chaucer WBT 1
bon adj. *OF & L* Chaucer *HF* 1
bon nɪ. 1a *OE* c1150 PDidax. RoᴍA 47
bon n2. 1a *ON* ?c1200 Orm. BD 15
bond n. 2a *ON* 1126 Peterb.Chron. BD
35

bonde n2. & adj. 1a *fr. bonde nɪ.*
(?a1300) Tristrem MᴋT 9
bonde-folk n. 3a, bonde n2. & adj. *(fr.
bonde n2. & folk n.)* Chaucer PᴀʀsT 2
bonde-man n. 1 *(fr. bonde nɪ. & man n.)*
c1250 Owl & N. *PᴀʀsT* 2
bor n. 1b *OE* c1150 Hrl.MQuad. MᴋT
27
boras n. c *L & OF, fr. Ar.* Chaucer GP 2
bord n. 3a f *OE* (?c1175) PMor. (Lamb)
BD 20
bordel nɪ. a *OF* c1300 SLeg.Lucy (Ld)
PᴀʀsT 2
bordure n. d *OF* (?c1350) Libeaus RoᴍA
47
bore nɪ. a *OE* (c1300) NHom.(1) Pilgr.
Tʀ 1
Boreas n. *L* Chaucer *Bo* 2
borgh n. 2a a *OE* (?a1200) Lay.Brut Tʀ
13
borwen v. 1a *OE* (c1200) Vices & V.(1)
Lᴀᴅʏ 11
borwing ger. 1a *(fr. borwen v.)* (c1250)
Prov.Hend. *PᴀʀsT* 1
bosom n. 1b *OE* ?c1200 Orm. Tʀ 6
bost n. 2a *AF* c1300 SLeg.Mich. (Ld)
SNT 12
bosten v. 1a *AF* (?c1350) Ywain Bo 4
bot nɪ. 1d *OE* (c1200) Vices & V.(1) Tʀ 5
bote nɪ. 2c *OE* 1131 Peterb.Chron. BD 26
bote n2. 1 *OF* c1300 Horn (Ld) *GP* 2
botel nɪ. 1a *OF* c1380 Firumb.(1) SᴜᴍT 4
botel n2. *OF* Chaucer *MᴀɴcPʀo* 1
boteler nɪ. 1a *OF; ML* (c1250) Gen.&
Ex. HF 2
boteles adjɪ. 1b *OE* a1375 WPal. *Tʀ* 1
bothe num. 3e *OE* a1126 Peterb.Chron.
Gᴇɴᴇʀᴀʟ 343
botme n. 4a *OE* (a1325) Cursor RoᴍA 11
botme-les adj. a *fr. botme n.* (?c1380)
Cleanness Tʀ 2
boue nɪ. 7e *OE* a1200 Body & S.(2)
RoᴍA 31
bouen vɪ. 5a c *OE* a1121 Peterb.Chron.
RoᴍA 12

bough n. 1b *OE* c1150 Hrl.HApul.
RomA 11

bouk n. 1c *OE* c1175 Bod.Hom. *KnT* 1

boun adj. 1a *ON* ?c1200 Orm. *FranT* 1

bounde n. 1a *OF; L* (?a1300) KAlex.
MkT 16

bounden v. *fr. bounde n.* Chaucer *AST* 1

bounte n. 3b *OF* c1275 Ken.Serm. RomA
69

bountevous adj. 1a *cp. OF* Chaucer TR
2

bour n. 5 *OE* a1121 Peterb.Chron. RomA
9

bourde n. 1a *OF* (?c1300) Amis
MancPro 1

bourden vi. b *OF* (c1303) Mannyng HS
PF 2

box n1. a *OE (fr. L)* c1350 Cmb.Ee.4.20
Nominale KnT 3

box n2. 1 *OE (fr. L)* c1150 PDidax. CkT
3

box n3. *? cp. box n2.* (?c1300) Bevis *LGW*
1

boxtre n. a, box n1. *(fr. box n1. & tre n.)*
Chaucer PF 2

bracer n. b *OF* Chaucer *GP* 1

bragot n. *Welsh* (a1387) Trev.Higd. *MilT*
1

brain n. 1a *OE* c1150 Hrl.MQuad. HF 5

bran n. 1a *OF* (a1325) Cursor RvT 3

brand n. 4b *OE* (1103–15) in Fransson
Surn. MkT 6

bras n. 1a *OE* a1200 Wor.Aelfric Gloss.
HF 16

brasile n. a *ML & OF* (c1325) Recipe
Painting(1) in Archaeol.J.1 *EpiNPT* 1

brat n. *OE (fr. Celtic)* Chaucer *CYT* 1

braun n. 1a *OF* a1325 Gloss.Bibbesw.
(Arun) KnT 7

braunch n. 1 *OF* c1300 SLeg.MLChr.
(Ld) RomA 23

braunchen v. 1b *fr. braunch n.* a1375
WPal. *SQT* 1

brech n. 1a *OE* (?a1200) Lay.Brut PardT
4

bred n1. 1a *OE* (?c1175) PMor. (Lamb)
RomA 18

brede n1. *OE* c1150 PDidax. *HF* 1

brede n2. 5b b *OE* (c1200) Vices & V.(1)
RomA 14

breden v3. 2a *OE* (?a1200) Lay.Brut Tr 7

bred-ful adj. b *ON* (?a1200) Trin.Hom.
HF 3

breid n1. 3 *cp. OE & OI* (?a1200)
Lay.Brut RomA 2

breiden vi. 9b *OE* a1121 Peterb.Chron.
MkT 13

breken v. 23b *OE* c1120 Leges Hen.I in
Liebermann Gesetze 1 RomA 71

brekere n. 1a *fr. breken v.* a1225
Lamb.Hom. *PF* 1

brekinge ger. 1c *(fr. breken v.)* (c1280)
SLeg.Pass. (Pep) *ParsT* 6

brekke n. *cp. MDu.* Chaucer *BD* 1

brembel n. 1 *OE* ?c1125 Dur-C.Gloss.
ThoP 1

breme adv. a *fr. breme adj.* c1325 Lenten
ys come Tr 2

breme n. a *OF* Chaucer *GP* 1

brennen v. 1a *OE* a1121 Peterb.Chron.
RomA 108

brenninge ger. 6b *(fr. brennen v.)*
(a1250) Bestiary RomA 8

brenningli adv. *fr. brennen v.* (c1303)
Mannyng HS Tr 2

brer n. 1a *OE* ?c1200 Orm. RomA 4

brest n1. 3 *OE* (c1125)
Vsp.D.Hom.Fest.Virg. BD 57

bresten v. 2a *OE & ON* c1150 PDidax.
BD 40

bresting ger. 2 *(fr. bresten v.)* Chaucer
FranT 1

brest-plate n. a *(fr. brest n1. & plate n.)*
(1358) Reg.Edw.Blk.Pr. *KnT* 1

breth n1. 1b *OE* (?a1200) *Ancr. RomA
22

brethen vi. 1b *fr. breth n1.* (?a1200)
Lay.Brut *Bo* 1

breuen v. 2b *OE* (c1250) Gen.& Ex.
MkT 1

breu-hous n. b *(fr. breuen v. & hous n.)* (?a1387) PPl.C (Hnt) *MILT* 1

briben v. a *cp. OF* Chaucer *CKT* 2

briberie n. a *OF* (a1387) Trev.Higd. *FRT* 1

brid n. 3a a *OE* a1200 Wor.Aelfric Gloss. *ROMA* 62

brid-ale n. 1a *OE* ?c1200 Orm. *CKT* 1

bride n1. 4 *OE* ?c1200 Orm. LGW 5

bridel n. 1a c *OE* c1175 HRood *ANEL* 23

bridelen v. 3 *OE* ?c1200 Orm. *TR* 4

brige n. b *OF* (c1385) Usk TL (Skeat) *MEL* 1

brigge n. 1a *OE* a1121 Peterb.Chron. *RVT* 1

bright adj. 1a *OE* a1121 Peterb.Chron. *ROMA* 132

bright n. *fr. bright adj.* (c1250) Gen.& Ex. *TR* 1

brighte adv. 1a *cp. OE* a1121 Peterb.Chron. *ROMA* 21

brightnesse n. 1a *OE* c1175 Bod.Hom. *SNT* 6

brike n2. *ONF (CF)* (a1338) Mannyng Chron.Pt.1 *MKT* 1

brimme n. 1 *akin to MHG* (?a1200) Lay.Brut *LGW* 1

brim-ston n. 2a *LOE* (c1125) Vsp.D.Hom.Elucid *GP* 8

bringen v. 1b *OE* 1123 Peterb.Chron. *ROMA* 281

bringer n. c *fr. bringen v.* (c1340) Rolle Psalter (UC 64) *WBT* 1

brinke n. 1a *prob. ON & MLG* (?c1225) Horn *ROMA* 6

bristel n. a *cp. OE* (?c1300) Bevis *GP* 2

bristled ppl. a *fr. <bristel n.>* (?a1200) Lay.Brut. *BO* 1

Brit n. a *OE* (?a1200) Lay.Brut *HF* 1

Britaine n. 1 *OF* a1200 Sanctus beda *ROMA* 10

Britoun n. & adj. 1a *cp. OE; L; OF* (?a1200) Lay.Brut MLT 8

broche n1. 2a *OF* (?a1200) *Ancr. ROMA* 16

brod adj. 1a *OE* 1122 Peterb.Chron. *ROMA* 32

brod n2. 1a *OE* c1250 Owl & N. *LGW F* 1

brode adv. 2 *OE* a1300 I-hereth nu one *HF* 7

broilen v1. a *OF* c1350 MPPsalter *GP* 1

brok n2. *cp. OI* Chaucer *FRT* 1

brok n3. 2 *OE* ?c1125 Dur-C.Gloss. (Cokayne) *KNT* 3

brokage n. 2 *AF* (c1378) PPl.B. (Ld) *MILT* 1

brokken v. *cp. brok n4.* (a1333) Shoreham Poems *MILT* 1

brom n. 1a *OE* ?c1125 Dur-C.Gloss. (Cokayne) *ROMA* 2

brotel adj. b *cp. OE* ?a1325 Swet ihc hend *BO* 9

brotelnesse n. d *fr. brotel adj.* Chaucer *TR* 5

brother n. 1a *OE* a1121 Peterb.Chron. *BD* 161

brotherhede n. 1b *fr. brother n.* (?c1300) Amis *GP* 3

brouded ppl. 2 *fr. breiden v1. & OF* Chaucer *MKT* 3

brouding ger. *(fr. brouden v.)* Chaucer *KNT* 1

broue n. 2 *OE* (?a1200) Lay.Brut *ROMA* 10

brouken v. 2a *OE* c1150 Hrl.HApul. *HF* 5

broun adj. 4b *OE; OF* ?c1125 Dur-C.Gloss. (Cokayne) *ROMA* 12

brutal adj. *OF* Chaucer *BO* 1

buf interj. *no etym.* Chaucer *SUMT* 1

buffet n2. 1a *OF* (?a1200) *Ancr. PARST* 1

bugle n1. 1a *OF* (?a1300) KAlex. *FRANT* 1

bukke n. 1a a *OE* a1131 Peterb.Chron. *BD* 4

bulle n. 1b *OF & L* c1300 SLeg.Becket (Hrl) *CLT* 7

bulten v1. 1a *OF* ?c1200 Orm. *NPT* 1

Burdeux n. *OF* Chaucer *PARDT* 1

Burdeux-ward n. MED Suppl. *(fr.*

Burdeux n. *& -ward suf.)* Chaucer *GP*
1

burdoun n2. *OF* (?c1300) Caiphas GP 2
burel n1. 1a *OF* (1307) Execution Frase
WBPRO 5
burgeis n. 1a *OF* (?a1200) *Ancr. TR 3
burgh n1. 2b *OE* (1100–7) Chart.St.Paul
in RHS ser.3.58 *WBT* 1
Burgoine n. & adj. 1a *OF* (a1325)
Glo.Chron.B. *ROMA* 1
burnen v. 1 *OF* Chaucer HF 6
burnet n1. & adj. a *OF* (?a1200)
Trin.Hom. *ROMA* 1
bush n1. 1a a *OE & ML* ?1250 Somer is
comen & ROMA 17
busshel n1. 1a *OF & ML* c1330 Why
werre BO 8
but conj. 1a a *OE* a1121 Peterb.Chron.
GENERAL 2850
but n3. *fr. but conj.* Chaucer *PARST* 1
buter-flie n. 1a *OE* (c1250) Floris MERT
3
buttok n. 1a *OE* c1300 SLeg.Mich. (Ld)
MILT 5
buxom adj. 2a *fr. bouen v1.* ?c1200 Orm.
LADY 5
buxomli adv. a *fr. buxom adj.* a1250
Lofsong Louerde *CLT* 1
buxumnesse n. a *fr. buxom adj.* (?c1200)
HMaid. *TRUTH* 1
c n. 2a *no etym.* (1340) Ayenb. TR 3
cable n. a *AF & ML* (?a1200) Lay.Brut
VENUS 1
cacchen v. 1b *AF; cp. CF* (?a1200) *Ancr.
ROMA 92
cadence n. *OF* Chaucer *HF* 1
cage n. 1a *OF* (?a1200) *Ancr. HF 14
cainard n. *prob. AF* (c1300) Havelok
WBPRO 1
caitif adj. 2c *AF & CF* c1300 NHom.(1)
Abp.& N. ROMA 10
caitif n. 2b *AF & CF* c1300 Body & S.(5)
ROMA 11
cake n. 1a *ON* ?c1200 Wor.Bod.Gloss.
GP 5

cakeling ger. *(fr. cakelen v.)* Chaucer *PF*
1
calcinacioun n. *ML & OF* (a1393)
Gower CA *CYT* 1
calcining ger. *fr. calcinen v.* * Chaucer
CYT 1
calculen v. b *OF & L* (c1378) PPl.B (Ld)
AST 3
calculer n. a *fr. calculen v.* (a1387)
Trev.Higd. *AST* 1
calculing ger. 1b *(fr. calculen v.)* Chaucer
TR 2
Calde n. a *L & OF* ?c1200 Orm. *MKT* 1
calender n. 1 *OF & L* (?a1200) Lay.Brut
ABC 6
calendes n. 1c *L* (?c1200) St.Juliana *TR*
2
calf n1. 1a *OE* ?c1200 Orm. MILT 3
calf n2. *ON* a1325 Gloss.Bibbesw. *GP* 1
calle n. 1a *OE* ?a1300 Gloss.Neckham *TR*
3
callen v. 1c *ON* (?c1200) St.Marg.(1)
ROMA 130
calme adj. *cp. It.* Chaucer *BO* 2
camel n. a *L & AF, CF* (c1250) Gen.&
Ex. *CLT* 1
camus adj. *OF* c1380 Firumb.(1) *RVT* 2
candel n. 1a a *OE; also L & OF* ?a1160
Peterb.Chron. ROMA 7
candel-light n. 2c, candel n. *(fr. candle n.
& light n.)* c1300 Lay.Brut (Otho)
MILT 1
candel-stikke n. a *OE* a1121
Peterb.Chron. *PARST* 1
canel n1. 1a *OF & ML* (?a1200) Lay.Brut
ROMA 1
canel-boon n. b, canel n2. *(fr. canel n2. &
bon n1.)* a1325 Gloss.Bibbesw. *BD* 1
canevas n. 2b *AF & ML* (1367) in
Löfvenberg Contrib.Lex *CYT* 1
canked-ort n. *? fr. <cankred ppl. & ort
n.>* Chaucer *TR* 1
canker n1. 1a a *OE, L & OF* c1150
Hrl.HApul. *PARST* 1
Canker n2. *ML* Chaucer *BO* 19

canoun n1. 1a *OE & OF, fr. L* (a1325)
Cursor Ast 3

canoun n2. 1a *AF & CF* (?a1200)
Lay.Brut CYPRO 43

cantel n. 1a *AF* c1300 SLeg.Magd.(2)
(Ld) *KnT* 1

cap n. *OF* Chaucer *GP* 1

capel n. a *ON* (a1300) Cokaygne RvT 6

capen v. *OE* c1300 SLeg.Fran.(1) (Ld) TR
5

capitain n. 1a *OF* Chaucer MkT 3

capital adj. a *OF & L* (?a1200) *Ancr.
Ast* 4

Capitolie n. *OF & L* Chaucer *MkT* 2

capoun n. 1a *OE & OF* (a1250) Bestiary
LGW 4

cappe n. 1a *OE & ML* (?a1200) *Ancr.
GP 4

Capricorn n. *OF & L* (1373) *Lelamour
Macer Ast 25

captivite n. 2a *L* Chaucer *Bo* 1

carbuncle n. 1a *OF & L* (?c1200)
HMaid. RoMA 3

cardiacle a *cp. ML* (1373) *Lelamour
Macer *IntPardT* 1

cardinal n. 1a *L* a1126 Peterb.Chron.
WBPro 3

care n1. 5a *OE* a1150 Rwl.G.57.Gloss.
RoMA 61

careful adj. 4 *OE* (c1200) Vices & V.(1)
Lady 3

careine n. 2a *AF & CF* (?a1200) *Ancr.
MkT 5

caren v. 2 *OE* (?a1200) *Ancr. RoMA 6

cariage n. 4b *AF* Chaucer RoMA 4

Caribdis n. b *L & OF* Chaucer *TR* 1

carien v. 1c *AF* Chaucer MkT 23

cariinge ger. a *(fr. carien v.)* (a1382)
WBible(1) *PardT* 1

carike n1. *OF & ML; ult. Ar.* Chaucer
SumPro 1

carl n. 1d *ON* ?a1160 Peterb.Chron. GP
4

carole n. 3a *OF* ?a1300 Gloss.Neckham
RoMA 6

carolen v. a *OF* (c1303) Mannyng HS
RoMA 3

carole-wise n. 1d, carole n. *(fr. carole n. &
wise n2.)* Chaucer *LGW G* 1

caroling ger. b *fr. carolen v.* * (?a1300)
KAlex. *RoMA* 3

carpen v. 1a *ON* c1225 Wooing Lord *GP*
1

carpenter n. 1a *AF & OF* c1300 SLeg.
(Ld) KnT 34

cart n. 2 *OE & ON* a1150
Vsp.D.Hom.Nicod. HF 23

carte-hors n. 3b, cart n. *(fr. cart n. & hors
n.)* Chaucer *HF* 1

carter n. 2 *partly AF & CF & cart n.*
?c1200 Wor.Bod.Gloss. PF 8

cartwheel n. 6a, cart n. *(fr. cart n. & whel
n.)* (c1392) EPlanets *SumT* 2

cas n. 1a *OF, fr. L* a1250 Ancr. (Nero) BD
142

case n1. 1d *AF, OF (fr. L)* (a1325) Cursor
KnT 4

cast n. 3e *ON* (c1250) Floris MkT 6

castel n. 1a a *OE & AF, L & CF* a1121
Peterb.Chron. BD 28

castelen v. c *AF* Chaucer *ParsT* 1

castel-gate n. 1b a, castel n. *(fr. castel n. &
gate n1.)* (?a1300) Arth.& M. *HF* 1

casten v. 1a *ON* (?a1200) *Ancr. RoMA
178

castigacioun n. *L* Chaucer *Sted* 1

casting ger. 1a *(fr. casten v.)* (c1300)
Glo.Chron.A *Bo* 1

casuel adj. 1b *OF & L* (c1384) Doc. in
Bk.Lond.E. *Tr* 1

casuelli adv. a *fr. <casuel adj.>* Chaucer
HF 2

cat n. 1b *OE & OF* (?c1150) Prov.Alf.
(Trin-C) HF 9

catapuce n. b *OF & ML* (1373)
*Lelamour Macer *NPT* 1

catel n. 1a *AF* c1250 Serm.St.Nich. GP
27

Caton n. *OF* Chaucer MilT 12

Caunterbury-ward n. MED Suppl. *fr.*

The making of Chaucer's English

*Caunterbury n. & -ward suf.** not in MED *GP* 1

cause n. 4a *OF & L* (?a1200) *Ancr. ABC 357

causeles adj. b *(fr. cause n.)* Chaucer TR 2

causeles adv. b *fr.* <*causeles adj.*> Chaucer HF 14

causen vi. 1a *OF & ML* Chaucer HF 40

causer n1. a *fr. causen vi.* Chaucer *MARS* 1

cave n1. 1a *OF & L* (a1250) Bestiary BD 22

caverne n. a *OF & L* Chaucer *BO* 1

cavillacioun n. *L & OF* (?1388) Syng I wold *SUMT* 1

cedre n. 1 *OF (fr. L)* c1175 HRood ROMA 2

ceint n. a *OF (fr. L)* (c1300) Assump.Virg.(1) GP 2

celebrable adj. *OF* Chaucer *BO* 2

celebrite n. a *OF* Chaucer *BO* 1

celer n1. 1a *OF (fr. L)* (?a1200) *Ancr. BO 2

celerere n. a *OF, fr. L* ?a1300 Fox & W. *PROMKT* 1

celestial adj. 1 *OF* Chaucer HF 19

celle n. 1 *OE & OF, fr. L* a1131 Peterb.Chron. KNT 3

cendal n. 1 *OF* (?c1200) St.Juliana GP 1

censen v. b *fr. encensen vi.* Chaucer *MILT* 1

censer n1. a *fr.* <*encenser n.*> c1250 *St. Marg.(2) *MILT* 1

centaur n. a *[L]* Chaucer MKT 2

centorie n. a *L* c1150 Hrl.HApul. *NPT* 1

centre n. 3 *OF, fr. L* Chaucer BO 20

ceptre n. 1 *OF & L* (?a1300) KAlex. MKT 9

Cerberus n. *L, fr. Gr.* Chaucer MKT 4

cercle n. 5a *OF & L* a1121 Peterb.Chron. ROMA 66

cerclen v. 3 *fr. cercle n.* Chaucer ROMA 3

cerial adj. *L* Chaucer *KNT* 1

cerimonie n. 1a *L & OF* (a1382) WBible(1) *SQT* 1

certain adj. 1a *OF* c1300 SLeg.Becket (Hrl) BD 122

certain adv. 1a *(fr. certain adj.)* c1300 SLeg.Becket (Hrl) ROMA 98

certain n. 3 *fr. certain adj.* (c1303) Mannyng HS ABC 17

certainli adv. 1b *(fr. certain adj.)* c1300 SLeg.Inf.Chr. (Ld) ROMA 64

certes adv. a *OF* c1250 Owl & N. GENERAL 503

ceruse n. 1a *OF fr. L* Chaucer *GP* 1

cesar n. *L* Chaucer MKT 10

cesen v. 4a *OF* (?c1300) LFMass Bk. SNT 30

chacen v. 1b *OF* (?a1300) Tristrem ABC 28

chaf n. 2a *[OE]* ?c1200 Orm. LGW G 3

chaffare n. 1 *OE* (?a1200) *Ancr. CKT 9

chaffaren v. a *fr. chaffare n.* (1340)Ayenb. *MLT* 1

chaiere n. 2a *OF* (?c1225) Horn MKT 7

chaine n. 1b *OF (fr. L)* c1300 SLeg.Patr.Purg. (Ld) MKT 21

chainen v. 3a *fr. chaine n.* (a1376) *PPl.A(1) (Trin-C) *BUK* 1

chalaundre n. *OF* (a1300) Cokaygne ROMA 3

chalengen v. 2a *OF (fr. L)* (?a1200) *Ancr. BO 3

chalenginge ger. 1c *(fr. chalengen v.)* (1338) Mannyng Chron.Pt.2 *PHYT* 1

chalice n. 2a *OF & L* a1121 Peterb.Chron. *PARST* 1

chalk n. 1a *OE* a1200 Wor.Aelfric Gloss. *SQT* 5

chaloun n. *OF* Chaucer *RVT* 1

champartie n. 2a *OF (fr. ML) & AL* Chaucer *KNT* 1

champioun n. 1a *OF* (?a1200) *Ancr. MKT 9

chaped ppl. *fr. chape n.* Chaucer *GP* 1

chapele n. 1a *OF* (?c1200) St.Marg.(1) *GP* 1

258

chapelein n. 1 *OF* a1121 Peterb.Chron.
GP 2

chapelet n. 1a {2a} *OF* Chaucer {(a1387)
Trev.} *ROMA* 4

chapitre n. 1a *OF* (?a1200) *Ancr. PF 13

chap-man n. 1a a *OE* ?c1200 Orm. GP 6

chapmanhede n. *fr. chapman n.*
Chaucer MLT 2

char n2. 1a *OF* (a1325) Cursor MKT 10

charge n. 1b c *OF* (?a1200) *Ancr. ROMA
33

chargeaunt adj. 2 *OF* 1381
Pegge.Cook.Recipes MEL 2

chargen v. 1a *OF* c1300 SLeg. (Ld)
ROMA 24

char-hors n. 4, char n2. *(fr. char n2. &
hors n.)* Chaucer *TR* 1

chariote n. 1c *OF* c1380 Firumb.(1) *BO* 3

charitable adj. 2 *OF* (?a1200) *Ancr. TR
7

charite n. 2a *CF & NF* ?a1160
Peterb.Chron. BD 26

charme n. a *OF, fr. L* (?a1300) KAlex. TR
6

charmeresse n. *OF* (1340) Ayenb. *HF* 1

chartre n1. 2b *OF (fr. L)* (?a1200) *Ancr.
TR 3

chaste adj. 1a *OF (fr. L)* (?a1200) *Ancr.
SNT 19

chaste adv. a *fr. chaste adj.* (c1350)
Alex.& D. *MERT* 1

chasten v. 1 *adapted fr. OF* (?a1200)
Trin.Hom. *SQT* 1

chastisen v. 1b *fr. OF* (c1303) Mannyng
HS ABC 10

chastisinge ger. 1a *(fr. chastisen v.)*
(c1303) Mannyng HS ABC 5

chastite n. 1a *OF & L* (c1200) Vices & V.
(1) SNT 31

chastnesse n. *fr. chaste adj.* Chaucer
SNPRO 1

chateringe ger. a *fr. chateren v.* c1250
Owl & N. *BO* 1

chaucer n2. a *OF* (1226) Close R.Tower
2 *IntMLT* 1

chaumberere n. b *OF* (1340) Ayenb.
WBPRO 3

chaumberlein n. 1b *OF & AF* (?a1200)
*Ancr. *KNT* 1

chaumbre n. 3 *OF, fr. L* (?a1200) *Ancr.
BD 80

chaumbre-dore n. 9a, chaumbre n. *(fr.
chaumbre n. & dore n1.)* Chaucer
LGW 1

chaunce n. 2 *OF* c1300 SLeg.Becket (Ld)
ROMA 20

chauncel n. a *OF* (c1303) Mannyng HS
MILT 1

chaunge n. 1a *OF* (?a1200) *Ancr. TR 4

chaungeable adj. 2a *OF* c1250 Seinte
Mari moder BO 3

chaungen v. 1b *AF, CF* (?a1200) *Ancr.
ROMA 98

chaunginge ger. 1a *(fr. chaungen v.)*
(?a1200) *Ancr. BO 12

chaunte-cler n. *OF* ?a1300 Fox & W.
NPT 20

chaunten vi. a *OF* Chaucer MILT 2

chaunte-pleure n. *OF* Chaucer *ANEL* 1

chaunterie n1. 2a *OF* Chaucer GP 1

chef adj. 1 *(fr. chef n.)* c1300
SLeg.Edm.Abp. (Ld) BD 11

chef n. 1a *OF* c1300 SLeg.Becket (Ld) BO
5

chek interj. & n. 1a *OF* (?a1300) Guy(2)
BD 2

cheke n. 1a *OE* (?a1200) *Ancr. ROMA 14

cheker n1. 1c *OF* (c1250) Floris *BD* 1

chep n. 1b *OE* (?c1175) PMor. (Lamb)
HF 8

chepen v. 1c *OE* (?a1200) *Ancr. *WBPRO*
1

chere n1. 2a *OF* (?a1200) *Ancr. ROMA
170

cheri n. 2b *fr. AF* (?a1300) Guy(2) *ROMA*
1

cherishen v. 1a *OF* (?a1325)
Bonav.Medit.(1) MKT 10

cherishinge ger. a *fr. cherishen v.* * (a1325)
Cursor *TR* 1

cherl n. 4 *OE* 1103–20 Inst.Cnuti in
Liebermann Gesetze 1 ROMA 44
cherlish adj. b {a} *OE* Chaucer {(a1382)
WBible(1)} ROMA 2
cherubin n. 1 *L (ult. Heb.)* ?c1200 Orm.
GP 1
ches n. 1a *OF; ML* (?a1300) Tristrem BD
6
chese n. 1a *OE* 1131 Peterb.Chron. MILT
4
chesen v. 2b *OE* 1121 Peterb.Chron.
ROMA 81
chesinge ger. b *(fr. chesen v.)* a1225
Trin.Hom.Creed CLT 3
chest n. 1a *OE (ult. L)* c1175 Bod.Hom.
PARS T 1
cheste n. 4a *OE, L & ON* ?a1160
Peterb.Chron. TR 9
chesteine n. 1a *OF (L)* (?c1300) Bevis
ROMA 2
cheuen vi. 1a *OE* c1150 PDidax. MILT 1
chevalrie n. 4b *OF* c1300 SLeg.Magd.(2)
ROMA 19
chevalrous adj. a *OF* (?c1350) Ywain TR
2
chevauche n. a *OF* ?c1350 Ballad
Sc.Wars MARS 3
cheven v. 2 *OF* (c1300) SLeg.Becket
(Hrl) CYT 1
chevesel n. b {c} *OF* Chaucer {c1400
Brut-1333 (Rwl B.171)} ROMA 1
chevetaine n. 2 *OF (fr. L)* (c1280)
SLeg.Eust. (Jul) KNT 3
chevisaunce n. 1b *OF* c1300 11 Pains(2)
LGW 5
chevishen v. 3a *fr. OF* (a1325) Cursor
MARS 1
chiche-vache n. *OF* Chaucer CLT 1
chiden v. 1a *OE* (?c1150) Prov.Alf. (Trin-
C) BD 28
chideresse *fr. chidere n.* Chaucer ROMA 1
chidestere n. *fr. chidere n.* Chaucer
MERT 1
chidinge ger. a *(fr. chiden v.)* (c1303)
Mannyng HS HF 11

chierte n. 1a *OF* (?a1200) *Ancr. WBPRO
3
chiken n. 1 *OE* a1200 Hat.Gosp. ROMA
2
child n. 6a *OE* a1100 Chro.Tbr.B.4
ROMA 208
childhod n. 2b *OE* (?c1175) PMor.
(Lamb) ROMA 5
childish adj. *(fr. child n.)* (c1378) PPl.B
TR 2
childishli adv. *fr. childish adj.* Chaucer
TR 1
childli adj. a *OE* (c1125)
Vsp.D.Hom.Ges.Virg. BD 1
chilindre n. *ML & OF* Chaucer SHIPT
1
chimb n. *cp. OE, akin to OI* Chaucer
RVPRO 1
chimben v. a *fr. chimbe n.* (c1340) Rolle
Psalter RVPRO 1
chimene n. 4 *OF & NWF (fr. L)* (c1280)
SLeg.Pass. (Pep) BO 3
chin n. 1a *OE* c1150 PDidax. ROMA 4
chinche adj. & n. c *OF* ?a1300 Names
Hare MEL 2
chincherie n. *(fr. chinche n.)* Chaucer
MEL 1
chinen vi. a *OE* c1175 Bod.Hom. BO 1
chippe n. 2 *OE* (a1338) Mannyng
Chron.Pt.2 MILT 1
chirche n. 3 *OE & ON* 1121
Peterb.Chron. SNT 72
chirche-haue n. *fr. chirche n. & haue
n1.* *a1250 Ancr. (Nero) PARS T 2
chirken v. a *OE* Chaucer BO 2
chirkinge ger. *fr. chirken v.* * Chaucer
HF 3
chisel n. a *ONF* (a1382) WBible(1)
PARS T 1
chiteren v. 1 *imitative* (?a1200) *Ancr.
CYT 1
chiteringe ger. a *(fr. chitern v.)* (c1303)
Mannyng HS TR 1
chois n. 1 *OF* c1300 SLeg.John (Ld) PF
12

choppen vi. 1a *cp. OF & ML* (a1376)
PPl.A(1) (Vrn) *HF* 1

chorus n. *L* Chaucer *Bo* 2

chose n. *OF* Chaucer *WBPro* 2

choughe n. *cp. OF, OE, OHG, all
imitative* (?a1200) *Ancr. PF* 2

chuk n. *imitative* Chaucer *NPT* 1

chukken v. *cp. chuk n.* Chaucer *NPT* 1

cimenting ger. *fr. cimenten v.* * Chaucer
CYT 1

cinamome n. c *OF & ML* Chaucer
MilT 1

cink n1. *OF* Chaucer *IntMLT* 2

Cipres n1. a *L, fr. Gr.* Chaucer *MkT* 1

cipresse n. 1a *OF (fr. L)* c1175 HRood
RomA 3

Circes n. *L* c1150 Hrl.HApul. *HF* 6

circuite n. 1b *L & OF* (a1382) WBible(1)
KnT 1

circuler adj. c *OF* Chaucer *Bo* 1

circumscriben v. *L & OF* Chaucer *TR* 1

circumstaunce n. 1b *OF, & L* (?a1200)
Ancr. KnT 20

ciren v. 1b *OF* Chaucer *CYT* 1

cirurgie n. 1a *L & OF* (?c1300) Bevis GP
2

cirurgien n. 1a *OF* (c1300) Glo.Chron.
Mel 6

cisours n. (pl.) a *OF* Chaucer *HF* 1

cite n. 1a *OF* (?a1200) *Ancr. MkT* 87

citisein n. 1 *AF* (?a1300) Arth.& M. HF
7

citole n. a *OF* (a1338) Mannyng
Chron.Pt.1 *KnT* 1

citrinacioun n. *ML* Chaucer *CYT* 1

citrine adj. & n. 1a *L & OF* Chaucer
KnT 1

claimen v. 1b *OF* (?c1300) NPass. *TR* 9

clamour n. 1b *OF* Chaucer *KnT* 3

claper n2. 1 *OF* Chaucer *RomA* 1

clappe n. 1b *(fr. clappen v.)* (?a1200)
Ancr. HF 2

clappen v. 1 *OE* c1150 PDidax. *MilT* 10

clapping ger. c *(fr. clappen v.)* Chaucer
ClT 1

clare n1. *OF* (c1300) Havelok *Bo* 5

clarioun n. 1 *OF* (a1338) Mannyng
Chron.Pt.1 HF 12

clariouning ger. *fr. clariounen v.* *
Chaucer *HF* 1

claspen v. 1 *prob OE* Chaucer *GP* 1

clateren v. 2a *cp. MDu* c1330 Why werre
KnT 3

clatering ger. a *cp. OE* (?c1380)
Cleanness *KnT* 3

claue n1. 1a *OE* c1150 Wenne Wenne HF
8

clauen v. 1a *OE* c1250 Owl & N. HF 5

clause n. 1a *OF* (?a1200) *Ancr. KnT* 6

clei n. 1a *OE* c1300 SLeg.Inf.Chr. (Ld)
CYT 2

clemence n. a *OF* Chaucer *KnT* 1

clenchen v. 1a *cp. OE* c1250 Owl & N.
KnT 1

clene adj. 4a *OE* a1121 Peterb.Chron.
SNT 31

clene adv. 1a *OE* (?a1200) Trin.Hom.
RomA 13

clenli adv. 1b *OE* ?c1200 Orm. *MancT* 1

clennesse n. 2a *OE* a1150
Vsp.D.Hom.VA SNT 9

clensen v. 2a *OE* c1150 Hrl.HApul. GP 3

clepen v. 2a a *OE* 1121 Peterb.Chron.
RomA 268

cler adj. 3b *OF* (c1280) SLeg.Pass. (Pep)
RomA 94

cler adv. 3a *OF* (c1303) Mannyng
RomA 28

cleren v. 4c *fr. cler adj.* (?a1350) Nicod.(1)
Bo 5

clergeoun n. a *OF* c1330 SMChron. *PrT*
1

clergial adj. a *fr. clergie n.* (c1385) Usk
TL (Skeat) *CYT* 1

clergie n. 3b *OF* (?c1200) St.Kath.(1)
FrPro 1

clerk n. 1b *OE & OF, L* a1121
Peterb.Chron. *RomA* 122

clerli adv. 1b *fr. <cler adj.>* (c1280)
SLeg.Pass. (Pep) *Bo* 13

clernesse n. 1a *fr. cler adj.* c1300
SLeg.Patr.Purg. (Ld) SNPRO 26
cler-seinge adj. 2b, cler adv. *fr. cler adv. &*
seing ger. * Chaucer *BO* 1
cleue n. a *OE* c1250 Owl & N. *LGW* 3
cleven v1. 1a *OE* c1150 Hrl.HApul. *BO* 13
cleven v2. 1b *OE* (?a1200) Trin.Hom.
ROMA 7
clif n1. 1a *OE & L* c1175 Bod.Hom. BD 3
clift n. 2a *cp. OE* a1325 Gloss.Bibbesw.
BO 7
cliket n1. a *OF* (a1376) PPl.A(1) (Vrn)
MERT 5
climat n. 1b *OF & L* (?a1387) PPl.C
(Hnt) *AST* 9
climben v. 1c *OE* a1121 Peterb.Chron.
HF 22
climbing ger. b *(fr. climben v.)* Chaucer
TRUTH 1
clinken v. b *MDu.* a1325 Flem.Insur.
EPiMLT 2
clinking ger. *(fr. clinken v.)* Chaucer
PRONPT 1
clippen v1. 1a *OE* (?a1200) Lay.Brut TR 3
clippen v2. 1d *ON* ?c1200 Orm. MKT 3
clipping ger1. d *OE* (?a1200)*Ancr.
ROMA 1
cloddred ppl. a *fr. <cloddre n.>* (a1349)
Rolle MPass.(2) *KNT* 1
cloistre n. 1a *OF* a1225 Wint.Ben.Rule
SNPRO 5
cloistrer n. *OF* (a1325) Cursor GP 3
cloke n1. *OF* c1300 Lay.Brut (Otho) TR
4
clokke n. 1a *OF* (c1370) Fabric
R.Yk.Min. in Sur.Soc.35 AST 18
clom n1. a *OE or ON* c1350 Ayenb.App.
MILT 3
clos n. 3a *OF & ML* c1250 Glade us
maiden BO 3
closen v. 1b *fr. OF* (c1280) SLeg.Pass.
(Pep) ROMA 20
closet n. 1a *OF* Chaucer *TR* 5
closing ger. 2c {2b} *(fr. closen v.)* Chaucer
{(c1384) WBible(1)} *ROMA* 1

closure n. 1a *OF* Chaucer *PARST* 1
clote-leef n. b, clote n. *(fr. clote n. & lef.*
n1.) (1373) *Lelamour Macer *CYPRO*
1
cloth n. 1a a *OE* c1150 Hrl.HApul.
ROMA 65
clothen v. 2a *fr. cloth n.* ?c1200 Orm.
ROMA 58
clothing ger. 1a *(fr. clothen v.)* ?c1200
Orm. ROMA 32
clothles adj. *fr. cloth n.* (1357)
Gaytr.LFCatech. *PARST* 1
cloth-makyng n. 8c, cloth n. *(fr. cloth n.*
& making ger.) Chaucer *GP* 1
cloud n. 1a *OE* ?c1200 Orm. BD 22
cloudeles adj. *[fr. cloud n.]* Chaucer *BO*
2
cloudi adj. 1 *OE & cloud n.* ?c1200 Orm.
BO 4
clout n1. 6c *OE* a1200 Body & S.(2)
ROMA 5
clouten v1. 3a *fr. clout n1. & OE* (?a1200)
Ancr. ROMA 1
clove-gylofre n. 2a, clove n2. *(fr. clove n2.*
& gilofre n.) (?a1200) *Ancr. ROMA 2
clubbed adj. a *fr. clubbe n.* Chaucer
PROMKT 1
clustred ppl. 1b *fr. cluster n.* Chaucer *BO*
1
coagulat ppl. b *L* Chaucer *CYT* 1
cod n1. 2a *OE* 1131 Peterb.Chron. *PARD T*
1
coempcioun n. *ML* Chaucer *BO* 3
coeterne adj. *ML* Chaucer *BO* 1
cofre n. 1a *OF* c1250 Louerd asse thu ard
PF 9
cogge n1. 1a *AF* (a1333–52) Minot Poems
LGW 1
coi adj. & adv. b *OF (fr. L)* (a1338)
Mannyng Chron.Pt.2 LGW 3
coien v. *OF* (c1350) Alex.Maced. *TR* 1
coilons n. pl. *OF (fr. L)* Chaucer *PARD T*
1
coin n1. 2a c *OF* Chaucer FORMAGE 2
coin n2. *OF* (?c1350) Ywain *ROMA* 1

coinen v. 2 *OF* (a1338) Mannyng
Chron.Pt.2 *PARD T* 1
cok, cok! interj. *imitative* Chaucer *NPT*
1
cok n1. 5a *OE & OF (fr. ML)* a1250
Ancr. (Nero) PF 20
cok n5. (gen.) *veiled var. to god n1.*
Chaucer MANCPRO 2
cok n6. 1a *OE (fr. L)* (?a1200) Lay.Brut
KNT 15
cokenei n2. *derisive use of cokenai n1. or*
cp. F Chaucer *RVT* 1
cokewold n. 1a *cp. late OF* c1250 Owl &
N. MILPRO 7
cokkel n. 1a *OE* ?a1300 Wor.F.157.Gloss.
EPIMLT 1
cokkou n. 1a *cp. OF* a1300 Sumer is
icumen PF 10
col adj. 1a *OE* c1150 Hrl.HApul. *LGW G*
1
col n2. 2a *OE* c1150 Wenne Wenne MKT
19
col-blak adj. 4a, col n2. *(col n2. & blak*
adj.) c1250 Owl & N. KNT 2
cold adj. 1b *OE* c1150 PDidax. ROMA 73
cold n. 1c *fr. cold adj.* c1150 PDidax.
ROMA 24
colde adv. a *fr. cold adj.* a1200 Body &
S.(2) *BD* 1
colden v. 1b *OE* a1200 Body & S.(2) PF
9
coldnesse n. 3b *(fr. cold adj.)* (1373)
*Lelamour Macer AST 2
coler n. 3 *OF (fr. L)* (c1300)
Glo.Chron.A ROMA 6
colered ppl. *fr. coler n.* Chaucer *KNT* 1
colerik adj. 3a *OF & L* (1340) Ayenb.
GP 3
col-fox n. a *(fr. col n2. & fox n.)* Chaucer
NPT 1
collacioun n. 1a *L & OF* a1225
Wint.Ben.Rule BO 5
collateral adj. b *L & OF* (c1378) PPl.B
(Ld) *TR* 1
collecten v. 2b *fr. L* Chaucer *FRANT* 1

college n. 2 *OF & L* (?c1378)
Wycl.OPastor *RVT* 1
collusioun n. 1a *L & OF* (1389)
Lond.Gild Ret. in Bk.Lond.E. *STED* 1
Coloine n. a *OF* a1325 Flem.Insur. *GP* 1
colour n. 3a *OF & L* (?c1225) Horn
ROMA 43
colouren v. 1b *OF & L* Chaucer ROMA 3
colre n. 2b *OF & L (fr. Gr.)* (a1382)
WBible(1) *NPT* 2
colt n. 2 *OE* (?c1200) St.Juliana MILT 4
coltish adj. a *fr. colt n.* Chaucer *MERT* 1
columbine adj. & n. 1 *OF & L* Chaucer
MERT 1
comb n. 1a *OE* c1150 Hrl.MQuad. HF 2
combren v. 5a *fr. acombren v.* (c1300)
NHom.(1) Gosp. *BO* 1
combre-world n. b *fr. combren the world*
phr. Chaucer *TR* 1
combust ppl. c *L* Chaucer *TR* 3
come n1. 2a *OE* c1175 Bod.Hom. *SNT* 1
comedie n1. *L & OF (ult. Gr.)* Chaucer
TR 1
comen v. 1a a *OE* a1121 Peterb.Chron.
ROMA 945
comfort n. 2a *OF* (?a1200) *Ancr. ROMA
37
comforten v. 4a *OF & L* (c1280)
SLeg.Pass. (Pep) ROMA 24
comin n. b *L (fr. Gr.) & OF* c1150
Hrl.HApul. *THOP* 1
cominge ger. 2a *(fr. comen v.)* (c1280)
SLeg.Pass. (Pep) HF 16
comlili adv. a *(fr. comli adj.)* Chaucer
BD 1
comlinesse n. a *(fr. comlie adj.)* c1350
MPPsalter BD 3
commaundement n. 1 *OF* c1275
Ken.Serm. HF 34
commaunden v. 2b *OF* c1300
SLeg.Inf.Chr. ROMA 53
commaundour n. 1a *OF* (a1325) Cursor
MLT 1
commendable adj. a *L* (?c1350)
SVrn.Leg. *MEL* 1

commendacioun n. 2a *L* (?a1200) *Ancr.
PARST* 2

commenden v. 3b *L & OF* (c1340) Rolle
Psalter (UC 64) SNT 14

commeven v. 1a *OF* Chaucer BO 7

commissioun n. 1b *L & OF* (1344)
Anc.Pet.(PRO) GP 1

committen v. 1b b *L* Chaucer BO 4

communalte n. 1 *OF* c1300 SLeg.Becket
(Ld) *BO* 4

commune adj. 1a *OF & L* c1300 SLeg.
(Ld) BD 59

commune n. 3 *OF & ML* c1300
SLeg.Edm.Abp. (Ld) BO 5

communeli adv. 1a *(fr. commune adj.)*
(?c1300) Guy(1) ROMA 12

communen v. 3a *OF* (c1303) Mannyng
HS SQT 2

communes n. 1a a *(fr. commune n.)*
(a1338) Mannyng Chron.Pt.2 *KNT* 1

communioun n. 3 *L & OF* (a1382)
WBible(1) *PARST* 1

compaignable adj. a *OF* (c1340) Rolle
Psalter (UC 64) SHIPT 2

compaignie n. 2b *OF* (?c1150) Prov.Alf.
(Trin-C) ROMA 118

comparisoun n. 1b *OF* (1340) Ayenb.
MKT 21

comparisounen v. 2a *OF* (1340) Ayenb.
BO 1

compas n. 4c *OF* c1300 SLeg.Inf.Chr.
(Ld) ROMA 32

compassement n. 1a *OF* (?a1300) KAlex.
LGW 1

compassen v. 2c *AF, CF* c1300
SLeg.Inf.Chr. (Ld) ROMA 8

compassinge ger. 2e *(fr. compassen v.)*
(a1325) Cursor ROMA 4

compassioun n. 2a *L & OF* (1340)
Ayenb. MKT 19

compellen v. 2b *L & OF* (?c1350)
SVrn.Leg. BO 4

comper n. b *OF* a1375 WPal. GP 2

compilatour n. a *L & OF* Chaucer *AST*
1

compleinen v. 4a *OF* Chaucer PITY 55

compleininge ger. 1b *(fr. compleinen v.)*
Chaucer ANEL 9

compleinte n. 1a *OF* Chaucer BD 34

complete adv. b *fr.* <*complete ppl.*>
Chaucer *TR* 1

completen v. 3a *fr.* <*complete ppl.*>
Chaucer MERT 2

complexioun n. 3a a *L & OF* (1340)
Ayenb. HF 9

compline n. 1a *OF, fr. ML* (?a1200)
Ancr. RVT 2

comporten v. *L & OF* Chaucer *TR* 1

composicioun n. 1c *L & OF* (a1382)
WBible(1) KNT 3

compotent adj. a *fr. L* Chaucer *BO* 1

compouned ppl. {4} *fr. compounen v.* *
Chaucer {(a1387) Trev.Higd.} HF 11

compounen v. 1b *L & OF* Chaucer *BO*
2

comprehenden v. 6a *L, & OF* (c1340)
Rolle Psalter (UC 64) BD 38

compressen v. 1b *L & OF* Chaucer *BO* 1

conceite n. 2a *fr. conceiven v.* Chaucer
BO 8

conceiven v. 1a *OF* (?c1280)
SLeg.Advent, etc. (Eg) ROMA 17

concentrik adv. *ML & OF* Chaucer *AST*
4

concepcioun n. 2 *L* (a1325) Cursor BO 3

concluden v. 2a *L* (a1325) Cursor SNT
26

conclusioun n. 2a *L & OF* Chaucer
SNT 80

concorde n. 1a *OF, & L* (a1325) Cursor
TR 4

concorden v. *OF & L* Chaucer *TR* 1

concubine n. a *OF & L* (c1300)
Glo.Chron.A MKT 2

concupiscence n. *L & OF* (?c1350)
SVrn.Leg.Barlaam *PARST* 9

condempnen v. 2b *L & OF* (1340)
Ayenb. *BO* 1

condescenden v. 1 *L & OF* (1340)
Ayenb. AST 5

condicional adj. *L & OF* Chaucer Bo 3

condicioun n. 4a *OF & L* (a1333) Shoreham Poems BD 55

conduit n. 1b *OF* c1300 SLeg. (Ld) RomA 2

confederacie n. 2 *AF* Chaucer Bo 1

confederen v. 1b *OF & ML* Chaucer *Pity* 2

confermen v. 2 *OF (& L)* ?a1250 (?939) Chart in Birch Cart.Sax. HF 16

confessen v. 2a *OF & ML* (c1378) PPl.B (Ld) Bo 18

confessioun n. 2a *L & OF* (c1378) PPl.B (Ld) Bo 39

confessour n. 1 *L & OF* (c1200) Vices & V(1) SumT 10

confiteor n. *L* (?a1200) *Ancr. *ParsT* 1

confiture n. *OF & L* Chaucer *PardT* 1

conformen v. 2a *OF & L* (c1340) Rolle Psalter (UC 64) ClT 3

confounden v. 2a *AF & L* c1300 SLeg.Nich. (Ld) 307 ABC 23

confused ppl. 1a *L* (a1338) Mannyng Chron.Pt.2 SNT 7

confusioun n. 1c *L & OF* c1300 SLeg. (Ld) ABC 24

congeien v. 2a *OF* (a1338) Mannyng Chron.Pt.2 *Tr* 1

congelen v. 2a *L & OF* Chaucer *HF* 1

congregacioun n. 1b *L & OF* Chaucer HF 9

coning n. 3 *OF* (?c1175) PMor. (Trin-C) RomA 2

conjecten v. 1a *L & OF* Chaucer Bo 6

conjectinge ger. a *(fr. conjecten v.)* (c1384) WBible(1) *Mel* 2

conjecture n. 1c *L & OF* (c1384) WBible(1) *ClT* 1

conjoinen v. 1a *OF* Chaucer Bo 12

conjoining ger. *conjoinen v.* * Chaucer *SNPro* 1

conjunccioun n. 1a *L & OF* Chaucer Bo 9

conjuracioun n. 3 *L & OF* Chaucer Bo 3

conjuren v. 1a *L & OF* (c1280) SLeg.Pass. (Pep) *Tr* 4

connen v. 1a *OE* 1123 Peterb.Chron. RomA 835

conning ppl. 2 *fr. connen v.* (c1300) NHom.(1) Abp.& N. RomA 6

conninge ger. 2 *(fr. connen v.)* (?c1300) Spec.Guy HF 29

conningli adv. a *fr. conning ger.* (1357) Gaytr.LFCatech. LGW 2

conqueren v. 4d *OF* (?c1200) HMaid. MkT 8

conquering ger. a *(fr. conqueren v.)* (c1340) Rolle Psalter (UC 64) *PF* 1

conquerour n. 1a *OF* (?c1300) Reinbrun MkT 16

conqueste n. 2 *OF & ML* (a1325) Cursor KnT 3

conscience n. 2a *OF, & L* (?a1200) *Ancr. SNPro 35

consecraten v. 2c *fr. L* Chaucer *MkT* 1

consentaunt adj. & n. 1a *OF* (a1382) WBible(1) *Phyt* 1

consentement n. a *OF* (?a1300) Arth.& M. *ParsT* 1

consenten v. 2c *L & OF* (?a1200) *Ancr. Bo 23

consentinge ger. 2b *(fr. consenten v.)* (1340) Ayenb. Mel 13

consequence n. 2a *OF* Chaucer Bo 7

consequent n. 1a *OF, & L* Chaucer *Mel* 2

conservacioun n. a *L & OF* Chaucer Bo 1

conservatif adj. a *OF* Chaucer *HF* 1

conserven v. 1a *OF & L* Chaucer SNT 10

consideracioun n. 2a *L & OF* (?c1350) Mirror St.Edm.(4) *ParsT* 2

consideren v. 2a *L & OF* Chaucer HF 89

consistorie n. 2 *L & OF* (?a1300) Tristrem *Tr* 3

consolacioun n. 3 *OF & L* Chaucer *Tr* 3

conspiracie n. a *prob. AF* (1357) Gaytr.LFCatech. MkT 2

conspiren v. 2 *L & OF* (a1376) PPl.A(1)
(Vrn) *PR*T 1

constable n. 2b *OF, fr. late L* (?c1200)
SWard *MLT* 17

constablesse n. a *OF* Chaucer *MLT* 1

constaunce n. 1a *OF, fr. L* (1340) Ayenb.
CLT 5

constaunt adj. a *L & OF* Chaucer *CLT* 3

constellacioun n. 2a *OF, & L* c1330 7
Sages(1) *TR* 6

constreinen v. 1a *OF, fr. L* (?a1325)
Bonav.Medit.(1) *BO* 49

constreininge ger. 1 *(fr. constreinen v.)*
Chaucer *BO* 2

constreinte n. 2b *OF* Chaucer *TR* 2

construen v. 2a *L* (a1376) PPl.A(1) (Vrn)
TR 3

consul n. a *L* Chaucer *BO* 3

consuler n. *(fr. consul n.)* Chaucer *BO* 2

consumen v. 6 *L & OF* Chaucer *BO* 4

contagioun n. b *L & OF* Chaucer
SNPRO 1

contagious adj. 2b *L & OF* Chaucer *BO*
1

conteinen v. 4b *OF* c1300 SLeg.Becket
(Ld) *BO* 23

contek n. 1a *AF* c1300 SLeg.Becket (Ld)
BO 4

contemplacioun n. 1 *L & OF* (?a1200)
Ancr. HF 3

contemplatif adj. 1b *L & OF* (a1340)
Rolle Psalter (UC 64) *BO* 1

contemplaunce n. *for rime's sake*
Chaucer *SUMT* 1

contenaunce n. 1a *OF & CF* (c1250)
Floris *ROMA* 49

continence n. 2a *OF & L* (c1378) PPl.B
(Ld) *WBPRO* 3

continuacioun n. a *L & OF* Chaucer *BO*
1

continuaunce n. 1 *OF* (a1349) Rolle
MPass.(2) *TR* 2

continuel adj. 1 *OF & L* a1325
MS.Rawl.B.520 lf.57 *BO* 5

continuelli adv. 1a *fr. <continuel adj.>*

c1300 SLeg.Edm.Abp. (Hrl: Horst)
SN*PRO* 4

continuen v. 3b *L & OF* (c1340) Rolle
Psalter (Ld) ABC 16

continuinge ger. a *(fr. continuen v.)*
Chaucer *PARST* 1

contract n. 1 *L & OF* (a1333) Shoreham
Poems *FRT* 1

contracten v. b *fr. <contract ppl.>*
Chaucer *PARST* 1

contraire adj. & adv. 1c *OF* Chaucer
BD 3

contrarie adj. 1 *L* (1340) Ayenb. ROMA
15

contrarie n. 1 *L* c1275 Ken.Serm. PITY 49

contrarien v. 3a *ML & OF* (c1340) Rolle
Psalter (UC 64) *BO* 5

contrarious adj. 4a *ML & OF* c1300
SLeg.Fran.(1) (Ld) *BO* 17

contrariousete n. c *OF, & ML* (c1340)
Rolle Psalter (UC 64) *PARST* 1

contree n. 3 *OF* (?a1250) Serm.Atte
wrastlinge ROMA 108

contre-folk n. 8, contree n. *(fr. contree n.
& folk n.)* (c1300) Glo.Chron.A
LGW 1

contre-houses n. 8, contree n. *(fr. contree
n. & hous n.)* Chaucer *ANEL* 1

contre-ward adv. *(fr. contree n. & -ward
suf.)* Chaucer *LGW* 1

contricioun n. 1 *L & OF* (c1303)
Mannyng HS MEL 29

contrit adj. *L* (?1300) Stations Rome(1)
PARST 2

contubernial adj. *L* Chaucer *PARST* 1

contumacie n. *L & OF* (?a1200) *Ancr.*
PARST 1

contumax adj. *L & OF* (?a1387) PPl.C
PARST 1

contumelie n. a *L & OF* Chaucer *PARST*
1

conveien v. 1a *AF & CF* (a1325) Cursor
KNT 4

convenient adj. 2 *L* Chaucer *BO* 5

convers n3. *It.* * Chaucer *TR* 1

conversacion n. 3 *L & OF* 1340 Ayenb.
MEL 1
conversen vi. b *L & OF* Chaucer *BO* 1
converten v. 2a *L & OF* c1300 SLeg. (Ld)
SNT 15
convertible adj. a *L & OF* (c1385) Usk
TL (Skeat) *CKT* 1
convicten v. 1a (c1340) Rolle Psalter
(UC 64) ABC 3
cop n. 1b *OE* (?a1200) Lay.Brut HF 5
cope n. 1a *ML* (?a1200) Lay.Brut ROMA 5
coper n. 1a *OE (fr. L)* c1275 Ancr. (Cleo:
Morton) HF 7
copie n. 2a *OF & ML* (a1338) Mannyng
Chron.Pt.2 *TR* 1
corage n. 1b *OF* (?a1300) KAlex. ROMA
94
corageous adj. 2 *OF* c1300
SLeg.Magd.(2) (Ld) MKT 3
coral ni. 1b *OF & L* (a1300) Cokaygne
KNT 3
corbet n. b *OF* Chaucer *HF* 1
cord n. 1 *fr. accord n.* (1340) Ayenb. *HF* 1
corde n. 1a a *OF* c1300 SLeg.And. (Hrl)
SNPRO 6
corden vi. 1b *fr. accorden v.* (a1325)
Cursor *TR* 1
cordewane n. *OF* Chaucer *THOP* 1
cordial n. a *fr.* <*cordial adj.*> Chaucer
GP 1
Coribant n. *L* Chaucer *BO* 2
cormeraunt n. *OF* c1330 Orfeo *PF* 1
corn n. 2a a *OE* 1121 Peterb.Chron. BD
41
cornemuse n. *OF* Chaucer *HF* 1
corner ni. 3a *OF* (c1280) SLeg.Pass.
(Pep) HF 4
corni adj. a *fr. corn n.* Chaucer
INTPARDT 2
corniculer n. *L* Chaucer *SNT* 1
corolarie n. a *L* Chaucer *BO* 3
coroune n. 1a *OF & L* a1121
Peterb.Chron. BD 41
corounen vi. 1a a *OF* ?c1200 Orm.
ROMA 14

corour n. 2c *OF* (?a1300) KAlex. *HF* 1
corporal adj. 2 *L & OF* Chaucer *PARST*
2
correccioun n. 4a *L & OF* (c1340) Rolle
Psalter (UC 64) BO 10
correcten v. 4a *fr. L* (1345–6) Grocer
Lond. ABC 12
corrigen v. a *L & OF* Chaucer *BO* 2
corrosif adj. 1a *L & OF* Chaucer *CYT*
1
corrumpable adj. *OF* Chaucer *KNT* 1
corrumpen v. 3a *L & OF* (1340) Ayenb.
BO 6
corrumping ger. *(fr. corrumpen v.)*
Chaucer *BO* 1
corrupcioun n. 4a *L & OF* (1340)
Ayenb. PF 8
corrupten v. 4a *fr. L* (1340) Ayenb. KNT
13
cors n. 1a *OF & L* c1275 Ken.Serm. PITY
20
cor-seint n. a *OF* (c1303) Mannyng HS
HF 1
cosinage n. b *OF* (1340) Rolle Psalter
(UC 64) *SHIPT* 3
cosine n. 1a *OF* (?c1225) Horn BO 28
cost n2. 3a *OF* (?c1200) St.Marg.(1)
MKT 18
costage n. 1a *OF* a1325 Of Rybaudy
WBPRO 5
coste n. 1a *OF* c1125 Dur-C.Gloss. AST 4
costeien v. 1a {2} *AF* Chaucer {(a1382)
WBible(1) Prol. Kings} ROMA 1
costen v. 2b *OF* (a1325) Cursor TR 7
cost-leue adj. a *fr. cost n2. & -leue suff.*
(a1387) Trev.Higd. *PARST* 3
costret n. a *OF* c1382 WBible(1) (DC
369(1)) *LGW* 1
cotage n. *OF* Chaucer *NPT* 2
cote ni. 1b *OE* a1200 Wor.Aelfric Gloss.
KNT 3
cote n2. 1a *OF* c1330 Why werre ROMA
11
cote-armure n. a *fr. cote n2. & armure n.*
(c1378) PPl.B (Ld) HF 7

cou n. 1a a *OE* a1200 Wor.Aelfric Gloss.
PardPro 4

couard adj. 1 *OF* c1275 Ancr. (Cleo:
Mac.) PF 7

couard n. 1a *fr. <couard adj.>* (a1250)
Harrow H. RvT 3

couardie n. *OF* Chaucer *KnT* 1

couardise n. 1a *OF* (?a1300) KAlex. *Tr* 2

couardli adv. *fr. couard n.* a1375 WPal.
Tr 1

couche n. 1a *OF* (1340) Ayenb. LGW F
4

couchen v. 2b *OF* (?a1300) Arth.& M.
PF 12

couching ger. b *(fr. couchen v.)* Chaucer
Ast 1

cough n. a *fr. <coughen v.>* (c1300)
Glo.Chron.A *MerT* 1

coughen v. a *cp. OE* a1325
Gloss.Bibbesw. *Tr* 4

counseil n. 1b *OF (L)* a1126
Peterb.Chron. BD 185

counseilen v. 3a *AF, CF* (c1280)
SLeg.Pass. (Pep) ABC 44

counseiler n. 2a *AF; CF* (?a1200) *Ancr.
Bo* 33

counseiling ger. 2 *(fr. counseilen v.)*
(?a1300) Arth.& M. WBPro 27

counten v. 2c *AF; CF* Chaucer BD 7

countesse n. a *AF; CF, ML* ?a1160
Peterb.Chron. LGW F 2

counting-bord n. 2b, counting ger. *fr.*
counting ger. *& bord n.* Chaucer *ShipT*
1

countour n1. 1a *AF; CF (fr. L)* (c1300)
Glo.Chron.A BD 4

countour-dore n. 3c, counter n. *(counter
n1. & dore n1.)* Chaucer *ShipT* 2

countour-hous n. 3c, counter n. *(fr.
counter n1. & hous n.)* Chaucer *ShipT*
1

countrefeten v. 3a *fr. <coutrefet adj.>*
c1300 SLg.Cross (Ld) BD 18

countrepeisen v. a *AF; CF* Chaucer HF
2

countrepleten v. 2, countre- pref. *AF*
(c1378) PPl.B. (Ld) *LGW F* 1

countretaille n. c *OF* c1390 Heil starre
ClT 1

countrewaiten v. 2, countre- pref. *(fr.
countre pref. & waiten v.)* Chaucer
Mel 2

coupable adj. & n. 2 *OF & L* (c1280)
SLeg.Pass. (Pep) Bo 4

coupe n2. *OF (fr. L)* (a1376) *PPl.A(1)
(Trin-C) ParsT* 1

couple n. 1a a *OF* (?c1280)
SLeg.Concep.Virg. (Ashm) *Tr* 1

couplen v. 4 *OF* (?a1200) *Ancr.* Bo 3

couren v. 2a *prob. ON* a1300 Vncomly in
Roma 1

cours n. 3a *OF & L* c1300 SLeg.Inf.Chr.
(Ld) SNT 41

courser n. 1 *OF* (?c1300) Guy(1) Tr 13

court n1. 6a *OF* ?a1160 Peterb.Chron.
Roma 36

courteis adj. & n. 1a *AF & CF* a1300 11
Pains (Jes-O) *Roma* 11

courteisie n. 1 *AF (CF)* (?a1200) *Ancr.
Roma* 33

courteisliche adv. b *fr. courteis adj.* c1300
SLeg.Becket (Hrl) *Roma* 10

courte-pi n. *MDu.* Chaucer {(c1378)
PPl.B (Ld)} *Roma* 3

court-man n. 5b a, court n1. *fr. court n1.
& man n.* Chaucer *MerT* 1

couth adj. (& n.) 1a *OE* a1131
Peterb.Chron. HF 6

coveiten v. 2 *OF* a1250 Ancr. (Nero) Bo
25

coveiting ger. 1a *(fr. coveiten v.)* (a1333)
Shoreham Poems *LGW* 1

coveitise n. 1 *OF* c1300 Body & S.(5)
Roma 54

coveitour n. *OF* (?c1350) Mirror
St.Edm.(4) *Mars* 1

coveitous adj. 1c *OF* c1250
Serm.St.Nich. *Roma* 7

covenable adj. 1a *OF* c1275 Ken.Serm.
Bo 24

covenabli adv. b *fr. covenable adj.*
(?c1350) Mirror St.Edm.(4) BO 2

covenaunt n. 1a *OF* (c1300)
Glo.Chron.A ROMA 12

covent n. 2b *OF & L* (?a1200) *Ancr.
SUMT 14

cover-chef n. 1c *OF* c1300 SLeg.Pilate
(Hrl) PF 6

covercle n. a *OF* Chaucer *HF* 1

coveren v1. 10b *OF* (?c1150) Prov.Alf.
(Trin-C) MKT 42

coveren v2. 3a *fr. OE & fr. OF* (c1250)
Gen.& Ex. TR 2

covertli adv. 2a *fr. covert adj.* Chaucer
ROMA 1

coverture n. 1a *OF* (?a1200) *Ancr.
ROMA 4

covine n. 1a *OF* (c1303) Mannyng HS
BO 2

crabbed ppl. c *fr. crabbe n1.* (a1376)
PPl.A(1) (Vrn) *CLT* 1

cracching ger. a *(fr. cracchen v.)* c1330 7
Sages(1) *KNT* 1

cradel n. 1a *OE* (?a1200) *Ancr. SNT 10

craft n1. 8b *OE* 1131 Peterb.Chron.
ROMA 62

crafti adj. 2a *OE* c1150 Hrl.HApul. BD 7

craftili adv. c *OE* (?c1200) St.Kath.(1)
ROMA 8

crag n. 1a *Celt.* (a1325) Cursor *BO* 1

craken v. 1a *OE* (?a1200) Lay.Brut RVT 2

craking ger. 3 *(fr. craken v.)* c1300 SLeg.
(Ld) *PARST* 1

crammen v. a *OE* a1325 Of Rybaudy HF
2

crampe n1. 1a *OF (ult. Gmc.)* (c1378)
PPl.B (Ld) *TR* 1

crampishen v. b *OF* Chaucer *ANEL* 1

crane n1. 1a *OE* ?c1200 Stw.57 Gloss. *PF*
1

crasen v. 1b *OF; ult. Gmc.* Chaucer BD 2

craven v. 3b *OE* (c1200) Vices & V.(1)
TR 2

creacioun n. 2 *L* c1390 I wolde witen
FRANT 1

creat ppl. a *L* Chaucer BO 4

creatour n. 1a *L & OF* c1300
SLeg.Becket (Ld) SNPRO 9

creature n. 2b *L & OF* (c1280)
SLeg.Pass. (Pep) ROMA 122

creaunce n. 1a *OF* (?c1300)
St.Patr.Purg.(1) ABC 3

creauncen v. *OF* Chaucer *SHIPT* 3

creaunt adj. & n. b *fr. <recreaunt adj.>*
a1250 Ancr. (Nero) *PARST* 1

crede n2. *OE; ult. L* a1225
Lamb.Hom.Creed TR 2

credence n. 2b *OF* (a1338) Mannyng
Chron.Pt.2 SNT 6

credible adj. 1 *L* Chaucer *BO* 1

crepel n. 1a *OE* (?c1200) HMaid. *TR* 1

crepen v. 2b *OE* 1131 Peterb.Chron. BD
30

crepuscule n. *L & OF* Chaucer *AST* 2

cresse n. 1a *OE* ?c1125 Dur-C.Gloss.
MILT 1

creste n1. 2a *OF & L* (?a1350) Siege
Troy(1) *THOP* 1

crevace n. b *OF* (?a1350) Castleford
Chron. HF 2

crie n. 5a *OF* (c1280) SLeg.Pass. (Pep) PF
9

crien v. 5b *OF* (?a1200) *Ancr. BD 154

criing ger. 1a *(fr. crien v.)* (?a1300)
Arth.& M. BO 4

crike n1. 1a *ON* (c1250) Gen.& Ex. BO 3

crime n. 2 *OF & L* c1250 Louerd asse thu
ard SNT 2

crinkled ppl. *cp. <cringle n.> & MDu.*
Chaucer *LGW* 1

crisp adj. 1 *L* c1300 SLeg. (Ld) ROMA 4

cristal adj. 1b b {1a} *fr. cristal n.* Chaucer
{(?c1380) Pearl} ROMA 4

cristal n. 1a *L, OF & OE* (c1250) Floris
ROMA 4

Criste-masse n. 1a *OE* (1100)
Chart.St.Paul in RHS ser 3.58
INTMLT 2

Cristen adj. & n. 1a *OE* a1121
Peterb.Chron. SNT 27

Cristendom n. 1c *OE* (1100)
Chart.St.Paul in RHS ser.3.58 SNT 8
Cristenli adv. *fr. cristenli adj.* (1357)
Gaytr.LFCatech. *MLT* 1
Cristianite n. 2b *L & OF* a1300 Floris
(Vit) *MLT* 1
cristnen n. 1a *OE* c1175 Bod.Hom. SNT
6
Cristofre n. a *OF & ML; ult Gr.* c1300
SLeg.Chris (Ld) *GP* 1
crois n. 5 *OF* (?a1200) *Ancr. ABC 16
crok n. 1a *OE & ON* a1200
Gloss.Sidonius *LGW* 1
croked ppl. 4c *OE* (?a1200) *Ancr.
ROMA 11
crokedli adv. a *fr. croked ppl.* (?a1325)
Bonav.Medit.(1) *ANEL* 1
crokke n. a *OE* a1250 Ancr. (Nero)
TRUTH 2
crome n. 1a *OE* c1150 PDidax. *SNPRO* 1
crone n. a *AF* Chaucer *MLT* 1
cronicle n. a *AF* (c1303) Mannyng HS
NPT 1
crop n. 2a *OE* c1150 Hrl.HApul. ROMA
9
cros n. 1b c *OE & ON* (?a1200) *Ancr.
ABC 10
cros-line n. 9b, cros n. *(fr. cros n. & line
n1.)* Chaucer AST 1
crosselet n2. a *fr. cros n.* Chaucer *CYT*
9
crossen v. 1 *fr. cros n.* (?a1200) *Ancr. AST
1
crou n. *fr. <crouen v.>* (?a1200)
Trin.Hom. *MILT* 1
crouchen v1. a *fr. crouche n.* (?a1200)
*Ancr. MILT 2
crouden v1. 1c *OE* (?c1225) Horn HF 3
crouding ger1. a *(fr. crouden v1.)*
Chaucer HF 2
croue n. 2e *OE* a1200 Wor.Aelfric Gloss.
PF 14
crouen v. 1a *OE* c1250 Judas TR 8
crouinge ger. *(fr. crouen v.)* (c1384)
WBible(1) *NPT* 2

croupe n. 1a *OF* (?a1300) Arth.& M.
FRT 1
crouper n. a *AF, CF* Chaucer CYPRO 2
crucifien v. 1a *OF* (a1325) Cursor *PARST*
2
crude adj. a *L* Chaucer *CYT* 1
cruel adj. 4 *OF, fr.L* ?c1200
Wor.Bod.Gloss. ABC 89
cruelli adv. b *(fr. cruel adj.)* Chaucer
MKT 8
cruelte n. 1 *OF* (?a1200) *Ancr. ROMA
26
crul adj. a *cp. MDu.* (?a1300) KAlex. GP
2
cubite n. 1b *OE & L* (a1338) Mannyng
Chron.Pt.1 MKT 2
cucurbite n. c *OF & L* Chaucer *CYT* 1
culpoun n. a *AF* (c1350) Ywain KNT 2
culter n. a *OE; ult. L* c1300 Body & S.(5)
MILT 4
culver n. 1a *OE; ult. L* ?c1200 Orm.
LGW 1
Cupide n. a *OF* (c1350) Alex.& D.
ROMA 17
cuppe n. 1a *OE & OF; L* c1150 PDidax.
KNT 7
curacioun n. a *OF* Chaucer BO 4
curat n. a *ML* (?1382) Wycl.Pet.Parl. GP
7
cure n1. 3a *OF & L* c1300 SLeg.Becket
(Hrl) PITY 45
curen v2. 2b *OF & L* (c1378) PPl.B (Ld)
BO 7
curfeu-tyme n. 2b, curfeu n. *(fr. curfeu n.
& time n.)* Chaucer *MILT* 1
curious adj. 1d *ML & OF* (1340) Rolle
Psalter (Ld) ROMA 13
curiousite n. 2b *OF & L* (?c1378)
Wycl.OPastor HF 5
curiousli adv. c *fr. curious adj.* (1340)
Ayenb. *FRANT* 1
curre n. *akin to OI, MLG* (?a1200)
*Ancr. LGW F 1
curs n. 1a *OE* a1121 Peterb.Chron. GP
6

cursed ppl. 3a *fr. cursen v.* ?c1200 Orm. MKT 58

cursedli adv. a *fr. cursed ppl.* Chaucer MKT 3

cursednesse n. 1a *fr. cursed ppl.* (c1303) Mannyng HS Bo 16

cursen v. 3a *OE* ?a1160 Peterb.Chron. TR 15

cursing ger. 2a a *(fr. cursen v.)* a1121 Peterb.Chron. GP 6

curtine n. 1a *OF* (?c1300) Bevis PF 3

custume n. 1a *OF* (?a1200) Trin.Hom. Bo 6

cut n2. 1a *fr. cutten vi.* (a1325) Cursor GP 8

cutten vi. 7a *OE* a1300 Serm.Lithir lok Bo 13

cuttinge ger. 3 *fr. cutten vi.* c1350 Cmb.Ee.4.20 Nominale Bo 1

daffe n. a *? c1330 Why werre RVT 1

daggen vi. *fr. <dagge n1.>* (c1378) PPl.B (Ld) PARST 1

daggere n. *AL; prob fr. OF* Chaucer GP 4

dagginge ger. *(fr. daggen vi.)* Chaucer PARST 1

dagoun n. a *? Chaucer SUMT 1

dai n. 3b *OE* 1121 Peterb.Chron. ROMA 744

daie n. 1a *OE* (?a1200) Trin.Hom. NPT 1

daierie n. a *formed in AF fr. daie n.* c1300 SLeg.Bridget(1) (Ld) GP 2

daies-ie n. 1a *fr. dai n. & eie n1.* a1300 Hrl.978 Vocab LGW F 14

dai-light n. a *(fr. dai n. & light n.)* (?1150) Prov.Alf. (Mdst) CYT 1

dai-sterre n. a *OE* c1250 Owl & N. Bo 2

dale n. 1 *OE & ON* ?c1200 Orm. PF 4

daliaunce n. 2 *fr. dalien v. or AF* (a1349) Rolle MPass.(2) LGW F 11

damage n. 1a *OF* (?a1300) Arth.& M. Bo 17

damageous adj. *OF* Chaucer PARST 1

damascene adj. as n. a *L* Chaucer MKT 1

dame n. 1b *OF, fr. L* (?a1200) *Ancr. ROMA 77

damisele n. 2a *AF, OF, L* (?c1225) Horn ROMA 5

dampnable adj. (& adv.) 2 *ML & OF* (c1303) Mannyng HS MKT 7

dampnableli adv. a *fr. dampnable adj.* Chaucer MEL 2

dampnacioun n. 2 *ML & OF* (?c1300) Spec.Guy ABC 7

dampnen v. 2b *OF & ML* ?c1200 Orm. BD 26

dappel-grai adj. & n. *fr. <dappeld grai phr.> or cp. OI* Chaucer THOP 1

daren v. 1a *OE* (?c1200) St.Kath.(1) SHIPT 1

dart n. 1 *OF, ult. Gmc.* (?a1300) Tristrem LADY 11

darten v. 1a *fr. dart n.* Chaucer TR 1

daswen v. *akin to <dasen v.>* a1325 Wyth was hys HF 2

date n2. 5 *fr. L* c1330 SMChron. WBPRO 2

date-tree n. 2a, date n1. *(fr. date n1. & tre n.)* Chaucer {(c1390) Susan} ROMA 1

dauen v. 1a *OE* (?a1200) Lay.Brut MKT 7

dauinge ger. 1a *OE* (?a1200) *Ancr. TR 1

daun n. 2 *AF, CF* a1300 Vncomly in ROMA 59

daunce n. 1a a *OF* (?a1300) KAlex. ROMA 34

dauncen v. 1a *OF* (?a1300) KAlex. ROMA 65

daunger n. 1d *AF, CF* a1250 Ancr. (Nero) ROMA 19

daungerous adj. 2a *OF* (?a1200) *Ancr. ROMA 11

dauninge ger. a *fr. daunen v.* * (c1250) Gen.& Ex. BD 8

daunten v. 1a *OF (fr. L)* (?a1300) KAlex. ROMA 11

de n. 1b *OF* (?a1300) KAlex. TR 12

de prep. *OF* ?a1160 Peterb.Chron. ROMA 4

debat n. 1a *OF* (a1325) Cursor BD 11

debaten vi. 2a *OF* Chaucer Bo 4

debonaire adj. & n. 1a *CF, NF* (?a1200) *Ancr. ROMA 25

debonaireli adv. *fr. debonaire adj. & n.* Chaucer BD 11

debonairete n. *OF* (?a1200) *Ancr. BD 11

deceite n. 1a *AF* (?a1300) KAlex. Bo 12

deceivable adj. 3a *AF* (c1303) Mannyng HS PF 10

deceivaunce n. a *AF* (a1338) Mannyng Chron.Pt.2 Bo 1

deceiven v. 1a *AF* (c1300) NHom.(1) Abp.& N. HF 42

deceiving ger. *(fr. deceiven v.)* (?c1350) SVrn.Leg. *ROMA* 1

Decembre n. *OF* 1122 Peterb.Chron. HF 6

declamen v. *L* Chaucer TR 1

declaracioun n. 2b *OF & L* Chaucer Bo 10

declaren v. 3b *L & OF* (a1338) Mannyng Chron.Pt.2 PITY 37

declaring ger. 1 *(fr. declaren v.)* (?c1378) Wycl.OPastor Bo 2

declinacioun n. 2 *L & OF* Chaucer AST 24

declinen v. 6 *OF* (1376) *PPl.A(1) (Trin-C) Bo 5

decoped ppl. *cp. OF* Chaucer *ROMA* 1

decre n. 2b *OF* (c1303) Mannyng HS MKT 8

ded adj. 2a a *OE* a1121 Peterb.Chron. ROMA 194

ded n. b *fr. OE* ?c1200 Orm. *SCOG* 1

dede n. 1a a *OE* a1121 Peterb.Chron. ROMA 129

deden v. d *OE* Chaucer *HF* 1

dedicat ppl. a *L* Chaucer PARST 1

dedli adj. 1c *OE* (c1200) Vices & V.(1) ROMA 59

dedli adv. 2a *OE* (?a1200) *Ancr. BD 6

deduit n. *OF* c1300 SLeg.Brendan (Hrl: Wright) *KNT* 1

def adj. (& n.) 1a *OE* ?c1200 Orm. SNT 7

defacen v. 2a *OF* (1340) Ayenb. HF 6

defamacioun n. a *OF & ML, CL* (c1303) Mannyng HS *FRT* 1

defame n. 1a *OF* Chaucer MKT 4

defamen v. 1 *OF & L* (c1303) Mannyng HS HF 6

defaute n. 3a *OF* a1250 Ancr. (Nero) BD 38

defendaunt n. 3 *AF* Chaucer PARST 1

defenden v. 3a *OF & L* c1250 *St.Marg.(2) ABC 56

defendour n. 1a *OF* (c1300) Glo.Chron.A Bo 2

defense n. 1a a *OF* (c1300) Glo.Chron.A ROMA 17

defet ppl. (& n.) 1a *OF* Chaucer *TR* 2

defeten v. 1b *fr.* <*defet ppl.*> Chaucer Bo 1

defien vi. 1c *OF* (?a1300) KAlex. (Auch) KNT 12

defoulen v. 2d *fr. foulen vi. & OF* (c1280) SLeg.Pass. (Pep) Bo 26

degre n. 2a *OF* (?c1200) HMaid. ROMA 301

deien v. 1a *OE* (c1325) Recipe Painting(1) in Archaeol.J.1 Bo 9

deier n. *fr. deien v.* (c1325) Recipe Painting(1) in Archaeol.J.1 GP 1

deinen vi. 1a *OF & L* c1300 SLeg.Cross (Ld) MKT 12

deinous adj. *fr.* <*disdeinous adj.*> (a1338) Mannyng Chron.Pt.2 TR 2

deinte adj. 1b *fr. deinte n.* c1300 SLeg.Nich. (Ld) TR 8

deinte n. 1c *AF & CF* a1250 Ancr. (Nero) ANEL 16

deintevous adj. c *fr. deinte n.* (a1387) Trev.Higd. CLT 2

deis n. 2b *AF & CF* c1300 SLeg.Cuth. (Ld) HF 7

deite n. 1 *OF* (?c1300) Spec.Guy TR 7

deken n. 1a *OE, fr. L* 1122 Peterb.Chron. SNT 2

del n2. 1a *OE* a1121 Peterb.Chron. ROMA
48

delaie n. 2a *OF* (a1250) Harrow H. TR 9

delaien v1. 1a *OF* c1300 SLeg.11000 Virg.
(Ld) TR 2

delectable adj. {b} *OF & L* Chaucer
{(a1396) *Hilton SP} ROMA 1

delen v. 1a *OE* a1131 Peterb.Chron. TR 11

deliberacioun n1. 1c *OF & L* Chaucer
BO 14

deliberen v. b *L & OF* Chaucer TR 3

delicacie n. 3a *ML & ?OF* Chaucer MKT
3

delicat adj. 2a *L* Chaucer MKT 10

delice n. 2a *OF* (?a1200) *Ancr. SNPRO
26

delicious adj. 1a *OF* (?a1300) KAlex. BO
2

deliciousli adv. b *fr. delicous adj.* c1300
SLeg.MLChr. (Ld) MERT 3

delie adj. *OF* Chaucer BO 1

delitable adj. a *OF* c1300 SLeg.Brendan
(Ld) ROMA 9

delitabli adv. *fr. delitable adj.* Chaucer
BO 1

delite n1. 1a *OF* (?a1200) *Ancr. ROMA
83

deliten v. 1a *OF* (?a1200) *Ancr. ROMA
35

delitous adj. *OF* Chaucer ROMA 2

deliveraunce n. 1a *OF* c1300 SLeg. (Ld)
TR 1

delivere adj. 1b *OF* c1300
SLeg.Edm.Abp. (Hrl) ROMA 2

deliveren v. 1b *OF* (?a1200) *Ancr. PF 38

deliverliche adv. a *fr. deliver adj.* a1375
WPal. TR 2

delivernesse n. a *fr. delivere adj.* (a1382)
WBible(1) MEL 2

deluge n. a *OF* Chaucer BO 3

delven v. 1a *OE* c1150 Hrl.HApul. BD 10

delver n. a *OE* (a1376) PPl.A(1) (Vrn) BO
1

demaunde n. 1a *AF; CF* (c1280)
SLeg.Pass. (Pep) SNT 10

demeine n1. 1a *OF (fr. L)* (?a1300)
Arth.& M. *MKT* 1

demeinen v. 1b *OF* (?a1300) KAlex. *HF* 1

demen v. 3b *OE* c1175 Bod.Hom. ROMA
136

deming ger. 1a *(fr. demen v.)* (c1303)
Mannyng HS *BO* 1

demoniak adj. & n. b *L & OF* Chaucer
SUMT 2

demonstracioun n. 2a *L & OF* Chaucer
HF 4

demonstratif adj. & n. a *L & OF*
Chaucer *SUMT* 1

den n1. 1c *OE* c1175 Body & S.(1) MKT 2

Dene-marche n. *OE* (?a1200) Lay.Brut.
WBPRO 1

denien v. 1b *OF (fr. L)* a1325 MS
Rwl.B.520 lf.56 BO 19

denticle n. *L* Chaucer *AST* 1

dep adj. 1a a *OE* a1150 Rwl.G.57.Gloss.
BD 18

dep n. 1a *OE* (c1250) Prov.Hend. BO 2

de-par-dieux adv. *OF* c1300
SLeg.Becket (Ld) TR 4

departen v. 2a *OF* (c1250) Floris HF 85

departinge ger. 1b *fr. departen v.*
(?a1200) *Ancr. PF 10

depe adv. 4 *OE* ?c1200 Orm. ROMA 29

depeinten v. 1b *fr. OF* (?a1200) *Ancr.
ROMA 12

depli adv. 2a *OE* ?c1200 Orm. BO 1

depnesse n. 1a *OE* c1150 PDidax. BO 3

depraven v. 1a *L & OF* (a1376) PPl.A(1)
(Vrn) MARS 1

depressioun n. c *ML & OF* Chaucer *AST*
1

depriven v. a *ML & OF* (a1338)
Mannyng Chron.Pt.2 ABC 3

der n. 3c *OE* 1123 Peterb.Chron. ROMA 8

deraie n. 1a *AF & CF* (?a1300) KAlex.
PARST 1

dere adj1. 3a *OE* ?a1160 Peterb.Chron.
ROMA 270

dere adv. 1b *OE* (?c1175) PMor. (Lamb)
ABC 25

dereinen v. 2a *OF* c1225 Wooing Lord
KNT 4

dereling n. 1c *OE* (?c1150) Prov.Alf.
(*Glb-James) MILT 1

deren v. 1a *OE* c1150 Hrl.HApul. MKT 4

dere-worthe adj. 2a *OE* c1175
Bod.Hom.(2) BO 3

deriven v. a *L & OF* Chaucer KNT 2

derk adj. 1c *OE* a1121 Peterb.Chron.
ROMA 54

derk n. 1b *fr. derk adj.* (?c1225) Horn BD
3

derken v. 3a *OE* c1300 SLeg.Becket (Ld)
BO 11

derkliche adv. 2a *fr. derk adj.* (c1378)
PPl.B (Ld) HF 1

derknen v. c *fr. derken v.* Chaucer BO 1

derknesse n. 4 *fr. derk adj.* (a1325)
Cursor SNT 32

derne adj. 4a *OE* a1121 Peterb.Chron.
MILT 3

derthe n. 1a *prob. OE* (c1250) Gen.& Ex.
HF 2

descenden v. 1e *OF & L* (?a1300) Arth.&
M. ROMA 44

descensioun n. c *L & OF* Chaucer AST 2

descensorie n. *ML* Chaucer CYT 1

descent n. 1b *OF* (?a1300) Arth.& M. TR
1

descripcioun n. 1a *L & OF* Chaucer
ROMA 10

descriven v. 2b *OF (fr. L)* a1250 Ancr.
(Nero) ROMA 24

descrivinge ger. c *(fr. descriven v.)*
(c1300) Glo.Chron.A PARST 1

desert n1. 1 *OF* (c1300) Glo.Chron.A BO
22

desert n2. 1a *ML & OF* (?a1200) *Ancr.
SNPRO 6

desert ppl. 1a *L & OF* (c1250) Gen.& Ex.
HF 2

deserven v. 1a *OF & L* c1225 Ancr. (Tit:
Morton) ROMA 60

desespeiren v. c *OF* Chaucer LADY 1

desesperat ppl. *L & OF* Chaucer HF 1

desesperaunce n. a *OF* (?a1200) *Ancr.
TR 2

desir n. 1a *OF* (?a1300) Arth.& M. PITY
65

desiren v. 1a a *OF* (?c1200) HMaid.
ROMA 174

desiringe ger. a {b} *(fr. desiren v.)*
Chaucer {(c1378) PPl.B (Ld)} ROMA 6

desirous adj. 1a *OF* (?a1300) KAlex. BO
9

deske n. a *ML* Chaucer FRANT 1

deslave adj. a *OF* (?c1384) Wycl.50
HFriars PARST 2

desolate adj. 3c *L* (?1350)
SVrn.Leg.Barlaam ANEL 9

despeir n. 1 *AF (CF)* (c1300) NHom.(1)
Abbess BO 12

despeiren v. 3 *fr. OF* (1340) Ayenb. PITY
16

desperacioun n. 2 *L & OF* Chaucer
ABC 2

despisen v. 2a *OF* c1300 SLeg.Inf.Chr.
(Ld) ROMA 48

despit n. 2b *OF* c1300 SLeg.Becket (Ld)
ROMA 47

despitous adj. 3a *OF* Chaucer ROMA 12

despitousli adv. 1b *fr. <despitous adj.>*
(?c1350) Ywain MKT 7

despoilen v. 2c *OF* (?a1200) *Ancr. BO 8

despoilinge ger. b *(fr. despoilen v.)*
Chaucer BO 1

desputeison n. a *OF* c1300 SLeg. (Ld)
BO 4

destinable adj. *OF* Chaucer BO 1

destinal adj. *?ML or fr. destine n.*
Chaucer BO 6

destine n. 1 *OF* (c1350) Alex.& D. HF 39

destrer n. *OF* (?a1300) Arth.& M. THOP
1

destroien v. 1 *OF & L* (?a1200) *Ancr.
ROMA 55

destroiere n. a *OF* (a1382) WBible(1)
PARST 1

destruccioun n. 3a *OF & L* (?c1300)
Guy(1) BD 26

determinate adj. a *L* Chaucer AST 3
determinen v. 7b *L & OF* Chaucer HF
6
deth n. 1a *OE* a1121 Peterb.Chron. ROMA
309
detraccioun n. 2 *L & OF* (1340) Ayenb.
PARST 4
dette n. 4a *OF & L* (?a1200) *Ancr. BO
16
detteles adj. *fr. dette n.* Chaucer *GP* 1
dettour n. 1a *AF (CF) & L* (?a1200)
*Ancr. WBPRO 4
deu n. 1 *OE* ?c1200 Orm. ROMA 4
deus n1. *OF & L* c1225 Ancr. (Tit:
Morton) SUMT 2
devel n. 5 *OE* c1150 Hrl.HApul. HF 100
devel-wei n. 6b, devel n. *(fr. devel n. &
wei n.)* (?c1200) St.Juliana *LGW* 1
dever n. 1a *AF, CF* (a1333) Shoreham
Poems TR 5
devis n. 3a *OF* c1300 SLeg. (Ld) ROMA
10
devisen v. 5 *OF* (?c1225) Horn ROMA 118
devisinge ger. c *(fr. devisen v.)* Chaucer
KNT 1
devocioun n. 1 *L & OF* (?a1200) *Ancr.
ROMA 24
devouren v. 1a *fr. OF (L)* (a1333)
Shoreham Poems SNPRO 17
devourer n. b *fr. OF & devouren v.* (1384)
WBible(1) *LGW* 2
devout adj. 1a *OF & L* (?a1200) *Ancr.
ABC 5
devoutli adv. 1 *fr. devout adj.* (1340)
Ayenb. BD 4
diademe n. 3a *OF & L* c1300
SLeg.Becket (Ld) GENT 5
diamaunt n. a *OF* c1325 Ichot a burde in
a KNT 1
diametre n. a *OF; ult.Gr.* (a1387)
Trev.Higd. *AST* 1
Diana n. a *L.* (?a1200) Lay.Brut *PF* 15
diapren v. b *OF* Chaucer ROMA 2
diche n. 1b *OE & ON* (?c1150) Prov.Alf.
(Trin-C) RVT 4

dichen v. 1a *fr. diche n.* c1300
SLeg.Fran.(1) (Ld) KNT 3
dien v. 1a a *ON* c1175 HRood ROMA 310
diete n. 3a *ML & OF* (?a1200) *Ancr. GP
5
difference n. 1b *L & OF* (1340) Ayenb.
SNT 18
differren v. 2a *L & OF* Chaucer *BO* 1
difficulte n. 1 *OF & L* Chaucer BO 8
diffinen v. 2a *ML & OF* Chaucer HF 6
diffinicioun n. 2c *ML & OF* (c1384)
WBible(1) *WBPRO* 1
diffinishen v. *OF* Chaucer *BO* 8
diffinitif adj. *OF* Chaucer *PHYT* 1
diffusioun n. *L & OF* Chaucer *TR* 1
digestible adj. a *OF* Chaucer *GP* 1
digestif adj. & n. 2a *L & OF* Chaucer
NPT 1
digestioun n. 1a *L & OF* Chaucer *SQT*
1
diggen v. 1a *AF* (?a1200) *Ancr. BO* 1
dighten v. 1c c *OE* a1121 Peterb.Chron.
ROMA 20
digne adj. 2a *OF & L* c1300 SLeg.Becket
(Ld) HF 35
digneli adv. c *fr. digne adj.* (a1333)
Shoreham Poems BO 3
dignite n. 1a *OF* (?a1200) *Ancr. MKT
69
digression n. *L & OF* Chaucer *TR* 1
diinge ger. a *fr. dien v.* (c1300)
Glo.Chron.A MKT 5
dilatacioun n. a *L & OF* Chaucer *MLT*
1
diligence n. 1b a *OF & L* (1340) Ayenb.
SNPRO 36
diligent adj. 1a *OF & L* (1340) Ayenb.
TR 8
diligentli adv. a *fr. diligent adj.* (1340)
Ayenb. BO 3
dim adj. 1a b *OE* c1175 Bod.Hom. TR 2
diminucioun n. 1c *L & OF* (c1303)
Mannyng HS *TR* 1
dimmen v. 2a *OE* a1200 Body & S.(2)
BO 1

dinen v2. 1 *OF* (c1300) Glo.Chron.A TR 11

diner n. 1a *OF* (c1300) Glo.Chron.A TR 6

dint n. 1c d *OE* ?c1200 Orm. *HF* 1

diocise n. *ML & OF; ult. Gr.* (a1338) Mannyng Chron.Pt.1 *GP* 1

direct adj. c *L & OF* Chaucer *AST* 3

direct adv. { } *fr. <direct adj.>* Chaucer {(c1392) EPlanets} VENUS 2

directen v. 1b *fr. L* Chaucer *TR* 1

disarmen v. b *OF* Chaucer *BO* 1

disavauncen v. a *OF* Chaucer *TR* 1

disaventure n. *OF* Chaucer *TR* 4

disblamen v. *OF* Chaucer *TR* 1

discernen v. 3d *L & OF* Chaucer HF 8

discerning ger. *(fr. discernen v.)* Chaucer *BO* 1

dischargen v. 3b *OF* (a1338) Mannyng Chron.Pt.2 *PARST* 3

dischevele adj. & ppl. *OF* Chaucer PF 5

disciple n. 1a *OE, L & OF* c1175 Bod.Hom. BO 7

discipline n. 1 *L & OF* (c1200) Vices & V.(1) CYT 3

disclaundre n. 1a *fr. <esclaundre n.>*, *sclaundre n.* c1300 SLeg.Becket (Hrl) *TR* 1

disclaundren v. 1a *fr. <esclaundren v.>*, *sclaundren v.* c1300 SLeg. (Ld) LGW 4

discolouren v. 2 *OF & L* c1380 Firumb.(1) *CYPRO* 1

discomfiten v. 1a *fr. OF* (?a1200) *Ancr.* BO 4

discomfiting ger. a *(fr. discomfiten v.)* Chaucer *KNT* 1

discomfiture n. 1a *OF* (a1338) Mannyng Chron.Pt.1 ROMA 4

discomfort n. 2a *OF* c1350 MPPsalter TR 5

discomforten v. 1a *OF* (c1300) Glo.Chron.A *KNT* 1

disconsolate adj. 2a *ML* Chaucer *TR* 1

discordable adj. c *OF & L* Chaucer BO 3

discordaunt adj. a *L & OF* Chaucer BO 3

discorde n. 1a *OF & L* c1230 *Ancr.* (Corp-C) HF 12

discorden v. 1a *L & OF* (a1325) Cursor BO 7

discours n. *L* Chaucer *BO* 1

discoveren v. 4a *OF* (?c1300) Bevis BD 18

discovert n. a *OF* (?a1300) KAlex. *PARST* 1

discrecioun n. 1c *ML & OF* (c1303) Mannyng HS MKT 25

discrete adj. b *OF & L* Chaucer TR 17

discreteli adv. *fr. <discrete adj.>* Chaucer MKT 6

discussen v. 1a *fr. ML* (c1380) Wycl.Papa PF 2

disdeine n. 1b *OF* c1300 SLeg.John (Ld) ROMA 17

disdeinen v. 1b *OF* (a1338) Mannyng Chron.Pt.1 BO 2

disencresen v. 2a *fr. encresen v.* Chaucer *BO* 1

disese n. 1a *OF* (a1338) Mannyng Chron.Pt.2 ROMA 26

disesen v. 2 *OF* (c1384) WBible(1) *TR* 4

disfigurat adj. *L* Chaucer *PF* 1

disfigure n. *fr. figure n.* Chaucer *WBT* 1

disfiguren v. 2 *OF* (?c1375) NHom.(3) Leg. TR 4

disgise adj. 2a *OF* c1330 SMChron. (Auch) *PARST* 1

disgisen v. 2a a *OF* (?a1300) KAlex. TR 2

disgisenesse n. a *fr. disgise adj.* Chaucer *PARST* 1

disgising ger. 1a *(fr. disgisen v.)* (a1349) Rolle MPass.(2) *PARST* 1

dish n. 2a *OE & L* c1175 HRood *WBPRO* 1

disheriten v. 1a a *OF* c1300 SLeg. (Ld) KNT 4

dish-metes n. 6, dish n. *(fr. dish n. & mete n1.)* (c1353) Winner & W. *PARST* 1

dishoneste adj. a *OF* Chaucer CLT 6
dishoneste n. 1 *OF* Chaucer PARST 1
dishonour n. a *OF* (?a1300) Arth.& M.
TR 7
disjointe n. a *OF* Chaucer TR 5
dismaien v. 1a a *fr. amaien v.*, <*esmaien v.*> c1300 SLeg.Inf.Chr. (Ld) BO 1
dismal n. & adj. a *OF* (c1300)Songs
Langtoft BD 1
dismembren v. 1a *OF* (c1300)
Glo.Chron.A PARST 2
dismembring ger. b *(fr. dismembren v.)*
Chaucer PARST 1
disobeien v. c *OF* Chaucer CLT 2
disobeissaunt adj. a *OF* Chaucer PF 2
disordeine adj. a *OF* (1340) Ayenb. BO 3
disordinate adj. b *ML* Chaucer PARST 3
disordinaunce n. b *OF* Chaucer HF 5
disparage n. b *OF* (a1333) Shoreham
Poems CLT 1
disparagen v. 1 *OF* c1375 WPal. RVT 2
dispenden v. 1b *OF* a1300 Worldes blis
ne last MKT 14
dispendour n. a *OF* (c1384) WBible(1)
MEL 1
dispensacion n. 2 *L & OF* Chaucer BO 2
dispense n. 2a *OF* (?a1300) KAlex.
ROMA 18
dispensen v. 1b *L & OF* (?c1350)
SVrn.Leg.Barlaam BO 2
displaien v. 1 *AF (CF)* (?a1300) Arth.&
M. KNT 1
displesaunce n. 1a *OF* (a1349) Rolle 10
Com. TR 5
displesaunt adj. a *OF* Chaucer PARST 3
displesen v. 1a *OF* (c1378) PPl.B (Ld) BO
23
disponen v. 1 *L* Chaucer BO 8
disport n. 1a *AF; CF* (c1303) Mannyng
HS HF 23
disporten v. 2b *AF; CF* Chaucer HF 9
disposen v. 7a *OF* (1373) *Lelamour
Macer BO 13
disposicioun n. 1a *L & OF* Chaucer HF
17

dispreisen v. *OF* (a1325) Cursor ROMA
3
dispreisinge ger. a *(fr. dispreisen v.)*
Chaucer MEL 2
disputen v. 1b *L & OF* c1300 SLeg.Kath.
(Ld) BD 6
disputinge ger. a *fr. disputen v.* * (?c1200)
St.Kath.(1) BO 1
dissencioun n. a *L & OF* (a1325) Cursor
STED 3
disseveraunce n. 1a *OF* Chaucer BO 2
disseveren v. 1c b *OF* c1275 Ken.Serm.
PITY 8
dissimulacioun n. 1 *L & OF* Chaucer
HF 2
dissimulen v. 1 *L & OF* Chaucer SNT 5
dissimuler n. a *fr. dissimulen v.* Chaucer
FORT 2
dissimulinge ger. a *(fr. dissimulen v.)*
Chaucer TR 3
dissolven v. 1b *L* Chaucer BO 3
distaf n. a *OE* a1200 Wor.Aelfric Gloss.
MKT 4
distaunce n. 1b *OF & L* c1300
SLeg.Becket (Ld) HF 6
distaunt adj. b *L& OF* Chaucer AST 2
disteinen v. 2a *OF* Chaucer TR 5
distemperaunce n. 2 *ML & OF* (1340)
Ayenb. BO 3
distemperen v. 1a *ML & OF* Chaucer
SUMT 4
distillen v. 4b *L & OF* (?c1378)
Wycl.OPastor TR 1
distinccioun n. 1c *L & OF* (?a1200)
*Ancr. BO 1
distincten v. 3b *fr. L & OF* c1300
SLeg.Inf.Chr. (Ld) PARST 1
distinctli adv. a *fr. L* (a1382) WBible(1)
AST 1
distinguen v. 1a *L & OF* (c1340) Rolle
Psalter (UC 64) BO 1
distourbaunce n. 1a *OF* (c1280)
SLeg.Pass. (Pep) MARS 1
distourben v. 2c *OF & L* (?a1200) *Ancr.
BO 23

distourbinge ger. 1b *(fr. distourben v.)* c1300 SLeg.MLChr. (Ld) *VENUS* 1

distracten v. 1b *fr. L* (c1340) Rolle Psalter (UC 64) *BO* 1

distreinen v. 3b *OF* c1300 SLeg.Becket (Hrl) PF 15

distresse n. 1a *OF* (c1280) SLeg.Pass. (Pep) ROMA 64

distroublen v. 2b *OF* (c1303) Mannyng HS *BD* 1

disturnen v. *OF* Chaucer *TR* 1

dite n. 1a *OF* ?a1325 Heil seint michel HF 8

diurnal adj. *L* Chaucer *MLT* 1

diurne adj. *L* Chaucer *MERT* 1

diverse adj. 3a *L & OF* c1275 Ken.Serm. ROMA 107

diverseli adv. 2a *fr. diverse adj.* c1330 Why werre ROMA 10

diversen v. 1a *OF* ?a1325 The grace of ihu *TR* 1

diversite n. 3a *OF* (c1340) Rolle Psalter (UC 64) BO 9

dives n. *L* (c1378) PPl.B *SUMT* 1

dividen v. 1a b *L* (?a1325) Bonav.Medit.(1) ROMA 37

divinacioun n. 1a *L & OF* Chaucer (a1382) WBible(1) *BO* 2

divinaille n. a *OF* Chaucer *PARST* 1

divine adj. 1b *L & OF* Chaucer MKT 65

divine n. 2a *L & OF* (?c1300) Arth.& M. *TR* 3

divinen v. 3d *L & OF* (a1338) Mannyng Chron.Pt.1 HF 15

divineresse n. *OF* Chaucer *TR* 1

divininge ger. a *fr. divinen v.** (a1349) Rolle 10 Com BO 2

divinistre n. *fr. divinen v.* Chaucer *KNT* 1

divinite n. 2a *OF* c1300 SLeg.Edm.Abp. (Hrl) SNT 10

divinour n. 2b *OF* (a1376) *PPl.A(1) (Trin-C) BO* 1

divisioun n. 5 *L & OF* (?c1350) SVrn.Leg. BO 18

do n. 1b *OE* a1200 Wor.Aelfric Gloss. ROMA 2

doctour n. 1a *L & OF* (a1376) PPl.A(1) (Trin-C) SNT 8

doctrine n. 3a *L & OF* Chaucer BO 15

doere n. 1a *fr. don vi.* Chaucer *BO* 3

dogge n. 1a *OE* (?a1200) *Ancr. ROMA 7

doggerel adj. a *fr. dogge n.* Chaucer *THOP* 1

doinge ger. 7a *(fr. don vi.)* (?1348) Rolle FLiving ROMA 16

doke n. 1a *OE* (?a1300) Arth.& M. PF 4

dokke n. 3 *OE* a1300 Hrl.978 Vocab. *TR* 1

dokken v. 2a *fr. <dok n.>* (?c1378) Wycl.OPastor. *GP* 1

dolfin n. 1a *OF* (c1350) Alex.& D. *HF* 1

dom n. 1a a *OE* c1175 Bod.Hom. ROMA 35

domb adj. 1a *OE* ?c1200 Orm. SNT 8

domesman n. 1a *(fr. dom n. & man n.)* (?c1175) PMor. (Lamb) MKT 3

dominacioun n. 2c *OF & L* (a1325) Ipotis MKT 7

don adj. 2 *OE* (a1325) Cursor ROMA 3

don n. a *fr. don adj.* Chaucer *MANCPRO* 1

don vi. 1d a *OE* a1121 Peterb.Chron. GENERAL 1679

don v2. *fr. do on phr.* (?a1350) 7Sages(2) *TR* 2

dong n1. 4 *OE* (?a1200) *Ancr. GP 8

dong-carte n. 5, donge n1. *(fr. dong n1. & cart n.)* Chaucer *NPT* 1

dongen v. a *fr. dong n1.* Chaucer *NPT* 1

donghil n. 1a, dong-hep, -hil n. *fr. dong n1. & hille n.* (c1280) SLeg.Eust. *PF* 1

dongoun n. 2b *OF; ult. Gmc.* (c1300) NHom.(1) Pilgr. KNT 2

dore n1. 2c *OE* (?c1150) Prov.Alf. (Mdst) ROMA 59

dormaunt adj. & n. 1b *OF* (?c1300) Amis (Suth) *GP* 1

dortour n. *OF* c1300 SLeg. (Ld) *SUMT* 1

doseine n. 1 *OF* (?a1300) KAlex. *GP* 1

Chaucer's words

doser n. 1 *OF* (?c1378) Wycl.OPastor *HF* 1

dotage n. a *fr. doten v.* (?c1380) Cleanness RVPRO 4

dotard n. *fr. dote n.* Chaucer WBPRO 3

doten v. 1a *prob.OE* (?a1200) *Ancr. ROMA 5

double adj. 5b *OF* (?a1200) *Ancr. HF 14

doublen v. 2b *OF* c1300 SLeg.Brendan (Ld) BO 4

doublenesse n. 1b *fr. double adj.* Chaucer ANEL 5

doucet adj. & n. 2b *OF* Chaucer *HF* 1

douen v2. 1a *OF* (a1376) PPl.A(1) (Trin-C) *TR* 1

douere n. 1 *OF* (a1387) Trev.Higd. *CLT* 2

doughter n. 1a *OE* a1121 Peterb.Chron. SNPRO 127

doughti adj. & n. 2a *OE* ?c1200 Orm. ROMA 5

doun adv. 1a *OE* a1121 Peterb.Chron. GENERAL 263

doun n. 1 *ON* Chaucer BD 2

doun prep. b *fr. doun adv.* Chaucer BD 2

doune n. 1a *OE* a1150 Vsp.DHom. *THOP* 1

doun-right adv. 1a *fr. doun adv. & right adj. & adv.* (?a1200) Lay.Brut *MANCT* 1

doun-ward adv. 4a *fr. doun adv. & -ward suff.* c1175 Bod.Hom. ROMA 11

doun-ward prep. *fr. doun-ward adv.* Chaucer *TR* 1

doutaunce n. a *OF & ML* (?a1300) KAlex. *TR* 3

doute n. 4 *OF* (?a1200) *Ancr. ABC 70

douteles adj. *fr. doute n.* Chaucer *BO* 1

douteles adv. *fr. doute n.* Chaucer SNPRO 29

douten v. 2c *OF* (*fr. L*) (?a1200) *Ancr. ROMA 40

doutous adj. 3 *OF* ?a1325 The grace of ihu BO 5

doutremer phr. as adj. *OF* Chaucer *BD* 1

douve n. 1a *OE* (?a1200) Trin.Hom. ROMA 10

draf n. 1a *OE* (?a1200) Lay.Brut LGW G 2

draf-sak n. 3, draf n. *(fr. draf n. & sak n.)* Chaucer *RVT* 1

dragoun n. 1a *OF & L* c1250 *St.Marg.(2) MKT 11

drake n2. a *cp. LG, HG & OHG* (c1300) Havelok PF 3

drasti adj. c *OE* Chaucer *THOP* 2

drauen v. 2a b *OE* a1131 Peterb.Chron. ROMA 103

draught n. 1b *prob. OE* (?a1200) Lay.Brut ROMA 16

drecchen v. 1a *OE* a1121 Peterb.Chron. *TR* 4

drecchinge ger. 1a *OE* (?c1200) HMaid. *TR* 2

drede n. 1a *fr. dreden v.* (?a1200) Lay.Brut ROMA 193

dredeful adj. 2a *fr. drede n.* (?a1200) *Ancr. MKT 21

dredefulli adv. 1b *fr. dredeful adj.* (?a1300) Arth.& M. *TR* 2

dredeles adv. b *fr. drede n.* Chaucer *BD* 14

dreden v. 1b *fr. adreden v.* ?c1200 Orm. ROMA 112

drem n2. 1a *OE & ON* (c1250) Gen.& Ex. ROMA 70

dremen v2. 1a *fr. dremen v1. & drem n2.* (c1250) Gen.& Ex. ROMA 23

dreming ger2. b *fr. dremen v2.* (c1303) Mannyng HS *NPT* 1

drenchen v. 4b *OE* (?c1175) PMor. (Trin-C) BD 37

drenchinge ger. 1a *(fr. drenchen v.)* (?c1300) Guy(1) KNT 4

dreri adj. 1a *OE* ?c1200 Orm. HF 7

279

drerinesse n. b *OE* (?c1200) SWard. Bo
3

dressen v. 1a *OF* (?a1300) KAlex. RomA
32

drie adj1. 7g *OE* c1150 Hrl.HApul.
RomA 24

drie n1. 1a *OE* (?a1200) Trin.Hom.
MkT 4

drien v1. 3a *OE* c1150 Hrl.HApul. MkT
9

drien v2. 3a *OE* a1121 Peterb.Chron. HF
12

drinke n. 1b *OE* c1150 PDidax. MkT 49

drinkeles adj. a *fr. drinke n.* a1225
Lamb.Hom. *TR* 1

drinken v. 1a b *OE* c1150 PDidax. RomA
88

drinkinge ger. 1a *(fr. drinken v.)* ?c1200
Orm. *ParsT* 4

driven v. 1b c *OE* a1121 Peterb.Chron.
RomA 71

drivere n. d *fr. driven v.* Chaucer *Bo* 1

drogge n. *OF* Chaucer *GP* 1

dronke-leue adj. a *OE* (a1376) PPl.A(1)
(Vrn) SumT 5

dronken ppl. 1b *OE* (?c1150) Prov.Alf.
(Mdst.) MkT 28

dronkenesse n. 1b *OE* c1175 Bod.Hom.
TR 13

drope n1. 3d *OE* c1150 Hrl.HApul.
RomA 14

droppen v. 1a *OE* c1150 PDidax. Bo 8

droppinge ger. 1b *(fr. droppen v.)* (a1333)
Shoreham Poems MEL 2

droughte n. 1 *OE* ?c1200 Orm. Bo 5

drounen v1. 1a b *prob. ON* a1325
Gloss.Bibbesw. *CYT* 1

droupen v. 1a *ON* a1300 Loke to thi
louerd *GP* 1

drovi adj. *OE* (a1250) Bestiary *ParsT* 1

druerie n. 1c *OF* (?a1200) *Ancr. RomA*
1

druggen v. *prob. OE* Chaucer *KnT* 1

dubben v. 1a *OE & OF* (?a1200)
Lay.Brut *ParsT* 1

ducat n. a *ML & OF* Chaucer *HF* 1

Duch adj. & n. 1 *MDu.* (c1333–52)
Minot Poems *HF* 1

duchesse n. a *OF* (?a1300) Stations
Rome(1) KnT 6

due adj. 2b *OF* ?c1350 Why werre Bo 9

duelie adv. 1d *fr. due adj.* Chaucer *Bo* 1

duete n. 1b *AF* (1377) Tenants in
Som.Dor.NQ 13 TR 7

duk n. 2a *OF & L* a1131 Peterb.Chron.
RomA 39

dul adj. 2 *OE* c1225 St.Kath.(1) (Tit) BD
10

dulcarnoun n. *ML, fr. Ar.* Chaucer *TR* 2

dullen v. 3a *fr. <dul adj.>* (?c1200)
St.Kath.(1) Bo 9

dulnesse n. c *fr. dul adj.* (1357) Gaytr.
LFCatech. *BD* 1

durabilite n. *cp. OF & L* Chaucer *Bo* 1

durable adj. a *L & OF* Chaucer *ParsT*
1

duracioun n. *OF* Chaucer HF 2

duren v. 1a *L & OF* c1250 *Body & S.
ABC 35

duresse n. 2a *OF* c1330 Why werre TR 2

during ppl. as adj. d *fr. duren v.* (?c1280)
SLeg.Advent, etc. (Eg) TR 2

during prep. *fr. during ppl.* Chaucer
LGW G 4

duringe ger. a *(fr. duren v.)* Chaucer *Bo*
1

durren v. 1a a *OE* ?a1160 Peterb.Chron.
RomA 203

durring don phr. & cpd. *fr. durren v.*
Chaucer *TR* 1

dusken v. a *OE* (?c1200) HMaid. Bo 2

dust n. 1b *OE* c1150 PDidax. Bo 2

dwale n. 3 *OE* (?c1150) Prov.Alf. (Trin-
C) *RvT* 1

dwellen v. 1a *OE* ?c1200 Orm. RomA
204

dwellinge ger. 1 *(fr. dwellen v.)* (c1300)
Havelok BD 17

dwinen v. a *OE* c1150 Hrl.HApul. *RomA*
1

ebbe n. 1a a *OE* a1121 Peterb.Chron. *SQT* 1

ebben v. 1 *OE* (?a1200) Trin.Hom. Bo 3

Ebraik adj. *late L* Chaucer HF 3

Ebreu n. 2 *OF, fr. L* (?a1200) *Ancr. AST* 1

ecclesiast n. 2 *ML, fr. Gr.* Chaucer GP 3

ecco n. c *L, OF* (1340) Ayenb. *CLT* 1

ech pron. 1a *OE* (1100) Chart.St.Paul in RHS ser.3.58 ABC 115

ech on pron. phr. b *OE* a1175 Bod.Hom. BD 16

echinus n. *L* Chaucer Bo 1

eclipse n. 1 *L, OF* (c1280) SLeg.Pass. (Hrl: C.Brown) Bo 2

ecliptik adj. & n. 1a *L* Chaucer *AST* 24

edifice n. *OF* Chaucer Bo 5

edifien v. 2a *OF* (a1338) Mannyng Chron.Pt.1 Bo 1

effect n. 1c *L, OF* (?c1350) SVrn.Leg. Pity 76

effectual adj. 1a *L, OF* Chaucer *SUMT* 1

efficient adj. a *L & OF* Chaucer Bo 2

eft adv. 2 *OE* a1121 Peterb.Chron. BD 41

eft-sones adv. 5 *OE* c1150 PDidax. MKT 25

egal adj. 1a *OF, fr. L* Chaucer Bo 3

egalite n. a *OF* Chaucer Bo 2

egalli adv. 3b *fr. egal adj.* Chaucer Bo 2

egge n2. 1a *OE* ?c1200 Orm. TR 2

eggement n. *fr. eggen v1.* Chaucer *MLT* 1

eggen v1. 1b *ON* ?c1200 Orm. RomA 2

egging ger1. a *(fr. eggen v1.)* ?c1200 Orm. *MERT* 1

Egipcien n. & adj. 2 *OF* c1290 SLeg. (Ld) MKT 2

Egipte n. *OE; L* a1225 Lamb.Hom. BD 6

egle n. 2b *OF, fr. L* (a1338) Mannyng Chron.Pt.1 MKT 22

egre adj. 3b *OF* c1275 Fox & W. RomA 7

egremoine n. *OF, L* Chaucer *CYT* 1

egren v. *OF* (a1338) Mannyng Chron.Pt.1 Bo 1

ei interj. b *L; OF* c1225 Mirie it is TR 18

ei n1. 1b a *OE* c1150 PDidax. NPT 2

eie n1. 1a a *OE* a1126 Peterb.Chron. RomA 259

eied ppl. 1a *fr. eie n1.* Chaucer TR 1

eighte card. num. 1a *OE* a1121 Peterb.Chron. BD 5

eighte-tene card. num. 1a *OE* (?a1200) Lay.Brut *MILT* 1

eighte-tenthe ord. num. a *OE* (1258) Procl.Hen.III in PST (1868) *INTMLT* 1

eighethe ord. num. 1b *OE* a1175 Bod.Hom.Dom.Quadr. TR 2

eilen v. 1 *OE* c1150 Hrl.HApul. BD 22

either conj. a *OE* (c1250) Gen.& Ex. RomA 29

either pron. 1c *OE* a1121 Peterb.Chron. HF 19

ek adv. & conj. 1 *OE* a1121 Peterb.Chron. GENERAL 928

eken v. 1a *OE* a1121 Peterb.Chron. HF 7

elacioun n. 1a a *OF, L* (?c1350) Mirror St.Edm.(4) *PARST* 2

elat adj. a *L* Chaucer *MKT* 1

elboue n. 1 *OE* a1200 Wor.Aelfric Gloss. *LGW F* 1

elde n. 3 *OE* c1150 PDidax. RomA 20

elde-fader n. 1 *(fr. elde n. & fader n.)* (1155) Chart.Hen.II in Hall ME 1 Bo 1

elden v1. 2 *fr. elde n.* ?c1200 Orm. RomA 5

eldre n. 2a *OE* ?c1200 Orm. MKT 10

ele n3. 1 *OE* ?c1200 Stw.57.Gloss. HF 2

eleccioun n. 3a *AF, L* c1290 SLeg.Edm.Abp. (Ld) PF 7

element n. 1a a *L, OF* c1290 SLeg.Mich. (Ld) BD 11

elenge adj. 1a *OE* c1290 SLeg.Brendan (Ld) WBT 2

elevacioun n. 1b {1a} *L, OF* Chaucer {(a1398) *Trev.Barth.} AST* 2

elevat ppl. c *L* Chaucer *AST* 1

elf n. 1 *OE* Chaucer *MILT* 4

elf-queene n. 2d, elf n. *fr. elf n. & queene n2.* Chaucer WBT 5

elixir n. 1b *ML & OF (fr. Ar.)* (a1393) Gower CA *CYT* 1

ellebre n. *OF; L* c1150 Hrl.HApul. *NPT* 1

elles adj. 1a *fr. elles adv.* ?c1200 Orm. BD 30

elles adv. 3 *OE* a1175 Bod.Hom. GENERAL 319

elleswher adv. 1 *OE* (c1200) Vices & V.(1) ROMA 12

elleven card. num. 1a *OE* c1150 PDidax. *ParsPro* 1

elme n. 1a *OE* ?a1300 St.J.List Trees ROMA 3

elongacioun n. a *L* Chaucer *AST* 1

eloquence n. 3 *OF, L* Chaucer BD 5

elvish adj. a *fr. elve n.* (?a1200) Lay.Brut PROTHOP 3

em n1. 1 *OE* a1121 Peterb.Chron. *TR* 18

embatailled adj. *fr. <embataillen v2.>* Chaucer *ROMA* 1

embaumen v. 1b {1a b} *OF* Chaucer {(c1378) PPl.B (Ld)} ROMA 2

embelif adj. *OF* Chaucer *AST* 8

embelif adv. a *(fr. embelif adj.)* Chaucer *AST* 2

embelishen v. 2b *OF* Chaucer BO 2

embiben v. 3 *L* Chaucer *CYT* 1

embocen v. 2 *OF* Chaucer *LGW* 1

embosen v. *fr. OF* Chaucer *BD* 1

embracen v. 2a b *OF* c1350 MPPsalter BO 31

embracing ger. a *(fr. embracen v.)* Chaucer *PARST* 2

embrouden v. 1a *fr. OE & OF* c1380 Firumb.(1) HF 6

embrouding ger. *(fr. embrouden v.)* Chaucer *PARST* 1

embushement n. 1 *OF* (a1338) Mannyng Chron.Pt.1 *MEL* 1

Emeleward n. MED Suppl *CLPRO* 1

emelle prep. 1 *(fr. emelle adv.)* (a1325) Cursor *RVT* 1

emeraude n. *OF, fr. L* (?a1300) *KAlex.* ROMA 3

emisperie n. *OF & L, fr. Gr.* Chaucer TR 3

empeiren v. 1c *OF* Chaucer BO 4

emperesse n. 1 *OF* ?a1160 Peterb.Chron. ROMA 9

emperie n. 1 *OF, fr. L* (c1300) Glo.Chron.A BO 1

emperour n. 1 *OF, fr. L* (?a1200) *Ancr.* ROMA 28

emplastren v. 1c *OF & ML* Chaucer *MERT* 1

empoisonere n. *OF* Chaucer *PARDT* 1

empoisounen v. a *OF* a1375 WPal. MKT 4

empoisouning ger. *(fr. empoisounen v.)* Chaucer BO 3

emprenten v. 4 *OF, fr. L* Chaucer BO 8

emprenting ger. 4 *(fr. emprenten v.)* Chaucer *FRANT* 1

emprise n. 1 *OF* (a1325) Cursor BD 19

empten v. 1a *OE* ?c1200 Wor.Bod.Gloss. BO 5

empti adj. 5 *OE* a1175 Bod.Hom. BO 8

enamoured ppl. 1 *OF* (?c1300) Guy(1) *LGW* 2

encens n. 1 *OF; ML* (c1280) SLeg.Pass. TR 5

encensen vi. 1a *<fr. encens n.>; OF, ML* (?c1280) SLeg.Advent., etc (Eg) SNT 3

enchargen v. a *OF* Chaucer BO 1

enchauntement n. *OF* c1290 SLeg.Jas. (Ld) BD 5

enchaunten v. 1a *OF* (c1378) PPl.B (Ld) BO 3

enchaunteresse n. *OF* Chaucer BO 1

enchauntour n. *OF* c1290 SLeg.Jas. (Ld) *PARST* 2

enchesoun n. 2a *OF, fr. L* (?a1200) *Ancr.* TR 8

enclinen v. 8b *OF; L* (a1325) Cursor BD 34

enclining ger. 2 *(fr. enclinen v.)* Chaucer *HF* 1

enclosen v. 1a *OF* (a1338) Mannyng
Chron.Pt.1 ROMA 17

encombraunce n. 2 *fr.* *<encombren v.>*;
OF (?a1300) Arth.& M. *MERT* 1

encombren v. 2a *OF* (a1338) Mannyng
Chron.Pt.2 ROMA 6

encombrous adj. 3 *OF* Chaucer HF
2

encorporing ger. *(fr. encorporen v.)*
Chaucer *CYT* 1

encountren v. 1a *OF* c1300
SLeg.Brendan (Hrl: Wright) *BO* 1

encountring ger. 2 *(fr. encountren v.)*
Chaucer *BO* 1

encres n. 1a *fr. encresen v.* Chaucer
SNPRO 13

encresen v. 3a *AF, CF; L* (a1333)
Shoreham Poems PITY 44

endamagen v. 1 *OF* Chaucer *BO* 2

ende n1. 3 *OE* a1121 Peterb.Chron.
ROMA 196

endeles adj. 3a *OE* a1175 Bod.Hom. *BO*
8

endeles adv. 2 *fr. endeles. adj.* (?c1380)
Pearl *TR* 1

endelong adv. 1 *fr. OE* (?a1200) Lay.Brut
HF 4

endelong prep. 1 *fr. endelong adv.*
(?c1200) St.Marg.(1) KNT 5

enden v. 1a a *OE* a1175 Bod.Hom. ROMA
35

endenting ger. a *(fr. endenten v.)* (a1382)
WBible(1) *PARST* 1

ender n. b *fr. enden n.* (c1384) WBible(1)
TR 3

endetted ppl. b *OF* (?a1200) *Ancr. CYT*
1

endinge ger. 1c *OE* a1175 Bod.Hom. BO
3

enditement n. a *AF* (c1303) Mannyng
HS *PARST* 1

enditen v. 1c *AF; AL* (c1303) Mannyng
HS SNPRO 47

enditinge ger. 1a *(fr. enditen v.)* (c1350)
Alex.& D. VENUS 4

endouten v. a *(fr. douten v.)* Chaucer
ROMA 1

enduren v. {3a} *OF; L* Chaucer {c1380
Firumb.(1)} ROMA 79

enduring ger. *(fr. 'enduren' v.* Chaucer
BO 1

enemi n. 1a *OF* (?c1225) Horn ROMA 70

enemite n. 2a *OF* (1382) WBible(1)
MARS 3

enfamined ppl. a *OF* Chaucer *LGW* 1

enforcen v. 3b *OF* (a1338) Mannyng
Chron.Pt.1 BO 38

enfortunen v. *OF* Chaucer *MARS* 1

enfourmen v. 1b *OF; L* (?a1325)
Bonav.Medit.(1) BO 8

Engelond n. 1 *OE* a1121 Peterb.Chron.
KNT 9

engendren v. 1b *OF* c1330 SMChron.
(Auch) PF 20

engendring ger. 1a *(fr. engendren v.)*
(c1378) PPl.B HF 4

engendrure n. 4 *OF* (a1333) Shoreham
Poems PF 10

engin n. 1b *OF; L* c1275 St.Eust. ROMA
9

enginen v. 2b *OF* c1290 Body & S.(5)
NPT 1

English adj. 1 *OE & AF* ?a1150
Chron.Tbr.B.1 *HF* 1

English n. 1a *OE & AF* a1121
Peterb.Chron. ROMA 23

engreggen v. c *OF* (a1382) WBible(1)
PARST 1

enhabiten v. 4 *OF, L* c1350 MPPsalter
BO 8

enhauncen v. 1a a *AF & CF* (c1280)
SLeg.Pass. (Pep) MKT 14

enhauncing ger. b *(fr. enhauncen v.)*
(c1350) NHom.(2) PSanct. *AST* 1

enhorten v. *OF; L* (a1382) WBible(1)
KNT 2

enjoinen v. 1c *OF; L* (?a1200) *Ancr.*
MEL 6

enlacen v. b *OF* Chaucer BO 3

enluminen v. 1b *OF* Chaucer ROMA 5

enluting ger. *fr. L* Chaucer *CYT* 1

enointen v. 4a *fr. OF* (c1303) Mannyng HS ROMA 5

enqueren v. 1b *OF, ML, CL* c1290 SLeg.Cross. (Ld) ABC 20

enquering ger. *(fr. enqueren v.)* Chaucer *MLT* 1

ensaumple n. 2b *AF* c1290 SLeg.Fran.(1) (Ld) ROMA 66

ensaumplere n. 1a *(fr. ensaumple n.)* Chaucer *BO* 1

enselen v. 1a *OF* (a1338) Mannyng Chron.Pt.2 *TR* 2

ensigne n. 2a *OF; L* Chaucer *ROMA* 1

enspiren v2. 3a *L, OF* (c1340) Rolle Psalter (UC 64) *TR* 4

ensuren v. 2d *OF* (a1376) PPl.A(1) (Vrn) HF 2

entaille n1. 1a *OF* c1290 SLeg.Patr.Purg. (Ld) *ROMA* 2

entaillen v1. a {a} *OF* Chaucer {c1390 Mayden Modur} *ROMA* 2

entalenten v. *OF* Chaucer *BO* 1

entamen v. a *OF* (a1338) Mannyng Chron.Pt.1 *ABC* 1

entechen v. a *OF* Chaucer *BO* 4

entencioun n. 2b *OF; L* Chaucer HF 32

entendement n. 1b *OF* Chaucer HF 2

entenden v. 3b *OF, L* c1290 SLeg.John (Ld) *ROMA* 22

entente n. 1a *OF; ML* (?a1200) *Ancr. ROMA* 160

ententif adj. 1a *OF* Chaucer *ROMA* 14

ententifli adv. a *fr. ententif adj.* * (?c1280) SLeg.Concep.Virg. (Ashm) HF 3

enterchaungeable adj. *OF* Chaucer *BO* 2

enterchaungen v. 1c *OF* Chaucer *BO* 8

enterchaunging ger. c *(fr. enterchaungen v.)* Chaucer *BO* 3

entercomunen v. 1b *AF* Chaucer *TR* 1

entercomuning ger. a *fr. entercomunen v.* * Chaucer *BO* 1

enterditen v. 1a *fr. <enterdit n.> & OF* c1290 SLeg.Becket (Ld) *PARST* 2

enterlacen v. b *OF* Chaucer *BO* 1

enterli adv. 1a *fr. <entere adj. & adv.>* (c1340) Rolle Psalter (UC 64) *PARST* 2

entermedlen v. 1a *AF, CF* Chaucer *ROMA* 3

entermes n. b *OF* (1340) Ayenb. *PF* 1

entermeten v. 3a *OF, AF; L* (?a1200) *Ancr.* PF 6

enterparten v. *OF* Chaucer *TR* 1

enticement n. a *OF* (?a1300) Arth.& M. *PARST* 1

enticen v. 1 *OF* (c1280) SLeg.Pass. (Pep) *PARST* 1

enticere n. *fr. enticen v.* Chaucer *PARST* 1

enticing ger. a *(fr. enticen v.)* (a1325) Ipotis *PARST* 2

entitelen v. 1a *OF, ML* Chaucer *PF* 1

entrailles n. 1a *OF, ML* (?a1300) *KAlex. BO* 5

entre n. 6a *OF* (c1300) Glo.Chron.A ROMA 10

entren v. 1b *OF* (c1280) SLeg.Pass. (Pep) ROMA 40

entriken v. {a} *L; OF* Chaucer {(a1393) Gower CA} ROMA 2

entringe ger. 3 *(fr. entren v.)* (?a1300) Arth.& M. *BO* 6

entune n. cp. *<tune n.> & <entunen v.>* Chaucer *BD* 1

entunen v. a cp. *<tune n.> & OF* Chaucer *TR* 2

envenimen v. 1 *OF* c1290 SLeg.Inf.Chr. (Ld) ROMA 5

enveniming ger. *(fr. envenimen v.)* Chaucer *MERT* 2

envie n. 1a *OF* (c1280) SLeg.Pass (Pep) ROMA 61

envien v1. 1a *OF, fr. ML* (a1382) WBible(1) *WBPRO* 1

envien v2. *OF, fr. L* Chaucer BD 4

envined ppl. *OF* Chaucer *GP* 1

envious adj1. 2 *AF* (c1303) Mannyng HS ROMA 10

enviroun adv. 7 *AF* (a1382) WBible(1) *LGW F* 1

Chaucer's words

environen v. 6 *fr.* <*enviroun adv.*>; *OF* c1350 MPPsalter ROMA 8

envirouninge ger. a *(fr. environen v.)* Chaucer *BO* 5

envolupen v. *OF* Chaucer *PARD T* 1

epicicle n. *OF & L, fr. Gr.* Chaucer {(a1398) *Trev.Barth.} *AST* 1

Epicurien n. *[L]* Chaucer *BO* 3

epistel n. 2 *OE, OF; L* a1175 Bod.Hom. HF 14

equacioun n. 2 *AF; L* Chaucer AST 8

equal adj. 1 *L* Chaucer AST 8

equalli adv. a *(fr. equal adj.)* Chaucer *SUM T* 2

equator n. *L* Chaucer *AST* 1

equinox n. 2 *OF; L, ML* Chaucer *AST* 1

equinoxial adj. *OF, fr. L* Chaucer AST 12

equinoxial n. 1 *OF, fr. L* Chaucer AST 36

equite n. 1a *OF* (a1333) Shoreham Poems BO 5

er adv. 4b *OE & ON* a1121 Peterb.Chron. BO 6

er conj1. 1a a *fr. er adv.* a1121 Peterb.Chron. GENERAL 268

er prep. 1a *fr. er adv.* a1121 Peterb.Chron. GENERAL 66

ere n1. 1 *OE* c1150 PDidax. ROMA 64

ere n2. a *OE; OHG* (?a1200) *Ancr. BO 2

erect adj. *L* Chaucer *INTMLT* 1

eren v1. 1a *OE* a1175 Bod.Hom. HF 3

erende n. 1 *OE* a1175 Bod.Hom. BD 2

erest adj. sup. 1a *OE* c1150 PDidax. SNT 11

erest adv. 2 *OE* a1121 Peterb.Chron. ROMA 30

erl n. 1b *OE* a1121 Peterb.Chron. ROMA 11

erli adv. 2b *OE* (?c1150) Prov.Alf. ROMA 12

ermen v. *OE* Chaucer BD 2

Ermin n. & adj. *no etym.* Chaucer *MKT* 1

ernest n. 1b *OE* a1175 Bod.Hom. HF 20

ernestful adj. *fr. ernest n.* Chaucer TR 2

erratik adj. & n. *OF, L* Chaucer *TR* 1

erraunt adj. f *AF* Chaucer BD 2

erren v1. 3a *OF, L* a1300 Vncomly in SNT 19

errour n1. 3 *OF, L* (?a1300) Arth.& M. ABC 24

errour n2. b *cp. OF* (?a1200) *Ancr. PF 2

erthe n1. 6b *OE* a1121 Peterb.Chron. ROMA 118

ertheli adj. 1a *fr. erthe n1.; OE* a1150 Vsp.D.Hom. ROMA 34

erthen adj. a *fr. erthe n1.* (?a1200) *Ancr. CYT* 1

escapen v. 1a a *CF, AF, NF* c1290 SLeg.Becket (Ld) SNT 33

eschaufen v. 1a *OF* Chaucer BO 10

eschaufinge ger. a *(fr. eschaufen v.)* Chaucer *PARS T* 2

eschaunge n. 2a *AF* (c1378) PPl.B (Ld) HF 7

escheu adj. 1 *OF* (?a1200) *Ancr. MERT 2

escheuen v. 2b a *OF* (?c1300) LFMass Bk. SNPRO 45

escheuinge ger. *(fr. escheuen v.)* Chaucer PF 3

ese n. 1a *OF* (?a1200) *Ancr. LADY 64

esement n. 1 *OF, AL* (a1338) Mannyng Chron.Pt.1 *RVT* 2

esen v. 2a *OF* (c1290) SLeg. (Ld) ROMA 18

esi adj. 9c *OF* (?a1200) Trin.Hom. BD 17

esili adv. 1 *fr. esi adj.* (c1290) SLeg. (Ld) HF 12

esing ger. a *fr. esen v.* Chaucer TR 1

espace n. *OF* Chaucer *MEL* 1

espece n. MED Suppl. *no etym.* not in MED *PARS T* 1

especial adj. 2 *OF* (c1385) Usk TL (Skeat) TRUTH 4

espiaille n. a *OF* Chaucer FRT 2

espirituel adj. a *OF* Chaucer ROMA 17

essoine n. 1b *OF* (c1300) Glo.Chron.A
PARST 1

est n. 5a g *OE* 1121 Peterb.Chron. BD 72

establisshen v. MED Suppl. *[OF]*
Chaucer BO 18

estat n. 10a *AF, CF & L* (?a1200) *Ancr.
ROMA 124

estatli adj. 2a *fr. estat n.* Chaucer MKT 4

estatute n. MED Suppl. *no etym.* not in
MED *BO* 1

estern n. 1 *OE* a1121 Peterb.Chron.
PARST 2

estimacioun n. 1a *OF, L* (1375) Award
Blount in ORS 7 *BO* 3

estre n. pl. 3c *OF* (?a1200) Lay.Brut
ROMA 5

estward adv. 1b *OE* a1121 Peterb.Chron.
TR 8

et cetera *L* c1150 Hrl.MQuad. AST 4

eten v. 2a *OE* ?1160 Peterb.Chron. ROMA
77

eternal adj. 1 *L, OF* Chaucer SNPRO 3

eternalli adv. 1b *fr. eternal adj.* * Chaucer
ABC 8

eterne adj. 2 *OF, L* Chaucer ABC 27

eternite n. 1 *OF* Chaucer *BO* 7

ethe adv. 2 *OE* (c1125)
Vsp.D.Hom.Fest.Virg *BO* 1

ethe pred. adj. 2b *OE* a1121
Peterb.Chron. *TR* 1

Ethiopien n. *OF* (c1250) Gen.& Ex.
PARST 1

etik n1. b *OF; LL, fr. Gr.* Chaucer *LGW*
F 1

etinge ger. 1 *(fr. eten v.)* ?c1200 Orm.
PARST 5

eu n. 1a *OE* a1200 Wor.Aelfric Gloss.
ROMA 3

Eurus n. *L, fr. Gr.* Chaucer *BO* 2

evangelie n. 2b *L* Chaucer {(c1378)
PPl.B} ROMA 3

evangelist n. 1a *L, OF* (?c1200)
St.Juliana PRT 4

even adj. 16c *OE* (?c1175) PMor. (Trin-
C) ROMA 23

even adv. 5b *OE* c1150 Hrl.MQuad.
ROMA 37

even n. 1b *OE* a1121 Peterb.Chron.
ROMA 33

evene-Cristene n. 16c, even adj. *(even adj.
& cristen n.)* (?c1175) PMor.(Trin-C)
PARST 5

evenforth prep. a *f. even adv. & forth
adv.* (?c1280) SLeg.OT Hist (Ld 622)
TR 5

evening n1. *OE* (?a1200) Lay.Brut AST 3

evenli adj. 2 *OE* ?c1200 Orm. *BO* 3

evenli adv. 10d *OE* (c1200) Vices &
V.(1) *BO* 2

even-song n. 1 *OE* (?a1200) *Ancr. GP 2

even-sterre n. *OE* (a1250) Bestiary *BO* 1

even-tide n. 1 *OE* (?a1200) *Ancr. LGW
2

ever adv. 1a *OE* a1121 Peterb.Chron.
GENERAL 446

everi pron. 3f *OE* ?a1160 Peterb.Chron.
GENERAL 728

everich-on pron. 2a *(fr. everi pron. & on
pron.)* (?c1200) SWard ROMA 51

everi-del n. & adv. 2 *(fr. everi pron. &
del n2.)* (a1250) Bestiary ROMA 19

everiwhere adv. *OE* (?c1200) St.Kath.(1)
PITY 5

ever-lasting ppl. a *(fr. ever adv. & lasten
vi.)* c1225 St.Marg.(1) (Roy) *MEL* 1

ever-mor adv. 4f *OE* a1200 Body & S.(2)
BD 84

evidence n. 5 *OF, fr. L* (c1378) PPl.B
(Ld) AST 1

evidentli adv. *(fr. evident adj.)* Chaucer
BO 3

exaltacioun n1. 4 *L* 1389 Nrf.Gild Ret.
WBPRO 4

exaltat adj. *L* Chaucer WBPRO 1

exametron n. MED Suppl. *[L; fr. Gr.]*
Chaucer PROMKT 1

examinacion n. 1 *L & OF* Chaucer *MEL*
1

examinen v. 2 *OF, L* (c1303) Mannyng
HS BO 11

Chaucer's words

examining ger. c *(fr. examinen v.)* (a1387) Trev.Higd. MEL 1

exceden v. 3 *L, OF* Chaucer Bo 3

excellence n. 1 *OF; L* (?c1350) SVrn.Leg. PITY 17

excellent adj. 1 *OF; L* (a1349) Rolle MPass.(1) (Cmb L1: Horst.) Bo 16

excepcioun n. 3 *OF & L* (a1382) WBible(1) LGW 3

excess n. 4 *OF, & L* (a1382) WBible(1) TR 7

exciten v. 2b *L, OF* (c1340) Rolle Psalter (UC 64) Bo 9

exciting ger. *(fr. exciten v.)* (a1387) Trev. Higd. PARST 1

excusable adj. a *L & OF* Chaucer TR 1

excusacioun n. 2 *L, & OF* (1345–6) Grocer Lond. LGW G 3

excuse n. a *OF* Chaucer ANEL 2

excusen v. 3 *OF, L* c1225 Ancr. (Tit: Morton) BD 37

execucioun n. 2 *L, AF* Chaucer Bo 8

executen v. 2 *OF, & L* Chaucer TR 2

executour n. 1 *AF, ML* c1290 SLeg. (Ld) SUMT 1

executrice n. c *AF & ML* Chaucer TR 1

exempt ppl. 2a *OF, & L* Chaucer Bo 1

exercen v. *OF, L* Chaucer Bo 1

exercise n. 4a *OF* (c1340) Rolle Psalter (UC 64) Bo 3

exercisen v. 4 *fr. exercise n.* Chaucer Bo 9

exercising ger. 2a *(fr. exercisen v.)* Chaucer Bo 2

exercitacioun n. b *L & OF* Chaucer Bo 1

exil n1. 1c *OF (L)* (a1325) Cursor Bo 7

exiled ppl. *fr. exilen v.* * (?c1300) LFMassBk. Bo 13

exilen v. 1c *OF, ML* (a1325) Cursor ABC 15

exiling ger. a *(fr. exilen v.)* Chaucer Bo 2

existence n. a *OF* Chaucer HF 1

Exodus n. *L, OF* (?a1200) *Ancr. PARST 1

exorcisacioun n. *ML* Chaucer HF 1

expans adj. *L* Chaucer FRANT 1

expellen v. 3 *L* Chaucer KNT 1

experience n. 1b *OF; L* Chaucer HF 22

expert ppl. adj. 2 *L, OF* (c1384) WBible(1) TR 6

exposicioun n. 2a *OF; L* c1390 Treat.Mass. PARST 1

expounen v. 3a *AF; L* (c1340) Rolle Psalter SNPRO 11

expres adj. 1 *L, OF* (a1393) Gower CA HF 2

expresse adv. a *L* (?c1380) Pearl WBPRO 8

expresseli adv. {d} *fr. expresse adv.* Chaucer {(a1393) Gower CA} PARDT 1

expressen v. 6a *ML, OF* (c1384) WBible(1) TR 12

expulsif adj. b *OF & ML* Chaucer KNT 1

extenden v. 7a *L* (a1338) Mannyng Chron.Pt.2 MLT 1

extorcioun n. a *OF; ML* (a1325) Cursor STED 6

f n. a *no etym.* (a1387) Trev.Higd. AST 15

fable n. 2c *OF, L* (?a1300) *KAlex. ROMA 15

face n. 1a *OF; L, ML* c1290 SLeg.Becket (Ld) ROMA 137

facioun n. 1a *OF; L* (?c1300) Bevis ROMA 7

facound adj. *OF, L* Chaucer PF 1

facounde n. a *OF, L* c1330 St.Mary Magd.(1) BD 3

faculte n. 2a *OF* Chaucer HF 5

fade adj. 1 *OF* c1290 SLeg.Mich. (Ld) ROMA 2

faden v1. 3b *OF* (?a1325) Bonav.Medit.(1) ROMA 4

fader n. 1a *OE* a1121 Peterb.Chron. ROMA 189

fader-in-laue n. *(fr. fader in laue phr.)* Chaucer Bo 2

fadme n. pl. 1a *OE* a1175 HRood ROMA 4

faile n. 2 *OF* c1275 Sirith ROMA 13

failen v. 4a *OF* (?a1200) *Ancr. ROMA 80

failinge ger. 5 *(fr. failen v.)* (c1340) Rolle Psalter (UC 64) BO 3

fain adj. 1a b *OE* (?a1200) Lay.Brut ROMA 24

fain adv. *fr. fain adj.* (?a1200) Lay.Brut ROMA 46

fair adj. 1a a *OE* a1175 Bod.Hom. ROMA 300

fair n. a *OE* a1225 Trin.Hom.Creed. KNT 4

faire adv. 5 *OE* ?a1160 Peterb.Chron. ROMA 68

faire n. *OF* c1250 Prov.Alf. TR 1

fairie n. 2b *OF* (?a1300) *KAlex. WBT 11

fairnesse n. 2a *OE* a1175 Bod.Hom. BD 12

fal n. 1a *OE* ?c1200 Orm. TRUTH 4

falding n. 2 *cp. OI* (1374) Pat.R.Edw.III GP 2

fallen v. 19a *OE* c1150 PDidax. ROMA 334

falling ppl. 1a *fr. fallen v.* c1150 Hrl.MQuad. TR 2

fallinge ger. 1a *fr. fallen v.* (c1280) SLeg.Pass. (Pep) MKT 7

fals adj. 7b *L, OF* ?c1200 Orm. ROMA 226

fals adv. b *(fr. fals adj.)* a1300 Thu schald o WBT 2

fals n. 1a *OE, fr. L* a1126 Peterb.Chron. HF 2

falsen v. 1 c *OF; L* (?a1200) *Ancr. BD 12

falshede n. 2a *fr. fals adj.* c1290 SLeg.Jas. CYT 5

falsli adv. 1b *fr. fals adj.* (?a1200) *Ancr. MKT 26

falsnesse n. 1a *fr. fals adj.* (c1300) Glo.Chron.A ANEL 13

falteren v. 1b *cp. OI* Chaucer MLT 1

falwe adj2. a *OE* (?a1200) Lay.Brut. HF 2

falwe n. 1 *OE* ?a1300 Gloss.Neckham WBPRO 1

fame n1. 1b *OF* (?a1200) *Ancr. SNPRO 81

familiarite n. 1 *OF & L* (?a1200) *Ancr. BO 2

familier adj. 1a *OF, & L* Chaucer BO 5

familier n. 1a *fr. <familier adj.>* c1225 Ancr. (Tit: W & H) BO 8

famine n. a *OF* (a1376) PPl.A(1) HF 3

famous adj. 1a *AF, & L* Chaucer HF 6

famous adv. *(fr. famous adj.)* Chaucer HF 1

fane n1. 2 *OE* (?a1350) Siege Troy(1) CLT 1

fanne n. 1 *OE, & L* a1325 Gloss.Bibbesw. MILT 2

fantasie n. 1b *OF, L, fr. Gr.* (c1350) Alex.Maced. BD 28

fantastik adj. 1a *L, OF* Chaucer KNT 1

fantom n. 1 *OF; L* a1250 Ancr. (Nero) HF 3

fare n1. 1a *OE* a1121 Peterb.Chron. PITY 23

fare-carte n. 8b, fare n1. *(fr. fare n1. & carte n.)* Chaucer TR 1

faren v. 1a *OE* a1121 Peterb.Chron. ROMA 147

farewel interj. 10b a, faren v. *(fr. fare wel phr.)* Chaucer BD 32

farmacie n. *OF, & ML* Chaucer KNT 1

farsen v. 2 *OF* (c1340) Rolle Psalter (UC 64) LGW 2

fast adj. 2d *OE* a1150 Hrl.HApul. ANEL 5

faste adv. 2e *OE* c1150 Hrl.HApul. ROMA 226

fasten n. 1a *OE & ON* a1175 Bod.Hom. TR 1

fasten v1. 8 *OE* ?a1160 Peterb.Chron. WBPRO 1

fasten v2. 2b *OE* c1150 PDidax. ROMA 19

fastinge ger2. 1a *(fr. fasten v2.)* ?c1200 Orm. ROMA 9

fastnen v. 8 *OE* a1121 Peterb.Chron. Bo 6

fat adj. 4a *OE* c1150 PDidax. ROMA 12

fatal adj. 2 *L & OF* Chaucer BO 5

fate n. 2a *OF, L* Chaucer TR 3

fatten v. 1a *OE* (?a1200) *Ancr. SUMT 1

fattish adj. a *fr. fat adj.* Chaucer BD 1

fauconer n. 1a *OF* Chaucer FRANT 1

faucoun n. 1a *OF; L* c1250 Owl & N. ROMA 17

faun n. 1a *L* Chaucer TR 2

faunen vi. 2 *OE* c1225 Ancr. (Tit: Morton) BD 1

favour n. 5a *OF & L* (?a1300) *KAlex. MKT 17

favourable adj. 1a *OF* (a1376) PPl.A(1) (Vrn) HF 2

favouren v. 1b *OF* (c1350) Alex.& D. BO 1

fe n2. 1d *AF, CF* c1290 SLeg.Becket (Ld) BD 6

feble adj. 8 *OF (fr. L)* ?c1200 Wor.Bod.Gloss. ROMA 31

feblenesse n. 1 *fr. feble adj.* (?c1280) SLeg.Nativ. (Eg) HF 1

feblesse n. a *OF* (?a1200) *Ancr. BO 10

febliche adv. b *fr. feble adj.* c1290 SLeg.Jas. (Ld) TR 1

februarie n. *L* a1150 Vsp.DHom. AST 3

fecche n. 1 *CF & L* (?c1320) Fasc.Mor. in EASBrown TR 1

fecchen v. 1a *OE* a1121 Peterb.Chron. SNT 19

fecching ger. *(fr. fecchen v.)* Chaucer TR 1

feden v. 1a *OE* (c1125) Vsp.D.Hom.Fest.Virg. ROMA 16

feding ger. 1b *(fr. feden v.)* (?a1325) Bonav.Medit.(1) PARST 1

feffen v. 1a *AF; CF* c1290 SLeg.Magd.(2) (Ld) BO 4

feinen v. 6a *OF (fr. L)* c1290 SLeg. BD 54

feining ger. 4 *(fr. feinen v.)* Chaucer BD 3

feint adj. 1a *OF* c1290 SLeg.Inf.Chr. (Ld) ROMA 1

feinten v. 3a *fr. feint adj.* (?a1300) Guy(2) BD 4

feinting ger. a *(fr. feinten v.)* (?a1300) Guy(2) CLT 1 .

feire n. 1a *OF (fr. ML)* (c1250) Floris TR 3

feith n. 8e *AF (fr. L)* (a1250) Harrow.H. ROMA 108

feithed ppl. *(fr. feith n.)* Chaucer TR 1

feithful adj. 1a *fr. feith n.* (a1325) Cursor SNPRO 8

feithfulli adv. 3b *fr. feithful adj.* (?a1325) Bonav.Medit.(1) HF 15

fel adj. 1a *OF* c1290 SLeg. (Ld) ROMA 11

fel n1. 1a *OE* c1150 PDidax. TR 1

felaue n. 3 *ON* (c1200) Vices & V.(1) ROMA 80

felauship n. 2 *fr. felaue n.* (c1200) Vices & V.(1) BD 14

felauships v. 3b *fr. felauship n.* Chaucer BO 4

feld n. 1a *OE* a1121 Peterb.Chron. BD 45

felde-fare n. a *fr. OE* ?a1300 St.J.List Trees PF 2

fele indef. num. 1b *OE* a1121 Peterb.Chron. ROMA 11

fele-fold adj. a *OE* (?a1200) Lay.Brut BO 1

felen vi. 3a *OE* a1175 Bod.Hom. ROMA 118

felicite n. 2a *OF* Chaucer ABC 19

felinge ger1. 1a *(fr. felen vi.)* (?a1200) *Ancr. BD 14

felingli adv. c *fr. felen vi.* (a1382) WBible(1) KNT 2

fellen v. 3a a *OE* (?a1200) Lay.Brut ROMA 3

felliche adv. 1a *fr. fel adj.* c1290 SLeg. (Ld) BO 1

felnesse n. 1a *fr. fel adj.* (?c1350) Mirror St.Edm.(4) BO 1

felonie n. 4 *OF* (c1250) Floris ROMA 27

The making of Chaucer's English

felonous adj. e *OF* (a1338) Mannyng
Chron.Pt.1 BO 18
feloun adj. 1a a *OF* (c1250) Floris *TR* 1
feloun n1. 2 *fr. feloun adj.* c1290
SLeg.Becket (Ld) BO 3
femele adj. & n. 1a *OF & ML* (a1333)
Shoreham Poems BO 3
Femenie n. *OF* Chaucer *KNT* 2
feminine adj. & n. 3 *OF & L* (?c1350)
SVrn.Leg. *HF* 1
femininite n. a *fr. feminine adj.* Chaucer
MLT 1
fen n1. 1a a *OE* a 1121 Peterb.Chron. *RVT*
3
fen n3. *ML (fr. Ar.)* Chaucer *PARDT* 1
fend n. 1a *OE* a1121 Peterb.Chron. ROMA
55
fendlich adj. 1 *OE* (?a1200) Lay.Brut BD
7
fenel n. 1 *OE (fr. ML)* c1150 Hrl.HApul.
ROMA 1
fenix n. a *OE & ML; OF (ult. Gr.)* a1150
Vsp.D.Hom. *BD* 1
fer adj1. 3 *OE* 1131 Peterb.Chron. HF 10
fer adv. 1a *OE* a1175 Bod.Hom. ROMA
99
fer n1. 1b *OE* a1225 Lamb.Hom.Pentec.
BD 61
ferde n1. d *prob. fr. for fered phr.*
(?a1300) Guy(2) BD 5
fere n1. 1a *OE* a1175 Bod.Hom. PF 6
fere n2. 1 *OE* (c1250) Gen.& Ex. *HF* 1
fered ppl. a *fr. feren v1.* ?c1200 Orm. TR
3
feren v1. 1 *OE* ?c1200 Orm. *TR* 1
fer-forth adv. 2a *fr. fer forth phr.* c1290
SLeg.Becket (Ld) SNPRO 29
ferforthli adv. b *fr. fer-forth adv.*
Chaucer TR 4
ferful adj. 1a *fr. fer n1.* (a1382) WBible(1)
TR 2
ferli adj. 1a *OE* ?c1200 Wor.Bod.Gloss.
(Hat 113) *RVT* 1
ferm adj. 2a *OF (fr. L)* (c1378) PPl.B
(Ld) *BO* 5

ferme adv. b *fr. <ferm adj.>* (c1340)
Rolle Psalter (UC 64) ROMA 4
ferme n2. 3a *OF* (c1300) Glo.Chron.A
GP 1
fermeli adv. d *fr. ferm adj.* Chaucer BO 9
fermen v3. b *OF & L* (c1303) Mannyng
HS *BO* 1
fermentacioun n. *L* Chaucer *CYT* 1
fermerer n. *fr. enfermerer n.* c1390
NHom.Monk fr. Death *SUMT* 1
fermour n. a *cp. OF* (c1384) WBible(1)
LGW F 1
fern- adj. b *OE* a1175 Bod.Hom. *TR* 1
fern adv. a *OE* (?a1200) Lay.Brut *SQT* 1
fern n1. a *OE* c1150 Hrl.HApul. BO 2
fern-asshen n. b, fern n1. *(fr. fern n1. &*
asshe n2.) Chaucer *SQT* 1
ferrene adj. a *fr. ferrene adv.* (?a1200)
Lay. Brut BO 2
fers adj. 1a *OF (L)* c1290 SLeg.Chris.
ROMA 14
fers n. a *OF (fr. Ar.)* Chaucer *BD* 6
fersli adv. 2b *fr. fers adj.* (?a1325)
Bonav.Medit.(1) *TR* 1
fert n. b *cp. OHG* Chaucer MILT 9
ferthe num. 1a *OE* a1131 Peterb.Chron.
ROMA 43
ferther adj. 2b *OE* (c1353) Winner & W.
MERT 2
ferther adv. 1a *OE* (?a1300) Tristrem
ABC 20
ferther-over adv. *(ferther adv. & over*
adv.) Chaucer *AST* 1
ferthest adj. & adv. a *(fr. ferther adj.)*
(c1378) PPl.B (Ld) *BO* 1
ferthing n. 1a *OE* (c1280) SLeg.Pass.
(Pep) GP 3
ferting ger. *OE* Chaucer MILT 1
fervent adj. 4a *OF, & L* (1340) Ayenb.
PARST 1
ferventli adv. 2a *fr. fervent adj.* Chaucer
TR 1
fesaunt n. 1a *AF; CF* (?a1300) Arth.&
M. *PF* 1
fese n. *(fr. fesen v.)* Chaucer *KNT* 1

feste n. 2d *OF & L* (?a1200) *Ancr. BD
78

festen v. a *OF* (c1300) Havelok KNT 7

festinge ger. *(fr. festen v.)* (c1378) PPl.B
(Ld) *TR* 2

festivalli adv. b *fr. <festival adj.>*
Chaucer *BO* 1

festli adj. a *fr. feste n.* Chaucer *SQT* 1

fet n. 1a *AF, CF (fr. L)* (a1376) *PPl.A(1)
(Trin-C) *CLT* 1

feter n. 1a *OE* c1290 SLeg. (Ld) BO 3

feteren v. a *OE* (?a1200) *Ancr. MKT 5

fether n. 1a *OE* c1150 PDidax. ROMA 19

fether-bed n. 3a, fether n. *(fr. fether n. &
bed n1.)* c1300 Lay.Brut (Otho)
ROMA 2

fetheren v1. 3a *OE* a1250 Ancr. (Nero)
ROMA 6

fetis adj. a *AF, CF* (?a1350) 7 Sages(2)
ROMA 10

fetisli adv. a {b} *(fr. fetis adj.)* Chaucer
{a1375 WPal.} ROMA 10

fetten v. 2b *OE* (?a1200) Trin.Hom.
ROMA 20

feture n1. 2b *OF* a1375 WPal. MANCT 2

feue indef. pron. 1a *OE* a1121
Peterb.Chron. ROMA 43

fever n. 1 *OE & OF (both fr. L)* c1150
Hrl.HApul. BO 6

fi interj. 2a *OF & L* (c1300)
Glo.Chron.A BD 24

fichen v1. 1b *OF* c1350 MPPsalter *BO* 9

fifte ord. num. 1a *OE* ?c1200 Orm.
ROMA 21

fif-tene card. num. 1a *OE* (c1200) Vices
& V.(1) GP 2

fifti card. num. 1a *OE* a1121
Peterb.Chron. BD 5

fige n. 1a *OF* (?a1200) *Ancr. ROMA 2

fight n. 2a *OE* a1121 Peterb.Chron. HF
3

fighten v. 4 *OE* 1122 Peterb.Chron. MKT
37

fightinge ger. 4 *(fr. fighten v.)* (?a1200)
*Ancr. KNT 3

figure n. 6a *OF & L* (?a1200) *Ancr.
ROMA 41

figuren v. 2a *OF & L* (1389) Wycl.25 Art.
AST 2

figuringe ger. b *fr. figuren v.* *Chaucer
SNPRO 2

fikelnesse n. a *fr. fikel adj.* Chaucer *STED*
1

file n1. 2 *OE* (c1125) Vsp.D.Hom.Elucid.
KNT 1

filen v1. 1a *OE & OF* (?a1200) *Ancr. PF
2

filet n. 1 *OF* a1325 Lord that lenest *MILT*
1

fille n1. a *OE* (?a1200) Trin.Hom. LADY
10

fillen v. 5 *OE* (c1125)
Vsp.D.Hom.Fest.Virg. HF 5

filth n. 2a a *OE* (?a1200) *Ancr. ABC 18

fin adj. 3a *OF, ML* (c1250) Gen.& Ex.
ROMA 40

fin n1. a *OE* (?c1200) St.Marg.(1) *PF* 1

fin n2. 2a *OF, L* (c1250) Gen.& Ex.
ROMA 32

final adj. 2d *OF, L* Chaucer TR 6

finalli adv. 2b *fr. <final adj.>* Chaucer
HF 33

finch n. a *OE* ?c1200 Stw.57.Gloss.
ROMA 3

finden v. 1a *OE* a1121 Peterb.Chron.
ROMA 402

findere n. 2b *fr. finden v.* (?a1300)
*KAlex. BD 2

finding ger. 1a *(fr. finden v.)* (?a1300)
Arth.& M. *MILT* 1

fine adv1. 2 *fr. fin adj.* c1330 Orfeo TR
2

finen v1. 2a *OF* (?c1225) Horn TR 5

finen v3. 1a *fr. fin adj.; OF* (1340) Ayenb.
ROMA 1

finger n. 1a *OE* a1121 Peterb.Chron.
ROMA 20

fingering ger. b *fr. fingeren v.* *Chaucer
LGW F 1

finishen v. 1a *fr. OF* a1375 WPal. *BO* 1

fiole n. a *ML & OF* (?c1380) Cleanness *CYT* 1

fir n. 1b c *OE* a1121 Peterb.Chron. ABC 155

fir-brond n. 1a *(fr. fir n. & brand n.)* c1300 Lay.Brut (Otho) PF 2

firen v. 2 *fr. fir n.* (?c1200) St.Marg.(1) *LGW* 1

firi adj. 1 *fr. fir n.* c1290 SLeg.Brendan (Ld) LADY 11

fir-makinge n. fir n., MED Suppl. *fr. fir n. & makinge ger.* * not in MED *KNT* 1

firmament n. 2 *L & OF* (c1250) Gen.& Ex. BD 16

firre n1. a *OE* (a1325) Cursor PF 2

fir-red adj. 1b b, fir n. *(fr. fir n. & red adj.)* Chaucer *GP* 1

first adv. 1a *OE* a1121 Peterb.Chron. ROMA 248

first ord. num. 1a *OE* ?c1200 Orm. ROMA 133

fish n. 1a *OE* a1175 Bod.Hom. HF 19

fishen v. 1a *OE* ?c1200 Orm. MKT 6

fishere n. 1a *OE* (?a1200) Lay.Brut *MARS* 1

Fisshstrete n. 5 cc, fish n. *(fr. fish n. & strete n2.)* Chaucer *PARDT* 1

fist n1. 1 *OE* (?a1200) Lay.Brut TR 6

fit n1. c *OE* (?a1300) Arth.& M. *THOP* 1

fit n2. b *fr. fit n1.?* (a1376) PPl.A(1) (Vrn) RVT 3

fithele n. *OE* (?a1200) Lay.Brut *GP* 1

five card. num. 2 *OE* a1121 Peterb.Chron ROMA 47

fix ppl. & adj. 2a *L* Chaucer TR 25

fixe ppl. & adv. c *L* Chaucer AST 5

fixen v. 1a *fr.* <*fix ppl.*> Chaucer ABC 5

flake n1. a *cp. OE, & OI* a1325 Gloss.Bibbesw. *HF* 1

flanke n. a *CF, Pic.* (?a1300) Arth.& M. *SHIPT* 1

flat adj. 2 *cp. OI* (?c1300) Bevis BD 2

flat n1. 2 *fr. flat adj.* Chaucer *TR* 1

flateren v1. a *OF* (?a1200) *Ancr. BD 12

flaterer n. *fr. flateren v1.* c1350

Gloss.Bibbesw. (Hrl 740: Koch) MEL 12

flaterie n. *OF* c1330 7 Sages(1) ROMA 20

flatering ger. a *(fr. flateren v1.)* (?a1200) *Ancr. BD 5

flatour n. *OF* (1340) Ayenb. *NPT* 1

flaume n. 2b *AF, CF; L* (c1303) Mannyng HS ABC 14

Flaundres-ward n. MED Suppl. *fr. Flaundres n. & -ward suf.* * not in MED *SHIPT* 1

Flaundrish adj. *fr. Flaundres n.* Chaucer *GP* 1

fle n. a *OE* c1150 Hrl.HApul. *MANCPRO* 1

fleing ger2. 1a *(fr. flen v2.)* c1290 SLeg.Becket (Ld) *BO* 1

flekked ppl. adj. *cp. MDu. & OF* (a1387) Trev.Higd. MERT 2

flemen v1. 1a *OE* 1131 Peterb.Chron. *SNPRO* 4

flemer n. *fr. flemen v1.* Chaucer *MLT* 1

fleming ger. *(fr. flemen v1.)* (a1325) Cursor *TR* 1

Fleming n. a *OFris.* ?a1150 Chron.Tbr.B.1 CKPRO 3

flen v1. 1a a *OE* c1150 Hrl.MQuad. ABC 102

flen v2. 1b *OE* (?a1200) Lay.Brut *PARST* 1

fles n. e *OE* (?a1200) *Ancr. BO 9

flesh n. 1a a *OE* c1150 PDidax. ROMA 57

flesh-hook n. 2c b, flesh n. *(fr. flesh n. & hok n.)* a1300 Uncomly in *SUMT* 1

fleshi adj. 1b *fr. flesh n.* Chaucer *BD* 1

fleshliche adj. 3a *OE* a1175 Bod.Hom. *TR* 17

fleshliche adv. b *OE* ?c1200 Orm. *PRT* 4

fleten v1. 1d *OE* ?c1200 Orm. *PITY* 26

flex n. 1a *OE* a1325 Gloss.Bibbesw. (Arun) *GP* 1

flie n1. 2 *OE* ?c1200 Stw.57.Gloss. PF 14

flien v. 1a a *OE* a1175 Bod.Hom. ROMA 38

flight n1. 1a *OE* ?c1200 Orm. MKT 7

flight n2. 1a *OE* (?a1200) Lay. Brut PF 3

fliinge ger. b *(fr. flien v.)* c1290 11
Pains(2) *BO* 1

flikeren v. c *OE* (?a1200) *Ancr. TR 2

flint n. 1a a *OE* a1200 Wor.Aelfric Gloss.
FORMAGE 2

flitten v. 1a *ON* a1200 Body & S.(2) BD
10

flo n. a *LOE* a1121 Peterb.Chron. *MANCT*
1

flod n. 2a *OE* 1126 Peterb.Chron. MKT
26

flok n1. 2a *OE* ?c1200 Orm. ROMA 2

flok-mele adv. *(fr. flok n1. and -mele
suf.)* (c1384) WBible(1) *CLT* 1

flor n. 1a *OE* a1200 Body & S.(2) HF 12

floren n. a *OF* (c1303) Mannyng HS
KNT 6

florishen v. 4a *OF* (?a1300) Rich. (Auch)
BO 3

florishing ger. 1 *(fr. florishen v.)* (c1303)
Mannyng HS HF 2

floteren v. 1a *OE* c1290 SLeg.Mich. (Ld)
BO 2

flotri adj. *fr. floteren v.* Chaucer *KNT* 1

flouen v. 2a *OE* (c1125)
Vsp.D.Hom.Fest.Virg. BO 8

flour n1. 1a a *OF* (?a1200) *Ancr. ROMA
125

flour n2. 2c *fr. flour n1.* (?c1225) Horn
RVT 4

flour-de-lice n. 2b *AF* a1325 Flem.Insur.
GP 1

flouren v1. 2a *fr. flour n1.; OF* (?a1200)
*Ancr. ANEL 6

flouret n. *OF* Chaucer *ROMA* 1

flouri adj1. a *fr. flour n1.* Chaucer BD 3

flouroun n. *OF* Chaucer *LGW F* 3

floute n. *OF* a1325 Gloss.Bibbesw. *HF* 1

flouten v. *OF* Chaucer *GP* 1

flouter n. *OF* (1268) in Thuresson ME
Occup.Terms *ROMA* 1

fnesen v. a *OE* c1150 PDidax. *MANCPRO*
1

fnorten v. a *cp. OE* Chaucer RVT 2

fo n. 1a *OE* (?a1200) Lay.Brut ABC 59

fodder n. a *OE* (?a1200) Lay.Brut BO 2

fode n1. 1a a *OE* ?c1200 Orm. SUMT 6

foinen v. b *fr. <foin n1.>* c1380 Firumb.
KNT 3

foisoun n. 1a *OF* (a1300) *KAlex. ROMA
3

fol adj. 2 *OF* (?a1200) *Ancr. ROMA 9

fol n. 1a *OF* ?c1200 Wor.Bod.Gloss.
ROMA 76

fold n1. 1a *OE* a1200 Wor.Aelfric Gloss.
KNT 2

folde n1. 2 *fr. folden v2.* c1250 Owl & N.
TR 1

folde n2. *fr. mani a fold phr.* (c1303)
Mannyng HS BD 14

folden v2. 1a *OE* (?a1200) *Ancr. BO 8

foleien v. b *OF* (1357) Gaytr. LFCatech.
BO 2

folen v1. *fr. fole n.* (a1387) Trev.Higd.
FRT 1

fol-hardi adj. *OF* a1250 Ancr. (Nero)
PROMKT 1

fol-hardinesse n. *fr. fol-hardi adj.*
(c1340) Rolle Psalter (UC 64) PF 3

folie n. 1a *OF* (?a1200) *Ancr. BD 90

folili adv. a *fr. folie n.* (?a1300) Tristrem
SNT 7

folish adj. 1b *fr. fol adj.* (a1325) Cursor
BO 4

folk n. 3a *OE* a1121 Peterb.Chron. ROMA
625

fol-large adj. a *OF* (c1300) Glo.Chron.A
BO 4

fol-largesse n. *OF* Chaucer *PARST* 1

folwen v. 2c *OE* a1150 Rwl.G.57.Gloss.
ROMA 125

fom n. 1b *OE* c1150 Hrl.MQuad. KNT 3

fo-man n. 1a *OE* (?a1200) *Ancr. MKT 7

fomi adj. 1 *OE* Chaucer KNT 2

fonden v. 3a *OE* c1150 Hrl.HApul.
ROMA 18

fongen v. 4b a *fr. fon v.* ?c1200 Orm.
MLT 1

fonne n. a *orig. unknown* (a1325) Cursor
RVT 1

font-ful n. *(fr. font n. & -ful suffr.)*
Chaucer *MLT* 1

font-ston n. 1 *(fr. font n. & ston n.)*
a1200 Body & S.(2) *MLT* 1

for conj. 1a *fr. for prep.* a1123
Peterb.Chron. GENERAL 2645

for prep. 1a *OE* a1121 Peterb.Chron.
GENERAL 3372

forage n. *OF; AL* (a1333) Shoreham
Poems RvPRO 3

for as muche adv. phr. & conj. 2a *(fr.*
for as muche phr.) c1290 SLeg.Becket
(Ld) BO 5

forbeden v. 1a a *OE* a1121 Peterb.Chron.
PF 45

forberen v. 1a *OE* c1150 PDidax. BO
13

forbering ger. c *(fr. forberen v.)* (?a1300)
KAlex. PARST 3

forbi adv. & conj. 1b *(fr. fore prep. & bi*
adv.) (?a1300) Arth.& M. *TR* 6

forbi prep. 3a *fr. forbi adv.* (c1250)
Gen.& Ex. *TR* 1

forbod n. a *OE* (c1200) Vices & V.(1)
LGW G 1

forbreken v. b *OE* a1131 Peterb.Chron.
BO 1

forbrused ppl. a *cp. OE & AF, CF*
Chaucer *MKT* 1

force n. 8b *OF* (?a1300) Arth.& M.
ROMA 66

forcracchen v. *fr. for- prefr. & cracchen v.*
Chaucer *ROMA* 1

forcutten v. a *fr. for- prefr. & cutten vt.*
(a1387) Trev.Higd. *MANCT* 1

ford n. 1a *OE* a1200 Wor.Aelfric Gloss.
BO 1

fordon v. 1b *OE* a1121 Peterb.Chron.
PITY 16

fordriven ppl. 2 *OE* (a1250) Bestiary *BO*
1

fordronken ppl. *OE* (?a1200) Lay.Brut
PARDT 1

fordwinen v. a *LOE* c1150 Hrl.HApul.
ROMA 1

fore n. 1a *OE* (?a1200) Lay.Brut WBPRO
2

fore-bisnen v. a *(fr. fore-bisne n.)* (a1250)
Bestiary *TR* 1

forein adj. 2 *OF* (c1250) Floris BO 19

forein n. 3 *fr. forein adj.* (c1303)
Mannyng HS *LGW* 1

fore-knouen v. *fr. fore adv. & knouen v.*
Chaucer *TR* 1

fore-knouing ger. *fr. fore-knouen v.* *
Chaucer *BO* 1

fore-said ppl. a *(fr. fore adv. & seien vt.)*
a1175 Bod.Hom. PF 65

fore-seing ger. a *(fr. fore-sen v.)* Chaucer
TR 1

fore-sight n. 1 *(fr. fore adv. & sighte n.)*
(a1325) Cursor *TR* 1

forest n. 2a *OF* (c1300) Glo.Chron.A BD
17

forever adv. 15a, for prep. *(fr. for prep. &*
ever adv.) a1375 WPal. *MARS* 1

fore-ward adv. 3b *fr. fore-ward adj.*
(?c1300) Amis BO 5

fore-ward n. 1 *OE* a1121 Peterb.Chron.
TR 12

fore-witen v. b *OE* Chaucer HF 4

fore-witer n. *fr. fore-witen v.* Chaucer *BO*
1

fore-witing ger. *(fr. fore-witen v.)* (c1385)
Usk TL (Skeat) *NPT* 1

forfered ppl. *fr. forferen v.* ?c1200 Orm.
SQT 1

forfeten v. 1a *fr. <forfet ppl.>* c1350
MPPsalter *PARST* 1

forge n. a *OF* Chaucer *MILT* 1

forgen v. 5 *OF* (a1325) Cursor PF 9

forgon v. 2a *OE* a1131 Peterb.Chron.
ROMA 25

forhed n. 1a *OE* (?a1200) *Ancr. ROMA 8

forken v. 1a *fr. forke n.* (a1325) Cursor *GP*
1

forkerven v. 1a *OE* c1150 Hrl.HApul.
MANCT 1

forlesen v. 1a *OE* a1121 Peterb.Chron. BO
9

forleten v. 5a *OE* a1121 Peterb.Chron.
HF 51

forleven vi. b *fr. for- pref1. & leven vi.*
(?c1200) St.Juliana PHYT 1

forlinen v. *OF* Chaucer BO 2

forloine n. *OF* Chaucer BD 1

forlosen v. 1a *OE* a1175 Bod.Hom. TR 2

formal adj. 4c *L, OF* Chaucer MEL 1

formalli adv. 2a *fr. <formal adj.>*
Chaucer BO 2

forme adj. 1a a *OE* a1121 Peterb.Chron.
MEL 1

forme n. 2a *L, OF* (?a1200) *Ancr. ROMA
60

formel adj. & n. a *OF* Chaucer PF 7

formen v. 1c *L & OF* c1290 SLeg.Mich.
(Ld) ROMA 22

former adj. 2 *fr. forme adj.* (a1375)
Octav.(2) FORMAGE 2

formere n. 1 *fr. formen v. & OF (L)*
(?a1325) Bonav.Medit.(1) PHYT 1

formest adj. (sup.) 1a *fr. forme adj.*
(?a1200) Lay.Brut BD 1

forn-cast ppl. *(fr. fore adv. & casten v.)*
Chaucer TR 3

fornicacioun n. 1c *L & OF* (c1303)
Mannyng HS FRPRO 5

forpampred ppl. *fr. for- pref1. &
pamperen v.* * Chaucer FORMAGE 1

forpassing ppl. *cp. OF* Chaucer TR 1

forpinen v. a *(fr. for- pref1. & pinen v.)*
(?a1200) Lay.Brut ROMA 4

forsaken v. 1a *OE* ?c1200 Orm. ROMA 38

forshapen ppl. 3 *OE* (?a1200) *Ancr. TR
1

forshright ppl. MED Suppl. *fr. for- pref1.
& skriken v.* * not in MED TR 1

forsleuthen v. a *cp. forsleuen v. & sleuth
n.* (a1325) Glo.Chron.B NPT 2

forsluggen v. *fr. for pref1. & sluggen v.* *
(a1333) Shoreham Poems PARST 1

forsongen ppl. *(fr. for- pref1. & singen
v.)* Chaucer ROMA 1

forsoth adv. 2a *OE* (?a1200) *Ancr. PF
32

forster n. 1a *OF* (c1300) Glo.Chron.A
BD 2

forstraught adj. *cp. distraught adj.*
Chaucer SHIPT 1

forsweren v. 2b *OE* ?1130 Chron.Tbr.B.4
HF 7

forswering ger. 1 *(fr. forsweren v.)* (1340)
Ayenb. HF 5

forth adv. 1a *OE* a1121 Peterb.Chron.
GENERAL 291

forth-bi adv. *fr. forth bi phr.* Chaucer TR
1

for-thi pronominal adv. & conj. 1a *OE*
a1121 Peterb.Chron. BO 49

forthinken v. 3 *OE* c1225 St.Juliana
ROMA 4

forth-right adv. 3a *fr. forth right phr.*
?c1200 Orm. ROMA 1

forth-ward adv. 3b *OE* ?c1200 Orm. AST
3

forth-with adv. 2 *fr. forth with phr.*
(a1325) Cursor TR 2

fortitude n. a *L.* a1175 Bod.Hom. PARST
2

forto adv. & particle (with inf.) 1 *fr. for
adv. & to vbl. particle* a1131
Peterb.Chron. ROMA 3

fortreden v. *OE* a1225 Trin.Hom. BO 2

fortuit adj. *L* Chaucer BO 2

fortuna major n. *L* Chaucer TR 1

fortunat adj. {1c} *L* Chaucer {(a1387)
Trev.Higd.} BO 11

fortune n. 1b *OF; L* (a1325) Cursor BD
227

fortunel adj. *OF* Chaucer BO 1

fortunen v. 3a *OF; L* Chaucer BD 4

fortunous adj. a *ML, OF* Chaucer BO
8

forwaked ppl. a *(fr. for pref1. & waken
v.)* c1325 Bytuene mersh BD 2

forwe n. 1 *OE* (a1250) Bestiary BO 2

forwelked ppl. *(fr. for pref1. & welken
vi.)* Chaucer ROMA 1

forwepen v. 1 *(fr. for- pref1. & wepen v.)*
Chaucer BD 1

forweren v. b *OE* (?a1200) Lay.Brut
ROMA 1

for-whi pronominal adv. & conj. 2a
OE a1121 Peterb.Chron. BD 40

forwrappen v. *(fr. for- pref1. & wrappen
v.)* Chaucer PARDT 2

foryelden v. 1a *OE* a1175 Bod.Hom.
LGW F 2

foryetelnesse n. a *fr. <foryetelful adj.>;*
OE (?a1200) Trin.Hom. PARST 1

foryeten v. 1a *OE* (?c1175) PMor. (Lamb)
ROMA 56

foryetful adj. a *fr. foryeten v.* (c1384)
WBible(1) CLT 1

foryeting ger. 1a *(fr. foryeten v.)* (1340)
Ayenb. BO 3

foryeven v. 3a *OE* a1121 Peterb.Chron.
ABC 45

foryevenesse n. 1b *OE* a1121
Peterb.Chron. MEL 11

foryeving ger. a *(fr. foryeven v.)* Chaucer
LGW 1

foryift n. b *(fr. foryeven v. & yifte n.)*
(?a1300) *KAlex. LGW 1

fostren v. 1a a *OE* (c1125)
Vsp.D.Hom.Fest.Virg. ROMA 20

fostring ger. a *(fr. fostren v.)* (?c1200)
HMaid. SUMT 1

fot n. 14t *OE* (c1125)
Vsp.D.Hom.Fest.Virg. ROMA 90

fot-brede n. *(fr. fot n. & brede n2.)*
Chaucer HF 1

fother n. 1 *OE* a1121 Peterb.Chron. KNT
2

fot-hot adv. a *?fr. with fot hot phrase*
(?c1300) Guy(1) BD 2

fot-man n. 1a *(fr. fot n. & man n.)*
(c1300) Glo.Chron.A KNT 1

fot-mantel n. 11 l, fot n. *(fr. fot n. &
mantel n.)* Chaucer GP 1

foudre n. *OF* Chaucer HF 1

foul adj. 1b b *OE* c1150 Hrl.HApul.
ROMA 120

foul n. 2a *OE* 1131 Peterb.Chron. ROMA
49

foule adv. 1b *OE* c1150 Hrl.HApul.
ROMA 17

foulere n. a *OE* a1200 Wor.Aelfric Gloss.
LGW F 2

foun n. a *OF* (a1338) Mannyng
Chron.Pt.1 BD 2

foundacioun n. 2a *L, OF* Chaucer *LGW*
1

foundement n. 3a *OF, & L* c1290 11
Pains(2) HF 6

founden v1. 1 *OE* a1121 Peterb.Chron.
ANEL 2

founden v2. 1d *OF & L* c1290
SLeg.Fran.(1) (Ld) BD 9

foundren v1. 2 *OF* (a1338) Mannyng
Chron.Pt.2 KNT 1

four num. 1b a *OE* 1122 Peterb.Chron.
ROMA 39

fourte-night n. 2 *fr. four-tene night phr.*
(?a1200) Lay.Brut TR 5

fourti num. as adj. 3a *OE* a1126
Peterb.Chron. BD 10

fox n. 1a *OE* c1150 Hrl.MQuad. MKT 22

fraccioun n. c *AF & L* Chaucer AST 2

frainen v. 1c *OE, OI* ?c1200 Orm. SNT 4

fraknes n. pl. *cp.* *OI* Chaucer KNT 1

framen v2. 1a *fr. <frame n2.>* (?a1300)
Rich. (Auch) TR 1

frank n2. *OF* Chaucer SHIPT 10

frankelein n. a *AF* (c1300) Glo.Chron.A
GP 5

frape n. 1a *OF* (a1338) Mannyng
Chron.Pt.1 TR 1

fraternite n. 1a *OF & L* (a1338) Mannyng
Chron.Pt.2 GP 1

fraude n. 3 *OF (fr. L)* (1345–6) Grocer
Lond. BO 10

fraughten v. 1a *MDu.* a1375 WPal. *MLT*
1

Fraunce n. a *OF* a1121 Peterb.Chron.
ROMA 9

fraunchise n. 1c *OF* c1290 SLeg. (Ld)
ROMA 8

fre adj. 3a a *OE* a1121 Peterb.Chron.
ROMA 110

fre adv. 2a *fr. fre adj.* c1250 Louerd asse thu ard PF 4

fredom n. 3a a *OE* a1121 Peterb.Chron. MᴋT 28

frele adj. 3a *OF (fr. L)* (?c1350) SVrn.Leg. Bo 4

frelete n. 2a *OF (fr. L)* (c1340) Rolle Psalter (UC 64) WBPʀᴏ 6

freli adv. 3a *OE* a1121 Peterb.Chron. SNPʀᴏ 18

frelnesse n. 1b *fr. frele adj.* Chaucer Bo 1

fremed adj. b *OE* (?c1175) PMor. (Lamb) Tʀ 4

frend n. 1b *OE* a1121 Peterb.Chron. RoᴍA 235

frendli adj. 1a *OE* Chaucer BD 18

frendli adv. *OE* (1155) Chart.Hen.II in Hall EME BD 5

frendshipe n. 2 *OE* (1155) Chart.Hen.II in Hall EME HF 17

frenesie n. {a} *OF & L* Chaucer {(?a1387) PPl.C (Hnt)} Tʀ 2

frenetik adj. a *OF & L* (a1376) PPl.A(1) (Vrn) Tʀ 1

frenge n. a *OF* Chaucer HF 2

Frensh adj. 2a *OE* a1121 Peterb.Chron. GP 3

frere n. 4b *OF* (?a1200) *Ancr. GP 74

fresen v. 1 *OE* c1250 Owl & N. PᴀʀsT 1

fresh adj. 3b *OE & OF* c1150 PDidax. RoᴍA 113

freshe adv. 2b *fr. fresh adj.* (a1325) SLeg.Cec. (Ashm) KɴT 7

freshen v. b *fr. fresh adj.* c1290 SLeg. (Ld) RoᴍA 1

freshli adv. 1c *fr. fresh adj.* (?a1325) Bonav.Medit.(1) BD 5

fret n2. a *OF* Chaucer LGW F 3

freten v1. 1a a *OE* a1131 Peterb.Chron. RoᴍA 13

freten v2. 1d *fr. OF* (a1376) PPl.A(1) (Vrn) LGW 1

fri-dai n. 1b *OE* a1131 Peterb.Chron. KɴT 5

frien v3. 1 *OF* c1290 SLeg.(Ld) GP 2

Frise n1. *cp. OE, & ML* c1300 Lay.Brut (Otho) RoᴍA 2

frogge n. 1a *OE* (?c1200) SWard RoᴍA 1

from adv. 1a *OE, & ON* c1150 Hr.HApul. SNT 35

from prep. 1a a *OE & ON* a1121 Peterb.Chron. GENERAL 849

frost n. 1a *OE* a1121 Peterb.Chron. Tʀ 4

frosti adj. b *fr. frost n.* Chaucer Aɴᴇʟ 6

froten v. 2a *OF* c1330 Orfeo Tʀ 2

frothen v. c *fr. <frothe n.>* (?c1380) Cleanness KɴT 1

frounce n1. 1a *OF* (c1378) PPl.B (Ld) Bo 1

frounceles adj. *fr. frounce n1.** Chaucer RoᴍA 1

frouncen v. 1a *OF* (a1325) Cursor RoᴍA 2

frounen v. 1 *OF* Chaucer CʟT 1

frount n. 1a *OF & L* c1290 SLeg.Becket (Ld) Bo 1

fructifien v. 1a *OF* (1340) Ayenb. Bo 2

fructuous adj. 1 *OF & L* (a1382) WBible(1) PᴀʀsPʀᴏ 1

fruit n. 1a *OF* ?c1200 Wor.Bod.Gloss. RoᴍA 53

fruitestere n. *fr. fruiter n.** Chaucer PᴀʀᴅT 1

fruitful adj. 1b *fr. fruit n.* c1390 Hilton ML PᴀʀsT 1

fugitif adj. a *L & OF* Chaucer HF 1

ful adj. 1b *OE* a1121 Peterb.Chron. GENERAL 245

ful adv. 1b *OE* a1121 Peterb.Chron. GENERAL 1108

ful-fillen v. 6c *OE* (?a1200) Trin.Hom. RoᴍA 60

ful-filling ger. 1a *(fr. ful-fillen v.)* (1340) Ayenb. Bo 2

fulle n1. 2a *fr. ful adj.* a1200 Body & S. BD 13

fulli adv. 1b *OE* ?c1200 Orm. MᴋT 60

fulsomnesse n. a *fr. fulsom adj.* Chaucer SǫT 1

fume n. 3a *OF & L* Chaucer NPT 2

fumetere n. *OF* (1373) *Lelamour Macer. *NPT* 1

fumigacioun n. c *L & OF* Chaucer *HF* 1

fumosite n. 2a *OF & L* Chaucer SQT 2

funeral adj. 1 *L* Chaucer TR 4

furial adj. *OF & L* Chaucer *SQT* 1

furie n. 2 *OF & L* Chaucer BO 12

furious adj. 2 *OF & L* Chaucer ANEL 3

furlong n. 1a *OE* (?a1300) Arth.& M. HF 13

furlong-wei n. 1b, furlong n. *(fr. furlong n. & wei n.)* Chaucer *LGW G* 1

furnaise n. 5 *OF* (?c1200) St.Juliana MKT 9

furre n. a *prob. fr. <furrer n.>* ?c1375 7 Sages(2) *ROMA* 1

furren v. 1b *OF* (?a1300) *KAlex. ROMA 3

furring ger. b *(fr. furren v.)* Chaucer *PARST* 1

further adv. 1c *OE* a1121 Peterb.Chron. PITY 28

furtheren v. 1a *cp. OE* ?c1200 Orm. HF 15

furthering ger. 1 *(fr. furtheren v.)* Chaucer HF 3

further more phr. & adv. 1a *fr. further adv. & more adv.* ?c1200 Orm. WBPRO 11

fusible adj. *OF* Chaucer *CYT* 1

fustian n. a *OF* (?a1200) Trin.Hom. GP 1

future adj. a *L & OF* Chaucer *BO* 5

future n. a *L* Chaucer BO 7

gabben v. 2a *ON* (?c1150) Prov.Alf. (Jes-O) BD 6

gabbere n. a *fr. gabben v. & OF* a1325 MS.Raw.B.520 lf.256 *PARST* 1

gable n1. b *ON & OF* (?c1350) SVrn.Leg. *MILT* 1

gadeling n. a *OE* (?c1150) Prov.Alf. (Mdst) *ROMA* 1

gaderen v. 1c *OE* a1121 Peterb.Chron. BO 19

gaderinge ger. 1a *(fr. gaderen v.)* ?a1160 Peterb.Chron. *MEL* 1

gai adj. 3b *OF, fr. Gmc.* (?c1300) Amis ROMA 41

gai adv. a *fr. gai adj.* (a1338) Mannyng Chron.Pt.2 MILT 2

gaillard adj. 2 *OF* Chaucer MILT 2

gaioler n. a *OF* (c1300) SLeg.Kath. (Ld) KNT 13

gaitris n. a *cp. gate-triu n.* Chaucer *NPT* 1

galauntine n. *OF* Chaucer FORMAGE 2

galaxie n. *L, fr. Gr.* Chaucer HF 2

galen v. b *OE* (?a1200) Lay.Brut WBPRO 2

Galien n. b *L, fr. Gr.* Chaucer BD 4

galingale n. 1a *OF, fr. Ar.* (a1300) Cokaygne *GP* 1

galle n1. 1a *OE* c1150 Hrl.HApul. SNPRO 9

galle n2. 2c *OE* (c1333–52) Minot Poems *WBT* 1

galoche n. a *OF* (c1353) Winner & W. *SQT* 1

galoun n. a *OF & ML* (?c1225) Horn *MANCPRO* 1

galpen v. c *cp. MDu.* (?a1300) KAlex. *SQT* 2

galwe n. 2a *OE* (?a1200) *Ancr. MKT 3

game n. 2a b *OE* (?c1175) PMor. (Trin-C) BD 63

gamen v. a *OE & game n.* (?a1200) *Ancr. GP* 1

gang n. 1a *OE & ON* c1150 Hrl.HApul. *PARST* 1

gap n. a *ON* a1325 Gloss.Bibbesw. *KNT* 2

gapen v. 1a *ON* (?c1200) St.Marg.(1) MKT 8

gapinge ger. b *(fr. gapen v.)* Chaucer BO 1

gardin n. 1a *OF* (c1280) SLeg.Pass. (Pep) ROMA 61

gardin-ward n. 2b, gardin n. *(fr. gardin n. & -ward suff.)* Chaucer MILT 2

gargate n. *OF* (?a1300) KAlex. *NPT* 1

gar-lek n. 1a *OE* c1150 PDidax. *GP* 1

garnement n. c *OF* (?a1300) KAlex.
ROMA 2

garnisoun n. a *OF* (a1338) Mannyng
Chron.Pt.1 *MEL* 4

gasen v. a *ON* Chaucer *CLT* 1

gastli adj. *fr.* <*gast adj*> c1300
SLeg.Chris. (Hrl) *KNT* 1

gastnesse n. a *fr. gast. adj.* Chaucer *BO* 1

gate n1. 6c *OE* a1121 Peterb.Chron.
ROMA 39

gat-tothed adj. *fr. gate n1. (& toth n.)*
Chaucer GP 2

gaude n. 1b *cp.* <*gaudi n.*> (c1333–52)
Minot Poems TR 3

gauded ppl. *fr. gaude n. & gaudi n.*
Chaucer *GP* 1

gaudi adj. *ML & OF* (c1325) Recipe
Painting(1) in Archaeol.J.1 *KNT* 1

gauren v. *ON* (c1200) Vices & V.(1)
MKT 6

geaunt n. & adj. 1a *OF & OE & L* c1300
Horn (Ld) MKT 10

gein n. a *ON & OF* (?c1200) St.Marg.(1)
ANEL 1

geinen v. 1b *ON* ?c1200 Orm. TR 4

gelden v. 2b *ON* ?c1200 Wor.Bod.Gloss.
(Hat 115) *MKT* 1

gelding n. 2a *ON* (a1382) WBible(1)
(Bod 959) GP 1

gemetrie n. 1a *OF* c1330 7 Sages(1) *KNT*
1

gemetrien n. a *OF* Chaucer *BO* 1

Gemini n. *L* Chaucer AST 8

gemme n. 1b *L & OF* a1300 A Mayde
Cristes MKT 10

gendre n. 2a *OF* (?c1350) SVrn.Leg. *HF* 1

Gene n. a *cp. OF* (?a1300) KAlex. CLT 2

generacioun n. 3c *OF* (a1325) Cursor BO
4

general adj. & n. 2b *L & OF* (?a1200)
*Ancr. ABC 36

generalli adv. a *fr. general adj.* (1340)
Ayenb. TR 21

Genesis n. *OE & L & OF* (?a1200)
*Ancr. *PARST* 1

gent adj. b *OF* c1250 On leome ROMA
4

gentil adj. 1a *OF & L* (?a1200) *Ancr.
ROMA 117

gentil n. {1a} *fr. gentil adj.* Chaucer
{(?c1380) Cleanness} ANEL 5

gentilesse n. 2a *OF* (?a1300) KAlex. PITY
80

gentilli adv. 1c *fr.* <*gentil n.*> *& gentil
adj.* (?a1200) Ancr. TR 7

gentil-man n. 2 *(fr. gentil adj. & man n.
& indef. pron.)* (?c1150) Prov.Alf.
(Trin-C) *LGW* 3

gentilnesse n. 1a *fr. gentil adj.* (a1325)
Cursor MARS 2

gentrie n. 1a *OF* (c1303) Mannyng HS
LGW F 8

gentrise n. 2a *OF* (?a1200) *Ancr. *PARST*
1

gere n. 5b *ON* ?c1200 Orm. BD 14

gerful adj. *fr. gere n.* Chaucer TR 2

geri adj. a *fr. gere n.* Chaucer *KNT* 1

gerlond n. 1c *OF* (?c1300) NPass.(1)
ROMA 16

germain adj. 1b *OF* (?c1300) Guy(1) *MEL*
1

gerner n. a *OF* (?a1200) *Ancr. ROMA 3

gessen v. 1a *cp. MDu., MLG & OI* (1303)
Mannyng HS ROMA 71

gessinge ger. a *(fr. gessen v.)* c1350
Ayenb.App. *BO* 3

gest n. 1c *ON* (c1125)
Vsp.D.Hom.Fest.Virg. HF 14

geste n1. 2c *OF & ML* (?c1225) Horn HF
15

gesten v2. *fr. geste n.* Chaucer *PARSPRO* 1

gestour n. *fr.* <*gesten v2.*> (a1338)
Mannyng Chron.Pt.1 HF 2

get n1. 1a *OF* c1330 Why werre GP 2

get n2. 2c *AF* Chaucer *NPT* 1

geten v1. 1a a *ON* ?c1200 Orm. ROMA
117

getinge ger1. 2a a *(fr. geten v1.)* (c1303)
Mannyng HS BO 11

gibete n. 1a *OF* (?a1200) *Ancr. *HF* 1

gide n. 1a *OF* (a1376) PPl.A(1) (Vrn)
SNPro 8
giden v. 1a *OF* Chaucer TR 16
gideresse n. *fr.* *<giden v.>* Chaucer *BO*
1
gidinge ger. a *fr. giden v* * Chaucer BO 2
gien v. 3c *OF, fr. Gmc.* c1300 SLeg. (Ld)
SNT 18
gigge n2. *cp.* *<gigen v.>* Chaucer *HF* 1
gigging ger. *fr.* *<gige n1.>* Chaucer *KNT*
1
gilde-halle n. a *OE* (1280) in Rymer's
Foedera (1816–69) GP 1
gilden v. 1a *OE* (?a1300) Arth.& M. BD
6
gile n3. 3b *OF* (?c1150) Prov.Alf. (Trin-C)
ROMA 7
gilour n. a *OF* c1300 SLeg. (Ld) *RvT* 1
gilt n1. 1a *OE* c1175 Bod.Hom. ABC 49
gilti adj. 1a *OE* a1125 Vsp.A.Hom. SNT
8
giltif adj. a *fr. gilt n1.* c1330 7 Sages(1) BO
3
giltles adj. 1a *fr. gilt n1.* ?c1200 Orm.
LGW 22
ginge-bred n. a *OF & ML* 1381 Pegge
Cook.Recipes *THOP* 1
gingivere n. a *OF & ML & OE* c1150
PDidax. *ROMA* 1
ginglen v. *?imitative* Chaucer GP 1
ginne n. 1a *OF* ?c1200 Orm. ROMA 6
ginnen v. 3b b *OE & beginnen v.* (?c1150)
Prov.Alf. (*Glb-James) GENERAL 692
ginninge ger. 1a *(fr. ginnen v.)* a1300
PMor. (McC) HF 4
gipser n. *OF* Chaucer GP 1
girdel n. 1a *OE* c1150 Hrl.MQuad.
ROMA 8
girdel-stede n. *(fr. girdel n. & stede n1.)*
(?a1300) Arth.& M. *ROMA* 1
girden v1. 1a *OE* (?a1200) Ancr. MARS 3
girden v2. 1a *OE* (?a1200) Lay.Brut *MKT*
1
girle n. *?OE* c1300 SLeg.Becket (Ld) GP
2

gise n. 3b *OF* c1300 Lay.Brut (Otho)
ROMA 29
giser n. b *OF* (1373) *Lelamour Macer
BO 1
giste n2. a *OF* (?a1200) *Ancr. TR 1
gite n3. *OF* c1390 Disp.GM & Devil
RvT 2
giterne n. *OF* (?1350–75) Origo Mundi
in Norris Anc.Corn.Drama MILT 5
giterninge ger. *fr. giternen v.* * (c1383)
Wycl.Leaven Pharisees *MILT* 1
glad adj. 2a *OE* a1121 Peterb.Chron.
ROMA 133
gladen v. 3a *OE* c1175 Bod.Hom. ROMA
37
gladere n. a *fr. gladen v.* (a1382)
WBible(1) *KNT* 1
gladli adv. 1 *OE* ?c1200 Orm. BD 43
gladnesse n. 1a *OE* c1175 HRood ROMA
43
gladsom adj. 2 *fr. glad adj.* (1382)
WBible(1) *PRONPT* 1
glaire n. a *OF* (?c1380) Pearl *CYT* 1
glaren v. a *cp. MDu.* c1275 Ken.Serm.
HF 2
glas n. 5a *OE* c1150 PDidax. BD 21
glasen v. 3d *fr. glas n.* (c1303) Mannyng
HS BD 2
glasinge ger. b *(fr. glasen v.)* Chaucer
BD 1
gle n1. 2b *OE* (?c1175) PMor. (Trin-C)
ABC 5
glede n2. 2 *OE* (?c1150) Prov.Alf. (Glb)
TR 11
gledi adj. *fr. glede n2.* Chaucer *LGW F* 1
glem n. 1a *OE* (?a1200) *Ancr. *LGW G* 1
glenen v. 2a *OF* c1330 The siker sothe
LGW F 1
glenten v. 3a *ON* (c1250) Gen.& Ex. *TR*
1
gleuen v2. 1d *OF* Chaucer HF 2
gliden v. 1a *OE* a1200 Sanctus Beda SNT
9
glimsinge ger. a *(fr. glimsen v.)* Chaucer
MERT 1

Chaucer's words

gliteren v. 1a *ON & OE* (?a1300) Arth.&
M. Bo 4

glorie n. 2b *OF* ?c1200 Wor.Bod.Gloss.
(Jun) ROMA 57

glorifien v. 1a *OF* (1340) Ayenb. HF 9

glorious adj. 1b *OF & L* c1275
Ken.Serm. ABC 16

glose n. 1a *ML & OF* c1300
SLeg.Inf.Chr. (Ld) BD 12

glosen v. 3a *ML & OF* (c1300)
Glo.Chron.A MKT 12

glosinge ger. 1c *(fr. glosen v.)* (c1300)
Glo.Chron.A SUMT 1

glotonie n. a *OF* (?a1200) *Ancr. PF
22

glotonous adj. a *OF* (c1350) Alex.& D.
BO 1

glotoun n. a *OF* (?a1200) *Ancr. PF 3

glouen vi. 1a *OE* ?c1200 Orm. Bo 6

glove n. 3b *OE & ON* c1150 Hrl.HApul.
ROMA 3

gnat n. b *OE* (?a1200) *Ancr. TR 3

gnauen v. 1a a *OE* a1200 Body & S.(2)
TR 7

gnauinge ger. a *(fr. gnauen v.)* a1325
SLeg. (Corp-C) PARST 1

gnodden v. a *cp. OE* (?a1200) *Ancr.
FORMAGE 1

gnof n. *?cp.* EFris. Chaucer MILT 1

gobet n. 1a *OF* (?a1325) Bonav.Medit.(1)
BO 3

god adj. 6a *OE* a1121 Peterb.Chron.
ROMA 620

god adv. a *fr. god adj.* (?a1200) Lay.Brut
ROMA 2

God, god n1. 10a c *OE* (1100)
Chart.St.Paul ROMA 1510

god n2. 1b *OE* a1121 Peterb.Chron.
ROMA 338

goddesse n. *fr. god n1.* (?a1350) Siege
Troy(1) BD 43

god-fader n. a *OE* a1200 Body & S.
PARST 1

godhede n1. 1a *fr. god n1.* (?a1200) *Ancr.
BO 3

godli adj2. 1b *OE* (?c1150) Prov.Alf.
(Mdst) BD 34

godli adv2. 1a *prob. OE* (?a1200)
Lay.Brut BD 26

godlihede n. c *fr. godli adj2.* Chaucer
BD 7

god-man phr. & n. 1a *fr. god adj. & man
n. & indef. pron.* a1121 Peterb.Chron.
LGW 2

godnesse n2. 3c *OE* (c1125)
Vsp.D.Hom.Fest.Virg. ABC 76

god-sibbe n. 2a *OE* a1300 Trin-C.Prov.
WBPRO 6

goinge ger. 1b *(fr. gon v.)* a1250 Ancr.
(Nero) BO 9

gold adj. 1c *fr. gold n.* (?a1200) Lay.Brut
MKT 2

gold n. 1c *OE* a1121 Peterb.Chron. ROMA
149

gold-bete adj. 3e, gold n. *(fr. gold n. &
beten vi.)* (?a1300) KAlex. ANEL 2

golde n. b *OE* a1325 Gloss.Bibbesw.
(Arun) *KNT* 1

golden adj. 1a *fr. gold n.* c1300 Lay.Brut
(Otho) MKT 7

gold-finch n. a *OE* c1250 Owl & N.
CKT 1

gold-hewen adj. 3e, gold n. *(gold n. &
heuen v2.)* Chaucer KNT 1

goldles adj. *fr. gold n.* Chaucer SHIPT
1

gold-smith n. a *OE* (?a1200) *Ancr. CYT
2

gold-smithrie n. b *fr. gold-smith n.*
Chaucer KNT 1

gold-tressed adj. 5b, gold n. *(fr. gold n. &
tressen v.)* Chaucer TR 1

gole n2. *OF* Chaucer PF 1

golet n. a *OF* Chaucer PARDT 1

goliardeis n. *AF* (c1303) Mannyng HS
GP 1

Golias n. a *ML* (?c1200) St.Juliana MLT
1

gomme n. b *OF & L* (a1325) Cursor
LGW F 1

gon v. 5b b *OE* a1121 Peterb.Chron. RoмA 753

gonen v. a *OE* c1250 *St.Marg.(2) MancPro 1

gonne n. 1a *prob. ON* (?a1300) KAlex. HF 2

gore n2. 3a *OE* c1250 Owl & N. MɪLT 2

gos n. 4a *OE* c1150 Hrl.HApul. PF 14

gos-hauk n. a *OE* (1300) Court R.Lond. PF 2

gosish adj. *fr. gos. n.* Chaucer *TR* 1

gospel n. 2a *OE* 1123 Peterb.Chron. SNT 16

gos-somer n. a *fr. gos n. & somer n1.* ?a1300 St.J.List Trees *SQT* 1

gost n. 3a *OE* a1150 Vsp.D.Hom. ABC 48

gostli adj. 2a *OE* a1150 Vsp.D.Hom. *ParsT* 6

gostli adv. 1a *OE* c1175 Bod.Hom.Dom.Quadr. SNPro 2

got n. 1c a *OE & ON* c1150 Hrl.HApul. GP 2

goter n1. 3a *OF & ML* (c1340) Rolle Psalter (UC 64) Bo 3

Gothes n. pl. a *L & OE* Chaucer *Bo* 1

goune n. c *OF & ML* ?a1325 Heil seint Michel GP 5

goune-clooth n. e, goune n. *(fr. goune n. & cloth n.)* Chaucer *SUMT* 2

gounfanoun n. 1a *OF, fr. Gmc.* (?a1300) Arth.& M. *RoмA* 1

gourde n. 1d *AF* (c1303) Mannyng HS *MancPro* 2

goute n1. c *OF & ML* (?a1200) *Ancr. NPT* 1

governail n. 3b *OF* (?c1350) Mirror St.Edm.(4) Bo 2

governaunce n. 3a *OF* (c1303) Mannyng HS BD 59

governement n. 1a *OF* Chaucer HF 10

governen v. 1a a *OF* (?c1280) SLeg.Advent, etc. (Eg) BD 73

governeresse n. 1a *OF* Chaucer ABC 2

governinge ger. 3a *(fr. governen v.)* (?c1300) LFMass Bk. Bo 5

governour n. 3b *OF & L* (?a1300) KAlex. MкT 21

grace n. 1a *OF* (c1200) Vices & V.(1) RoмA 261

graceles adj. c *fr. grace n.* Chaucer TR 2

gracious adj. 1b *OF & L* (c1303) Mannyng HS TR 5

graciousli adv. a *fr. gracious adj.* (c1303) Mannyng HS *SHIPT* 1

graciousnesse n. b *fr. gracious adj.* Chaucer *LGW* 1

grain n. 3a *OF* c1300 SLeg.John (Ld) RoмA 14

grame n. 3a *OE* c1175 Bod.Hom. ANEL 5

gramerci n. & interj. b *OF* c1300 SLeg.Inf.Chr. (Ld) TR 2

gramere n. 1a *OF* (a1387) Trev.Higd. *PRT* 1

grape n1. 2a *OF* (c1250) Gen.& Ex. Bo 4

grapenel n. *cp. OF* Chaucer *LGW* 1

gras n. 1a *OE* (?c1150) Prov.Alf. (Mdst) RoмA 22

graspen v. b *?OE* (c1350) Alex.& D. TR 2

graunge n. d *OF* (c1300) Havelok HF 3

graunt adj. b, gramerci n. & interj. *OF* c1300 SLeg.Inf.Chr. (Ld) BD 13

graunt n. 1a *OF* (?a1200) *Ancr. RoмA 4

graunten v. 1b *OF* (?c1225) Horn RoмA 134

grauntinge ger. a *(fr. graunten v.)* (1340) Ayenb. Bo 2

grave n1. a *OE* (c1250) Gen.& Ex. TR 9

gravel n. a *OF* (?c1225) Horn RoмA 3

graven v1. 3c *OE* (?a1200) Lay.Brut BD 29

gre n1. 1a *OF* (?a1300) Stations Rome(1) *MERT* 1

gre n2. 2a *OF* c1300 SLeg.Inf.Chr. (Ld) RoмA 7

Grece n. a *L* (?a1300) KAlex.(Auch) BD 14

gredi adj. 2 *OE* c1175 Bod.Hom. Bo 6

gredili adv. b *OE* a1200 Body & S.(2)
PARST 1
gref n. 2b *AF & CF* (?a1200) Ancr. TR 8
gre-hound n. a *OE* (?a1200) *Ancr. GP 1
grei adj. & n. 1a *OE & ON* (?a1200)
*Ancr. ROMA 16
greithen v. 1a a *ON* ?c1200 Orm. ROMA
4
Grek adj. *fr. Grek n.* (?a1300) KAlex. TR
4
Grek n. 1a *OE* c1150 Hrl.HApul. BD 69
Grekish adj. & n. 1a *OE* ?c1200 Orm.
BO 3
grene adj. 1a *OE* c1150 Hrl.HApul.
ROMA 70
grene n1. c *fr. grene adj.* (?a1200)
Lay.Brut ROMA 32
grenehede n. c *fr. grene adj.* a1325
Gloss.Bibbesw. MLT 1
grene-wode n. 2b, grene adj. *(fr. grene
adj. & wod n2.)* (?a1300) KAlex. FRT
1
grenish adj. a *fr. grene adj.* Chaucer HF
1
grennen v. 1e *OE* (c1150) Prov.Alf. (Trin-
C) ROMA 1
grese n. 1a *AF* c1300 SLeg. (Ld) GP 3
gret adj. & adv. & n. 1a a *OE* c1150
Hrl.HApul. ROMA 860
greten v2. 1b *OE* (1100) Chart.St.Paul in
RHS ser.3.58 BD 18
gretli adv. b *fr. gret adj.* (?a1200)
Trin.Hom. ROMA 44
gretnesse n. 1c *OE* c1150 Hrl.HApul.
ROMA 7
grevaunce n. 1a *OF* (?a1300) Arth.& M.
ABC 19
greve n1. 1d *OE* a1121 Peterb.Chron. BD
6
greven v. 3a a *OF* (?a1200) *Ancr. ROMA
40
grevous adj. 2c *AF* c1300 SLeg.Lucy (Ld)
ROMA 26
grevousli adv. a *fr. grevous adj.* (c1303)
Mannyng HS BO 10

griffoun n2. a *OF* (c1350) Octav.(1) KNT
1
grille adj. 1a *OE* ?c1200 Orm. ROMA 1
grim adj. 1a *OE* c1175 Bod.Hom. HF 5
grimli adv. 1b *OE* (?a1200) Lay.Brut
ROMA 1
grimnesse n. *OE* c1175 Bod.Hom. PARST
1
grinden v1. 1a *OE* c1150 PDidax. HF 15
grindinge ger. 2 *(fr. grinden v1.)* c1150
PDidax. RVT 2
gripen v. 2b *OE* (?c1150) Prov.Alf. (Mdst)
ROMA 3
gris adj. *OF* Chaucer CYPRO 1
gris n2. *OF* c1250 *Body & S.(4) GP 1
grisel n. *OF* (a1393) Gower CA SCOG 1
grisli adj. & n. 1c *OE* a1150
Vsp.D.Hom.Nicod. MKT 18
groin n1. 1a *OF* (?c1300) Bevis PARST 1
groin n2. *OF* Chaucer TR 1
groininge ger. a *(fr. groinen v.)* c1300
SLeg.Mich. (Hrl: Wright) KNT 1
grom n. 1b *prob. OE* (?a1200) *Ancr.
ROMA 2
gronen v. 1a *OE* a1175 Bod.Hom. HF 13
groninge ger. a *OE* a1200 Body & S.(2)
NPT 1
gropen v. 1b *OE* (c1125)
Vsp.D.Hom.Elucid. LGW 9
grot n1. b *OE* c1225 SWard (Roy) FRPRO
1
grot n3. 1a *MDu.* (a1376) PPl.A(1) (Trin-
C) TR 5
grouen v. 3a *OE* c1150 Hrl.HApul.
ROMA 22
ground n. 15c *OE* a1121 Peterb.Chron.
ROMA 56
grounden v. 6b *fr. ground n.* (?a1200)
Lay.Brut BD 3
grove n1. a *OE* (?a1200) Lay.Brut KNT 13
grubben v. b *prob. OE* (a1325) Cursor
FORMAGE 1
grucchen v. 1a *OF* (?a1200) *Ancr. TR 16
grucchinge ger. 1a *(fr. grucchen v.)*
(?a1200) *Ancr. WBPRO 5

gruel n. 2a *OF* (c1353) Winner & W. *TR* 1

gruffe n. & adj. & adv. c *ON* Chaucer *TR* 3

grunten v. 2 *OE* a1250 Ancr. (Nero) *MKT* 1

guerdonen v. a *OF* Chaucer BO 7

guerdoninge ger. a *fr. guerdonen v.* * Chaucer PF 3

guerdoun n. a *OF* Chaucer ROMA 25

gut n. 1a a *OE* c1300 SLeg.Edm.Abp. (Ld) *MKT* 2

ha interj. *cp. L & OF* (?a1325) Bonav.Medit.(1) HF 11

haberdasher n. *AF* (1377) Plea & Mem.R.Lond.Gildh. *GP* 1

habergeoun n. a *OF* (?a1300) Arth.& M. KNT 5

habit n. 1c *OF* (?a1200) Ancr. MKT 16

habitacioun n. 1 *L & OF* Chaucer MKT 5

habitacle n. 2b *OF & L* Chaucer HF 2

habiten v. 1 {2} *OF* Chaucer {(c1378) PPl.B (Ld)} *ROMA* 1

hacche n. 3d *OE* a1121 Peterb.Chron. *LGW* 1

hail n. 1a *OE* a1121 Peterb.Chron. HF 5

hainous adj. a *OF* Chaucer *TR* 1

hait interj. *?* Chaucer *FRT* 3

hakeneie n. 1a *prob. fr. Borough of Hackney* (?c1300) Bevis ROMA 2

hakken v. 1a *OE* (?a1200) Trin.Hom. TR 2

halen v. 1a a *OF, fr. Gmc.* (?a1200) Lay.Brut ABC 4

half adj. 2a *OE* c1150 Hrl.HApul. BD 10

half adv. 1b *OE* c1150 Hrl.MQuad. ROMA 31

half n. 5a b *OE* a1121 Peterb.Chron. ROMA 49

half-god n. 4, half adj. *(fr. half adj. & God, god n1.)* Chaucer *LGW F* 1

half-wei adv. *fr. half adj. & wei n.* c1330 7 Sages(1) *RVPRO* 1

hali-dai n. & phr. 1a *OE* c1175 Bod.Hom. LGW F 5

halk n. 1a *OE* (?c1225) Horn ROMA 4

halle n. 1e *OE* (?a1200) Lay.Brut BD 51

halouen v. b *OF* Chaucer *BD* 1

hal-peni n. 1a *fr. half n. & peni n.* c1275 Ancr. (Cleo Morton) *SUMT* 1

hals n. 1a *OE* c1150 PDidax. HF 6

halsen v1. 1a *OE* c1175 HRood *PRT* 1

halten v. 1b *OE* c1325 Heye louerd BD 2

halven-dele n. 1a *OE* (?a1200) Lay.Brut *TR* 2

halwe n. 1b *OE* a1121 Peterb.Chron. BD 11

halwen v. 3a *OE* a1121 Peterb.Chron. SNT 4

hamelen v. a *LOE fr. ON* (?a1200) Lay.Brut *TR* 1

hamer n. 1a *OE* (c1125) Vsp.D.Hom.Elucid. BD 3

hamperen v. c {b} *?fr. <hamper n.>* Chaucer {(a1375) WPal.} *ROMA* 1

hanselin n. *OF* Chaucer PARST 1

hap n. 1a *ON* (?1200) Lay.Brut BD 34

happen v1. 1a *fr. hap n.* (c1303) Mannyng HS ROMA 41

happenen v. 2b *fr. happen v1. & -en suf4.* (?c1380) Cleanness *LGW F* 1

happi adj. & adv. 1a *fr. hap n.* Chaucer HF 5

hard adj. 4b *OE* a1126 Peterb.Chron. ROMA 64

hard n. 1b *fr. hard adj.* ?c1200 Orm. *TR* 1

harde adv. 2b *OE* (?c1175) PMor. (Lamb) BO 12

harden v. 1d *OE* c1150 Hrl.Hapul. BO 2

hard-herted adj. a *fr. hard-hert adj. & n.* (?a1200) Lay.Brut BO 2

hardi adj. 1a c *OF (fr. Gmc.)* (?a1200) Ancr. ROMA 30

hardili adv. 3a *fr. hardi adj.* (?a1200) Ancr. ROMA 22

hardiment n. *OF* Chaucer *TR* 1

hardinesse n. 1a *fr. hardi adj.* (?a1300) KAlex. MKT 15

hardinge ger. a *(fr. harden v.)* Chaucer *SQT* 1

hardnesse n. 1b *OE* c1150 Hrl.MQuad.
Bo 7

hare n. 2b *OE* ?c1125 Dur-C.Gloss. HF 9

harlot n. 1a *OF* (?a1200) Ancr. RoмA 7

harlotrie n. 2 *fr. harlot n.* (a1376)
PPl.A(1) (Trin-C) GP 6

harm n. 1a *OE* a1121 Peterb.Chron.
RoмA 171

harmen v. 1a *OE* (?a1200) Trin.Hom.
BD 5

harmful adj. a *fr. harm n.* (1340) Ayenb.
BD 1

harmfullie adv. *fr. harmful adj.* Chaucer
Bo 1

harminge ger. a *(fr. harmen v.)* (a1325)
Cursor *Tr* 1

harmles adj. 1a *fr. harm n.* (c1280)
SLeg.Pass. (Pep) *LGW* 1

harneis n. 1a *OF* (?a1300) Arth.& M.
KnT 15

harneisen v. c *OF* (?a1300) KAlex. *GP* 1

harou interj. & n. b *OF* (?a1300)
Arth.& M. MiLT 8

harpe n. 1a *OE & OF, fr. Gmc.* a1200
Body & S.(2) HF 12

harpen v. 1a *OE & OF, fr. Gmc.* (?a1200)
Lay.Brut *Tr* 1

harpere n. a *OE & OF, fr. Gmc.* (?c1225)
Horn HF 4

harpe-stringes n. 1c, harpe n. *OE*
Chaucer *HF* 1

harpinge ger. a *OE* (?a1200) Lay.Brut
GP 1

hasard n. 1a *OF, fr. Ar.* (c1300) Havelok
PardT 4

hasardour n. a *OF* (c1303) Mannyng HS
PardT 7

hasardrie n. *OF* (c1300) Glo.Chron.A
PardT 4

hasel n. 1a *OE & ON* (?a1200) Lay.Brut
KnT 1

haselwode n. 2b, hasel n. *(fr. hasel n. &
wod n2.)* Chaucer *Tr* 3

haspe n. a *OE & ON* a1200 Wor.Aelfric
Gloss. *MiLT* 1

haste n. 2a *OF, fr. Gmc.* (?c1225) Horn
Tr 11

hasten v. 1c *OF* (c1280) SLeg.Pass. (Pep)
RoмA 28

hastif adj. 2a *OF* c1300 SLeg.Becket (Ld)
Tr 8

hastiflie adv. 1a *fr. hastif adj.* c1300 SLeg.
(Ld) MLT 3

hastifnesse n. b *fr. hastif adj.* (c1338)
Mannyng Chron.Pt.2 *Mel* 3

hastilie adv. 1a *fr. <hastie adj.>* (c1300)
Glo.Chron.A RoмA 46

hat n. 1a a *OE & ON* a1200 Wor.Aelfric
Gloss. PF 9

hate n. c *prob. fr. OE* c1175 Bod.Hom.
RoмA 37

hateful adj. a *fr. hate n.* Chaucer Bo 8

haten v. 1c *OE* c1175 Bod.Hom. RoмA
46

hatrede n. b *fr. hate n. & -reden suf.*
a1225 Vsp.A.Hom. *Bo* 1

hauberk n. b *OF fr. Gmc.* c1300
SLeg.Edm.Abp. (Ld) Mars 6

haue n1. a *OE & ON* c1250 Owl & N.
PardT 1

haue n2. c *OE* c1250 *St.Marg.(2) Tr
4

haue-bake n. d, haue n2. *fr. haue n2. &
bake ppl.* Chaucer *IntMLT* 1

haue-thorn n. 2a *OE* c1150 Hrl.HApul.
KnT 1

hauk n1. 1b *OE* (c1200) Vices & V.(1) Tr
14

hauken v1. a *fr. hauk n1.* (c1350) Alex.&
D. *ClT* 1

hauking ger1. a *(fr. hauken v1.)* (?a1300)
KAlex. Tr 2

haunche-bon n. 1d, haunche n. *(fr.
haunche n. & bon n1.)* Chaucer *MiLT*
2

haunt n. 1b *OF* (?a1300) KAlex. GP 3

haunten v1. 4a *OF* (?c1200) HMaid. Bo
12

hautein adj. & n. 1a *OF* (c1300)
Glo.Chron.A PF 4

The making of Chaucer's English

haven n1. 1a *OE & ON* (?a1200)
Lay.Brut ABC 9
haven v. 4a a *OE* (1100) Chart.St.Paul in
RHS ser.3.58 GENERAL 4715
haven-side n. 2a, haven n1. *(fr. haven n1.*
& side n.) Chaucer *NPT* 1
havinge ger. b *(fr. haven v.)* c1350
MPPsalter BO 4
he pron1. 1a a *OE* a1121 Peterb.Chron.
GENERAL 5853
hed n1. 1a b *OE* a1121 Peterb.Chron.
ROMA 226
hed n2. 2a *fr. heden v1.* c1300
SLeg.Dunstan (Ld) ROMA 68
heden v1. 2a *fr. hed n1.* c1230 Ancr.
(Corp-C) *TR* 1
hegge n. a *OE* c1250 Owl & N. ROMA
6
hei interj. 1a *prob. imitative* (?c1200)
St.Kath.(1) *LGW* 1
hei n. 1a *OE* a1200 Wor.Aelfric Gloss.
ROMA 9
heien v. 1a a *fr. OE* ?c1200 Orm. *BO* 1
heigh adj. 2a a *OE* a1121 Peterb.Chron.
ROMA 260
heighe adv. 1a *OE* a1200 Body & S.(2)
ROMA 74
heighli adv. 3d *fr. heigh adj.* c1150
Hrl.HApul. *TR* 3
heighnesse n. 1b *fr. heigh adj. & OE*
c1175 Bod.Hom. LADY 4
heighte n. 3a *OE* c1230 Ancr. (Corp-C)
ROMA 48
heil interj. a *(fr. heil adj.)* (c1200) Vices
& V.(1) MILT 3
heir n. 1b *AF & L* (?c1225) Horn BD 18
heironer n. *OF* Chaucer *TR* 2
heironseu n. b *OF* Chaucer *SQT* 1
heiroun n. 1a *OF; fr. Gmc.* c1300 Orfeo
PF 2
hei-sugge n. *OE* c1250 Owl & N. *PF* 1
helden v. 1a b *OE* a1200 Body & S.(2)
HF 2
hele n1. 1a *OE* c1150 Hrl.MQuad. ABC
39

hele n3. 1a *OE* c1150 Hrl.MQuad. ROMA
5
heleles adj. *fr. hele n1.* Chaucer *TR* 1
helen v1. 1a *OE* c1150 Hrl.HApul. BD
21
helen v2. 2a *OE* (?c1175) PMor. (Lamb)
WBT 3
helinge ger1. f *(fr. helen v1.)* c1225
St.Marg.(1) (Roy) *TR* 1
helle n. 1a *OE* a1121 Peterb.Chron.
ROMA 128
helle-pit n. 2a, helle n. *(fr. helle n. & pit*
n.) ?c1200 Orm. *BD* 1
helm n. a *OE & ON* (?a1200) Lay.Brut
ANEL 12
helmen v. *OE* (?a1200) Lay.Brut MKT 2
help n. 1a *OE* a1131 Peterb.Chron. ROMA
53
helpen v. 3b *OE* c1150 PDidax. ROMA
187
helpinge ger. 1a *(fr. helpen v.)* (?a1200)
Lay.Brut BO 7
helples adj. a *fr. help n.* (c1200) Vices &
V.(1) LGW 3
helplich adj. a *fr. help n.* ?a1325 The
grace of god *TR* 1
hem n. a *OE* a1200 Gloss.Sidonius *BO* 1
hem pron. pl. 1 *OE* a1121 Peterb.Chron.
GENERAL 1354
hempen adj. *fr. hemp. n.* Chaucer
{(1392) *MS Wel.564} ROMA* 1
hem-self pron. 1c *OE* a1131
Peterb.Chron. SNT 61
hem-ward adv. 4d, hem pron. pl. *(fr. hem*
pron. pl .& -ward suf.) (c1250) Gen.&
Ex. *BO* 2
hen n1. 2b *OE* ?c1125 Dur-C.Gloss.
(Cokayne) GP 9
hen n2. a *OF* (?a1200) Lay.Brut *CYT* 1
hende adj. 1a *OE* (?a1200) Lay.Brut
ROMA 15
henne adv. 1a *OE* a1121 Peterb.Chron.
TR 6
hennes adv. 1a *fr. henne adv.* (?c1225)
Horn ROMA 13

306

hennes-forth adv. a *fr. hennes adv. & forth adv.* a1375 WPal. HF 6

henten v. 3c *OE* (?a1200) Trin.Hom. ROMA 56

henter n. *fr. henten v.* Chaucer BO 1

hep n. 1a *OE* c1175 Bod.Hom. ROMA 11

hepe n2. a *OE* ?c1125 Dur-C.Gloss.(Cockayne) THOP 1

hepen v. 2b *OE* ?c1200 Orm. BO 2

her adv. 1a a *OE* a1121 Peterb.Chron. GENERAL 402

her n. 1b *OE & ON* (?c1150) Prov.Alf. (Trin-C) ROMA 59

her-abouten adv. a *fr. her adv. & abouten adv.* (c1200) Vices & V.(1) MILT 1

her-after adv. 1d *OE* a1121 Peterb.Chron. ROMA 12

her-after-ward adv. b *fr. her-after adv.* c1300 SLeg. (Ld) TR 3

heraud n. 1c *AF* (?c1300) Guy(1) HF 5

herauden v. *OF* Chaucer HF 1

her-ayenes adv. c *fr. her adv. & ayen adv.* a1250 Ancr. (Nero) TR 3

herbe n. 1a *OF & L* c1300 SLeg.Brendan (Hrl: Horst.) HF 30

herber n1. a *OF* ?a1300 Thrush & N. TR 2

herbergage n. 1a *OF* (a1387) Trev.Higd. CKPRO 4

herbergeour n. 2b *OF* a1225 Lamb.Hom. MLT 1

herberwe n. 1e *OE* (c1125) Vsp.D.Hom.Fest.Virg. GP 6

herberwen v. 1e *fr. herberwe n.* (c1125) Vsp.D.Hom.Fest.Virg. ROMA 2

herberwinge ger. d *(fr. herberwen v.)* (a1325) Cursor CKPRO 1

her-bi adv. 1a *fr. her adv. & bi prep.* (?c1200) HMaid. MKT 5

her-biforen adv. e *OE* c1150 Hrl.HApul. BD 51

Hercules n. a *L, fr. Gr.* (?a1200) Lay.Brut BD 28

herde n1. a *OE & ON* (?a1200) Ancr. LGW 1

herde n2. 2a *OE* a1121 Peterb.Chron. SNT 4

herde n3. a *OE* (?a1200) Ancr. ROMA 1

herde-gromes n. 3a, herde n2. *(fr. herde n2. & grom n.)* Chaucer HF 1

herdesse n. *fr. herde n2.* Chaucer TR 1

here n2. 1a *OE & OF, fr. Gmc.* (?a1200) Ancr. ROMA 6

here pron. poss. pl. 1a a *OE* a1121 Peterb.Chron. GENERAL 987

hered ppl. b *fr. her n.* Chaucer KNT 1

heremite n. 1a *ML & OF* (c1200) Vices & V.(1) HF 1

heren v. 5b *OE* a1121 Peterb.Chron. ROMA 461

hereos n. *ML* Chaucer KNT 1

heres pron. a *fr. here pron.* a1225 Vsp.A.Hom. BO 2

heresie n. 1a *OF & L* (?a1200) Ancr. LGW F1

herien v1. a *OE* (c1125) Vsp.D.Hom.Fest.Virg. SNPRO 18

herien v2. 1a *OE* a1121 Peterb.Chron. KNT 4

heriinge ger. 1b *cp. OE* c1175 Bod.Hom. TR 3

heringe ger. 3a *OE* a1200 Body & S.(2) BO 5

her-inne adv. a *fr. her adv. & in prep.* (?a1200) Trin.Hom. KNT 2

heritage n. 2a a *OF* (?a1200) Ancr. ROMA 21

herken v. a *prob. fr. herkenen v.* (c1200) Vices & V.(1) HF 13

herkenen v. 1a a *OE* (c1125) Vsp.D.Hom.Fest.Virg. ROMA 95

herkeninge ger. a *OE* (?a1200) Ancr. BO 1

her-mele n. 4b, her n. *(fr. her n. & -mele suf.)* Chaucer AST 1

hernia n. 1a *L* Chaucer PARST 1

her-of adv. 3a *fr. her adv. & of prep.* ?c1200 Orm. ROMA 19

her-on adv. 2b *fr. her adv. & on prep.*
(c1200) Vices & V.(1) *HF* 1

herre n1. 2a *OE* c1150 PDidax. *GP* 1

herre n2. 1a *OE & MDu.* (?a1200)
Lay.Brut *TR* 1

herse n. a *OF & ML* (?a1300) Interl.CG
PITY 2

hert n. 1e *OE* c1150 Hrl.HApul. BD 20

herte n. 4c (c1125)
Vsp.D.Hom.Fest.Virg. ROMA 918

herte-blod n. a *fr. herte n. & blod n1.*
(?a1200) Lay.Brut KNT 3

herteles adj. a *OE* (a1338) Mannyng
Chron.Pt.1 TR 2

hertelie adj. 1a *(fr. hertelie adv.)* (a1338)
Mannyng Chron.Pt.1 LGW 3

hertelie adv. 1a *cp. herte n. & OE*
(?a1200) Ancr. BD 16

herte-rote n. b *fr. herte n. & rote n4.*
a1225 Trin.Hom ROMA 2

herte-spoon n. 1d a, herte n. *fr. herte n. &*
spon n. Chaucer *KNT* 1

hert-hunting n. 1e, hert n. *(fr. hert n. &*
hunting ger.) Chaucer *BD* 1

her-to adv. a *fr. her. adv. & to prep.*
(1100) Chart.St.Paul in RHS ser.3.58
BD 7

her-toforen adv. a *fr. her adv. & toforen*
prep. (c1200) Vices & V.(1) BD 2

her-upon adv. a *fr. her adv. & upon prep.*
a1225 Lamb.Hom. TR 8

her-withal adv. b *fr. her adv. & with-al*
adv. (?c1325) NHom.(3) Leg. *HF* 2

Hesperus n. *L, fr. Gr.* Chaucer *BO* 3

heste n1. 1e *OE* a1121 Peterb.Chron.
MKT 27

hete n1. 2b *OE* c1150 PDidax. ROMA
34

heten v. 1a *OE* c1150 Hrl.HApul. *PF* 1

heterli adv. c *? fr. OE & ON* (?a1200)
Ancr. *LGW* 1

heth n. 1a *OE & ON* (?a1200) Lay.Brut
GP 3

hethen adj. & n. 1a *OE & ON* a1121
Peterb.Chron. GP 9

hethen adv. 1c *ON* (?c1150) Prov.Alf.
(Mdst) *RVT* 1

hethenesse n. 1b *OE* (c1200) Vices &
V.(1) GP 2

hething n. 1a *ON* ?c1200 Orm. *RVT* 1

heu n. 1a *OE* a1121 Peterb.Chron. ROMA
68

heue n1. a *OE* ?c1200 Orm. *MERT* 1

heuen v1. 1f *OE* a1200 Body & S.(2)
KNT 2

heuen v2. 3 *fr. heu n. & OE* c1175
Bod.Hom. ROMA 6

heven n. 4a *OE* 1121 Peterb.Chron.
ROMA 211

heven v. 1b *OE* ?c1200 Orm. BO 12

hevenish adj. a *OE* Chaucer HF 5

hevenishli adv. *fr. hevenish adj.* Chaucer
KNT 1

hevenli adj. 1a *OE* a1121 Peterb.Chron.
BO 3

hevi adj. 2b a *OE* a1121 Peterb.Chron.
ROMA 42

hevi n. a *fr. hevi adj.* (c1250) Floris *PF* 1

hevien v. 2a *OE* (?a1200) Trin.Hom. BO
1

hevinesse n. 2b a *OE* (?a1200) Ancr.
ROMA 51

hiden v. 1a *OE* a1121 Peterb.Chron.
ROMA 112

hider adv. 1a *OE* a1121 Peterb.Chron.
ROMA 17

hidere n. *fr. hiden v.* Chaucer BO 2

hider-to adv. b *fr. hider adv. & to prep.*
(?a1200) Ancr. BO 3

hider-ward adv. 1a *OE* (?a1200) Lay.Brut
SHIPT 2

hidous adj. 1a *OF* (c1303) Mannyng HS
ROMA 7

hidousli adv. a *fr. hidous adj.* (1340)
Ayenb. HF 2

hie n2. a *fr. hien v.* ?c1200 Orm. TR 5

hien v. 1a *OE* ?c1200 Wor.Bod.Gloss. BD
23

hiene n. *ML & OF* (1340) Ayenb. FORT
1

highten v2. 1a *? fr. hight n. & highten v1.*
(?a1200) Trin.Hom. Bo 2

hille n. 3 *OE* (?c1175) PMor. (Trin-C)
RomA 15

him pro. 1a a *OE* a1121 Peterb.Chron.
General 2521

him-self pron. 2a *OE* a1121
Peterb.Chron. General 247

himself-ward n. MED Suppl. *(fr. himself
pron. & -ward suf.)* Chaucer Bo 1

him-ward n. 7c, him pron. *(fr. him pron.
& -ward suf.)* c1250 Owl & N. Bo 2

hinde n. d *OE* ?c1125 Dur-C.Gloss. BD
3

hinder adj1. 2b *prob. fr OE* c1300
SLeg.Brendan (Ld) GP 3

hindren v. 1 *OE* (?a1200) Trin.Hom.
RomA 4

hine n. 2a *OE* a1200 Body & S.(2) GP 2

hipe n. 2a *OE* c1150 Hrl.HApul. BD 3

hire n. 1a *OE* (?a1200) Ancr. ABC 11

hire pron1. 1a a *OE* a1131 Peterb.Chron.
General 1736

hire pron2. 1a *OE* a1121 Peterb.Chron.
General 1088

hiren v. 1a *OE* (?a1200) Ancr. PrT 1

hires pron. b *fr. hir pron1.* (?a1200)
Lay.Brut BD 7

hire-self pron. 1a *OE* (?c1150) Prov.Alf.
(Trin-C) RomA 74

hirne n. 1b *OE* 1131 Peterb.Chron.
FranT 2

his pron1. 2a *OE* (1100) Chart.St.Paul in
RHS ser.3.58 General 5011

his pron2. 2a *fr. his pron1. & OE* a1121
Peterb.Chron. BD 13

historial adj. a *L & OF* Chaucer LGW
G 2

hit pron. 1a *OE* a1121 Peterb.Chron.
General 4069

hit-self pron. b *fr. hit pron. & self pron.*
a1121 Peterb.Chron. Bo 27

hitten v. 1a *LOE, fr. ON* (?a1200)
Lay.Brut TR 4

hive n. b *OE* a1131 Peterb.Chron. HF 5

ho interj. 3 *OF & ON* (a1325) Cursor TR
5

ho n. b *fr. ho interj.* Chaucer TR 2

hoche-pot n. b *OF, fr. Gmc.* 1381 Pegge
Cook.Recipes MEL 1

hod n. 2a *OE* (?a1200) Lay.Brut BD 18

hodles adj. *fr. hod n.* Chaucer BD 1

hogge n1. 1a *OE, ?fr. Celt.* (?a1300)
KAlex. PardT 2

Hogge n3. *dim. of Roger* (a1376)
PPL.A(1) (Trin-C) CkPro 1

hok n. 2a *OE* (?c1200) St.Marg.(1) Bo 6

hoker n. b *OE* (?c1150) Prov.Alf. (Trin-
C) RvT 1

hokerliche adv. a *fr. hoker n.* (?a1200)
Lay.Brut ParsT 1

hold n2. 6a *OE* ?c1200 Orm. RomA 7

holden v1. 7a a *OE* a1121 Peterb.Chron.
RomA 358

holdere n. f *fr. holden v1.* (c1383)
Wycl.Leaven Pharisees TR 1

holdinge ger. 5b *(fr. 'holden' v1.)*
(?a1200) Ancr. HF 3

hole adj2. 1a a *OE* c1150 Hrl.HApul.
RomA 48

hole adv. b *fr. hole adj2.* (c1300) Havelok
BD 10

hole n2. 3b *OE* (c1200) Vices & V.(1)
RomA 24

hole n3. 2a *fr. hole adj2.* (c1200) Vices &
V.(1) KnT 1

holi adj2. 4a a *OE* a1121 Peterb.Chron.
ABC 132

holiliche adv1. a *fr. holi adj2.* ?c1200
Orm. Bo 4

holinesse n2. 2a *OE* ?c1200 Orm.
SNPro 13

holli adv. 2c *fr. hole adj2.* (?c1300)
Guy(1) RomA 29

holme n2. b *fr. holin n.* Chaucer PF 2

holnesse n2. c *fr. hole adj2.* (c1340) Rolle
Psalter (Ld) Bo 2

holour n. a *OF* (?c1200) HMaid.
WBPro 4

holsom adj. 1b *OE* ?c1200 Orm. PF 6

holsomnesse n. b *fr. holsom adj.* (?a1200)
Trin.Hom. MEL 1

holt n. a *OE* a1200 Wor.Aelfric. Gloss.
TR 2

holwe adj. 2f *fr. holgh n. & hole adj1.*
?c1200 Wor.Bod.Gloss. (Hat 115) HF 5

holwenesse n. b *fr. holwe adj.* Chaucer
TR 1

hom adv. 2a *OE* a1121 Peterb.Chron. BD
77

hom n. 1a *OE* a1131 Peterb.Chron. BD 21

homage n. 4 *OF* (?c1225) Horn BD 2

hom-cominge n. *fr. hom-come n.*
Chaucer TR 5

homicide n. a *OF* c1230 Ancr. (Corp-C)
MKT 23

homli adj. 2d *fr. hom n.* (?1348) Rolle
FLiving ROMA 5

homli adv. a *fr. hom n.* (?a1325)
Bonav.Medit.(1) BO 5

homlinesse n. b *fr. <homli adj.>* (c1340)
Rolle Psalter (Hat) CLT 2

hom-ward adv. 1a *OE* c1175 Bod.Hom.
BD 18

hond-brede n. *OE* (?a1350) Siege Troy(1)
MILT 1

honde n. 2b *OE & ON* a1121
Peterb.Chron. ROMA 273

hondlen v. 1a *OE* a1200 Body & S.(2)
TR 5

hond-werk n. c *OE* a1200 Body & S.(2)
FRT 1

honeste adj. 3a *OF* c1300 Horn Child
BO 21

honeste n. 3a *OF* (a1338) Mannyng
Chron.Pt.2 PITY 14

honestete n. c *fr. honeste adj.* (a1333)
Shoreham Poems BO 6

honestliche adv. d *fr. honeste adj.* (1340)
Ayenb. SNT 5

hongen v. 1a b *OE & ON* c1150
Hrl.HApul. ROMA 69

honginge ger. 1b a *(fr. hongen v.)* (a1325)
Cursor KNT 2

honi n. 1a *OE* c1150 Hrl.HApul. MKT 16

honi-comb n. a *OE* a1300 I-hereth nu
one MILT 2

honied ppl. *fr. honi n.* (?c1350)
SVrn.Leg. BO 1

honi-swete adj. *fr. honi n. & swete adj.*
c1390 Talking LGod MERT 1

honour n. 2a *OF* (?a1200) Trin.Hom.
ROMA 199

honourable adj. 1a *(fr. honour n.)*
(a1338) Mannyng Chron.Pt.2 ROMA
21

honouren v. 1a *OF* (c1250) Floris HF 32

hope n1. 2a *OE* ?c1200 Orm. ABC 71

hopen vi. 1b *OE* c1175 Bod.Hom. ROMA
52

hoppen v. 1b *OE* (?a1200) Trin.Hom. TR
4

hoppere n. d *?OE* (c1250) Gen.& Ex.
RVT 2

hoppestre n. *OE* Chaucer KNT 1

hor adj. 1b *OE* (?a1200) Lay.Brut ROMA
11

hord n1. 1a b *OE* (c1125)
Vsp.D.Hom.Fest.Virg. TRUTH 6

hore n1. 1a *OE* c1150 Hrl.HApul MARS 1

horn n. 5a *OE* a1131 Peterb.Chron. BD
27

horned adj. & ppl. 1a *(fr. horn n.)*
(?a1300) KAlex. TR 1

horoscopum n. a *L* Chaucer AST 5

horrible adj. 1a *OF* (?a1300) Arth.& M.
MKT 39

horribli adv. a *fr. horrible adj.* (c1340)
Rolle Psalter (UC 64) MKT 3

horrour n. c *OF & L* a1325
Gloss.Bibbesw. PARST 2

hors n. 1a *OE* a1121 Peterb.Chron. ROMA
80

horsli adj. *fr. hors n.* Chaucer SQT 1

hos adj. a *OE* c1250 Owl & N. BD 2

hose n. 1a *OE* a1200 Wor.Aelfric Gloss.
HF 10

hospiteler n. a *OF* (a1338) Mannyng
Chron.Pt.2 PARST 1

hoste n1. 1a *OF* (1265) BLewes MKT 25

hoste n2. 1b *OF* (c1250) Floris GP 61

hostel n. 1 *OF* (c1250) Gen.& Ex. HF 1

hostelrie n. a *OF* Chaucer KNT 9

hostesse n. 1a *OF* c1300 SLeg.Magd.(2) (Ld) Bo 2

hostiler n. 1 *AF & OF & ML* c1300 SLeg.Cuth. (Ld) GP 5

hostilment n. *OF* Chaucer Bo 2

hot adj. 1b *OE* c1150 Hrl.HApul. ROMA 64

hot n1. 1a *OE* ?c1200 Orm. PF 5

hote adv. 1a *OE* (?a1300) KAlex. TR 6

hoten v1. 3a a *OE* (1100) Chart.St.Paul in RHS ser.3.58 ROMA 128

hotte n. a *OF, fr. Gmc.* (a1325) Cursor HF 1

hou conjunctive adv. 4b *OE* a1121 Peterb.Chron. GENERAL 557

hou interj1. 2a {2c} *OF* Chaucer {(c1378) PPl.B (Ld)} BD 6

hou interrog. adv. 1b a *OE* (c1125) Vsp.D.Hom.Fest.Virg. GENERAL 164

hou-ever adv. b *?fr. hou adv. & ever adv.* (1392) *MS Wel.564 FRANT 1

hou-gates adv. a *(fr. hou-gate adv.)* (?c1350) Mirror St.Edm.(4) RVT 1

houlen v. c cp. *MDu. & AF* (a1250) Bestiary Bo 2

hound n. 4c *OE* ?c1120 Dur-C.Gloss. BD 36

houndes-fish n. a *fr. hound n. & fish n.* (c1350) Alex.& D. MERT 1

houne n2. *fr. hine n.* Chaucer TR 1

houpen v. b *OF & OE* (c1376) PPl.A(1) (Trin-C) NPT 1

houre n. 1b a *OF & L* (?a1200) Ancr. ROMA 101

hous n. 1a a *OE* a1121 Peterb.Chron. SNT 225

hous-bonde n. 2a *LOE, fr. ON* (?a1200) Lay.Brut SNT 119

houselen v. a *OE* ?c1200 Orm. PARST 1

hous-hold n. 1a a *fr. hous n. & hold n2.* Chaucer Bo 4

hous-holdere n. a *fr. hous-hold n.* Chaucer GP 1

hous-holding ger. *fr. hous-hold n.* Chaucer ROMA 1

housinge ger. 1d *(fr. housen v.)* (a1325) Cursor MERT 1

houve n. a *OE* c1230 Ancr. (Corp-C) TR 3

hoven v1. 1a *?OE* (a1250) Bestiary TR 3

huge adj. 1 *fr. OF* (?c1150) Prov.Alf. (Trin-C) BD 11

humanite n. 2 *OF & L* (1384) WBible(1) CLT 1

humble adj. a *OF* c1275 Ken.Serm. PITY 48

humblen v. b *fr. humble adj.* c1380 Firumb.(1) PARST 2

humblesse n. c *OF* Chaucer ABC 20

humbli adv. a *fr. humble adj.* c1380 Firumb.(1) TR 5

humblinge ger. *(fr. humblen v.)* Chaucer HF 1

humiliacioun n. a *L & OF* Chaucer PARST 1

humilite n. b *OF* (?a1300) Arth.& M. SUMT 27

hummen v. c *prob. imitative* Chaucer TR 1

humour n. 3a *L & OF* (1340) Ayenb. KNT 8

hundred card. num. 1a *OE & ON* a1121 Peterb.Chron. ROMA 53

hunger n. 1b *OE* a1126 Peterb.Chron. ROMA 20

hungrie adj. 1a *OE* (c1125) Vsp.D.Hom.Fest.Virg. Bo 3

hunte n. a *OE* a1131 Peterb.Chron. BD 7

hunten v. 1a *OE* a1131 Peterb.Chron. BD 14

huntere n. a *fr. hunten v.* (c1250) Gen.& Ex. ROMA 4

hunteresse n. *fr. huntere n.* Chaucer HF 3

huntinge ger. a *OE* (?a1200) Lay.Brut ROMA 13

hurlen v. 1b a *prob. imitative* (?a1200)
Ancr. *MLT* 1
hurt n. 1a *(fr. hurten v.)* (?a1200)
Lay.Brut *SQT* 2
hurtelen v. 1b *fr. hurten v.* (a1338)
Mannyng Chron.Pt.1 B0 4
hurten v. 5c *?OF, fr. Gmc.* ?c1200 Orm.
R0MA 23
hurtinge ger. 2a *(fr. hurten v.)* (?a1200)
Ancr. *PARST* 1
hus-bondrie n. 1a *fr. hous-bonde n.* c1300
SLeg.Magd.(2) (Ld) R*V*T 5
hust adj. a *prob. imitative* Chaucer B0 6
iben v. 2a *fr. ben v.* (?c1175) PMor.
(Lamb) HF 12
iberen vi. 2a a *OE* (c1125)
Vsp.D.Hom.Fest.Virg. HF 21
ibouen v. 1c *OE* a1121 Peterb.Chron. B0 1
ibringen v. 1a *OE* a1121 Peterb.Chron.
B0 18
ich pron. 1a *OE* a1121 Peterb.Chron.
GENERAL 6786
idel adj. 1a *OE* c1175
Bod.Hom.Dom.Quadr. BD 35
idel n. 1b a *OE* (c1125)
Vsp.D.Hom.Fest.Virg. B0 15
idelli adv. b *OE* (a1333) Shoreham Poems
PARDPRO 1
idelnesse n. 2c *OE* (?c1150) Prov.Alf.
(Jes-O) R0MA 24
idiote n. b *L & OF* (a1325) Cursor T*R* 2
idolastre n. a *OF* Chaucer M*K*T 6
idolatrie n. a *OF & ML* (c1250) Gen. &
Ex. *PARST* 1
idole n. 1a *L & OF, ult Gr.* (c1250)
Gen.& Ex. BD 6
idouten v. b *fr. douten v.* c1300
SLeg.Inf.Chr. (Ld) B0 1
idre ni. a *OF & L, ult. Gr.* Chaucer B0 2
idus n. a *L & OF* a1126 Peterb.Chron.
SQT 1
if conj. 1b a *OE* a1121 Peterb.Chron.
GENERAL 1365
i-faith interj. 8c, feith n. *(fr. in prep. &
feith n.)* a1375 WPal. R*V*T 2

ifere adv. 1a *fr. ifere n1. & n2.* (?a1200)
Lay.Brut R0MA 33
ifinden v. 1a *OE* c1175 HRood BD 16
igaderen v. 1a *OE* a1121 Peterb.Chron.
B0 1
ignoraunce n. a *L & OF* (?a1200) Ancr.
B0 15
ignoraunt adj. a *L & OF* Chaucer B0 1
igon v. 4a *OE* c1175 Bod.Hom. SNT 14
igreten v. 1a *OE* (?a1200) Lay.Brut BD 1
ihalwen v. 2a *OE* a1121 Peterb.Chron.
LGW 1
ihenten v. b *OE* (?c1200) HMaid. SNT 2
ihered ppl. adj. *(fr. her n.)* a1150
Rwl.G.57.Gloss. *MILT* 1
iheren v. 2a a *OE* a1121 Peterb.Chron. T*R*
3
ihevien v. a *OE* c1150 PDidax. B0 1
iholden v. 2a a *OE* a1121 Peterb.Chron.
HF 7
ikepen v. 3a *OE* (?a1200) Ancr. *LGW* 1
ikissen v. *OE* (?a1200) Lay.Brut T*R* 1
iknitten v. a *OE* (?a1200) Lay.Brut LADY
3
iknouen v. 1a *OE* c1150 PDidax. BD 23
ile ni. 1a *OF; AF* (?c1225) Horn HF 12
ileden v. 2b *OE* c1150 Hrl.HApul. B0 5
ileien v. 1c *OE* c1175 Body & S.(1) M*K*T
4
ileven vi. 1a *OE* c1175 HRood B0 5
ilich adj. 1a *OE* c1150 Hrl.HApul. K*N*T 8
iliche adv. 1a *OE* c1150 Hrl.HApul. BD
31
ilke pron. 1a *OE* a1121 Peterb.Chron.
R0MA 61
ille adj. 1c *ON* (?c1175) PMor. (Lamb)
R*V*T 3
ille hail phr. b *ON* a1300 Uncomly in
R*V*T 1
illusioun n. 1a *L & OF* c1350 MPPsalter
HF 7
image n. 1a *OF* (?c1200) St.Kath.(1)
R0MA 36
imagerie n. 1a *OF* c1350 MPPsalter *HF* 2
imaginable adj. *L* Chaucer B0 4

imaginacioun n. 1d *OF* (1340) Ayenb. BD 31

imaginatif adj. 4b *ML & OF* (c1378) PPl.B (Ld) Bo 2

imaginen v. 1a *OF* (a1340) Rolle Psalter (UC 64) Bo 21

imagininge ger. 1a *(fr. imaginen v.)* Chaucer Bo 4

imaken v. 1b *OE* a1121 Peterb.Chron. HF 24

imenen v. a *OE* c1175 Bod.Hom. *HF* 1

imengen v. 1a *OE* c1150 Hrl.HApul. KNT 1

imeten v3. 2a *OE* a1121 Peterb.Chron. TR 3

immevable adj. b {b} *fr. mevable adj.* Chaucer {(c1385) Usk TL (Skeat)} *Bo* 1

immoevablete n. *fr. moevablete n.* Chaucer *Bo* 1

immortal adj. a *OF & L* Chaucer PF 6

imne n. 1b *OE & OF & ML* (?a1200) Ancr. *LGW F* 1

impacience n. a *OF & L* (?a1200) Ancr. Bo 6

impacient adj. a *OF* (c1378) PPl.B (Ld) Bo 5

imparfit adj. 1a *fr. parfit adj.* (c1378) PPl.B (Ld) Bo 9

impe n. 1c *OE* (?a1200) Ancr. *PROMKT* 1

imperfeccioun n. a *L & OF* Chaucer *PARST* 1

imperial adj. b *OF & L* Chaucer HF 3

impertinent adj. a *L & OF* Chaucer *CLPRO* 1

impetren v. a *OF & L* Chaucer *Bo* 1

implien v. a *OF* Chaucer *Bo* 1

importable adj. a *L & OF* Chaucer MKT 2

imposen v. *fr. L* Chaucer *Bo* 1

imposicioun n. 1a *L & OF* Chaucer *Bo* 1

impossible adj. 2 *OF* (a1325) Cursor HF 8

impossible n. a *fr. impossible adj.* Chaucer TR 5

impressen v. 1c *OF & L* Chaucer Bo 6

impressioun n. 4b *L & OF* Chaucer HF 7

imprudent adj. *L* Chaucer *MLT* 1

impudence n. *L* Chaucer *PARST* 1

impudent adj. *L* Chaucer *PARST* 1

in adv. 2c b *OE* a1121 Peterb.Chron. ROMA 78

in n. 3b *OE* a1121 Peterb.Chron. KNT 7

in prep. 1a *OE & L & ON & OF* a1121 Peterb.Chron. GENERAL 6528

inceste n. a *OF & L* (?a1200) Ancr. *PARST* 1

inche n. 1a *OE, fr. L* (?a1200) Lay.Brut BD 1

inclinacioun n. 1a *L & OF* Chaucer *WBPRO* 1

incominge ger. a *(fr. incomen v.)* ?a1325 Swet ihc hend *TR* 1

inconstaunce n. *L & OF* Chaucer *SUMT* 1

inconvenient n. c *OF* Chaucer *Bo* 1

incubus n. a *L* (?a1200) Lay.Brut *WBT* 1

incurable adj. c *L & OF* (c1340) Rolle Psalter (UC 64) *MKT* 1

inde adj2. b *OF* (?a1300) Arth.& M. *ROMA* 1

Inde n1. a *OF* (?a1200) Ancr. ROMA 13

indeterminate adj. a *L* Chaucer *AST* 1

indifferentli adv. b *fr. <indifferent adj.>* Chaucer *Bo* 1

indigence n. b *OF & L* (c1385) Usk TL (Skeat) *INTMLT* 2

indignacioun n. 1a *L & OF* c1350 MPPsalter Bo 2

indulgence n. 2b *OF & L* (a1376) PPl.A (Trin-C) WBPRO 2

induracioun n. b *ML* Chaucer *CYT* 1

inequale adj. a *L* Chaucer KNT 15

inestimable adj. a *L & OF* Chaucer *Bo* 1

infecten v. 4a *fr. L & OF* Chaucer Bo 7

in-fere adv. 2, fere n2. *(fr. in prep. & fere n2.)* a1375 WPal. TR 7

infernal adj. b *OF & L* Chaucer TR 4

infinite adj. 1b *OF & L* Chaucer Bo 12

infinite n. b *OF & L* (c1378) PPl.B (Ld)
Bo 2

infirme adj. *OF & L* Chaucer Bo 1

infirmite n. 1b *OF & L* (?c1350)
SVrn.Leg. Bo 2

influence n. 1c *OF* Chaucer TR 3

informacioun n. 1a *L & OF* Chaucer Bo
1

infortunat adj. 2a *L* (c1390) Gower CA
1st Concl. AST 3

infortune n. b *OF* Chaucer Bo 7

infortunen v. b *OF* Chaucer TR 1

infortuninge ger. *(fr. infortunen v.)*
Chaucer AST 1

ingot n. *fr. OF* Chaucer CYT 7

inhelden v. *fr. helden v.* (?c1380)
Cleanness TR 1

inimen v. 1a *OE* a1121 Peterb.Chron. PF
3

iniquite n. 2a *OF* (?a1300) Arth.& M.
KNT 6

injure n. *OF* Chaucer TR 1

injurie n. a *AF* (c1384) WBible(1) MEL 4

inke n. a *OF* c1250 *St.Marg. (2) TR 6

inli adv. 3a *OE* (c1125)
Vsp.D.Hom.Fest.Virg. ROMA 5

inne adv. a *OE* c1150 Hrl.HApul. ROMA
9

inne prep. 1a *OE* a1121 Peterb.Chron.
MKT 19

innen v2. a *OE* (c1280) SLeg.Pass. KNT 1

innerest adj. sup. a *fr. innere adj. comp.*
?c1200 Orm. Bo 2

innocence n. a *OF* (1340) Ayenb. SNT
22

innocent adj. a *OF* (1340) Ayenb. Bo 4

innocent n. 1a *OF* (c1200) Vices & V.(1)
Bo 17

inobedience n. a *OF & L* (?a1200) Ancr.
PARST 1

inobedient adj. 1a *OF* c1330 Adam &
E.(1) PARST 1

inordinate adj. c *L* (?1348) Rolle FLiving
PARST 1

inough adj. d *OE* c1150 PDidax. PF 18

inough adv. a *OE* a1200 Body & S.(2)
ROMA 68

inough n. e *OE* ?a1160 Peterb.Chron.
ROMA 48

in principio phr. *L* Chaucer GP 2

inquisitif adj. a *ML* Chaucer MILPRO 1

insetten v. 2b *fr. setten v.* Chaucer Bo 1

insight n. 1a *OE* ?c1200 Orm. Bo 3

insolence n. 2 *L & OF* Chaucer PARST 1

insolent adj. c *L* Chaucer PARST 1

insonder adv. 2a *fr. in sonder phr.* (c1300)
NHom.(1) Peter & P. TR 1

instaunce n. 2a *OF* Chaucer Bo 3

instede adv. a, in stede of prep. *fr. in prep.*
& stede n1. (?a1200) Ancr. LGW F 1

instrument n. b *L & OF* c1300
SLeg.Brendan (Hrl: Wright) BD 31

insufficient adj. b *L & OF* (c1385) Usk
TL (Skeat) SUMT 2

intellect n. a *L & OF* Chaucer SNT 2

intelligence n. 1a *OF & L* Chaucer Bo 9

intercepten v. a *fr. L* Chaucer AST 1

interesse n. 2a *ML & AF* Chaucer FORT
1

interminable adj. *L & OF* Chaucer Bo
4

interrogacion n. a *L & OF* Chaucer
MILT 1

intervalle n. a *OF & L* (a1325) Cursor
MEL 1

in-til prep. 1 *fr. in adv. & til prep.* ?c1200
Orm. ROMA 1

in-to prep. 2a *OE* 1121 Peterb.Chron.
GENERAL 322

introduccioun n. b *L & OF* Chaucer
CYT 1

introductorie n. *ML* Chaucer AST 1

invisible adj. a *L & OF* (c1340) *Rolle
Psalter (Sid) MKT 3

invocacioun n. a *L & OF* Chaucer HF 1

in-ward adj. 2b *OE* ?c1200 Orm. Bo 2

in-ward adv. 3a *OE* (?a1200) Ancr. TR 6

in-wardli adv. 2a *OE* ?c1200 Orm. TR 1

inwith prep. 2a *(fr. in prep. & with*
prep.) ?c1200 Orm. Bo 16

Chaucer's words

ipassen v. 1b b *fr. passen v.* c1300
SLeg.Inf.Chr. (Ld) Bo 4
ipocras n. c *OF* Chaucer BD 2
ipocrisie n. *OF & L, fr. Gr.* (?a1200)
Ancr. PardPro 3
ipocrite n. *OF & L, fr. Gr.* (?a1200)
Ancr. RomA 5
ipreien v. 1a *fr. preien v1.* (a1387)
Trev.Higd. ClT 1
ire n. 1a *L & OF* c1300 Horn (Ld) RomA
98
ireden v. 2d *OE* (c1125)
Vsp.D.Hom.Fest.Virg. Tr 1
iren adj. a *OE* a1200 Wor.Aelfric Gloss.
HF 2
iren n. 2a *OE* c1150 Hrl.HApul. RomA
20
irennen v. 1a *OE* (c1200) Vices & V.(1)
Tr 10
irous adj. 1a *OF* (?a1300) KAlex. SumT
10
irreguler adj. a *OF* Chaucer ParsT 1
irreverence n. a *OF & L* (a1349) Rolle 10
Com. ParsT 2
is n. a *OE* a1225 Lamb.Hom.DD HF 1
isechen v. 2c *OE* a1121 Peterb.Chron.
Anel 3
iseien v. 2b *OE* a1121 Peterb.Chron. BD
3
isen v1. 2a a *OE* a1121 Peterb.Chron.
ABC 33
isenden v. 1a b *OE* a1121 Peterb.Chron.
HF 7
isetten v. 5a *OE* a1121 Peterb.Chron. Bo
14
ishapen v. 2b *OE* (?c1150) Prov.Alf. (Jes-
O) MkT 6
isheden v. 1a *OE* c1175 Bod.Hom. Bo 4
ishen v. 1a *OF* (a1338) Mannyng
Chron.Pt.2 Bo 3
ishenden v. 1b *OE* a1200 Body & S.(2)
FrT 1
isheuen v. 1 *OE* c1175 Bod.Hom. Bo 4
ishriven v. c *OE* c1175
Bod.Hom.Dom.Quadr. GP 3

isouen v. 1b a *OE* (?c1150) Prov.Alf. (Jes-
O) HF 2
ispeden v. 1a *OE* (?a1200) Lay.Brut Bo 3
ispeken v. 3a *LOE* (c1200) Vices & V.(1)
Tr 2
issue n. 2a *OF* (?a1300) KAlex. Bo 5
istinten v. a *OE* ?c1200 Wor.Bod.Gloss.
WBPro 1
istonden v. 1b *OE* (?a1200) Lay.Brut Tr 1
iswounen v. *fr. swounen v.* (?a1300)
KAlex. LGW 1
Itaille n. *OF & L* (?a1200) Lay.Brut HF
19
itaken v. 1b a *fr. taken v.* (?a1200)
Lay.Brut MkT 17
itechen v. 1 *OE* (?a1200) Lay.Brut SNT 8
itellen v. 2 *OE* c1175 Bod.Hom. Tr 6
ithen v. a *OE* c1175 Bod.Hom. Tr 2
iturnen v. 1b *prob. OE* c1175 Bod.Hom.
BD 5
ivel adj. 1a *OE* a1121 Peterb.Chron. Pity
20
ivel n. 4a *OE* a1121 Peterb.Chron. Bo 53
ivele adv. 2a *OE* (?c1150) Prov.Alf. (Jes-
O) RomA 31
ivi n. 1d *OE* ?c1125 Dur-C.Gloss. Tr 3
ivorie n. a *OF* (?a1300) Tristrem BD 4
iwar adj. 2a *OE* (?c1175) PMor.(Trin-C)
Tr 1
iwaxen v. a *OE* c1175 HRood BD 4
iwenden v. 2a *OE* c1150 Hrl.HApul. HF
1
iwerken v. 2c *OE* a1121 Peterb.Chron.
BD 16
iwinden v. 1a *OE* c1150 Hrl.MQuad. Ros
1
iwinnen v. 1a *OE* a1121 Peterb.Chron.
HF 8
iwis adv. & adj. & n. 2 *OE* c1150
Hrl.HApul. RomA 155
iwiten v1. 1b *OE* c1150 Hrl.MQuad. Bo
6
iworthen v. 2a *OE* a1121 Peterb.Chron.
BD 1
j n. b *no etym.* Chaucer Ast 1

315

jade n. a *?AF* Chaucer *PRONPT* 1
jagounce n. a *OF* Chaucer *ROMA* 1
jai n. a *OF* (?a1300) KAlex. PF 6
jakke n1. b *AF* (c1300) NHom.(1) Pilgr.
CKPRO 4
Jame n. a *OF* (?a1200) Ancr. HF 11
jangle n. b *OF, fr. Gmc.* (c1280)
SLeg.Pass. (Pep) HF 4
janglen v. 1a *OF* c1300 SLeg.MLChr.
(Ld) PF 8
janglere n. a *OF* (c1303) Mannyng HS
PF 4
jangleresse n. *OF* Chaucer WBPRO 3
janglerie n. *OF* Chaucer TR 2
janglinge ger. 1a a *fr. janglen v.* *c1225
St.Juliana SQT 4
Jankin n. *fr. Jan var. of John n.* c1250
LSSerm. *EPIMLT* 1
januarie n. a *L & OF* a1150 Vsp.D.Hom.
AST 41
jape n. 1a *fr. <japen v.>* (c1333–52)
Minot Poems ROMA 30
japen v. 1b *prob. OF* (c1378) PPl.B (Ld)
TR 17
japere n. a *fr. japen v* (c1378) PPl.B (Ld)
TR 5
japerie n. b *fr. jape n.* (?c1350) SVrn.Leg.
MERT 2
jape-worthi adj. *fr. jape n. & worthi adj.*
Chaucer *BO* 1
jargoun n. *OF* (c1350) Alex.& D. *MERT*
1
jargouning n. *fr. jargounen v.* * Chaucer
ROMA 1
jaspre n. a *AF* (?c1300) St.Patr.Purg.(1)
PF 4
jaumbeus n. pl. *?AF* c1380 Firumb.(1)
THOP 1
jaunis n. a *OF, AF* (c1303) Mannyng HS
ROMA 1
jelous adj. 1a *OF* (?a1200) Ancr. ANEL
23
jelousie n. a *OF* (?a1200) Ancr. HF 36
Jesu n. d *L* c1175 Bod.Hom. SNT 128
Jeu n. 1b *OF, AF* (?a1200) Ancr. MKT 22

jeuel n. 3a *OF* c1300 SLeg.Becket (Ld)
KNT 4
Jeuerie n. 1c *AF & CF* (?a1200) Ancr. HF
4
je-vous-di interj. *OF* (?a1300) Arth.&
M. SUMT 2
jo v. *?OF* Chaucer *TR* 1
jocounde adj. 1b *OF* (c1395) WBible(2)
CYPRO 2
jogelerie n. b *AF & OF* (a1325) Cursor
FRANT 1
jogelour n. 1b *AF & OF* (?a1200) Ancr.
ROMA 4
joie n. 1a *OF* (?a1200) Ancr. ROMA 220
joien v. 4b *OF* ?c1250 Somer is comen &
HF 1
joiful adj. 1a *fr. joie n.* c1250 *St.Marg.(2)
BO 8
joinant adj. a *OF* Chaucer *KNT* 1
joinen v1. 3 *OF* c1300 SLeg.Cuth. (Ld)
BD 27
joinen v2. a *fr. enjoinen v.* (c1303)
Mannyng HS *PARST* 1
joininge ger1. 3a *(fr. joinen v1.)* Chaucer
HF 1
jointlie adv. a *fr. <joint adj.>* (?c1300)
LFMass Bk. *AST* 1
jointure n. 2a *OF* Chaucer *BO* 1
joious adj. a *OF* c1300 SLeg.Magd.(2)
(Ld) *MEL* 1
joli adj. 1a *OF* c1300 SLeg.Swithin (Hrl)
ROMA 43
jolili adv. a *fr. joli adj.* (?a1300) KAlex.
CKT 2
jolinesse n. b *fr. joli adj.* Chaucer WBT
2
jolite n. 1d *OF* c1300 SLeg. (Ld) ROMA
19
Jon n. a *AF* (c1378) PPl.B (Ld) *PROMKT*
2
jordan n. a *ML & CL* Chaucer
INTPARDT 1
jossa n. *?fr. OF* Chaucer *RVT* 1
joue n. 2b *OF* Chaucer HF 2
jouken v. c *OF* (c1378) PPl.B (Ld) *TR* 1

journei n. 6b *OF* (?a1200) Ancr. RoMA 3
Jove n. a *L* Chaucer HF 33
jubbe n. 1a *origin uncertain* Chaucer MiLT 2
jubile n. 1 *OF & L* (a1382) WBible(1) (Bod 959) SUMT 1
Judas n. 1a *L; ult Heb.* (a1376) PPl.A(1) (Trin-C) FRT 7
judicial adj. 1a *L & OF* (a1382) WBible(1) AST 1
juge n. 2a *OF* (c1303) Mannyng HS ABC 62
juge n2. MED Suppl. *?fr. juge n1.* * not in MED PARST 2
jugement n. 5b *OF* a1250 Ancr. (Nero) PF 49
jugen v. 5c *AF* (?a1200) Ancr. HF 20
juil n. a *OF & L* a1121 Peterb.Chron. AST 4
juin n. *OF & L* a1121 Peterb.Chron. AST 3
jumperen v. *?imitative* Chaucer TR 1
Juno n. *L* (c1350) Alex.& D. BD 19
juparten v. b *fr. jupartie n. & OF* Chaucer TR 1
jupartie n. 4b *OF* ?a1300 Sirith BD 12
Jupiter n. a *L & OF* (?a1200) Lay.Brut SNT 29
jupon n. *OF fr. Ar.* (c1353) Winner & W. KNT 2
jurisdiccioun n. b *ML & OF* (a1325) Cursor FRT 4
juste adj. 4c *L & OF* Chaucer HF 20
justen v. 3b *OF* (c1250) Gen.& Ex. TR 8
justes n. pl. 2a *OF* (c1300) Glo.Chron.A KNT 1
justice n. 2a *OF* ?a1160 Peterb.Chron. ABC 22
justinge ger. a *(fr. justen v.).* (?a1300) Arth.& M. LGW 1
justli adv. 2c *fr. <juste adj.>* (a1338) Mannyng Chron.Pt.2 AST 5
juwise n. 1a *OF* (c1303) Mannyng HS KNT 2
kechel n. a *OE* ?c1200 Orm. SUMT 1

keie n1. 1a a *OE* c1175 Body & S.(1) ANEL 11
kemben v. 1a *OE* c1150 Hrl.MQuad. RoMA 13
kempe adj. *?ON* Chaucer KNT 1
kene adj. 4b *OE* a1200 Body & S.(2) MKT 13
kene adv. c {b} *fr. kene adj.* Chaucer {c1390 NHom.Narrat.} LADY 3
keneliche adv. a *OE* (?c1150) Prov.Alf. (Jes-O) HF 1
kennen v1. 3c *OE* (?c1150) Prov.Alf. (Trin-C) BD 3
kep n. 1a *fr. kepen v.* (c1250) Gen.& Ex. BD 44
kepen v. 17a *OE* a1131 Peterb.Chron. RoMA 225
kepere n. 2a *fr. kepen v.* (?a1300) Guy(2) Bo 5
kepinge ger. 3a *(fr. kepen v.)* (a1325) Cursor Bo 16
kerven v. 3b a *OE* c1150 PDidax. RoMA 25
kervere n. 2a *fr. kerven v.* (a1376) PPl.A(1) (Trin-C) KNT 1
kervinge ger. 1a *(fr. kerven v.)* (?a1200) Ancr. HF 5
kichene n. 1a *OE, fr. L* (?a1200) Lay.Brut WBT 1
kide n. 1a *ON* ?c1200 Orm. MiLT 2
kiken v1. c *?ON* (c1384) WBible(1) WBT 1
kiken v2. a *MDu.* Chaucer MiLT 2
killen v. 1a *?OE* (?a1200) Lay.Brut MKT 5
kimelin n. *ML* c1350 Of alle the witti MiLT 2
kin n. 1e *OE* c1150 Hrl.HApul. RoMA 21
kinde adj. 2a *cp. OE* (c1250) Gen.& Ex. HF 24
kinde n. 7b *OE* a1121 Peterb.Chron. RoMA 104
kindelen v1. 1a *cp. OI* ?1200 Orm. KNT 2
kindeli adj. 1a *OE* (?c1200) St.Kath.(1) BD 7

kindeli adv. 1c *cp. OE* (?a1200) Ancr. BD 9

kindenesse n. 3a *fr. kinde adj.* c1300 SLeg.Patr. (Ld) TR 8

king n. 1a a *OE* a1121 Peterb.Chron. ROMA 276

kingdom n. 4a *OE* c1250 Ure fadir that hart TR 1

kinrede n. 1a *LOE* c1200 Wor.Serm. in EGSt.7 BO 25

kirtel n. 1a *OE* ?c1200 Orm. ROMA 4

kissen v. 1d *OE* c1175 HRood. ROMA 80

kissinge ger. a *(fr. kissen v.)* (c1250) Floris (Cmb) ROMA 4

kite n. b *OE* (?a1300) KAlex. PF 5

kithen v. 1c *OE* (1100) Chart.St.Paul in RHS ser.3.58 HF 17

knakke n. 1a *cp. <knakken v.>* Chaucer BD 2

knarre n. 1a *prob. OE & MDu., MLG* c1250 Owl & N. GP 1

knarri adj. a *fr. knarre n.* Chaucer KNT 1

knave n1. 1a *OE* (?a1200) Lay.Brut ROMA 27

knavish adj. *fr. knave n1.* Chaucer MANCT 1

kne n. 1a a *OE* c1150 Hrl.HApul. ROMA 39

kneden v. a *OE* c1150 Hrl.MQuad. ROMA 2

knedinge ger. b *(fr. kneden v.)* Chaucer MILT 4

knedinge-tubbe n. b, knedinge ger. *(fr. knedinge ger. & tubbe n.)* Chaucer MILT 1

knelen v. 2a *OE* ?c1200 Orm. TR 26

knelinge ger. *(fr. kenelen v.)* ?c1200 Orm. PARST 1

knif n. 2a *LOE (fr. ON) & ON* c1150 PDidax. TR 25

knight n. 1a *OE* a1126 Peterb.Chron. ROMA 201

knighthode n. 1d *fr. knight n. & -hede suf.* (?c1225) Horn MKT 10

knightli adj. a *fr. knight n.* (c1384) WBible(1) TR 1

knightli adv. a *fr. knight n.* Chaucer LGW 1

knitten v. 2a *OE* c1150 Hrl.HApul. ROMA 29

knittinge ger. 1b *(fr. knitten v.)* (c1380) Wycl.Papa BO 3

knobbe n. a *prob. MLG* (1373) *Lelamour Macer GP 1

knokke n. a *fr. knokken v.* (c1333–52) Minot Poems NPT 1

knokken v. 1b *OE & ON* c1150 Hrl.HApul. ROMA 12

knokkinge ger. e *(fr. knokken v.)* (?a1300) Rich.(Auch) PARST 1

knoppe n1. 1b *OE* (c1353) Winner & W. ROMA 6

knotte n. 2a *OE & ON* (?c1200) St.Kath.(1) BO 5

knotteles adj. *fr. knotte n.* Chaucer TR 1

knotti adj. 1c *fr. knotte n.* (?c1200) St.Kath.(1) ROMA 3

knouen v. 1c *OE* (?c1150) Prov.Alf. (Trin-C) ROMA 561

knouere n. c *fr. knouen v.* c1350 MPPsalter BO 1

knouinge ger. 2d *(fr. knouen v.)* (?a1200) Ancr. ROMA 45

knouleche n. 9 *fr. <knouen v.> & -leche suf.* a1121 Peterb.Chron. BO 4

knoulechen v. 5c *fr. knouen v. & -lechen suf.* (?c1200) St.Kath.(1) MEL 4

knoulechinge ger. 2b *cp. LOE* (?a1200) Ancr. BD 3

labbe n. a *fr. <labben v.>* Chaucer TR 2

labben v. *MLG* (?a1387) PPl.C (Hnt) EpiMERT 1

label n. f *OF* (?c1300) Bevis AST 35

laberinthe n. *L, fr. Gr.* Chaucer HF 1

laborous adj. 1a *OF & L* Chaucer FRT 1

labour n. 3a *L & OF* c1300 SLeg.Becket (Hrl) ABC 67

labouren v. 1a *OF* (a1376) PPl.A(1) (Trin-C) TR 13

labourere n. 1b *AF & OF* ?c1350 Why
werre KNT 2
lacche n. a *fr. lacchen vi.* a1325
Gloss.Bibbesw. *ROMA* 1
lacerte n. *L* Chaucer *KNT* 1
lache adj. c *OF* (?c1300) KAlex. *BO* 1
lachesse n. a *AF & CF* (a1376) PPl.A(1)
PARST 1
laddere n. 1a *OE* c1175 Bod.Hom. *ROMA*
8
ladel n. a *OE* c1300 SLeg. KNT 2
laden v. 4a *OE* ?c1200 Orm. *TR* 1
ladie n. 2a *OE* a1121 Peterb.Chron.
ROMA 361
ladishipe n. a *fr. ladie n.* (?a1200) Ancr.
ANEL 1
lai n2. b *OF* a1250 Cristes milde moder
ROMA 13
lainere n. *OF, fr. Gmc.* c1330 Degare
KNT 1
lak n. 2a *prob. OE* a1300 Hit bilimpeth
BD 26
lake n1. 1a *OE & L & OF* a1121
Peterb.Chron. PF 3
lake n2. *fr. MDu., MLG* Chaucer *THOP*
1
lakken v. 1c *prob. fr. <lak n.>* a1225
Vsp.A.Hom. *ROMA* 41
lakkinge ger. b *(fr. lakken v.)* c1350
MPPsalter *ROMA* 1
lambish adj. *fr. lomb n.* Chaucer
FORMAGE 1
lame adj. c *OE* a1150 Vsp.D.Hom. ABC
2
lamentacioun n. c *OF & L* (a1382)
WBible(1) KNT 4
lane n. a *OE* (?c1300) Bevis *CYPRO* 1
langage n. 2a *OF* (c1280) SLeg.Pass.
(Pep) HF 15
langour n. b *OF* c1300 SLeg. (Ld) *ROMA*
12
languishen v. a *OF* (a1325) Cursor HF
10
languishinge ger. *(fr. languishen v.)*
(?1348) Rolle FLiving *ANEL* 5

lanterne n. 4a *OF & L* c1250
Serm.St.Nich. *TR* 4
lapidarie n. 2 *L & OF* Chaucer *HF* 1
lappe n. 1a *OE* c1300 SLeg.Lucy (Ld)
SNPRO 11
lappen v. 1b *fr. lappe n.* ?a1325 The grace
of godde *MARS* 1
lap-winke n. 1 *OE* (1340) Ayenb. *PF* 1
large adj. 1a *OF* (?a1200) Ancr. *ROMA* 73
large adv. 3 *OF* (a1325) Cursor ABC 3
large n. 4b *OF* (?a1350) Nicod.(1) HF 6
largelie adv. 2 *fr. large adj.* (?a1200)
Ancr. *BO* 6
largenesse n. 3b *fr. large adj.* (c1303)
Mannyng HS *PARST* 1
largesse n. 1a *OF* (?a1200) Ancr. *ROMA*
17
larke n. 1a *OE* ?c1200 Stw.57.Gloss.
ROMA 9
las interj. *[fr. alas interj.]* MED Suppl.
TR 1
las n. 1a *OF* c1230 Ancr. (Corp-C) *ROMA*
8
lasen v. 1a *OE* (?a1200) Ancr. *MILT* 1
laser n1. b *OF & ML; ult. Gr.* (?c1300)
Amis GP 3
lashe n. a *prob. fr. lashen v.* (?a1300)
Arth.& M. PF 2
lasinge ger. 1 *(fr. lasen v.)* Chaucer *KNT*
1
last n2. e *OE* Chaucer *SHIPT* 1
laste adj. sup. 1a *prob. fr. laste adv. sup.*
?c1200 Orm. *ROMA* 164
laste adv. sup. 1a *OE* ?c1200
Wor.Bod.Gloss. *TR* 6
lasten vi. 5b *OE* 1122 Peterb.Chron. BD
59
lastinge ger1. b *(fr. lasten vi.)* (?1348)
Rolle FLiving *BO* 1
lastinge ppl. adj. a *fr. lasten vi.* (?a1200)
Trin.Hom. SNPRO 2
lastinge prep. *fr. lastinge ppl. adj.* (a1325)
Cursor *LGW G* 1
late adj. 1a *OE* (?a1200) Trin.Hom. *BO* 4
late adv. 2c *OE* c1175 Bod.Hom. BD 17

latere adj. comp. 1a *OE* c1175 Bod.Hom. Bo 6

latere adv. comp. 1a *OE* ?c1200 Orm. *PARST* 1

late-rede adj. *OE* (c1280) SLeg.Pass. (Pep) *PARST* 1

lathe n1. a *ON* (c1250) Gen.& Ex. HF 2

Latin adj. a *L & OF* ?c1200 Orm. HF 4

Latin n. 1a *L & OF* ?c1200 Orm. ANEL 15

latitude n. 2a *L & OF* Chaucer AST 62

latoun n. & adj. a *OF* (?a1300) Tristrem GP 5

laude n1. b *OF & L* (1340) Ayenb. HF 12

laue n. 6a b *LOE* a1121 Peterb.Chron. BD 99

laueful adj. 2a *ON* c1300 Lay.Brut (Otho) Bo 3

lauefulli adv. b *fr. laueful adj.* (a1325) Cursor *PARST* 3

laughen v. 1b *OE* ?c1200 Orm. ROMA 57

laughinge ger. d *(fr. laughen v.)* (c1300) Glo.Chron.A *PARST* 1

laughter n1. a *OE* a1200 Wor.Aelfric Gloss. BD 4

laumpe n. a *OF* (c1200) Vices & V.(1) LGW 3

launcegai n. a *OF & Ar.* Chaucer *THOP* 2

launcen v. 1a *OF* (?c1300) Guy(1) *HF* 1

launchen v. 2a *OF* (?a1300) KAlex. *SUMT* 1

launde n. a *OF* (?a1300) Arth.& M. PF 3

laure n. *OE, fr. L* c1150 Hrl.HApul. *HF* 1

laureate adj. *L* Chaucer MKT 2

laurel n. 1b *L* (1373) *Lelamour Macer *NPT* 1

laurer n. a *OF* (a1325) Cursor ROMA 13

laurer-crowned adj. c, laurer n. *(fr. laurer n. & corounen v1.)* Chaucer ANEL 2

laven v. 1a *OE, fr. L* (?a1200) Trin.Hom. Bo 2

lavendere n1. a *OF & lavanderie & ML* c1325 Heye louerd *LGW F* 1

lavour n. b *OF* (1340) Ayenb. *WBPRO* 1

laxatif n. 1b *OF & ML* (1373) *Lelamour Macer KNT 4

leche n3. 1a *OE* c1150 Hrl.HApul. ABC 19

leche-craft n. 1a *OE* c1150 PDidax. TR 2

lechere n. a *fr. lechen v2.* Chaucer *BO* 1

lecherie n. 1a a *OF* (?a1200) Ancr. MKT 35

lecherous adj. 1c *prob. fr. lechour n. & lecherie n.* (c1300) Glo.Chron.A GP 4

lechour n. a *OF, fr. Gmc.* (?a1200) Trin.Hom. WBPRO 9

led n. 1a a *OE* (?a1200) Lay.Brut SNT 8

leden adj. a *OE* (c1384) WBible(1) *CYT* 1

leden n. 1 *OE* c1150 Hrl.HApul. *SQT* 3

leden v1. 6a *OE* a1121 Peterb.Chron. ROMA 132

ledere n1. 2a *OE* c1300 SLeg. (Ld) Bo 4

lef adj. & adv. 1a a *OE* a1121 Peterb.Chron. ROMA 125

lef n1. 1a *OE* c1150 Hrl.HApul. ROMA 44

lef n2. 3a *OE* c1175 Bod.Hom. ROMA 18

lefful adj2. a *fr. leve n2* Chaucer SNPRO 25

lefsel n. 1b, lef n1. *OE* c1175 Bod.Hom. RVT 2

leg n. 1a *ON* c1300 Lay.Brut (Otho) KNT 9

lege adj. 1a *AF & CF, fr. Gmc.* (c1300) Glo.Chron.A LGW F 5

lege n2. 2a {2a} *(fr. lege adj.)* (c1378) PPl.B (Ld) {Chaucer} LGW F 4

legende n. 1a *OF & ML* (?a1325) Bonav.Medit. (1) SNPRO 16

legioun n. 1a *OF & L* (?a1200) Lay.Brut *MKT* 1

lei n. 2a *OF* (?c1200) St.Kath.(1) TR 6

leien v1. 1b c *OE* a1121 Peterb.Chron. ROMA 130

leien v2. *fr. leie n2.* c1325 Dream Bk.(1) *WBT* 1

leiser n. 2a *OF* (?a1300) KAlex. ROMA 30

leit n1. a *OE* (?a1200) Lay.Brut *PARST* 1

lek n. 1d *OE* c1150 PDidax. ROMA 7

lemman n. 1a *OE* (?a1200) Lay.Brut
RoMA 24

lende n. 1a *OE* c1150 Hrl.HApul. *MILT*
2

lene adj1. 1b *OE* (?a1200) Lay.Brut
RoMA 15

lenen v1. 1b *OE* (?a1200) Ancr. TR 4

lenen v3. 2b *OE* (?c1175) PMor. (Lamb)
RoMA 20

lenenesse n. b {b} *fr. lene adj1.* Chaucer
{(a1382) WBible(1)} *RoMA* 1

lengere adj. comp. a *OE* c1175 HRood.
HF 24

lengere adv. comp. 1d *fr. leng adv. &
lengere adj. comp. ?c1200* Orm. RoMA
88

lengest adj. sup a *OE* c1300 SLeg.Mich.
(Ld) *BO* 1

lengest adv. sup. a *OE* (?c1150) Prov.Alf.
(Mdst) *PF* 1

lengthe n. 2b a *OE* 1122 Peterb.Chron.
RoMA 31

lengthinge ger. a *(fr. lengthen v.)*
(?a1387) PPl.C (Hnt) *AST* 1

lenten n. 2a *OE* a1121 Peterb.Chron.
WBPRo 4

leonine adj. a *L & OF* Chaucer *MKT* 1

leopard n. 1a *OF & L, ML* ?a1300
St.Eust. RoMA 3

lepen v. 1b c *OE* ?c1200 Orm. RoMA 20

leren v. 1b b *OE* a1121 Peterb.Chron. HF
36

lernen v. 1b *OE* c1175 Bod.Hom. BD 67

lerninge ger. 2b *OE* Chaucer SNT 5

lese adj. 1a a *OE* a1200 Wor.Aelfric
Gloss. *RoMA* 1

lese n1. b *OE* c1300 SLeg.Brendan (Hrl:
Horst) HF 2

lese n2. 1a *OE* ?c1200 Orm. HF 5

lesen v4. 1b c *OE* (?c1150) Prov.Alf. (Trin-
C) RoMA 115

lesinge ger2. 2a a *OE* a1131
Peterb.Chron. RoMA 25

lesinge ger3. 1a *(fr. lesen v4.)* (?a1300)
KAlex. MKT 5

lesse adj. comp. 5a *OE* ?c1125 Dur-
C.Gloss. (Cokayne) RoMA 46

lesse adv. 1a a *OE* (?c1175) PMor. (Lamb)
RoMA 44

lesse n1. 1a a *OF* (?a1300) Arth.& M.
SNPRo 3

lesse n2. 2a a *fr. lesse adj. comp.* (?c1150)
Prov.Alf. (Mdst) RoMA 15

lessen v. 1b *fr. lesse adj. comp.* (?c1200)
St.Kath.(1) *TR* 1

lessoun n. 1b a *OF* (?a1200) Ancr. ABC 7

leste adj1. 2b a *OE* (c1125)
Vsp.D.Hom.Gest.Virg. RoMA 60

leste adv. 1c *OE* (?a1200) Trin.Hom.
RoMA 8

leste conj. 1a *OE* (c1200) Vices & V.(1)
RoMA 69

leten v. 2a *OE* a1121 Peterb.Chron.
RoMA 473

lether n. 1a *OE* (?a1200) Ancr. *MILT* 1

lette n. a *fr. letten v.* (?a1200) Trin.Hom.
TR 7

lette-game n. *fr. letten v. & game n.*
Chaucer *TR* 1

letten v. 1a *OE* a1121 Peterb.Chron.
RoMA 50

lettre n. 5 *OF & L* (?c1150) Prov.Alf.
(*Glb-James) RoMA 107

lettrure n. b *OF* c1330 Adam & E.(1)
MKT 3

letuarie n. a *OF & ML* (?a1200) Ancr.
TR 4

leued adj. e *OE* a1121 Peterb.Chron.
SNT 31

leuedli adv. 1b *fr. leued adj.* Chaucer
SNT 4

leuednesse n. d *fr. leued adj.* Chaucer PF
5

leve n2. 1d *OE* a1121 Peterb.Chron. BD
88

level n. a *OF* (1340) Ayenb. *AST* 1

leven n. a *?OE* (c1250) Gen.& Ex.
WBPRo 1

leven v1. 3a *OE* a1131 Peterb.Chron.
RoMA 95

leven v3. b *OE* c1175 Bod.Hom. Tr 9

leven v4. 2b *OE* c1150 Hrl.MQuad. BD 37

liard adj. & n. 2a *OF* (1265) BLewes *FrT* 1

libelle n. a *OF & L* (c1300) Glo.Chron.A *FrT* 1

liberal adj. 1a *OF & L* (?a1350) 7 Sages(2) Mel 2

liberte n. 2b *OF* Chaucer MkT 25

Libie n. b *L* Chaucer HF 5

libra n. a *L* Chaucer Ast 17

librarie n. a *AF & CF* Chaucer Bo 2

licence n. 1a *OF* (a1376) PPl.A(1) (Trin-C) Bo 9

licenciate adj. *ML* Chaucer GP 1

liche-wake n. 1d, lich n. *(fr. lich n. & wake n.)* Chaucer KnT 1

licoris n. a *OF & L & ML* (?a1200) Lay.Brut RomA 5

licour n. 1a *OF & L* (?a1200) Ancr. Tr 3

lie n1. a *OE* c1175 Bod.Hom. HF 13

lie n2. *OF* Chaucer HF 2

lien v1. 3b *OE* a1121 Peterb.Chron. RomA 254

lien v2. 1a a *OE* (?c1150) Prov.Alf. (Trin-C) RomA 65

liere n1. a *OE* a1225 Lamb.Hom. Tr 4

lif n. 1b a *OE* a1121 Peterb.Chron. RomA 459

lifli adj. 1b *OE* c1175 Bod.Hom. Bo 2

lifli adv. e *OE* Chaucer BD 2

lif-lode n. 3a *OE* (?a1200) Trin.Hom. *ParsT* 1

lift adj. 1a *cp. OE* (?a1200) Lay.Brut RomA 11

liften v. 4a *ON* ?c1200 Orm. Bo 4

liftinge ger. a *(fr. liften v.)* c1350 MPPsalter *MancPro* 1

ligeaunce n. 1a *OF* (1377) Death Edw.III *MLT* 1

light adj1. 1b *OE* 1122 Peterb.Chron. SNT 3

light adj2. 1a a *OE* a1150 Rwl.G.57.Gloss. RomA 51

light n. 1b a *OE* a1121 Peterb.Chron. RomA 78

lighte adv1. a *fr. light adj1. & OE* (?c1200) HMaid. RomA 1

lighte adv2. 1b *fr. light adj2. & OE* (?c1150) Prov.Alf. (Jes-O) Bo 5

lighten v1. 2a *OE* ?a1160 Peterb.Chron. ABC 12

lighten v2. 1a c *OE* c1150 Hrl.HApul. HF 12

lightles adj. b *fr. light n.* Chaucer Tr 1

lightli adv. 6a *fr. light adj2.* a1121 Peterb.Chron. SNPro 57

lightnen v1. 1d *fr. lighten v1.* (a1325) Cursor Bo 2

lightnesse n1. 2b *fr. light adj1.* (c1250) Gen.& Ex. PF 2

lightnesse n2. 1a *fr. light adj2.* a1225 Lamb.Hom. Bo 5

lightninge ger. b *fr. lightnen v1.* * (c1280) SLeg.Pass. (Pep) *ParsT* 1

lightsom adj2. c *fr. light adj2.* Chaucer RomA 1

liinge ger2. a *(fr. lien v2.)* (1340) Ayenb. *RvPro* 1

lik adj. 1b *OE & ON* ?c1200 Orm. RomA 61

like adv. 1a c *OE* (a1325) Cursor HF 3

like conj. b *fr. like adv.* (?c1380) Cleanness Mars 1

like prep. 1a *fr. lik adj. & <like adv.>* ?c1200 Orm. General 124

liken v1. 1a e *OE* a1150 Rwl.G.57.Gloss. RomA 132

likerous adj. 3b *?AN* c1325 Iesu suete is PF 12

likerousli adv. a *fr. likerous adj.* (a1333) Shoreham Poems *MkT* 1

likerousnesse n. b *fr. likerous adj.* Chaucer WBPro 6

likinge ger1. 3a *OE* (c1200) Vices & V.(1) RomA 13

likinge ppl. adj. 1a *fr. liken v1.* c1325 Iesu suete is RomA 5

likli adj. 2a *OE & ON* (a1325) Cursor TR 8

liklihode n. 1a *fr. likli adj. & -hede suf.* Chaucer CLT 2

liklinesse n. 1a *fr. likli adj.* Chaucer CLT 1

liknen v2. 1a *fr. <liken v2.>* (c1280) SLeg.Pass. BD 16

liknesse n. 3a *OE* c1175 Bod.Hom. HF 12

lilie n. 1c *OE, fr. L* c1150 Hrl.HApul. ROMA 15

liltinge-horn n. *fr. <lilting ger.> & horn n.* Chaucer *HF* 1

lim n1. 2a *OE* a1126 Peterb.Chron. ROMA 26

lim n2. 1a a *OE* c1150 PDidax. LGW 5

limaille n. *OF* Chaucer CYT 6

limen v1. 1a *OE* (?a1200) Ancr. TR 2

limer n. *OF* Chaucer BD 2

limitacioun n. 3 *OF* Chaucer WBT 1

limiten v. 1b *OF* Chaucer MEL 1

limitour n. a *fr. limiten v.* (c1378) PPl.B (Ld) GP 7

limrod n. 4c, lim n2. *(fr. lim n2. & rodde n.)* Chaucer MKT 1

linage n. 1a *OF* (?a1300) Arth.& M. ROMA 25

linde n. 2 *OE* c1250 Owl & N. ROMA 3

line n1. 1b *OE (fr. L) & L & OF* (?c1225) Horn TR 121

linen v1. c *fr. lin n.* Chaucer GP 1

line-right n., adj., adv. b *fr. line n1. & -right suf.* Chaucer AST 3

linx n. *L* (1340) Ayenb. BO 1

lioun n1. 1d *OF & OE & L* c1150 Hrl.MQuad. ROMA 54

liounesse n. 1a *OF* (?c1300) Bevis LGW 4

lippe n1. 1a *OE* c1150 PDidax. KNT 7

lire n2. a *OE* (?c1200) HMaid. THOP 1

lisse n. a *OE* (?a1200) Lay.Brut HF 4

lissen v. 1a *fr. lisse n. & OE* c1300 SLeg. (Ld) BD 5

list n1. a *OE* c1175 Bod.Hom. WBPRO 1

list n2. 1b *fr. listen v1.* (?a1200) Lay.Brut BD 10

liste n2. 2b *OE & OF, ML (fr. Gmc.)* (?c1280) SLeg.Nativ.(Eg) ABC 15

listen v1. 1a c *OE* c1150 PDidax. ROMA 337

listen v2. a *OE* (c1125) Vsp.D.Hom.Fest.Virg. THOP 2

litarge n. a *OF; ult. Gr.* Chaucer GP 2

litargie n. a *ML & OF* (1373) *Lelamour Macer BO 2

lite adj1. 1a *OE* c1150 PDidax. ROMA 39

lite adv. *(fr. lite adj1.)* (?a1200) Ancr. BD 9

lite n3. 2a *(fr. lite adj1.)* (?c1175) PMor (Lamb) BD 34

litel adj. 1a e *OE* a1121 Peterb.Chron. ROMA 183

litel adv. 1a *(fr. litel adj.)* a1126 Peterb.Chron. BD 72

litel n. 1b b *(fr. litel adj.)* a1121 Peterb.Chron. ROMA 24

litel what phr. 1 *fr. litel adj. & what pron.* a1121 Peterb.Chron. BO 1

litestere n. a *fr. liten v1. & -estre suf.* Chaucer FORMAGE 1

lith n1. a *OE* c1150 Hrl.HApul. BD 2

lithe adj. b *OE* c1150 Hrl.HApul. HF 1

lithen v2. 1a *OE* c1150 Hrl.HApul. TR 1

litherli adv. a *OE & LOE* a1200 Body & S.(2) MILT 1

liven v1. 1c *OE* a1121 Peterb.Chron. ROMA 216

livere n1. a *OE* c1150 Hrl.HApul. SUMT 1

livere n2. a *fr. liven v1.* (c1378) PPl.B (Ld) MLT 1

livere n3. 3a *OF* (?c1300) Amis GP 1

livinge ger. 1b *(fr. liven v1.)* (?a1300) KAlex. SNT 15

livinge ppl. adj. 1c *(fr. liven v1.)* c1150 Hr.MQuad. BO 3

lo interj. 1c *OE* a1121 Peterb.Chron. ROMA 227

lode n. 2a *OE* ?c1200 Orm. KNT 1

lode-sterre n. a *fr. lode n. & sterre n.*
Chaucer T R 3

lod-man n. a *OE* Chaucer *LGW* I

lod-manage n. a *fr. lod-man n.* Chaucer
GP I

lof n2. a *OE* a1121 Peterb.Chron. *MLT*
I

lofsom adj. 1a *OE* ?c1200 Orm. *TR* 2

loft n. 2a *ON* a1225
Vsp.A.Hom.Init.Creat. T R 2

logge n2. 2d *OF* c1300 SLeg.Mich. (Ld)
NPT I

loggen v. 1b *OF* (?a1200) Ancr. *NPT* 3

logginge ger. 1a *(fr. loggen v.)* (a1325)
Cursor *NPT* I

logike n. b *L & OF; ult. Gr.* c1150
PDidax. *GP* I

lok n1. 1a *OE* a1200 Gloss.Sidonius
ADAM 6

lok n4. 1a a *fr. loken v2.* (?a1200)
Trin.Hom. BD 29

loken v1. 1a *ON* (c1300) Glo.Chron.A
WBPRO 2

loken v2. 5a *OE* a1121 Peterb.Chron.
ROMA 222

lokinge ger. 1a a *(fr. loken v2.)* (?a1200)
Ancr. ROMA 41

lollere n. I *fr. lollen v. & <Lollard n.>*
(c1378) PPl.B (Ld) *EpiMLT* 2

lomb n. 1a *OE* ?c1200 Orm. ABC 14

Lombard n. & adj. 3b *OF* (?a1300)
KAlex. *SHIPT* I

Lombardie n. *OF* (?a1200) Lay.Brut
LGW F 7

lombe-skynnes n. 6b, lomb n. *(fr. lomb
n. & skin n1.)* Chaucer ROMA I

lond n. 1a *OE* a1121 Peterb.Chron.
ROMA 95

London n. a *OE; ult. Celt.* a1121
Peterb.Chron. GP 7

lone n1. 2 *ON* (?c1150) Prov.Alf. (Mdst)
SUMT 2

long adj1. 1a *OE* a1121 Peterb.Chron.
ROMA 176

long adj2. a *OE* ?c1200 Orm. *CYT* 2

longe adv. 2a *OE* a1121 Peterb.Chron.
ROMA 153

longe n. a *OE* c1150 Hrl.MQuad. *KNT* I

longen v1. 2b *OE* ?c1200 Orm. BD 10

longen v3. 6a *(fr. long adj2.)* (?c1225)
Horn ROMA 25

longitude n. b *L & OF* Chaucer *AST* 27

loppe n1. a *OE* c1350 MPPsalter *AST* 2

lop-web n. a, loppe n1. *(fr. loppe n1. &
web n.)* Chaucer *AST* I

lord n. 2b *OE* a1121 Peterb.Chron.
ROMA 491

lorden v. a *fr. lord n.* (1340) Rolle Psalter
(UC 64) *MARS* I

lordinge n. 7a *OE* ?c1200 Orm. MKT 22

lordli adv. a *fr. lordli adj.* (c1350)
Alex.Maced. *RVPRO* I

lordshipe n. 3c *OE* a1225
Lamb.Hom.VA ROMA 45

lore n1. b *OE* (?a1300) Arth.& M. *HF* I

lore n2. 3c *OE* c1150 Vsp.D.Hom. SNT
34

lorel n. *fr. loren ppl. of lesen v4.* (?c1350)
Libeaus BO 2

los adj. 3a *ON* (?a1200) Ancr. HF 7

los n1. 3a *OE & ON* (?a1200) Lay.Brut
BD 16

los n2. 1b *OF & L* c1300 SLeg.Edm.Abp.
(Ld) ROMA 19

losen v2. 6 *OE* a1121 Peterb.Chron.
ROMA 106

losenge n. a *OF* Chaucer ROMA 2

losenger n. c *OF* (?a1300) KAlex. ROMA
6

losengerie n. b *OF* (c1303) Mannyng HS
PARST I

loste n. b *(fr. losen v2.)* (a1338) Mannyng
Chron.Pt.1 BO I

lot n1. 2b *OE* ?c1200 Orm. LGW 4

loten v1. a *OE* (?a1200) Trin.Hom. SNT
I

loth adj. 1a *OE & ON* a1121
Peterb.Chron. ROMA 26

loth adv. *fr. loth adj.* (c1340) Rolle
Psalter *TR* I

loth n. ɪb *OE* cɪɪ50 Hrl.HApul. LGW 2

lothli adj. ɪa *OE & ON* aɪɪ3ɪ
Peterb.Chron. *WBT* ɪ

loud adj. ɪb *OE* aɪɪ2ɪ Peterb.Chron. HF
ɪ0

loude adv. ɪc *OE* (?cɪɪ50) Prov.Alf. (Trin-
C) BD 4ɪ

loue adj. ɪa a *ON* cɪɪ75 Body & S.(ɪ)
ROMA 42

loue adv. ɪb a *fr. loue adj.* (?aɪ200) Ancr.
ROMA 38

loue n3. 2a *fr. loue adj.* (?cɪɪ75) PMor.
(Lamb) ROMA 9

louke n2. *? <cp. louk n.>* Chaucer *CKT*
ɪ

louli adj. b *fr. loue adj.* Chaucer ANEL 3

louli adv. ɪ *fr. loue adj.* (?cɪ300) Guy(ɪ)
TR 7

lounesse n. 2c *fr. loue adj.* (?aɪ200) Ancr.
BO 2

louren v. ɪb a *cp. MDu. & MHG* (?cɪ225)
Horn HF 2

lousi adj. a *fr. louse n.* (?cɪ350) Ywain
FRT ɪ

louten vɪ. 2c *OE* ?cɪ200 Orm. ROMA 5

love nɪ. ɪb f *OE* aɪɪ2ɪ Peterb.Chron.
ROMA 676

love-dai n. b *(fr. love nɪ. & dai n.)* cɪ300
SLeg.Edm.Abp. (Ld) HF 2

love-daunce n. 4b, love nɪ. *(fr. love nɪ. &
daunce n.)* Chaucer *HF* ɪ

love-drinke n. 4b, love nɪ. *(fr. love nɪ. &
drinke n.)* (?aɪ300) Tristrem *WBPRO* ɪ

love-drueri n. 4b, love nɪ. *(fr. love nɪ. &
druerie n.)* (cɪ300) Havelok *THOP* ɪ

love-knotte n. 4c, love nɪ. *(fr. love nɪ. &
knotte n.)* Chaucer *GP* ɪ

loveli adj. ɪa *OE* (?aɪ200) Trin.Hom.
MILT ɪ

love-likinge n. 4c, love nɪ. *(fr. love nɪ. &
likinge gerɪ.)* cɪ390 Talking LGod
THOP ɪ

love-longinge n. 4d, love nɪ. *(fr. love nɪ.
& longinge gerɪ.)* (?aɪ300) Tristrem
MILT 4

loven vɪ. ɪa *OE* aɪɪ2ɪ Peterb.Chron.
ROMA 367

lovere n2. ɪa *fr. loven vɪ.* cɪ250 Ful feir
flour ROMA 83

love-tidinges n. 4f, love nɪ. *(fr. love nɪ. &
tidinge n.)* cɪ250 Owl & N. *HF* ɪ

lovinge gerɪ. {a} *OE* Chaucer {ɪ372
Undo thi dore} ROMA ɪ6

luce n. a *OF* ɪ38ɪ Pegge Cook.Recipes
GP ɪ

Lucifer n. a *L* (cɪ303) Mannyng HS
MKT 7

lucre n. b *L* Chaucer *PRT* 2

lullen v. a *imitative* aɪ325 Gloss.Bibbesw.
MLT 3

luna n. a *L & OF* (ɪ392) *MS Wel.564
CYT 2

lunarie nɪ. b *ML* (ɪ373) *Lelamour
Macer *CYT* ɪ

lure nɪ. c *OF* (cɪ300) Glo.Chron.A
LGW 3

luren vɪ. a *OF* (cɪ378) PPl.B (Ld)
WBPRO ɪ

lurken v. a *ON* (cɪ300) Havelok ROMA
5

lushe-burgh n. a *fr. <Luxemburg n.>*
(cɪ378) PPl.B (Ld) *PROMKT* ɪ

lust n. 2c *OE* aɪɪ50 Rwl.G.57 Gloss.
ROMA ɪ02

lusten v. ɪd *fr. lust n. & OE* cɪɪ75
Bod.Hom. ROMA ɪɪ

lusti adj. 2c *fr. lust n.* (?cɪ200)
St.Kath.(ɪ) ROMA 53

lustihede n. a *fr. lusti adj.* Chaucer BD 4

lustili adv. 2b *fr. lusti adj.* (?cɪ200)
St.Juliana ROMA 8

lustinesse n. ɪa *fr. lusti adj.* Chaucer
ROMA 4

lute nɪ. a *OF, fr. Ar.* Chaucer PARDT 2

luxurie n. a *OF* (ɪ340) Ayenb. BO 7

luxurious adj. a *OF, AF* (?aɪ300) Arth.&
M. *BO* ɪ

mace n. a *OF* (cɪ300) Glo.Chron.A TR 6

Macedone adj. & n. b *L* (?aɪ300) KAlex.
BD 3

mad adj. 4 *OE* c1275 Ancr. (Cleo: Morton) T*R* 8

ma-dame n. & phr. 1a *OF* c1300 SLeg.Oxf.Scholar (Hrl) HF 29

madden v. b *fr. mad adj.* (a1325) Cursor R*O*MA 5

madere n. 1a *OE & ON* c1150 Hrl.HApul. F*ORM*AGE 1

madnesse n. b *fr. mad adj.* (c1394) WBible(1) CYT 2

madrian n. *OF* Chaucer P*RO*M*K*T 1

mafai interj. 8e, feith n. *(fr. min pron. & feith n.)* (a1250) Harrow.H. T*R* 1

mageste n. a *OF* c1300 SLeg.Edm.Abp. (Hrl) R*O*MA 15

magicien n. *OF* Chaucer M*K*T 4

magike n. *OF* Chaucer HF 9

magistrat n. b *L* Chaucer B*O* 1

magnanimite n. a *OF* (1340) Ayenb. SNP*RO* 2

magnesia n. *ML, fr. Gr.* Chaucer CYT 2

magnificence n. 1 *OF* (1340) Ayenb. SNP*RO* 5

magnifien v. a *OF* (a1382) WBible(1) (Bod 959) P*ARS*T 1

magnifiinge ger. a *fr. magnifien v.** Chaucer HF 1

Mahoun n. 1a *OF* (?a1200) Lay.Brut M*LT* 2

mai n1. b *OE* ?c1200 Orm. T*R* 3

Mai n2. 1a *OF & L* ?a1114 Chron.Dom.A.9 R*O*MA 43

maide n. & adj. 1a *OE* (?a1200) Lay.Brut R*O*MA 74

maiden n. 1a *OE* (c1125) Vsp.D.Hom.Fest.Virg. R*O*MA 52

maidenhede n. 2a *OE* ?c1200 Orm. ABC 20

maille n. 1a *OF* (?a1300) Guy(2) T*R* 2

maime n. a *OF; AF* (?a1300)KAlex. P*ARS*T 1

maimen v. 1a *OF* (c1300) Glo.Chron.A W*B*T 1

maintenaunce n. 1a *OF* (1333) Shoreham Poems W*B*T 1

maintenen v. 3a *OF* (?c1300) LFMass Bk. R*O*MA 6

maister n. 1b *OF & OE, fr. L* (?c1150) Prov.Alf. (*Glb-Spelman) M*K*T 59

maisterful adj. a *fr. maister n.* (?c1380) Pearl T*R* 1

maister-hunte n. 1f, maister n. *(fr. maister n. & hunte n.)* Chaucer BD 1

maister-strete n. 1g, maister n. *(fr. maister n. & strete n2.)* Chaucer LGW 2

maister-toun n. 1g, maister n. *fr. maister n. & toun n.** (?a1300) KAlex. LGW 1

maister-tour n. 1g, maister n. *(fr. maister n. & tour n1.)* Chaucer SQT 1

maistresse n. 2b *OF* (?a1300) Tristrem ABC 16

maistrie n. 1a *OF* (?a1200) Ancr. R*O*MA 27

make n1. 1a *OE* c1175 Bod.Nativ.Virg. SNT 28

makeles adj. a *fr. make n1.* (?c1200) St.Marg. T*R* 1

maken v1. 3a *OE* a1121 Peterb.Chron. R*O*MA 1090

maken v2. a *fr. make n1.* ?a1300 Thrush & N. T*R* 1

makere n. 1 *fr. maken v1.* (1340) Ayenb. SNP*RO* 20

makinge ger. 8c *(fr. maken v1.)* a1121 Peterb.Chron. T*R* 7

Makomete n. b *ML & OF* (?a1200) Lay.Brut M*LT* 2

maladie n. a *OF* c1275 Ken.Serm. B*O* 43

malapert adj. b *OF* (?a1300) KAlex. T*R* 1

male adj2. 1a *OF* (1378) PPl.B (Ld) P*ARS*T 1

male n1. 2a *OF* (1373) *Lelamour Macer B*O* 2

male n2. 1a *OF* (?a1200) Lay.Brut GP 5

malefice n. a *L & OF* Chaucer B*O* 2

malencolie n. 3 *OF & ML, CL; ult. Gr.* (c1303) Mannyng HS BD 8

malencolik adj. 1a *OF & ML, fr. Gr.* Chaucer K*N*T 1

malencolious adj. 2d *OF* Chaucer *HF* 1
malice n. 1b *OF* (c1300) Glo.Chron.A
ROMA 29
malicious adj. 1a *OF* c1225 Ancr. (Tit.)
HF 1
malignite n. a *OF* c1390 Psalt.Mariae(1)
PARST 1
malisoun n. a *OF* (c1250) Floris CYT 5
malkin n. a *fr. Matilda prop. n.* c1250
LSSerm. NPT 1
malliable adj. *OF & ML* Chaucer *CYT*
1
malt n. 1a *OE* a1200 Wor.Aelfric Gloss.
RvT 3
maltalent n. a *OF* (?a1300) KAlex. ROMA
2
malvesie n. *OF & ML* Chaucer *SHIPT* 1
man n. 1a e *OE* (1100) Chart.St.Paul in
RHS ser.3.58 GENERAL 2357
manace n. 1a *OF* (c1303) Mannyng HS
MKT 5
manacen v. 3b *OF* (c1300) NHom.(1)
Abp.& N. Bo 6
manacinge ger. *(fr. manacen v.)*
(c1333–42) Minot Poems *KNT* 1
mane n. a, techel n. *L, fr. Gr.; ult Aram*
a1150 Vsp.D.Hom. *MKT* 2
maner n1. 1a *AF & CF* c1300
SLeg.Becket (Ld) *BD* 1
manere n. 1b a *OF (esp. AF)* (?a1200)
Ancr. ROMA 496
manes n. pl. b *L* Chaucer *TR* 1
manhede n. 1b *fr. man n.* (?a1200) Ancr.
MKT 10
mani adj. & n. 1a a *OE* a1121
Peterb.Chron. GENERAL 542
mania n. *L* Chaucer *KNT* 1
manifeste adj. *L* Chaucer *BO* 3
manifeste adv. a *L* Chaucer *AST* 1
manifesten v. *fr. manifeste adj.* Chaucer
BO 1
mani-fold adj. 1a *OE* a1121
Peterb.Chron. *PROV* 1
man-kinde n. 1a *fr. man n. & kinde n.*
a1225 Stond wel moder ABC 55

manli adj. 1 *prob. OE* (c1200) Vices &
V.(1) MKT 12
manli adv1. 2 *OE & ON* (?a1200)
Lay.Brut TR 4
mannish adj. 1 *OE* (c1125)
Vsp.D.Hom.Fest.Virg. TR 4
mansioun n1. 1a *L & OF* (1340) Rolle
Psalter (UC 64) HF 8
man-slaughter n. 1 *fr. man n. &*
slaughter n. (a1325) Cursor FORMAGE
9
mansuete adj. a *OF & L* Chaucer *TR* 1
mansuetude n. *L & OF* Chaucer *PARST*
1
mantel n. 1a *OF & L & OE, fr. L* (c1200)
Vices & V.(1) ROMA 6
Mantoan n. *L* Chaucer *LGW* 1
mapel n. a *OE* ?a1300 St.J.List Trees
ROMA 2
mappe-mounde n. *OF & ML* Chaucer
ROS 1
marble n. 1a *OF* a1200 Annot.Cld.OT
ROMA 5
marchaundise n. 1b *OF & AF* (a1250)
Harrow.H BO 8
marchaunt n. 1a *OF & AF* ?c1200
Wor.Bod.Gloss. FORMAGE 34
marche n1. a *AF & CF* ?c1200 Orm. TR
11
marcial adj1. a *ML* Chaucer *TR* 1
marcien adj1. a *?ML* Chaucer *WBPRO* 1
mareis n. sg. & pl. a *OF* (a1338)
Mannyng Chron.Pt.2 BO 3
margine n. b *L & OF* (?a1350) Castleford
Chron. *AST* 1
mariage n. 1b *OF* c1300 SLeg.Edm.Abp.
(Ld) SNT 62
mari-bon n. a *fr. marwe n1. & bon n1.*
Chaucer *GP* 1
Marie n. 1a b *OE & L, OF* c1175
Bod.Hom. HF 15
Marie n2. 2, Egipcien n. and adj. *L, OF**
c1290 SLeg. (Ld) *MLT* 1
marien v. 1a *OF* (c1300) Glo.Chron.A
MKT 5

mariner n. a *AF & CF* (c1250) Floris (Auch) Bo 3

marke n1. 5d *OE* ?c1200 Orm. Bo 7

marke n2. 2a *LOE & OI & OF, ML (fr. Gmc.)* a1121 Peterb.Chron. PARDPRO 3

marken v1. 1a *OE & ON* c1175 Bod.Hom. HF 12

market n1. 1a *?LOE & ON & OF* a1121 Peterb.Chron. WBPRO 2

market-betere n. 4a, market n1. *fr. market n1. & beter n1.* * Chaucer *RVT* 1

market-place n. 4c, market n1. *(fr. market n1. & place n.)* (a1393) Gower CA *MERT* 1

markis n. a *OF* (?c1300) Guy(1) *CLT* 33

markisesse n. *fr. markis n.* Chaucer *CLT* 4

marle-pit n. c, marle n. *(fr. marle n. & pit n.)* Chaucer *MILT* 1

Marmorike adj. *L* Chaucer *BO* 1

Mars n. b *L* c1300 SLeg.Mich. (Ld) ANEL 61

marshal n. 1b *OF, fr. Gmc.* (1258) Procl.Hen.III in PST (1881) GP 2

Marte n. a *L* (c1350) Alex.& D. HF 10

Martin n. a *OF* a1121 Peterb.Chron. *SHIPT* 1

martir n. 1a *OE (fr. L) & OF* ?a1160 Peterb.Chron. SNPRO 8

martirdom n. a *OE* c1175 Bod.Hom. SNT 5

martire n. b *OF & ML* (c1300) NHom.(1) Gosp. *TR* 1

martiren v. 1 *OE & OF & ML* (c1200) Vices & V.(1) *KNT* 1

marwe n1. 1a a *OE* c1150 PDidax. Bo 3

masculine adj. & n. c *OF & L* (?c1350) SVrn.Leg. *BO* 1

mase n. a *(fr. amased ppl.)* c1300 SLeg.Judas (Hrl) TR 3

masednesse n. *fr. masen v.* Chaucer *CLT* 1

maseline n. *OF* ?a1300 St.Eust. *THOP* 1

masen v. 1a *fr. amased ppl.* a1325 SLeg.Brendan BD 6

masken v. *fr. <maske n.>* Chaucer *TR* 1

masonrie n. {b} *OF* Chaucer {?c1375 NHom.(3) Pass.} ROMA 2

mast n1. a *OE* (?a1200) Lay.Brut. BD 5

mast n2. b *OE* (?a1200) Lay.Brut FORMAGE 2

masti adj. *fr. mast n2.* Chaucer *HF* 1

mat adj. 1b *OF; ult. Persian* (?a1200) Ancr. ANEL 6

mat interj. & n. a *OF* (?a1300) Arth.& M. BD 2

matere n. 5c a *L & OF* (?a1200) Ancr. ROMA 159

material adj. 2a *L & OF* (c1340) Rolle Psalter (UC 64) MEL 3

material n. *fr. material adj.* Chaucer *BO* 2

matin n. b *OF* c1250 Ful feir flour *WBT* 1

matrimoine n. 1a *OF & L* (c1300) NHom.(1) Gosp. *KNT* 5

Maudelaine n. 1a *OF & L* (?a1325) Bonav. Medit.(1) LGW F 6

maue n. 1a *OE* c1150 Hrl.HApul. MLT 3

maugre prep. a *fr. maugre n.* (1265) BLewes BD 19

maumet n. 1a *OF* (?a1200) Lay.Brut *PARST* 3

maumetrie n. 1a *fr. maumet n.* (c1303) Mannyng HS MLT 2

maunciple n. b *OF* (?a1200) Ancr. GP 13

maundement n. 2a *OF & ML* (c1300) Glo.Chron.A FRPRO 3

mauntelet n. a *OF* Chaucer *KNT* 1

mavis n. sg. & pl. *OF* Chaucer ROMA 2

me pron2. 1c *OE* a1121 Peterb.Chron. GENERAL 1934

mede n1. *OE* c1150 PDidax. *KNT* 4

mede n2. a *OE* c1150 Hrl.HApul. ROMA 15

Mede n3. a *L* (?a1300) KAlex. *MKT* 1

mede n4. 2a *OE* a1150 Vsp.D.Hom. ANEL 49

mediacioun n. a *ML & OF* (a1387) Trev.Higd. AST 6

mediatour n. a *L* (c1350) NHom.(2) PSanct. *PARST* 2

medicine n. 2a b *L & OF* (?a1200) Ancr. ABC 15

meditacioun n. a *L & OF* (?a1200) Ancr. *PARSPRO* 2

medle adj. a *fr. medle n2.* (c1303) Mannyng HS *GP* 1

medlen v. 2a g *OF* a1300 Weole thu art HF 23

medler n. b *OF* Chaucer *ROMA* 1

medlinge ger. 4c *(fr. medlen v.)* (?a1350) Nicod.(1) ROMA 4

medwe n. 1b *OE* a1121 Peterb.Chron. ROMA 4

megre adj. a {a} *OF* Chaucer {(c1378) PPl.B (Ld)} *ROMA* 2

meine n. 1c *AF & CF* (c1250) Floris (Cmb) ROMA 33

mek adj. 1a *ON* ?c1200 Orm. SNPRO 27

meken v. 1c *fr. mek adj.* ?c1200 Orm. *MEL* 1

mekli adj. a *fr. mek adj.* (?c1280) SLeg.Advent, etc (Eg) *WBPRO* 1

mekli adv. 1a *fr. mek adj.* ?c1200 Orm. TR 15

meknesse n. 1a *fr. mek adj.* ?c1200 Orm. Bo 5

mel n2. 4 *OE* a1121 Peterb.Chron. BD 4

mele n1. 1a *OE* c1150 Hrl.HApul. RvT 8

melodie n. 2a *L & OF; ult. Gr.* c1300 SLeg.Brendan (Ld) ROMA 26

melodious adj. *ML* Chaucer *TR* 1

melten v. 1a d *OE* c1150 PDidax. ROMA 9

mel-tid n. 2b, mel n2. *(fr. mel n2. & tide n.)* (?a1200) Trin.Hom. *TR* 1

membre n. 1a *OF* (?c1280) SLeg.Advent, etc. (Eg) ROMA 25

memorial adj. a *OF & L* Chaucer *ANEL* 1

memorie n. 2c *L & OF* c1250 *St.Marg.(2) BD 21

mencioun n. 1b *OF* c1300 ll Pains (2) MKT 16

menden v. 4a <*fr. amenden v.*> (?a1200) Trin.Hom. *TR* 2

mendinaunt n. c *AF* (a1376) PPl.A (Trin-C) *SUMT* 2

mene adj2. 3 *OF* (1340) Ayenb. ANEL 16

mene n3. 6 *OF; AF* (?c1300) Caiphas ABC 18

menelich adj2. *fr. mene adj2.* Chaucer *BO* 1

menen v1. 1a *OE* c1175 HRood ROMA 120

mene-while n. & adv. 1a *fr. mene adj2. & whil n.* a1375 WPal. *BO* 1

meninge ger1. 3a *(fr. menen v1.)* (c1303) Mannyng HS TR 4

meni-ver n. a *AF* (c1250) Floris (Cmb) *ROMA* 1

Menouresse n. b {a} *fr. Menour n. & ML* Chaucer {(1395) EEWills} *ROMA* 1

mercenarie n. *L* Chaucer *GP* 1

Mercenrike n. c, Merce n. *OE & ML* c1330 SMChron. *NPT* 1

merci n1. 1a *OF* (?a1200) Ancr. ABC 150

merciable adj. b *OF* (?a1200) Ancr. ABC 9

merciful adj. a *fr. merci n1.* (1340) Ayenb. *MLT* 1

Mercurie n. a *OF & L* c1150 Hrl.HApul. HF 20

mere n1. 1a *OE* (?a1200) Ancr. GP 6

mere-maide n. 1 *fr. mere n2. & maide n. & adj.* c1350 Cmb.Ee.4.20 Nominale *NPT* 1

mere-maiden n. b *fr. mere n2. & maiden n.* Chaucer ROMA 3

meridian adj. c *L & OF* Chaucer *AST* 5

meridian n. 1a *OF & L* (?c1350) SVrn.Leg. *AST* 5

meridional adj. 1 *OF & L* (c1386) Almanac (1647) 50 AST 37

merite n. 3a b *L & OF* (?a1200) Ancr. SNPRO 16

meritorie adj. 1 *L & OF* (c1378) PPl.B (Ld) *PARST* 2

merlioun n. a *AF* Chaucer *PF* 2

mershi adj. *fr. mersh n.* (a1382) WBible (1) (Bod 959) *SUMT* 1

merveille n. 1b *OF* c1300 SLeg.Inf.Chr. (Ld) ROMA 21

merveillen v. 1a *OF* (?a1300) KAlex. *BO* 9

merveillous adj. 1b a *OF* c1300 SLeg.Inf.Chr. (Ld) ROMA 8

mes n1. c {a} *OF, fr. L* Chaucer {c1390 Susan} ROMA 1

mesel n. 1a *OF & ML* c1300 SLeg. (Ld) *PARST* 1

meselrie n. a *OF* (a1325) Cursor *PARST* 1

message n1. 2c *OF* c1300 SLeg.Becket (Ld) SNT 16

messager n. 1b *OF* (?a1200) Ancr. BD 28

messagerie n. *OF* Chaucer *PF* 1

messe n1. 1b c *OF & ML & OE* a1121 Peterb.Chron. BD 12

messe-dai n. 4d, messe n1. *(fr. messe* n1. *& dai n.)* ?c1200 Orm. *NPT* 1

mesuage n. *AF & AL* Chaucer *RVT* 1

mesurable adj. 2a *OF* (?a1300) KAlex. GP 5

mesurablie adv. b *fr. mesurable adj.* (a1382) WBible(1) (Bod 959) *MEL* 1

mesure n. 6a *OF* (?a1200) Trin.Hom. ROMA 30

mesuren v. 5b *OF* (a1325) Cursor ABC 8

mesuringe ger. a {a} *(fr. mesuren v.)* Chaucer {(a1398) *Trev.Barth.} ROMA 1

met n. 1b *OE* c1175 HRood *PARST* 1

metal n. b *OF* (c1250) Gen.& Ex. ROMA 15

Metamorphoseos n. *fr. Gr.* Chaucer *INTMLT* 1

mete adj. 3a *OE* (?c1300) NPass. BD 5

mete n1. 1b e *OE* ?c1125 Dur-C.Gloss. ANEL 60

meteli adj. a *fr. mete adj.* (a1325) Cursor ROMA 1

meten v3. 1a *OE* c1150 Hrl.MQuad. ROMA 47

meten v4. 1a *OE* (?a1200) Lay.Brut ROMA 65

metinge ger3. 1b *OE* c1275 Ken.Serm. BD 1

metinge ger4. 1a *OE* (c1300) NHom.(1) Gosp. TR 2

metre n. 2a *OF & L* (a1338) Mannyng Chron.Pt.1 LGW F 3

meue n1. 3a *OF* a1375 WPal. TR 8

meuen v1. a *OF* c1380 Firumb.(1) *TR* 1

mevable adj. 6 *OF* a1325 SLeg. (Corp-C) BO 13

mevement n. a *OF* Chaucer *BO* 2

meven v. 1b a *OF & AF* c1275 Ken.Serm. HF 68

mevere n. 1a *fr. meven v.* Chaucer HF 4

mevinge ger. 1a a *(fr. meven v.)* Chaucer HF 50

meward n. s. v. -ward suf. *(fr. me pron2. &-ward suf.)* (a1338) Mannyng Chron.Pt.2 BO 3

mid adj. & pref. 2 *OE* (?a1200) Lay.Brut *BD* 1

mid n. 1b *OE* c1175 HRood HF 2

mid-dai n. 1a *OE* c1150 Hrl.HApul. *AST* 9

middel adj. 1d *OE* ?c1200 Orm. ANEL 9

middel n. 2a *OE* (?a1200) Lay.Brut ROMA 9

Middelburgh n. 6, middel adj. *(fr. middel adj.)* Chaucer *GP* 1

middes n. 1d *OE* (a1325) Cursor HF 2

mid-night n. 1b *OE* c1175 Bod.Hom. TR 12

mid-ward n1., adj. & adv. 2a *OE* a1121 Peterb.Chron. *CYT* 1

Mighel-messe n. a *fr.* <*Mighel n.*> *& messe* n1. a1121 Peterb.Chron. *SCOG* 1

might n. 1a *OE* (c1125) Vsp.D.Hom.Fest.Virg. ROMA 175

mighti adj. 1a *OE* c1175 Bod.Hom. ROMA 98

mightili adv. 1a *OE* (?a1200) Ancr. MKT 8

Milan n. a *It. & OF* Chaucer *MKT* 1

milde adj. 1b *OE & ON* ?a1160 Peterb.Chron. *TR* 1

mile n1. 1a *OE, fr. L* a1121 Peterb.Chron. ROMA 20

mile-wei n. 2b, mile NI. *(fr. mile IN. &*
wei n.) (1370) Fabric R.Yk.Min. in
Sur.Soc.35 *AST* I

milioun num. (as n.) *OF* (a1376)
PPl.A(1) (Trin-C) *SumPro* I

milk n. 1a *OE* (c1125)
Vsp.D.Hom.Fest.Virg. RomA 14

milki adj. b *fr. milk n.* Chaucer *HF* I

milk-sop n. 1b b, milk n. *(fr. milk n. &*
soppe NI.). Chaucer *ProMkT* I

milne n. 1a *OE* (?a1200) Ancr. FormAge
II

milnere n. a *fr. milne n.* (a1376) PPl.A(1)
(Trin-C) GP 39

milne-ston n. a *OE* a1225 Vsp.A.Hom.
Tr I

min pron. 1a *OE* (1100) Chart.St.Paul in
RHS ser.3.58 GENERAL 2745

minde NI. 2 *OE* c1175 Bod.Hom. BD 79

minen v. 1a a *OF* (?a1300) Rich. (Auch)
Tr 3

Minerve n. *L* (c1350) Alex.& D. BD 4

ministre n. 2a a *L & OF* c1300
SLeg.Fran.(1) (Ld) SNPRO 8

ministren v. 3a *OF & L* (a1338) Mannyng
Chron.Pt.2 *Bo* I

minnen VI. 1e *ON* ?c1200 Orm. *Scog* I

Minotaure n. *L, fr. Gr.* Chaucer KNT 4

minour n. 1 *OF* a1300 A Mayde Cristes
KnT I

minstral n. 2 *ML & OF* (?a1200) Ancr.
RomA 5

minstralsie n. 1a *AF & AL* (?a1300)
Guy(2) HF 12

minte NI. b *OE, fr. L & OF & L* c1150
Hrl.HApul. *RomA* I

minten v. 1d *OE* ?a1160 Peterb.Chron.
Bo I

minute NI. {1a} *ML* Chaucer {(c1378)
PPl.B (Ld)} *AST* 19

miracle n. 1b b *OF & L* ?a1160
Peterb.Chron. SNT 21

mire NI. 1b *ON* ?a1300 II Pains(1) GP 5

mirie adj. 3d *OE* c1175 Bod.Hom. RomA
73

mirie adv. 1a *OE* (?a1200) Lay.Brut
RomA 11

mirili adv. 1b *OE* (?a1350) 7 Sages(2)
RomA 13

mirinesse n. *OE* (a1325) Cursor *Bo* I

mirour n. 1a *OF* (c1250) Floris (Auch)
RomA 30

mirre n. a *OE (fr. L) & L & OF* c1150
Hrl.HApul. *KnT* I

mirthe n. 4a *OE* (?c1150) Prov.Alf.
(Mdst) RomA 42

mirtheles adj. *fr. mirthe n.* Chaucer *PF*
I

mis adj. c *fr. mis n. & mis pref.* (?a1200)
Ancr. HF 6

mis n. 3 *OE & ON* (?c1175) PMor.
(Lamb) *LGW G* I

misaccounten v. *fr. accounten v.* Chaucer
Tr I

misaventure n. d *fr. aventure n. & OF*
(?c1225) Horn RomA 9

misavisen v. *fr. avisen v.* c1390 II Pains(3)
WBPro I

misbeden v. *fr. beden v.* c1250 Owl & N.
KnT I

misberen v. b *fr. beren* VI. c1300
SLeg.Becket (Hrl) *Mel* I

misbileve n. 2a *fr. bileve n.* (c1200) Vices
& V.(1) *CYT* I

misbileven v. 2a *fr. bileven* VI. (?c1200)
St.Marg.(1) ABC 2

miscarien v. b *fr. <carien v.>* (c1300)
NHom.(1) Abp.& N. *GP* I

mischaunce n. 1a *OF* (c1300)
Glo.Chron.A RomA 50

mischef n. 1b a *OF* (?a1300) Arth.& M.
RomA 28

misconceiven v. *fr. conceiven v.* Chaucer
MerT I

misconstruen v. *fr. construen v.* Chaucer
Tr I

miscounting ger. *fr. miscounten v.* * not
in MED *RomA* I

misdede n. 1b *OE* a1150 Rwl.G.57.Gloss.
FrT 3

misdemen v. b *fr. demen v.* Chaucer HF
3

misdeparten v. *fr. departen v.* Chaucer
INtMLT 1

misdoere n. a *fr. <doer n.>* (?a1300)
KAlex. *MEL* 2

misdoinge ger. a *(fr. misdon v.)* a1225
Lamb.Hom.Pater. *MEL* 1

misdon v. 1c *OE* ?a1160 Peterb.Chron.
PROMKT 2

misdrauinge ger. *fr drauinge ger.*
Chaucer *BO* 1

mi-self pron. 1a *fr. me pron2. & self pron.*
& OE (?a1200) Lay.Brut ROMA 70

misentrechaungen v. *fr. enterchaungen*
Chaucer *BO* 1

misericorde n. 1a *OF* (?a1200) Ancr.
ABC 17

miserie n. b *OF* Chaucer MKT 3

misese n. 1 *OF* (?a1200) Ancr. BO 8

misesed ppl. a *fr. misese n.* Chaucer
PARST 1

misfallen v. a *fr. fallen v.* (c1303)
Mannyng HS *KNT* 1

misforyeven v. *fr. foryeven* Chaucer *TR* 1

misgien v. *fr. gien v.* Chaucer *MKT* 1

misgon v. a *fr. gon v.* (c1280) SLeg.Pass.
RvT 4

misgovernaunce n. b *fr. governaunce*
Chaucer *MKT* 1

mishap n. b *fr. hap n.* a1250 Ancr.
(Nero) *MKT* 1

mishappen v. 1a *fr. happen vi.* (a1338)
Mannyng Chron.Pt.1 KNT 3

mishappi adj. *fr. happi adj.* Chaucer
MEL 1

misknouen v. b *fr. knouen v.* (?a1300)
Guy(2) *BO* 1

misknouinge ger. *(fr. misknouen v.)*
Chaucer *BO* 1

misleden v. 2a *fr. leden vi.* ?c1200
Wor.Bod.Gloss. BO 4

misledinge ger. c *(fr. misleden v.)* (a1325)
Cursor *BO* 1

mislien v. *fr. lien vi.* Chaucer *MILT* 1

misliken vi. 1a *OE* (?c1175) PMor.
(Lamb) *LGW* 1

misliven v. *fr. liven vi.* (?c1375)
NHom.(3) Leg. *TR* 1

mismetren v. *fr. <metren v.>* Chaucer
TR 1

misseien v. 1a *fr. seien vi.* (?a1200) Ancr.
ROMA 8

missen vi. 1a a *OE & ON* ?c1200 Orm.
LADY 10

missette ppl. *fr. setten v.* a1325 SLeg.
(Corp-C) *BD* 1

missitten v. b *fr. sitten v.* a1325
Gloss.Bibbesw. (Arun) ROMA 2

misspeken v. a *fr. speken v.* Chaucer TR 2

misspendinge ger. *(fr. spenden v.)*
(?c1384) Wycl.50 HFriars *PARST* 1

mist n1. 1a a *OE* c1175 Bod.Hom. HF 3

mistaken v. 1a *fr. taken v. & ON* (a1338)
Mannyng Chron.Pt.1 ROMA 4

mister n. 3a *OF* (?a1200) Ancr. ROMA 4

misterie n2. a *ML & OF* Chaucer *PARST*
2

misti adj1. a *fr. mist n1.* c1325 Dream
Bk.(1) *TR* 1

mistiden v. *OE* c1250 Owl & N. *MEL* 1

mistihede n. *fr. misti adj1.* Chaucer
MARS 1

mistili adv. *fr. misti adj2.* (a1382)
WBible(1) Pref.Jer. (Bod 959) *CYT* 1

mistristen v. d *fr. tristen v.* Chaucer
PARDPRO 1

mistrust n. a *fr. trust n.* Chaucer *TR* 2

mistrusten v. 1b *fr. trusten v.* (a1382)
WBibel(1) (Bod 959) TR 6

misturnen v. 1d *fr. turnen v.* c1325 Dream
Bk.(1) *BO* 3

misusen v. 1b *fr. usen v. & OF* Chaucer
BO 3

miswandringe ppl. *fr. wandringe ger.*
Chaucer *BO* 2

miswei n. *fr. wei n.* Chaucer *BO* 2

miswenden v. 1a *OE* c1175 Bod.Hom. *TR*
1

miswriten v. *fr. writen v.* Chaucer *TR* 1

mitaine n. a *OF & ML* Chaucer
PardPro 2

mite n1. *OF* (1373) *Lelamour Macer
WBPro 1

mite n2. b *MDu., MLG* a1375 WPal.
SNT 11

mitre n. b *L & OF; ult. Gr.* (c1303)
Mannyng HS *Gent* 3

mixen n. a *OE* (?a1200) Ancr. *ParsT* 1

mo adj. 3a *OE* ?c1200 Orm. RomA 88

mo adv. 1 *OE* c1150 Hrl.HApul. RomA
55

mo n. 2a *OE* a1121 Peterb.Chron. *Lady*
37

mocchen v. *prob. imitative* a1325 Of
Rybaudy *Tr* 1

mocioun n. 2a *L & OF* Chaucer *Tr* 2

mod n. 1b *OE* (?c1150) Prov.Alf. (Mdst)
Knt 2

mode n. a *OF & L* Chaucer *Bo* 1

moder n. 1a *OE* (c1125)
Vsp.D.Hom.Fest.Virg. ABC 100

modifien v. d *OF* Chaucer *Knt* 1

moeble adj. b *OF* (a1338) Mannyng
Chron.Pt.2 *Ast* 1

moeble n. b *OF* (a1338) Mannyng
Chron.Pt.2 SNT 5

moevablete n. *fr. mevable adj.* Chaucer
Bo 1

Moises n. a *OE, fr. L; ult. Heb* (?c1200)
St.Juliana ABC 7

moisoun n. b {a} *OF* Chaucer {(a1376)
PPl.A(1) (Trin-C)} *RomA* 1

moiste adj. 1d *OF* (1373) *Lelamour
Macer. *Bo* 9

moiste n. b *OF* Chaucer RomA 4

moisti adj. c *fr. moiste adj.* Chaucer
MancPro 1

moisture n. 2a *OF* (c1350) NHom.(2)
PSanct. RomA 2

mokeren v. *(fr. moker n.)* Chaucer *Bo* 2

mokerere n. *fr. mokeren v.* (c1303)
Mannyng HS *Bo* 1

moleste n. *OF* (?a1300) KAlex. *Bo* 2

mollificacioun n. a *ML* Chaucer *Cyt* 1

molloke n. a *fr. molle n2.* Chaucer
RvPro 3

moment n. a *L & OF* Chaucer *Bo* 8

mon n1. 1a *fr. OE* (?a1200) Ancr. HF 13

mone n1. 1c *OE* a1121 Peterb.Chron.
RomA 77

Mone-dai n. a *OE* a1131 Peterb.Chron.
Knt 5

moneie n. 1c *OF* (c1300) Glo.Chron.A
Bo 22

monk n. 1a *OE, fr. L* 1121 Peterb.Chron.
LGW F 31

monstre n. a *OF & L* (a1325) Cursor BD
10

monstruous adj. a *OF & L* Chaucer *Bo*
1

month n. 1b *OE* a1121 Peterb.Chron. *Tr*
29

moral adj. 1a *L & OF* (c1340) Rolle
Psalter (UC 64) *Tr* 7

moralite n. 2a *OF & L* Chaucer *Mkt* 7

mordaunt n. *OF* Chaucer {c1400
Femina} *RomA* 1

more adj. comp. 9a a *OE* (c1125)
Vsp.D.Hom. Fest.Virg. *General* 164

more adv. 5a *OE* a1131 Peterb.Chron.
General 350

more n1. 1a *OE* c1150 PDidax. *Tr* 1

more n3. 3b a *OE* a1131 Peterb.Chron.
General 130

more-over adv. b *fr. more adv. & over
adv.* (c1250) Gen.& Ex. BD 12

mor-male n. *OF* Chaucer *GP* 1

morn n. 2a *OE* a1121 Peterb.Chron. GP
2

mornen v. 1a a *OE* (?a1200) Lay.Brut *Bo*
6

morninge ger. 1a *(fr. mornen v.)* (?a1200)
Ancr. *Bo* 5

morninge n. 1b *fr. morn n.* c1250 Owl &
N. *Bo* 7

Morpheus n. *L* Chaucer *BD* 4

morsel n. 1a b *OF & ML* (c1280)
SLeg.Pass. (Pep) GP 6

mortal adj. 6a *L & OF* Chaucer *Pity* 43

mortalli adv. a *(fr. mortal adj.)* Chaucer MLT 2

morter n1. 1a *OE, fr. L, & OF & L* c1150 Hrl.HApul. TR 2

morther n1. 1a *OE & OF, fr. Gmc. & ML, fr. Gmc.* c1175 Bod.Hom. ROMA 11

mortheren v. 1a *OE & OF & ML* ?c1200 Orm. BD 12

mortherer n. a *fr. mortheren v.* (a1325) Cursor PF 5

mortheringe ger. a *(fr. mortheren v.)* Chaucer KNT 1

mortificacion n. b *ML & OF* Chaucer PARST 1

mortifien v. 1a *OF* (a1382) WBible(1) (Bod 959) CYT 5

mortreues n. a *OF* (1378) PPl.B (Ld) GP 1

morwe n. 2c *OE* (?c1150) Prov.Alf. (Trin-C) ROMA 84

morwe-song n. 2c, morwe n. *(fr. morwe n. & song n.)* Chaucer GP 1

morwe-tide n. 1c *(fr. morwe n. & tide n.)* (c1250) Floris (Cmb) ROMA 4

mosel n. b *OF* Chaucer KNT 1

most adj. sup. & n. 1a c *fr. <mo adj.>* a1121 Peterb.Chron. ROMA 44

most adv. sup. 1c *fr. <mo adv.> & OE* a1121 Peterb.Chron. GENERAL 132

mot n1. a *OE* c1300 SLeg. (Ld) TR 1

mot n2. *OF* (?a1300) Tristrem BD 1

moten v2. 1a a *OE* a1121 Peterb.Chron. GENERAL 470

moteren v. b *L* a1325 Gloss.Bibbesw. TR 1

motif n. a *OF & ML* (a1376) PPl.A (Trin-C) MLT 2

motle n. a *prob. fr. mot n1.* Chaucer GP 1

motthe n. 1a *OE* c1225 HMaid. WBPRO 3

moue n2. b *OF* (c1303) Mannyng HS HF 3

mouen v3. 2a b *OE* a1121 Peterb.Chron. GENERAL 2302

mouinge ger3. *(fr. mouen v3.)* Chaucer BO 9

moulen v. a *ON* (?a1200) Ancr. RVPRO 2

mount n1. b *OE (fr. L) & AF & CF & L* a1121 Peterb.Chron. KNT 6

mountaine n. a *OF* (?a1200) Lay.Brut MKT 16

mountaunce n. b *OF* c1300 SLeg. (Hrl) ROMA 7

mounten v. 1c *OF* c1300 SLeg.Becket (Hrl) HF 1

mous n. 1a *OE* a1225 Lamb.Hom. HF 12

moustre n. e *OF* Chaucer BD 1

mouth n. 1a a *OE* c1150 Hrl.HApul. ROMA 67

muable adj. *OF* Chaucer BO 2

muche adj. 1a *fr. muchel adj.* c1200 Wor.Serm. in EGSt.7 BD 51

muche adv. 1a *fr. muchel adv.* (?c1200) St.Juliana ROMA 32

muche n. 1a a *fr. muchel n.* (?a1200) Ancr. ROMA 89

muchel adj. 1 *OE & ON* a1121 Peterb.Chron. ROMA 44

muchel adv. 2b a *OE* ?a1160 Peterb.Chron. BD 28

muchel n. 1a a *OE* a1121 Peterb.Chron. BD 35

muet adj. 1c *OF & L* (c1378) PPl.B (Ld) TR 1

multiplicacioun n. a *OF & ML* (?c1350) Mirror St.Edm.(4) HF 3

multiplien v. 1b a *OF* (?c1150) Prov.Alf. (Trin-C) HF 21

multipliing ger. 1b *(fr. multiplien v.)* (a1382) WBible(1) (Bod 959) PARDPRO 2

multitude n. c *OF & L* (1340) Rolle Psalter (UC 64) BO 11

murmuracioun n. a *L & OF* Chaucer PARST 1

murmure n. b *OF & L* Chaucer HF 10

murmuren v. b *OF & L* (a1325) Cursor SQT 2

murmuringe ger. *(fr. murmuren v.)*
Chaucer HF 2

muscle nɪ. a *OE, fr L* (1364) Plea &
Mem.R.Lond.Gildh Bo 2

Muse n. a *L & OF; ult. Gr.* Chaucer HF
13

musen v. 1b c *OF* (1340) Ayenb. ROMA 6

musicien n. a *OF* Chaucer Bo 1

musike n. 1 *OF & L; ult Gr.* (c1250)
Gen.& Ex. PF 7

mutabilite n. 1b *OF & L* Chaucer Bo 4

mutable adj. a *L* Chaucer Bo 1

mutacioun n. *L & OF* Chaucer Bo 5

n. d *no etym.* Chaucer AST 1

nacioun n. 1a *OF & L* (?a1300) KAlex.
HF 8

naddre n. 2a *OE* c1150 Hrl.HApul. Bo 4

nadir n. *ML, fr. Ar.* Chaucer HF 18

nai adv. b *fr. nai interj.* (a1325) Cursor
MEL 1

nai interj. 1a *ON* ?c1200 Orm. BD 155

nai n. c *fr. nai interj.* (?a1300) Tristrem
BD 7

nail n. 1a *OE* c1150 PDidax. BD 14

nailen v. 1b *OE* c1175 Bod.Hom. KNT 4

naiten v2. *ON* Chaucer Bo 2

naked adj. 1b *OE* (c1125)
Vsp.D.Hom.Fest.Virg. ROMA 38

nakednesse n. *fr. naked adj.* (c1384)
WBible(1) CLT 2

naken v. a *fr. nake adj. & naked adj.*
a1350 Songs Langtoft (Roy 20.A.11) Bo
1

naker n. a *OF & ML; ult. Kurdish*
(c1333–52) Minot Poems KNT 1

nale n. 2a, ale n. *(fr. ale n.)* ?a1300 Jacob
& J. FRT 1

name n. 1a a *OE* a1121 Peterb.Chron.
ROMA 225

namelesse adj. b *fr. name n.* c1330 Len
puet Bo 1

nameli adv. 1a *fr. name n.* (?a1200)
Trin.Hom. ROMA 58

nappen v. b *OE* (?a1200) Trin.Hom.
MANCPRO 1

narcotik n. *ML & OF* Chaucer KNT 2

narwe adj. 1d *OE* c1150 Hrl.MQuad.
LGW 7

narwe adv. 1a *OE* (?a1200) Lay.Brut
ANEL 8

natal adj. c *L* Chaucer TR 1

natif adj. a *OF & L* Chaucer TR 1

nativite n. 2c *OF & L* a1121
Peterb.Chron. MKT 6

natural adj. 2b *L & OF* (c1250) Gen.&
Ex. HF 38

naturalli adv. 2a *fr. natural adj.* c1275
Ken.Serm. Bo 15

nature n. 2b *L & OF* c1275 Ken.Serm.
ROMA 160

nave n. a *OE* a1325 Gloss.Bibbesw.
(Arun) SUMT 2

naveie n. a *AF* (?a1350) Siege Troy(1) Bo
1

navele n. 1a *OE* c1150 Hrl.HApul. KNT
1

navie n. 2a *OF* (a1338) Mannyng
Chron.Pt.2 HF 3

Nazarene n. & adj. c *L* ?c1200 Orm.
PARST 2

ne adv. 1a *OE & OF & L* a1121
Peterb.Chron. GENERAL 1247

ne conjɪ. 1a b *OE* a1121 Peterb.Chron.
GENERAL 1130

nece n. d *OF* c1300 Evang. TR 80

necessarie adj. e *L & OF* Chaucer Bo 30

necessarie n. a *L & OF* (c1340) Rolle
Psalter (UC 64) MLT 2

necessen v. *L* Chaucer Bo 1

necessite n. a *OF & L* Chaucer ROMA
96

necligence n. a *L & OF* (c1340) Rolle
Psalter (UC 64) ADAM 14

necligent adj. a *L & OF* Chaucer PF 8

necligentli adv. b *fr. necligent adj.*
(?1348) Rolle FLiving PARST 1

nede adv. b *OE* c1175 Bod.Hom. ROMA
17

nede nɪ. 3c *OE* a1121 Peterb.Chron.
ROMA 149

nedeful adj. 1a *fr. nede n1.* (c1200) Vices & V.(1) IntMLT 4

nedefulli adv. b *fr. nedeful adj.* (c1340) Rolle Psalter (UC 64) *TR* 3

nedeles adj. c *fr. nede n1.* c1300 SLeg.Becket (Ld) *ParsT* 2

nedeles adv. b *fr. nedeles adj.* (?c1200) St.Kath.(1) *TR* 5

nedeli adv2. a *fr. nede n1.* ?c1200 Wor.Bod.Gloss. Bo 6

neden v2. 2b *fr. nede n1. & LOE* ?c1200 Orm. RomA 103

nedes adv. b *fr. nede adv.* * 1131 Peterb.Chron. RomA 69

nedes-cost adv. *fr. nedes adv. & cost n1.* Chaucer *LGW* 1

nedi adj. 1b *fr. nede n1.* a1225 Lamb.Hom. Bo 11

nedle n. 1a *OE* a1200 Wor.Aelfric Gloss. RomA 3

neigh adj. 1a *OE* c1150 Wenne Wenne Bo 9

neigh adv. 5a *OE* c1175 Body & S.(1) RomA 77

neigh prep. 1b *OE* a1121 Peterb.Chron. BD 13

neighebor n. a *OE* a1121 Peterb.Chron. HF 54

neighen v1. 2a *OE* ?c1200 Orm. TR 2

neither conj. 1a *OE* c1150 PDidax. RomA 88

neither pron. a *OE* (c1250) Floris (Cmb) HF 8

nekke n. 1a a *OE* c1150 PDidax. RomA 44

nekke-bon n. a *fr. nekke n. & bon n1.* (?a1300) Arth.& M. NPT 3

Nembrot n. *L; ult. Heb.* (c1250) Gen.& Ex. *FormAge* 1

nemnen v. 2a *OE* (c1125) Vsp.D.Hom.Fest.Virg. MLT 4

Neptunus n. *L* Chaucer TR 4

ner adj. a *fr. ner adv2.* (c1300) Glo.Chron.A TR 2

ner adv2. 1a *OE* (?a1200) Lay.Brut RomA 23

ner prep. a *fr. ner adv2.* (?a1200) Lay.Brut LGW F 3

nerre adj. 1a *OE* ?c1200 Wor.Bod.Gloss. BD 6

nerre adv. 2b *OE & ON* ?c1200 Orm. RomA 8

nerve n. b *ML & CL* Chaucer TR 1

nest n. 1a *OE* (?a1200) Ancr. HF 6

net n1. 3 *OE* ?c1200 Orm. RomA 14

net n2. c *OE* a1121 Peterb.Chron. GP 1

net-herde n. a *fr. net n2. & herde n2.* (c1384) WBible(1) MEL 1

nethere adj. 1a *OE & ON* c1150 Hrl.MQuad. Bo 9

netle n. 1a *OE* c1150 Hrl.HApul. TR 2

neue adj. 1a *OE* a1121 Peterb.Chron. RomA 119

neue adv. 2b *fr. neue adj. & OE* (c1280) SLeg.Pass.(Pep) RomA 48

neue n. a *fr. neue adj.* (c1200) Vices & V.(1) MkT 13

neue-fangel adj. a *fr. neue adv. & <fangel adj.>* (c1250) Prov.Hend. SQT 2

neue-fangelnesse n. a *fr. neue-fangel adj.* Chaucer ANEL 4

Neue-gate n. *fr. neue adj. & gate n1.* Chaucer *CkT* 1

neuen v. 2c *OE* c1150 Hrl.HApul. BD 4

neuli adv. 3a *fr. neue adj.* (c1200) Vices & V.(1) RomA 3

nevenen v. 1a *ON* (c1250) Floris (Auch) HF 8

never adv. 1a *OE* a1121 Peterb.Chron. GENERAL 633

never-a-del n. & adv. a *fr. never adv. & a indef. art. & del n2.* (c1250) Gen.& Ex. *PardT* 1

never-mo adv. a *fr. never adv. & <mo adv.>* a1131 Peterb.Chron. Bo 8

never-more adv. a *fr. never adv. & <more adv.>* 1123 Peterb.Chron. LGW 2

never-the-les adv. *fr. never adv. & the*

def. art. & lesse adv. (a1325) Cursor LADY 5

never-the-mo adv. a *fr. never adv. & the def. art. & mo adv.* (?c1300) Guy(1) MERT 1

neveu n. 1f *OF* (a1250) Harrow.H. HF 5

Newe-Thought 5, neue adj. *(fr. neue adj. & thought n.)* Chaucer ROMA 1

nexte adj. 1c *OE* (?a1200) Ancr. HF 26

nexte adv. 2b *OE* (?a1200) Ancr. ROMA 14

nexte prep. 1a *OE* (c1200) Vices & V.(1) ROMA 34

nice adj. 1a *OF* c1300 SLeg.Magd.(2) (Ld) ROMA 46

niceli adv. e *fr. nice adj.* (a1338) Mannyng Chron.Pt.2 TR 1

nicete n. 4d *OF* (a1338) Mannyng Chron.Pt.2 ROMA 10

Nicholas n. b *OE (fr. L) & OF; ult Gr.* c1300 SLeg.Nich. (Hrl) MILT 41

nifle n. c *AF* Chaucer SUMT 1

nigard adj. a *fr. <nigard n.>* Chaucer ROMA 1

nigard n. a {a} *fr. ON* Chaucer {(c1384) WBible(1)} ROMA 5

nigardie n. a *fr. nigard n.* Chaucer FORT 2

night n. 1b a *OE* a1121 Peterb.Chron. ROMA 314

night-cappe n. 6a, night n. *fr. night n. & cappe n.* Chaucer MERT 1

nighten v. a *fr. night n.* (c1303) Mannyng HS PF 2

nighter-tale n. *ON* (c1300) Havelok GP 1

nightin-gale n. a *fr. <nighte-gale n.>* c1250 Owl & N. ROMA 15

night-spel n. 6d, night n. *(fr. night n. & spel n.)* Chaucer MILT 1

nigromancien n. *OF* (c1303) Mannyng HS PARST 1

nigromauncie n. b *OF & ML* (?a1300) Arth.& M. PARST 1

nillinge ger. *fr. willing ger.* Chaucer BO 2

nimen v. 1a c *OE* a1121 Peterb.Chron. ROMA 9

nimphe n. *L, fr. Gr.* Chaucer TR 2

nin num. 1a *OE* c1150 PDidax. PF 7

nintene num. b *OE* (?a1200) Lay.Brut LGW F 1

ninthe num. 1 *OE* c1175 HRood TR 3

ninti num. 1b *OE* (c1250) Gen.& Ex. PARST 1

no adj. 1b a *OE* a1131 Peterb.Chron. GENERAL 1429

no adv. 1a a *OE* a1121 Peterb.Chron. GENERAL 121

no conji. 2b a *fr. no adv.* a1121 Peterb.Chron. ROMA 31

no interj. b *fr. no adv.* (?a1200) Ancr. BD 33

noble adj. 1a *OF* (?a1200) Ancr. ROMA 150

noble n1. a *fr. noble adj.* (c1300) Glo.Chron. MERT 1

noble n2. a *fr. noble adj. & AF* (c1378) PPl.B (Ld) HF 7

nobleie n. 3a *OF* c1300 SLeg.Becket (Ld) SNT 7

nobleli adv. 2a *fr. noble adj.* c1300 SLeg.Edm.Abp. (Ld) BO 1

noblen v. *fr. noble adj* Chaucer SNPRO 1

noblesse n. 1a *OF* (?a1200) Ancr. ROMA 34

nodden v. a *?MLG* Chaucer MANCPRO 1

Noe n. a *L* (?a1200) Lay.Brut MILT 9

noious adj. b *fr. <anoious adj.>* (c1340) Rolle Psalter (UC 64) HF 2

noise n. 1f *OF* (?a1200) Ancr. ROMA 44

noisen v. 2c *OF & fr. noise n.* Chaucer BO 1

nokked adj. *fr. <nokke n.>* Chaucer ROMA 1

nombre n. 1e *AF & CF & L* c1300 SLeg.Edm.Abp. (Hrl) ROMA 57

nombren v. 1a *OF* (c1300) Glo.Chron.A BD 6

no-mo adj. *fr. no adv. & mo adj. & OE* (?a1200) Lay.Brut GP 1

no-mo adv. *fr. no adv. & mo adv.* a1225 Lamb.Hom. *SQT* 1

no-mo n. b *fr. no adj. & mo n. & OE* a1225 Trin.Hom.Creed SNT 7

no-more adj. a *fr. no adv. & more adj. comp.* c1150 PDidax. T*R* 6

no-more adv. a *fr. no adv. & more adv.* ?c1200 Orm. M*K*T 45

no-more n. a *fr. no adj. & more n3. & OE* c1175 HRood SNT 80

non adj. 1b a *OE* a1121 Peterb.Chron. G*ENERAL* 350

non adv1. a *fr. non adj.* a1200 Body & S.(2) L*ADY* 33

non n. d *OE (fr. L) & L & OF* ?a1160 Peterb.Chron. T*R* 16

non pron. 3b *OE* a1121 Peterb.Chron. G*ENERAL* 134

non-certain n. & adj. a *fr. non adj. & certain n. & adj.* (c1350) NHom.(2) PSanct. T*R* 2

nones n1. 1a *fr. to than anes phr.* ?c1200 Orm. R*O*MA 25

nonne n. 1a *OE (fr. L) & L & OF* a1121 Peterb.Chron. GP 4

nonnerie n. b *fr. nonne n.* (?c1280) SLeg.Concep.Virg. (Ashm) *RvT* 2

non-pouer n. a *OF* (c1378) PPl.B (Ld) *BO* 1

nor conj. c *fr. ne adv. & or conj.* (c1250) Floris (Suth) R*O*MA 60

Nor-folk n. a *OE* a1300 Hundreds Engl. GP 1

norice n. 1a *OF* (?a1200) Ancr. SNP*RO* 14

norishen v. 1a *fr. OF* c1300 SLeg.Inf.Chr. (Ld) B*O* 22

norishinge ger. 2a *(fr. norishen v.)* c1300 SLeg.Mich. (Ld) B*O* 13

norri n. a *OF* (?a1300) KAlex. B*O* 3

nortelrie n. *fr. norture n. by jocular distortion* Chaucer *RvT* 1

north adj. 1a *OE* a1131 Peterb.Chron. A*ST* 16

north adv. a *OE* a1126 Peterb.Chron. HF 11

north n. 1a *fr. north adj.* ?c1200 Orm. B*O* 13

northerne adj. 1a *OE* (?a1200) Lay.Brut *KNT* 1

North-humbre-lond n. a *fr. North-humbre n.* (?a1200) Lay.Brut *MLT* 2

north-north-west n. a *fr. north adv. & north-west n.* Chaucer *PF* 1

north-ward adv. a *fr. north n. & -ward suf.* c1300 SLeg.Brendan (Ld) HF 11

norture n. 2a *OF* (?a1300) Arth.& M R*O*MA 3

nose n1. 1a *OE* c1150 Hrl.HApul. R*O*MA 25

nose-thirl n. *fr. nose n1. & thirl n.* (?a1300) KAlex. GP 2

nos-kinnes adj. b *fr. no-kin adj. & nones-kinnes adj.* ?c1350 Why werre (Peterh) HF 1

not adj. a *OE* a1325 SLeg. (Corp-C) GP 1

not adv. 1a *fr. nought adv.* (c1250) Floris (Vit) G*ENERAL* 2303

not n. *(fr. nought n.)* Chaucer B*O* 2

nota interj. *L* Chaucer *AST* 5

notabilite n. a *OF & ML* (?c1350) SVrn.Leg. NPT 1

notable adj. 1a *OF* (1340) Rolle Psalter (UC 64) A*ST* 4

notarie n. b *OF & L* (c1303) Mannyng HS P*ARS*T 1

note n1. 4a *OE* ?c1125 Dur-C.Gloss. (Cokayne) R*O*MA 2

note n2. 1a *OE* (?a1200) Trin.Hom. *RvT* 1

note n3. 1b *OF & L* c1300 Lay.Brut (Otho) R*O*MA 18

noteful adj. *fr. note n2.* (a1325) Cursor B*O* 2

note-muge n. a *cp. ML & OF* (?a1300) KAlex. R*O*MA 2

noten v2. 1a *OF* (?a1200) Ancr. A*ST* 8

no-the-lesse adv. a *OE* a1150 Rwl.G.57.Gloss. R*O*MA 158

no-thing adv. 1a *fr. <no-thing pron.>* a1121 Peterb.Chron. R*O*MA 59

no-thing pron. 1d *OE* (?c1175) PMor. (Lamb) ROMA 115

notificacioun n. b *OF* Chaucer BO 1

notifien v. e *OF* Chaucer TR 4

notus n. a *L, fr. Gr.* Chaucer BO 2

not-with-stondinge prep. *cp. <not-with-stondinge adv.>* (?c1378) Wycl.OPastor VENUS 1

nou adv. 1a *OE* a1121 Peterb.Chron. GENERAL 1230

nou conj. *fr. nou adv.* c1175 Bod.Hom. BD 6

nou n. *fr. nou adv.* c1175 Bod.Hom. BD 17

nou-a-daies adv. a *fr. <nou-a-dai adv.> & <adaies adv.>* (a1376) PPl.A(1) (Trin-C) CLT 2

nouche n. *AF* Chaucer HF 3

nouel n1. 1 *OF* (?c1390) Gawain FRANT 1

nought adj. c *OE* (?c1200) St.Juliana LGW 1

nought adv. 1b *OE* a1121 Peterb.Chron. GENERAL 501

nought pron. 3a *OE* 1123 Peterb.Chron. GENERAL 139

nou-the adv. 1a *OE* (?c1175) PMor. (Lamb) TR 2

nouther conj. 1g *OE* a1121 Peterb.Chron. BD 7

novelrie n. a *OF* (c1303) Mannyng HS HF 3

novelte n. 1b *OF* (c1384) WBible(1) CLT 1

Novembre n. *L & OF* (?c1200) St.Kath.(1) AST 2

novice n. b *OF* (1340) Ayenb. PROMKT 1

no-wher adv. 3a *OE* c1175 HRood ROMA 22

o interj. a *L & OF* (?a1200) Lay.Brut ABC 299

o num. 2a a *fr. on num.* (?a1200) Trin.Hom. ROMA 195

o prep2. 2b a *fr. on prep.* a1131 Peterb.Chron. ROMA 31

obedience n. b *OF* (c1200) Vices & V.(1) PARST 4

obedient adj. 1a *OF* (?a1200) Ancr. HF 7

obeien v. 1b *OF* (?a1300) KAlex. ABC 35

obeisaunce n. {1a} *OF* Chaucer {(a1382) WBible(1)} PITY 18

obeisaunt adj. b *OF* (c1300) Glo.Chron.A BO 7

obeishen v. 2 *fr. OF* (a1338) Mannyng Chron.Pt.1 LGW 1

objecte adj. a *L* Chaucer BO 2

obligacioun n. a *OF & L* (c1300) Glo.Chron.A STED 3

obligen v. b *OF* (?c1280) SLeg.Concep.Virg. (Ashm) TR 4

obsequi n2. b *OF & L* Chaucer KNT 1

observaunce n. c *OF & L* a1250 Ancr. (Nero) ANEL 23

observen v. b *OF* Chaucer AST 5

obstacle n. c *OF & L* (c1340) Rolle Psalter (UC 64) KNT 3

obstinate adj. a *L & OF* (?1387) Wimbledon Serm. GP 1

occasioun n. 3c *OF & L* (a1382) WBible(1) (Bod 959) LGW 10

occean n. 1a *OF* c1300 SLeg.Brendan (Ld) BO 2

occident n. b *OF & L* Chaucer MKT 2

occidental adj. *OF & L* Chaucer AST 1

occupacioun n. 1a *OF* a1325 MS Rwl.B.520 lf.38b BO 3

occupien v. 9a a *OF & L* a1325 MS.Rwl.B.520 lf.80 PITY 10

october n. a *L & OF* a1121 Peterb.Chron. AST 2

octogamie n. *fr. L* Chaucer WBPRO 1

odde adj. 2 *ON* (c1280) SLeg.Pass. AST 1

odious adj. 2 *OF & L* (a1382) WBible(1) (Bod 959) SUMT 1

odour n. 2a *OF & L* (a1300) Cokaygne KNT 5

of adv. 1d *OE* a1121 Peterb.Chron. BD 36

of prep. 17a *OE* (1100) Chart.St.Paul in RHS ser.3.58 GENERAL 11382

ofcasten v. *fr. casten v.* Chaucer PF 1

offenden v. 1a *OF & L* (?1350–75) Origo Mundi in Norris Anc.Corn.Drama LADY 14

offense n. 1b *OF & L* (?1350–75) Origo Mundi in Norris Anc.Corn.Drama Bo 15

offensioun n. 1c *OF & L* Chaucer Bo 2

offertorie n. a *L* (c1350) NHom.(2) Corp.Chr. *GP* 1

office n. 1a *L & OF* (c1250) Gen.& Ex. MKT 35

officer n. 2a *OF* (a1338) Mannyng Chron.Pt.2 SNT 12

offren v. 3c *L & OF & OE, fr. L* a1121 Peterb.Chron. TR 13

offringe ger. 2d *OE* ?c1200 Orm. GP 5

of-shouven v. *fr. shouven v.* Chaucer *RVPRO* 1

ofspring n. 1a *OE* (?c1175) PMor. (Lamb) KNT 2

ofte adj. ofte-sithes adv. *fr. ofte adv* c1175 Bod.Hom. ROMA 46

ofte adv. a *OE* a1121 Peterb.Chron. GENERAL 218

often adj. often-time adv. *fr. often adv.* Chaucer SNPRO 8

often adv. *fr. ofte adv.* (c1250) Gen.& Ex. HF 28

ofte-time adv. *fr. ofte adv. & time n.* Chaucer TR 2

ofthaued ppl. *fr. thauen v.* Chaucer *HF* 1

oile n. 2a *CF & AF & L* (?a1200) Ancr. KNT 5

oinement n. 2a *OF* (c1280) SLeg.Pass. (Pep) GP 3

oinyon n. 3 *OF & L* (a1300) Cokaygne *GP* 1

oistre n. a *OF & L* (1364) Plea & Mem.R.Lond.Gildh. Bo 3

oke n. 1a *OE & ON* a1200 Wor.Aelfric Gloss. ROMA 17

olde adj. 3a *OE* a1121 Peterb.Chron. ROMA 306

olde n. 1a a *fr. olde adj.* a1150 Rwl.G.57 Gloss. MKT 7

olifaunt n. *OF* (?a1300) Arth.& M. *BO* 1

olive n. 1c *L & OF* (?a1200) Trin.Hom. *PF* 1

olivere n. a *OF* (?a1300) KAlex. ROMA 5

omelie n. *OF & ML; fr. Gr.* (a1387) Trev.Higd. *PARST* 1

omnipotente adj. b *OF & L* (?a1300) Guy(2) WBPRO 2

on adv1. 1a *OE* a1121 Peterb.Chron. ROMA 33

on adv2 d *OE* a1121 Peterb.Chron. *SQT* 1

on num. 3a *OE* a1121 Peterb.Chron. ROMA 89

on prep. 18a *OE* (1100) Chart.St.Paul in RHS ser.3.58 GENERAL 1151

on pron. 5b a *OE* a1121 Peterb.Chron. GENERAL 269

onde n1. b *OE* c1150 Hrl.HApul. *ROMA* 1

onen v. d *fr. on num.* (a1333) Shoreham Poems BO 3

ones adv. 4a *fr. OE* 1131 Peterb.Chron. ROMA 73

on-fire adj. 12b, fir n. *(fr. on prep. & fir n.)* (c1303) Mannyng HS TR 3

on-huntinge adv. b, huntinge ger. *(fr. on prep. & huntinge ger.)* (?c1225) Horn *BD* 1

oninge ger. 1a *(fr. onen v.)* (1340) Ayenb. *BO* 1

onli adj. 2b *OE* (c1200) Vices & V.(1) ROMA 73

onli adv. 1b a *fr. onli adj.* (c1280) SLeg.Pass. ROMA 115

on-live adv. 20a, on prep. *fr. on prep. & lif n.* * (?a1200) Lay.Brut LADY 6

on-lofte adv. 3b a, loft n. *fr. on prep. & lofte n.* * c1250 Seinte Mari moder HF 9

onward adv. a *fr. on adv.* Chaucer *KNT* 1

open adj. 1a e *OE* a1200 Body & S.(2) ROMA 28

open adv. a *fr. open adj.* (c1280) SLeg.Pass. (Pep) *SNT* 1

open-ars n. *fr. open adj. & ars n.* c1350 Cmb.Ee.4.20 Nominale *RVT* 1

openen v. 1f b *OE* c1150 Hrl.HApul.
ROMA 18
open-heded adj. *fr. open adj. & heden*
vi. Chaucer *WBPRO* 1
openinge ger. 5a *OE* (?a1200) Ancr.
ROMA 1
openli adv. 2a d *OE* a1121 Peterb.Chron.
ROMA 33
operacioun n. 1a *OF & L* Chaucer AST 6
opie n. a *L, fr. Gr.* Chaucer KNT 2
opinioun n. 1c *L & OF* (a1325) Cursor
HF 53
opportunite n. c *OF & L* Chaucer BO 2
opposen v. b *OF* Chaucer BO 2
opposicioun n. e *L & OF* Chaucer
FRANT 1
opposite adj. *OF* Chaucer AST 2
opposite n. 1a *OF* Chaucer KNT 4
oppressen v. 2a *OF* Chaucer SNPRO 11
oppressioun n. d *OF* (1334) RParl. TR 7
or conj. 1a b *fr. other conj. & outher conj.*
?c1200 Orm. GENERAL 2113
oracle n. a *L & OF* Chaucer *HF* 1
oratorie n. a *OF & L* (?a1325) ADAM &
E.(2) KNT 4
oratour n. a *L & OF* Chaucer BO 1
ord n. a *OE* a1200 Wor.Aelfric Gloss.
MKT 5
ordal n. a *OE* Chaucer *TR* 1
ordeinen v. 1c *OF & L* (c1250) Floris
(Suth) BO 34
ordeinour n. a *OF* c1300 SLeg.Dunstan
(Hrl) BO 2
ordene adj. c *OF* (a1338) Mannyng
Chron.Pt.2 BO 3
ordeneli adv. *fr. ordene adj.* (1340)
Ayenb. BO 1
ordinate adj. 2d *L* Chaucer BO 2
ordinatli adv. a *fr. ordinate adj.* (c1384)
WBible(1) *PARST* 1
ordinaunce n. 4 *OF* (?a1300) Arth.& M.
SNT 49
ordre n. 9a *OF* (?a1200) Ancr. ROMA 78
ordren v. 2 *fr. ordre v.* (?c1200) SWard
PARST 3

ordure n. a *OF* Chaucer BO 11
ore n1. a *OE* c1300 SLeg.Magd.(2) (Ld)
BO 2
ore n2. 4a *OE* c1175 Bod.Hom. *MILT*
1
ore n3. 1a *fr. OE & AF* (?a1200) Ancr.
WBT 1
orfrei n. pl. *OF* (c1250) Floris (Auch)
ROMA 3
organe n. 1a *OF & L* (?a1300) KAlex.
SNT 2
orientale adj. d *OF & L* Chaucer LGW
F 2
oriente n. c *OF* Chaucer MKT 5
originale adj1. 1e *OF & L* (a1325) MS
Rwl.B.520 65b *PARST* 3
originale n. f *OF & ML* (c1350)
NHom.(2) PSanct. LGW 2
orisonte n. 1a *OF & L & ML* Chaucer
TR 66
orisoun n. 1e *fr. OF* (?a1200) Ancr. SNT
17
orloge n. a *OF & L; ult. Gr.* (?a1375)
Abbey HG PF 2
orphelin n. b *OF* Chaucer BO 1
orpiment n. b *OF* (1392) *MS Wel.564
CYT 3
osanna interj. a *L; ult. Heb.* (a1325)
Cursor SNPRO 2
ote n. 2b *OE* a1126 Peterb.Chron. SUMT
2
oth n. 1a c *OE* a1121 Peterb.Chron. ANEL
35
other adj. 1a a *OE* a1121 Peterb.Chron.
GENERAL 497
other adv. 1a *fr. other pron.* a1121
Peterb.Chron. *TR* 1
other conj. 2c *OE* a1131 Peterb.Chron.
BD 12
other pron. 1b *OE* a1121 Peterb.Chron.
GENERAL 210
other-weies adv. a *fr. other adj. & wei n.*
(?a1200) Lay.Brut BO 10
other-while adv. a *OE* c1150 PDidax. BO
4

The making of Chaucer's English

other-wise adv. 1a a *fr. other adj. & wise n2.* ?c1200 Orm. PF 4

ou interj. ?*imitative* (c1250) Floris (Suth) BO 2

ouen adj. 2b c *OE* a1121 Peterb.Chron. GENERAL 238

ouen v. 1a c *OE* a1121 Peterb.Chron. ROMA 210

ought adv. 1a *OE* ?c1200 Orm. ROMA 26

ought pron. 1a *OE* c1150 Hrl.MQuad. ROMA 55

oul n. a *OE* a1200 Wor.Aelfric Gloss. SUMT 1

oule n. 1a *OE* a1200 Wor.Aelfric Gloss. PF 8

ounce n. 1a *OF & L & OE* c1150 Hrl.HApul. ROMA 13

ounde adj. c *AF* Chaucer HF 1

ounded adj. c *fr. ounde adj.* Chaucer TR 1

oundinge ger. *cp. ounde adj. & ounded adj.* Chaucer PARST 1

oure pron. 4a *OE* a1121 Peterb.Chron. GENERAL 586

oures pron. 1c *fr. oure pron.* (c1303) Mannyng HS PARDT 2

oure-self pron. 1a *fr. oure pron. & self adj., n. & pron.* (a1325) Cursor BO 2

ournement n. 1a *OF* (?a1200) Ancr. LGW 1

outbreken v. 1 *fr. breken v.* (c1300) Glo.Chron.A PITY 1

outcasten v. 1a *fr. casten v.* (c1280) SLeg.Pass. (Pep) BO 5

oute adv. 1b a *OE* a1121 Peterb.Chron. GENERAL 588

oute interj. c *fr. oute adv. & outen v.* (c1174) Wace Roman de Rou MILT 4

outen v. 2c *OE* (c1250) PROV.Hend. TR 5

outfliinge ger. *(fr. outflien v.)* Chaucer HF 1

outher adj. b *OE* (1303) Mannyng HS KNT 2

outher conj. 1b *OE* a1121 Peterb.Chron. ROMA 36

outhes n. ? *fr. LOE* c1250 Owl & N. KNT 1

outlaue n. a *OE* a1121 Peterb.Chron. MANCT 3

outlondish adj. <*fr. outlond n.*> c1300 Horn FORMAGE 1

outrage n. 2b *OF* c1300 SLeg.Kenelm (Ld) ROMA 19

outrageous adj. 1 *OF* (c1300) NHom.(1) Abp.& N. ROMA 18

outrageousli adv. a *fr. outrageous adj.* (c1340) Rolle Psalter (UC 64) RVT 1

outraien v. 2d ?*AF* (?a1300) Rich. (Auch) BO 2

outraious adj. b *fr.* <*outrai n.*> & *AF* Chaucer BO 1

outraunce n2. b *OF* Chaucer WOMNOB 1

outre adj. comp. 1a a *fr. oute adj. & OE* (?a1200) Ancr. SNT 2

outreli adv. 1a *fr. outre adj. comp.* ?c1200 Orm. BD 46

outreste adj. sup. 2a *fr. outre adj. comp.* (c1200) Vices & V.(1) BO 11

outridere n. a *fr. ridere n.* (?a1387) PPl.C (Hnt) GP 1

outtaken prep. 1a *fr* <*outtaken v.*> (a1325) Cursor ROMA 2

outwarde adj. 1a *OE* c1150 Hrl.HApul. CLT 4

outwarde adv. 3b *OE* (?a1200) Ancr. ROMA 11

oven n. 1a *OE* a1200 Wor.Aelfric Gloss. PARST 1

over adv. 2b *OE* a1121 Peterb.Chron. BD 30

over prep. 3a *OE* (1100) Chart.St.Paul in RHS ser.3.58 GENERAL 155

over-al adv. 1a *OE* a1126 Peterb.Chron. ROMA 20

overbiden v. a *OE* a1121 Peterb.Chron. WBT 1

overblouen v. b *fr. blouen v1.* Chaucer LGW 1

Chaucer's words

overbord adv. *fr. bord n.* (?a1300)
Tristrem *LGW* 1

overcasten v. 3d *fr. casten v.* (?a1200)
Ancr. *KnT* 1

overcomen v. 1a *OE* a1121 Peterb.Chron.
RomA 39

overcomere n. a *fr. overcomen v.* (?1348)
Rolle FLiving *Bo* 2

overdon v. 1c *OE* c1175 Bod.Hom.
CYPro 1

overest adj. a *fr. over adv.* (a1382)
WBible(1) (Bod 959) *GP* 1

overgilden v. a *OE* ?c1200 Orm. *RomA* 1

overgon v. 5a *OE* a1121 Peterb.Chron. *Bo*
3

overgret adj. *fr. gret adj., adv. & n.*
Chaucer *RomA* 5

overhard adj. b *fr. hard adj.* (c1303)
Mannyng HS *Mel* 1

overhaste n. *fr. haste n.* Chaucer *Tr* 1

overhasteli adv. *fr. hastelie adv.* Chaucer
Mel 1

overheighe adv. c *fr. heighe adv.* c1225
Ancr. (Tit) *Bo* 1

overhot adj. b *fr. hot adj.* (1392) *MS
Wel.564 *CYT* 1

overistraued ppl. *fr. streuen v.* Chaucer
Bo 1

overkerven v. *fr. kerven v.* Chaucer *Ast* 3

overladen v. *fr. laden v.* Chaucer *LGW* 1

overlarge adj. b *fr. large adj.* Chaucer
Mel 1

overlargeli adv. b *fr. largelie adv.*
Chaucer *Mel* 1

overleden v. 1a *fr. leden v1.* (?a1200)
Ancr. *ProMkT* 1

overlien v. b *fr. lien v1.* a1225
Lamb.Hom. *ParsT* 1

overlight adj. a *fr. light adj2.* Chaucer
Bo 1

over-lippe n. 1b, over adj. *(fr. over adj. &
lippe n.)* a1325 Gloss.Bibbesw. (Arun)
GP 1

overloken v. a *fr. loken v2.* Chaucer *BD*
1

overlonge adv. *fr. long adj1.* c1250 Owl
& N. HF 2

overloue adv. a *fr. loue adv.* Chaucer *Bo*
2

overmacchen v. b *fr. macchen v.* a1375
WPal. *MerPro* 1

overmuche adv. *fr. muche adv.* (c1303)
Mannyng HS HF 2

overmuchel adj. *fr. muchel adj.* (c1303)
Mannyng HS *Mel* 2

overmuchel adv. *fr. <muchel adv.>*
(?c1150) Prov.Alf. (Trin-C) *Bo* 4

overnight adv. *fr. night n.* (c1303)
Mannyng HS *Tr* 1

overold adj. *fr. olde adj.* Chaucer *Bo* 1

overpassen v. 1a a *fr. passen v.* (c1300)
Glo.Chron.A *Bo* 2

overrechen v. 1a *fr. rechen v1.* (a1325)
Cursor *Tr* 1

overriden v. 1a *OE* c1300 SLeg. (Ld)
KnT 1

overshaken v. b *fr. shaken v.* (?c1300)
St.Patr.Purg.(1) *PF* 3

oversheten v. b *fr. sheten v.* Chaucer *BD*
1

overskippen v. a *fr. skippen v.* Chaucer
BD 1

oversloppe n. *OE* Chaucer *CYPro* 1

overspreden v. 1b *OE* (?a1200) Lay.Brut
Tr 5

overspringen v. *fr. springen v.* Chaucer
FranT 1

overstrecchen v. a *fr. strecchen v.*
Chaucer *Bo* 1

overswift adj. a *fr. swifte adj.* Chaucer
Bo 1

overswimmen v. *fr. swimmen v.* Chaucer
Bo 1

overt adj. a *fr. OF* c1330 Degare *HF* 1

overtaken v. 5c *fr. taken v.* (?c1200)
St.Juliana *BD* 2

overthrouen v. 1a *fr. throuen v1.* (?a1300)
Arth.& M. *MkT* 9

overthrouinge ger. a *(fr. overthrouen v.)*
(?a1300) Arth.& M. *Bo* 3

343

The making of Chaucer's English

overthrouinge ppl. a *fr. overthrouen v.*
Chaucer BO 5
overthwert adj. 1c *fr. thwert adj.* (c1303)
Mannyng HS *BD* 1
overthwert adv. 1a *fr. thwert adv.* (c1300)
Havelok ROMA 3
overthwert prep. *fr. thwert prep.* c1380
Firumb.(1) *AST* 3
overtimeli adv. *fr. timeli adv.* (1303)
Mannyng HS *BO* 1
overturnen v. 3b *fr. turnen v.* (?a1200)
Ancr. *BO* 1
overwhelven v. 1a *fr. whelven v.* Chaucer
BO 1
o-wher adv. a *OE* a1121 Peterb.Chron.
BD 6
oxe n. 1a a *OE* ?c1200 Orm. M KT 12
Oxenford 5b, oxe n. *OE* (c1190)
EPNSoc.23 (Oxf) GP 10
oxe-stal n. *fr. oxe n. & stalle n.* c1250 Of
one stable *CLT* 1
p n. a *no etym.* Chaucer *BO* 1
pacience n. 1a *OF & L* (?a1200) Ancr. PF
58
paciente adj. a *OF* c1350 Apoc. in LuSE
29 TR 21
paciente n. 1a *OF* Chaucer TR 4
pacientli adv. a *fr. paciente adj.* (c1350)
NHom.(2) PSanct. MARS 13
page n1. 1c *OF* c1300 Horn (Ld) K NT 13
paie n. b *OF* c1300 Body & S.(5) PF 3
paiement n. c *OF* ?c1375 NHom.(3) Pass.
WBPRO 2
paien adj. *OF* (?c1225) Horn *K NT* 1
paien n. a *OF* (?c1225) Horn TR 7
paien v. 1a *OF* (?a1200) Ancr. BD 46
paillet n. a *AF* Chaucer TR 1
pain-demeine n. *AF* Chaucer *THOP* 1
paire n1. 1a f *OF & ML* (c1250) Floris
(Cmb) ROMA 17
pake n. 1b *cp. MDu., MLG & OI*
(?a1200) Ancr. *LGW G* 1
palais n. 1b *OF & L* (?c1225) Horn ABC
44
palais-chaumbre n. 1e, palais n. *(fr. palais*

n. *& chaumbre n.)* Chaucer FORMAGE
1
palais-wal n. *(fr. palais n. & wal n1.)*
MED Suppl. *HF* 1
palais-ward n. *(fr. palais n. & -ward*
suf.) MED Suppl. TR 1
pale adj. 2a *OF* (a1325) Cursor ROMA 53
pale adv. *fr. pale adj.* Chaucer LGW 2
pale n. 1a *L & OF* a1200 Wor.Aelfric
Gloss. *HF* 1
palefrei n. a *OF & ML* (?a1200)
Trin.Hom. K NT 5
palen v3. b *OF* Chaucer *BO* 1
palesie n. a *fr. OF* c1300 SLeg.Jas. (Ld)
ROMA 1
palestral adj. *fr. <palestre n.>* Chaucer
TR 1
palinge ger2. b *(fr. pallen v2.)* Chaucer
PARST 1
palis n. a *OF & ML* (?c1350) Ywain BO
4
Palladion n. *OF & L* Chaucer TR 3
pallen v1. b *fr. <apallen v.>* ?a1325 Elde
makith me MANCPRO 1
palme n. b *OE (fr. L) & OF & L* a1200
Wor.Aelfric Gloss. SNT 3
palmere n. a *AF & CF* (?c1225) Horn GP
1
palpable adj. b *L & OF* Chaucer *HF* 1
Pan n. *L, fr. Gr.* Chaucer *BD* 1
panade n. *prob. AL or AF* Chaucer *RVT*
2
pandare n. b *It.* Chaucer TR 191
paniere n. a *OF* (c1300) Havelok HF 2
pannage n. a *AF* Chaucer FORMAGE 1
panne n1. 1a *OE* c1150 Hrl.MQuad.
K NT 10
papejaie n. a *OF & ML; ult. Ar.* c1325
Ichot a burde in a ROMA 6
papire n. a *OF & L* (?c1380) Cleanness
TR 4
papir-whit adj. b, papire n. *(fr. papire n.*
& whit adj.) Chaucer LGW 1
par prep. b *OF & L* (a1250) Harrow.H.
LGW 14

parable n. b *OF & L; fr. Gr.* c1250
Serm.St.Nich. *WBPRO* 2

paradise n. 1a *OF & L* a1200
Annot.Cld.OT *ROMA* 33

parage n. 1a *OF* c1250 *Body & S.(4)
WBPRO* 2

parais n. a *OF* (?a1200) Ancr. *ROMA* 1

par amoure adv. phr. b *AF* (c1250)
Floris (Vit) *TR* 7

paramoure n. 1d *fr. par amoure adv. phr.*
(a1325) Cursor *TR* 10

paraventure adv. 1a *OF* c1300
SLeg.Becket (Ld) BD 63

Parcas n. pl. *L* Chaucer *TR* 1

parcel n. 1a i *OF & ML* (c1303)
Mannyng HS *PITY* 5

parcener n. a *OF* (c1300) Glo.Chron.A
BO 1

parchemin n. c *OF & ML* (c1250) Floris
(Suth) *BO* 2

parde interj. a *OF* (c1250) Floris (Suth)
BD 76

pardoner n. a *OF* (a1376)) PPl.A (Trin-
C) HF 14

pardoun n. 1b *OF & ML* c1300
SLeg.Becket (Ld) GP 7

paregal adj. a *OF* (a1325) Cursor *TR* 1

parementes n. pl. b *OF & ML* Chaucer
KNT 3

parentele n. b *OF* Chaucer *PARST* 1

par fei interj. a *AF & CF* c1300
SLeg.John (Ld) HF 8

parfit adj. 6a *OF & L* c1300
SLeg.Fran.(1) (Ld) *PITY* 69

parfitli adv. 2a *fr. parfit adj.* (c1303)
Mannyng HS *ROMA* 13

Paris n1. a *OF* Chaucer *ROMA* 6

parishe n. b *OF* c1300 SLeg.Becket (Ld)
GP 11

parishen n1. *OF* (?a1200) Ancr. *GP* 2

park n. 1e *OF* a1300 Chart. in Birch
Cart.Sax. PF 3

parlemente n. 2b *fr. OF & ML* c1300
SLeg.Becket (Ld) *TR* 14

parlour n. 2b *OF* (?a1200) Ancr. *TR* 1

Parnaso n. *It.* Chaucer HF 4

parodie n. a *fr. OF or ML* Chaucer *TR* 1

part n. 1a c *OF* (c1250) Floris (Cmb)
LADY 67

parten v. 5b *OF* (?a1200) Ancr. BO 14

partenere n. 1a *fr. parcener n. & part n.*
c1300 SLeg. (Hrl) *PARST* 1

Parthes n. pl. *L, fr. Gr.* (a1325)
Glo.Chron.B BO 2

participacioun n. *OF & L* Chaucer *BO* 3

particuler adj. a *L & OF* (a1387)
Trev.Higd. CLPRO 2

partie adj. a *fr. OF* Chaucer *KNT* 1

partie n. 1b *OF* c1300 SLeg.Brendan
(Ld) PF 84

partinge ger. c *(fr. parten v.)* (c1250)
Floris (Cmb) *TR* 2

partles adj. a *fr. part n.* (1340) Rolle
Psalter (UC 64) *BO* 1

partriche n. a *OF* c1300 SLeg.John (Ld)
HF 2

parvise n. a *OF* Chaucer *GP* 1

pase n1. 3g *OF & L* (c1280) SLeg.Pass.
(Pep) *ROMA* 32

passage n. 3a *OF & ML* (?c1225) Horn.
ROMA 2

passaunt adj. a *OF* (?c1300) Bevis *KNT* 1

passed ppl. adj. a *fr. passen v.* (a1325)
Cursor BO 5

passen v. 6c *OF* (?a1200) Ancr. *ROMA*
191

passinge ppl. adj. 1a *(fr. passen v.)*
(a1338) Mannyng Chron.Pt.1 MERPRO
2

passioun n. 1a *OF & L* (?a1200) Ancr.
ABC 28

paste n2. a *OF* (a1300) Cokaygne *CKPRO*
1

pasture n. 1a *OF & L* (?a1300) KAlex.
MERT 4

patente n1. d *fr. <patente adj.>* (a1376)
PPl.A(1) (Trin-C) GP 2

pater n. *L* (?c1300) LFMass Bk. SUMT 5

pater-noster n. 1a *ML & OF* c1175
Bod.Hom. *MILT* 2

path n. ıc *OE* (?cıı75) PMor.(Trin-C) RomA 17

patriarke n. a *OF & L, fr. Gr.* cı200 Wor.Serm. in EGst.7 *PardPro* ı

patrimoine n. b *OF & L* (1340) Ayenb. *ParsT* ı

patrone n. a *OF & ML* Chaucer *BD* ı

patroun n. ıb *OF & ML* cı300 SLeg.Becket (Hrl) Anel 2

paue n. a *OF* (?aı300) Arth.& M. *HF* ı

paume n. ıa *OF* cı300 SLeg.Edm.Abp. (Hrl) *TR* ı

paunche n. a *OF* (1373) *Lelamour Macer *PF* ı

paunter n. b *OF* cı300 SLeg.Mich. (Ld) RomA 2

pavement n. a *OF & L* (cı250) Floris (Vit) IntMLT 4

paven v. b *OF* cı325 Flem.Insur. RomA 3

pax n. b *ML* (?cı300) LFMass Bk *ParsT* ı

pece n. 8 *OF & ML* (?aı200) Ancr. HF 7

peche n. a {b} *OF & ML* Chaucer {aı400 Lanfranc} *RomA* ı

pecuniale adj. *L & OF* Chaucer *FrT* ı

Pegase n. a *L* Chaucer *SqT* ı

peine n. 2c *OF* (cı280) SLeg.Pass. (Pep) RomA 252

peinen v. 5b *fr. OF & peine n.* (?cı300) Guy(ı) RomA 22

peinten v. ıc *OF* cı250 Owl & N. RomA 51

peintinge ger. c *(fr. peinten v.)* (?aı200) Ancr. *RomA* 2

peintour nı. ıa *OF* aı325 SLeg. (Corp-C) *TR* ı

peinture n. b *OF* (?aı200) Ancr. RomA 2

peitrel nı. a *OF* (?aı325) Otuel & R. CyPro 2

pekke n. 2a *ML* (1381) Doc. in Morsbach Origurk *RvT* ı

pekken v. c *cp. piken* vı. *& MLG* (?aı300) Rich. (Auch) *NPT* ı

pel nı. c *OF* (cı303) Mannyng HS *HF* ı

pelote n. b *OF & ML* Chaucer *HF* ı

penaunce n. 2a *AF & CF* (cı280) SLeg.Pass. (Pep) ABC 58

penaunte n. a *OF* (aı325) Cursor *ProMkT* ı

pencel nı. a *OF* cı300 Lay.Brut (Otho) *TR* ı

pencel n2. *OF & ML* (cı325) Recipe Painting(ı) in Archaeol.J.ı *KnT* ı

peni n. ıa *OE* aıı2ı Peterb.Chron. RomA 18

penible adj. a *OF, AF* Chaucer MkT 3

penitence n. a *OF & L* (?aı200) Trin.Hom. ABC 46

penitencere n. *OF* (?aı375) Abbey HG *ParsT* ı

penitent n. ıa *fr. penitente adj.* Chaucer ABC 3

penitente adj. a *L & OF* (1341) Doc. in HMC Rep.9 App.ı ABC 4

penne n. 3c *L & OF* (?cı280) SLeg.Advent, etc. (Eg) TR 4

penner n. *L* (cı395) WBible(2) *MerT* ı

penoun n. a *OF* cı380 Firumb.(ı) *KnT* ı

peple n. 5a *OF, AF* (cı280) SLeg.Pass. (Pep) RomA 169

peplish adj. *fr. peple n.* Chaucer *TR* ı

per n. ıb *OF, AF* (cı250) Floris (Suth) RomA 10

perceiven v. ıb *AF* (cı300) NHom.(ı) Martin AM *AsT* ı

percen v. ıa b *OF, AF* (cı300) Glo.Chron.A PF 15

perche n2. ıa *OF* cı300 SLeg.Chris. (Ld) RomA 5

perchen v. a *OF* Chaucer *HF* ı

percinge ger. a *(fr. percen v.)* (cı385) Usk TL (Skeat) *Thop* ı

perdurable adj. b *OF & ML* Chaucer Bo 26

perdurablete n. *OF* Chaucer *Bo* 2

perdurabli adv. *fr. <perdurable adj.>* cı275 Ken.Serm. *Bo* 4

pere nı. ıa *OE* cı300 SLeg.Becket (Ld) RomA 3

peregrine adj. *OF* Chaucer *SqT* ı

pere-jonette n. *fr. pere n1. & <jonette n.>* (?a1387) PPl.C (Hnt) *MILT* 1

perfeccioun n. 1d *OF & L* (?a1200) Ancr. *BO* 15

performen v. 2b *AF & CF* c1300 SLeg.Inf.Chr. (Ld) *ROMA* 47

performinge ger. b *(fr. performen v.)* Chaucer *PARST* 1

peril n. 2a *OF* (?a1200) Ancr. *BO* 61

perilous adj. 1a *OF* c1300 SLeg.Patr.(Ld) *ROMA* 22

perilousli adv. a *fr. perilous adj. & <perilous adv.>* (1340) Ayenb. *MEL* 1

perishen v. 1b *fr. OF* c1275 Ken.Serm. *BO* 8

peritorie n. *ML & AF* (1373) *Lelamour Macer *CYPRO* 1

perle n2. 3b *OF & ML* (1340) Ayenb. *MKT* 6

perled adj. a *fr. perle n.* Chaucer *MILT* 1

permutacioun n. a *OF & L* (a1376) PPl.A(1) (Trin-C) *TR* 2

perpendiculere adj. & adv. b *OF* Chaucer *AST* 2

perpetuelle adj. & adv. 1a *OF & L* (c1340) Rolle Psalter (UC 64) *BO* 7

perpetuelli adv. a *fr. perpetuelle adj. & adv.* Chaucer *SNT* 9

perrie n. a *AF* a1300 Hrl.978 Vocab. *MKT* 8

perse n1. & adj. b *OF* Chaucer *ROMA* 3

Perse n2. a *OE (fr. L) & L & OF* c1150 Hrl.HApul. *MKT* 1

persecucioun n. a *OF & L* (c1340) Rolle Psalter *SUMT* 1

perseli n. b *OF, AF & OE, fr. ML* a1300 Hrl.978 Vocab. *CKPRO* 1

Perses n. pl. *OF & L* Chaucer *MKT* 1

perseveraunce n1. 2a *OF & L* (1340) Ayenb. *BD* 4

perseveren v. a *OF & L* Chaucer *TR* 6

perseveringe ger. *(fr. perseveren v.)* Chaucer *SNPRO* 1

Persien n. *OF* (?a1300) KAlex. *MKT* 4

persoune n1. 1a *OF & L* (?a1200) Ancr. *SNT* 59

persoune n2. 1 *(fr. persoune n1.)* c1250 LSSerm. *GP* 11

perspectif n. a *ML* (a1387) Trev.Higd. *SQT* 1

persuasioun n. *OF & L* Chaucer *HF* 1

perte adj. 1 *fr. <apert adj.>* (c1250) Gen.& Ex. *RVT* 1

pertinacie n. *L* (c1385) Usk TL (Skeat) *PARST* 2

pertinent adj. 2c *OF & L* Chaucer *MEL* 1

perturbacioun n. a *OF & L* Chaucer *BO* 5

perturben v. a *OF & L* Chaucer *TR* 2

perturbinge ger. b *(fr. perturben v.)* Chaucer *SUMT* 1

perverse adj. a *OF & L* Chaucer *BD* 1

perverten v. 1b *OF & L* Chaucer *BO* 4

pervinke n. a *OE, fr. L* (?c1300) St.Patr.Purg.(1) *ROMA* 2

pes interj. *fr. pesen v. & pes n.* (?a1300) KAlex. *PF* 12

pes n. 5b c *OF* ?a1160 Peterb.Chron. *ABC* 84

pese n. 1a *OE* c1150 Hrl.HApul. *LGW* 1

pesible adj. 1a *OF* (a1338) Mannyng Chron.Pt.1 *BO* 4

pestilence n. 1a *OF & L* (c1303) Mannyng HS *BO* 13

Peter n. 1a *OE & L; ult. Gr.* a1121 Peterb.Chron. *HF* 18

peticioun n. 1a *OF & L* (a1338) Mannyng Chron.Pt.2 *LGW G* 1

petre n. sal-petre n. *(fr. sal-petre n.)* c1330 SMChron. *CYT* 1

Pharao n. *L; ult. Heb.* c1175 HRood *BD* 4

phares n. *L, fr. Gr; ult. Aram.* Chaucer *MKT* 2

pharise n. a *L & OE* ?c1200 Orm. *PARST* 1

Phebus n. a *L, fr. Gr.* Chaucer *MKT* 59

Philistienes n. pl. *L* (a1325) Cursor *MKT* 1

philologie n. *L, fr. Gr.* Chaucer *MERT* 1
philomene n. a *ML* Chaucer *LGW* 3
philosophical adj. a *fr. philosophe n.*
Chaucer *TR* 1
philosophie n. a *OF & L* (c1300)
Glo.Chron.A HF 39
philosophre n. a *fr. OF & L* c1330
SMChron. SNPRO 40
phisicien n. b *OF* (?a1200) Ancr. BD 12
phisike n. 1e *OF & L* (c1300)
Glo.Chron.A BO 9
Phisiologus n. *L* Chaucer *NPT* 1
phislias n. *?fr. phisike n.* Chaucer
EPIMLT 1
phitonesse n. *OF & ML* Chaucer HF 2
Phitoun n. *L* Chaucer *MANCT* 2
picchen v. 1a *OE* (?a1200) Lay.Brut ABC
2
piche n1. 1d *OE (fr. L) & L & OF, AF*
c1150 PDidax. *MILT* 2
pie n1. a *OF* c1250 Owl & N. HF 9
pie n2. a *ML* (1376) PPl.A (Trin-C) *GP* 1
Pierides n. pl. *L* Chaucer *INTMLT* 1
piete n. a *OF* c1325 Nou skrynketh *TR* 4
pigge n. a *?OE* a1250 Ancr. (Nero) GP 3
pigges-nie n. *fr. pigge n. & eie n1.*
Chaucer *MILT* 1
pike n2. a *prob. fr. pike n1.* 1381 Pegge
Cook.Recipes *TR* 3
piken v1. 2 *OE & ON* c1225 Ancr. (Tit)
TR 5
piken v2. *? fr. MDu.* Chaucer *TR* 1
pike-purs n. 8c, piken v1. *fr. piken v. &*
purs n. * Chaucer *KNT* 1
pikerel n. b *fr. pike n2.* Chaucer *MERT* 1
Pilate n. *L* a1250 Creed (Blickling)
MILPRO 1
pilche n. e *fr. OE* (?a1200) Ancr. *PROV* 1
pilen v1. 3a *OE (fr. L) & OF & ML*
(?a1200) Ancr. LGW 8
pilere n. 1a *OF & ML* ?c1200
Wor.Bod.Gloss. BD 18
pilgrim n. 1b *OF* (c1200) Vices & V.(1)
HF 6

pilgrimage n. 1b *OF* c1275 Ken.Serm.
HF 13
pilour n1. a *OF & pilen v1.* (c1333–52)
Minot Poems KNT 3
pilwe n. b *OE (fr. L) & L* c1150
Hrl.MQuad. BD 4
pilwe-beer n. g, pilwe n. *(fr. pilwe n. &*
bere n3.) Chaucer *GP* 1
piment n. c *OF & L* 1150 PDidax. BO 2
pin n. 4a *OE, fr. L* a1200 Gloss.Sidonius
GP 16
pinacle n. c *fr. OF & L* (?c1300) Guy(1)
HF 3
pinchen v. 2d *OF* c1230 Ancr. (Corp-C)
FORT 4
pine n1. a *prob. OE* (c1125)
Vsp.D.Hom.Elucid. MKT 21
pine n2. a *fr. OE & OF & L* c1150
Hrl.HApul. *ROMA* 2
pinen v. 1c *OE* (c1125)
Vsp.D.Hom.Elucid. ANEL 4
pine-tree n. a, pine n2. *(fr. pine n2. & tre*
n.) c1150 Hrl.HApul. *ROMA* 3
pipe n1. 3a *OE, fr. L* a1200 Wor.Aelfric
Gloss. HF 7
pipen v. c *OE* c1250 Owl & N. HF 8
pipere n. a *OE* a1200 Wor.Aelfric Gloss.
HF 2
pirie n. a *OE, prob. fr. ML* (?a1300)
KAlex. *MERT* 3
Pisces n. *L* Chaucer AST 10
pisse n. *fr. pissen v.* (a1387) Trev.Higd.
WBPRO 2
pisse-mire n. a *fr. <pisse n.> & mire n2.*
(?c1350) Mirror St.Edm.(4) *SUMT* 1
pissen v. a *OF* c1300 SLeg.Jas. (Ld) MILT
5
pit n. 2a *OE & MDu.* c1175 HRood HF
9
pitaunce n. a *OF & ML* (?a1200) Ancr.
GP 1
pite n. 1b *OF* a1250 Ancr. (Nero) *ROMA*
122
pithe n. 1a *OE* c1150 PDidax. *ROMA* 2

pitous adj. 1a *OF* c1300 SLeg.Magd.(2) (Ld) RomA 56

pitousli adv. b *fr. pitous adj.* c1300 SLeg.Becket (Hrl) RomA 53

place n. 1a *OF & ML* (?a1200) Ancr. RomA 329

placebo n. 1a *L* (?a1200) Ancr. SumT 2

plage n1. 1a *L* (a1382) WBible(1) (Bod 959) AST 3

plaine adj. 1b b *OF* (?a1300) KAlex. RomA 19

plaine adv. 2a *fr. plaine adj.* (a1325) Cursor RomA 11

plaine n. 1c *OF* (c1300) Glo.Chron.A RomA 5

plainlie adv. 1d *fr. plaine adj.* (?a1350) 7 Sages(2) Bo 13

plainnes n. b *fr. plaine adj.* (?a1300) Guy(2) Bo 1

plane n1. *OF* Chaucer {(a1382) WBible(1)} RomA 2

planen v1. 3 *fr. <plane n2.> & OF & L* (a1325) Cursor SumT 1

planete n1. 1a *OF & L* c1300 SLeg.Mich. (Ld) BD 60

planteine n. 1a *OF, AF* a1300 Hrl.978 Vocab. CYPRo 1

plastre n. 1a *OE (fr. ML) & OF* c1150 Hrl.HApul. SQT 1

plat adj. a *OF* (?a1300) KAlex. KnT 2

plat adv. 1a *fr. plat adj.* (c1280) SLeg.Pass. (Pep) MkT 6

plat n. a *OF* Chaucer SQT 1

plate n. 4a *OF & ML* c1250 Judas KnT 13

platen v. *OF* Chaucer HF 1

platlie adv. a *fr. plat adj.* Chaucer TR 5

plaunte n1. 1b {1a} *OE (fr. L) & L* Chaucer {(a1376) PPl.A(1) (Trin-C)} RomA 4

plaunten v. 1b *OE (fr. L) & OF & L* ?a1160 Peterb.Chron. Bo 6

ple n. a *OF* c1250 Owl & N. PF 2

pleden v. a *OF* c1250 Owl & N. MEL 1

pledinge ger. *(fr. pleden v.)* c1250 Owl & N. BD 3

pledour n. a *fr. pleden v. & OF* ?a1300 Sayings St.Bede RomA 1

plegge n1. a *OF & ML* (1348) Doc. in Welch Hist.Pewterers Lond. MEL 1

pleie n. 1c *OE* (?a1200) Trin.Hom. RomA 37

pleien v1. 1a a *OE* (c1200) Vices & V.(1) RomA 145

pleiinge ger. 1a *fr. pleien v1* (?c1225) Horn RomA 9

plein adv. *fr. pleine adj.* (a1338) Mannyng Chron.Pt.1 KnT 3

pleine adj. 1c *OF & L* (?a1300) Rich. (Auch) ABC 10

pleinen v. 4b *OF* c1230 Ancr. (Corp-C) RomA 90

pleininge ger. a *(fr. pleinen v.)* c1300 SLeg.Inf.Chr. (Ld) BD 3

pleinli adv. b *fr. pleine adj.* Chaucer PF 18

pleinte n. 1a *OF* (?a1200) Ancr. PITY 20

pleinten v1. a *fr. pleinte n.* a1325 SLeg. (Corp-C) TR 1

pleiten v. c *fr. <pleit n.>* c1330 Le Freine Bo 3

plenere adv. *AF & CF* (a1325) Cursor LGW 1

plente n. 1b *OF* a1250 Ancr. (Nero) RomA 21

plentevous adj. e *OF* (c1300) Glo.Chron.A Bo 9

plentevousli adv. d *fr. plentevous adj.* (1340) Ayenb. Bo 4

plesaunce n1. 1a *OF* c1350 MPPsalter BD 96

plesaunte adj. 1b *OF* c1350 MPPsalter RomA 12

plesen v. 1a *OF* (c1303) Mannyng HS RomA 52

plesinge ger. c *(fr. plesen v.)* (a1376) PPl.A(1) (Trin-C) MLT 1

plesire n. 1d *OF* Chaucer LADY 1

pleten v. 2a *OF* (?c1280)
SLeg.Nativ.M.&C. (Stw) Bo 3
pletinge ger. b *(fr. pleten v.)* (1340)
Ayenb. *PF* 1
plicchen v. *OE* c1300 SLeg.Lucy (Ld)
MkT 4
plien v1. 1b *OF* (?c1380) Patience CLT 2
plien v2. d *fr. applien v.* (?c1380)
Cleanness TR 1
plight n. 1a *OE & AF* c1175 Bod.Hom.
ANEL 16
plighten v. a *OE* (?a1200) Lay.Brut ANEL
11
plough n. 2 *LOE (fr. ON) & ON* 1131
Peterb.Chron. KnT 6
plough-man n. a *fr. plough n. & man n.*
c1300 SLeg. (Ld) GP 2
ploume n. b *OE; fr. L* c1150 PDidax.
ROMA 1
ploungi adj. *fr. plungen v.* Chaucer Bo 2
plukken v. 2a *OE* (?c1300) Reinbrun TR
2
plumage n. *OF* Chaucer SQT 1
plumet n. b *OF* (c1384) WBible(1) AST 1
plum-rule n. b, plum n. *(fr. plum n. & reule n.)* Chaucer AST 1
plungen v. 1a *OF* c1380 Firumb.(1) Bo 9
Pluto n. *L* c1330 Orfeo HF 10
po-cok n. 1a *fr. <po n.> & cok n1.* ?c1200
Stw.57.Gloss. PF 4
poesie n. 1a *OF; ult. Gr.* (c1378) PPl.B
(Ld) TR 1
poete n. a *OF & L, fr. Gr.* (a1325) Cursor
BD 11
poetical adj. *? fr. poete n.* Chaucer HF 2
poetrie n. a *OF & ML* Chaucer HF 6
Poileis adj. *prob. AF* Chaucer SQT 1
poinaunt adj. a *OF* Chaucer GP 5
point-devis n. 6a, devis n. *fr. OF* Chaucer
MiLT 2
pointe n1. 5c *OF, AF* (?a1200) Ancr.
ROMA 120
pointel n. a *OF* (a1325) Cursor Bo 3
pointen v1. 1b a *OF* (c1300)
Glo.Chron.A ROMA 4

poisoun n. a *OF* (?c1200) HMaid. MkT
10
pok n. b *OE* (c1280) SLeg.Pass. PARDPRO
1
poke n. a *OE & ON* (c1300) Havelok
MiLT 2
poken v1. a *cp. MDu., MLG* (?a1300)
Guy(2) TR 2
poket n. b *AF* (1392) *MS Wel.564 CYT
1
pol-axe n. a *fr. pole n2. & axe n1.*
Chaucer KnT 2
pol-cat n. a *?AF* Chaucer PARDT 1
pole n1. a *L & OF* Chaucer Bo 37
pole n2. a *OE, fr. L* a1325 SLeg.Blase
(Corp-C) LGW 1
policie n. 1a *OF* (1385) Usk TL (Skeat)
PARDT 1
Polimia n. *L, fr. Gr.* Chaucer ANEL 1
polishen v. 1a *fr. OF & ML* (a1325)
Cursor SUMT 2
pollucioun n. c *OF & L* (a1349) Rolle 10
Com. PARST 1
polluten v. d *fr. L* Chaucer Bo 1
pome-garnete n. a *OF & ML* (?c1300)
Reinbrun ROMA 1
pomel n. 1a *OF & ML* (c1250) Floris
(Suth) KnT 1
pomele adj. *OF & ML* Chaucer GP 2
pompe n. b *OF & L* (?c1300) Spec.Guy.
MkT 7
pompous adj. c *OF & L* Chaucer MkT 2
pope n. a *OE (fr. L) & OF & L* a1121
Peterb.Chron. BD 22
pope-holi adj. b {a} *fr. pope n. & holi
adj2.* Chaucer {(a1387) Trev.Higd.}
ROMA 1
popelote n. *prob. OF* Chaucer MiLT 1
popet n. c *prob. OF* (?a1300) KAlex.
ProTHOP 1
poplere n. *OF & ML* Chaucer ROMA 2
poppen v2. *prob. OF* Chaucer {c1400
St.Anne(1)} ROMA 1
poppere n. *fr. <poppen v1.>* Chaucer
RVT 1

porche n. 1a *OF* c1300 SLeg. (Ld) *Bo* 2

porcioun n. 1a *OF & L* (a1325) Cursor
Bo 9

porisme n. *ML, fr. Gr.* Chaucer *Bo* 2

porphirie n. *OF* Chaucer *CYT* 1

port n2. 2 *OE (fr. L) & OF* (?1200)
Lay.Brut *TR* 2

port n4. 1a *OF* (?a1300) Guy(2) RomA 7

portatif adj. 1a *OF* (c1378) PPl.B (Ld)
AST 2

porter n. 1a *OF* (c1250) Floris (Cmb)
SNPro 7

port-hors n. a *OF* (c1378) PPl.B (Ld)
ShipT 2

Portingale n. *cp. OF & ML* a1375 WPal.
EpiNPT 1

portraien v. 1a *OF, AF* (c1250) Floris
(Suth) RomA 8

portraiinge ger. b *(fr. portraien v.)*
Chaucer *KnT* 1

portraiour n. a *OF* Chaucer *KnT* 1

portraiture n. a *OF, AF* Chaucer RomA
9

pose n. *OE, LOE* c1300 SLeg.Dunstan
(Hrl) RvT 2

posen v. 1b *OF* (a1325) MS.Rawl.B.520
lf.56 *Bo* 5

posicioun n. a *OF & L* Chaucer *Bo* 1

positif adj. a *OF & L* (a1325) Cursor
KnT 1

possessen v. b *OF* Chaucer *Bo* 1

possessioun n. 1b *L & OF* (1340) Ayenb.
Bo 19

possessiouner n. b *fr. possessioun n.*
(c1378) PPl.B (Ld) *SumT* 1

possibilite n. 1c *OF & L* Chaucer TR 5

possible adj. 1a *OF & L* (?1350–75)
Pass.Christi in Norris
Anc.Corn.Drama BD 14

possibli adv. *fr. possible adj.* Chaucer
AST 1

post n1. 1d *OE* a1200 Wor.Aelfric Gloss.
TR 3

potage n. 1a *OF* (?a1200) Ancr. PardPro
2

pote n1. 1b *OE* (c1200) Vices & V.(1) HF
11

potente n. a {a} *OF* Chaucer {(a1376)
PPl.A(1) (Trin-C)} RomA 3

potestate n. 2 *OF & L* (a1325) Ipotis
SumT 1

pouche n. 1d *OF* a1325 Prov.Hend.
(Cmb Gg) HF 3

poudre n1. 2b *fr. OF* c1300
SLeg.Magd.(2) (Ld) HF 10

poudre-marchant n. 5b b, poudre n1. *(fr.
poudre n1. & marchant n.)* Chaucer
GP 1

poudren v. 3a *OF* (a1300) Cokaygne
RomA 1

pouere n. 1c *OF* c1300 SLeg.Becket (Ld)
RomA 132

Poule n. 1a *OF & OE (fr. L)* a1150
Vsp.D.Hom. GP 32

pounde n1. 2a *OE, fr. L* a1121
Peterb.Chron. RomA 17

poune n1. *AF* Chaucer *BD* 1

pounsoned ppl. *fr. pouncen v.* Chaucer
ParsT 1

pounsoninge ger. *fr. pounsonen v.**
Chaucer *ParsT* 1

poupen v. *imitative* Chaucer NPT 2

pouren v1. a *?OE* (?c1225) Horn RomA
10

pouren v2. a *OF* (?c1300) Amis RomA
4

pouringe ger1. *(fr. pouren v1.)* (1340)
Ayenb. *TR* 1

pouse n. a *OF & L* (a1338) Mannyng
Chron.Pt.1 *TR* 1

pouste n. 1a *AF & CF* c1250 *St.Marg.(2)
Bo 1

poveraile n. a *AF* (c1300) Glo.Chron.A
GP 1

poverte n. 1b *OF (AF)* (?a1200) Ancr.
RomA 38

povre adj. 3b *AF & CF* (?c1150) Prov.Alf.
(Trin-C) RomA 93

povre n. *fr. povre adj.* Chaucer *Fort*
1

povreli adv. 2a *fr. povre adj.* c1230 Ancr.
(Corp-C) ROMA 5

practike n. c *OF & ML; ult Gr.* (a1387)
Trev.Higd. AST 3

practisoure n. a *fr. practisen v.* (c1378)
PPl.B (Ld) *GP* 1

prauncen v. 2a *?fr. <pranken v.> &*
dauncen v. c1380 Firumb.(1) *TR* 1

preamble n. *OF & ML* Chaucer *WBPRO*
1

preambulacioun n. *fr. preamble n.*
Chaucer *WBPRO* 1

precedent adj. a *OF & L* Chaucer *AST* 1

precepte n. 1a *OF & L* Chaucer MKT 2

prechen v. 1a *OF* (?a1200) Ancr. SNT 31

prechinge ger. a *(fr. prechen v.)* a1300 I-
hereth nu one SNT 9

prechour n. 1a *OF* (?a1200) Ancr.
WBPRO 1

preciouse adj. 1a *OF* (c1280) SLeg.Pass.
(Pep) ROMA 56

preciouslie adv. a *fr. preciouse adj.*
(?c1350) SVrn.Leg.Barlaam *TR* 2

preciousnesse n. a *fr. preciouse adj.*
Chaucer BO 2

predestinacioun n. a *OF & L* (c1340)
Rolle Psalter (UC 64) *BO* 1

predestinaten v. 2c *fr. L* Chaucer *BO* 1

predestine n. *fr. destine n.* Chaucer *TR* 1

predicacioun n. a *L & OF* (c1303)
Mannyng HS EpiMLT 4

preface n. a *fr. OF & L* Chaucer SNT 1

prefect n. b *OF & L* (?c1350) SVrn.Leg.
SNT 2

preferren v. 1a *OF & L* (a1393) Gower
CA *WBPRO* 1

pregnaunt adj. d *L & OF* Chaucer *TR* 1

preie n2. 4 *OF* (?c1225) Horn ABC 9

preien v1. 1b b *OF* (?c1225) Horn ROMA
347

preiere n2. 2a e *OF* c1300 SLeg. (Ld)
ROMA 60

preiinge ger. 1 *(fr. preien v1.)* (c1303)
Mannyng HS ROMA 3

preisen v. 2b *OF* (?a1200) Ancr. ROMA
60

preisere n. b *fr. preisen v. & AF* (a1382)
WBible(1) (Bod 959) *MEL* 1

preisinge ger. 2a *(fr. preisen v.)* (?a1200)
Ancr. HF 22

prelate n. 1a *OF & ML* (?a1200) Lay.Brut
GP 2

premisse n. 3 *OF & ML* Chaucer BO 3

prenostike n. b *ML* Chaucer FORT 1

prente n. 1a *OF* c1300 SLeg.MLChr.
WBPRO 1

prenten v. 3c *fr. prente n.* (c1380)
Wycl.Papa *TR* 1

prentis n. b *fr. apprentis n.* (a1325)
Cursor CKT 6

prentished n. *fr. prentis n.* (c1378) PPl.B
(Ld) *CKT* 1

preparaten v. 2a *L* (1392) *MS Wel.564
CYT 1

prescience n. a *OF & L* Chaucer BO 39

presence n. 2a *OF & L* c1330 7 Sages
ABC 45

presentarie adj. *L* Chaucer *BO* 3

presente adj. 1b *OF & L* (c1303)
Mannyng HS ROMA 43

presente adv. b *fr. presente adj.* Chaucer
PF 4

presente n1. 1c *fr. presente adj. & OF*
(?a1300) Arth.& M. ROMA 3

presente n2. a *OF & ML* (?a1200) Ancr.
ROMA 4

presenten v. 1a *OF & L* c1300
SLeg.Becket (Ld) PF 7

presentinge ger. e *(fr. presenten v.)*
(?1383) Wycl.Curse *LGW* 1

presentli adv. b *fr. presente adj.* Chaucer
BO 1

president n. 1a *OF & L* (a1382)
WBible(1) (Bod 959) *TR* 1

presse n. 3 *OF & CL & ML* (?a1200)
Ancr. MKT 26

pressen v. 4d *OF & L* (a1325)
MS.Rawl.B.520 lf.81 PITY 17

prest adj. 2 *OF* (c1280) SLeg.Pass. (Pep) PF 7

prest n3. 1a a *OE, fr. L; ult. Gr.* a1121 Peterb.Chron. SNT 95

presthede n. 1c *fr. prest n3. & OE* a1225 Wint.Ben.Rule *PARST* 1

presumen v. 2b *L & OF* (c1378) PPl.B (Ld) MERT 2

presumpcioun n. 1c *OF & L* a1250 Ancr. (Tit) MKT 11

pretenden v. 1a a *L & OF* (?1382) Wycl.Pet.Parl. *TR* 1

preterit adj. b *OF* (1340) Ayenb. *BO* 1

preterit n. *OF & L* Chaucer *BO* 5

pretorie n. c *OF & L* (a1325) Cursor *BO* 1

preve n. 1b *OF* (?a1200) Ancr. HF 24

preven v. 1a *OF* (?a1200) Ancr. BD 70

previdence n. a *ML & OF* Chaucer *BO* 1

Priapus n. *L* Chaucer PF 2

pricasour n. *fr. priken v.* Chaucer GP 1

pride n2. 1a a *LOE* c1200 Wor.Serm. in EGSt.7 ROMA 59

pridelesse adj. *fr. pride n2.* Chaucer LADY 2

priden v. 2a *fr. <pride n2.>* (?c1150) Prov.Alf. (Trin-C) *PARST* 5

prien v. c *cp. OE* (1307) Execution Fraser TR 7

prike n. 2a *OE* a1200 Body & S.(2) HF 41

priken v. 2a *OE* c1150 PDidax. ROMA 27

prikinge ger. 1a *OE* a1200 Body & S.(2) BO 5

prime adj. 2b *OF & L* Chaucer *TR* 1

prime n. 1b a *OE & OF & ML* (c1200) Vices & V.(1) TR 20

primere n. *ML* (?a1387) PPl.C. (Hnt) *PRT* 2

primerole n. 1a *OF* (?c1300) St.Patr.Purg.(1) *MILT* 1

prince n. 2b *OF* (?a1200) Ancr. SNT 26

princesse n. c *OF* Chaucer ABC 2

principal adj. 1d *OF & L* c1300 SLeg.Kenelm (Ld) BD 11

principallie adv. a *fr. principal adj.* (a1325) Cursor *PARST* 2

principle n. d *cp. OF & L* Chaucer BO 4

prioresse n. a *ML & OF* c1300 SLeg.Edm.Abp. (Ld) GP 3

pris n1. 4 *OF* (?a1200) Ancr. ROMA 48

prise n1. a *OF & ML (chiefly AL)* (c1300) Glo.Chron.A *PARST* 1

prisen v1. b *OF* Chaucer ROMA 2

prisoner n2. 1a *OF & ML* (?1350–75) Pass.Christi in Norris Anc.Corn.Drama TR 8

prisoun n. 1b *OF & ML* a1121 Peterb.Chron. SNPRO 61

prisoun-steue n. *(fr. prisoun n. & steue n2.)* not in MED *HF* 1

prive adj1. 2c *OF* (?a1200) Ancr. ROMA 40

prive adv. *fr. prive adj1.* (?a1300) Tristrem HF 6

prive n. 2b *OF* (?a1200) Ancr. MERT 2

privelie adv. 2d *fr. prive adj1.* a1250 Ancr. (Tit) ROMA 93

privete n. 1a *fr. prive adj1. & OF* (?a1200) Ancr. ROMA 27

privilege n. e *OF & L* ?a1160 Peterb.Chron. MEL 1

privilegen v. a *OF & ML* (a1387) Trev.Higd. *PARST* 1

probleme n. a *OF & L, fr. Gr.* (a1382) WBible(1) (Bod 959) *SUMT* 1

proceden v. 5a *OF & L* Chaucer SNT 19

proces n. 3h *OF & L* (a1338) Mannyng Chron.Pt.2 BD 24

processioun n. 1a *OF & L* a1121 Peterb.Chron. WBPRO 2

procreacioun n. a *OF & L* Chaucer *MERT* 1

procuratour n. d *OF & L* c1300 SLeg.Magd.(2) (Ld) *FRT* 1

procuren v. 1b *OF & L* c1300 SLeg.Becket (Ld) *PARST* 1

procuringe ger. a *(fr. procuren v.)* c1330 SMChron. (Auch) *PARST* 2

The making of Chaucer's English

professioun n. 2a *OF & L* (?a1200) Ancr.
SumT 3

profitable adj. 1d *OF & AL* (?c1300)
Spec.Guy Bo 14

profite n1. 1b d *OF & L* (?c1300)
Spec.Guy HF 39

profiten v. 2b *fr. profite n1. & OF* c1330 7
Sages(1) SNT 6

profre n. 2b *AF & ML* a1375 WPal.
LGW 3

profren v. 2c *OF & AF* c1300
SLeg.Faith(1) (Ld) SNT 16

progenie n. 1a *OF & L* (a1325) Cursor
ParsT 1

progressioun n. b *OF & L* Chaucer Bo 3

prohemie n. *L* (a1382) WBible(1) (Bod
959) ClPro 1

proinen v. a *OF* c1390 Susan MerT 1

prolacioun n. b *L* Chaucer Bo 1

prolixite n. a *OF & L* Chaucer HF 3

prollen v. *?fr. <prolongen v.> or proloinen
v.* Chaucer CYT 1

prologe n. a *OF & L* (a1325) Cursor TR 2

pronouncen v. c *OF & L* (a1338)
Mannyng Chron.Pt.2 PF 4

pronouncere n. *fr. pronouncen v.*
Chaucer Bo 1

prophecie n. 1a *OF & L; ult. Gr.*
(?a1200) Ancr. TR 2

prophete n. 2a *OF & L; ult.Gr.* c1200
Wor.Serm. in EGSt.7 LGW 22

propinquite n. b *OF & L* Chaucer Bo 1

proporcionable adj. *OF; ML* Chaucer
Bo 1

proporcionel n. *fr. proporcional adj.*
Chaucer FranT 1

proporcioun n. 4 {4} *OF & L* Chaucer
{(a1382) WBible(1) (Bod 959)}
RomA 9

proporciounen v. 1b *fr. <proporcioun
n.> & OF* (?c1350) SVrn.Leg. SQT 1

proposicioun n. 2a *OF & L* (c1340)
Rolle Psalter Bo 4

propre adj. 2b a *OF & L* c1300
SLeg.Magd.(2) (Ld) MkT 66

propre n. 1b *fr. propre adj.* (a1338)
Mannyng Chron.Pt.1 Bo 2

proprelie adv. 5a *fr. <propre adj.>*
(?a1200) Ancr. Bo 17

proprete n. 4a b *OF & L* (c1303)
Mannyng HS Bo 11

proscripcioun n. *L* Chaucer Bo 1

prose n. d *OF & L* (?a1300) Stations
Rome(1) Prol. LGW F 7

prosen v. *fr. prose n.* Chaucer SCOG 1

Proserpine n. *L* Chaucer HF 5

prosperite n. 1a *fr. OF & L* (?a1200)
Ancr. MkT 41

proteccioun n. a *OF & L* c1350
MPPsalter KnT 5

protestacioun n. a *OF & L* (1382)
Knighton Chron.Contin. TR 5

prou n. 1b *OF* c1300 SLeg.Aug.Cant.
(Ld) HF 8

proud adj. 4a *OE (fr. OF) & OF* (?c1150)
Prov.Alf. (Trin-C) RomA 48

proud n. a *fr. <proud adj.>* (?c1175)
PMor. (Trin-C) TR 2

proud-herted adj. {a} *fr. proud adj. &
herted adj.* Chaucer {(c1378) PPl.B
(Ld)} RomA 1

proudli adv. 3a *fr. proud adj.* (c1200)
Vices & V.(1) SNT 4

prouesse n. 1c *OF* (?c1225) Horn RomA
11

proverbe n. a *OF & L* (c1303) Mannyng
HS MkT 26

proverben v. *fr. proverbe n. & ML*
Chaucer TR 1

province n. a *OF & L* (a1338) Mannyng
Chron.Pt.2 Bo 2

provost n. g *OE (fr. L) & OF* a1121
Peterb.Chron. Bo 4

provostrie n. a *fr. provost n. & OF*
Chaucer Bo 2

prudence n. 2a *OF & L* (1340) Ayenb.
TR 51

prudent adj. a *OF & L* (a1382)
WBible(1) (Bod 959) IntMLT 4

Prusse n. 1a *OF & AL* Chaucer BD 3

Psalme n. 1a d *L & ML & OE & OF; ult.*
Gr. a1150 Vsp.D.Hom. S∪MT 2

publican n1. a *OF & L* ?c1200 Orm.
P∧RST 1

publishen v. 1b *fr. OF* (a1338) Mannyng
Chron.Pt.2 Bo 6

puffen v. 1a *OE* (?a1200) Ancr. HF 1

pul n. a *fr. pullen v.* (a1338) Mannyng
Chron.Pt.1 PF 1

puli n. a *OF & ML* (1392) *MS Wel.564
SQT 1

pullen v. 3a *OE* c1300 SLeg.Cross. (Ld)
R○M∧ 16

pulpit n. a *OF & L* (a1338) Mannyng
Chron.Pt.2 S∪MT 2

pultrie n. b *OF & ML* (1345–6) Grocer
Lond. GP 1

punishement n. a *OF* (c1385) Usk TL
(Skeat) MEL 1

punishen v. 3a *fr. OF* (c1303) Mannyng
HS Bo 20

punishinge ger. 2a *(fr. punishen v.)*
Chaucer Bo 4

purchase n. 1a *AF & CF* (c1300)
Glo.Chron.A GP 3

purchasen v. 3d *AF & CF* c1300
SLeg.11000 Virg. (Ld) BD 17

purchasinge ger. 1a *(fr. purchasen v.)*
(?a1300) KAlex. Bo 3

purchasour n. *AF & CF* (1303)
Mannyng HS GP 1

pure adj. 1b *OF & L* (c1250) Floris
(Auch) R○M∧ 22

pure adv. a *fr. pure adj.* c1300
SLeg.Kenelm (Ld) BD 4

pureli adv. 1a *fr. pure adj.* c1300 SLeg.
(Hrl) BD 4

puren v. 1a *OF* (c1325) Recipe Painting(1)
in Archaeol.J.1 WBPR○ 2

purfiled ppl. a *fr. <purfile n.>* ?c1325 As I
stod on GP 1

purgacioun n. 2b *OF & L* (a1382)
WBible(1) (Bod 959) WBPR○ 1

purgatorie n. 1a *OF & ML* (?a1200)
Ancr. KNT 5

purgen v1. 3a *AF & L* c1300 SLeg.Becket
(Ld) SNT 9

purpos n. 1a *AF & CF* c1300 SLeg. (Ld)
R○M∧ 78

purposen v. 3a *OF* Chaucer Bo 24

purpure adj. c *(fr. purpure n.)* (a1333)
Shoreham Poems Bo 6

purpure n. 1d *OE (fr. L) & AF* (?a1200)
Lay.Brut R○M∧ 5

purse n. 1b *OE, fr. ML* (?a1200) Ancr.
R○M∧ 22

purseuen v. 5d *AF & CF* (1280)
SLeg.Pass. (Pep) Bo 6

pursevaunte n. a *?AF & CF* Chaucer HF
1

pursuite n. 3b *AF & CF* (c1383)
Wycl.Leaven Pharisees TR 3

purveiable adj. a *fr. purveien v. & OF*
Chaucer Bo 1

purveiaunce n. 1a *AF & CF* c1300 SLeg.
(Hrl) Bo 66

purveien v. 2d *AF & CF* c1300
SLeg.Becket (Ld) Bo 27

purveiinge ger. f *(fr. purveien v.)* (1340)
Ayenb. TR 2

pushen v. a *OF* (?c1225) Horn TR 2

putour n. *OF* (?a1387) PPl.C (Hnt)
P∧RST 1

putrie n. *OF* (c1383) Wycl.Leaven
Pharisees P∧RST 2

putten v. 1b a *OE* (?a1200) Lay.Brut.
R○M∧ 203

quaile n. a *OF & ML* Chaucer PF 2

quaken v. 1a a *OE* (?a1200) Lay.Brut
R○M∧ 36

quakinge ger. 2a *(fr. quaken v.)* (c1300)
Glo.Chron.A ANEL 1

quakke n. *prob. imitative* Chaucer RVT 1

qualite n. 2a *OF & L* c1300 SLeg.Mich.
(Ld) Bo 11

qualm n1. 1a *OE* a1126 Peterb.Chron.
R○M∧ 3

qualm n2. *? cp. EFris.* Chaucer TR 1

quantite n. 7 *OF & L* (a1325) Cursor PF
27

quappen v. a *Cp. MDu., MLG* (a1382)
WBible(1) (Bod 959) T*R* 3

quarte n. 1d *OF* ?a1325 Heil seint Michel
GP 2

quartere n. 3e *OF & ML* c1300
SLeg.Nich. (Ld) BD 15

quede adj. a *fr. quede n1.* (?a1200)
Lay.Brut C*K*P*RO* 2

queinte adj. 1c *OF* (?a1200) Ancr. R*O*M*A*
29

queinte adv. *fr. queinte adj.* (?a1350)
Castleford Chron. HF 1

queinte n. 2a *fr. queinte adj.* (?a1300)
Tristrem M*I*L*T* 3

queintise n. 1a *OF* (?c1280)
SLeg.OTHist. (Ld 622) R*O*M*A* 3

queintlie adv. 1a *fr. queinte adj.* c1300
SLeg. (Ld) R*O*M*A* 3

queke interj. a *imitative* (1342) The fals
fox PF 4

queken v. a *fr. queke interj. & MDu.*
a1325 Gloss.Bibbesw. PF 1

quellen vi. 1a *OE* (c1125)
Vsp.D.Hom.Fest.Virg. T*R* 4

quemen v. 1b b *OE* a1200 Body & S.(2)
T*R* 3

quenchen v. 1a *fr. OE* (?c1175) PMor.
(Lamb) T*R* 15

quene n1. a *OE* (?c1150) Prov.Alf. (*Glb-
James) M*ANC*P*RO* 1

quene n2. 1a b *OE* a1121 Peterb.Chron.
R*O*M*A* 138

querele n. 1a *OF & L* (1340) Ayenb. B*O* 2

querne n2. 1b *OE & ON* a1200
Wor.Aelfric Gloss. HF 3

queste-mongere n. 1b b, queste n. *(fr.
queste n. & mongere n.)* (c1378) PPl.B
(Ld) P*ARS*T 1

questioun n. 2a *L & OF* a1200 Sanctus
Beda SNT 23

quethen v. 1a *OE* a1121 Peterb.Chron.
GENERAL 1177

quiete n. a *L & OF* (?a1300) Arth.& M.
ABC 16

quik adj. 5e *OE* ?c1125 Dur.-C Gloss. BD
12

quiken v. 2b *OE* c1175 Bod.Hom. SNT
15

quikenen v. 1a *fr. quiken v.* (c1300)
NHom.(1) Peter & P. P*ARS*T 1

quiknesse n. a *fr. quik adj.* (?a1200)
Ancr. BD 1

quik-silver n. a *OE* Chaucer GP 9

quinible adj. b *fr. L* Chaucer M*I*L*T* 1

quir-boili n. *fr. CF, AF & OF* Chaucer
T*HOP* 1

quishin n. 1a *OF* (a1350) Isumb. T*R* 2

quistroun n. *OF* (?a1300) KAlex. R*O*M*A*
1

quite adj. 1a *OF & ML* (?a1200) Ancr.
SNP*RO* 11

quiten v. 1b *OF* (?a1200) Ancr. R*O*M*A* 47

quitli adv. a *fr. quite adj.* (?a1300)
Guy(2) K*N*T 1

quoniam n. *L* Chaucer WBP*RO* 1

rabbi n. b *L & OF; ult. Heb.* (a1325)
Cursor S*UM*T 1

radevore n. *?OF* Chaucer LGW 1

rafle n1. *OF & ML* Chaucer P*ARS*T 1

rafter n. a *OE* a1200 Wor.Aelfric Gloss.
K*N*T 1

rage n. 2 *OF* (c1300) Glo.Chron.A
R*O*M*A* 18

ragen v. 4b *OF* c1250 *Body & S.(4) GP
3

ragerie n. a *OF* (a1393) Gower CA
WBP*RO* 2

raied adj. *fr. raie n2.* Chaucer BD 1

railen v2. b *fr. raile n.* Chaucer T*R* 1

raines n. *fr. OF* Chaucer BD 1

rake n1. a *OE* a1325 Gloss.Bibbesw. GP 1

rakel adj. a *fr. raken v2.* c1300
SLeg.Inf.Chr. (Ld) T*R* 7

rakelen v. *fr. rakel adj.* Chaucer T*R* 1

rakelnesse n. *fr. rakel adj.* Chaucer
M*ANC*T 2

raken vi. 1a *ON* (c1250) Gen.& Ex.
M*K*T 1

Chaucer's words

rake-stele n. b, rake n1. *(fr. rake n1. & stele n3.)* Chaucer *WBT* 1

raket n. a *?OF* Chaucer *TR* 1

ram n. 1a *OE* c1150 Hrl.HApul. *LGW* 6

rammish adj. *fr. ram n.* Chaucer *CYT* 1

rancour n. b *OF & L* (?a1200) Ancr. ROMA 13

rank adj. 1a *OE* ?c1200 Orm. *PARST* 1

ransaken v. b *ON* (c1250) Gen.& Ex. MARS 2

rape n1. b *fr.* <*rapen v1.*> (a1220) Giraldus Des.Kambriae in RS 21.6 ADAM 1

rape n2. c *AF & AL* (a1325) Cursor *TR* 1

rapen v2. d *L* (a1338) Mannyng Chron.Pt.2 *CYT* 1

rascaile n. 1a *OF* (a1338) Mannyng Chron.Pt.2 *TR* 1

rasoure n. c *OF & ML* c1300 SLeg. (Ld) MKT 4

rat n. a *OE* (c1378) PPl.B (Ld) PARDT 2

raten v2. *OF* Chaucer *MILT* 1

rathe adv. b *OE* a1121 Peterb.Chron. HF 6

rathere adj. comp. a *fr. rathe adj.* (c1300) Glo.Chron.A BO 4

rathere adv. comp. 3c *OE* c1150 PDidax. BD 95

raue adj. 1a *OE* c1150 Hrl.HApul. *PARST* 2

raumpen v. 2b a *OF* (a1325) Cursor PROMKT 1

raunsoun n. 1c *OF* (?a1200) Ancr. KNT 6

raunsouninge ger. a *(fr. raunsounen v.)* (a1325) Cursor *PARST* 1

raven n. 2b *OE, LOE* c1150 Hrl.HApul. HF 4

raven v1. a *OF* a1325 SLeg.11000 Virg. (Corp-C) TR 2

ravine n. 2 *OF* (?1348) Rolle FLiving PF 6

ravinge ger. a *(fr. raven v1.)* Chaucer FRANT 1

ravinour n. b *OF* (?c1350) SVrn.Leg. BO 2

ravishen v. 1b *fr. OF* (c1300) Glo.Chron.A PF 28

ravishinge ger. b *(fr. ravishen v.)* (a1325) Cursor *TR* 2

real adj1. 1b *OF* (?c1300) Guy(1) ABC 12

realte n1. 2a *OF* a1375 WPal. FORT 1

reaume n. 1a *OF* c1300 SLeg.Becket (Ld) ROMA 18

rebatinge ger. a *(fr. rebaten v.)* Chaucer WOMNOB 1

rebekke n2. *? fr. L* Chaucer FRT 1

rebel adj. a *OF & L* (c1300) Glo.Chron.A MKT 12

rebellen v. d *OF & L* (1340) Ayenb. INTSQT 3

rebellinge ger. b *(fr. rebellen v.)* (c1340) Rolle Psalter (UC 64) KNT 1

rebellioun n1. c *L & OF* (c1340) Rolle Psalter (UC 64) PARST 1

rebounden v. 1b *OF* (?c1380) Cleanness TR 1

rebuken v. 1a *AF* c1330 Le Freine PARST 1

recchen v1. 1b *OE* c1175 Bod.Hom. NPT 1

recchen v2. 1c *OE* 1123 Peterb.Chron. ROMA 68

receite n. 2a *OF* (a1349) Rolle MPass.(2) CYT 3

receiven v. 1d *OF* (?a1300) Guy(2) ABC 84

receivinge ger. 1c *(fr. receiven v.)* (a1382) WBible(1) (Bod 959) PARST 2

rechasen v2. b *OF & ML* Chaucer BD 1

recheles adj. 4a *OE* c1175 Bod.Hom. ROMA 10

rechelesnesse n. a *OE* (c1378) PPl.B (Ld) PARST 4

rechen v1. 1a *OE* (?a1200) Ancr. ROMA 8

reclaimen v. 1a *OF & ML* (a1325) Cursor MANCPRO 1

reclaiminge ger. b *(fr. reclaimen v.)* Chaucer LGW 1

recomforten v. 1a *OF* (c1378) PPl.B (Ld)
TR 5

recommaunden v. 1c *OF* c1380
Firumb.(1) TR 7

recommenden v. 1e *ML* Chaucer SNT
2

recompensacioun n. b *OF & ML*
Chaucer HF 3

reconcilen v. 6b a *L & OF, AF* (c1350)
NHom.(2) PSanct. MEL 10

reconciliacioun n. b *L & OF* (c1350)
NHom.(2) PSanct. *MEL* 1

reconcilinge ger. c *fr. reconcilen v.* *
(c1340) Rolle Psalter (UC 64) MEL 2

reconisaunce n. 2b *OF* a1325
MS.Rawl.B.520.lf.31b *SHIPT* 1

recorde n. 6b *OF & ML* (?c1300)
Reinbrun BD 4

recorden v. 6 *OF & L* (?a1200) Ancr. PF
18

recours n. 4a *OF & L* Chaucer BO 5

recoveren v2. 1e *OF* (?a1300) Arth.& M.
ROMA 12

recoveringe ger. 1a *(fr. recoveren v2.)*
Chaucer BO 1

recreaunt adj. a *OF* (?a1300) Guy(2) TR
3

red adj. 1b a *OE* a1121 Peterb.Chron.
ROMA 95

red n1. 1a b *OE* a1121 Peterb.Chron.
ROMA 38

red n2. a *fr. red adj.* (?a1200) Ancr.
ROMA 13

red n3. 1e *OE* (?a1200) Lay.Brut HF 2

reddour n. e *OF* a1375 WPal. *FORT* 1

redempcioun n. 1a *OF & L* (c1340) Rolle
Psalter (UC 64) TR 3

reden v1. 2a b *OE* a1121 Peterb.Chron.
ROMA 181

reden v2. a *OE* c1150 Hrl.MQuad. *TR*
1

redere n1. b *OE* (?c1200) St.Marg.(1) PF
2

redi adj1. *fr. red n1.* (c1280) SLeg.Pass.
(Pep) *TR* 1

redi adj3. 5a *fr. OE* c1200 Wor.Serm. in
EGSt.7 ROMA 75

redili adv2. 2a *fr. redi adj3.* a1300
Serm.Lithir lok ROMA 14

redles adj. c *OE* a1250 Lofsong Louerde
PITY 1

rednesse n. e *OE* Chaucer BO 3

redoutable adj. b *OF* Chaucer BO 1

redouten v. a *OF* Chaucer BO 3

redoutinge ger. *(fr. redouten v.)* Chaucer
KNT 1

redresse n. a *OF* (1385) in Rymer's
Foedera (1709) TR 2

redressen v. 2 *OF* (c1350) NHom.(2)
PSanct. ABC 15

reducen v. 3 *L & OF* (?c1378) Wycl.O
Pastor. BO 1

ref n1. a *OE* (?a1200) Lay.Brut *FRT* 1

refecten v. *fr. L* Chaucer BO 1

referren v. a *L & OF* Chaucer BO 18

refiguren v. a *fr. <figuren v.> or L*
Chaucer TR 1

refleccioun n. 3b *L & OF* Chaucer HF
2

refreiden v. b *OF (chiefly AF)* Chaucer
TR 4

refreine n. *OF* Chaucer TR 1

refreinen v2. 2b *OF* (?c1350) SVrn.Leg.
PARST 4

refreininge ger1. *fr. <refreine n.>*
Chaucer *ROMA* 1

refreshen v. 2b *OF* (1375) Canticum
Creat. BO 7

refreshinge ger. 1a *(fr. refreshen v.)*
(a1382) WBible(1) (Bod 959) *PARST* 2

refuge n. a *OF* Chaucer *KNT* 1

refuse adj. a *?fr. OF* Chaucer TR 1

refusen v. 2a *OF* (?a1300) KAlex. BO 13

refute n. c *OF* (a1349) Rolle MPass.(2)
ABC 8

regale adj. *L* Chaucer BO 1

regale n. a *OF & ML* (a1338) Mannyng
Chron.Pt.1 *LGW* 1

regalie n. {a} *L* Chaucer {(a1393) Gower
CA} *PITY* 1

regarde n. b *OF* (1348) Doc. in Welch
Hist.Pewterers Lond. HF 10
regioune n. 1a *OF & L* (?a1300) KAlex.
HF 41
registre n. 1a *OF & ML* (c1378) PPl.B
(Ld) *KNT* 1
regne n1. 2a *OF* (?c1225) Horn ROMA 53
regnen v. 2a *OF* (?c1280) SLeg.Advent,
etc. MKT 14
rehersaille n. a *fr. rehersen v.* Chaucer
CYT 1
rehersen v. 1a *OF* c1300 SLeg.Inf.Chr.
(Ld) BD 39
rehersinge ger. 1e *(fr. rehersen v.)* (a1325)
Cursor BO 4
reie n. *MDu.* Chaucer *HF* 1
rein n1. 1a a *OE, LOE* a1121
Peterb.Chron. MKT 30
reine n1. 1a *OF & AL* (?a1300) Arth.&
M. HF 7
reine n2. 1a *OF* c1150 PDidax. *PARST* 1
reinen v1. 1a *OE* c1175
Bod.Hom.Dom.Quadr. TR 12
reisen v1. 2b *ON* ?c1200 Orm. BD 8
reisen v2. *MDu., MLG* Chaucer *GP* 1
rejoien v. 1 *OF* (a1333) Shoreham Poems
TR 1
rejoisen v. 1a *fr. OF* (c1303) Mannyng
HS ABC 17
rejoisinge ger. {a} *(fr.rejoisen v.)* Chaucer
{(?c1384) Wycl.50 HFriars} BO 3
reken v2. a *MDu.* (?a1300) Arth.& M.
RVPRO 1
reken v3. a *OE* c1150 Hrl.HApul. *LGW* 1
rekenen v. 1b *OE & LOE* ?c1200 Orm.
ROMA 57
rekeninge ger. 4a *(fr. rekenen v.)* c1325
Weping Haveth ABC 13
relai n. *OF* Chaucer *BD* 1
relefe n. 1a *OF, AF, ML, AL* (?a1200)
Ancr. *MLT* 1
relenten v. b *AF* (1392) *MS Wel.564
CYT 1
reles n2. 1a *OF* (a1325) Glo.Chron.B
ABC 2

relesen v1. 1 *OF, AF* (c1300)
Glo.Chron.A MKT 10
relesinge ger. a *(fr. relesen v1.)* Chaucer
BO 2
releven v. 2d *OF & L* Chaucer ABC 10
relevinge ger. b *(fr. releven v.)* (c1385)
Usk TL (Skeat) *PARST* 3
religioun n. 1b *OF & L, ML* (c1200)
Vices & V.(1) ROMA 6
religious adj. 1b *OF & L* (c1200) Vices
& V.(1) TR 4
relik n. 1a *OF* (?a1200) Ancr. TR 9
remede n. a *OF* Chaucer *TR* 1
remedie n. 3a *OF & L* (?a1200) Ancr.
ROMA 52
remembraunce n. 1d *OF* (?a1300)
Arth.& M. ROMA 52
remembren v. 1d *OF* (a1338) Mannyng
Chron.Pt.2 ROMA 68
remenaunt n. 2a *OF* (?a1300) Arth.& M.
ROMA 36
remeven v. 1a *OF* (?a1325) Bonav.
Medit.(1) BO 9
remissioun n. 2a *L & OF* (?a1200) Ancr.
SNT 7
remorden v. c *OF & L* Chaucer BO 2
remorse n. *OF & ML* Chaucer *TR* 1
remounten v. 1d *AF* Chaucer *BO* 1
remuable adj. a *OF* Chaucer BO 2
remuen v. 1b *OF* (c1280) SLeg.Pass.
(Pep) BO 4
ren n. b *fr. rennen v1.* (c1250) Gen.& Ex.
RVT 1
renabli adv. a *fr. renable adj.* (?c1300)
Bevis *FRT* 1
Renarde n. *OF* Chaucer *LGW* 1
renden v2. 1e *OE* (?a1200) Lay.Brut HF
20
renegate n. a *ML* Chaucer LGW G 2
reneien v1. 1b *OF* c1300 SLeg. (Ld) SNT
9
reneiinge ger. *(fr. reneien v1.)* (a1325)
Cursor *PARST* 1
reneuen v1. 3d *fr. neuen v.* (c1350)
NHom.(2) PSanct. *ADAM* 1

renge n2. b *OF* (?c1200) HMaid. *KNT* 1

rengen v. 1a *OF* (?a1200) Ancr. *ROMA* 1

rennen vi. 9a *fr. OE & ON* a1121
Peterb.Chron. ROMA 89

rennere n. 2a *fr. rennen vi.* (a1325)
Cursor *FRPRO* 1

renninge ger1. 1d *(fr. rennen vi.)* (c1300)
Glo.Chron.A ROMA 3

renome n. a *OF, NF, AF* Chaucer BO 2

renomen v. a *OF, AF* (a1325) Cursor *BO*
4

renoun n. 1e *OF, AF* (?a1300) Tristrem
ROMA 65

renouncen v. 1a *OF & L* Chaucer *BO* 1

renovelaunce n. *OF* Chaucer *HF* 1

renovelen v. a *OF* (a1333) Shoreham
Poems BO 5

rente n. 1b *OF & ML* ?a1160
Peterb.Chron. BD 19

renten v2. a *fr. renden v2.* a1325
SLeg.Geo.(1) (Corp-C) ROMA 3

rentinge ger. *(fr. renten v2.)* Chaucer
KNT 1

repaire n1. 1c *OF* (a1338) Mannyng
Chron.Pt.1 WBT 2

repairen v. 2a *OF* (?a1300) Tristrem
MKT 15

reparacioun n. 3 *OF & L* Chaucer *HF* 1

repelen v. 1a *OF, AF* Chaucer *TR* 2

repen vi. 1d *OE* (?c1175) PMor. *LGW F* 1

repentaunce n. 1a *OF* c1300 SLeg.Becket
(Ld) BD 15

repentaunt adj. a *OF* c1230 Ancr. (Corp-
C) GP 9

repenten v. 1a a *OF* c1300 SLeg.Brendan
(Hrl: Horst) ROMA 42

repentinge ger. a *(fr. repenten v.)*
(?a1300) KAlex. MARS 3

replecioun n. a *OF & L* Chaucer *NPT* 2

replenishen v. b *fr. OF, AF* Chaucer BO
3

replete adj. & ppl. e *OF & L* (c1384)
WBible(1) PARDT 2

replicacioun n. a *OF, AF & L* Chaucer
PF 3

replien vi. 2a *OF* (a1382) WBible(1)
(Bod 959) LGW F 3

reporte n. c *OF* Chaucer TR 2

reporten v. 1b *OF* Chaucer TR 7

reportoure n. b *OF* Chaucer *GP* 1

reprehenden v. a *L* (1340) Rolle Psalter
(Ld) BO 2

reprehensioun n. *L & OF* Chaucer *TR* 1

representen v. 2a *OF & L* (1389) Wycl.25
Art. *VENUS* 1

repressen v. d *fr. OF & L* Chaucer ABC
3

repressioun n. *OF & ML* Chaucer *TR* 1

reprevable adj. a *fr. repreven v. & OF*
(c1340) Rolle Psalter (UC 64) STED 3

repreve n. 1d *OF, AF* (a1338) Mannyng
Chron.Pt.1 TR 11

repreven v. 1c *OF, AF* (c1303) Mannyng
HS ROMA 28

reprevinge ger. b *(fr. repreven v.)* c1330
SMChron. (Auch) *PARST* 2

reproche n. b *OF, AF* c1350 MPPsalter
PARST 1

repugnen v. 2b *OF & L* Chaucer *BO* 1

reputacioun n. b *OF & L* (?c1350)
SVrn.Leg. BO 6

requerable adj. *OF* Chaucer *BO* 1

requeren v. 3b *OF & L* Chaucer BO 42

requeste n. b *OF* (a1338) Mannyng
Chron.Pt.2 SNT 20

res n. 2a *OE* (?a1200) Lay.Brut *TR* 1

resalgar n. *AL* (1392) *MS Wel.564 *CYT*
1

rescouen v. 1a *OF, AF* (?c1300) Guy(1)
BO 5

rescouinge ger. b *(fr. rescouen v.)*
Chaucer *PARST* 1

rescous n. b *OF, AF* (a1338) Mannyng
Chron.Pt.1 TR 3

resemblable adj. *OF* Chaucer {(a1393)
Gower CA} *ROMA* 1

resemblaunce n. a *OF* (a1393) Gower
CA *WBPRO* 1

resemblen vi. 1a *OF* (1340) Ayenb. BO 3

resen vi. a *OE* (?a1200) Lay.Brut *KNT* 1

reserven v. 3b *OF & L* (1357)
Gaytr.LFCatech. Bo 2
residence n. a *OF & ML, AL* (?c1378)
Wycl.OPastor *CYPRO* 1
resignen v. d *OF & L* Chaucer ABC 4
resisten v. b *OF & L* Chaucer *BO* 2
resistence n. 2a *OF & L, AL* (?c1350)
SVrn.Leg. TR 2
resolven v. 1a *L & OF* Chaucer *BO* 4
resonable adj2. 6 *OF* (c1303) Mannyng
HS ROMA 21
resonabli adv. 1b *fr. resonable adj2.*
(c1378) PPl.B (Ld) Bo 5
resorte n. 3a *OF* Chaucer TR 1
resoun n2. 1a a *OF* (?a1200) Ancr. ROMA
240
resounen v1. 1c *OF* Chaucer Bo 3
resouninge ger. a *fr. resounen v2.* *
Chaucer Bo 3
respecte n. 2b *OF & L* (?c1380) Pearl TR
3
respite n. 1a *OF, AF* (c1250) Floris
(Auch) ROMA 10
respiten v. 1c *OF* c1330 7 Sages ANEL 2
resport n. *prob. OF* Chaucer TR 2
reste n1. 4a *OE, LOE* a1121
Peterb.Chron. ABC 109
resten v1. 1a *OE* c1175 HRood ROMA
27
resting ppl. adj. c, restinge-place n. *(fr.
resten v1.)* (a1338) Mannyng
Chron.Pt.1 *BD* 1
resting-while n. 1b, restinge ger1. *(fr.
resten v1. & whil n.)* Chaucer *BO* 1
restles adj. b {b} *OE* Chaucer {(?c1380)
Cleanness} ROMA 4
restoren v. 1a *OF & AL* (c1300)
Glo.Chron.A MKT 13
restreinen v. 2b *fr. OF* (a1349) Rolle
Com.LG (Rwl) MKT 25
resurreccioun n. 1b *OF* c1300
SLeg.Brendan (Ld) *LGW F* 1
retentif adj. b *OF & ML* Chaucer *PARS T*
1
retenue n. 2a *OF* Chaucer KNT 3

rethor n. a *L & OF; ult Gr.* (?c1350)
SVrn.Leg. SQT 2
rethorien adj. *OF* Chaucer *BO* 1
rethorien n. a *OF* Chaucer *BO* 2
rethorike n. 1a *OF & L* c1330 7 Sages(1)
HF 7
retraccioun n. b *L & OF* Chaucer *PARS T*
1
retreten v2. b *fr. OF* Chaucer *BO* 1
retrograde adj. a {a} *L & OF* Chaucer
{(1392) *MS Wel.564} *AST* 4
returnen v. 2a *OF & ML* (a1325)
MS.Rawl.B.520 lf.55b ROMA 40
returninge ger. a *(fr. returnen v.)*
Chaucer BO 3
reue n2. 4b *OE, LOE* (?a1200) Ancr.
ROMA 10
reuen v1. 6 *OE* (?c1150) Prov.Alf. (Mdst)
LADY 48
reuful adj. 1c *fr. <reue n1.>* (?a1200)
Ancr. PF 4
reufulli adv. d *fr. reuful adj.* (?c1200)
St.Marg.(1) *TR* 3
reule n. 1a *OF* (?a1200) Ancr. FORT 33
reulen v. 2a *OF* (?a1200) Ancr. BO 11
reuli adj1. d *OE* (c1200) Vices & V.(1)
BO 1
reuthe n. 1a *fr. ON* (c1200) Vices & V.(1)
ROMA 84
reutheles adj. *fr. reuthe n.* c1330 Len
puet LADY 4
reve n. 1a *OE* (?c1175) PMor. (Lamb) GP
11
revel n1. b *OF* a1375 WPal. KNT 19
revelacioun n. 1a *L & OF* (c1303)
Mannyng HS HF 4
reveloure n. *fr. revelen v1.* Chaucer CKT
3
revelous adj. *OF* Chaucer *SHIP T* 1
revelrie n. *fr. revel n1.* Chaucer *RVT* 1
reven v. 1b *OE* ?a1160 Peterb.Chron.
SNT 31
revengen v. 1c *OF* Chaucer *BO* 1
reverberacioun n. a *AL & OF* Chaucer
SUM T 1

reverence n. 1c *OF & L* (c1280)
SLeg.Pass.(Pep) PITY 72
reverencen v. b *fr. reverence n.* (?c1375)
NHom.(3) Leg. BO 5
reverente adj. 1a *L & OF* Chaucer BO 6
reverentli adv. a *fr. <reverente adj.>*
(?c1350) SVrn.Leg. CLT 2
reverie n1. a *OF* c1350 Of alle the witti
ROMA 1
reverse n. 1 *OF* (?c1350) Mirror St.Edm.
(4) VENUS 6
revesten v. 1b *OF & L* c1300
SLeg.Brendan (Ld) TR 1
revilen v. c *OF* (c1303) Mannyng HS
PARS T 1
revoken v. e *OF & L* (?c1350) SVrn.Leg.
TR 2
revolucioun n. 1a *OF & L* Chaucer
MARS 2
reward n. 2b *AF, NF & ML* (a1338)
Mannyng Chron.Pt.2 PF 11
riban n. b *OF, AF & ML, AL* ?c1325 As I
stod on HF 1
ribaning n. *fr. riban n.* Chaucer ROMA
1
ribaudie n. a *OF* (c1280) SLeg.Pass.
(Pep) RvPRO 3
ribbe n1. a *OE* c1175 Bod.Hom. WBPRO
2
ribibe n. b *OF; ult. Ar.* Chaucer FRT 1
ribible n. a *prob. fr. <ribibe n.>* c1330
Why werre MILT 2
riche adj. 1c *OE & OF (fr. Gmc.) & ON*
a1121 Peterb.Chron. ROMA 102
riche adv. *fr. riche adj.* (c1250) Gen.&
Ex. HF 4
richeli adv. 2 *OE* (?a1200) Lay.Brut
ROMA 14
richesse n. 1a *OF* (?a1200) Trin.Hom.
ROMA 156
ridelen v2. b *cp. OF* Chaucer ROMA 2
riden v. 2b *OE* a1121 Peterb.Chron. BD
164
ridere n. b *LOE* (?a1200) Lay.Brut PARS T
1

ridinge ger. 4a *(fr. riden v.)* ?c1200 Orm.
CKT 3
rie n. a *OE* a1325 Gloss.Bibbesw. SUM T 1
riet n. a {b} *L* Chaucer {(1392) EPlanets}
AST 15
right adj. 1a *OE* a1121 Peterb.Chron.
ROMA 95
right n. 1a *OE* a1121 Peterb.Chron.
ROMA 82
righte adv. 6 *OE* a1121 Peterb.Chron.
GENERAL 875
rightful adj. 2c *fr. right n.* a1121
Peterb.Chron. ROMA 34
rightfulli adv. a *fr. rightful adj.* (c1300)
Glo.Chron.A HF 15
right-wise adj. 1b *OE* c1175 Bod.Hom.
LGW F 3
right-wisnesse n. 2c *OE* (c1125)
Vsp.D.Hom.Fest.Virg. BO 13
rigour n. 2 *OF & L* (1392) *MS Wel.564
FRAN T 1
rime n3. b *OF* ?c1200 Orm. BD 18
rimeien v. *OF* Chaucer FRANPRO 1
rimen v1. a *OF* c1300 SLeg.Magd.(2)
(Ld) ROMA 14
riming ger. *(fr. rimen v1.)* Chaucer
INTMLT 2
rinde n1. 3b *OE* c1150 Hrl.HApul. TR 2
ring n. 1a *OE* c1150 Hrl.HApul. BD 42
ringen v2. 1a *OE* 1131 Peterb.Chron. BD
22
riote n. 5 *OF, AF* (?a1200) Ancr. CKT 4
rioten v. a *OF* Chaucer CKT 1
riotour n. a *OF, AF* (1389) Lond. Gild
Tert. in Bk.Lond.E. PARD T 5
riotous adj. 1c *OF* (1340) Ayenb. CKT 2
ripe adj. 3a *OE* (c1200) Vices & V.(1)
RvPRO 6
ris n1. a *OE* (?a1200) Lay.Brut ROMA 2
risen v. 9a *OE* ?a1160 Peterb.Chron.
ROMA 115
rishe n. 1b *OE* (c1250) Gen.& Ex. ROMA
2
risinge ger. 1c *(fr. risen v.)* (?a1200)
Trin.Hom. BO 2

rite n. 1a *L* (a1333) Shoreham Poems TR 6
riven v2. 1f *ON* a1250 Mon may longe
HF 7
rivere n. 2a *OF, AF* (?c1225) Horn ROMA
25
ro n1. a *OE* ?c1200 Stw.57.Gloss. ROMA
5
robben v. 1a *OF, OPic.* (?a1200) Ancr.
ROMA 5
robbere n. a *OF, AF* (?a1200) Ancr.
MKT 2
robberie n. a *OF, AF* (?a1200)
Trin.Hom. *ROMA* 1
robe n. 1a *OF* ?c1200 Wor.Bod.Gloss.
ROMA 12
Robert n. 1a *OF & ML; ult. Gmc.*
(a1376) PPl.A(1) (Trin-C) *FRT* 1
Robin n. 1a *OF* (a1376) PPl.A(1) (Trin-
C) TR 4
roche n2. 1a *OF* (?c1225) Horn BD 31
Rochelle n. a *OF* (a1376) PPl.A(1) (Trin-
C) *PARDT* 1
rode n1. c *OE* (?a1200) Ancr. MILT 2
rode n5. 2c b *OE* a1121 Peterb.Chron.
BD 6
rodi adj. d *OE* (?a1200) Ancr. ROMA 7
rof n. 1e *OE* c1175 Body & S.(1) BD 10
roial adj. 2a *OF* (c1250) Floris (Suth)
MKT 32
roialli adv. a *fr. roial adj.* Chaucer KNT
10
roialte n. b *OF* Chaucer MLT 3
roilen v1. 2a *OF* ?a1325 Heil seint Michel
BO 1
roine n. *OF* Chaucer *ROMA* 1
roinouse adj. b {a} *OF* Chaucer {(c1378)
PPl.B (Ld)} *ROMA* 1
roke n2. 1a *OE* ?c1200 Stw.57.Gloss. *HF*
1
roket n1. a *OF* c1300 SLeg. (Ld) *ROMA* 3
rokken v. 1b *prob. OE* (c1125)
Vsp.D.Hom.Fest.Virg. *RVT* 1
rolle n. 1b f *OF* (?a1200) Ancr. *PARDT* 1
rollen v2. 1b *OF* a1325 SLeg.Pilate
(Corp-C) BO 11

rom n. *no etym.* Chaucer *PARSPRO* 1
Romain adj. a *OF & L* (a1325) Cursor
MKT 5
Romain n. a *OF & L & OE* c1150
Hrl.HApul. BD 17
romaunce n. e *OF, AF* (c1300) Havelok
ROMA 9
Rome n. 2a *OE & OF & L* 1123
Peterb.Chron. ROMA 61
romen v. 1d *prob. OE* (?a1200) Lay.Brut
BD 32
Rome-ward n. 1a, Rome n. (*fr. Rome n.
& -ward suf.*) (a1338) Mannyng
Chron.Pt.1 *MLT* 1
ron n3. b *OE* a1300 Hwi ne serue *ROMA*
1
rop n2. 1a *OE* ?a1160 Peterb.Chron.
LGW 1
rore n2. *MDu.* Chaucer *TR* 1
roren v1. 1a *OE* (?c1200) St.Juliana HF 8
roringe ger1. a (*fr. roren v1.*) (?c1200)
SWard *MERT* 1
rosarie n. c *L* (a1387) Trev.Higd. *CYT* 1
rose n1. b *OE & OF & L* c1150
Hrl.HApul. ROMA 37
rose-leef n. 6a, rose n1. (*fr. rose n1. & lef
n1.*) a1325 Add.46919 Cook.Recipes
ROMA 2
rosene adj. c *OE & OF* (1351–2) in
Antiq.50 ROMA 6
rosere n. a *OF, AF* (c1300) Havelok
ROMA 3
rosi adj. a *fr. rose n1.* 1381 Dc.257
Cook.Recipes *TR* 3
roste n1. a *OF* (?c1300) Amis *GP* 1
rosten v. 1a *OF* (c1280) SLeg.Pass. (Pep)
GP 5
rote n1. a *OF* (?a1300) Tristrem *GP* 1
rote n2. b *origin unknown* (?c1300)
Caiphas GP 4
rote n4. 9 *ON & LOE* (*fr. ON*) a1131
Peterb.Chron. ROMA 37
roteles adj. *fr. rote n4.* Chaucer *TR* 1
roten adj. 1a a *ON* c1300 Body & S.(5)
SNPRO 10

roten vi. 1b a *OE* c1150 PDidax. *CKT* 1
roten-herted adj. 2b, roten adj. *(fr. roten adj. & herted adj.)* Chaucer *PARST* 1
rouel n1. *OF; ult ON* (?c1300) Reinbrun *THOP* 1
rouen vi. e *OE* (?c1150) Prov.Alf. (Mdst) *TR* 2
rouere n. *fr. rouen vi.* Chaucer *BO* 1
roughe adj. 7 *OE* c1150 PDidax. ROMA 6
rouken v. b *fr. ruke n.* (?a1200) Ancr. *KNT* 1
roum adj. a *OE* (?c1150) Prov.Alf. (Trin-C) AST 3
roum n2. 1a *OE* ?c1200 Orm. *LGW* 1
rounci n. c *OF, AF & ML, AL* (c1300) Havelok *GP* 1
rounde adj. 1a *OF, AF* c1300 SLeg.Mich. (Ld) ROMA 21
rounde adv. 1a *fr. rounde adj.* c1300 SLeg.Becket (Ld) KNT 5
rounde n. 5 *fr. OF, AF & <rounde adj.>* (?a1200) Ancr. *BO* 1
roundel n. 1f *OF & ML, AL* c1300 SLeg.Becket (Ld) HF 6
rounden v. b *OF* Chaucer *GP* 1
roundnesse n. 1a *fr. rounde adj.* Chaucer *BO* 4
rounen v. 1a *OE* (?a1200) Trin.Hom. HF 14
rouninge ger. 1a *(fr. rounen v.)* (?a1200) Lay.Brut *HF* 1
route n1. 1c *OF, AF* ?c1225 Ancr. (Cleo) ROMA 45
routen v2. a *OE* (?c1300) Bevis BD 3
routen v3. *OE* (a1325) Ipotis HF 2
routen v8. a *OF* a1325 SLeg. (Corp-C) *MLT* 1
routinge ger2. *(fr. routen v2.)* Chaucer *RVT* 2
routinge ger3. *(fr. routen v3.)* Chaucer *HF* 1
rubben v. 2a *cp. LG, EFris.* a1325 SLeg.Geo.(1) (Corp-C) ADAM 3

rubie n. a *OF* (?c1300) St.Patr.Purg.(1) ROMA 15
rubifien v. a *OF* Chaucer *CYT* 1
rubriche n. 1b *OF & L* (?c1300) LFMass Bk. *WBPRO* 1
ruddoke n. a *OE* ?c1200 Stw.57.Gloss. *PF* 1
rude adj. 2c *OF* (?c1300) NPass. ROMA 14
rudeli adv. 2b *fr. rude adj.* a1375 WPal. GP 2
rudenesse n. c *fr. rude adj.* Chaucer TR 3
ruf n2. *no etym.* Chaucer *PARSPRO* 1
ruggen v. 1a *ON* (c1300) Songs Langtoft *LGW* 1
ruggi adj. a *prob. ON* Chaucer *KNT* 1
ruine n. a *OF & L* c1175 Bod.Hom. HF 4
rumbel n. a *fr. <rumbelen v.>* Chaucer *KNT* 2
rumbelen v. c *MDu., MLG & ON* Chaucer MKT 4
rumbelinge ger. a *(fr. rumbelen v.)* Chaucer *SUMT* 1
rumour n. a *OF & L* Chaucer *BO* 4
rung n. b *OE* a1300 Gloss.Bibbesw. (Seld) *MILT* 1
rusen v. a *OF* (a1338) Mannyng Chron.Pt.1 *BD* 1
rushen v. 1a *AF, OF* c1380 Firumb.(1) *KNT* 1
russel n. b *OF* Chaucer *NPT* 1
rusten v. a *fr. rust n.* (?a1200) Ancr. GP 3
rusti adj. a *OE* a1225 Wint.Ben.Rule ROMA 2
sable n. e *OF & ML, AL* (?a1325) Otuel & R. *MARS* 1
sachel n1. a *OF & L* (c1340) Rolle Psalter (UC 64) *BO* 1
sacrament n. 1a *OF & L* (?a1200) Ancr. *BO* 12
sacren v. 1a *OF & L* (?a1200) Ancr. KNT 2
sacrifice n. 1a *OF, AF & L* c1275 Ken.Serm. BD 21

sacrificen v. a *fr. sacrifice n.* c1300 SLeg.
(Ld) SNT 4
sacrifien v. a *OF* (?a1300) KAlex. *LGW* 1
sacrifiinge ger. a *(fr. sacrifien v.)* (?a1300)
KAlex. *BO* 1
sacrilege n. a *OF* (c1303) Mannyng HS
BO 4
sacrilegie n. b *L* (a1325) Ipotis *BO* 1
sad adj. 1a *OE* (?a1200) Lay.Brut BD 29
sad adv. e *fr. sad adj.* (a1338) Mannyng
Chron.Pt.2 *CLT* 1
sadel n. a *OE* (?a1200) Lay.Brut KNT 7
sadel-boue n. a *OE* (?c1150) Prov.Alf.
(Mdst) *KNT* 1
sadli adv. 4e *fr. sad adj.* (a1325) Cursor
KNT 8
sadnesse n. 2b *fr. sad adj.* (a1333)
Shoreham Poems LADY 5
saffroun n. 1c *OF & AL; ult. Ar.* (?a1200)
Trin.Hom. *THOP* 1
safrounen v. *fr. saffroun n.* (c1303)
Mannyng HS *PARDPRO* 1
sagittarie n. a *OF, AF & L* Chaucer *AST*
4
saillour n. a *OF* Chaucer *ROMA* 1
sak n. 4a *OE & ON & OF & L* (?a1200)
Trin.Hom. *ROMA* 6
sake n. 2b *OE* a1121 Peterb.Chron. LADY
36
sakken v. 1a *fr. sak n.* (c1303) Mannyng
HS *RVT* 1
sal n. 1 *L & OF* c1330 SMChron. (Auch)
CYT 5
Salomon n. a *L & OF; ult. Heb.* (?c1150)
Prov.Alf.(Trin-C) KNT 75
saloue n. a *OE, ON* (1373) *Lelamour
Macer *WBPRO* 1
salt adj. 1d *OE* ?c1200 Orm. TR 20
salt n1. 1c *OE* c1150 Hrl.HApul. SUMT 2
salu adj. a *OE* Chaucer *ROMA* 1
saluen v. b *OF* (?a1300) KAlex. TR 16
saluinge ger. *(fr. saluen v.)* Chaucer TR
2
salutacioun n. a *OF & L* (c1384)
WBible(1) *SHIPT* 1

salve n1. 1a *OE* c1150 Hrl.HApul. TR 3
Samaritane n. a *fr. OE & L* (a1325)
Cursor *WBPRO* 2
same adj. 1c *ON* ?c1200 Orm. BD 223
same pron. 2a *fr. same adj.* (c1303)
Mannyng HS ABC 28
samite n. b *OF & ML* (?a1300) KAlex.
ROMA 3
Sampsoun n. a *OE (fr. L) & L, ML; ult
Gr.* (?a1200) Ancr. BD 17
sand n. 1f *OE* a1150 Vsp.D.Hom. HF
14
sanden v. *fr. sand n.* Chaucer *TR* 1
sanguine adj. a *OF & L* (1373)
*Lelamour Macer KNT 2
sanguine n. b *OF & L* Chaucer *GP* 1
saphire n. a *OF & L, AL* (c1250) Floris
(Cmb) ROMA 2
sapience n. f *OF & L* (a1376) PPl.A(1)
(Trin-C) SNPRO 17
Sarasineis adj. a *OF* (?a1300) Rich.
(Auch) *ROMA* 1
sarge n. b *OF & ML* (a1382) WBible(1)
(Bod 959) *KNT* 1
sarplere n. *AF & ML, AL* c1380
Firumb.(1) *BO* 1
Satan n. a *L, OE & OF; ult. Heb.* c1225
St.Juliana (Roy) *MLT* 3
Satanas n. a *L, OE & OF; ult. Heb.*
(c1175) PMor. (Trin-C) MKT 11
Sater-dai n. a *OE* a1150 Vsp.D.Hom.
AST 6
satin n. b *OF & ML, AL* Chaucer ROMA
3
satire n. a *OF & L, fr. Gr.* Chaucer *TR* 1
satisfaccioun n. 1a *OF & L* (a1325)
Cursor *BO* 9
Saturne n. b *L & OF* c1300 SLeg.Mich.
(Ld) HF 19
saturnine adj. a *ML & OF* Chaucer *HF*
1
sauce n. b *OF & ML, AL* (1340) Ayenb.
FORMAGE 5
saucefleume adj. a *fr. <saucefleume n.>*
Chaucer *GP* 1

saue n2. 4a *OE* (?c1150) Prov.Alf. (Trin-
C) HF 14

sauf adj. 3a *OF & L* (c1280) SLeg.Pass.
(Pep) ANEL 12

sauf adv. vouche-sauf v. *fr. sauf adj.* c1330
KTars. ABC 22

sauf prep. 1a a *fr. sauf adj.* (?c1300) Amis
BD 90

sauf-garde n. c *OF* Chaucer TR 1

saufli adv. 1a *fr. sauf adj.* (c1280)
SLeg.Pass. (Pep) HF 8

sauns prep. a *OF* (?a1300) Tristrem HF 3

sauter n. 1e *OE & OF* (?a1200) Ancr.
ROMA 1

sautrie n. a *OF & L* (?c1300) Reinbrun
GP 4

savacioun n. 2a *OF & L* (?a1200) Ancr.
ABC 30

save n1. b *prob. fr. salvie n. or L* (1373)
*Lelamour Macer KNT 1

saven v. 1b *OF & L* (?a1200) Ancr. ABC
118

saveour n. 2a *OF* (?a1300) Arth.& M.
PARST 2

saverous adj. *OF* Chaucer ROMA 1

savinge ger. 1c *(fr. saven v.)* (c1280)
SLeg.Pass. (Pep) BO 1

savinge prep. 1a *fr. saven v.* Chaucer BD
7

savour n. 1b b *OF* (?a1200) Ancr. ROMA
21

savouren v. 7a *OF* (?a1250) Serm.Atte
wrastlinge TRUTH 4

savourie adj. d *OF* (?c1200) St.Kath.(1)
TR 1

savouringe ger. 2b *(fr. savouren v.)*
(c1384) WBible(1) PARST 3

savourli adv. a *fr. savour n.* Chaucer
MILT 1

scabbe n. 1a *prob. ON* c1275 Ken.Serm.
ROMA 2

scaffold n. 2b *AL* Chaucer KNT 2

scalden v. 4a *AL & OF, ONF* (?a1200)
Ancr. KNT 2

scale n1. 1a *ML* (?c1300) Guy(1) PF 1

scale n2. 3 *L & ML* Chaucer AST 2

scalle n. b *prob. ON* (a1325) Cursor
ADAM 1

scallede adj. e *fr. scalle n.* (1340) Ayenb.
GP 1

scant adj. a *fr. ON* (?a1350) Castleford
Chron. ABC 1

scantite n. *fr. scant adj.* Chaucer PARST 1

scantnesse n. c *fr. scant adj.* Chaucer
PARST 3

scapen v1. 2a a *fr. <escapen v.> & OF, AF*
(?c1225) Horn TR 8

scapinge ger. a *(fr. scapen v1.)* (?a1300)
Arth.& M. BO 1

scarlet adj. a *fr. scarlet n.* c1300
SLeg.Inf.Chr. (Ld) WBPRO 2

scarlet n. 2c *OF, AF & ML* c1250 Thene
latemeste dai (Clg) GP 2

scarmuche n. *OF* (?c1380) Cleanness TR
3

scarmuching ger. *(fr. scarmuchen v.)*
Chaucer LGW 1

scarse adj. 1c *OF, (chiefly) ONF* c1300
SLeg. (Ld) FORMAGE 2

scarsete n. 1a *AF, ONF* (?a1300) KAlex.
VENUS 3

scarsli adv. b *fr. scarse adj.* (c1300)
Glo.Chron.A BD 9

scarsnesse n. 2a *fr. scarse adj.* (a1325)
Cursor PARST 1

scateren v. 3 *prob. OE* ?a1160
Peterb.Chron. BO 3

scathe n. 3b *ON* (a1250) Bestiary TR 4

scathles adj. *fr. <scathe n.>* ?c1200 Orm.
ROMA 1

science n. 1a a *OF & L, ML* (c1340) Rolle
Psalter (UC 64) HF 46

sclate n. b *fr. OF* (c1340) Rolle Psalter
(UC 64) MercB 1

sclaundre n. 3a *AF, OF* (c1280)
SLeg.Pass. (Pep) HF 10

sclaundren v. 1a *AF, OF* (?c1280)
SLeg.Concep.Virg. (Ashm) CYPRO 3

sclave n2. *OF & ML* c1300 SLeg.Becket
(Ld) TR 1

Chaucer's words

sclendre adj. 1a *AF* Chaucer ROMA 6

scochoun n. 1a *AF* (c1353) Winner & W.
ROMA 1

scole n2. 6a *OE, fr. L* a1150 Vsp.D.Hom.
BO 17

scoleien v. *AF* Chaucer GP 1

scoleiing ger. *(fr. scoleien v.)* Chaucer
WBPRO 1

scole-matere n. 2d, scole n2. *(fr. scole n2.
& matere n.)* Chaucer FRPRO 1

scolere n. c *OE & OF & ML* c1300
SLeg.Edm.Abp. (Hrl) GP 3

scole-termes n. 2d, scole n2. *(fr. scole n2.
& terme n.)* Chaucer MERT 1

scoleward n. 2a, scole n2. *fr scole n2. & -
ward suf.* * Chaucer PRT 1

scome n. a *fr. MDu., MLG* (1340)
Ayenb. BO 1

scoren v. d *fr. score n.* Chaucer SHIPT 1

scorklen v. b *? fr. scorcnen v. by
dissimilation* Chaucer BO 1

scorn n. 1a *OF, AF/ONF* ?c1200 Orm.
HF 12

scornen v. 3a *OF, AF/ONF* (?c1150)
Prov.Alf. (Trin-C) BD 21

scornere n. c *fr. scornen v.* (c1303)
Mannyng HS PF 5

scorninge ger. a (fr. scornen v.) (?a1200)
Lay.Brut TR 3

scorpioun n. 1a *OF, AF & OE & L* c1150
Hrl.HApul. BD 10

Scot n1. b *fr. OE, LOE* a1126
Peterb.Chron. MLT 1

scot n3. *?ON* Chaucer GP 2

Scotlond-ward n. b, Scot-lond n. *(fr.
Scotlond n. & -ward suf.)* Chaucer
MLT 1

scouren v2. a *prob. MDu., MLG*
(?a1200) Ancr. ROMA 2

scourge n. b *AF, OF* (?a1200) Ancr. CLT
2

scourgen v. a *fr. scourge n.* c1300
SLeg.Fran.(1) (Ld) PARST 1

scourginge ger. b *(fr. scourgen v.)*
(?a1200) Ancr. MARS 2

scrapen v. b *ON* ?c1225 Ancr. (Cleo)
ADAM 1

scrippe n. b *ON* (?c1225) Horn HF 3

scripture n. 1a *L* (a1325) Cursor BO 4

scrite n. a *OF, AF & L* (c1300)
Glo.Chron.A TR 2

scrivein n. a *OF, AF* (c1303) Mannyng
HS ADAM 1

scrivenish adv. *fr. scrivein n.* Chaucer TR
1

sculle n. a *? fr. ON* (?a1200) Ancr. RVT 2

se n1. 3a *OE, LOE* a1121 Peterb.Chron.
ROMA 127

se n2. 2a *OF* c1300 SLeg.Becket (Ld)
MKT 5

sechen v. 5a *OE & ON* a1121
Peterb.Chron. ROMA 145

sechinge ger. 1a *(fr. sechen v.)* (?c1300)
Guy(1) BO 1

second num. 1a *OF & L* (c1300)
Glo.Chron.A SNT 44

seconde n. a *ML* Chaucer AST 2

secondli adv. a *fr. second num.* (a1382)
WBible(1) (Bod 959) TR 3

secre adj. b *OF* Chaucer MKT 26

secre n. c *fr. <secre adj.>* (c1300)
Glo.Chron.A MKT 6

secreli adv. a *fr. secre adj.* Chaucer CLT 5

secrenesse n. b *fr. secre adj.* Chaucer
MLT 1

secret adj. g *fr. L* (c1378) PPl.B (Ld) TR 3

secret n. b *L* Chaucer BO 2

secte n. 2d *OF, AF & L* (?c1350)
SVrn.Leg. HF 4

seculere adj. 1c *OF & L* c1300
SLeg.Becket (Hrl) MERT 3

seculere n. b *fr. seculere adj.* c1300
SLeg.Becket (Ld) PARST 1

sed n. 1a d *OE* a1126 Peterb.Chron.
ROMA 22

seden v. 1c *fr. sed n. & LOE* Chaucer
ANEL 1

sed-foul n. 1a f, sed n. *(fr. sed n. & foul
n.)* Chaucer PF 2

sege n2. 1a *OF* (?a1200) Ancr. BO 12

seien vi. 1a a *OE* a1121 Peterb.Chron. GENERAL 2815

seile n. 1a *OE* (?a1200) Lay.Brut BO 13

seilen v. 1a a *OE* (?a1200) Lay.Brut HF 29

seilinge ger. a *(fr. seilen v.)* (a1338) Mannyng Chron.Pt.2 *PF* 1

seinge ger. c *(fr. sen vi.)* (?a1325) Bonav.Medit.(1) *TR* 1

seinte adj. 2a *OF* (c1125) Vsp.D.Hom.Euclid. BD 201

seinte n. 1a *OE & OF & L* ?c1200 Orm. ROMA 18

Seint-Jame n. b, Jame n. *OF* (c1300) NHom.(1) Pilgr. *GP* 1

seintuarie n. 2a a *OF, AF & L, AL* (a1325) Cursor BO 3

seisen v. 1a a *OF & ML, AL* (1265) BLewes PF 3

selde adj. a *fr. selde adv.* (?a1200) Ancr. *CLT* 1

selde adv. a *fr. OE* (?c1175) PMor. (Trin-C) ROMA 13

seldene adv. c *OE* (?c1150) Prov.Alf. (Trin-C) LGW F 2

sele n1. 2a *OE* c1175 Bod.Hom. *RVT* 1

sele n3. 2d *OF* (?c1200) HMaid. TR 6

selen v. 3a *OF, AF* (?a1200) Ancr. TR 3

self adj., n. & pron. 3a a *OE* a1121 Peterb.Chron. HF 21

seli adj. 1a *fr. OE* c1175 Bod.Hom. HF 44

selili adv. b *fr. OE* ?c1200 Orm. BO 1

selinesse n. a *fr. seli adj.* (a1325) Cursor *TR* 3

sellen v. 2c *OE* a1126 Peterb.Chron. ROMA 26

sellere n. a *fr. sellen v.* (?a1200) Trin.Hom. *GP* 1

semblable adj. 1a *OF* c1300 SLeg.Becket (Ld) BO 25

semblaunce n. 1b *OF, AF* (a1325) SLeg.Cec. (Ashm) ROMA 4

semblaunt n. 1b *OF* (?a1200) Ancr. ROMA 15

seme n1. 1f *OE* a1225 Vsp.A.Hom.Init.Creat. *PARST* 1

semeli adj. 3a *ON* (?a1200) Ancr. ROMA 10

semeli adv. 2a *fr. semeli adj.* (?c1200) St.Marg.(1) ROMA 4

semelihede n. a *fr. semeli adj.* Chaucer *ROMA* 2

semelinesse n. b *fr. semeli adj.* Chaucer *LGW* 1

semen v2. 11b *fr. ON* ?c1200 Orm. ROMA 244

semi adj. *prob. fr. semeli adj.* Chaucer MILT 2

semicope n. *fr. cope n.* Chaucer *GP* 1

seminge ger. c *(fr. semen v2.)* Chaucer BD 3

sen vi. 3a *OE or LOE* a1121 Peterb.Chron. ROMA 1113

senate n. a *OF & L* (?a1200) Lay.Brut BO 9

senatorie n. a *OF* Chaucer BO 1

senatour n. c *OF & L* (?a1200) Lay.Brut MKT 23

senden v2. 1a *OE* a1121 Peterb.Chron. ROMA 181

Seneciens n. pl. *OF* Chaucer BO 1

sengen v. *OE* (1340) Ayenb. WBPRO 2

sengle adj. 4 *OF & L, AL* (?a1300) KAlex. MERT 2

sengli adv. a *fr. sengle adj.* (a1338) Mannyng Chron.Pt.1 BO 1

senith n. a *ML, AL; ult. Ar.* (a1387) Trev.Higd. *AST* 21

sense n. a *OF & L* (a1382) WBible(1) Pref.Jer. (Bod 959) *PARST* 1

sensibilite n. e *OF* Chaucer BO 1

sensible adj. 4b *OF & L* (c1380) Wycl.Papa BO 12

sensualite n. a *OF* (c1340) Rolle Psalter (UC 64) *PARST* 9

sentement n. b *OF & ML* Chaucer TR 5

sentence n. 2a *OF & L* (?a1200) Ancr. SNPRO 96

Septembre n. a *L, OE & OF* a1121
  Peterb.Chron. *AST* 2
septentrional adj. a *L & OF* Chaucer
  AST 2
septentrione n. c *L & OF, AF* Chaucer
  M*K*T 2
sepulcre n. 1b *L & OF & L OE* (?a1200)
  Trin.Hom. *WBPRO* 1
sepulture n. 1 *L & OF* (a1333) Shoreham
  Poems T*R* 7
serchen v. 1c *OF* (?a1300) KAlex. *WBT* 2
sergeaunt n. 1a *OF* (?a1200) Trin.Hom.
  SNT 12
serie n. *fr. L* Chaucer *KNT* 1
seriousli adv. b *prob. fr. ML* Chaucer
  MLT 1
serment n. d *OF* (?c1280) SLeg.Advent,
  etc.(Eg) *FRANT* 1
sermoun n. 2a *OF, AF & L* (c1200) Vices
  & V.(1) T*R* 9
sermounen v. b *OF, AF* a1225
  Lamb.Hom. *PARDT* 1
sermouninge ger. a *(fr. sermounen v.)*
  (a1325) Cursor K*N*T 4
serpent n. 1a *OF & L* (a1300) Cokaygne
  M*K*T 19
servage n. 3 *OF & ML* (?c1280)
  SLeg.OTHist. (Ld 622) BD 13
servaunt n. 1a *OF, CF, AF* (?a1200)
  Ancr. P*I*TY 72
serven v. 15a *OF, (chiefly)AF & L* c1175
  Bod.Hom. R*O*MA 136
servisable adj. a *OF & ML* a1375 WPal.
  GP 4
servise n. 3b *OF, NF* (c1200) Vices &
  V.(1) R*O*MA 95
servitour n. b *OF* (a1338) Mannyng
  Chron.Pt.2 S*U*MT 1
servitute n. b *L & OF* Chaucer CLT 2
sesoun n. 1d *OF, AF* (?a1300) KAlex.
  R*O*MA 28
sessioun n. c *OF, AF & L, AL* Chaucer
  GP 1
sete n2. 1b *OE; ult ON* ?c1200 Orm.
  M*K*T 16

setewale n. a *OF, AF & AL; ult Ar.*
  (?a1200) Ancr. R*O*MA 3
sethen vi. 1e *OE* a1150 Vsp.D.Hom. GP
  4
setlen v. 1a *OE* ?c1200 Orm. *MERT* 1
setten v. 17a *OE* a1121 Peterb.Chron.
  R*O*MA 278
settinge ger. 10b *(fr. setten v.)* (c1303)
  Mannyng HS *AST* 1
seu n1. a *OE & OF* c1150 Hrl.HApul.
  SQT 1
seuen vi. 4c *OF* (?a1200) Trin.Hom. BD
  7
seuen v2. 3 *OE* (?a1200) Ancr. R*O*MA 6
seur adj. 1a b *OF* c1250 Owl & N. M*E*L 2
seur adv. e *fr. seur adj.* (?a1350) Siege
  Troy(1) T*R* 2
seurli adv. a *fr. seur adj.* (?c1300) Bevis
  S*H*IPT 2
seurte n. 3a *OF* (?c1300) Bevis HF 13
seven num. 1a a *OE* a1150 Vsp.D.Hom.
  ABC 33
seventene num. a *OE* c1150 Hrl.MQuad.
  EPINPT 1
seventhe num. 1a *fr. <seven num.>* a1121
  Peterb.Chron. HF 5
sexe n. *OF & L* Chaucer BO 1
sexteine n. a *AL fr. ML* (c1303) Mannyng
  HS S*U*MT 2
shade n. b *OE* c1150 Hrl.HApul. HF 2
shadwe n. 1b *fr. OE* c1175 Bod.Hom.
  R*O*MA 22
shadwen v. 1a *OE* (1340) Ayenb. R*O*MA 3
shadwi adj. b *fr. shadwe n.* Chaucer BO
  1
shadwinge ger. b *OE* a1150 Vsp.D.Hom.
  R*O*MA 1
shafte n2. 1a *OE* (?a1200) Lay.Brut
  R*O*MA 4
shaken v. 3a *OE* a1150 Vsp.D.Hom.
  R*O*MA 18
shale n. a *OE* (?a1200) Lay.Brut HF 1
shalemie n. *OF* Chaucer HF 1
shame n. 3a *OE* a1150 Vsp.D.Hom.
  R*O*MA 118

shamefaste adj. 1a *OE* ?c1200 Orm.
RomA 8

shamefastnesse n. 2 *OE* (?a1200)
Trin.Hom. GP 4

shamefulle adj. a *fr. shame n.* (?a1200)
Ancr. RomA 6

shamen v. 1a a *OE* a1150 Vsp.D.Hom.
HF 7

shape n. 6a *OE* ?c1200 Orm. RomA 22

shapen v. 3b *OE* a1150 Vsp.D.Hom. PITY
89

shapli adj. a *fr. shape n.* (a1382)
WBible(1) (Bod 959) TR 2

share n1. *OE* (c1300) Glo.Chron.A
MiLT 1

sharp adj. 10a *OE* a1150 Vsp.D.Hom.
RomA 44

sharpe adv. b *fr. OE* c1250 Owl & N.
HF 6

sharpen v. b *fr. sharp adj. & OE* c1225
Body & S.(2) MiLT 1

sharpli adv. 5b *fr. OE & sharp adj.* c1150
Hrl.HApul. GP 3

sharpnesse n. 3a *fr. OE & sharp adj.*
c1150 Hrl.HApul. BO 1

shaue n. a *OE, LOE* ?a1300 Thrush &
N. TR 3

shaven v. 1a *OE* c1150 Hrl.MQuad.
RomA 8

shavinge ger. 2b *(fr. shaven v.)* (c1353)
Winner & W. CYT 1

she pron. 1a *prob. fr. OE* ?a1160
Peterb.Chron. GENERAL 2580

she-ape n. 3b, she pron. *(fr. she pron. &
ape n.)* Chaucer PARST 1

shede n. b *OE* ?c1200 Orm. KNT 2

sheden v. 6d *OE, LOE* c1150 Hrl.HApul.
MKT 7

shef n. 1b *OE* ?c1200 Orm. HF 4

Sheffeld n. *fr. OE* Chaucer RVT 1

sheld n. 1a *OE* a1150 Vsp.D.Hom. BO 17

shelden v. 1b *OE* c1150 Hrl.HApul. HF
14

shelfe n. a *OE* Chaucer MiLT 1

shelle-fishe n. 1c, shelle n. *OE* Chaucer
BO 3

shenchen v. b *OE* (c1125)
Vsp.D.Hom.Fest.Virg. MERT 1

shenden v. 1a *OE* ?c1200 Orm. RomA 30

shendshipe n. 1b *fr. <shende n.>* (?a1250)
Serm.Atte wrastlinge PARST 1

shene adj. 2a *OE* ?c1200 Orm. RomA 26

shene adv. a *fr. schene adj.* (?a1200) Ancr.
TR 2

shep n. 1a *OE* a1150 Vsp.D.Hom. KNT
18

shep-herde n. 1a *OE* ?c1200 Orm.
RomA 5

shere n1. a *OE* (c1300) Havelok MKT 4

sheren v. 1a *OE* (?a1200) Lay.Brut MKT 5

sheringe-hok n. a, shering ger. *(fr.
sheringe ger. & hok n.)* Chaucer LGW 1

shete n2. d *OE* a1150 Vsp.D.Hom. SNT
7

sheten v. 1a *OE* a1150 Vsp.D.Hom.
RomA 9

shetere n. a *OE* c1300 SLeg. (Hrl) PF 1

shethe n1. a *OE* a1150 Vsp.D.Hom. TR 4

sheuen v1. 11b *OE* a1131 Peterb.Chron.
RomA 259

sheuinge ger. 5a *OE* a1150 Vsp.D.Hom.
BO 4

she-wolf n. 3b, she pron. *(fr. she pron. &
wolf n.)* Chaucer MANCT 1

shiften v. 2 *OE* ?c1200 Orm. SNT 2

shimeringe ger. *(fr. shimeren v.)* (?c1380)
Pearl. RVT 1

shine n1. a *OE* c1225 Wor.Aelfric Gloss.
KNT 2

shinen v. 1a a *OE* a1150 Vsp.D.Hom.
RomA 78

shininge ger. 2 *(fr. shinen v.)* c1300
SLeg. (Hrl) BO 11

ship n. 1a a *OE* a1121 Peterb.Chron. ABC
69

shipe n. *OE* (1340) Ayenb. ANEL 2

shipene n. a *OE* (?c1280) SLeg.Nativ.
(Eg) KNT 2

ship-man n. a *OE* 1122 Peterb.Chron. HF 5

shire n. a *OE* a1121 Peterb.Chron. GP 4

shir-reve n. a *OE* (1100) Chart.St.Paul in RHS ser.3.58 *GP* 1

shirte n. a *OE* (?a1200) Trin.Hom. MκT 20

shiten v. b *OE* (?a1300) KAlex. *GP* 1

shitten v. 1a *OE* (c1200) Vices & V.(1) RomA 32

shittinge ger. a {a} *(fr. shitten v.)* Chaucer {(c1384) WBible (1)} *RomA* 1

shivere n. b *perh. OE* (?a1200) Lay.Brut *SumT* 1

shiveren v. a *fr. shivere n.* (a1338) Mannyng Chron.Pt.1 *KnT* 1

sho n. 1a *OE* a1150 Vsp.D.Hom. RomA 9

shon v. a *OE* a1150 Vsp.D.Hom. RomA 3

shond n1. a *OE* (?c1150) Prov.Alf. (Mdst) HF 2

shoppe n. a *OE* (c1300) Glo.Chron.A CκPro 5

short adj. 1a *OE* a1150 Vsp.D.Hom. RomA 41

short n. b *fr. short adj.* (c1340) Rolle Psalter (UC 64) Tr 9

shorte adv. 3c *fr. short adj.* ?a1325 Swet ihc hend SNT 4

shorten v. 2a b *OE* a1225 Lamb.Hom. Tr 5

shortli adv. 1b *fr. short adj. & OE* (c1125) Vsp.D.Hom.Fest.Virg. RomA 99

shortnesse n. 2b *fr. short adj.* (c1384) WBible(1) *ParsT* 1

short-sholdred adj. 1b, short adj. *(fr. short adj. & shulder n.)* Chaucer *GP* 1

shot n. 1a *OE* (c1300) Glo.Chron.A Tr 3

shot-windoue n. *fr. windoue n.* Chaucer *MilT* 2

shour n. 1a *OE* a1150 Vsp.D.Hom. Tr 10

shoute n1. b *?fr. ON* ?c1375 NHom.(3) Pass. *NPT* 1

shouten v. e *fr. shoute n1.* Chaucer HF 3

shoutinge ger. *(fr. shouten v.)* Chaucer PF 3

shouven v. 1i *OE* a1150 Vsp.D.Hom. RomA 10

shouvinge ger. d *(fr. shouven v.)* (c1300) Glo.Chron.A *MancPro* 1

shreden v. a *OE* c1150 PDidax. *CLT* 1

shreue n. 1a *prob. OE* (?c1225) Horn HF 133

shreued adj. 1a *fr. shreue n.* (c1280) SLeg.Pass. (Pep) HF 7

shreuedli adv. a *fr. shreued adj.* c1330 Why werre *SumT* 1

shreuednesse n. c *fr. shreued adj.* c1300 SLeg.Kenelm (Ld) HF 21

shreuen v. a *fr. shreue n.* (a1338) Mannyng Chron.Pt.2 WBPro 6

shrift n. 2a *OE, LOE* a1150 Vsp.D.Hom. BD 22

shrifte-fader n. 1e, shrift n. *(fr. shrift n. & fader n.)* (?a1200) Ancr. *FrT* 1

shrille adj. a *? fr. shille adj.* (?c1380) Cleanness *NPT* 1

shrimpe n. c *prob fr. MLG, MDu.* Chaucer *ProMκT* 1

shrine n. a *OE (fr. L) & L, AL & OF* a1121 Peterb.Chron. Tr 6

shrinen v. a *fr. shrine n.* c1300 SLeg.Becket (Ld) ParдT 2

shrinken v. 1a *OE* c1150 Wenne Wenne Bo 2

shriven v. 2a *OE* ?c1200 Orm. Tr 32

shroud n. 1b *OE* a1121 Peterb.Chron. *RomA* 1

shrouden v. 1 *fr. shroud n.* (a1325) Cursor *RomA* 1

shulder n. 1a a *OE* a1150 Vsp.D.Hom. RomA 17

shulder-bon n. a *fr. shulder n. & bon n1.* a1325 Gloss.Bibbesw. PardPro 2

shulen v1. 3a e *OE* a1121 Peterb.Chron. General 2542

sibbe adj. f *OE* a1150 Vsp.D.Hom. RomA 2

sibbe n2. b *fr. OE.* (?c1175) PMor. (Lamb) *MEL* 1

sibille n. a *L, OE & OF* (?a1200) Lay.Brut HF 2

sicamoure n. a *L & OF* (c1350) NHom.(2) PSanct. *HF* 1

siclatoun n. a *OF, (chiefly) AF & AL* (?c1200) St.Juliana *THOP* 1

side n. 2a *OE* a1150 Vsp.D.Hom. ROMA 155

sien vi. a *OE* c1150 Hrl.HApul. *TR* 1

siften v. b *OE* a1150 Vsp.D.Hom. *CYT* 1

sighe n. b *fr.* sighen *v.* Chaucer *KNT* 1

sighen v. 1a *fr.* siken *v2.* (c1250) Gen.& Ex. *TR* 1

sighte n. 1a *OE* c1175 Bod.Hom. ROMA 115

signal n. b *OF* Chaucer HF 2

signe n. 3 *OE & OF & L, AL* (?a1200) Ancr. ABC 118

signet n1. a *OF* (?c1380) Pearl *TR* 1

signifer n. *L* Chaucer *TR* 1

signifiaunce n. b *OF* c1275 Ken.Serm. ROMA 5

significacioun n. 1c *OF, AF & L* (a1325) Cursor BO 3

significaunce n. {b} *OF & L* Chaucer {a1400 Newberry Lapid} *PARST* 1

Significavit n. *ML* Chaucer GP 1

signifien v. 1a *OF* c1275 Ken.Serm. MKT 11

sik adj. 1c *OE, LOE* a1121 Peterb.Chron. ROMA 52

sik n. *fr.* sik *adj.* (a1325) Cursor *WBPRO* 1

sike n. a *fr.* siken *v2.* (?a1200) Ancr. PF 22

siken v2. 1d *OE, LOE* ?c1200 Orm. ROMA 47

siker adj. 4b b *OE, fr. L* a1150 Vsp.D.Hom. ROMA 29

siker adv. a *fr.* siker *adj.* (?c1150) Prov.Alf. (Mdst) *TR* 5

sikeren v. b *fr.* siker *adj.* (?c1280) SLeg.Nativ.M&C (Stw) *LGW* 1

sikerli adv. 1a *fr. <siker adj.>* (c1125) Vsp.D.Hom.Elucid. ROMA 35

sikernesse n. 2b *fr. <siker adj.>* (c1125) Vsp.D.Hom.Elucid. BD 28

sikinge ger. 1a *(fr.* siken *v2.)* c1300 SLeg.Brendan (Ld) *TR* 1

sikli adj. b *fr.* sik *adj.* a1375 WPal. TR 3

siknesse n. 1b *OE* c1150 Hrl.HApul. BD 22

silence n. 1a *OF & L* (?a1200) Ancr. WBT 3

silke n. 1a *OE* (?a1200) Ancr. ROMA 14

sillable n. *OF* Chaucer {(a1382) WBible(1) Pref.Her. (Bod 959)} HF 2

sille n1. b *OE* c1225 Wor.Aelfric Gloss. *MILT* 1

silver adj. a *fr.* silver *n.* (c1303) Mannyng HS ROMA 3

silver n. 3b *OE* a1121 Peterb.Chron. ROMA 34

similitude n. 4b *OF & L* Chaucer SNT 4

simonial n. *OF* Chaucer *PARST* 1

simonie n. a *OF & L* (?a1200) Ancr. FRT 5

simphonie n. a *OF & L* c1300 SLeg. (Ld) *THOP* 1

simple adj. 1a *OF* (?a1200) Ancr. ROMA 24

simplesse n. b *OF* (1340) Ayenb. ROMA 3

simpli adv. 1 *fr.* simple *adj.* (c1300) Glo.Chron.A HF 6

simplicite n. a *OF* Chaucer BO 15

sin conj. a *fr.* sitthen *conj.* (c1250) Floris (Suth) GENERAL 240

sin prep. *fr.* sitthen *prep.* (a1325) Cursor PF 7

sineu n. 1a *OE, LOE* c1150 Hrl.HApul. *PARST* 1

sinful adj. 1a *OE* a1150 Vsp.D.Hom. ABC 24

sinfulli adv. *fr.* sinful *adj.* ?c1200 Orm. MKT 7

singen v. 3b *OE* 1122 Peterb.Chron.
ROMA 202
singere n. a *fr. singen v.* (c1303) Mannyng
HS *PARDT* 1
singinge ger. a *(fr. singen v.)* a1300
Serm.Lithir lok ROMA 10
singularite n. 1b *OF* c1230 Ancr. (Corp-
C) *BO* 2
singulere adj. 2c *OF & L* (c1340) Rolle
Psalter (UC 64) HF 13
singulerli adv. 1a *fr. singulere adj.* (c1340)
Rolle Psalter (UC 64) *BO* 2
sinken v. 1c *OE* ?c1200 Orm. ABC 19
sinne n. 1a *OE* (c1125)
Vsp.D.Hom.Elucid. ROMA 445
sinnen v. a *OE* a1150 Vsp.D.Hom.VA
PHYT 30
sinnere n. a *fr. sinnen v.* (1340) Ayenb.
MEL 6
sinninge ger. *(fr. sinnen v.)* a1250 Ancr.
(Nero) *PARST* 3
sippen v. *perh. fr. OE* Chaucer *WBPRO* 1
sire n. 1a *OF* (?a1200) Lay.Brut ROMA
222
siren n. b *L & OF* (1340) Ayenb. *ROMA* 1
Sirie n. a *L & OE (fr. L)* a1150
Vsp.D.Hom. *MLT* 8
Sirien adj. a *OF & OE* a1150
Vsp.D.Hom. MKT 7
Sirius n. *L* Chaucer *BO* 1
sis n. a *OF* Chaucer MKT 2
siser n. *L, AL* (a1325) Cursor *MKT* 1
site n2. b *L & OF* Chaucer HF 4
sith n. 4a *OE* a1121 Peterb.Chron. ROMA
14
sithe n. a *OE* (c1300) Havelok *LGW* 1
sitten v. 1a *OE* (c1125)
Vsp.D.Hom.Fest.Virg. ROMA 247
sitthe adv. a *fr. OE, LOE* c1175 Body &
S.(1) ROMA 8
sitthe conj. 1a *OE.*(?a1200) Lay.Brut
GENERAL 144
sitthe prep. b *fr. sitthe adv. or sitthe conj.*
c1300 Lay.Brut (Otho) ROMA 3

sitthen adv. a *OE* a1121 Peterb.Chron.
ROMA 11
sitthen conj. 1a *OE* a1121 Peterb.Chron.
TR 6
sitthen prep. c *fr. sitthen adv. or sitthen
conj.* a1121 Peterb.Chron. *TR* 1
sittinge ger. 5a *(fr. sitten v.)* (?a1200)
Ancr. *BO* 7
sive n. a *OE* c1225 Wor.Aelfric Gloss.
CYT 1
six num. 1a *OE* a1121 Peterb.Chron.
ROMA 9
sixte num. 1a *OE* a1150 Vsp.D.Hom. HF
7
sixti num. a *OE* a1121 Peterb.Chron.
MKT 7
skie n. 1b *ON* (a1250) Bestiary HF 2
skil n. 7a *ON* (c1125)
Vsp.D.Hom.Elucid. HF 15
skilful adj. c *fr. skil n.* (a1325) Cursor BD
10
skilfulli adv. c *fr. <skilful adj.>* (c1300)
NHom.(1) John Bapt. SNT 4
skillinge ger. a *(fr. skillen v.)* Chaucer
BO 1
skin n1. 2c *ON & OE (fr. ON)* ?c1200
Orm. MKT 16
skippen v. 1c *?ON* (?a1300) KAlex. BO 9
skriken v. a *imitative in origin* (?a1200)
Trin.Hom. TR 7
skrikinge ger. a *(fr. skriken v.)* ?a1300
Fiftene toknen *TR* 1
slak adj. a *OE* a1225 Wor.Aelfric Gloss.
BO 5
slaken vi. 5a *OE* (?a1200) Ancr. ROMA 15
slaknesse n. a *fr. slak adj.* (1340) Ayenb.
PARST 1
slaughter n. 1a *ON* (c1300) NHom.(1)
Gosp. BO 6
sledde n. a *MDu., MLG* ?a1325 Elde
makth me *BO* 1
sleere n. *fr. slen. v.* (a1349) Rolle 10 Com.
KNT 1
sleigh adj. 1a *ON* ?c1200 Orm. BD 18

sleighli adv. c *fr. sleigh adj.* (?a1200)
Lay.Brut TR 11
sleight n. 1e *ON* (?a1200) Trin.Hom.
ROMA 33
slen v. 1a *OE, LOE* a1150 Vsp.D.Hom.
ABC 307
slep n. 1d *OE* a1121 Peterb.Chron. ROMA
58
slepen v. 1a *OE, LOE* a1150 Vsp.D.Hom.
ROMA 124
slepere n. a *OE* a1150 Vsp.D.Hom. *NPT*
1
slepi adj. d *fr. slep n.* (?a1200) Ancr. HF
2
slepinge ger. a *(fr. slepen v.)* c1250
Serm.St.Nich. ROMA 15
slepinge-time n. f, slepinge ger. *(fr.
slepinge ger. & time n.)* (1370) Fabric
R.Yk.Min. in Sur.Soc.35 *LADY* 1
slet n1. a *?OE* (a1300) Cokaygne LGW
2
sleuthe n. a *OE* a1150 Rwl.G.57.Gloss.
PARS T 1
sleve n. a *OE* (?a1200) Ancr. ROMA 9
sliden v. 1a *OE* (?c1150) Prov.Alf. (Trin-
C) BD 17
slider adj. a *OE* (c1200) Vices & V.(1)
KNT 2
slik adj. 2c *ON* (c1300) NHom.(1)
Magd. *RVT* 4
slike adj. d *?OE* (c1300) Havelok ROMA
2
slingen v. 2c *prob. ON* (?c1200)
St.Juliana *MANCT* 1
slinge-stone n. 1a, slinge n. *(fr. slinge n.
& ston n.)* Chaucer *TR* 1
slinken v. *OE* Chaucer *TR* 1
slippen v. 2f *prob. MLG* (c1303)
Mannyng HS *LGW* 1
slitten v. d *? fr. OE* c1150 Hrl.HApul.
MKT 3
slivere n. *fr. sliven v1.* Chaucer *TR* 1
slo n. c *OE* c1250 On hire is al ROMA 2
slogardie n. *fr. <slogard n.>* Chaucer
SNPRO 3

slomber n. a *fr. slomberen v.* (a1338)
Mannyng Chron.Pt.1 *MIL T* 1
slomberen v. a *? fr. MDu.* (a1250)
Bestiary *TR* 1
slomberinge ger. a *(fr. slomberen v.)*
c1350 MPPsalter TR 3
slombri adj. *fr. slomber n.* Chaucer
PARS T 1
sloppe n. b *?OE* (c1303) Mannyng HS
PARS T 1
slou adj. 2c *OE* ?c1200 Orm. ROMA 11
slough n1. a *OE* (?c1200) St.Kath.(1)
FRT 3
slouthe n. a *fr. slou adj.* a1150
Rwl.G.57.Gloss. BD 22
sluggi adj. *perh.fr. ON* (?a1200) Ancr.
PARS T 1
sluttish adj. *fr. <slutten.>* Chaucer
CYPRO 1
smal adj. 1a *OE* c1150 Hrl.HApul. ROMA
111
smale adv. 1a *OE* c1150 Hrl.HApul. AST
6
smalish adj. *fr. smal adj.* Chaucer *ROMA*
1
smateren v. a *cp. bismotered ppl., smoterli
adj., <smotri adj.>, smotten v.*Chaucer
PARS T 1
smel n. 4a *LOE* (c1200) Vices & V.(1)
ROMA 6
smellen v. 1b *?OE* (?a1200) Ancr. ROMA
10
smellinge ger. 1a *(fr. smellen v.)* (?c1200)
HMaid CYT 3
smert adj. 1a *LOE* (?a1200) Lay.Brut
ROMA 31
smerte adv. a *fr. smert adj.* a1225
Trin.Hom. TR 4
smerte n. 1a *?OE* (?c1175) PMor. (Lamb)
MKT 7
smerten v. 1b *OE* (?c1150) Prov.Alf.
(Trin-C) ABC 29
smilen v. 1b *?ON* (c1303) Mannyng HS
ROMA 13
smilere n. *fr. smilen v.* Chaucer *KNT* 1

smilinge ger. *(fr. smilen v.)* Chaucer *GP* 1

smiten v. 11 *OE* c1150 PDidax. ROMA 62

smith n. a *OE & fr.* *<smithen v.>* (c1125) Vsp.D.Hom.Elucid KNT 3

smithen v. a *OE* (?a1200) Lay.Brut *MILT* 1

smok n. a *OE* (?a1200) Trin.Hom. ROMA 9

smoke n. 1a *OE* ?a1160 Peterb.Chron. HF 7

smoken v. b *OE, LOE* ?a1160 Peterb.Chron. BO 3

smoki adj. a *fr. smoke n.* c1300 SLeg.Brendan (Hrl: Wright) *TR* 1

smokles adj. *fr. smok n.* Chaucer *CLT* 1

smoterli adj. a *cp. smotten v., <smotri adj.>, bismotered ppl. & smateren v.* Chaucer *RVT* 1

smothe adj. b *LOE* c1330 Orfeo ROMA 12

smothenesse n. *fr. smothe adj.* Chaucer *BO* 1

snake n. a *OE* c1150 Hrl.HApul. *BO* 1

snare n. 2b *OE & ON* (c1300) NHom.(1) Martin AM ROMA 11

sneuen v. 1a *OE* c1250 Owl & N. *GP* 1

snibben v. a *ON* (?a1250) Serm.Atte wrastlinge GP 3

snou n. 1b *OE* a1121 Peterb.Chron. ROMA 12

snouen vi. 1a *fr. snou n.* (?a1300) KAlex. *ROMA* 1

snouish adj. *fr. snou n.* Chaucer *TR* 1

snoute n. 2a *?OE* (?c1225) Horn SHIPT 2

snou-whit adj. a *OE* a1150 Vsp.D.Hom. CLT 2

snurten v. a *?ON* Chaucer *ROMA* 1

so adv. 1a a *OE* a1121 Peterb.Chron. GENERAL 2962

sobbe n. *fr. sobben v.* Chaucer *TR* 2

sobben v. a *perh. fr. MDu. or MLG* (c1200) Vices & V.(1) BO 2

sobbinge ger. *(fr. sobben v.)* (c1300) Havelok TR 2

sobre adj. 1a *OF* (1340) Ayenb. BD 13

sobreli adv. 1b *fr. sobre adj.* (1340) Ayenb. PF 17

sobrenesse n. 1 *fr. <sobre adj.>* (a1325) Cursor PARD T 2

socour n. 3c *fr. socours n. & AF* (c1250) Floris (Cmb) ROMA 24

socouren v. 3a *OF, AF, NF* c1275 Ken.Serm. *TR* 1

sodein adj. b *OF, AF* (?c1300) LFMass Bk. BO 19

sodeinli adv. a *fr. <sodein adj.>* (c1280) SLeg.Pass. (Pep) BD 77

softe adj. 4a *OE* a1121 Peterb.Chron. ROMA 39

softe adv. 3c *OE* (?a1200) Lay.Brut BD 44

softenen v. 2b *fr. soften v.* Chaucer *LGW* F 1

softli adv. 6c *fr. OE & softe adj.* (?a1200) Ancr. SNT 32

softnesse n. 5c *OE* a1150 Vsp.D.Hom. *PARS T* 1

sojournen v. a *OF, (chiefly) AF* c1300 SLeg.Becket (Ld) ROMA 15

sokene n. 2b *OE* a1121 Peterb.Chron. *RVT* 1

sokingli adv. a *fr. soken v.* Chaucer *MEL* 1

sol n1. a *L & OF* (1392) *MS Wel.564 *CYT* 2

solas n. 1b *OF & L* c1300 SLeg.Becket (Ld) ROMA 21

solasen v. 2a *OF, AF & ML* (c1280) SLeg.Pass. (Pep) ROMA 7

sole adj1. 1a *OF & L* Chaucer *MERT* 1

soleine adj. 2c *AF* Chaucer BD 3

solempne adj. 1d *OF & L* (a1333) Shoreham Poems BD 9

solempneli adv. b *fr. <solempne adj.>* a1325 *MS Rawl.B.520 lf.30b SNT 6

solempnite n. 3 *OF* c1300 SLeg.Becket (Ld) KNT 5

solere n. 1a *OE & OF & L* c1250 *Body & S.(4) *RVT* 1

solide adj. a *OF & L* Chaucer *AST* 2

solitarie adj. a *L & OF, AF* (c1340) Rolle
Psalter (UC 64) Bo 5

solitude n. a *OF & L* (?1348) Rolle
FLiving *MARS* 1

solstice n. *OF & L* (c1250) Gen.& Ex.
AST 2

solucioun n. 1a *OF & L* Chaucer *BO* 1

som adj. 1d *OE* a1121 Peterb.Chron.
GENERAL 321

som pron. 2a a *OE* a1121 Peterb.Chron.
GENERAL 172

som-del adv. b *fr. som-del n.* c1150
Hrl.HApul. ROMA 17

som-del n. c *OE* (c1125)
Vsp.D.Hom.Fest.Virg. *PF* 1

somer n1. 1a *OE* a1121 Peterb.Chron.
ROMA 42

somme n2. 1b *OF & L* c1300
SLeg.Becket (Ld) Bo 20

somnen v. 4a *OF, AF & ML, AL*
(?a1200) Lay.Brut *FRT* 8

somnour n. e *OF, AF* (c1280) SLeg.Pass.
(Pep) GP 49

somouns n. a *OF, AF* (?c1280)
SLeg.Nativ. (Eg) *FRT* 1

sompnolence n. *OF & L* Chaucer *PARST*
1

som-thing phr. & n. c *fr. som adj. &
thing n.* a1150 Vsp.D.Hom. ROMA 4

som-time adv. 1a *fr. som adj. & time n.*
(?a1200) Ancr. ROMA 123

som-what adj. *fr. som-what pron.*
Chaucer Bo 4

som-what adv. 1a *fr. som-what pron.*
?c1200 Orm. ROMA 31

som-what pron. 1a *fr. som adj. & what
pron.* ?c1200 Orm. LADY 45

som-wher adv. a *fr. som adj. & wher adv.*
?c1200 Orm. *FRANT* 1

Son-dai n. a *fr. OE* a1121 Peterb.Chron.
KNT 7

sonde n. 3 *OE* a1150 Vsp.D.Hom. SNT
11

sondri adj. 1c *OE* c1175 Bod.Hom.
ROMA 54

sone adv. 1a a *OE* a1121 Peterb.Chron.
ROMA 203

sone n. 1a *OE* a1121 Peterb.Chron. ROMA
145

sone-in-laue n. *fr. sone n. & in laue phr.*
(a1382) WBible(1) (Bod 959) CLT 2

song n. 1c *OE* a1150 Vsp.D.Hom. ROMA
103

sonne n. 1a a *OE* a1121 Peterb.Chron.
ROMA 271

sonne-bem n. 1a *OE* c1175 Bod.Hom.
WBT 1

sonnish adj. *fr. sonne n.* Chaucer *TR* 2

sopere n1. a *OF, AF* (c1250) Floris
(Cmb) *TR* 16

sophie n. *L* (?c1200) St.Juliana *MEL* 1

sophime n. b *OF & L* (c1383)
Wycl.Leaven Pharisees CLPRO 2

sophistrie n. a *OF & ML, AL* (1340)
Ayenb. *LGW F* 1

soppe n1. b *OE & OF* (a1338) Mannyng
Chron.Pt.1 GP 2

sorceresse n. *OF* Chaucer HF 2

sorcerie n. a *OF & ML* (?a1300) KAlex.
MLT 3

sore adj1. c *OF, AF* Chaucer *BD* 1

sore adj2. 4a *OE* a1150
Vsp.D.Hom.Nicod. PITY 23

sore adv. 2b *OE* a1121 Peterb.Chron.
ROMA 121

sore n1. 2a *OE, LOE* a1121 Peterb.Chron.
ROMA 10

soren v1. *OF* Chaucer HF 6

sori adj. 1a *OE, LOE* a1121 Peterb.Chron.
ROMA 50

sori adv. b *fr. sori adj.* (c1250) Gen.& Ex.
BO 1

sort n1. 2b *OF & L* (?c1380) Patience *TR*
8

sorte n. 1b *OF, AF* Chaucer RVT 4

sorten v1. b *fr. sort n1. or L & OF*
Chaucer *TR* 1

sorwe n. 4e *OE* (c1125)
Vsp.D.Hom.Elucid. ROMA 314

sorweful adj. 4b *OE* a1121 Peterb.Chron.
ROMA 79

sorwefulli adv. a *fr. sorwerful adj.*
(?a1200) Ancr. ANEL 18

sorwen v. 1a *OE* ?c1200 Orm. BO 17

sorwinge ger. b *fr. sorwen v.* (?c1300)
Guy(1) *BD* 1

sot n2. a *OE* c1150 Hrl.MQuad. *TR* 1

sote adj. 2b *OE* (c1125)
Vsp.D.Hom.Fest.Virg. ROMA 29

sote adv. d *OE* (?a1200) Ancr. LGW 2

soth adj. 1a *OE* a1150 Vsp.D.Hom. ABC 65

soth n. 3c *OE* a1131 Peterb.Chron. ROMA 197

sothe adv. a *OE* a1150 Vsp.D.Hom. BO 7

sothfast adj. 2b *OE* a1126 Peterb.Chron.
BO 9

sothfastli adv. c *fr. sothfast adj.* a1150
Vsp.D.Hom. *BO* 1

sothfastnesse n. 2a *OE* a1150
Vsp.D.Hom. SNT 20

sothli adv. 1a *OE* a1150 Vsp.D.Hom.
ROMA 114

sothnesse n. 1a *fr.* soth *n.* or soth *adj.*
a1300 I-hereth nu one SNT 5

soti adj. *fr. sot n2.* c1250 Owl & N. *NPT*
1

sotil adj. 1a a *OF* c1300 SLeg.Inf.Chr.
(Ld) ROMA 37

sotilli adv. 1a a *fr. sotil adj.* (a1333)
Shoreham Poems ROMA 22

sotilte n. 1c *OF* c1300 SLeg. (Ld) HF 20

sotten v. a *fr. <sot adj.>* c1175 Bod.Hom.
CYT 1

soudan n. a *OF & ML, AL* (c1300)
Glo.Chron.A *MLT* 13

soudanesse n. *fr. soudan n.* Chaucer
MLT 6

souden v1. 2b *OF* (1373) *Lelamour
Macer *PRT* 1

soue n2. 1a *OE* ?c1200 Stw.57.Gloss. BO 8

souen v1. 1a *OE* a1150 Vsp.D.Hom.
ROMA 13

souere n. a *fr. OE & souen v1.* a1225
Trin.Hom. SNT 2

souken v. 1a c *OE* a1150 Vsp.D.Hom.
RVT 4

soule n. 1b c *OE, LOE* a1121
Peterb.Chron. ABC 219

soulen v. a *OE* Chaucer SNT 1

soun n. 2b *OE (fr. L) & OF, AF & L*
?c1225 Ancr.(Cleo) BD 59

sounde adj. 1b *fr. OE or isound adj.*
?c1200 Orm. BO 8

sounden v1. a *OF* Chaucer *TR* 1

sounden v2. 2a *fr. sounde adj.* (a1325)
Cursor ROMA 2

sounen v. 2d *OF, AF & L* (?c1225) Horn
ROMA 27

souninge ger. 2a *(fr. sounen v.)* Chaucer
BD 1

soupen v2. b *OF, AF* c1300 SLeg.Becket
(Hrl) *TR* 7

souple adj. 1a *OF* (c1300) Glo.Chron.A
MKT 2

sour adj. 3a *OE* ?c1200 Orm. BO 2

sourden v. a *OF* Chaucer *PARST* 7

soure adv. b *fr. sour adj.* (c1300) Havelok
THOP 2

sours n. 2a *OF, AF* Chaucer HF 7

soutere n. a *OE, fr. L* a1150 Vsp.D.Hom.
RVPRO 1

south adj. a *OE* c1175 Bod.Aelfric OT
AST 18

south adv. a *OE* a1126 Peterb.Chron. HF
10

south n2. 1a *fr. south adj.* ?c1200 Orm.
MKT 15

southerne adj. 1c *OE* ?c1125 Dur-
C.Gloss. *PARSPRO* 1

southward adj. b *OE* (1307) Execution
Fraser *AST* 4

southward adv. a *OE* (?a1200) Lay.Brut
AST 3

souvenaunce n. *OF* Chaucer *WOMNOB* 1

soverain adj. 2c *OF* (1340) Ayenb. MKT
125

soverain n. 1a *OF, AF* (c1280) SLeg.Pass.
(Pep) ABC 12

soverainli adv. 1a *fr. soverain adj.*
(?a1350) Trental St.Gre.(1) BO 3

soverainte n. 2a *OF, AF* Chaucer TR 6

space n. 5a *fr. OF, AF & L, ML* c1300
SLeg. (Ld) ROMA 76

spade n. a *OE* c1225 Wor.Aelfric Gloss.
GP 1

Spaine n. a *fr. OF, AF* (?a1200) Lay.Brut
HF 5

Spainol n. b *fr. OF, AF* c1350 Of all the
witti *WBPRO* 1

spanne n. 1b *OE* (c1280) SLeg.Pass.
(Pep) *GP* 1

span-neue adj. *ON* (c1300) Havelok TR
1

sparen v. 1b a *OE* a1150 Vsp.D.Hom.
ROMA 34

spar-hauk n. a *OE* (a1325) Cursor PF 5

sparinge ger. d *fr. sparen v.* (c1378) PPl.B
(Ld) *PARST* 1

sparke n. a *OE* a1150 Vsp.D.Hom. LADY
4

sparkle n. 1a *fr. sparke n. & -el suf1.* c1300
Body & S.(5) BO 3

sparklen v. a *fr. sparke n. & -el suf3.*
(?a1200) Ancr. *KNT* 1

sparre n. a *OE & MDu. or MLG & ON*
(a1325) Cursor *KNT* 2

sparthe n. a *ON* (?a1350) Castleford
Chron. *KNT* 1

sparwe n. a *OE* (?a1200) Lay.Brut PF 3

speche n. 1a *fr. OE & speken v.* a1150
Vsp.D.Hom. ROMA 112

specheles adj. a *fr. speche n. & OE* c1300
SLeg.Fran.(1) (Ld) *TR* 2

speciale adj. 1a *fr. OF, AF & L* (?a1200)
Ancr. HF 8

speciale n. 1a *fr. speciale adj.* c1300
SLeg.Dunstan (Ld) TR 15

specialli adv. a *fr. speciale adj.* (c1300)
Glo.Chron.A GP 18

spectacle n. a *OF & L* (c1340) Rolle
Psalter (UC 64) *WBT* 1

speculacioun n. c *OF & L* Chaucer BO 1

spede n. 1e *OE* a1150 Vsp.D.Hom. PF 4

spedeful adj. 1a *fr. spede n.* (a1349) Rolle
MPass.(2) BO 3

speden v. 1a *OE* a1121 Peterb.Chron.
ROMA 60

spedili adv. b *fr. <spedi adj.> & OE*
(a1376) PPl.A(1) (Trin-C) SHIPT 2

speken v. 4a *OE* ?a1114 Chron.Dom.
ROMA 493

spekinge ger. 1b *(fr. speken v.)* (c1280)
SLeg.Pass. (Pep) PF 7

spel n. c *OE* a1150 Vsp.D.Hom. *THOP* 1

spenden v. 2a *OE* (?c1200) St.Kath.(1)
ROMA 31

spendere n. *fr. spenden v.* (?a1387) PPl.C
(Hnt HM 137) *MEL* 1

spense n2. a *AF & AL* (c1350) Gamelyn
SUMT 1

spere n1. 1e *OE* 1130–5 Leges
Edw.Conf. in Liebermann Gesetze
HF 35

spere n3. 1a a *OF, AF & L, ML* (?a1300)
Arth.& M. PF 16

speren v1. 1 *MLG & MDu. & ON*
?c1200 Orm. *TR* 1

sperme n. 1b *L* Chaucer *MKT* 1

speuen v. a *OE* c1150 Hrl.HApul. MLT
2

speuinge ger. a *fr. speuen v.* (1373)
*Lelamour Macer *PARST* 1

spice n1. 1a *fr. OF, AF (fr. L)* (?a1200)
Ancr. ROMA 10

spice n2. 1e *fr. L, AL & OF* (?a1200)
Ancr. BO 33

spicen v. b *fr. spice n1.* a1325
Gloss.Bibbesw. (Arun) GP 3

spicerie n. 1d *OF, AF & ML, AL*
(?c1200) NPass. KNT 5

spie n. 1a *fr. OF* (c1250) Floris (Cmb)
HF 2

spien v1. 1a *fr. OF* (c1250) Gen.& Ex.
SNT 5

spillen v. 1e *OE* a1126 Peterb.Chron.
ABC 25

spinnen v. 1e *OE* (c1250) Prov.Hend. TR
4

spinninge ger. a *(fr. spinnen v.)* c1300
SLeg. (Ld) *WBPRO* 1

spire n1. a *OE* c1250 Owl & N. *TR* 1

spirit n. 1a *fr. L & OF, AF* (c1250)
Gen.& Ex. BD 55

spiritual adj. 1a *L & OF, AF* (c1303)
Mannyng HS *PARST* 6

spiritualli adv. 1b *fr. spiritual adj.* (1340)
Ayenb. *PARST* 2

spitous adj. 1b *fr. spite n2.* (?a1325)
Cursor *ROMA* 1

spitousli adv. 1c *fr. spitous adj.* (c1280)
SLeg.Eust. (Jul) MILT 2

spitten v1. 3 *OE* c1150 PDidax. TR 5

spittinge ger. 1b *fr. spitten v1.* (a1325)
Cursor *PARST* 1

spoke n. b *OE* (?c1200) St.Juliana *SUMT*
4

spon n. 1a *OE* c1300 SLeg. (Ld) WBPRO
3

spore n2. 2c *OE* a1121 Peterb.Chron. TR
4

spot n1. 3b *OE* (c1200) Vices & V.(1) TR
2

spotten v. 1b *fr. spot n1.* (c1250) Gen.&
Ex. *TR* 1

spousaille n. 2a *fr. OF, AF* (?c1300) Bevis
CLT 2

spouse n. 3c *OF* (c1200) Vices & V.(1)
SNT 10

spousen v. 4a *fr. OF, AF* (c1200) Vices &
V.(1) CLPRO 2

sprai n1. b *OE, LOE* (c1250) Floris
(Cmb) *THOP* 1

spreden v. 1a *OE* ?c1200 Orm. ROMA 30

sprengen v. a *OE* c1150 Hrl.HApul. BO
4

spring n. 1a *OE* (c1125)
Vsp.D.Hom.Fest.Virg. ROMA 8

springen v. 6a *OE* a1150 Vsp.D.Hom.
ROMA 59

springinge ger. 1d *fr. springen v.* (a1325)
Cursor CLPRO 2

spurnen v. 1a *OE* a1150 Vsp.D.Hom. TR
4

squaimous adj. b *fr. AF & <esquaimous
adj.>* c1330 Le Freine *MILT* 1

squame n. b *OF & L* c1225
Wor.Bod.Gloss. *CYT* 1

square adj. 1c *fr. AF & OF* (a1325)
Cursor ROMA 7

square n. 1a *fr. OF & AL* (c1250) Floris
(Cmb) AST 2

squier n. 1b *fr. OF, AF* (?c1225) Horn TR
27

squieren v. *fr. squier n.* Chaucer *WBPRO*
1

squirel n. c *OF, AF* c1330 7 Sages ROMA
3

stabilite n. a *OF* (?a1349) ?Rolle Ihesu
god sone BO 1

stable adj. 3a *fr. OF, AF & L* (?c1150)
Prov.Alf. (Trin-C) ROMA 34

stable adv. 1a *fr. stable adj.* c1300
SLeg.Becket (Ld) BO 1

stable n. a *fr. OF & L* (?c1225) Horn
ROMA 5

stablenesse n. 2d *fr. stable adj.* (a1325)
Cursor BO 6

stabli adv. 1a *fr. stable adj.* c1300
SLeg.Patr. (Ld) BO 2

stablishen v. 8 *fr. OF* a1325 *MS Rawl
B.520 lf.57 BO 2

stadie n. b *fr. AF & L* Chaucer BO 1

staf n. 1d a *OE, LOE* a1121 Peterb.Chron.
ANEL 17

staf-slinge n. a *fr. staf n. & slinge n.*
Chaucer *THOP* 1

stage n. 1a *OF* (c1250) Floris (Cmb) *HF* 1

stake n. 2a *OE* (?a1200) Lay.Brut KNT 6

stakeren v. a *ON* (a1325) Cursor *LGW* 1

stale adj1. a *OF* c1300 Horn (Ld) *THOP* 1

stalke n1. b *prob. fr. stale n3.* a1325
Gloss.Bibbesw. ROMA 7

stalken v. a *fr. OE* c1300 Horn (Ld) BD
6

stalle n. 1a *OE & OF, AF & ML, AL*
c1200 Wor.Serm. in EGSt.7 TR 7

stallen v. 2f *fr. OF & stalle n.* (a1325)
Cursor *HF* 1

stamin n. b *OF & ML & L* (?a1200)
Ancr. LGW 2

stampen v. 1a *prob. OE* (c1200) Vices &
V.(1) HF 2

stank n. a *OF, AF & ML* (a1325) Cursor
PARST 1

stare n2. a *OE* ?c1200 Stw.57.Gloss. *PF* 1

staren v. 3 *OE* (?c1200) St.Marg.(1) SNT
6

stark adj. 2e *OE* a1150 Vsp.D.Hom.
MKT 3

stat n. 10a a *fr. OF, AF & L* (?a1200)
Ancr. *GP* 1

statli adj. 2a *fr. stat n.* Chaucer *LGW* 1

statue n. a *OF & L* Chaucer MKT 7

stature n. 1a *fr. OF & L* (a1325) Cursor
ROMA 10

statute n. 1a *fr. OF & L* c1300
SLeg.Becket (Ld) PF 9

staunchen v. 1b *fr. OF, AF* (?a1325)
ADAM & E.(2) *BO* 3

stede n1. 1a a *OE* a1121 Peterb.Chron.
ROMA 18

stede n2. 1c *OE* (?c1150) Prov.Alf. (Mdst)
TR 25

sted-fast adj. 1c *OE* ?c1200 Orm. BD 37

sted-fast adv. a *fr. stedfast adj.* (a1325)
Cursor *BO* 1

sted-fastli adv. 1a *fr. sted-fast adj.*
(?a1200) Ancr. SNT 6

sted-fastnesse n. 5a *fr. OE & sted-fast
adj.* ?c1225 Ancr.(Cleo) ANEL 18

steire n. 1a *OE* (?a1200) Trin.Hom. TR 5

stele n3. 1a *OE* (?a1200) Lay.Brut ROMA
19

stelen v. 1a *OE* a1150 Vsp.D.Hom.
ROMA 47

stelinge ger. a *fr. stelen v.* c1330 7 Sages(1)
PARST 1

stellifien v. a *prob. OF* Chaucer HF 3

stemen v. a *OE* a1150 Vsp.D.Hom. *GP* 1

step n. 1b *OE* a1150 Vsp.D.Hom. BO 5

stepe adj. 1a *OE* (?c1200) Orm. *GP* 2

steppen v. 1a *OE* a1150 Vsp.D.Hom.
RVT 3

stere n1. a *OE* c1225 Wor.Aelfric Gloss.
KNT 1

stere n2. 2a *OE* a1150 Vsp.D.Hom.VA
BO 4

stere n3. b *OE* (c1250) Gen.& Ex. HF 4

stereles adj. b *OE* a1150 Vsp.D.Hom.VA
TR 2

steren v1. 2c *OE* a1150 Vsp.D.Hom. TR
4

steresman n. a *OE* ?c1200 Orm. *HF* 1

sterling n. a *prob. fr. AF or ML* (c1300)
Glo.Chron.A HF 2

sterne adj. 1a *OE* a1121 Peterb.Chron. BO
11

sternli adv. c *fr. OE & sterne adj.*
(?a1200) Lay.Brut HF 3

sterre n. 1a b *OE* a1121 Peterb.Chron.
ROMA 128

sterred adj. a *fr. sterre n.* c1225
St.Marg.(1) (Roy) *AST* 1

sterri adj. *fr. sterre n.* Chaucer PF 2

stert n2. a *fr. sterten v.* (?a1200) Ancr. TR
2

stertelen v. a *OE* c1300 Body & S.(5)
KNT 2

sterten v. 1a b *OE* (?a1200) Lay.Brut
ROMA 62

sterven v. 1b b *OE* a1126 Peterb.Chron.
ROMA 64

steuard n. 1b *OE* a1121 Peterb.Chron. GP
4

steue n1. a *fr. OF* Chaucer *GP* 1

steue n2. 3 *fr. OF, AF* (a1300) Cokaygne
TR 4

stevene n1. 1d *OE* a1121 Peterb.Chron.
BD 9

stevene n2. 2b *OE* (?c1200) St.Juliana
MARS 3

sti n. a *OE* (?a1200) Ancr. *SUMT* 1

stibourne adj. a *cp. stubbe n.* Chaucer
WBPRO 2

stien v. 1a c *OE* (c1125)
Vsp.D.Hom.Elucid. *Bo* 2

stif adj. 1a *fr. OE* (?a1200) Lay.Brut
Rom A 4

stifli adv. 2a *fr. stif adj.* c1300
SLeg.Becket (Ld) *WBPro* 1

stiken v. 3b *OE* (c1125)
Vsp.D.Hom.Elucid. Rom A 16

stikinge ger. 3c *(fr. stiken v.)* Chaucer
ParsT 1

stikke n. 3a *OE* a1121 Peterb.Chron.
Rom A 9

stile n1. a *OE* (c1333–52) Minot Poems
Sq T 3

stile n2. a *OF & L* (a1325) Cursor ClPro
4

stillatorie n. *AL* Chaucer *CyPro* 1

stille adj. 1a *OE* a1150 Vsp.D.Hom. Pity
20

stille adv. 2b *OE* a1150 Vsp.D.Hom. BD
68

stillen vi. 2b *OE* c1175 Bod.Hom. Tr 3

stilnesse n. c *OE* a1150 Vsp.D.Hom. Bo
2

stingen v. 1d *OE* c1150 Hrl.MQuad. BD
13

stink n. 1b *fr. stinken v.* (c1250) Gen.&
Ex. ABC 7

stinken v. 2a b *OE* a1150 Vsp.D.Hom.
Mkt 13

stinten v. 1a d *OE* ?c1200 Orm. Rom A
96

stintinge ger. a *(fr. stinten v.)* (a1338)
Mannyng Chron.Pt.2 *Bo* 1

stiren v. 5a *OE* c1150 Hrl.HApul. HF 18

stiringe ger. 3a *fr. OE* a1150
Vsp.D.Hom. HF 3

stirop n. 1a *OE* c1225 Body & S.(2)
EpiMLT 2

stith n1. *fr. ON* (c1300) Havelok *KnT* 1

Stoiciens n. pl. *fr. OF* Chaucer *Bo* 5

stok n1. 2a *OE* ?c1200 Orm. Bo 6

stoken v2. b *fr. OF* (a1325) Cursor *KnT* 1

stokken v. a *fr. stok n1.* a1325
Gloss.Bibbesw. (Arun:Owen) *Tr* 1

stol n. 1b *OE* a1121 Peterb.Chron. LGW
2

stole n. 2a *OE & L* a1121 Peterb.Chron.
Mer T 1

stomak n. 1a *L, ML & OF, AF* a1325
Add.46919 Cook.Recipes Bo 4

stomblen v. 1a *prob. ON* (?a1300) Guy(2)
Kn T 1

ston n. 14a *OE, LOE* a1126
Peterb.Chron. Rom A 118

stonden vi. 5b *OE* a1121 Peterb.Chron.
Rom A 301

stonen vi. 1a *fr.* <*astonen n.*> ?c1200
Orm. *Pars T* 1

ston-wal n. a *OE* c1175 Bod.Aelfric OT
LGW 1

stoppen v. 1b *OE* (?a1200) Ancr. TR 3

store adj. 1b b *LOE & ON* (?a1200)
Lay.Brut *Mer T* 1

store n1. 1a *fr. OF, AF* (c1300)
Glo.Chron.A LGW 7

storen v. 3 *fr.* <*astoren v.*> (?a1200)
Lay.Brut *Ship T* 1

storial adj. a *fr. historial adj.* Chaucer
LGW 2

storie n1. 1a *fr. AF & L* a1250 Ancr.
(Nero) Rom A 81

stork n. a *OE* a1150 Vsp.D.Hom. *PF* 1

storm n. 1a *OE* a1121 Peterb.Chron. HF
3

stormi adj. 1a *fr. storm n.* a1150
Vsp.D.Hom. Rom A 3

stot n. 1b *LOE & AL* c1250 Owl & N.
GP 2

stounde n. 1b c *OE* a1121 Peterb.Chron.
HF 24

stoundmele adv. a *OE* (?a1200)
Trin.Hom. *Tr* 1

stoupen v. 3b *OE* (?a1200) Lay.Brut Tr 6

stoure n2. 1b *OF, (chiefly) AF* (c1300)
NHom.(1) Gosp. Rom A 2

stoute adj. 1a *OF, AF* c1300 SLeg.Becket
(Hrl) Tr 7

straken vi. *Gmc.* (?a1325) Bonav.Medit.
BD 1

stranglen v. 2a *OF & L* (?c1280)
SLeg.OTHist. (Ld 622) Bo 6

stranglinge ger. d *fr. stranglen v.* (a1382)
WBible(1) Pref.Jer. (Bod 959) KnT 3

strau n. 1a *OE & ON* a1150 Vsp.D.Hom.
BD 21

straunge adj. 1e *fr. OF, AF* (c1280)
SLeg.Pass. (Pep) RoMA 46

straungeli adv. a *fr. straunge adj.* (a1382)
WBible(1) (Bod 959) *Tr* 2

straungenesse n. a *fr. straunge adj.*
Chaucer SHIPT 2

straungere n. h *fr. OF, AF* (a1338)
Mannyng Chron.Pt.1 Bo 4

strecchen v. 1a *OE* (?a1200) Lay.Brut
RoMA 24

streight adj. a *fr. strecchen* ?c1325 A
levedy and my RoMA 8

streight adv. c *fr. streight adj. & strecchen*
v. (?a1325) Bonav.Medit.(1) HF 18

streinen v1. 1a *fr. OF, AF* c1300
SLeg.Becket (Hrl) Bo 15

streinen v2. 1b {d} *fr. distreinen v.*
Chaucer {(c1384) WBible(1)} RoMA 1

streit adj. 8a *AF* (?a1200) Lay.Brut
RoMA 17

streit n. h *fr. streit adj.* (?a1349) ?Rolle
Heyle Ihu my MLT 1

streite adv. 5b *fr. streit adj.* (?a1300)
KAlex. Bo 5

streitnesse n. 6a *fr. streit adj.* (c1340)
Rolle Psalter (UC 64) AST 1

strem n. 6a *OE* (c1125)
Vsp.D.Hom.Fest.Virg. RoMA 31

stremen v. 2a *fr. strem n.* ?c1225 Ancr.
(Cleo) *Tr* 1

stren n. 1 *OE* (?c1150) Prov.Alf. (Mdst)
CLT 1

streng n. 3a *OE* c1150 PDidax. PF 6

strengere adj. comp. 7b *OE, LOE* a1121
Peterb.Chron. MKT 13

strengest adj. sup. 1a *OE* (?a1200)
Lay.Brut *Tr* 2

strengthe n. 1e *OE* a1121 Peterb.Chron.
RoMA 94

strengthen v. 4a *fr. strengthe n.* (?a1200)
Ancr. Bo 3

strepen v. 4b *OE* (?a1200) Trin.Hom. Bo
8

strete n2. 3a a *OE, LOE; ult. L* a1150
Vsp.D.Hom.VA ABC 23

streuen v. 4a *OE* a1150 Vsp.D.Hom.
LGW F 3

strife n. 1c *OF, AF* (?a1200) Ancr. HF 31

strike n1. a *OE* (a1382) WBible(1) (Bod
959) AST 8

strike n2. e *fr. striken v. & AF, ONF &*
AL (a1338) Mannyng Chron.Pt.1 GP
1

striken v. 11a *OE* ?c1200 Orm. FRT 3

striven v. 6a *OF* (c1200) Vices & V.(1)
PF 28

strivinge ger. 1a *(fr. striven v.)* (?a1200)
Lay.Brut Bo 5

strogelen v. a *origin unknown* Chaucer
MERT 3

strogelinge ger. a *(fr. strogelen v.)*
Chaucer MLT 1

stroiere n. a *fr. <destroiere n.> or stroien*
v. (a1325) Cursor PF 1

stroke n. 1a *OE* c1300 Horn (Ld) SNT
29

stroken v. a *OE* c1150 PDidax. Tr 4

stronde n1. 1b a *OE, LOE* (?1058–1066)
Chart.in Kemble Codex Dipl. HF 11

strong adj. 7a *OE* a1121 Peterb.Chron.
RoMA 91

stronge adv. 8b *OE* a1121 Peterb.Chron.
RoMA 3

strongli adv. 3a *OE* 1123 Peterb.Chron.
Bo 5

strother n1. b *prob. *OE* (1232) in Mawer
PNNhb.& Dur. RVT 1

strouten v. a *OE* a1300 Serm.Lithir lok
MILT 1

strumpet n. a *origin uncertain* c1325 Lord
that lenest Bo 1

stubbe n. c *OE* c1250 Owl & N. KNT 1

stuble n. a *OF, AF* (c1300) Glo.Chron.A
CKPRO 1

studie n. 2a *fr. OF, AF & L* c1300
SLeg.Edm.Abp. (Hrl) HF 24

studien v. 1b *fr. OF, AF & L, ML* (c1125)
Vsp.D.Hom.Fest.Virg. BO 11

studiinge ger. a *(fr. studien v.)* (c1125)
Vsp.D.hom.Fest.Virg. MILT 2

stuffen vi. 1b *OF, AF & AL* (?a1350)
Castleford Chron.Lear CLT 1

sturdi adj. 1 *OF, AF* c1300 Horn (Ld)
BO 7

sturdili adv. a *fr. sturdi adj.* Chaucer
MARS 2

sturdinesse n. a *fr. sturdi adj.* (c1384)
WBible(1) CLT 1

suasioun n. b *OF & L* Chaucer BO 1

subdeken n. a *OE (fr. L) & L* (c1303)
Mannyng HS PARST 1

subget adj. 2a *fr. subget n. & L & OF, AF*
(a1338) Mannyng Chron.Pt.1 BO 18

subget n. 1a *L & OF, AF* c1330 7 Sages(1)
BO 9

subjeccioun n. 2b *L & OF, AF* Chaucer
MKT 7

sublimatori n. *prob. fr. ML* Chaucer
CYT 1

sublimen v. b *L & OF* (1392) *MS
Wel.564 CYT 1

subliminge ger. *(fr. sublimen v.)*
Chaucer CYT 1

submissioun n. b *L & OF, AF* Chaucer
MEL 1

submitten v. 1a *L* Chaucer BO 8

substaunce n. 2b *L & OF, AF* (?a1300)
Arth.& M. ABC 32

suburbe n. a *L, AL & OF* c1350
MPPsalter CYPRO 1

subverten v. a *L & OF* (a1382) WBible(1)
Pref.Jer. (Bod 959) PARST 1

succeden v. a {b} *OF, AF & L* (c1384)
WBible(1) {Chaucer} AST 5

succedent adj. b *L* Chaucer AST 1

successioun n. 1b *OF, AF & L* a1325 *MS
Rawl.B.520 BO 2

successour n. a *OF, AF & L* (c1300)
Glo.Chron.A MLT 2

sufferable adj. 2b *OF, AF & AL* (c1303)
Mannyng HS WBPRO 1

sufferaunce n. 4a *OF, AF & L* c1300
SLeg.Pass. (Hrl) BO 17

sufferaunt adj. a *OF, AF* (?c1300)
Spec.Guy BD 2

sufferen v. 8b i *OF, AF & L* (?a1200)
Ancr. ROMA 173

sufferinge ger. 4 *(fr. sufferen v.)* (c1340)
Rolle Psalter (UC 64) BO 5

sufficient adj. 2a *L & OF, AF* (1322)
Satutes Realm BO 4

sufficientli adv. a *fr. sufficient adj.*
(c1340) *Rolle Psalter (Sid) MEL 1

suffisaunce n. 3b *OF, AF* Chaucer BD 35

suffisaunt adj. 1a *OF, AF* (c1340) Rolle
Psalter (UC 64) BO 22

suffisauntli adv. a *fr. suffisaunt adj.*
(c1340) Rolle Psalter (UC 64) BO 4

suffisen v. 2a *OF & AF* a1325 *MS
Rawl.B.520 BD 79

suggestioun n. 1b *L & OF, AF* (c1340)
Rolle Psalter (UC 64) MKT 3

sugre n. a *ML, AL & OF, AF* a1325
Add.46919 Cook.Recipes TR 3

sugren v. 1c *fr. sugre n.* Chaucer TR 1

sukkenie n. *OF; ult Gmc.* Chaucer
ROMA 1

sulphur n. a *L & OF, AF* Chaucer HF 1

superfice n. a *OF* Chaucer BO 3

superfluite n. {1a} *OF* Chaucer {(a1387)
Trev.Higd.} BO 13

superlatif adj. a *OF & L* Chaucer MERT
1

supersticious adj. a *L & OF, AF*
Chaucer FRANT 1

supplicacioun n. c *L & OF, AF* Chaucer
BO 2

supplien v2. *OF* Chaucer BO 1

supportacioun n. a *L, AL & OF*
Chaucer MEL 1

supporten v. c *OF & L* (c1384)
WBible(1) MEL 2

supposen v. 1c *OF* (c1303) Mannyng HS
MKT 21

supposinge ger. d *(fr. supposen v.)* (c1385) Usk TL (Skeat) CLT 3

supprisen v. a *fr. AF* (?a1349) ?Rolle Mercy es maste TR 2

surcot n. a *OF, AF, ONF* c1330 Degare *GP* 1

surfet n. 2a *OF, AF* (a1325) Cursor *PARST* 1

surmounten v. 3b *OF, AF* a1325 SLeg.Bridget(2) (Corp-C) ROMA 14

surname n. a *fr. name n.* (?a1300) Arth.& M. *LADY* 1

surplis n. a *OF, AF* c1230 Ancr. (Corp-C) MILT 2

surplus n. 2c *OF, AF* (a1382) WBible(1) (Bod 959) *TR* 1

surquidrie n. a *OF, AF/ONF, AF* a1250 Ancr. (Nero) TR 3

sursanure n. *OF, AF* Chaucer *FRANT* 1

surveiaunce n. *AF* Chaucer *PHYT* 1

suspecioun n. 1a b *L & OF, AF* c1300 SLeg. (Ld) BO 13

suspecious adj. 1b *OF, AF; L* (1340) Ayenb. *CLT* 1

suspect adj. 1a c *L & OF* (a1325) Cursor *CLT* 3

suspect n. a *ML* Chaucer CLT 5

sustenaunce n. 1a a *OF, AF & L* c1300 SLeg.Becket (Hrl) LGW 6

sustenen v. 2a *OF, AF* (c1280) SLeg.Pass. (Pep) ROMA 35

suster n. 1a *OE & ON* a1121 Peterb.Chron. SNT 71

sute n. 3a *OF, AF* c1300 SLeg.Jas. (Ld) BD 3

swalwe n. 1a *OE, LOE* a1150 Vsp.D.Hom. PF 3

swan n. 1a *OE* ?c1200 Stw.57.Gloss. ANEL 7

swap n. b *fr. swappen v.* Chaucer *HF* 1

swappen v. d *origin unknown; perh. imitative* a1375 WPal. SNT 4

swarm n. a *OE* c1350 Cmb.Ee.4.20.Nominale TR 3

swarmen v. a *fr. swarm n.* (?c1380) Cleanness SUMPRO 3

swartish adj. *fr. swart adj.* Chaucer *HF* 1

swei n2. a *fr. sweien v2.* Chaucer BO 4

swein n. c *ON* a1131 Peterb.Chron. RVT 2

swellen v. 4b *OE* c1150 PDidax. BO 11

swellere n. *fr. swellen v.* Chaucer *BO* 1

swellinge ger. 3a *fr. swellen v.* a1325 Add.15236 Recipes(2) BO 3

swelten v. 1a *OE* 1123 Peterb.Chron. TR 6

swenchen v. a *OE* a1121 Peterb.Chron. *HF* 1

swepen v. b *fr. OE* a1325 Gloss.Bibbesw. CLT 3

sweren v. 4a *OE* a1121 Peterb.Chron. ROMA 154

swerere n. b *fr. sweren v.* c1300 SLeg.Mich. (Ld) *PARST* 1

sweringe ger. b *fr. sweren v.* (c1200) Vices & V.(1) PARDT 13

swete adj. 1f *OE* a1150 Vsp.D.Hom. ROMA 159

swete adv. b *fr. swete adj.* ?c1200 Orm. TR 5

swete n2. 1a *fr. OE & swete adj.* (?c1200) HMaid. *PF* 1

sweteli adv. 2c *fr. OE & swete adj.* ?c1200 Orm. BD 5

Swete-lokyng n. 8, swete adj. *(fr. swete adj. & lokinge ger.)* Chaucer *ROMA* 3

sweten v1. 1a *OE* a1150 Vsp.D.Hom. SNT 12

swetenesse n. 2 *OE* a1150 Vsp.D.Hom. ROMA 25

sweti adj. *fr. swete n1.* Chaucer *FORMAGE* 1

sweven n. a *OE* a1150 Vsp.D.Hom. ROMA 25

sweveninge ger. b *fr. swevenen v.* * (?c1225) Horn *ROMA* 2

swich adj. 1a f *OE* a1121 Peterb.Chron GENERAL 835

swich pron. 1a *OE* a1121 Peterb.Chron. TR 5

swifte adj. 1a *OE* a1150 Vsp.D.Hom.
RomA 32

swifte adv. a *fr. swifte adj.* c1380
Firumb.(1) HF 2

swiftli adv. a *OE* a1150 Vsp.D.Hom. PF
4

swiftnesse n. b *OE* c1175 Bod.Hom. *BO* 3

swimmen v. 1a *OE* a1150 Vsp.D.Hom.
PF 5

swine n. 3 *OE* (c1100) Herbarium in
MS.Bodl.130 lf.42b HF 8

swines-hed n. 2a, swine n. *(fr. swine n. &*
hed n1.) Chaucer *RVT* 1

swink n. 1a *OE* c1150 PDidax. GP 4

swinken v. 1a *OE* (c1125)
Vsp.D.Hom.Fest.Virg. SNPRO 15

swinkere n. a *fr. swinken v.* (1340)
Ayenb. *GP* 1

swire n. 1a *OE* a1150 Vsp.D *ROMA* 1

swithe adv. 1a d *OE* a1121 Peterb.Chron.
HF 18

swiven v. a *OE* Chaucer M1LT 7

swolwe n. d *fr. swolwen v. & OE* (a1338)
Mannyng Chron.Pt.1 *LGW* 1

swolwen v. 1a *OE* c1150 Hrl.HApul. HF
7

sword n. 1a *OE* a1121 Peterb.Chron. SNT
77

swot n. 3a *OE* a1150 Vsp.D.Hom.
CYPRO 1

swoue n. b *fr. <aswouen pred. adj. &*
adv.> (c1250) Gen.& Ex. BD 9

swough n1. b *fr. swouen v1.* (a1350)
Isumb. HF 5

swoune n. a *fr. <a-swoune pred. adj. &*
adv.> (c1250) Floris (Suth) *FRANT* 1

swounen v. a *fr. swouen v2.* (?a1200)
Ancr. BD 17

swouninge ger. a *(fr. swounen v.)*
(?c1225) Horn CLT 3

t n. a *no etym.* ?c1200 Stw.57
Abecedarium Bo 2

tabarde n1. a *OF* (c1300) Songs Langtoft
GP 3

tabernacle n. 2a *OF & L* (c1250) Gen.&
Ex. HF 3

table n. 1c *OF, L, ML & OE (fr. L)* a1150
Vsp.D.Hom. RomA 44

tabour n. b *OF & ML; ult Pers.* c1300
SLeg. (Ld) Bo 2

tabouren v. a *OF & tabour n.* (c1378)
PPl.B (Ld) *LGW* F 1

tache n3. 1c *OF* (1340) Ayenb. HF 3

taffata n. *ML, AL; ult. Pers.* Chaucer *GP*
1

tail n. 1a a *OE* c1150 Hrl.MQuad. BD 18

taillage n. *OF* c1300 SLeg.Becket (Ld)
FORMAGE 3

taille n. 1d *OF* c1230 Ancr. (Corp-C) GP
2

taillinge ger. a *(fr. taillen v.)* (a1376)
PPl.A(1) (Trin-C) *SHIPT* 1

takel n. 3 *MLG & MDu.* (c1250) Gen.&
Ex. *GP* 1

taken v. 3a b *LOE fr. ON* a1131
Peterb.Chron. RomA 705

takinge ger. 8b *fr. taken v.* (?a1200) Ancr.
Bo 7

tal adj. e *fr. OE* (a1325) Cursor *MARS* 1

talbot n. c *prob. LOE, fr. OF* 1381 Dc.257
Cook.Recipes *NPT* 1

tale n. 9a *OE* (c1125)
Vsp.D.Hom.Elucid. RomA 248

talen v. 2 *OE* a1150 Vsp.D.Hom. TR 4

talent n. 2d *OE & OF & L* c1300
SLeg.Inf.Chr. (Ld) Bo 17

talken v. a *prob. fr.tal- & -ke suf.* (?a1200)
Lay.Brut RomA 4

talkere n. a *fr. talken v.* Chaucer *PARST* 1

talkinge ger. d *(fr. talken v.)* c1300
SLeg.Inf.Chr. (Ld) NPT 2

tame adj. 3b *OE* (?a1200) Ancr. ANEL 7

tape n. *fr. LOE* Chaucer *MILT* 1

tapeten v. *fr. tapete n.* Chaucer *BD* 1

tapicer n. a *OF & ML* Chaucer *GP* 1

tappe n1. a *OE, LOE* (1340) Ayenb.
RVPRO 3

tappestere n. b *OE* Chaucer GP 2

tare n1. 1b *?cp. MDu., MLG* (?a1300)
Arth.& M. KnT 3

targe n1. a *OE & OF* (c1300)
Glo.Chron.A ABC 5

tarien v1. 2b *origin unknown* (?a1325)
Bonav.Medit.(1) MkT 35

tariinge ger1. a *fr. tarien v1.* (c1350)
Alex.& D. RomA 19

Tarse n. a *OF* (?c1300) Guy(1) KnT 1

tart adj. a *OE* a1150 Vsp.D.Hom. *GP* 1

tartar n1. a *ML* Chaucer GP 3

Tartar n2. a *OF & ML* Chaucer SqT 2

Tartarie n. a *OF & ML* Chaucer BD 2

tasse n2. a *OF, AF & ML* (?a1300)
Arth.& M. KnT 3

tasselen v. a {b} *fr. tassel n.* Chaucer
{(?a1370) Winner & W.} RomA 2

taste n1. 2a *OF & AL* (a1325) Cursor *PF*
1

tasten v. 1b *OF* c1300 SLeg.Inf.Chr. (Ld)
SNT 5

tastinge ger. 4 *fr. tasten v.* (?a1300)
KAlex. ParsT 1

Taur n. *L & AF* Chaucer LGW 8

taverne n. 1a *OF, AF* c1300 SLeg. (Ld)
GP 6

tavernere n. a *OF* (?c1300) Bevis PardT
2

techel n. a *L, fr. Gr.; ult Aramaic* a1150
Vsp.D.Hom. MkT 2

techen v. 4b *OE* (c1125)
Vsp.D.Hom.Elucid. RomA 93

techinge ger. 2b *fr. techen v. & OE* c1175
Bod.Hom. SNPro 8

te he interj. *prob. imitative* Chaucer
MilT 1

teien v. 1b *OE* a1150 Vsp.D.Hom. GP 2

teine n. *ON* Chaucer CYT 9

tellen v. 7e *OE* a1121 Peterb.Chron.
RomA 888

tellinge ger. 1c *fr. tellen v.* (?a1300)
Arth.& M. ThoP 1

teme n2. b *OF & L* (a1325) Cursor
PardPro 2

temen v1. 2b *OE* c1175 Bod.Hom. HF 1

temperaunce n. 1b *OF, AF & L* (1340)
Ayenb. FranT 1

tempere n. 1e {1d} *fr. tempre adj. or
tempren v.* Chaucer {(a1387)
Trev.Higd.} RomA 1

tempest n. 1a *OF & L* c1275 Ken.Serm.
ABC 28

tempesten v. c *OF* Chaucer Bo 2

tempestous adj. *OF & L* Chaucer TR 1

temple n1. 1c b *OE (fr. L) & OF & L*
a1131 Peterb.Chron. ABC 69

temple n2. b *OF* c1330 *St.Marg.(2)
(Auch) TR 1

temple-dore n. 1b b, temple n1. *(fr.
temple n1. & dore n1.)* c1300 SLeg.
(Ld) PF 1

temporal adj. 2a *OF, AF & L* (?a1350)
Castleford Chron.Lear Bo 30

tempren v. 3a *OE & OF & L, AL* ?c1200
Orm. PF 4

temps n. *OF & L* Chaucer CYT 1

temptacioun n. 2a *L & OF, AF* (?a1200)
Ancr. MLT 13

tempten v. 2a *L & OF, AF* (?a1200) Ancr.
FrT 16

temptere n. b *fr. OF & tempten v.*
(?c1350) SVrn.Leg. FrT 1

ten num. 1a a *OE* a1121 Peterb.Chron.
RomA 31

tenden v2. c *OF & L* (c1350) NHom.(2)
PSanct. Bo 2

tender adj. 1a *OF, AF* (?a1200) Ancr.
RomA 35

tender-herted adj. 6b, tender adj. *(fr.
tender adj. & herted adj.)* Chaucer TR 1

tenderli adv. 2a *fr. tender adj.* (a1325)
Cursor RomA 26

tendernesse n. 2a *fr. tender adj.* (a1325)
Cursor TR 3

tene n2. 1a *OE* a1150 Vsp.D.Hom.
RomA 14

tenour n. 1a *OF & L* (?a1300) KAlex.
LGW 1

tente n1. 1b *OF & ML* (c1300)
Glo.Chron.A ABC 12

tenthe num. 1a *fr.* *OE* a1150
Vsp.D.Hom. HF 9

tentifli adv. *fr. tentife adj.* (c1350)
NHom.(2) PSanct. CLT 1

tercel n. *OF, AF* Chaucer *PF* 7

tercelet n. *OF* Chaucer PF 9

tercian adj. *L & OF, AF* Chaucer NPT 1

tere n. 1c a *OE* a1150 Vsp.D.Hom. PITY
93

teren v2. 1a *OE* c1175 Bod.Hom. ROMA
10

teri adj. *fr. tere n.* Chaucer TR 1

terin n. *OF* Chaucer ROMA 1

Termagaunt n. *OF* (?a1200) Lay.Brut
THOP 1

terme n. 4c *OF, AF* (?a1200) Ancr.
ROMA 35

terme-dai n. 4a, term n. *(fr. terme n. &
dai n.)* c1300 SLeg.Cross (Ld) BD 1

terminen v. 1a *OF & L* a1325
MS.Rawl.B.520 lf.30b PF 1

terrestre adj. b *OF, AF* (?a1300) KAlex.
MERT 1

testament n. 2a *L, OF, AF* c1300 SLeg.
(Ld) WBPRO 4

teste n1. a *OF, AF & L, ML* Chaucer
CYT 1

tester n2. *OF & ML* Chaucer KNT 1

testif adj. *fr. OF* Chaucer TR 2

tete n. 1a *OF & OE* c1150 Hrl.HApul.
MILT 1

teuel n. b *OF, AF* Chaucer HF 2

texte n. 3b *OF, AF & L* Chaucer BD 25

textuel adj. *?AL* Chaucer MANCT 3

thakken v. b *OE* c1150 PDidax. MILT 2

than conj. 8a *OE* a1121 Peterb.Chron.
GENERAL 589

thank n. 1d a *OE, LOE* a1150
Vsp.D.Hom. ROMA 34

thanken v. 1b e *OE* a1121 Peterb.Chron.
ROMA 81

thankinge ger. 1a *fr. thanken v.* (c1280)
SLeg.Pass. (Pep) MEL 1

thanne adv. 2a a *OE* a1150 Vsp.D.Hom.
GENERAL 1017

that conj. 6a *OE* (1100) Chart.St.Paul in
RHS ser.3.58 20 GENERAL 6133

that def. art. & adj. 1c a *OE* (1100)
Chart.St.Paul in RHS ser.3.58
GENERAL 828

that pron. 1a a *OE* (1100) Chart.St.Paul
in RHS ser.3.58 GENERAL 943

that rel. pron. 1a a *OE* a1121
Peterb.Chron. GENERAL 5177

the adv. 1a *OE* a1150 Vsp.D.Hom.
GENERAL 203

the def. art. 1a a *LOE* a1121
Peterb.Chron. GENERAL 12143

the pron2. 2a a *OE* a1121 Peterb.Chron.
GENERAL 879

theatre n. b *L & OF* Chaucer BO 4

Theban adj. b *fr. L* Chaucer ANEL 7

Theban n. *L* (?a1300) KAlex. ANEL 7

Thebes n. a *OF* (?a1300) KAlex. HF 37

Thebes-ward n. a, Thebes n. *(fr. Thebes n.
& -ward suf.)* (?a1300) KAlex. KNT 2

thedom n. a *fr. then v.* c1330 7 Sages(1)
SHIPT 1

thef n2. 1a c *OE* a1121 Peterb.Chron.
ROMA 42

thefli adv. *fr. thef n2.* c1300
SLeg.Brendan (Ld) LGW 1

thefte n. 1a b *OE* (?a1200) Lay.Brut
ROMA 15

thei pron. 2b *ON & LOE* c1150 PDidax.
GENERAL 1714

then v. 1a *OE* a1150 Vsp.D.Hom. ROMA
20

thennes adv. 1a *fr. thenne adv.* ?a1250
PMor. (Dgb) ROMA 17

thennesforth adv. 5d, thennes adv. *(fr.
thennes adv. & forth adv.)* Chaucer BO
2

theologie n. a *L & OF; ult. Gr.* (a1376)
PPl.A.(1) (Trin-C) PARST 1

theorike n. a *ML & OF* Chaucer AST 2

ther adv. 1a a *OE* a1121 Peterb.Chron.
GENERAL 1518

ther-abouten adv. 1a *OE* a1121
Peterb.Chron. HF 5

ther-after adv. 1a *OE* a1121
Peterb.Chron. BD 5

ther-amonge adv. 1b b *fr. ther adv. &*
<amonges adv.> & amonges prep. a1121
Peterb.Chron. *ROMA* 1

ther-as adv. & conj. 3a a *fr. ther adv. &*
as conj. (?a1200) Ancr. SNPRO 7

ther-ayen adv. 2d *fr. ther adv. & ayein*
adv. & ayen prep. (c1200) Vices &
V.(1) FRT 1

ther-ayenes adv. 1a *fr. ther adv. & ayenes*
prep. (?c1200) St.Kath.(1) BO 4

ther-bi adv. 2a *OE* a1150 Vsp.D.Hom.
ROMA 30

ther-biforen adv. 1a *fr. ther adv. &*
biforen adv. & biforen prep. & LOE
(?a1200) Trin.Hom. RvT 7

ther-fore adv. 3a *fr. ther adv. & for prep.*
& LOE a1121 Peterb.Chron. GENERAL
316

ther-from adv. 2b *fr. ther adv. & fr. adv.*
& from prep. (?c1150) Prov.Alf. (Mdst)
ROMA 6

ther-inne adv. 1a *OE* a1121 Peterb.Chron.
ROMA 32

ther-of adv. 2a a *OE* a1126 Peterb.Chron.
ROMA 64

ther-on adv. 1a *OE* a1121 Peterb.Chron.
ROMA 11

ther-oute adv. 1c *OE* c1150 PDidax.
MKT 4

ther-to adv. 3b c *OE* a1121 Peterb.Chron.
GENERAL 103

ther-upon adv. 1a a *fr. ther adv. & upon*
adv. & upon prep. (c1200) Vices &
V.(1) PF 3

ther-while adv. & conj. 1c *prob. fr. OE*
(c1200) Vices & V.(1) TR 1

ther-whiles adv. & conj. 2a *prob. fr.*
therwhile adv. & conj. (a1250) Bestiary
BO 1

ther-with adv. 1a *OE* (?c1175) PMor.
(Trin-C) ROMA 83

ther-withal adv. 3 *fr. ther adv. & withal*

adv. & prep. a1300 A Mayde Cristes
ROMA 57

these adj. 1a c *fr. OE* a1150 Vsp.D.Hom.
GENERAL 519

these pron. 1a *fr. OE* (?a1200) Lay.Brut
ROMA 37

theu n1. 3b *OE* (c1125)
Vsp.D.Hom.Elucid. SNPRO 8

theuen v1. a *fr. theu n1.* ?c1200 Orm.
ROMA 4

the-ward n. 3a, the pron2. *(fr. the pron2.*
& -ward suf.) Chaucer BO 4

thider adv. 1a a *OE* 1121 Peterb.Chron.
SNT 20

thiderward adv. 1a a *OE* (?a1200)
Lay.Brut HF 3

thikke adj. 2b *OE* a1150 Vsp.D.Hom.
ROMA 24

thikke adv. 1 *fr. thikke adj. & OE* c1150
PDidax. ROMA 11

thikke n. b *fr. thikke adj.* (?a1216) Owl &
N. RvT 2

thilke adj. 1a a *fr. the def. art. & ilke*
pron. (?a1216) Owl & N. GENERAL 540

thilke pron. 2a *fr. the def. art. & ilke*
pron. (c1250) Floris (Cmb) HF 16

thin pron. 2c *OE* a1121 Peterb.Chron.
GENERAL 1524

thing n. 4a *OE* a1121 Peterb.Chron.
ROMA 1773

thinken v1. 1a *OE* a1121 Peterb.Chron.
ROMA 176

thinken v2. 10b *OE* a1131 Peterb.Chron.
ROMA 269

thinkinge ger. 3 *fr. thinken v2.* (a1325)
Cursor PARST 1

thinne adj. 1a *OE* c1150 Hrl.HApul. BO 9

thinne adv. 1b *fr. thinne adj.* (?a1216)
Owl & N. GP 1

thinne n. b *fr. thinne adj.* c1325 In a fryht
RvT 1

thirlen v. 1c *OE* c1175 Bod.Hom. ANEL 4

thirst n. 1b *OE* a1150 Vsp.D.Hom.
ROMA 10

thirsten v. 1b *OE* a1150 Vsp.D.Hom.
MᴋT 4

this adj. 1a *OE* a1121 Peterb.Chron.
Gᴇɴᴇʀᴀʟ 2966

this pron. 1a a *OE* a1121 Peterb.Chron.
Gᴇɴᴇʀᴀʟ 986

thi-self pron. 2a *fr. thin pron. & self adj.,
n. & pron.* (?c1200) St.Juliana ABC 90

tho adv. 1a *OE* a1121 Peterb.Chron.
Gᴇɴᴇʀᴀʟ 246

tho def. art. & adj2. 1a a *OE* a1121
Peterb.Chron. BD 69

tho pron2. 1b *OE* a1121 Peterb.Chron.
BD 25

tholen v. 6a *OE* a1131 Peterb.Chron. FʀT
1

thonder n. 1a a *OE* a1121 Peterb.Chron.
HF 10

thonder-clappe n. a *fr. thonder n. &
clappe n.* Chaucer PᴀʀsT 1

thonder-dint n. 2d, dint n. *(fr. thonder n.
& dint n.)* Chaucer Tʀ 3

thonder-leit n. 1b, thonder n. *OE*
?a1300 Fiftene tokenen Bo 2

thondren v. 1 *OE* a1150 Vsp.D.Hom. Bo
2

thondrere n. *fr. thondren v.* Chaucer Bo
1

thondringe ger. b *(fr. thondren v.)* c1300
SLeg.Cross (Ld) HF 1

thorn n. 3a *OE* (c1125)
Vsp.D.Hom.Fest.Virg. ABC 9

thorp n. a *OE & ON* 1121 Peterb.Chron.
PF 5

thou pron. 1a *OE* 1121 Peterb.Chron.
Gᴇɴᴇʀᴀʟ 2141

though adv. 1a *OE & ON* a1150
Vsp.D.Hom. BD 1

though conj. 1a a *OE & ON* a1121
Peterb.Chron. Gᴇɴᴇʀᴀʟ 441

thought n. 1a a *OE* a1150 Vsp.D.Hom.
RᴏᴍA 197

thoughtful adj. a *fr. thought n.* ?c1200
Orm. CʟT 2

thoume n. 1a *OE* c1150 Hrl.MQuad. GP
6

thousand num. 3a *OE* a1121
Peterb.Chron. RᴏᴍA 90

thousandfold adj. b *OE* (?a1200) Ancr.
PF 1

thral adj1. 2b *fr. thral n1.* (c1200) Vices
& V.(1) Bo 12

thral n1. 1a *OE & ON* (c1200) Vices &
V.(1) BD 24

thraldom n. 1a *fr. thral n1.* (?a1200)
Lay.Brut Tʀ 14

thrallen v. a *fr. thral n1.* (?a1200)
Lay.Brut RᴏᴍA 3

thre num. 1b b *OE* a1121 Peterb.Chron.
RᴏᴍA 149

thred-bare adj. a *fr. threde n. & bar adj.*
(a1376) PPl.A (1) (Trin-C) GP 4

threde n. 1a *OE* c1150 Hrl.HApul. RᴏᴍA
9

threden v2. a *fr. threde n.* c1350
Cmb.Ee.4.20.Nominale RᴏᴍA 1

threpen v. c *OE* ?c1200 Orm. CYT 1

threshen v. b *OE, LOE* ?c1200 Orm. GP
1

thresh-wolde n. a *OE* c1225 Wor.Aelfric
Gloss. Bo 4

thresten v. 3a *OE* a1150 Vsp.D.Hom. Bo
10

threten v1. 2a *OE* a1150 Vsp.D.Hom. Tʀ
3

thretinge ger. e *(fr. threten v1. & OE)*
a1150 Vsp.D.Hom. CYPʀo 1

thrice adv. 1a *fr. thrie adv. & -es suf1.*
?c1200 Orm. PF 12

thrid num. 1a a *OE* a1121 Peterb.Chron.
RᴏᴍA 60

thrie adv. a *OE* c1150 Hrl.HApul. Tʀ 3

thrift n. b *ON* c1300 SLeg.Jas. (Hrl) HF
13

thrifti adj. a *fr. thrift n.* Chaucer ANᴇʟ
10

thriftili adv. a *fr. thrifti adj.* (?c1380)
Cleanness Tʀ 4

thringen v. 1a *OE* (?a1200) Ancr. ROMA 5

thritene num. 1a *OE* a1150 Vsp.D.Hom. *SUMT* 1

thriti num. a *OE* a1121 Peterb.Chron. MERT 4

thriven v. 1a *fr. ON* ?c1200 Orm. ROMA 28

throng n. b *fr. OE* (?a1300) Arth.& M. *KNT* 1

throstel n. a *OE* ?c1200 Stw.57.Gloss. ROMA 3

throstel-cok n. a *fr. throstle n. and cok n1.* ?a1300 Thrush & N. *THOP* 1

throte n. 1a *OE* c1150 Hrl.HApul. ROMA 29

throte-bolle n. a *OE* c1250 Thene latemeste dai *RVT* 1

throu n1. 1b c *OE* ?c1200 Orm. PITY 13

throu n2. a *fr. OE & ON* (?a1200) Trin.Hom. *TR* 2

throuen v1. 10c *OE* (c1200) Vices & V.(1) ROMA 20

thurgh prep. 1d *OE* a1121 Peterb.Chron. GENERAL 291

thurghdarten v. *(fr. thurgh prep. & darten v.)* Chaucer *TR* 1

thurgh-fare n. b *(fr. thurgh prep. & fare n1.)* Chaucer *KNT* 1

thurghgirden v. *(fr. thurgh prep. & girden v2.)* Chaucer KNT 2

thurgh-oute prep. 1a *OE* (?a1200) Lay.Brut ROMA 33

thurghpassen v. b *(fr. thurgh prep. & passen v.)* Chaucer BO 1

thurghpercen v. a *(fr. thrugh prep. & percen v.)* (?a1300) Arth.& M. *BO* 1

thurghsheten v. a *OE & (fr. thurgh prep. & sheten v.)* c1330 SMChron. *TR* 1

thurrok n. a *OE* Chaucer *PARST* 2

thurven v. 2a a *OE* a1150 Vsp.D.Hom.Nicod. ROMA 15

thus adv. 1a *OE* a1121 Peterb.Chron. GENERAL 888

thwitel n. a *prob. fr. thwiten v.* Chaucer *RVT* 1

thwiten v. a *OE* a1325 Gloss.Bibbesw. ROMA 2

tide n. 2a *OE* a1121 Peterb.Chron. ROMA 28

tiden v. 1b a *OE* 1123 Peterb.Chron. HF 8

tidif n. *origin unknown* Chaucer LGW F 2

tidinge n. 2a *LOE & ON* (?c1150) Prov.Alf. (Trin-C) HF 32

tigre n. a *OE & OF & L* (?a1300) KAlex. HF 9

tikel adj1. d *fr. tikelen v.* (a1338) Mannyng Chron.Pt.1 *MILT* 1

tikelen v. 2 *prob. fr. tiken v.* (a1338) Mannyng Chron.Pt.2 *WBPRO* 2

tikelnesse n. *fr. tikel adj1.* Chaucer *TRUTH* 1

til adv. 2a *fr. til prep.* ?c1200 Orm. *RVT* 1

til conj. 1a a *fr. til prep.* ?a1160 Peterb.Chron. GENERAL 308

til prep. 16a *OE & ON* c1150 Hrl.MQuad. ROMA 44

tile n2. 1a *OE; ult. L* (c1250) Gen.& Ex. BD 3

Tile n3. *L* Chaucer BO 1

tillen v1. 3 *OE* a1150 Vsp.D.Hom. *MEL* 1

tillere n. a *fr. tillen v1.* (c1250) Gen.& Ex. BO 1

tillinge ger1. 2 *fr. tillen v1. & OE* a1150 PDidax. BO 1

timber n1. 1a *OE* (c1200) Vices & V.(1) ROMA 5

timbester n. *fr. timber n1.* Chaucer *ROMA* 1

time n2. 2a c *OE* a1121 Peterb.Chron. ROMA 515

timeli adv. a *OE* (?a1200) Lay.Brut *PARST* 1

tin n1. a *OE* (?a1200) Trin.Hom. *CYT* 1

tine n1. *OF & L* Chaucer *ROS* 1

tinnen v1. *fr. tin n1.* Chaucer *HF* 1

tippen v2. a *prob. ON* (?c1380) Patience
SumT 3

tippet n. 1a *prob. fr.< tippe n1.>* (c1300)
Songs.Langtoft HF 3

tipto n. b, tippe n1. *fr. tippe n1. and to n.* *
Chaucer *NPT* 1

tirannie n. d *OF* Chaucer Pity 15

tiraunt n. 2c *OF, AF* c1300 SLeg.Becket
(Ld) MкT 25

Tire n3. b *L & OF & OE* a1150
Vsp.D.Hom. Bo 4

tirven v. a *?fr. OE* (c1300) Havelok *CYT*
2

tisheu n. b *OF, AF* Chaucer RomA 2

Titan n. a *L* Chaucer *TR* 1

titanos n. *L; ult. Gr.* Chaucer *CYT* 1

titering ger. *ON* Chaucer *TR* 1

tithe n1. *OE* (?a1200) Trin.Hom. GP 3

tithere n. *fr. tithen v2.* Chaucer *FRT* 1

title n. 1a a *OF, AF & L* (a1325) Cursor
MкT 3

titleles adj. *fr. title n.* Chaucer *MancT* 1

titlen v1. c *OF, AF* c1175 Bod.Aelfric
OT *ParsT* 1

to adj. b *fr. ton adj.* (a1325) Cursor *Bo* 3

to adv1. 1a *OE* a1150 Vsp.D.Hom. SNT 39

to adv2. a *OE* a1150 Vsp.D.Hom.
General 164

to n. 1b *OE* (?c1200) St.Juliana HF 5

to prep. 1a a *OE* a1121 Peterb.Chron.
General 3275

to vbl. particle. 1a c *OE* a1121
Peterb.Chron. General 5296

tobreken v. 7b *OE* a1121 Peterb.Chron.
HF 7

tobresten v. 1a *OE* a1150 Vsp.D.Hom.
ABC 6

tocleven v. a *OE* c1175 Bod.Aelfric OT
TR 1

todai adv. a *OE* a1121 Peterb.Chron.
RomA 12

todashen v. c *fr. <dashen v.>* (?a1200)
Lay.Brut RomA 2

tode n. b *OE* (?a1200) Ancr. *ParsT* 1

todrauen v. 1a *fr. drauen v.* (?a1200)
Lay.Brut *Bo* 3

todriven v. a *OE* a1150 Vsp.D.Hom.
LGW 1

toforen adv. 1 *OE* a1150
Vsp.D.Hom.Nicod. *Bo* 1

toforen prep. 1a *OE* a1121 Peterb.Chron.
Bo 12

togeder adv. 1a b *OE* a1121
Peterb.Chron. RomA 59

togederes adv. 1a *fr. togeder adv.*
(?a1200) Lay.Brut BD 8

togon v. a *OE* a1225 Vsp.A.Hom. *LGW*
1

to-hepe adv. 4d, hep n. *(fr. hep n.)* c1300
Lay.Brut (Otho) *Bo* 5

toheuen v. a *OE* (?a1200) Lay.Brut TR 4

token n. 1c *OE* a1121 Peterb.Chron.
LGW 5

toknen v. 2 *OE* a1150 Vsp.D.Hom. *Bo* 1

tokninge ger. 2a *fr. toknen v. & OE*
a1150 Vsp.D.Hom. Anel 5

tol n3. a *OE* (c1125) Vsp.D.Hom.Elucid.
TR 2

tollen v1. 1a *prob. OE* (?a1200) Ancr. Bo
2

tollen v2. b *fr. tol n1.* (?a1387) PPl.C
(Hnt HM 137) *GP* 1

Tolletan adj. *L* Chaucer *FranT* 1

tombe n. a *OF, AF* c1300 Lay. Brut
(Otho) WBPro 3

tomelten v. *fr. melten v.* a1250 Wooing
Lord *TR* 1

tomorn adv. 1a *OE* a1150 Vsp.D.Hom.
FrT 2

tomorwe adv. a *OE* (?a1200) Lay.Brut
Bo 39

ton pron. a *misanalysis of that on phr. or
the on phr.* (c1250) Gen.& Ex. *Bo* 13

tonge n1. 1e *OE* (c1125)
Vsp.D.Hom.Elucid. *ParsT* 1

tonge n2. 3a b *OE* a1121 Peterb.Chron.
RomA 98

tongen v. b *fr. tonge n2.* Chaucer BD 1

tonight adv. b *OE* (?a1200) Lay.Brut Tʀ 9

tonne n. 1a *OE* a1121 Peterb.Chron. PF 8

tonne-gret adj. 1d, tonne n. *(fr. tonne n. & gret adj.)* Chaucer KɴTɪ

top nɪ. 1a *OE* (?a1200) Lay.Brut HF 7

torasen v. b *<fr. rasen vɪ.>* c1300 SLeg. (Ld) CʟTɪ

torche n. b *OF* (c1250) Floris (Vit) BD 6

torde n. b *OE* c1150 Hrl.MQuad. PᴀʀᴅT 2

torenden v. 2a *OE* (?a1200) Ancr. RoᴍA 14

toret nɪ. c *OF & AL* Chaucer KɴT 2

torment n. 1a *OF, AF & L* c1300 SLeg. (Ld) RoᴍA 58

tormenten v. 1a *OF, AF* c1300 SLeg. (Ld) Bo 21

tormentinge ger. 1b *fr. tormenten v.* c1300 SLeg.Cross (Ld) CʟTɪ

tormentise n. *fr. torment n.* Chaucer MᴋTɪ

tormentour n. 1a *OF, AF* c1300 SLeg.Edm.King (Hrl) SNT 9

tormentrie n. 3 *OF & fr. torment n.* or *tormentour n.* (?c1375) NHom.(3) Leg. WBPʀo ɪ

tortuous adj. c *OF & L* Chaucer AsT 2

toscateren v. b *fr. scateren v.* (a1382) WBible(1) (Bod 959) SuᴍTɪ

toshaken v. 1 *OE* a1150 Vsp.D.Hom. LGW 2

toshiveren v. b *<fr. shiveren v.>* (?a1200) Trin.Hom. PFɪ

toshreden v. *fr. shreden v.* Chaucer KɴT ɪ

toslitered adj. *(fr. toslitten v.)* Chaucer RoᴍA ɪ

tosterten v. *fr. sterten v.* c1380 Firumb.(1) Tʀ ɪ

total adj. a *OF* Chaucer PᴀʀsTɪ

toteren v2. 1a *OE* a1150 Vsp.D.Hom. RoᴍA 7

toth nɪ. 3 *OE* a1150 Vsp.D.Hom. Bo 10

toth-ache n. 5a, toth nɪ. *OE* c1150 Hrl.HApul. RoᴍA ɪ

tother adj. 1c *fr. misanalysis of that def. art. & adj. & other adj.* (c1250) Gen.& Ex. Bo 5

tother pron. 2b *fr. misanalysis of that def. art. & adj. & other pron.*(c1250) Gen.& Ex. Bo 17

toti adj. a *prob. fr. toteren v.* Chaucer RvTɪ

totreden v. a *fr. to adv. & treden v.* (c1200) Vices & V.(1) PᴀʀsT ɪ

tou nɪ. b *prob. OE* (c1378) PPl.B (Ld) LGW 3

touail n. 1a *OF* (c1250) Floris (Cmb) RoᴍA 3

touche n. 1b *OF, AF* (c1300) Glo.Chron.A Tʀ ɪ

touchen v. 1a *OF, AF* (c1280) SLeg.Pass. (Pep) RoᴍA 44

touchinge ger. 1a *fr. touchen v.* c1300 SLeg.Lucy (Ld) Bo 5

touchinge prep. {1a b} *fr. touching ppl.* Chaucer {(?1384) Wycl.Church} Bo 22

tough adj. 1a *OE* (?a1200) Lay.Brut BD 6

tought adj. a *prob. OE* (?a1216) Owl & N. SuᴍTɪ

toun n. 1a *OE* a1121 Peterb.Chron. RoᴍA 190

tour nɪ. 1a *OF, AF & OE* a1121 Peterb.Chron. ABC 35

touret n. 1a *OF, AF* (?a1300) Guy(2) KɴTɪ

tournei nɪ. a *AF, OF* c1300 SLeg.Becket (Hrl) Tʀ ɪ

tourneiinge ger. a *fr. tourneien v.* (?a1300) KAlex. RoᴍA 4

tournement n. c *OF, AF* (?a1200) Ancr. Tʜoᴘ ɪ

toute n. b *prob. fr. touten v.* (a1300) Cokaygne MɪʟT 2

toward prep. 2a *OE* a1121 Peterb.Chron. RoᴍA 42

towardes prep. 1 *OE* a1121 Peterb.Chron.
HF 6

towinden v. *fr. winden vi.* (?a1200)
Lay.Brut *MARS* 1

toyere adv. a *OE.* (?a1200) Lay.Brut HF
3

trace n1. 2b *OF* ?c1250 Somer is comen
& Bo 5

tracen v. 1b *OF* Chaucer *PF* 1

tragedie n. a *OF & L* Chaucer *MKT* 10

tragedien n. *OF* Chaucer *BO* 1

traien v. 1a *OF, AF* a1300 I-hereth nu
one *LGW* 1

trailen vi. 1b *OF* a1300 Serm.Lithir lok
PARST 1

trailinge ger1. *fr. trailen vi.* ?a1300
Sayings St.Bern. *PARST* 1

trais n. a *OF* c1330 7 Sages(1) TR 2

traishen v. d *OF* (?c1300) Guy(1) HF 2

traitour n. 4d *OF, AF* (?c1200) HMaid.
ROMA 33

traitouresse n. a *OF, AF* (?c1350) Ywain
BD 2

traitourie n. b *AF* (c1303) Mannyng HS
HF 3

tranquillite n. 2c *OF* Chaucer *BO* 1

transferren v. a *L & OF* Chaucer *BO* 1

transfiguren v. a *L & OF* (a1325) Cursor
BO 2

transformen v. e *OF & L* Chaucer *BO* 4

transitorie adj. c *L & OF, AF* Chaucer
BO 5

translacioun n. 5b *L & OF, AF* Chaucer
SNPRO 4

translaten v. 2a *L & OF* (a1325) Cursor
BO 7

transmuen v. a *OF* Chaucer *TR* 2

transmutacioun n. 1c *L & OF, AF*
Chaucer HF 3

transporten v. a *OF & L* Chaucer *BO* 3

trappe n1. d *OE* ?c1200 Orm. *SNPRO* 5

trappe-dore n. *fr. trappe n1. & dore n1.*
Chaucer *TR* 1

trappen v2. a *fr. trappe n2.* Chaucer
KNT 2

trappour n. a *prob. fr. AL or AF*
Chaucer *KNT* 1

traunce n. b *OF, AF* Chaucer *MKT*
8

trauncen v2. *perh. ult. fr. L* Chaucer *TR*
1

travail n. 1a *OF, AF* c1275 Ken.Serm.
ROMA 32

travailen v. 1a a *OF, AF* c1275
Ken.Serm. *ROMA* 25

travailinge ger. 3b *fr. travailen v.*
(?c1300) Guy(1) *PARST* 1

trave n. b *ML, AL* Chaucer *MILT* 1

travers n. 1b *OF* (a1338) Mannyng
Chron.Pt.1 TR 2

tre n. 1a d *OE* a1121 Peterb.Chron.
ROMA 110

treble adj. a *OF, AF* (?c1280)
SLeg.OTHist. (Ld 622) *BO* 2

trecheri n. 1b *OF, AF* (?a1200) Ancr.
ANEL 8

trechour n1. a *OF, AF* a1300 King
conseilles *ROMA* 1

trede-foul n. 7d, foul n. (*fr. treden v. &
foul n.*) Chaucer *PROMKT* 2

treden v. 3b *OE* a1150 Vsp.D.Hom. HF
7

tredinge ger. 4 *fr. treden v.* (a1382)
WBible(1) (Bod 959) *PROMKT* 1

tregetour n. b *OF, AF* (a1325) Cursor
HF 4

trei n3. a *AF* (1387) PPl.C (Hrt.137)
PARDT 1

treisoun n. 3b *OF, AF* (?a1200) Ancr.
BD 17

tremblen v. 1b a *OF & ML* (c1303)
Mannyng HS *BO* 3

tremour n. *OF, AF* Chaucer *TR* 1

trench n. a *OF* Chaucer *SQT* 1

trenchaunt adj. a *OF, AF* c1380
Firumb.(1) *RVT* 1

trenden v. c *OE* (c1200) Vices & V.(1)
BO 1

trental n. a *ML, AL & OF* (?a1350)
Trental St.Greg.(1) *SUMT* 2

tresour n. 1a *OF, AF* ?a1160
Peterb.Chron. ROMA 40

tresourer n. b *OF, AF* a1250 SWard
(Tit) ABC 2

tresourie n. a *OF, AF.* c1300
SLeg.Becket (Ld) HF 2

trespas n. 2a *OF, AF* c1250 *Body &
S.(4) ROMA 24

trespassen v. 1a d *OF, AF* (?c1300)
LFMass Bk. MKT 14

trespassinge ger. b *fr. trespassen v.* (1375)
Canticum Creat. *LGW F* 1

trespassour n. b *OF, AF* (a1376) PPl.A
(Trin-C) *MEL* 3

tresse n. 1a *OF* c1300 11 Pains(2) ROMA
10

tressen v. c *OF, AF* (?a1300) KAlex.
ROMA 5

tressour n. a *OF, AF* ?a1300 Sayings
St.Bern *ROMA* 1

tretable adj. 2a *OF, AF & fr. treten v.*
(c1303) Mannyng HS BD 4

trete n2. 4a *fr. treten v.* (?c1350)
SVrn.Leg. MKT 6

treten v. 1b a *OF, AF* (c1300)
Glo.Chron.A MKT 25

tretis adj. a {a} *OF, AF* Chaucer {c1380
Firumb.(1)} ROMA 4

tretise n. 1a *AF* Chaucer TR 21

treue adj. 12a *OE* a1121 Peterb.Chron.
ROMA 202

treue adv. 1a *fr. treue adj.* (?c1225) Horn
BD 2

treue n1. 8 *OE & OF* a1150 Vsp.D.Hom.
TR 5

treuli adv. 1a *OE* (?a1200) Lay.Brut
ROMA 126

treu-love n. 1b *fr. treue adj. & love n1.*
(?c1200) HMaid. *MILT* 1

treuth n. 2e *OE* a1150 Vsp.D.Hom.
ROMA 196

triacle n. b *OF, AF* (a1300) Cokaygne
MLT 2

tribulacioun n. b *OF, AF & L* (?a1200)
Ancr. BO 15

tributarie adj. a *L* Chaucer BD 2

tribute n. a *OF, AF & L* (c1350) Alex.&
D. *BO* 1

tricen v. a *MDu.* Chaucer MKT 1

trie adj. b *OF* (a1300) Cokaygne *THOP* 1

triklen v. *origin uncertain* (c1350)
Octav.(1) *PRT* 1

trillen v1. a *prob. ON* (c1350) NHom.(2)
PSanct. SUMT 4

trine adj. b *L & OF* Chaucer *SNPRO* 1

trinite n. 2b *OF, AF* (?a1200) Lay.Brut
SUMT 3

trippe n3. *cp. MnE dial.* Chaucer *SUMT*
1

trippen v. c *OF* c1380 Firumb.(1) MILT
2

triste n. a *OF* (?a1200) Ancr. *TR* 1

triumphe n. 2 *L & OF* Chaucer MKT 4

Troian adj. *L & OF* Chaucer HF 7

Troian n1. *L & OF* (a1338) Mannyng
Chron.Pt.1 HF 14

Troianish adj. a *OE* (?a1200) Lay.Brut
HF 1

Troie n1. a *L & OF & OE* (?a1200)
Lay.Brut BD 98

Troieward n. a, Troie n1. *(fr. Troie n1. &
-ward suf.)* Chaucer *TR* 1

trompe n. 1 *OF, AF* (c1300)
Glo.Chron.A HF 24

trompen v. a *OF, AF* (a1325) Cursor HF
6

trompour n1. a *OF, AF* a1325 SLeg.
(Corp-C) *KNT* 1

tronchoun n. 1a *OF, AF* (c1300)
NHom.(1) Widow's Candle *KNT* 1

trone n2. 2b *OF, AF & L* (?c1200)
SWard. MKT 11

tropik n. *L* Chaucer *AST* 2

trot n1. d *OF* (?c1380) Cleanness *CYPRO*
1

trotten v. 1a *OF* (a1376) PPl.A (Trin-C)
WBPRO 2

troublable adj. *OF* Chaucer *BO* 1

trouble adj. c *OF, AF* (?a1300) KAlex.
LADY 8

Chaucer's words

troublen v. 3a *OF* (?a1200) Ancr. SNPro
15

troubli adj. e *prob. fr. trouble n.* Chaucer
Bo 1

troublinge ger. 2a *fr. troublen v.* c1350
MPPsalter Bo 1

trouen v. 1a *OE* a1150 Vsp.D.Hom.
RomA 185

trough n. a *OE* a1325 Gloss.Bibbesw.
MilT 4

trufle n. 1b *OF, AF* (?a1200) Trin.Hom.
ParsT 1

trussen v. 1b a *OF, AF* (?a1200) Ancr. GP
1

trust n. 1a *prob. ON* (?a1200) Lay.Brut
HF 17

trusten v. 1a *prob. ON* (?a1200) Ancr.
RomA 101

trustli adv. 2 *fr. trust n.* (?a1200)
Trin.Hom. RomA 1

tubbe n. a *prob. MDu., MLG* c1350 Of
all the witti MilT 5

tuft n. a *origin uncertain* (a1387)
Trev.Higd. GP 1

tuken v. 1a *OE & MDu., MLG* a1150
Vsp.D.Hom. LGW 3

tumbester n. *fr. tumben v.* (c1385) Usk
TL PardT 1

tumblen v. 1a *prob. AF* (c1300) Songs
Langtoft Bo 3

tumulte n. *OF & L* Chaucer Bo 1

turbacioun n. {b} *OF, AF & ML*
Chaucer {(a1388) Wallingford
Exafrenon} Bo 1

turf n. 1b *OE* (?a1200) Lay.Brut LGW F
2

Turk n. {a} *ML & OF* Chaucer {(a1387)
Trev.Higd.} RomA 1

Turkeis adj. a *OF, AF* Chaucer KnT 1

Turkie n. a *AF, AL* (?a1200) Lay.Brut
BD 2

turne n. 3b *OF, AF* (?a1200) Ancr.
PardT 2

turnen v. 1a *OE & OF* a1150
Vsp.D.Hom. RomA 170

turninge ger. 1c *fr. turnen v.* (?c1200)
HMaid. RomA 4

turtel n. a *OE* ?c1200 Orm. RomA 8

tusk n1. a *OE* c1150 Hrl.HApul. TR 2

tusked ppl. a *fr. tusk n.* Chaucer FranT
1

tutelere n. a *fr. tutelen v.* Chaucer LGW
F 1

tweifold adj. a *fr. twein num.* ?c1225
Ancr. (Cleo) CYPro 1

twein num. 1a a *OE* a1121 Peterb.Chron.
ABC 109

twelfth num. 1a *OE* a1150 Vsp.D.Hom.
Mars 1

twelve num. 1a *OE* 1121 Peterb.Chron.
RomA 35

twelve-month n. 1b *OE* a1131
Peterb.Chron. WBT 1

twenti num. 1b a *OE* a1121 Peterb.Chron.
RomA 53

twicchen v. 1a *?OE* c1300 SLeg.Lucy
(Hrl) TR 3

twies adv. 1a *fr. twie adv.* a1121
Peterb.Chron. BD 18

twig n. a *OE* c1150 Hrl.MQuad. HF 5

twine n. 1b *OE* (?a1200) Lay.Brut KnT 2

twinen v. 4 *fr. twine n.* (?a1200) Lay.Brut
TR 2

twinklen v. a *OE* c1300 Ne saltou neuer
Bo 2

twinklinge ger. 1a *fr. twinklen v.* a1300
Serm.Lithir lok Mars 2

twinnen v1. 1a a *fr. twinne num.* (?a1200)
Ancr. SNT 19

twinninge ger. 1c *fr. twinnen v1.* (?a1200)
Ancr. TR 1

twist n. 1 *prob. OE* a1300 Gloss.Bibbesw.
(Seld) TR 3

twisten v. 1b *prob. fr. < twist n. >* c1230
Ancr.(Corp-C) HF 7

twiteren v. *prob. imitative* Chaucer Bo 1

two num. 1a a *OE* a1121 Peterb.Chron.
RomA 345

two-foted adj. 1b c, two num. *(fr. two
num. & foted adj.)* Chaucer Bo 1

ugli adj. [ugly a.,adv. & sb.] *[fr. ON]* (c1250) Gen.& Ex. CLT 1

unable adj. [unable a.] *fr. able adj.* (?c1378) Wycl.OPastor. BO 5

unagreable adj. [unagreeable a.] *fr. agreable adj.* Chaucer BO 1

unapt adj. [unapt a.] *fr. apt adj.* Chaucer TR 1

unaraced adj. [unraced ppl. a1.] *fr. aracen v.* Chaucer BO 1

unarmen v. [unarm v.] *fr. armen v.* c1300 SLeg.John (Ld) SQT 1

unaspied adj. [unespied ppl. a.] *fr. aspien v.* Chaucer TR 1

unassaied adj. [unassayed ppl. a.] *fr. assaien v.* Chaucer BO 1

unavised adj. [unadvised a. & adv.] *fr. avisen v.* (?c1380) Pearl TR 3

unbetiden v. *fr. bitiden v.* Chaucer BO 3

unbinden v. [unbind v.] *fr. binden v.* a1150 Vsp.D.Hom. PF 20

unbirien v. [unburied ppl. a.] *fr. birien v.* (?c1200) St.Kath.(1) (Bod) FRANT 1

unbodien v. [unbody v.] *fr. bodi n.* Chaucer TR 1

unbokelen v. [unbuckle v.] *fr. bokelen v.* (?a1387) PPl.C (Hnt HM137) MILPRO 4

unboren adj. [unborn ppl. a.] *OE* (?c1150) Prov.Alf. (Mdst) TR 5

unboued adj. [unbowed ppl. a.] *fr. bouen vr.* Chaucer BO 1

unbreiden adj. [unbroided ppl. a.] *fr. breiden vr.* Chaucer TR 1

unbrent adj. [unburnt ppl. a.] *fr. brennen v.* c1300 SLeg. (Ld) HF 2

unbridelen v. [unbridled ppl. a.] *fr. bridelen v.* Chaucer TR 1

unbuxomnesse n. [unbuxomness] *fr. n.* (c1200) Vices & V.(1) WOMNOB 1

uncertain adj. [uncertain a.] *fr. certain adj.* (c1303) Mannyng HS BO 8

uncharitabli adv. [uncharitably adv.] *fr. charitableli adv.* Chaucer PARST 1

uncircumscript adj. [uncircumscript ppl. a.] *fr. <circumscriben v.>* Chaucer TR 1

uncle n. [uncle sb.] *OF* c1300 SLeg. (Ld) TR 19

unclene adj. [unclean a.] *fr. clene adj.* c1150 Hrl.HApul. MKT 2

unclosen v. [unclose v.] *fr. closen v.* (c1325) Recipe Painting(1) in Archaeol.J.1 LGW F 3

unclothen v. [unclothe v.] *fr. clothen v.* (c1300) Havelok BO 1

uncommitted adj. [uncommitted ppl. a.] *fr. <committen v.>* Chaucer PF 1

unconninge adj. [uncunning a.] *fr. <conning ppl.>* (1340) Ayenb. ROMA 7

unconninge ger. [uncunning sb.] *fr. conning ger.* c1300 SLeg.Becket (Ld) MEL 2

unconstreined adj. [unconstrained ppl. a.] *fr. constreinen v.* Chaucer PHYT 1

uncouplen v. [uncouple v.] *fr. couplen v.* (?c1300) Guy(1) MKT 1

uncouplinge ger. [uncoupling vbl. sb.] *(fr. uncouplen v.)* Chaucer BD 1

uncourteisli adv. [uncourteously adv.] *fr. courteisliche adv.* (a1338) Mannyng Chron.Pt.2 MERT 1

uncouth adj. [uncouth a. & sb.] *fr. <couth adj.>* a1121 Peterb.Chron. HF 8

uncouthli adv. [uncouthly adv.] *fr. uncouth adj.* c1175 Bod.Hom. ROMA 1

uncovenable adj. [uncovenable a.] *fr. covenable adj.* (?a1350) Castleford Chron. BO 3

uncoveren v. [uncover v.] *fr. coveren vr.* (a1325) Cursor BO 2

undefouled adj. [undefouled ppl. a.] *fr. defoulen v.* (c1350) NHom.(2) PSanct. BO 1

undepartable adj. [undepartable a.] *fr. departable adj.* Chaucer BO 1

under adv. [under adv.] *[OE]* (?c1225) Horn BD 11

under prep. [under prep.] *[OE]* a1121 Peterb.Chron. GENERAL 180

undergrouen v. [undergrown ppl. a.] *fr.*
grouen v. a1382 WBible(1) (Bod 959)
GP 1

underlinge n. [underling sb. & a.] *OE*
a1150 Vsp.D.Hom. *PARST* 2

undermel n. [undermeal] *OE* 1372 Als a se
(Adv) *WBT* 1

undern n. [undern sb.] *OE* 1122
Peterb.Chron. CLT 3

undernethen adv. [underneath prep., adv.,
a. & sb.] *OE* (?c1200) HMaid. Bo 2

undernethen prep. [underneath prep.,
adv., a. & sb.] *OE* a1121 Peterb.Chron.
KNT 1

undernimen v. [undernim v.] *OE* c1175
Bod.Hom. SNT 2

underpicchen v. [underpight pa. t. & pa.
pple.] *fr. under adv. & picchen v.*
(c1378) PPl.B (Ld) *MLT* 1

underputten v. [underput v.] *fr. under
adv. & putten v.* (a1250) Bestiary Bo 1

undersporen v. [underspore v.] *[fr. under
adv. & spore n2.]* Chaucer *MILT* 1

understonden v. [understand v.] *OE*
a1100 Jun.Aelfric Gloss. ROMA 166

understondinge ger. [understanding vbl.
sb.] *(fr. understonden v.)* 1325 Horn
(Hrl) BD 7

undertaken v. [undertake v.] *[fr. under
adv. & taken v.]* ?c1200 Orm. ROMA
27

undeserven v. [undeserved ppl. a.] *fr.*
deserven v. Chaucer *TR* 1

undevocioun n. [undevotion] *fr.*
devocioun n. (?1348) Rolle FLiving
PARST 1

undigne adj. [undigne a.] *fr. digne adj.*
(a1333) Shoreham Poems Bo 3

undiscomfited adj. [undiscomfited ppl. a.]
fr. discomfiten v. Chaucer Bo 1

undiscrete adj. [undiscreet a.] *fr. <discrete
adj.>* (a1382) WBible(1) (Bod 959)
CLT 2

undon v. [undo v.] *fr. don vi.* a1121
Peterb.Chron. ROMA 11

undoutous adj. [undoubtous a.] *fr.*
doutous adj. Chaucer Bo 1

unescheuable adj. [uneschewable a.] *(fr.*
escheuen v.) Chaucer Bo 1

unescheuabli adv. [uneschewable a.] *fr.*
unescheuable adj. Chaucer Bo 1

unethe adv. [uneathe adv., uneathes
adv.] *OE* a1150 Vsp.D.Hom. ROMA
65

unexercised adj. [unexercised ppl. a.] *fr.*
exercisen v. Chaucer Bo 1

unfamous adj. [unfamous a.] *fr. famous
adj.* Chaucer *HF* 1

unfeined adj. [unfeigned ppl. a.] *fr. feinen
v.* Chaucer SNT 4

unfeithful adj. [unfaithful a.] *fr. feithful
adj.* 1370–2 Y am by-wylt Bo 1

unfelingli adv. [unfeelingly adv.] *fr.*
felingli adv. Chaucer *TR* 1

unfesteli adj. [unfeastly a.] *fr. feste n.*
Chaucer *SQT* 1

unfeteren v. [unfetter v.] *fr. feteren v.*
(c1350) Gamelyn *TR* 1

unfolden v. [unfold vi.] *OE* (?c1150)
Prov.Alf. (Trin-C) Bo 6

unfoldinge ger. [unfolding vbl. sb.] *(fr.*
unfolden v.) Chaucer Bo 1

unfore-sein adj. [unforeseen ppl. a.] *fr.*
<fore-sen v.> Chaucer Bo 1

unforged adj. [unforged ppl. a.] *fr. forgen
v.* Chaucer *FORMAGE* 1

ungentil adj. [ungentle a.] *fr. gentil adj.*
Chaucer Bo 2

ungilti adj. [unguilty a.] *fr. gilti adj.* c1225
Wor.Gloss. (Corp-C 178) *TR* 1

ungoverned adj. [ungoverned ppl. a1.] *fr.*
governen v. Chaucer Bo 1

ungrobbed adj. [ungrubbed ppl. a.] *fr.*
grubben v. Chaucer *FORMAGE* 1

unhap n. [unhap sb.] *fr. hap n.* (?a1200)
Ancr. HF 4

unhappi adj. [unhappy a.] *fr. unhap n.*
(a1325) Cursor *TR* 3

unhappili adv. [unhappily adv.] *fr.*
unhappi adj. Chaucer *TR* 2

unhardi adj. [unhardy a.] *fr. hardi adj.*
(c1378) PPl.B (Ld) *RVT* 1

unhele n. [unheal] *OE* c1150 Hrl.HApul.
PHYT 1

unholi adj. [unholy a. & sb.] *OE* (c1378)
PPl.B (Ld) *PARST* 2

unholsom adj. [unwholesome a. & sb.] *fr.*
holsom adj. ?c1200 Orm. *TR* 1

unhoped adj. [unhoped ppl. a.] *fr. hopen*
vi. Chaucer *BO* 1

unhorsen v. [unhorse v.] *fr. horsen v.*
Chaucer *KNT* 1

unite n. [unity] *OF & L* (?c1300)
Spec.Guy *BO* 8

universalite n. [universality] *OF & L*
Chaucer *BO* 2

universe n. [universe] *[fr. OF (fr. L)]*
Chaucer *TR* 1

universel adj. [universal a. (adv.) & sb.]
OF & L Chaucer *BO* 10

universite n. [university sb.] *OF* c1300
SLeg.Edm.Abp. (Hrl) *BO* 2

unjoiful adj. [unjoyful a.] *fr. joiful adj.*
(c1350) Alex.Maced. *BO* 1

unjoinen v. [unjoin v.] *fr. joinen vi.*
(1340) Ayenb. *BO* 4

unkinde adj. [unkind a.] *OE* (?a1200)
Trin.Hom. ABC 17

unkindeli adj. [unkindly a.] *fr. unkinde*
adj. c1230 Ancr. (Corp-C) *PARST* 1

unkindeli adv. [unkindly adv.] *fr. unkinde*
adj. (?a1200) Ancr. HF 4

unkindenesse n. [unkindness] *fr. unkinde*
adj. (c1303) Mannyng HS ANEL 3

unkist adj. [unkissed ppl. a.] *fr. kissen vl.*
Chaucer *TR* 1

unknitten v. [unknit v.] *OE* (?c1200)
St.Kath.(1) *BO* 1

unknouable adj. [unknowable a. & sb.]
OE (?a1200) Trin.Hom. *BO* 1

unknouen v. [unknown ppl. a1. & sb.,
unknowing ppl. a.] *fr. knouen v.* (a1325)
Cursor HF 16

unkorven adj. [uncorven ppl. a.] *fr.*
kerven ppl. Chaucer *FORMAGE* 1

unlasen v. [unlace v.] *fr. lasen v.* (?a1300)
Guy(2) *BO* 1

unlefful adj2. [unleeful a.] *fr. <lefful*
adj2.> (?a1350) 7 Sages(2) *BO* 4

unlike adj. [unlike a. & sb.] *fr. lik adj.*
?c1200 Orm. *BO* 6

unlikli adj. [unlikely a. (& sb.)] *fr. likli*
adj. Chaucer LADY 2

unliklinesse n. [unlikeliness] *fr.*
<liklinesse n.> Chaucer *TR* 1

unloven v. [unlove v.] *fr. loven vi.*
Chaucer *TR* 1

unlust n. [unlust sb.] *OE* ?c1200 Orm.
PARST 1

unmanhede n. [unmanhood] *fr. manhede*
n. (a1325) Cursor *TR* 1

unmeke adj. [unmeek a.] *fr. mek adj.*
(?c1150) Prov.Alf. ROMA 2

unmesurable adj. [unmeasurable a., sb. &
adv.] *fr. mesurable adj.* (?c1350) Mirror
St.Edm.(4) MLT 4

unmete adj. [unmeet a.] *OE* c1200
Wor.Serm. in EGSt.7 ROMA 3

unmevable adj. [unmovable a. & sb.] *fr.*
mevable adj. Chaucer *BO* 2

unmevablete n. [unmovablety] *fr.*
moevablete n. Chaucer *BO* 1

unmighti adj. [unmighty a.] *OE* a1150
Vsp.D.Hom.Nicod. *BO* 4

unmirie adj. [unmerry a.] *OE* c1250 Owl
& N. *HF* 1

unnesten v. [unnest v.] *fr. nesten v.*
Chaucer *TR* 1

unoccupied adj. [unoccupied ppl. a.] *fr.*
occupien v. Chaucer *MEL* 1

unordren v. [unordered ppl. a1.] *fr. ordren*
v. Chaucer *PARST* 1

unparegal adj. [unparegal a.] *fr. paregal*
adj. Chaucer *BO* 1

unpinnen v. [unpin v.] *fr. <pinnen v.>*
c1300 Horn (Ld) *TR* 1

unpitous adj. [unpiteous a.] *fr. pitous adj.*
Chaucer *BO* 1

unplitable adj. [unplitable a.] *fr. unpliten*
v. Chaucer *BO* 1

Chaucer's words

unpliten v. [unplight v.] *fr. pleiten v.* Chaucer *BO* 2

unpreied adj. [unprayed ppl. a.] *fr. preien vi.* Chaucer *TR* 1

unprofitable adj. [unprofitable a.] *fr. profitable adj.* c1350 MPPsalter *BO* 3

unpunished adj. [unpunished ppl. a.] *fr. punishen v.* (c1340) Rolle Psalter (UC 64) *BO* 4

unpurveied ppl. adj. [unpurveyed ppl. a.] *fr. purveien v.* (?c1300) LFMassBk. *BO* 1

unreprevable adj. [unreprovable a.] *fr. reprevable adj.* (a1382) WBible(1) (Bod 959) *LGW* 1

unresounable adj. [unreasonable a.] *fr. resonable adj2.* (c1340) Rolle Psalter (UC 64) *FRANT* 1

unreste n. [unrest sb.] *fr. reste n1.* (c1340) Rolle Psalter (UC 64) *BO* 8

unresti adj. [unresty a.] *fr. unreste n.* (c1340) Rolle Psalter (UC 64) *TR* 1

unreverentli adv. [unreverently adv.] *fr. unreverent adj.* Chaucer *PARST* 1

unright n. [unright sb.] *fr. right n.* a1121 Peterb.Chron. *TR* 3

unrighte adv. [unright adv.] *fr. righte adv.* a1150 Vsp.D.Hom. *TR* 1

unrightful adj. [unrightful a.] *fr. rightful adj.* c1300 SLeg.Becket (Ld) *BO* 3

unrightfulli adv. [unrightfully adv.] *fr. unrightful adj.* c1350 MPPsalter *BO* 1

unsad adj. [unsad a.] *fr. sad adj.* (c1384) WBible(1) Rom.15.1 *CLT* 1

unsavouri adj. [unsavoury a.] *fr. savourie adj.* (?a1200) Ancr. *PARST* 2

unscience n. [unscience] *fr. science n.* Chaucer *BO* 1

unseli adj. [unseely a.] *OE* c1175 HRood SNT 14

unselinesse n. [unseeliness] *fr. selinesse n.* a1325 PROV.Hend. (Cmb Gg) *BO* 5

unset adj. [unset ppl. a.] *fr. setten v.* Chaucer *KNT* 1

unseuen v. [unsew v.] *fr. seuen v2.* (?a1200) Ancr. *PARST* 1

unshethen v. [unsheathe v.] *fr. <shethen v.>* (c1384) WBible(1) *TR* 1

unsheued adj. *fr. sheuen vi.* (1386) RParl.FM *PARST* 1

unshitten v. [unshut v., unshut ppl. a.] *fr. shitten v.* (?a1300) KAlex. *HF* 2

unsitting adj. [unsitting ppl. a.] *fr. sitten v.* Chaucer *TR* 1

unskilful adj. [unskilful a.] *fr. skilful adj.* (?1348) Rolle FLiving *TR* 1

unskilfulli adv. [unskilfully adv.] *fr. skilfulli adv.* (c1350) Alex.& D. *BO* 2

unslekked adj. [unslecked ppl. a.] *fr. slekken v.* Chaucer *CYT* 1

unsoft adj. [unsoft a.] *fr. softe adj.* a1300 Hwi ne serue *HF* 2

unsolempne adj. [unsolemn a.] *fr. solempne adj.* Chaucer *BO* 1

unsouen adj. [unsown ppl. a.] *fr. souen vi.* (c1350) Gamelyn *FORMAGE* 1

unsought ppl. adj. [unsought ppl. a.] *fr. sechen v.* (?a1200) Ancr. *PITY* 2

unspedeful adj. [unspeedful a.] *fr. <spedeful adj.>* (c1340) Rolle Psalter (UC 64) *BO* 1

unstable adj. [unstable a.] *fr. stable adj.* (?a1200) Ancr. *BO* 5

unstablenesse n. [unstableness] *fr. stableness n.* (?a1350) Castleford Chron. *BO* 1

unstaunchable adj. [unstanchable a.] *fr. staunchen v.* Chaucer *BO* 1

unstaunched adj. [unstanched ppl. a.] *fr. staunchen v.* Chaucer *BO* 1

unstedefast adj. [unsteadfast a.] *fr. <stedfast adj.>* & *OE* (?c1175) PMor. *BO* 2

unstedefastnesse n. [unsteadfastness] *fr. sted-fastness n.* (a1325) Cursor *LGW* G 3

unstraunge adj. [unstrange a.] *fr. straunge adj.* Chaucer *AST* 1

unsufferable adj. [unsufferable a. & adv.]

399

fr. sufferable adj. a1325 MS.Rawl.B.520
lf.31b *BO* 2

unswellen v. [unswell v.] *fr. swellen v.*
Chaucer *TR* 2

unswet adj. [unsweet a.] *fr. swete adj.*
(?a1300) Tristrem *HF* 1

unteien v. [untied ppl. a2.] *fr. teien v.*
(?c1300) Bevis *TR* 1

untellen v. [untold ppl. a.] *fr. tellen v.*
(a1325) Cursor *MILT* 2

unthank n. [unthank sb.] *OE* a1126
Peterb.Chron. *TR* 2

unthrift n. [unthrift sb.] *fr. thrift n. &*
<*unthriven v.*> (c1303) Mannyng HS
TR 1

unthrifti adj. [unthrifty a.] *fr. thrifti adj.*
& unthrift n. (1384) Appeal Usk in
Bk.Lond.E *TR* 1

unthriftili adv. [unthriftily adv.] *fr.*
<*unthrifti adj.*> (?c1380) Cleanness
CYT 1

until prep. [until prep. & conj.] *on prep.*
& til prep. ?c1200 Orm. BD 4

untim n. [untime sb.] *OE* a1126
Peterb.Chron. *PARS T* 1

unto conj. [unto prep. & conj.] *fr. unto*
prep. (c1303) Mannyng HS *PF* 1

unto prep. [unto prep. & conj.] *fr. on*
prep. & to prep. (c1300) Havelock
GENERAL 554

untormented adj. [untormented ppl. a.]
fr. tormenten v. Chaucer *TR* 1

untressed adj. [untressed ppl. a.] *fr. tressen*
ppl. Chaucer PF 3

untretable adj. [untreatable a.] *fr. tretable*
adj. Chaucer *BO* 1

untreu adj. [untrue a. & adv.] *[OE]*
[(a1250) Bestiary (Arun)] LADY 21

untreue adv. [untrue a. & adv.] *[fr. untreu*
adj.] [c1325 Lutel wot hit (Hrl)] *GP*
1

untreuth n. [untruth] *fr. treuth n.* (1340)
Ayenb. HF 11

untrust adj. [untrist sb.] *fr. trust adj.*
Chaucer *TR* 1

untrust n. [untrist sb.] *fr. trust n.* (?a1200)
Ancr. *MERT* 1

unusage n. [unusage] *fr. usage n.* Chaucer
BO 1

unwar adj. [unware a., sb. & adv.] *[OE]*
[(c1200) Vices & V.(1)] MKT 7

unwar adv. [unware a., sb. & adv.] *[OE]*
[(c1300) Glo.Chron.A] TR 3

unwarli adv. [unwarely adv.] *[OE]* [a1121
Peterb.Chron.] *BO* 1

unwelde adj. [unwield a.] *[OE]* [(a1250)
Bestiary] ROMA 2

unweldi adj. [unwieldy a.] *[fr. weldi adj.]*
[Chaucer] *MANCPRO* 1

unwemmed adj. [unwemmed ppl. a.]
[OE] [?c1200 Orm.] ABC 6

unwened adj. [unweened ppl. a.] *(fr.*
wenen v2.) Chaucer *BO* 1

unweri adj. [unweary a.] *[OE]* [(c1340)
Rolle Psalter] *TR* 2

unwis adj. [unwise a.] *[OE]* (?a1200)
Ancr. (Corp-C) ROMA 2

unwist adj. [unwist ppl. a.] *(fr. witen vi.)*
Chaucer *KNT* 11

unwit n. [unwit sb.] *[fr. wit n.]* [?c1200
Orm.] MARS 2

unwiten v. [unwit vi.] *[fr. unwit n.]*
Chaucer *BO* 3

unwitingli adv. [unwittingly adv.] *[fr.*
unwiting ppl. adj.] [Chaucer] *PARD T* 1

unworshipful adj. [unworshipful a.] *[fr.*
worshipful adj.] [Chaucer] *BO* 2

unworthi adj. [unworthy a., adv., sb.] *[fr.*
worthi adj.] [a1250 Wooing Lord
(Tit)] SNPRO 15

unworthili adv. [unworthily adv.] *[fr.*
unworthi adj.] [c1300
SLeg.Becket(Ld)] *BO* 1

unworthinesse n. [unworthiness] *[fr.*
unworthi adj.] [(c1340) Rolle Psalter]
BO 2

unwrappen v. [unwrap v.] *[fr. wrappen v.]*
Chaucer *BO* 2

unwreien v. [unwry v.] *[OE]* c1175
Bod.Hom. *TR* 1

Chaucer's words

unyolden adj. [unyolden ppl. a.] *(fr. yelden v.)* a1325 MS.Rawl.B.520 lf.29b *KNT* 2

up adv. [up advi.] *[OE]* [a1122 Peterb.Chron.] GENERAL 355

up prep. [up prepi.] *[OE]* a1225 Vsp.A.Hom.Init.Creat. BD 12

up-beren v. [upbear v.] *[fr. beren vi.]* [(?a1300) KAlex.] *TR* 1

upbounde adj. [up- prefix] *(fr. binden v.)* Chaucer *TR* 1

upbreiden v. [upbraid v.] *[OE]* [(?a1200) Ancr. (Corp-C)] ANEL 3

uphepinge ger. [upheaping vbl. sb.] *fr. uphepen v.* * Chaucer *BO* 1

upon adv. [upon adv.] *[fr. upon prep.]* ?c1200 Orm. ROMA 9

upon prep. [upon prep.] *[fr. up adv. & on prep.]* a1121 Peterb.Chron. GENERAL 631

uppe adv. [up adv2.] *[OE]* (?a1200) Lay.Brut *SQT* 1

upper adv. comp. [upper adv.] *[fr. up adv.]* Chaucer HF 4

upperest adj. [upperest a.] *[fr. upper adj.]* Chaucer *BO* 1

upright adj. [upright a. & sb.] *[OE]* [(?a1200) Ancr. (Corp-C)] BO 4

uprighte adv. [upright adv.] *[fr. upright adj.]* (c1250) Floris ROMA 24

uprisen v. [uprise v.] *(fr. risen v.)* [(a1325) Cursor] TR 5

uprist n. [uprist sb.] *fr. uprisen v.* * [(?c1225) Horn] *KNT* 1

up-so-doun adv. [upside down adv., sb. & a.] *(fr. up adv. & so adv. & doun adv.)* [c1330 Why werre] BO 7

upspringen v. [upspring v.] *(fr. springen v.)* [?c1200 Orm.] MARS 2

upstonden v. [upstanding ppl. a.] *(fr. stonden vi.)* [(?a1200) Lay.Brut] HF 1

upward adv. [upward adv., prep, a., & sb.] *[OE]* (?a1200) Lay.Brut HF 18

urinal n. [urinal sb.] *[OF]* [c1300 Lay.Brut (Otho)] INTPARDT 2

urine n. [urine sb1.] *[OF]* [c1330 7 Sages(1)] *WBPRO* 2

urne n. [urn sb.] *[L]* Chaucer *TR* 1

Ursa n. [Ursa] *[L]* Chaucer *BO* 1

us pron. [us pers. & refl. pron.] *[OE]* c1175 Bod.Hom. GENERAL 547

usage n. [usage sb.] *AF* (c1300) Glo.Chron.A ROMA 34

usaunce n. [usance] *OF* Chaucer ROMA 5

usaunt adj. [usant a.] *OF* c1380 Firumb.(1) RvT 2

usen v. [use v., used ppl. a.] *AF* a1250 Lofsong Lefdi (Nero) BD 79

usher n. [usher sb.] *AF* (c1280) SLeg.Pass. (Pep) *SQT* 1

usinge ger. [using vbl. sb.] *fr. usen v.* (c1340) Rolle Psalter VENUS 3

usure n. [usury sb.] *AF & ML* (c1280) SLeg.Pass. (Pep) ROMA 4

usurpen v. [usurp v.] *AF* a1325 MS.Rawl.B.520 lf.56 *AST* 1

us-ward adv. [usward adv., us pron.] *fr. us pron. & -ward suf.* Chaucer AST 3

utilite n. [utility sb.] *AF* Chaucer *AST* 1

vacacioun n. [vacation sb.] *[OF]* Chaucer *WBPRO* 1

valaunse n. *OF* Chaucer *MARS* 1

vale n. [vale sb1.] *[OF]* (a1325) Cursor *KNT* 1

valei n. [valley sb.] *[OF]* [(c1300) Glo.Chron.A] BD 6

Valence n1. [Valence 1] *OF* Chaucer *PF* 1

Valentine n. [Valentine sb.] *[OF]* Chaucer PF 7

valerian n. [valerian] *[OF]* Chaucer *CYT* 1

valeu n. [value sb.] *[OF]* [(c1303) Mannyng HS] ROMA 9

valour n. [valour] *[OF]* [(?a1300) Arth.& M.] ROMA 2

vanishen v. [vanish v.] *[OF]* [(c1303) Mannyng HS] SNT 7

vanishinge ger. [vanishing vbl. sb.] *[fr. vanishen v.]* Chaucer *KNT* 1

The making of Chaucer's English

vanite n. [vanity] *[OF]* [(?c1200)
HMaid.] Bo 18

vapour n. [vapour sb.] *AF (OF) & L*
(c1384) WBible(1) TR 3

variable adj. [variable a. & sb.] *[OF]*
[(a1387) Trev.Higd.] *STED* 1

variacioun n. [variation] *[OF]* Chaucer
KNT 1

variaunce n. [variance] *[OF]* Chaucer TR
6

variaunt adj. [variant a & sb.] *OF*
Chaucer Bo 2

varien v. [vary v.] *[OF]* Chaucer BD 6

vassalage n. [vassalage sb.] *OF* (c1303)
Mannyng HS KNT 2

vavasour n. [vavasour] *OF* (?a1300)
Arth.& M. *GP* 1

veil n. [veil sb1.] *OF* (c1250) Gen.& Ex.
GP 1

vein adj. [vain a. & sb.] *OF; L* (c1303)
Mannyng HS ROMA 20

vein n. [vain a. & sb.] *fr. vein adj.* (a1382)
WBible(1) (Bod 959) ABC 15

veine n. [vein sb.] *OF; L* (c1280)
SLeg.Pass. (Pep) ROMA 7

veine-blood n. [vein sb.] *fr. veine n. &
blod n1.* Chaucer *KNT* 1

veinglori n. [vainglory sb.] *fr. <vein adj.>
& glorie n.* c1230 Ancr. (Corp-C)
PARST 2

vele n. [veal sb1.] *OF* a1325 Add.46919
Cook.Recipes *MERT* 1

velvet n. [velvet sb.] *[ML]* Chaucer
ROMA 2

veneri n2. [venery1.] *OF* (?a1300)
Tristrem KNT 2

Venerien adj. [Venerien a. & sb.] *L and
-ien suf1.* (c1385) Usk TL (Skeat)
WBPRO 1

venesoun n. [venison] *OF* (?a1300)
KAlex. *PHYT* 1

vengeaunce n. [vengeance sb., adv., & a.]
[AF] (c1300) Glo.Chron.A ABC
56

vengeaunce-takinge ger. [vengeance sb.,

adv., & a.] *fr. vengeaunce n. & takinge
ger.* Chaucer *MEL* 5

vengen v. [venge v.] *[OF]* (?a1300) Rich.
(Auch) MEL 25

vengeresse n. [vengeress] *[OF]* Chaucer
Bo 1

venial adj. [venial a1. & sb.] *[OF]* [(a1325)
Cursor] *PARST* 21

venialli adv. [venially adv.] *[fr. venial adj.]*
[(c1340) Rolle Psalter] *PARST* 1

Venice n. [Venice] *[OF]* Chaucer HF 2

venim n. [venom sb. & a.] *[AF & OF]*
[(a1250) Bestiary (Arun)] ROMA 28

venimous adj. [venomous a.] *[OF]*
[(c1300) SLeg.Becket (Ld) ABC 5

venquishen v. [vanquish v.] *[OF]* [(a1338)
Mannyng Chron.Pt.1] ABC 8

ventosinge ger. [ventosing vbl. sb.] *[fr.
<ventosen v.>]* Chaucer *KNT* 1

Venus n. [Venus] *[L]* c1300 SLeg.Mich.
(Ld) ROMA 98

ver n. [ver sb1.] *OF* c1350 MPPsalter *TR* 1

verdegrece n. [verdigris] *[AF & OF]*
(c1325) Recipe Painting in Archaeol.J.1
CYT 1

verdit n. [verdict sb.] *[AF]* [(c1300)
Glo.Chron.A] PF 3

verie n. [verye] *[no etym.]* Chaucer *MILT*
1

verifien v. [verify v.] *[OF]* [(c1385) Usk
TL (Skeat)] *CYT* 1

vermin n. [vermin sb. (& a.)] *[AF & OF]*
[(?a1300) KAlex.] TR 3

vernage n. [vernage] *[OF]* Chaucer
MERT 2

vernicle n. [vernicle] *[AF & OF]* [(a1376)
PPl.A(1) (Trin-C)] *GP* 1

vernishen v. [varnish v.] *[OF]* Chaucer
RVT 1

verre n. [verre] *[OF]* [(a1382) WBible] TR
1

verrei adj. [very a., adv. & sb.] *[AF, OF]*
[c1275 Ken.Serm.] ROMA 207

verrei adv. [very a., adv. & sb.] *(fr. verrei
adj.)* [(?c1380) Patience] HF 5

402

verreilli adv. [verily adv. (& a.)] *[fr. verrei adj.]* [(c1303) Mannyng HS] ROMA 38

verreiment adv. [veriment adv., sb. & a.] *[OF]* [(?a1300) KAlex.] THOP 1

vers n. [verse sb.] *OF* (?a1200) Trin.Hom. BD 14

versefiour n. [versifier] *OF* (a1382) WBible(1) (Bod 959) MEL 1

versifien v. [versify v.] *OF* (c1378) PPl.B (Ld) PROMKT 1

vertu n. [virtue sb.] *OF & L* (?a1200) Ancr. ROMA 151

vertules adj. [virtueless a.] *fr. vertu n.* Chaucer TR 1

vertuous adj. [virtuous a.] *OF* (?a1300) Arth.& M. ROMA 33

vertuousli adv. [virtuously adv.] *fr. vertuous adj.* Chaucer WBT 3

vessel n. [vessel sb1.] *OF* (c1280) SLeg.Pass (Pep) MKT 18

vestement n. [vestiment] *OF & L* (?a1200) Ancr. KNT 2

vesture n. [vesture sb.] *OF & ML* (a1376) PPl.A(1) HF 2

viage n. [voyage sb.] *OF & AF* c1300 SLeg.Brendan (Hrl: Horst) HF 15

vicar n. [vicar, vicary sb1.] *AF, OF & L* (a1325) Cursor ABC 5

vice n. [vice sb1.] *OF & L* (c1300) Glo.Chron.A ROMA 97

vicious adj. [vicious a.] *AF, OF & L* Chaucer MKT 13

victorie n. [victory sb.] *AF; OF & L* (?c1300) Bevis SNPRO 28

victorious adj. [victorious a.] *AF* Chaucer BO 2

victour n. [victor sb1.] *OF, AF & L* (c1340) Rolle Psalter PF 1

vigil n. [vigil sb1.] *OF* a1250 Ancr. (Nero) TR 1

vigili n. [vigily] *AF & L* ?c1225 Ancr. (Cleo) GP 2

vigorous adj. [vigorous a.] *OF, AF & ML* (?a1300) Arth.& M. PARST 1

vigour n. [vigour sb.] *OF, AF & L* (?a1300) Arth.& M. BO 7

vile adj. [vile a., adv. & sb.] *OF* (c1280) SLeg.Pass. (Pep) BO 6

vileinie n. [villainy sb.] *OF & AN* c1230 Ancr. (Corp-C) ROMA 63

vileinous adj. [villainous a., villains a.] *OF* (c1303) Mannyng HS ROMA 14

vileinousli adv. [villainsly adv.] *fr. vileinous adj.* (a1338) Mannyng Chron.Pt.1 ROMA 3

village n. [village sb.] *OF* Chaucer SUMT 11

vine n. [vine sb.] *OF* c1300 SLeg.MPChr. (Ld) MKT 9

vinolent adj. [vinolent a.] *L* (c1384) WBible(1) WBPRO 2

violence n. [violence sb.] *OF & L* c1300 SLeg.Becket (Ld) HF 12

violent adj. [violent a.] *L & OF* Chaucer BO 2

violet n. [violet sb1.] *OF* (?a1300) Arth.& M. ROMA 3

virago n. [virago] *L* (a1325) Cursor MLT 1

virelai n. [virelay] *OF* Chaucer LGW F 2

virgin n. [virgin sb. & a.] *OF & L* (?a1200) Trin.Hom. ABC 5

virginite n. [virginity] *OF & L* (c1303) Mannyng HS SNPRO 13

Virgo n. [Virgo] *L* c1150 Hrl.HApud. AST 4

viritoot n. [viretote] *[OF]* Chaucer MILT 1

viritrate n. [viritrate] *[Of obscure origin]* Chaucer FRT 1

visage n. [visage sb.] *OF* (?a1300) KAlex. ROMA 41

visagen v. [visage v.] *fr. visage n.* (?a1300) KAlex. MERT 1

visible adj. [visible a. & sb.] *L & OF* (c1340) Rolle Psalter (UC 64) TR 1

visioun n. [vision sb.] *OF & L* c1300 SLeg.Fran.(1) (Ld) SUMPRO 2

visitacioun n. [visitation] *L & OF* (c1303)
Mannyng HS *WBPRO* 1

visiten v. [visit v.] *OF & L* (?a1200) Ancr.
TR 11

visitinge ger. [visiting vbl. sb.] *[fr. visiten
v.]* (a1325) Cursor TR 2

vitaile n. [victual sb.] *OF* (?a1300) KAlex.
Bo 18

vitailen v. [victual v.] *fr. vitaile n.* (?a1300)
Rich.(Auch) LGW 3

vitailer n. [victualler sb.] *OF* (c1378)
PPl.B (Ld) *CKT* 1

vital adj. [vital a. & sb.] *OF & L* Chaucer
KNT 1

vitremite n. [vitremyte] *?prob. L* Chaucer
MKT 1

vitriol n. [vitriol sb.] *OF & ML* Chaucer
CYT 1

voice n. [voice sb] *OF & L* c1300
SLeg.Patr. (Ld) ROMA 66

voide adj. [void a. & sb1.] *OF* c1300
SLeg.Becket (Ld) Bo 6

voide n. [voidee] *[AF]* Chaucer *TR* 1

voiden v. [void v.] *[AF & OF]* a1325 MS
Rawl.B.520 lf.30b ANEL 17

volage adj. [volage a.] *OF* Chaucer
ROMA 2

volatil n. [volatile sb. & a.] *OF & L*
a1325 Add.46919 Cook.Recipes *SHIPT*
1

volume n. [volume sb.] *OF & L* (a1382)
WBible(1) (Bod 959) INTMLT 2

voluntarie adj. [voluntary a., adv. & sb.]
OF; L Chaucer Bo 3

voluntarili adv. [voluntarily adv.] *fr.
voluntari adj.* Chaucer Bo 1

voluper n. [voluper] *? fr. volupen v.*
Chaucer MILT 2

voluptuous adj. [voluptuous a.] *OF*
Chaucer Bo 2

vomit n. [vomit sb.] *OF & L* (1373)
*Lelamour Macer *KNT* 1

vouchen v. [vouch v.] *OF* (c1303)
Mannyng HS ABC 22

vouchen-sauf phr. [vouchsafe v.] *fr.*

vouchen v. & sauf adj. c1330 KTars TR
9

vouen v. [vow v1.] *OF* (c1303) Mannyng
HS *PROMKT* 1

vulgar adj. [vulgar a.] *L; OF* Chaucer *AST*
3

vulgarli adv. [vulgarly adv.] *fr. <vulgar
adj.>* Chaucer *TR* 1

vulture n. [vulture sb.] *L & OF* Chaucer
Bo 2

wacche n. [watch sb.] *[OE]* [(c1200) Vices
& V.(1)] *MEL* 1

wachet n. [watchet sb. & a.] *[OF]*
Chaucer *MILT* 1

waden v. [wade v.] *[OE]* [(a1250)
Bestiary] MKT 4

wafer n. [wafer sb.] *[AF]* [(c1378) PPl.B
(Ld)] *MILT* 1

waferer n. [waferer sb.] *[AF]* [(a1376)
PPl.A(1) (Trin-C)] *PARDT* 1

wage n. [wage sb.] *[AF, OF]* [(a1338)
Mannyng Chron.Pt.21] MARS 5

waggen v. [wag v.] *[OE]* [(?a1200) Ancr.]
RVT 1

wagginge ger. [wagging vbl. sb.] *(fr.
waggen v.)* [(a1376) PPl.A(1) (Trin-C)]
TR 1

waimenten v. [wayment v.] *[OF]* [(c1375)
Canticum Creat] *PARST* 1

waimentinge ger. [wayment v.] *fr.
waimenten v.* * [(c1340) Rolle Psalter]
ROMA 7

wain n1. [wain sb1.] *OE* ?c1200 Orm. *Bo*
3

waiten v. [wait v1.] *[OF]* [(c1200) Vices &
V.(1)] SNPRO 46

waitinge ger. [waiting vbl. sb1.] *(fr.
waiten v.)* [(a1225) Trin.Hom.]
MANCT 1

waken v. [wake v., waking ppl. a.] *[OE]*
a1150 Vsp.D.Hom. BD 47

wake-plei n. [wake sb1.] *(fr. wake n1. &
pleie n.)* Chaucer *KNT* 1

waker adj. [waker a.] *[fr. waken v.]*
[(?a1200) Trin.Hom.] *PF* 1

wakinge ger. [waking vbl. sb.] *(fr. waken v.)* [a1225 Lamb.Hom.PaterN.] BD 5

waknen v. [waken v.] *[OE]* [?c1200 Orm.] NPT 1

wal n1. [wall sb1.] *[OE]* a1121 Peterb.Chron. ROMA 81

Walakie n. [Walach] *[L]* Chaucer BD 1

Wales n. *[OE]* c1300 SLeg.Kenelm (Ld) MLT 1

walet n. [wallet] *[?AF or OF]* (c1385) Usk TL (Skeat) GP 2

walk n1. [walk sb1.] *[fr. walken v1.]* (a1250) Bestiary TR 4

walken v1. [walk v1.] *[OE]* a1150 Vsp.D.Hom. ROMA 70

walkinge ger. [walking vbl. sb1.] *(fr. walken v1.)* (a1325) Cursor WBPRO 3

walled adj2. [walled ppl. a.] *fr.wallen v2.* (?a1300) Arth.& M. ROMA 6

walmen v. [walm v.] *[fr. walm n1. & ?OE]* Chaucer ROMA 1

walshnot n. [walsh-nut] *[?MDu.]* Chaucer HF 1

walwen v. [wallow v1.] *[OE]* [(?c1200) HMaid.] BO 11

wan adj. [wan a.] *[OE]* [(?c1200) HMaid.] TR 6

wandringe adj. [wandering ppl. a.] *[fr. wanderen v.]* (?c1200) HMaid. BO 6

wandringe ger. [wandering vbl. sb.] *(fr. wandren v.)* [(a1325) Cursor] GP 1

wanen v. [wane v.] *[OE]* [a1121 Peterb.Chron.] HF 5

wanhope n. [wanhope sb. & a.] *[fr. wan-pref. & hope n1.]* [(c1300) Glo.Chron.A] ROMA 11

wanten v. [want v.] *[prob. ON]* [?c1200 Orm.] PITY 13

wantinge ger. [wanting vbl. sb.] *[fr. wanten v.]* [(a1325) Cursor] SNPRO 2

wantoun adj. [wanton a. & sb.] *[fr. wan-pref. & touen v.]* [(a1325) Cursor] GP 3

wantounesse n. [wantonness sb.] *[fr. wantoun adj.]* [(a1376) PPl.A(1) (Trin-C)] GP 2

wantounli adv. [wantonly adv.] *[fr. wantoun adj.]* Chaucer SHIPT 1

wantrust n. [wantrust] *[fr. wan- pref. & trust n.]* Chaucer TR 2

warant n. [warrant sb1.] *[OF]* [(?c1200) St.Marg.] ROMA 1

waranten v. [warrant v.] *[OF]* a1300 Hwile wes seynte ROMA 3

ward n2. [ward sb2.] *[OE]* [(?a1200) Lay.Brut] BD 3

wardecors n. [wardecorps] *[AF]* [c1330 Otuel] WBPRO 1

wardein n. [warden sb1.] *[OF]* [(?c1200) Ancr.] TR 10

warderere interj. [warderere int.] *[AF]* Chaucer RVT 1

warderob n. [wardrobe] *[OF]* (a1325) Cursor PRT 1

ware adj. [ware a.] *[OE]* [?a1160 Peterb.Chron.] ROMA 78

ware n2. [ware sb3.] *[OE]* [a1225 PMor.] FORMAGE 4

wareli adv. [warely adv.] *[OE]* [(?a1200) Trin.Hom.] TR 1

waren v1. [ware v1.] *[OE]* [(c1250) Gen.& Ex.] BO 10

wariangle n. [wariangle] *[?OE]* Chaucer FRT 1

warien v. [wary v.] *[OE]* [(?a1200) Trin.Hom.] TR 3

warishen v. [warish v1.] *[OF]* [c1275 Ken.Serm.] BD 11

warishinge ger. [warish v1.] *(fr. warishen v.)* 1379 Glouc.Cath.MS.19 MEL 1

warisoun n. [warison] *[OF]* [(?a1300) KAlex.] ROMA 1

warm adj. [warm a.] *[OE]* [?c1200 Orm.] BD 9

warme adv. [warm adv.] *[OE]* (a1349) Rolle Com.LG ROMA 2

warmen v. [warm v.] *[OE]* [?c1200 Orm.] BO 2

warmnesse n. [warmness] *[fr. warm adj.]* Chaucer MERT 2

warnen vi. [warn vi.] *[OE]* c1175
Bod.Hom.Dom.2 Quadr. MKT 35

warnestoren v. [warnestore v.] *[fr.*
warnestore n.] a1375 WPal. BO 4

warnestoringe ger. [warnestore v.] *(fr.*
warnestoren v.) Chaucer *MEL* 2

warninge ger1. [warning vbl. sb1.] *[OE]*
[(a1325) Cursor] TR 2

warninge ger2. [warning vbl. sb2.] *[OE]*
Chaucer *ROMA* 1

warpinge ger. [warping vbl. sb1.] *[fr.*
warpen v.] Chaucer *AST* 1

wart n. [wart sb.] *[OE]* [(a1325) Cursor]
GP 1

washen v. [wash v.] *[OE]* c1150 PDidax.
ROMA 14

wasp n. [wasp sb.] *[OE]* Chaucer *PRT*
1

wast adj. [waste a.] *[OF]* [c1300
SLeg.Patr. (Ld)] *KNT* 1

wast n. [waist] *[?fr. OE]* [a1225
Lamb.Hom.] *ProTHOP* 1

waste n. [waste sb.] *[OF]* (?a1200)
Trin.Hom. WBPRO 7

wastel-bred n. [wastel sb.] *fr. wastel n. &*
bred n1. * a1325 Add.46919 Cook.
Recipes *GP* 1

wasten v. [waste v.] *[AF, ONF]* (?a1200)
Ancr. PF 23

waster n1. [waster sb1.] *[AF]* [(?a1370)
Winner & W.] *MERT* 1

wastinge ger. [wasting vbl. sb.] *[fr. wasten*
v.] [(a1325) Cursor] *MEL* 1

water n. [water sb.] *[OE]* a1121
Peterb.Chron. ROMA 79

water-foul n. [waterfoul] *[fr. water n. &*
foul n.] [(a1325) Cursor] PF 4

waterles adj. [waterless a.] *[OE]* [(a1325)
Cursor] *GP* 1

water-vessel n. [water sb.] *(fr. water n. &*
vessel n.) Chaucer *CYT* 1

Watringe ger. [watering vbl. sb.] *(fr.*
wateren v.) Chaucer *GP* 1

wau n. [waw sb1.] *[fr. OE]* [c1300
Lay.Brut (Otho)] ROMA 16

wax n1. [wax sb1.] *[OE]* [(?a1200)
Trin.Hom.] BO 10

waxen v1. [wax vi.] *[OE]* a1121
Peterb.Chron. ROMA 152

waxen v2. [wax v2.] *[fr. wax n1.]* [(c1378)
PPl.B (Ld)] *AST* 1

we pron. [we pron.] *[OE]* c1175
Bod.Hom. GENERAL 612

web n. [web sb.] *[OE]* [(c1200) Vices &
V.(1)] *AST* 1

webbe n. [webbe] *[OE]* a1325
Gloss.Bibbesw. (Arun: Owen) *GP*
1

wed n1. [weed sb1.] *[OE]* [(?a1200)
Trin.Hom.] *TR* 1

wed n2. [wed sb.] *[OE]* [a1121
Peterb.Chron.] KNT 2

wedden v. [wed v.] *[OE]* a1121
Peterb.Chron. SNT 97

weddinge ger. [wedding vbl. sb.] *[fr.*
wedden v.] [(c1250) Gen.& Ex.] MKT
19

wede n. [weed sb2.] *[OE]* ?c1200 Orm.
ROMA 7

weder n1. [weather sb.] *[OE]* [a1121
Peterb.Chron.] ROMA 11

wedercok n. [weathercock sb.] *(fr. weder*
n1. & cok n1.) [?a1300 Gloss.Neckam]
WOMUNC 1

wedlok n. [wedlock sb.] *[OE]* [?c1200
Orm.] LGW G 5

wegge n. [wedge sb.] *[OE]* a1150
Vsp.D.Hom. *AST* 1

weghte n1. [weight sb1.] *[OE]* [a1121
Peterb.Chron.] SNPRO 26

we-he interj. [wehee int. & sb.] *[echoic]*
[(a1376) PPl.A(1) (Vrn)] *RVT* 1

wei adv. [way adv.] *[fr. awei adv.]*
[(?a1200) Lay.Brut SNT 7

wei n. [way sb1.] *[OE]* [a1121
Peterb.Chron.] ROMA 319

weien vi. [weigh vi.] *[OE]* [(?c1175)
PMor. (Lamb)] MKT 8

weier n. [weigher] *[fr. weien vi.]* [(a1325)
Cursor] *AST* 1

weifaringe adj. [wayfaring ppl. a.] *[OE]*
(?a1200) Ancr. *BO* 1

weik adj. [weak a. & sb.] *[ON]* [(a1325)
Cursor] ROMA 10

weiken v. [weak v.] *[fr. weik adj.]*
Chaucer *TR* 1

weilawai interj. [wellaway int. & sb.] *[OE]*
[(?a1200) Lay.Brut] BD 35

weilen v. [wail v.] *[prob. ON]* [(?a1300)
Arth.& M.] LADY 18

weilinge ger. [wailing vbl. sb.] *[fr. weilen
v.]* [(?a1300) KAlex.] TR 3

weiven v1. & v2. [waive v1. & v2.] *[AF &
ON]* (c1300) Glo.Chron.A SNT 17

weke n. [week sb.] *[OE]* (c1125)
Vsp.D.Hom.Elucid. MKT 13

wel adj. [well a.] *[fr. wel adv.]* (c1125)
Vsp.D.Hom.Elucid. ROMA 42

wel adv. [well adv.] *[OE]* [a1121
Peterb.Chron.] GENERAL 1574

welcom adj. [welcome sb1, int. & a.] *[OE]*
[(?a1200) Lay.Brut] PF 24

welcomen v. [welcome v1.] *[OE]* [(?a1200)
Lay.Brut] TR 2

weld n1. [wield sb.] *[OE]* [?c1200 Orm.]
ROMA 2

weld n3. [weld sb1.] *[OE]* Chaucer
FORMAGE 1

welden v. [wield v.] *[OE]* [a1121
Peterb.Chron.] MKT 6

weldi adj. [wieldy a.] *[fr. welden v.]*
Chaucer *TR* 1

weldinge ger. [wielding vbl. sb.] *[fr.
welden v.]* [(?a1200) Lay.Brut] *MEL* 1

wele n1. [weal sb1.] *[OE]* (c1125)
Vsp.D.Hom.Elucid. BD 31

weleful adj. [wealful a.] *[fr. wele n1.]*
[(?c1200) HMaid.] BO 20

welefulnesse n. [wealful a.] *(fr. weleful
adj)* Chaucer BO 31

welfare n. [welfare sb.] *[fr. wel adv. & fare
n1.]* [(c1303) Mannyng HS] BD 7

wel-faringe adj. [well-faring ppl. a.] *(fr.
wel adv. & faren v.)* (1350) Apollonius
BD 1

welked adj. [welked ppl. a.] *[fr. welken
v1.]* [(c1250) Gen.& Ex.] WBPRO 2

welken n. [welkin] *[OE]* [a1121
Peterb.Chron.] BD 8

welken v1. [welk v1.] *[prob. fr. MDu.,
OHG]* [(c1340) Rolle Psalter (UC 64)]
BO 1

welle n. [well sb1.] *[OE]* [(?a1200)
Lay.Brut] ROMA 84

wellen v. [well v1.] *[OE]* [(?a1200) Ancr.]
TR 2

wel savoured phr. [savoured ppl. a.] *[fr.
savour n.]* Chaucer ROMA 1

welstreme n. [well-stream] *[OE]* [(?a1200)
Lay.Brut] *PF* 1

welth n. [wealth] *[fr. wel adv. or wele n1.]*
[(c1250) Gen.& Ex.] *PRONPT* 1

wel-willi adj. [well-willy a.] *(fr. wel adv.
& willi adj.)* Chaucer *TR* 1

wem n. [wem sb.] *[OE]* [(?a1200) Ancr.]
ROMA 2

wemles adj. [wemless a.] *[fr. wem n.]*
[a1300 Louerd crist ich] *SNPRO* 1

wench n. [wench sb.] *[fr. wenchel n.]*
[c1300 SLeg.Kath.(Ld)] MKT 19

wenden v. [wend v.] *[OE]* [?c1200 Orm.]
ROMA 317

wendinge ger. [wending vbl. sb.] *[fr.
wenden v.]* [(?a1300) KAlex.] BO 4

wene n. [ween sb.] *[OE]* [?c1200 Orm.]
ROMA 3

wenen v2. [ween v.] *[OE]* [?a1160
Peterb.Chron.] ROMA 233

weninge ger. [weening vbl. sb.] *[fr. wenen
v2.]* [a1300 I-hereth nu one] BO 2

went n. [went] *[fr. wenden v.]* [c1250
Gen.& Ex.] BD 8

wepen n. [weapon sb.] *[OE]* [?c1200
Orm.] ROMA 8

wepen v. [weep v. & weeping ppl. a.] *[OE]*
[a1121 Peterb.Chron.] ABC 184

wepinge ger. [weeping vbl. sb.] *[fr. wepen
v.]* [(?a1200) Trin.Hom.] ROMA 40

wepli adj. [weeply a.] *[fr. wepe n. or
wepen v.]* Chaucer BO 2

wer adv. [war, waur a. & adv.] *[ON]*
[?c1200 Orm.] *BD* 1

wer n2. [weir sb.] *[OE]* [a1121
Peterb.Chron.] PF 2

werble n. [warble sb1.] *[OF]* Chaucer *TR*
1

werd n. [weird sb.] *[OE]* [(a1325) Cursor]
B0 4

weren v1. [were v.] *[OE]* [a1121
Peterb.Chron.] *KNT* 1

weren v2. [wear v1.] *[OE]* [(?a1200)
Lay.Brut] ROMA 32

weri adj. [weary a.] *[OE]* c1150
Hrl.HApul. ROMA 31

werien v. [weary v.] *[OE]* c1150 PDidax.
CYT 1

werinesse n. [weariness] *[fr. <weri adj.>]*
a1150 Vsp.D.Hom. ROMA 4

weringe ger. [wearing vbl. sb1.] *(fr. weren
v1.)* (?a1200) Ancr. *PARST* 1

werk n. [work sb.] *[OE]* a1121
Peterb.Chron. ROMA 166

werken v. [work v. & working ppl. a.] *[OE]*
a1150 Vsp.D.Hom. ROMA 197

werker n. [worker] *[fr. werken v.]* (?c1350)
SVrn.Leg. MARS 3

werkinge ger. [working vbl. sb.] *(fr.
werken v.)* (c1280) SLeg.Pass. (Pep)
SNPRO 26

werk-man n. [workman] *[OE]* (?a1200)
Ancr. B0 7

wernen v. [warn v2.] *[OE]* [a1121
Peterb.Chron.] ROMA 13

werre n1. [war sb1.] *[LOE]* [?c1160
Peterb.Chron.] ABC 70

werre n2. [were sb3.] *[of doubtful origin]*
[(c1250) Gen.& Ex.] BD 3

werreien v. [warray v.] *[OF]* [(a1325)
Cursor] MKT 10

werreiour n. [warrior] *[ONF]* [(c1300)
Glo.Chron.A] *LGW* 1

werse adj. [worse a. & sb.] *[OE]* [a1121
Peterb.Chron.] BD 30

werse adv. [worse adv.] *[OE]* [?a1160
Peterb.Chron.] BD 5

werse n. [worse a. & sb.] *[fr. werse adj.]*
[?a1160 Peterb.Chron.] TR 5

werste adj. & n. [worst a. & sb.] *[OE]*
[(?c1175) PMor.] BD 18

wesel n. [weasel] *[OE]* [a1325
Gloss.Bibbesw. (Arun: Owen)] MILT
2

west adj. [west adv., sb1. & a.] *[fr. west
adv.]* [(c1378) PPl.B (Ld)] MKT 25

west adv. [west adv., sb1. & a.] *[OE]*
[?c1200 Orm.] BD 13

west n. [west adv., sb1. & a.] *[fr. west adv.]*
[(?a1200) Ancr.] B0 14

westen v1. [west v.] *[fr. west adv.]*
Chaucer PF 3

western adj. [western a. & sb1.] *[OE]*
(c1353) Winner & W. B0 3

westren v. [wester v.] *[fr. west adv.]*
Chaucer *TR* 1

westward adv. [westward adv., sb. & a1.]
[OE] [?a1160 Peterb.Chron.] KNT 5

wet adj. [wet a.] *[OE, ON]* a1150
Vsp.D.Hom. ROMA 12

wet n. [wet sb1.] *[OE]* [?c1200 Orm.]
MKT 2

wete adv. *(fr. wet adj.)* c1330 Orfeo *TR* 1

weten v. [wet v.] *[OE]* a1275 Stod ho HF
6

wether n. [wether] *[OE]* (c1250) Gen.&
Ex. TR 3

weven v1. [weave v1.] *[OE]* a1150
Vsp.D.Hom. B0 10

whal n. [whale sb.] *[OE]* a1150
Vsp.D.Hom. *SUMT* 1

whan adv. [when adv.] *[OE]* [?c1200
Orm.] GENERAL 1343

what adj. [pron., a1., adv., conj. int.] *[OE]*
[?c1200 Orm.] GENERAL 279

what adv. [what pron., a1., adv., conj. int.]
[OE] [?c1200 Orm.] GENERAL 101

what interj. [what pron., a1., adv., conj.
int.] *OE* [?c1200 Orm.] HF 50

what pron. [what pron., a1., adv., conj. int.]
[OE] [?a1160 Peterb.Chron.] GENERAL
566

what-so adj. [whatso pron. & a.] *[fr. OE.]*
[?c1200 Orm.] *BO* 1

what-so- ever adj. [whatsoever pron. & a.]
[fr. what-so pron. & adj. & ever pron.]
Chaucer BO 2

what-so-ever pron. [whatsoever pron. &
a.] *[fr. what-so adj. & ever adv.]*
[(c1250) Gen.& Ex.] BO 2

whel n. [wheel sb.] *[OE]* [?c1200 Orm.]
BD 21

whelen v2. [wheel v.] *[fr. whel n.]*
[(?a1200) Ancr.] *TR* 1

whelk n. [whelk2.] *[LOE]* (1373)
Lelamour Macer (Sln) GP 1

whelp n. [whelp sb.] *[OE]* [?c1200 Orm.]
BD 7

whennes adv. [whence adv., conj. (sb.)] *[fr.
whenne adv.]* (?c1225) Horn ROMA 27

wher adv. & conj. [where adv. & conj.]
[OE] [?c1200 Orm.] GENERAL 215

wher-as adv. [whereas rel. adv., conj.] *(fr.
wher adv. & as conj.)* [a1375 WPal.]
MKT 17

wher-bi adv. [whereby adv.] *[fr. wher adv.
& bi prep.]* [(?a1200) Trin.Hom.] BO
3

wher-for adv. [wherefore adv.] *[fr. wher
adv. & for prep.]* [(c1200) Vices &
V.(1)] ABC 98

wher-fro adv. [wherefro adv.] *[fr. wher
adv. & conj. & from prep.]* Chaucer TR
1

wher-in adv. [wherein adv.] *[fr. wher adv.
& in prep.]* [(?c1200) HMaid.] *CLT* 1

wher-of adv. [whereof adv.] *[fr. wher adv.
& of prep.]* [?c1200 Orm.] ROMA 14

wher-on adv. [whereon adv.] *[fr. wher
adv. & on prep.]* [(?a1200) Lay.Brut]
TR 2

wher-so adv. [whereso adv., conj.] *[fr. OE]*
[?a1160 Peterb.Chron.] ROMA 11

wher-thurgh adv. [wherethrough adv.] *[fr.
wher adv. & thurgh prep.]* [(?a1200)
Ancr.] *BD* 1

wher-to adv. [whereto adv.] *[fr. wher adv.*

& to prep.] [(?c1200) St.Marg.(1)]
BD 9

wher-with adv. [wherewith adv.] *[wher
adv. & with prep.]* [?c1200 Orm.] BO
9

whete n. [wheat sb.] *[OE]* [?c1200 Orm.]
RVT 8

whete-sed n. [wheat sb.] *(fr. whete n. &
sed n.)* Chaucer *WBPRO* 1

whether adj. [whether pron., adj., conj.]
[OE] [(c1300) Glo.Chron.A] *AST* 1

whether conj. [whether pron., adj., conj.]
[OE] [(?c1175) PMor.] GENERAL 104

whether pron. [whether pron., adj., conj.]
[OE] [(?a1200) Ancr.] BO 5

whether-so conj. [whetherso pron. &
conj.] *[fr. whether conj. & so adv.]*
(a1250) Bestiary LGW F 3

whet-ston n. [whetstone] *[OE]* a1225
Wor.Aelfric Gloss. *TR* 1

whetten v. [whet v.] *[OE]* [(?a1200)
Lay.Brut] LADY 3

whi adv. [whi adv.] *[OE]* (c1125)
Vsp.D.Hom.Elucid. GENERAL 232

whi interj. [whi adv.] *(fr. whi adv.)*
Chaucer TR 18

whi pron. [whi adv.] *(fr. whi adv.)*
(c1303) Mannyng HS BD 29

which adj. [which a. & pron.] *[OE]*
[?c1200 Orm.] GENERAL 307

which pron. [which a. & pron.] *[OE]*
[a1225 Lamb.Hom.] GENERAL 1296

whider adv. [whither adv.] *[OE]* [(c1200)
Vices & V.(1)] ABC 16

whiderward adv. [whitherward adv.] *[fr.
whider adv.]* [?c1200 Orm.] TR 3

whil conj. [while adv., conj.] *[fr. OE]*
[?a1160 Peterb.Chron.] GENERAL 153

whil n. [while sb.] *[OE]* [?c1200 Orm.]
ROMA 88

whil-er adv. [whilere adv.] *[fr. whil adv.]*
Chaucer *CYT* 1

whiles conj. [whiles sb. (advb. gen.), conj.
(prep.), adv.] *[fr. other-whiles adv.]*
[(a1250) Bestiary] ROMA 13

whilom adv. [whilom adv. (a.), conj.] *[OE]* a1121 Peterb.Chron. ROMA 75

whinen v. [whine v.] *[OE]* [a1300 Sayings St.Bede] *WBPRO* 1

whippe n. [whip sb.] *[fr. whippen v. & MLG]* [a1325 Gloss.Bibbesw.] SNT 5

whippel-tre n. [whippletree] *(fr. whippe n. & tre n.)* Chaucer *KNT* 1

whippen v. [whip v.] *[?fr. MLG]* [(?a1216) Owl & N.] *PARST* 1

whirlen v. [whirl v. & whirling ppl. a.] *[prob. fr. ON]* [c1300 SLeg.Patr. (Ld)] HF 5

whirling ger. [whirling vbl. sb.] *[fr. whirlen v.]* Chaucer *FORT* 1

whispering ger. [whispering vbl. sb.] *[fr. whisper v.]* Chaucer HF 2

whistle n. [whistle sb.] *[OE]* c1225 Wor.Aelfric Gloss. *RVT* 1

whistlen v. [whistle v.] *[OE]* [(?a1300) KAlex.] GP 2

whistlinge ger. [whistling vbl. sb.] *[OE]* [(?a1300) KAlex.] *KNT* 1

whit adj. [white a., white sb1.] *[OE]* [(c1200) Vices & V.(1)] ROMA 118

whiten v. [white vi.] *[OE]* c1150 Hrl.HApul. *TR* 1

whitnesse n. [whiteness] *[OE]* c1175 HRood *SNPRO* 1

who pron. [who pron.] *[OE]* [?c1200 Orm.] GENERAL 242

whom pron. [whom pron.] *[fr. OE]* [a1123 Peterb.Chron.] GENERAL 142

whom-so pron. [whomso pron.] *(fr. whom pron. & so adv.)* [(?a1200) Lay.Brut] *TR* 1

whos pron. [whose pron.] *[fr. OE]* [(c1200) Vices & V.(1)] PF 30

who-so pron. [whoso pron.] *[fr. OE]* [?a1160 Peterb.Chron.] GENERAL 138

whosoevere pron. [whosoever pron.] *[fr. who-so pron. & ever adv.]* [(?a1200) Ancr.] *BO* 4

wicch n2. [witch sb2.] *[OE]* [c1300 SLeg.Kath.(Ld)] *HF* 1

wicchcraft n. [witchcraft] *[OE]* [?c1200 Orm.] *FRT* 1

wid adj. [wide a.] *[OE]* [?c1200 Orm.] ROMA 34

wide adv. [wide adv.] *[OE]* [a1121 Peterb.Chron.] ROMA 15

wide-wher adv. [wide-where adv.] *[fr. wide adv. & wher adv.]* [?c1200 Orm.] TR 2

widnesse n. [wideness] *[OE]* [(?c1200) St.Marg.] *AST* 1

widwe n. [widow sb1.] *[OE]* [?c1200 Orm.] TR 26

widwehod n. [widowhood] *[OE]* [?c1200 Orm.] LGW G 2

wif n. [wife sb.] *[OE]* (c1125) Vsp.D.Hom.Elucid. BD 489

wifhod n. [wifehood] *[fr. wif n.]* Chaucer LGW F 11

wifles adj. [wifeless a.] *[OE]* [(a1325) Cursor] MERPRO 2

wifli adj. [wifely a.] *[OE]* Chaucer LGW 7

wight adj. [wight a.] *[ON]* [(?a1200) Lay.Brut] MKT 2

wight n. [wight sb.] *[OE]* [(?c1175) PMor. (Trin-C)] ROMA 409

wiket n. [wicket] *[AF]* [(c1225) Horn] ROMA 7

wikke adj. [wick a.] *[fr. OE]* [?a1160 Peterb.Chron.] ROMA 28

wikke adj. as n. [wick a.] *[fr. wikke adj.]* [(c1300) Glo.Chron.A] *TR* 2

wikked adj. [wicked a1.] *[fr. wikke adj.]* [c1300 Lay.Brut (Otho)] ROMA 152

wikkedli adv. [wickedly adv.] *[fr. wikked adj.]* [(c1303) Mannyng HS] HF 11

wikkednesse n. [wickedness] *[fr. wikked adj.]* [(a1325) Cursor] HF 48

wilde adj. [wild a. & sb.] *[OE]* [a1121 Peterb.Chron.] ROMA 41

wildernesse n. [wilderness] *[OE]* [(?a1200) Trin.Hom.] TR 4

wildli adv. [wildly adv.] *[fr. wilde adj.]* Chaucer *BD* 1

wildnesse n. [wildness] *[fr. wilde adj.]*
Chaucer FORMAGE 1

wile n. [wile sb.] *[origin obscure]* [a1131
Peterb.Chron.] BD 10

wilful adj. [wilful a1.] *[fr. wille n.]*
[(?a1200) Trin.Hom.] PF 5

wilfulhede n. [wilful a1.] *[fr. wilful adj.]*
Chaucer LGW G 1

wilfulli adv. [wilfully adv.] *[LOE]* [a1250
Wooing Lord] BO 11

wilfulnesse n. [wilfulness] *[fr. wilful adj.]*
[(?a1200) Trin.Hom.] TR 7

wili adj. [wily a.] *[fr. wile n.]* [(a1325)
Cursor] PROMKT 3

wille n. [will sb1.] *[OE]* [a1121
Peterb.Chron.] ROMA 210

willen v. [will v1.] *[OE]* [a1121
Peterb.Chron.] GENERAL 2299

willinge ger. [willing vbl. sb.] *[OE]*
[(1340) Ayenb.] BO 4

willingli adv. [willingly adv.] *[OE]*
Chaucer CLT 1

wilnen v. [wilne v.] *[OE]* c1175 HRood
BD 22

wilning ger. [wilning vbl. sb.] *[OE]*
[(?a1200) Ancr.] BO 1

wilwe n. [willow sb.] *[OE]* [a1325
Gloss.Bibbesw.] KNT 1

wimple n. [wimple sb.] *[LOE]* [(?a1200)
Trin.Hom.] LGW 7

wimplen v. [wimple v.] *[fr. wimple n.]*
[c1230 Ancr. (Corp-C)] BO 3

win n. [wine sb1.] *[OE]* [a1121
Peterb.Chron.] MKT 55

wincen v. [wince v1.] *[AF]* [c1300
SLeg.(Ld)] MILT 1

wind n1. [wind sb1.] *[OE]* [(c1200) Vices
& V.(1)] SNT 61

windas n. [windas] *[AF]* [(a1338)
Mannyng Chron.Pt.1] SQT 1

winden v1. [wind v1.] *[OE]* [?c1200
Orm.] SNPRO 14

windi adj1. [windy a.] *[OE]* a1150
Vsp.D.Hom. BO 1

windinge ger1. [winding vbl. sb1.] *[fr.*

winden v1. (a1382) WBible(1) (Bod
959) PARST 1

wind-mil n. [windmill sb.] *[fr. wind n1. &
milne n.]* [(c1300) Glo.Chron.A] HF 1

windoue n. [window sb.] *[ON]* [(?a1200)
Ancr.] BD 30

windren v. [wyndre v.] *[OF]* Chaucer
ROMA 2

Windsor n. [Windsor] *[no etym.]*
Chaucer ROMA 1

wing n. [wing sb.] *[ON]* [?c1200 Orm.]
HF 13

winged adj. [winged a.] *[fr. wing n.]*
Chaucer HF 3

winken v. [wink v1.] *[OE]* [(?a1200)
Ancr.] PITY 8

winnen v. [win v1.] *[OE]* [a1121
Peterb.Chron.] ROMA 114

winninge ger1. [winning vbl. sb1.] *[fr.
winnen v.]* [(?a1300) Tristrem] ROMA
9

winter n. [winter sb1.] *[OE]* [?a1160
Peterb.Chron.] ROMA 38

win-yevinge ger. yevinge ger. *(fr. win n.
& yevinge ger.)* Chaucer PARDT 1

wipen v. [wipe v.] *[OE]* [(c1200) Vices &
V. (1)] BO 7

wir n. [wire sb.] *[OE]* [(?a1200) Lay.Brut]
TR 4

wis adv. [wis adv.] *[fr. iwis adv. & adj. &
n.]* [?c1200 Orm.] BD 18

wisdom n. [wisdom] *[OE]* [?c1200 Orm.]
PITY 34

wise adj.& n. [wise a.] *OE* [a1121
Peterb.Chron.] ROMA 226

wise n2. [wise sb1.] *[OE]* [?1200 Orm.]
ROMA 231

wiseli adv. [wisely adv.] *[OE]* [?c1200
Orm.] TR 21

wise man n. [wise man] *[fr. wise adj. & n.
& man n.]* [(?a1200) Ancr.] TR 2

wish n. [wish sb1.] *[fr. wishen v.]* [(a1325)
Cursor] BD 1

wishen v. [wish v.] *[OE]* [(?a1200)
Trin.Hom.] BD 3

wisli adv. [wisly adv.] *[OE]* [?c1200 Orm.] ROMA 33

wissen v. [wis v1.] *[OE]* [(?c1150) Prov.Alf. (Jes-O)] ABC 8

wit n. [wit sb.] *[OE]* [?c1200 Orm.] ROMA 205

wite n2. [wite sb2.] *[OE]* [?c1200 Orm.] ANEL 4

witen v1. [wit v1.] *[OE]* [?a1160 Peterb.Chron.] GENERAL 759

witen v3. [wite v1.] *[OE]* [(?a1200) Ancr.] ROMA 16

with prep. [with prep.] *[OE]* [a1121 Peterb.Chron.] GENERAL 2342

with-al adv. [withal adv. & prep.] *[fr. with prep. & al lim. adj. & n.]* [?c1200 Orm.] ROMA 21

withdrauen v. [withdraw v.] *[fr. with- pref. & drauen v.]* [(?a1200) Ancr.] ROMA 25

withdrauinge ger. [withdrawing vbl. sb.] *[fr. withdrauen v.]* [(a1333) Shoreham Poems] PARST 1

withholden v. [withhold v.] *[fr. with- pref. & holden v1.]* [(c1200) Vices & V.(1)] ROMA 23

withholdinge ger. [withholding vbl. sb.] *[fr. withholden v.]* (a1382) WBible(1) (Bod 959) MEL 2

within-forth adv. [withinforth adv.] *[fr. withinne adv. & prep. & forth adv.]* c1380 Firumb.(1) BO 1

withinne adv. & prep. [within adv., prep.] *[LOE]* [1131 Peterb.Chron.] GENERAL 111

withouten adv. & prep. [without adv., prep. conj.] *[LOE]* [a1121 Peterb.Chron.] ROMA 435

without-forth adv. [withoutforth adv.] *[fr. withouten adv. & prep. & forth adv.]* [(1357) Gaytr.LFCatech.] BO 8

without-forth n. [withoutforth adv.] *(fr. withouten adv.)* Chaucer BO 3

withseien v. [withsay v.] *[OE]* [?c1200 Orm.] SNT 9

withstonden v. [withstand v.] *[OE]* [a1121 Peterb.Chron.] SNPRO 32

withstondinge ger. [withstanding vbl. sb.] *[fr. withstonden v.]* [(?a1300) KAlex.] BO 2

witnesfulli adv. [witnessfully adv.] *[fr. <witnesful adj.>]* Chaucer BO 1

witnesse n. [witness sb.] *[OE]* [a1121 Peterb.Chron.] ABC 27

witnessen v. [witness v.] *[fr. witnesse n.]* [(?c1300) Guy] SNT 16

witnessinge ger. [witnessing vbl. sb.] *[fr. witnessen v.]* [(a1325) Cursor] LGW F 5

wittinge ger1. [witting vbl. sb1.] *[ON & witen v1.]* [(a1325) Cursor] ROMA 8

wittingli adv. [wittingly adv.] *[fr. <witting ppl. adj.>]* [(1340) Ayenb.] PARST 3

wiven v. [wive v.] *[OE]* [(?a1200) Ancr.] CLT 2

wivere n. [wyver] *[OF]* [(?a1300) KAlex.] TR 1

wlatsom adj. [wlatsome a.] *[fr. wlat n.]* [(a1325) Cursor] MKT 2

wlispen v. [lisp v.] *[OE]* c1230 Ancr. (Corp-C) GP 1

wo adj. [woe int., adv., sb., a.] *(fr. wo adv.)* [(?a1200) Trin.Hom.] ROMA 4

wo adv. [woe int., adv., sb., a.] *[OE]* [(?c1175) PMor (Trin-C)] TR 9

wo n. [woe int., adv., sb., a.] *(fr. wo adv.)* [?c1200 Orm.] ROMA 335

wo-begon adj. [woe-begone a.] *(fr. wo n. & bigon v.)* [(?c1300) Guy(1)] ROMA 5

wod adj. [wood a. (sb2., adv.)] *[OE]* [?c1200 Orm.] ROMA 75

wod n1. [woad sb1.] *[OE]* [(?a1216) Owl & N.] FORMAGE 1

wod n2. [wood a. (sb2., adv.)] *[fr. wod adj.]* [a1300 II Pains (1)] ROMA 3

wode n. [wood sb1.] *[OE]* [a1121 Peterb.Chron.] ROMA 36

wode-binde n. [woodbine] *[OE]* [a1300 Hrl.978 Vocab.] KNT 2

wode-craft n. [woodcraft] *[fr. wod n2. & craft n1.]* Chaucer GP 1

wode-douve n. [wood-dove] *(fr. wod n2. & douve n.)* Chaucer THOP 1

woden vi. [wood vi.] *[fr. wod adj.]* (?c1350) Ywain SNT 3

wode-wale n. [woodwall] *[fr. wod n2. & ?wale n.]* [(?a1216) Owl & N.] ROMA 2

wodli adv. [woodly adv.] *[OE]* [(?a1200) Lay.Brut] KNT 2

wodnesse n. [woodness] *[OE]* [(c1340) Rolle Psalter] BO 12

woful adj. [woeful a.] *[fr. wo n.]* [(a1325) Cursor] ROMA 78

wofulli adv. [woefully adv.] *[fr. woful adj.]* Chaucer TR 1

wol n. [wool sb.] *[OE]* [c1300 SLeg.Kath.] ROMA 5

wolf n. [wolf sb.] *[OE]* [(?a1200) Lay.Brut] BO 16

wombe n. [womb sb.] *[OE]* [(?c1175) PMor.] BO 22

womman n. [woman sb.] *[OE]* (c1125) Vsp.D.Hom.Elucid. ROMA 358

wommanhode n. [womanhood & womanhead] *(fr. womman n.)* Chaucer LADY 15

wommanish adj. [womanish a.] *[fr. womman n.]* (a1382) WBible(1) (Bod 959) TR 1

wommanli adj. [womanly a.] *[fr. womman n.]* [(?a1200) Ancr.] PITY 15

wommanli adv. [womanly adv.] *[fr. womman n.]* [(c1300) Glo.Chron.A] BD 2

won n1. [wone sb2.] *[prob. ON]* [(?a1200) Ancr.] HF 3

won n2. [wone sb3.] *[fr. ON]* [(c1250) Floris (Cmb)] ROMA 5

wonden v. [wonde v.] *[OE]* a1121 Peterb.Chron. LGW 1

wonder adj. [wonder a.] *[fr. OE]* [(?a1200) Lay.Brut] ROMA 19

wonder adv. [wonder adv.] *[OE]* [?c1200 Orm.] ROMA 54

wonder n. [wonder sb.] *[OE]* (c1125) Vsp.D.Hom.Elucid. ABC 77

wonderful adj. [wonderful a.] *[LOE]* [(?a1200) Trin.Hom.] ROMA 8

wonderli adv. [wonderly adv.] *[OE]* [?a1160 Peterb.Chron.] HF 8

wondermost n. wonder n. *(fr. wonder n. & most adj. sup. & n.)* Chaucer HF 1

wondren v. [wonder v.] *[OE]* [?c1200 Orm.] ROMA 45

wondringe ger. [wondering vbl. sb.] *[fr. wondren v.]* [(a1325) Cursor] TR 3

wone n1. [wone sb1.] *[fr. OE]* [(?a1200) Ancr.] HF 11

wonen vi. [won v., wont pa. pple. & ppl. a.] *[OE]* (c1125) Vsp.D.Hom.Elucid. ROMA 102

wong n2. [wang1.] *[OE]* [(?a1300) Tristrem] RVT 1

wonger n. [wanger] *[OE]* Chaucer THOP 1

wongtoth n. [wang-tooth] *[fr. wong n2. & toth n.]* [a1325 Gloss.Bibbesw. (Arun:Owen)] MKT 1

woninge ger1. [wonning vbl. sb1.] *[OE]* [(?a1200) Trin.Hom.] ABC 2

word n. [word sb.] *[OE]* a1121 Peterb.Chron. ROMA 513

world n. [world sb.] *[OE]* (c1125) Vsp.D.Hom.Elucid. ROMA 356

worldli adj. [worldly a.] *[OE]* [?c1200 Orm.] MKT 37

worm n. [worm sb.] *[OE]* (c1125) Vsp.D.Hom.Elucid. ROMA 20

worm-foul n. [worm sb.] *(fr. worm n. & foul n.)* Chaucer PF 1

worshipe n. [worship sb.] *[OE]* a1121 Peterb.Chron. ROMA 34

worshipen v. [worship v.] *[fr. worshipe n.]* [(?a1200) Trin.Hom.] ROMA 6

worshipful adj. [worshipful a.] *[fr. worshipe n.]* [(1340) Ayenb.] ROMA 9

worsted n. [worsted sb.] *[fr. Worsted n. (parish)]* Chaucer GP 1

413

wort n1. [wort sb1.] *[OE]* [(?a1200)
Lay.Brut] CLT 3

wort n2. [wort sb2.] *[OE]* [a1325
Gloss.Bibbesw.] CYT 1

worth adj. [worth a.] *[OE]* [a1121
Peterb.Chron.] ROMA 58

worthen v. [worth v1.] *[OE]* [a1121
Peterb.Chron.] HF 13

worthi adj. [worthi a., adv., sb.] *[fr. worth
n.]* [(a1250) Bestiary] ROMA 184

worthili adv. [worthily adv.] *[fr. worthi
adj.]* [(c1340) Psalter] TR 4

worthinesse n. [worthiness] *[fr. worthi
adj.]* Chaucer ROMA 34

worthli adj. [worthly a.] *[OE]* [(?a1200)
Lay.Brut] THOP 1

wouen v. [woo v.] *[LOE]* [(?a1200) Ancr.]
TR 6

wouing ger. [wooing vbl. sb.] *[fr. wouen
v.]* [(?a1200) Ancr.] LGW 1

wound n. [wound sb.] *[OE]* (c1125)
Vsp.D.Hom.Elucid. ROMA 46

wounden v. [wound v. & wounded ppl. a.]
[OE] [?c1200 Orm.] ABC 21

wrappen v. [wrap v.] *[Of obscure origin]*
[(?a1325) Bonav.Medit.(1)] BO 12

wrappinge ger. [wrapping vbl. sb.] *[fr.
wrappen v.]* [(a1387) Trev.Higd.]
PARST 1

wrath n. [wrath sb.] *[OE]* [(c1200) Vices
& V.(1)] ROMA 29

wrathful adj. [wrathful a.] *[fr. wrath n.]*
[(?c1300) Spec.Guy] MEL 1

wrathli adv. [wrothly adv.] *[OE]* [?c1200
Orm.] BO 1

wratthen v. [wrath v.] *[fr. wrath n.]*
[?c1200 Orm.] BD 6

wrau adj. [wraw a.] *[of obscure origin]*
[(?a1200) Lay.Brut] MANCPRO 2

wraunesse n. [wraw a.] *(fr. wrau adj.)*
Chaucer PARST 1

wrecche adj. [wretch sb. & a.] *[OE]* [a1121
Peterb.Chron.] HF 8

wrecche n. [wretch sb. & a.] *[OE]* [?c1200
Orm.] BD 71

wrecched adj. [wretched a.] *[fr. wrecche
adj.]* [(c1200) Vices & V.(1)] HF 36

wrecchedli adv. [wretchedly adv.] *[fr.
wrecched adj.]* [(c1300) Glo.Chron.A]
MKT 4

wrecchednesse n. [wretchedness] *[fr.
wrecched adj.]* [(c1340) Rolle Psalter]
MKT 37

wrech n. [wreche sb.] *[OE]* [?c1200 Orm.]
MKT 10

wreien v. [wray v1.] *[OE]* [a1121
Peterb.Chron.] TR 5

wrek n. [wreck sb1.] *[AF]* ?c1350 Legal
Gloss. Jul. MLT 1

wreken v. [wreak v.] *[OE]* [a1121
Peterb.Chron.] ROMA 28

wreker n. [wreaker] *[fr. wreken v.]*
Chaucer PF 3

wrekinge ger. [wreak v.] *(fr. wreken v.)*
(1340) Ayenb. BO 1

wrench n1. [wrench sb1.] *[OE]* [a1121
Peterb.Chron.] CYT 1

wresten v. [wrest v.] *[OE]* [(?a1200)
Lay.Brut] TR 1

wrestlen v. [wrestle v.] *[OE]* [(?a1200)
Lay.Brut] MKT 5

wrestling ger. [wrestling vbl. sb.] *[fr.
wrestlen v.]* [(?a1200) Lay.Brut] PF
4

wreth n2. [wreath] *[OE]* [(?a1300)
KAlex.] KNT 1

wrien v1. [wry v1.] *[OE]* [(?c1175) PMor.
(Lamb)] ROMA 16

wrien v2. [wry v2.] *[OE]* [c1275 Hwenne
so wil wit] BD 4

wrighte n. [wright sb1.] *[OE]* (c1125)
Vsp.D.Hom.Elucid. GP 3

wringen v. [wring v.] *[OE]* [(?a1200)
Ancr.] HF 11

writ n. [writ sb.] *[OE]* [a1121
Peterb.Chron.] GP 13

writen v. [writen v.] *[OE]* [a1121
Peterb.Chron.] ROMA 207

writer n. [writer] *[OE]* c1175 Bod.Aelfric
OT BO 1

writhen v. [writhe vi.] *[OE]* [?a1160
Peterb.Chron.] ROMA 6

writhing ger. [writhing vbl. sb.] *[fr.
writhen v.]* Chaucer SQT 1

writinge ger. [writing vbl. sb.] *[fr. writen
v.]* [(?a1200) Ancr.] HF 10

wrong adj. [wrong a. & adv.] *[LOE]*
[?c1200 Orm.] BO 8

wrong adv. [wrong a. & adv.] *[LOE]*
[?c1200 Orm.] BD 5

wrong n2. [wrong sb2.] *[fr. <wrong adj.>]*
[a1126 Peterb.Chron.] BD 73

wrong-dede n. wrong adj. *(fr. wrong
adj. & dede n.)* Chaucer BO 1

wrongful adj. [wrongful a.] *[fr. wrong
n2.]* [(?c1300) Spec. Guy] BO 5

wrongfulli adv. [wrongfully adv.] *[fr.
wrongful adj.]* (a1349) Rolle MPass.(2)
(Upps) SNT 12

wrongli adv. [wrongly adv.] *[fr. wrong
adj.]* [(c1303) Mannyng HS] LGW G
1

wroten v. [wroot v.] *[OE]* [(?a1200)
Trin.Hom.] PARST 2

wroth adj. [wroth a.] *[OE]* [a1121
Peterb.Chron.] ABC 76

x n. [x] *[no etym.]* c1200 Stw.57
Abecedarium AST 2

yare adj. [yare a.] *[OE]* [(?a1200)
Lay.Brut] LGW 1

ye adv. [yea adv.] *[OE]* [?c1200 Orm.] BD
99

ye pron. [ye pers. pron. 2nd pers. nom.
(obj.), pl. (sing.)] *[OE]* a1121
Peterb.Chron. GENERAL 1647

yedding n. [yedding vbl. sb.] *[OE]* c1350
Of alle the witte GP 1

yeden v. [go v.] *[OE]* a1121 Peterb.Chron.
ROMA 5

yelden v. [yield v., yolden ppl. a.] *[OE]*
[a1121 Peterb.Chron.] ROMA 37

yelding ger. [yielding vbl. sb.] *[fr. yelden
v.]* [(1340) Ayenb.] GP 1

yellen v. [yell v.] *[OE]* [(?a1200) Lay.Brut]
KNT 2

yelpen v. [yelp v.] *[OE]* [?c1200 Orm.]
TR 2

yelwe adj. [yellow a. & sb.] *[OE]* [a1225
Lamb.Hom.] ROMA 18

yelwenesse n. [yellowness] *[fr. yelwe adj.]*
[(a1398) Trev.Barth.] PURSE 1

yeman n. [yeoman] *[prob. fr. yongman n.]*
[(?a1300) KAlex.] KNT 23

yemanli adv. [yeomanly adv.] *[fr. yeman
n.]* Chaucer GP 1

yemanri n. [s.v. yeomanry] *[fr. yeman n.]*
Chaucer RVT 1

yer n. [year] *[OE]* [1132 Peterb.Chron.]
ROMA 169

yerd n. [yard sb1.] *[OE]* [(c1300)
Havelok] ROMA 19

yerde n. [yard sb2.] *[OE]* [(?a1200)
Lay.Brut] PF 17

yern adj. [yern a.] *[OE]* [(?c1175) PMor.
(Lamb)] MILT 1

yerne adv. [yerne adv.] *[OE]* [a1121
Peterb.Chron.] HF 9

yernen v. [yearn vi.] *[OE]* [a1121
Peterb.Chron.] BD 3

yester-dai adv. [yersterday adv., sb.
& a.] *[OE]* [(c1250) Gen.& Ex.] TR
1

yester-dai n. [yersterday adv., sb. & a.]
[OE] Chaucer ROMA 2

yester-night n. [yesternight adv. & sb.]
[OE] [(?c1300) Bevis] TR 1

yet adv. [yet adv. & conj.] *[OE]* [a1121
Peterb.Chron.] GENERAL 744

yeven v. [give v.] *[OE]* [a1121
Peterb.Chron.] ROMA 466

yevere n. [giver] *[fr. yeven v.]* [(a1325)
Cursor] LGW 2

yevinge ger. [giving vbl. sb.] *[fr. yeven v.]*
[(?a1300) KAlex.] ANEL 8

yexen v. [yex, yesk v.] *[OE]* [c1300
SLeg.Becket (Ld)] RVT 1

yicchen v. [itch vi.] *[OE]* [(?a1200) Ancr.]
MILT 1

yifte n. [gift sb.] *[OE]* [(?a1200) Ancr.]
ROMA 44

yis adv. [yes adv.] *[OE]* [(c1200) Vices &
V.(1)] BD 38

yok n. [yoke sb.] *[OE]* [?c1200 Orm.] Bo 7

yon adj. [yon dem. a. & pron.] *[OE]*
[(a1325) Cursor] MARS 2

yond adv. [yond prep. & adv.] *(fr. yond
prep.)* (?c1225) Horn HF 13

yonder adj. [yonder adv. & a.] *[fr. OE]*
[Chaucer] HF 8

yonder adv. [yonder adv. & a.] *[OE]*
[c1300 Havelok] HF 12

yong adj. [young a.] *[OE]* [?c1200 Orm.]
ROMA 131

yonghede n. [younghede] *[fr. yong adj.]*
[?c1250 PMor. (Eg(1):Furn.)] ROMA 1

yor adv. [yore adv.] *[OE]* [(?a1200)
Lay.Brut] ABC 32

you pron. [you pers. pron., 2nd pers. obj.
(nom.) pl. (sing.)] *[OE]* [?c1200 Orm.]
GENERAL 1350

youling n. [yowling vbl. sb.] *[fr. <youlen
v.>]* [(?c1200) St.Juliana] KNT 1

your pron. [your poss. pron. & a.] *[OE]*
[a1121 Peterb.Chron.] GENERAL
1066

youres pron. [yours poss. pron.] *[OE]*
[(a1325) Cursor] BD 22

yourself pron. [yourself pron.] *(fr. your
pron. & self adj., n., & pron.)* [(c1350)
Alex.& D.(Bod)] BD 45

youth n. [youth] *[OE]* [(?a1200)
Trin.Hom.] ROMA 34

you-ward n. [-ward suffix] *[fr. you pron.]*
Chaucer Bo 1

Zeferus n. [Zephyr] *[L (fr. Gr.)]* Chaucer
BD 7

zel n. [zeal sb.] *[L (fr. Gr.)]* [(a1382)
WBible(1) (Bod 959)] TR 1

zodiak n. [zodiac sb.] *[OF]* (a1388)
Wallingford Exafrenon AST 37

References

Arnold, Mathew, "General Introduction." In Thomas Humphrey Ward (ed.), *The English Poets: Selections*, vol. I, pp. xvii–xlvii, London: Macmillan, 1880.
"The Study of Poetry." In R. H. Super (ed.), *The Complete Prose Works of Mathew Arnold: English Literature and Irish Politics*, pp. 161–88, Ann Arbor: University of Michigan Press, 1973.
Ashby, George, "Active Policy of a Prince." In Mary Bateson (ed.), *George Ashby's Poems*, pp. 12–41, EETS ES 76 (1899).
Attridge, Derek, *Peculiar Language*, Ithaca, NY: Cornell University Press, 1988.
The Rhythms of English Poetry, London: Longman, 1982.
Augustine, *De doctrina Christiana*, R. P. H. Green (ed. and trans.), Oxford: Clarendon Press, 1995.
Baugh, Albert, "The Chronology of Loan-words in English," *Modern Language Notes* 50 (1935), 90–3.
and Thomas Cable, *A History of the English Language*, 4th edn, London: Routledge, 1993.
Baum, Paull F., *Chaucer's Verse*, Durham, NC: Duke University Press 1961.
Bense, J. F., *A Dictionary of the Low-Dutch Element in the English Vocabulary*, London and The Hague: Nijhoff and Oxford University Press, 1926–39.
Benson, C. David, *Chaucer's Drama of Style*, Chapel Hill: University of North Carolina Press, 1986.
Benson, Larry D., *A Glossarial Concordance to the Riverside Chaucer*, 2 vols., New York: Garland Press, 1993.
Berndt, Rolf, "The Period of the Final Decline of French in Medieval England (14th and 15th Centuries)," *Zeitschrift für Anglistik und Amerikanistik* 20 (1972), 341–69.
Blake, Norman, *The English Language in Medieval Literature*, London: Methuen, 1977.
"The Literary Language." In Norman Blake (ed.), *The Cambridge History of the English Language*, vol. II (1066–1476), pp. 500–41, Cambridge: Cambridge University Press, 1992.
Bloomfield, Leonard, *Language*, New York: Henry Holt, 1933.
Bloomfield, Morton W. and Leonard Newmark, *A Linguistic Introduction to the History of English*, New York: Alfred A. Knopf, 1965.

References

Boccaccio, Giovanni, *Decameron*, Vittore Branca (ed.). In Vittore Branca (ed.), *Tutte le opere*, vol. 4, Verona: Arnoldo Mondadori, 1976.

Filocolo, Antonio Enzo Qualio (ed.). In Vittore Branca (ed.), *Tutte le opere*, vol. I, pp. 45–675, Verona: Arnoldo Mondadori, 1967.

Boethius, Anicius Manlius Severinus, *Philosophiae Consolationis Libri Quinque*, Karl Büchner (ed.), Heidelberg: Carl Winter, 1977.

Bradley, Henry, *The Making of English*, New York: Macmillan, 1904.

Bradshaw, Henry, *The Life of St. Werburge of Chester*, Carl Horstmann (ed.), EETS OS 88 (1887).

Brewer, Charlotte, "The Second Edition of the *Oxford English Dictionary*," *Review of English Studies*, new series 44 (1993), 313–42.

Brewer, Derek S., *Chaucer and His World*, New York: Eyre Methuen, 1978.

(ed.), *Chaucer: The Critical Heritage*. 2 vols., London: Routledge, 1978.

(ed.), *Geoffrey Chaucer: Writers and Their Background*, Athens: Ohio University Press, 1974.

"The Relationship of Chaucer to the English and European Traditions." In D. S. Brewer (ed.), *Chaucer and Chaucerians*, pp. 1–38, London: Thomas Nelson and Sons, 1966.

Brook, G. L. and R. F. Leslie (eds.), *Laȝamon's Brut*, 2 vols., EETS OS 250 (1963) and EETS OS 277 (1978).

Brusendorff, Aage, *The Chaucer Tradition*, London: Oxford University Press, 1925.

Bryan, W. F. and Germaine Dempster (eds.), *Sources and Analogues of Chaucer's Canterbury Tales*, Chicago: University of Chicago Press, 1941.

Burnley, David, *A Guide to Chaucer's Language*, Norman: University of Oklahoma Press, 1983.

"Chaucer's 'Termes,'" *Yearbook of English Studies* 7 (1977), 53–67.

"Lexis and Semantics." In Norman Blake (ed.), *The Cambridge History of the English Language*, vol. II (1066–1476), pp. 409–99, Cambridge: Cambridge University Press, 1992.

"Picked Terms," *English Studies* 65 (1984), 195–204.

Burrow, John A., *Ricardian Poetry: Chaucer, Gower, Langland and the Gawain-poet*. New Haven, CT: Yale University Press, 1971.

Caluwé-dor, Juliette de, "Chaucer's Contribution to the English Vocabulary: A Chronological Survey of French Loan-words," *North-Western European Language Evolution* 2 (1983), 73–91.

Carlyle, Thomas, *Past and Present*, London: Chapman and Hall, 1888.

Carter, Ronald and Walter Nash, "Language and Literariness," *Prose Studies* 6 (1983), 123–41.

Caxton, William, *The Prologues and Epilogues*, W. J. B. Crotch (ed.), EETS OS 176 (1927).

Cerquiglini, Bernard, *Éloge de la variante: Histoire critique de la philologie*, Paris: Seuil, 1989.

Chambers, R.W., *On the Continuity of English Prose*, EETS OS 191A (1932; rprt. 1963).

Champneys, A. C., *History of English: A Sketch of the Origin and Development of the*

References

English Language with Examples Down to the Present Day, London: Percival, 1893.

Chaucer, Geoffrey, *Boece*, F. J. Furnivall (ed.), Chaucer Society Publications, 1st series 75 (1886).

Boece, Richard Morris (ed.), EETS ES 5 (1868).

The Complete Works of Geoffrey Chaucer, W. W. Skeat (ed.), 6 vols., Oxford: Clarendon Press, 1894.

The Reeve's Prologue and Tale, Spearing, A. C. and J. E. Spearing (eds.), Cambridge: Cambridge University Press, 1979.

Troilus and Criseyde, B. A. Windeatt (ed.), New York: Longman, 1984.

Works, F. N. Robinson (ed.), Cambridge, MA: Houghton Mifflin, 1933.

Works, 2nd ed., F. N. Robinson (ed.), Cambridge, MA: Houghton Mifflin, 1957.

Chesterton, G. K., *Chaucer*, London: Faber and Faber, 1932.

Cicero, *Orator*. H. M. Hubbell (ed.), 2 vols., Cambridge, MA: Harvard University Press, 1939; rev. edn, 1962.

Clanchy, M. T., *From Memory to Written Record: England 1066–1307*, 2nd edn, Oxford: Blackwell, 1993.

Clemen, Wolfgang, *Chaucer's Early Poetry*, C. A. M. Sym (trans.), London: Methuen, 1963.

Coleridge, Samuel Taylor, *The Collected Works*, Kathleen Coburn (gen. ed.), vol. I, Barbara E. Rooke (ed.), Bollingen Series 75, Princeton, NJ: Princeton University Press, 1969.

Copeland, Rita, *Rhetoric, Hermeneutics, and Translation in the Middle Ages*, Cambridge: Cambridge University Press, 1991.

"Richard Rolle and the Rhetorical Theory of Levels of Style." In Marion Glasscoe (ed.), *The Medieval Mystical Tradition in England*, pp. 55–80, Cambridge: D. S. Brewer, 1984.

Crane, Susan, *Insular Romance*, Berkeley: University of California Press, 1986.

Dante Alighieri, *Inferno*. In *La Commedia secondo L'Antiqua Vulgate*, Giorgio Petrocchi (ed.), pp. 3–141, Turin: Einaudi, 1975.

De vulgari eloquentia, Pier Vincenzo Mengaldo (ed.). In *Opere Minori*, vol. II, pp. 3–237, Milan: Riccardo Ricciardi, 1979.

Literature in the Vernacular (De vulgari eloquentia), Sally Purcell (trans.), Manchester: Carcanet New Press, 1981.

David, Alfred, *The Strumpet Muse*, Bloomington: Indiana University Press, 1976.

Davis, Norman, "Chaucer and the English Language," *Geoffrey Chaucer: Conferenze organizatte dall'Accademia Nazionale dei Lincei*, Problemi Attuali di Scienza e di Culture, Quaderno 2434, pp. 58–84, Rome: Accademia Nazionale dei Lincei, 1977.

"Chaucer and Fourteenth-Century English." In Brewer (ed.), *Geoffrey Chaucer* pp. 58–84.

"Language and Versification." In Larry D. Benson (ed.), *The Riverside Chaucer*, 3rd edn, pp. xxix–xlv, Boston, MA: Houghton Mifflin, 1987.

De Man, Paul, "The Return to Philology." In *Resistance to Theory*, pp. 21–6, Minneapolis: University of Minnesota Press, 1986.

References

Dekeyser, Xavier, "Romance Loans in Middle English: A Reassessment." In Dieter Kastovsky and Alexander Szwedek (eds.), *Linguistics Across Historical and Geographical Boundaries: In Honour of Jacek Fisiak*, 2 vols., vol. I, pp. 253–64, Berlin: Mouton de Gruyter, 1986.

Derrida, Jacques, *De la grammatologie*, Paris: Minuit, 1967.
    Of Grammatology, Gayatri Chakravorty Spivak (trans.), Baltimore, MD: The Johns Hopkins University Press, 1974.

D'Evelyn, Charlotte (ed.), *The Latin Text of the Ancrene Riwle*, EETS OS 216 (1944).
    and Anna J. Mill (eds.), *The South English Legendary*, 2 vols., EETS OS 235 (1956) and 236 (1956).

Dinshaw, Carolyn, *Chaucer's Sexual Poetics*, Madison: University of Wisconsin Press, 1989.

Dobson, E. J., *The Origins of Ancrene Wisse*, Oxford: Clarendon Press, 1976.

Donaldson, E. Talbot, "Idiom of Popular Poetry in the Miller's Tale." In *Speaking of Chaucer*, pp. 13–29, London: Athlone Press, 1970 (first published 1951).

Donner, Martin, "Derived Words in Chaucer's Language," *Chaucer Review* 13 (1978–9), 1–15.

Douglas, Gavin, *Virgil's Aeneid*, D. F. C. Coldwell (ed.), 4 vols., Scottish Text Society Publications, 3rd series, 25, 27, 28, 30 (1957–64).

Dryden, John, "Preface" to *Fables Ancient and Modern*. In James Kinsley (ed.), *The Poems and Fables of John Dryden*, pp. 520–39, London: Oxford University Press, 1962.
    "To Her Grace The Dutchess Ormond." In James Kinsley (ed.), *The Poems and Fables of John Dryden*, pp. 539–43.

Dunbar, William, *The Goldyne Targe*. In James Kinsley (ed.), *The Poems of William Dunbar*, pp. 29–38, Oxford: Oxford University Press, 1979.

Edwards, A. S. G. and Derek Pearsall, "The Manuscripts of the Major Middle English Poetic Texts." In J. J. Griffiths and Derek Pearsall (eds.), *Book Production and Publishing in Britain, 1375–1475*, pp. 257–78, Cambridge: Cambridge University Press, 1989.

Eliason, Norman, *The Language of Chaucer's Poetry: An Appraisal of the Verse Style and Structure*, Anglistica 17, Copenhagen: Rosenkilde and Bagger, 1972.

Elliott, Ralph W. V., *Chaucer's English*, London: André Deutsch, 1974.

Empson, William, *The Structure of Complex Words*, London: The Hogarth Press, 1951; rprt. 1985.

Ewert, Alfred (ed.), *Gui de Warewic*, 2 vols., Paris: Champion, 1932.

Fischer, Olga, "Syntax." In Norman Blake (ed.), *The Cambridge History of the English Language*, vol. II (1066–1476), pp. 207–408, Cambridge: Cambridge University Press, 1992.

Fisher, John H., "A Language Policy for Lancastrian England," *Publications of the Modern Language Association* 107 (1992), 1168–80.
    "Chaucer and the French Influence." In Donald M. Rose (ed.), *New Perspectives in Chaucer Criticism*, pp. 177–91, Norman, OK: Pilgrim, 1981.
    "Chaucer's French: A Metalinguistic Inquiry," *Chaucer Yearbook* 1 (1992), 33–45.
    The Importance of Chaucer, Carbondale: Southern Illinois University Press, 1992.

References

Fleischman, Suzanne, "Philology, Linguistics and the Discourse of the Medieval Text," *Speculum* 65 (1990), 19–37.

Foster, Kenelm, *Petrarch: Poet and Humanist*, Edinburgh: Edinburgh University Press, 1984.

Frank, Robert Worth, "The *Reeve's Tale* and the Comedy of Limitation." In Stanley Weintraub and Philip Young (eds.), *Directions in Literary Criticism: Contemporary Approaches to Literature*, pp. 53–69, University Park: Pennsylvania State University Press, 1973.

Frantzen, Allen, *Desire for Origins*, New Brunswick, NJ: Rutgers University Press, 1991.

Furnivall, Frederick J. (ed.), *The Book of Curtesye*, EETS ES 3 (1868).

Trial-Forewards to My Parallel-Text Edition of Chaucer's Minor Poems, Chaucer Society Publications, new series 6 (London, 1871).

Galbraith, V. H., "Nationality and Language in Medieval England," *Transactions of the Royal Historical Society*, 4th series, 23 (1941), 113–28.

Gardner, John, *The Life and Times of Chaucer*, New York: Knopf, 1977.

Gaylord, Alan T., Scanning the Prosodists: An Essay in Metacriticism," *Chaucer Review* 11 (1976–7), 22–82.

"The Moment of *Sir Thopas*: Towards a New Look at Chaucer's Language," *Chaucer Review* 16 (1981), 311–29.

Görlach, Manfred, "Chaucer's English: What Remains to Be Done," *Arbeiten aus Anglistik und Amerikanistik* 3 (1978), 61–79.

Greenough, J. B. and G. L. Kittredge, *Words and Their Ways in English Speech*, New York: Macmillan, 1902.

and A. A. Howard and Beng. L. D'Ooge (eds.), *Allen and Greenough's New Latin Grammar*, Boston, MA: Ginn and Company, 1931.

Guillaume de Lorris and Jean de Meun, *Le roman de la rose*, Félix Lecoy (ed.), 3 vols., Les classiques français du moyen âge 92, 93, 98, Paris: Honoré Champion, 1965–70.

Hali Meiðhad, Bella Millett (ed.), EETS OS 284 (1982).

Hammond, Eleanor Prescott, *Chaucer: A Bibliographical Manual*, New York: Macmillan, 1908.

Hansen, Elaine Tuttle, *Chaucer and the Fictions of Gender*, Berkeley: University of California Press, 1992.

Hawes, Stephen, *The Pastime of Pleasure*, William Edward Mead (ed.), EETS OS 173 (1928).

Herbert, J. A. (ed.), *The French Text of the Ancrene Riwle*, EETS OS 219 (1944).

Hirsch, Jr., E. D., *Aims of Interpretation*, Chicago: University of Chicago Press, 1976.

Hoccleve, Thomas, *Regiment of Princes*. In Frederick J. Furnivall (ed.), *Hoccleve's Works*, vol. III, EETS ES 72 (1897).

Howard, Donald, *Chaucer and the Medieval World*, London: Weidenfeld and Nicolson, 1987 (published in the United States as *Chaucer: His Life, His Works, His World*, New York: Dutton, 1987).

Howe, Nicholas (rev.), "*The Cambridge History of the English Language*, vol. 2 (Norman Blake [ed.])," *Speculum* 71 (1996), 125–7.

References

Hudson, Anne, *A Premature Reformation*, Oxford: Oxford University Press, 1988.

Hulbert, J. R. (rev.), *"Chaucer's Romance Vocabulary* (J. Mersand)," *Philological Quarterly* 26 (1947), 302–6.

Hunt, Leigh, *Wit and Humor, Selected from the English Poets*, new edn, London: Smith and Elder, 1890.

Jakobson, Roman, *Language and Literature*, Krystyna Pomorska and Stephen Rudy (eds.), Cambridge, MA: Harvard University Press, 1987.

Jean de Meun, "'Boethius' *De Consolatione* by Jean de Meun," V. L. Dedeck-Héry (ed.), *Medieval Studies* 14 (1952), 165–275.

Jespersen, Otto, *Growth and Structure of the English Language*, 2nd edn (revised), Leipzig: B. G. Teubner, 1912.

Jones, Richard Foster, *The Triumph of the English Language*, London: Oxford University Press, 1953.

Jonson, Ben, "Timber or Discoveries." In Ian Donaldson (ed.), *Ben Jonson*, pp. 521–94, Oxford: Oxford University Press, 1985.

Justice, Steven, "Inquisition, Speech, and Writing: A Case from Late-Medieval Norwich," *Representations* 48 (1994), 1–29.

Kean, P. M., *Chaucer and the Making of English Poetry*, 2 vols. London: Routledge & Kegan Paul, 1972.

Ker, W. P., "Chaucer, 'House of Fame' (ii.417–26)," *Modern Quarterly of Language and Literature* 1 (1899), 38–9.

Kittredge, George Lyman, *Chaucer and His Poetry*, Cambridge, MA: Harvard University Press, 1915.

Knapp, Steven, *Literary Interest*, Cambridge, MA: Harvard University Press, 1993.

Kölbing, E. (ed.), *The Romance of Sir Beues of Hamtoun*, EETS ES 46 (1885), 48 (1886), and 65 (1894).

Langland, William, *The Vision of Piers Plowman*, W. W. Skeat (ed.), A-text: vol. I, EETS OS 28 (1867) and B-text: vol. II, EETS OS 38 (1869).

Lerer, Seth, *Chaucer and His Readers: Imagining the Author in Late-Medieval England*, Princeton, NJ: Princeton University Press, 1993.

Le Saux, Françoise, *Laʒamon's* Brut: *The Poem and Its Sources*, Cambridge: D. S. Brewer, 1989.

Lévi-Strauss, Claude, *Le cru et le cuit*, Paris: Plon, 1964.

    The Raw and the Cooked: Introduction to a Science of Mythology, John and Doreen Weightman (trans.), New York: Harper and Row, 1964.

Lewis, C. S., *Studies in Words*, Cambridge: Cambridge University Press, 1960.

    The Allegory of Love, Oxford: Oxford University Press, 1936.

Loomis, Laura Hibbard, "Chaucer and the Auchinleck MS." In P. W. Long (ed.), *Essays and Studies in Honor of Carleton Brown*, pp. 111–28, New York: New York University Press, 1940.

    "The Auchinleck Manuscript and a Possible London Bookshop of 1330–1340," *Publications of the Modern Language Association* 57 (1942), 595–627.

Lounsbury, T. R., *Studies in Chaucer: His Life and Writings*, 3 vols., New York: Harper and Brothers, 1892.

References

Lowes, John Livingston, *Geoffrey Chaucer and the Development of His Genius*, Boston, MA: Houghton Mifflin, 1934.

The Road to Xanadu, Boston, MA: Houghton Mifflin, 1927.

Lydgate, John, *The Fall of Princes*, Henry Bergen (ed.), 4 vols., EETS ES 121 (1924), 122 (1924), 123 (1924) 124 (1927).

The Life of Our Lady, J. Lauritis with R. Klinefelter and V. Gallagher (eds.), Duquesne Studies, Philological Series 2 (Pittsburg, 1961).

Troy Book, Henry Bergen (ed.), 4 vols., EETS ES 97 (1906), 103 (1906), 106 (1910), 126 (1935).

Machan, Tim William, *Techniques of Translation: Chaucer's Boece*, Norman, OK: Pilgrim, 1985.

Manly, J. M., "Chaucer and the Rhetoricians," *Proceedings of the British Academy* 12 (1926), 95–113.

Mannyng, Robert, *Handlyng Synne*, Frederick J. Furnivall (ed.), 2 vols., EETS OS 119 (1901) and 123 (1903).

The Story of England, Frederick. J. Furnivall (ed.), 2 vols., Rolls Series 87, London, 1887.

Marchand, Hans, *The Categories and Types of Present-Day English Word Formation*, 2nd edn, Munich: C. H. Beck'sche, 1969.

Marsh, George Perkins, *The Origin and History of the English Language*, rev. edn, New York: Scribner, 1885.

Matthew, F. D. (ed.), *The English Works of Wyclif*, EETS OS 74 (1880).

McKeon, Richard, "Rhetoric in the Middle Ages," *Speculum* 17 (1942), 1–32.

Mersand, Joseph, *Chaucer's Romance Vocabulary*, New York: Comet Press, 1937.

Middleton, Anne, "Chaucer's 'New Men' and the Good of Literature in the *Canterbury Tales*." In Edward Said (ed.), *Literature and Society*, Selected Papers from the English Institue, new series 3, pp. 15–56, Baltimore, MD: Johns Hopkins University Press, 1980.

"The Clerk and His Tale: Some Literary Contexts," *Studies in the Age of Chaucer* 2 (1980), 121–50.

Miles, Josephine, *Wordsworth and the Vocabulary of Emotion*, Berkeley: University of California Press, 1942; rprt. New York: Octagon Books, 1965.

Milton, John, *Poems Upon Several Occasions*, Thomas Warton (ed.), London: James Dodsley, 1785.

MLA International Bibliography [computer file], New York: Modern Language Association of America, 1981–Feb. 1997.

Moore, J. L., *Tudor-Stuart Views on the Growth, Status and Destiny of the English Language*, Studien zur Englischen Philologie 41 (Halle, 1910).

Mossé, Fernand, "On the Chronology of French Loan-words in English," *English Studies* 25 (1943), 33–40.

Mukarovsky, Jan, *The Word and Verbal Art*, John Burbank and Peter Steiner (ed. and trans.), New Haven, CT: Yale University Press, 1977.

Murray, J. A. H., "The President's Annual Address for 1880," *Transactions of the Philological Society, 1880–1*, (London, 1884), 117–74.

References

"The President's Annual Address for 1884," *Transactions of the Philological Society, 1882–4* (London, 1885), 501–642.

Murray, Katherine Maud Elisabeth, *Caught in the Web of Words: James A. H. Murray and the* Oxford English Dictionary, New Haven, CT: Yale University Press, 1977.

Muscatine, Charles, *Chaucer and the French Tradition*, Berkeley: University of California Press, 1957.

"Chaucer's Religion and the Chaucer Religion." In Ruth Morse and Barry Windeatt (eds.), *Chaucer Traditions: Studies in Honor of Derek Brewer*, pp. 249–62, Cambridge: Cambridge University Press, 1990.

Mustanoja, T. F., *A Middle English Syntax*, Mémoires de la Société de Helsinki 23, Helsinki, 1960.

Nietzsche, Friedrich, *Die Geburt der Tragödie*. In Giorgio Colli and Mazzino Montinari (eds.), *Sämtliche Werke*, vol. I, pp. 9–156, New York: Walter de Gruyter, 1967–77; rprt. 1988.

The Birth of Tragedy. In Walter Kaufmann (trans.), *Basic Writings of Nietzsche*, pp. 15–144, New York: Random House, 1968.

Zur Genealogie der Moral. In Giorgio Colli and Mazzino Montinari (eds.), *Sämtliche Werke.*, vol. V, pp. 245–412, New York: Walter de Gruyter, 1967–77; rprt. 1988.

On the Genealogy of Morals. In Walter Kaufmann (trans.), *Basic Writings of Nietzsche*, pp. 449–599, New York: Random House, 1968.

Ovid, *Metamorphoses*, 2 vols., Frank Justus Miller (ed. and trans.), G. P. Gold (rev.), Cambridge, MA: Harvard University Press, 1916; rev. edn, 1984.

Patterson, Lee, *Chaucer and the Subject of History*, Madison: University of Wisconsin Press, 1991.

"The 'Parson's Tale' and the Quitting of the 'Canterbury Tales,'" *Traditio* 34 (1978), 331–80.

Payne, Robert O., "Chaucer and the Art of Rhetoric." In Beryl Rowland (ed.), *Companion to Chaucer Studies*, pp. 42–64, Oxford: Oxford University Press, 1968; rev. edn, 1979.

The Key of Remembrance: A Study of Chaucer's Poetics, New Haven, CT: Yale University Press, 1963.

Pearsall, Derek, *John Lydgate*, London: Routledge and Kegan Paul, 1970.

Old English and Middle English Poetry, London: Routledge and Kegan Paul, 1977.

The Life of Geoffrey Chaucer, Oxford: Blackwells, 1992.

"The Origins of the Alliterative Revival." In Bernard S. Levy and Paul E. Szarmach (eds.), *The Alliterative Tradition in the Fourteenth Century*, pp. 1–24, Kent, OH: Kent State University Press, 1981.

Petrarch, *Scritti inediti*, Attilio Hortis (ed.), Trieste: Lloyd Austro-Ungarico, 1874.

Piramus, Denis, *La vie Seint Edmund Le Rei*, Hilding Kjellman (ed.), Göteborg, 1935; rprt. Geneva: Slatkine, 1974.

Pope, Alexander, *An Essay on Criticism*. In Pat Rogers (ed.), *Alexander Pope*, pp. 17–39, Oxford: Oxford University Press, 1993.

References

Pratt, Robert, "Chaucer Borrowing From Himself," *Modern Language Quarterly* 7 (1946), 259–64.

Puttenham, George, *The Arte of English Poesie*, Gladys Doidge Willcock and Alice Walker (eds.), Cambridge: Cambridge University Press, 1936; rprt. 1970.

Raymond, Darrell R. (ed.), *Dispatches from the Front: The Prefaces to the Oxford English Dictionary*, Waterloo, Ontario: Centre for the New Oxford English Dictionary, 1987.

Richards, I. A., *Principles of Literary Criticism*. London: K. Paul, Trench, Trubner, 1924.

— and C. K. Ogden, *The Meaning of Meaning*, New York: Harcourt, Brace, 1923.

Riffaterre, Michael, *Semiotics of Poetry*, Bloomington: Indiana University Press, 1978.

Robbins, Rossell Hope, "Geoffroi Chaucier Poète Français, Father of English Poetry," *Chaucer Review* 13 (1978–9), 93–115.

Robert of Gloucester, *The Metrical Chronicle*, William Aldis Wright (ed.), 2 vols., Rolls Series 86, London, 1857.

Robinson, Ian, *Chaucer and the English Tradition*, London: Cambridge University Press, 1972.

— *Chaucer's Prosody*, Cambridge: Cambridge University Press, 1971.

Roscow, G. H., *Syntax and Style in Chaucer's Poetry*, Cambridge: D. S. Brewer, 1981.

Rothwell, William, "The Role of French in Thirteenth-Century England," *Bulletin of The John Rylands University Library* 58 (1975–6), 445–66.

Rymer, Thomas, *A Short View of Tragedy*. In Curt A. Zimansky (ed.), *The Critical Works*, pp. 82–175, New Haven, CT: Yale University Press, 1956.

Said, Edward, *Beginnings: Intention and Method*, Baltimore, MD: Johns Hopkins University Press, 1975.

Saintsbury, George, *A History of English Prosody*, 2nd edn, 3 vols., New York: Russell and Russell, 1923 (first published: London, 1906).

Salter, Elizabeth, *English and International*, Derek Pearsall and Nicolette Zeeman (eds.), Cambridge: Cambridge University Press, 1988.

Scarry, Elaine, "The Well-Rounded Sphere: Cognition and Metaphysical Structure in Boethius's *Consolation of Philosophy*." In *Resisting Representation*, pp. 143–80, Oxford: Oxford University Press, 1994.

Schäfer, Jürgen, *Documentation in the O. E. D.: Shakespeare and Nashe as Test Cases*, Oxford: Oxford University Press, 1980.

Scheps, Walter, "Chaucer's Use of Nonce Words, Primarily in the *Canterbury Tales*," *Neuphilologische Mitteilungen* 80 (1979), 69–77.

Schipper, Jakob, *A History of English Versification*, Oxford: Clarendon Press, 1910.

Schlauch, Margaret, "Chaucer's Colloquial English: Its Structural Traits," *Publications of the Modern Language Association* 47 (1952), 1103–16.

Schless, Howard H., *Chaucer and Dante: A Revaluation*, Norman, OK: Pilgrim Books, 1984.

Scott, Walter Sir, "Life of John Dryden." In Sir Walter Scott (ed.), *The Works of John Dryden*, George Saintsbury (rev. and corr.), 18 vols., vol. I, Edinburgh: Paterson, 1882–93.

References

Shakespeare, William, *The Riverside Shakespeare*, G. Blakemore Evans (ed.), Boston, MA: Houghton Mifflin, 1974.

Shepherd, Geoffrey (ed.), *Ancrene Wisse: Parts Six and Seven*, Exeter: Short Run Press, 1985 (first published: 1959).

Sidney, Philip, *An Apology for Poetry*, Geoffrey Shepherd (ed.), London: Thomas Nelson and Sons, 1965.

Skeat, W. W., *A Popular Sketch of the Origin and Progress of the English Language*, London: Bell and Daldy, 1861.

(ed.), *The Lay of Havelok the Dane*, EETS ES 4 (1868).

Skelton, John, *Garlande or Chaplet of Laurell*. In John Scattergood (ed.), *John Skelton: The Complete English Poems*, pp. 312–58, Harmondsworth: Penguin, 1983.

Smith, Barbara Hernstein, *On the Margins of Discourse: The Relation of Literature to Language*, Chicago: University of Chicago Press, 1978.

Southey, Robert (ed.), *Select Works of the British Poets*, London: Longman, 1835.

Southworth, James G., *The Prosody of Chaucer and His Followers*, Oxford: Blackwell, 1962.

Spearing, A. C., *Medieval to Renaissance in English Poetry*, Cambridge: Cambridge University Press, 1985.

Speirs, John, *Chaucer the Maker*, London: Faber and Faber, 1951.

Spenser, Edmund, *Poetical Works*, J. C. Smith and E. de Selincourt (eds.), London: Oxford University Press, 1912.

The Faerie Queene, A. C. Hamilton (ed.), London: Longman, 1977.

Spurgeon, Caroline F. E., *Five Hundred Years of Chaucer Criticism and Allusion, 1357–1900*, 3 vols., Cambridge: Cambridge University Press, 1925.

Strang, Barbara M. H., *A History of English*, London: Methuen, 1970.

Strohm, Paul, *Hochon's Arrow: The Social Imagination of Fourteenth-Century Texts*, Princeton, NJ: Princeton University Press, 1992.

Sutherland, Ronald (ed.), *The Romaunt of the Rose and Le Roman de la Rose: A Parallel-Text Edition*, Oxford: Basil Blackwell, 1967.

Tatlock, J. S. P., *The Development and Chronology of Chaucer's Works*, Chaucer Society Publications, 2nd series 37 (London, 1907).

ten Brink, Bernhard, *Chaucer: Studien zur Geschichte siener Entwicklung und zur Chronologie seiner Schriften*, vol. I, Münster: Adolph Russell's, 1870.

Thompson, John, *The Founding of English Metre*, London: Routledge and Kegan Paul, 1961.

Tobler, Adolf and Lommatzsch, Erhard, *Altfranzösisches Wörterbuch*, 10 vols., Berlin: Weidmannsche, 1925–.

Tolkien, J. R. R. (ed.), *The English Text of the Ancrene Riwle: Ancrene Wisse*, EETS OS 249 (1962).

Trethewey, W. H. (ed.), *The French Text of the Ancrene Riwle*, EETS OS 240 (1958).

Turville-Petre, Thorlac, *The Alliterative Revival*, Cambridge: D. S. Brewer, 1977.

Ullmann, J., "Studien zu Richard Rolle de Hampole," *Englische Studien* 7 (1884), 415–72.

References

Usk, Thomas, *The Testament of Love*. In W. W. Skeat (ed.), *Chaucerian and Other Pieces*, pp. 1–145, Oxford: Clarendon Press, 1897.

Vising, Johan, *Anglo-Norman Language and Literature*, London: Oxford University Press, 1923.

Visser, F. Th., *An Historical Syntax of the English Language*, 3 parts in 4 vols., Leiden: Brill, 1963–73.

Wallace, David, *Chaucer and the Early Writings of Boccaccio*, Woodbridge: D. S. Brewer, 1985.

"Chaucer's Continental Inheritance: The Early Poems and *Troilus and Criseyde*." In Piero Boitani and Jill Mann (eds.), *The Cambridge Chaucer Companion*, pp. 19–37, Cambridge: Cambridge University Press, 1986.

"'When She Translated Was': A Chaucerian Critique of the Petrarchan Academy." In Lee Patterson (ed.), *Literary Practice and Social Change: 1380–1530*, pp. 156–215, Berkeley: University of California Press, 1990.

Wartburg, Walther v., *Französisches Etymologisches Wörterbuch*, 14 vols., Bonn: Fritz Klopp, 1928–61.

Warton, Thomas, *History of English Poetry*, London: Alex. Murray and Son, 1870.

Weisse, John A., *Origin, Progress and Destiny of the English Language and Literature*, New York: J. W. Bouton, 1878.

Wellek, René, *The Rise of English Literary History*, Chapel Hill: University of North Carolina Press, 1941.

Wilkins, Ernest Hatch, *Studies in the Life and Works of Petrarch*, Cambridge, MA: Medieval Academy of America, 1955.

Williams, Raymond, *Keywords*, London: Fontana, 1976.

Willinsky, John, *Empire of Words: The Reign of the* OED, Princeton, NJ: Princeton University Press, 1994.

Wilson, R. M., "English and French in England, 1100–1300," *History*, new series 28 (1943), 37–60.

The Lost Literature of Medieval England, London: Methuen, 1952.

Wimsatt, James, "Chaucer and French Poetry." In Brewer (ed.), *Geoffrey Chaucer*, pp. 109–36.

Chaucer and the Poems of "Ch.": in University of Pennsylvania MS French 15, Cambridge: D. S. Brewer, 1982.

"Guillaume de Machaut and Chaucer's *Troilus and Criseyde*," *Medium Aevum* 45 (1976), 277–93.

"Machaut's *Lay de Confort* and Chaucer's *Book of the Duchess*." In Rossell Hope Robbins (ed.), *Chaucer at Albany*, pp. 11–26, New York: Burt Franklin, 1975.

Wimsatt Jr., W. K., *The Verbal Icon*, Lexington: University of Kentucky Press, 1954.

Windeatt, B. A. (ed. and trans.), *Chaucer's Dream Poetry: Sources and Analogues*, Cambridge: D. S. Brewer, 1982.

Woodbine, George E. (ed.), Thorne, Samuel E. (trans. with revisions and notes), *Bracton: De legibus et consuetudinibus Angliae*, vol. II, Cambridge, MA: Harvard University Press, 1968.

Woodcock, E. C., *A New Latin Syntax*, Bristol: Bristol Classical Press, 1987 (first published, 1959).

References

Woods, Susanne, *Natural Emphasis: English Versification from Chaucer to Dryden*, San Marino, CA: Huntington Library, 1984.

Woolf, Virginia, *A Room of One's Own; Three Guineas*, Morag Shiach (ed.), Oxford: Oxford University Press, 1992.

Wordsworth, William, *Ecclesiastical Sonnets*, part 2, no. 31 ("Edward VI"). In Paul D. Sheats (ed.), *The Poetical Works of Wordsworth*, pp. 620–1, Boston, MA: Houghton Mifflin, 1982.

"Preface" to the *Lyrical Ballads* (1800 edition). In W. J. B. Owen and Jane Worthington Smyser (eds.), *The Prose Works of William Wordsworth*, 3 vols., vol. I, pp. 118–58, Oxford: Oxford University Press, 1974.

Zeeman, Elizabeth, "Continuity in Middle English Devotional Prose," *Journal of English and Germanic Philology* 55 (1956), 417–22.

Zupitza, Julius (ed.), *The Romance of Guy of Warwick*, 3 vols., EETS OS 42 (1883), 49 (1887), and 59 (1891)

Index

Index

Index

Index

Middle English, literary culture, 61–5, 69–77, 80–90; studies, 218–20; see also, eloquence, English, French, Latin
Middle Low German, 77 (and n. 78)
Middleton, Anne, 144 n. 23, 147 nn. 28–9
Midland Prose Psalter, 204
Miles, Josephine, 19 n. 30
Mill, Anna J., 69 n. 59
Miller, Frank Justus, 75 n. 76
Milton, John, 190–1 (and n. 40), 193
Modern Language Association Bibliography, 218
modes of language, see also style; "high,", 150–7; "low," 157–68
Moore, J. L., 195 n. 56
Morte D'Arthur, alliterative, 181
Mossé, Fernand, 71 n. 65
Mukarovsky, Jan, 19 (and n. 31)
Murray, J. A. H., 3 n. 3, 41, 199–201 (and n. 79), 203–4 n. 88, 206
Murray, Katherine Maud Elisabeth, 41 n. 55, 201 n. 81
Muscatine, Charles, 17, 50–1, 95–7 (and n. 8), 134, 138 n. 4, 218
Mustanoja, T. F., 43–4
myth, 194–5, 210–12

Nash, Walter, 20 n. 32
"native English," see etymology, polysyllabic words, words
Newmark, Leonard, 88 (and n. 101)
Nietzsche, Friedrich, 194, 211
Norman Conquest, 140–1, 151
novelty, see linguistic, novelty

OED, 1–3, 38, 41–2, 56–7, 58 n. 41, 88, 162–4, 183, 227–31; bias toward "great writers" in, 199–206; omissions from, 203–5; second edition, 206 (and n. 95)
Ogden, C. K., 19 n. 30
originality and origination, 182–3, 186–7, 189, 191, 193–4, 200–2, 209–11
Ormulum, 89
Ovid, 143 (and n. 21), 144 n. 22, 185–6 (and n. 24), 191–2, 195; *Metamorphoses*, 75 n. 76
Owl and the Nightingale, 165, 180–2, 218

Patterson, Lee, 96 (and n. 11), 102 n. 25, 168, 191 n. 45
Payne, Robert O., 96 n. 12, 139 (and nn. 5 and 7)
Pearsall, Derek, 46, 52, 92–3, 99–100 n. 21, 140 n. 12, 181 nn. 7–9, 210 n. 103
Percy, Thomas, *Reliques of English Poetry*, 199
Peterborough Chronicle, 89
Petrarch, 147–8 (and nn. 29–30), 171, 185
philology, 2–4
Piramus, Denis, 71

"poetic diction," 18, 24, 197–8; see also language, "literary"
"poetry," 13–19, 25–37, 146–7, 185–6, 214–17; English, 148, 171; "laureate," 147–9; as "poesye," 143–6 (and n. 23), 177
polysyllabic words; borrowed, 152–5, 167, 169, 172, 175; "native," 155–7, 172–3, 175
Pope, Alexander, *Essay on Criticism*, 188, 191
Pratt, Robert, 100 n. 22
proprietas, 67 (and n. 57); see also language, propriety in
Provençal, 198–9, see also French
Purcell, Sally, 142 nn. 18–19
Puttenham, George, *Arte of English Poesie*, 196 n. 58

Raymond, Darrell R., 41 n. 56, 204 n. 90
Read, Thomas, 184 n.19
Renaud de Louens, *Livre de Melibée et de Dame Prudence*, 137
rhetoric, 11, 18, 23–4, 67, 139; *occupatio*, 146
Rhetorica ad Herennium, 67 n. 57
rhetoricians, Latin, 152
rhyme in Chaucer, 31, 60–1, 153, 169, 172–6
Richard II, 72
Richards, I. A., 19 n.30
Riffaterre, Michael, 19 n. 31
Riverside Chaucer, 99–100 nn.20–1, 112 n. 36, 223–4
Robbins, Rossell Hope, 50
Robert of Canterbury, 142 n. 15
Robert of Gloucester, *Chronicle*, 62, 89, 140–2 (and n. 15), 203–4, 218–19
Robinson, F. N., 16
Robinson, Ian, 4, 46, 54 n. 30, 179 n. 2
Rogers, Pat, 188 n. 33
Rolle, Richard, *Psalter*, 62, 89, 204, 218; *Form of Living*, 204
Roman de la Rose, 60, 64, 80–6, 144; see also Jean de Meun
romance, as genre, 65–7, 72–3, 169, 176; language of, 66–7, 158; words, see words, Romance
Roscow, G. H., 45 n. 65
Rothwell, William, 71 n. 68
Rymer, Thomas, 198

Said, Edward, 211 (and nn. 104–5)
Saintsbury, George, 45–6
Salter, Elizabeth 69, see also as Zeeman, Elizabeth
Scarry, Elaine, 24 n. 38, 25 n. 42
Scattergood, John, 186 n. 26, 187 n. 28, 216 n. 110
Schäfer, Jürgen, 201 n. 80
Scheps, Walter, 131
Schipper, Jakob, 45
Schlauch, Margaret, 159 (and n. 48)
Schless, Howard, 143

433

Index

Scott, Walter, 190–1
Selincourt, E. de, 217 n. 111
Seven Sages of Rome, 62
Shakespeare, William, 136, 191, 193, 201
Sheats, Paul D., 190 n. 43
Shepherd, Geoffrey, 66 nn. 54–5, 184 n. 16
Sidnam, Jonathan, 184
Sidney, Phillip, 184
Skeat, W. W., 112 n. 36, 169 n. 53, 201 (and n. 83), 205–6 (and nn. 91–2), 209 n. 100
Skelton, John, *The Garland of Laurel*, 186–7 (and n. 26), 215
Smith, Barbara Hernstein, 20 (and n. 34)
Smith, J. C., 217 n. 111
Somnium Scipionis, Cicero's, 169
South English Legendary, 62, 68–9, 89, 218
Southey, Robert, 190
Southworth, James, 46
Spearing, A. C., 52, 127 n. 53, 169
Spearing, J. E., 127 n. 53
Speculum Vitae, 71
Speght, Thomas, 184, 215
Speirs, John, 53 (and n. 30)
Spenser, Edmund, 184, 187, 190 n. 40, 193; *The Faerie Queene*, 184 n. 20; *Shepheardes Calendar*, 217 (and n. 111); *Two Cantos of Mutabilitie*, 184 n. 20
Spivak, Gayatri Chakravorty, 180 n. 6, 183 n. 13
Spurgeon, Caroline F. E , 12 n. 7, 48 n. 2–3, 184 nn. 15, 17–19, and 21, 189 n. 36, 190 nn. 39 and 41, 196 n. 61, 197 n. 63, 198 n. 65, 199 n. 70, 216 n. 110
stanzaic structure, in Chaucer, 27–35; in Boethius's Latin, 34–5
Statius, 143 (and n. 21), 144 n. 22, 148 n. 30, 185 n. 24
Stowe, John, 215
Strang, Barbara, 56 n. 34
Strohm, Paul, 43 n. 59
style, 4, 16–18, 96–7, 138, *see also* modes of language; "high," 139, 149–52, 170, 172–4; levels of, 139–40; "plain," 139
Super, R. H., 192 n. 46, 193 n. 51, 199 n. 69
Sutherland, Ronald, 60 n. 45
syntax, in Boethius's Latin, 33–5; borrowed (Latinate), 34–5; Chaucer's, 29–35; history of, 43–5; in Jean de Meun's French, 33–5

Tatlock, J. S. P., 95 (and n. 7), 96 n. 11, 99 n. 20, 103
ten Brink, Bernhard, 92, 93 n. 5
"terms," 67–8 (and n. 58); "cherles," 149, 175; "ink-horn," 195–6 (and n. 58)
Thomas, Duke of Gloucester, 72
Thompson, John, 46 n. 69
Tobler, Adolf, 86 n. 98
Tolkien, J. R. R., 66 n. 54

Trethewey, W. H., 70 n. 63
Trevisa, John, translation of Higden's *Polychronicon*, 216
trilingualism, 71–3
Tristrem, Sir, 89
Turville-Petre, Thorlac, 181 n. 10
Tyrwhitt, Thomas, 48 (and n. 3)

Ullmann, J., 71 n. 68
Usk, Thomas, 71–2; *Testament of Love*, 212

vernacular, 147–8, 150; *see also* "eloquence," English, French, Italian, Latin, status of (vs. Middle English), manuscripts, Middle English
Vernon MS, *see* manuscripts
Verstegan, Richard, 197
Vices & Virtues, 89
Virgil, 143 (and n. 21), 144 n. 22, 185–6 (and n. 24), 191, 195
Vising, Johan, 71 n. 68
Visser, F. Th., 44–5
vocabulary, *see* words

Wace, *Roman de Brut*, 70 (and n. 64), 142 n. 15
Wadington, William, *Manuel des Pechiez*, 64, 87
Wallace, David, 51, 144 n. 22, 147 (and nn. 28–9)
Walter of Bibbesworth, English glosses to *Treatise of*, 204
Walton, John, 208 n. 97
Wartburg, Walther von, 86 n. 98
Warton, Thomas, 12, 189–90 (and n. 40), 198
Weightman, Doreen, 194 n. 53
Weightman, John, 194 n. 53
Weisse, John A., 12–13, 199
Wellek, René, 189 n. 38
Wilkins, Ernest Hatch, 148 n. 30
William of Shoreham, *Poems*, 62, 204
Williams, Raymond, 1
Willinsky, John, 206
Wilson, R. M., 52, n. 24, 71 n. 66
Wilson, Thomas, *Arte of Rhetorique*, 196 (and n. 60)
Wimsatt, James, 50 n. 14, 51 (and n. 18), 59
Wimsatt, W. K., 19 n. 31
Windeatt, Barry, 26–7 n. 44, 73 n. 75, 147 n. 29
Woodcock, E. C., 34 n. 48
Woods, Susanne, 46–7
Woolf, Virginia, 1
word study 1–2; *see also* lexical history
words, borrowed, 35–6, 39–40, 56–67, 69, 70–80, 97–8, 106, 121–6, 134, 154–5, 169–75 196–9, 208 n. 99, "inherited" borrowings, 74–7, 84–8, *see also*, polysyllabic words; boundaries of, 38, 57–8 (and n. 41), 227; density of in Chaucer's writings, 118–20; derived, 39–40, 78–90,110–12, 121–6, 129–31,

434

Index

CAMBRIDGE STUDIES IN MEDIEVAL LITERATURE

CABRINI COLLEGE LIBRARY
610 KING OF PRUSSIA RD.
RADNOR, PA 19087-3699

DEMCO